LAW AND SCIENCE

by

STEVEN GOLDBERG
Professor of Law
Georgetown University

LAWRENCE O. GOSTIN
Associate Dean for Research and Academic Programs
Professor of Law, Georgetown University
Director, Center for Law and the Public's Health

FOUNDATION PRESS
NEW YORK, NEW YORK
2006

© 2006 By FOUNDATION PRESS

       395 Hudson Street

       New York, NY 10014

       Phone Toll Free 1–877–888–1330

       Fax (212) 367–6799

       fdpress.com

Printed in the United States of America

ISBN–13: 978–1–58778–911–3

ISBN–10: 1–58778–911–6

 TEXT IS PRINTED ON 10% POST CONSUMER RECYCLED PAPER

S.G.

To Missy, Joe and Becky.

L.O.G.

To Jean, Bryn and Kieran.

*

PREFACE

This Reader is drawn from the third edition of Law, Science and Medicine, an influential text that has been widely used since its debut in 1984. We have added a new Chapter One, An Overview of Law and Science, and then provided those chapters from Law, Science and Medicine that are relevant to our topic.

The materials in this Reader can serve not only as the primary text in a course on law and science, but as a vital supplement for courses in science policy and the history of science. Too often students, whether in undergraduate or graduate programs, discuss legal and scientific issues without access to the actual judicial decisions, statutes, and other technical materials that are essential for meaningful analysis. This Reader can remedy that situation.

There are daily reminders of the currency and importance of the issues addressed here from gene therapy to clashes between science and religion; from the funding of basic research to the use of controversial scientific theories in high profile trials. Although such issues arise with increasing frequency—in courtrooms, legislative chambers, and executive agencies as well as in the popular and professional press—our society often seems perplexed about how to deal with them.

A major source of this problem is the lack of exposure that many people have to the values, methods, and assumptions of the legal and scientific communities. This has led to a particular gulf of misunderstanding between scientists and nonscientists. This gulf may widen as more complex issues are presented by the growing sophistication and powers of the physical and life sciences (from their theoretical underpinnings to their technological applications) and as well-publicized incidents make the public apprehensive about progress in science.

To be able to work across traditional boundaries, students of law and science, science policy, and the history of science need exposure to sophisticated materials from the legal and scientific disciplines—as well as from the humanities and the social sciences—presented within a structure that enables the students to unravel the issues, analyze their content, and construct a framework for their own future roles as informed citizens in a society seeking new relationships at the interface of law and science. Such are the objectives we attempt to fulfill in this book.

The overarching issue in this Reader is how ought society learn about and respond to the role of science in society. Five themes are explored:

• The use and misuse of scientific expertise in making public policy. What factors determine when an expert's views are invaluable and when they are irrelevant, and what weight should such views be given by the public and its representatives?

• Who decides: the need to find appropriate institutions to promote, to direct, and even to curtail science. What are the strengths and weaknesses of agencies, legislatures, courts, the executive, private groups, individual scientists, and lay people when the question is who should control science at the various stages of its development and use?

• The application of risk assessment or cost-benefit analysis to scientific issues. How, if at all, should these techniques guide those making public policy in the face of scientific uncertainty?

• The contrasting value systems of law and science. How can one reconcile science's ethic of progress toward verifiable truth, with the law's focus on individual rights and interests and its obligation to provide an orderly process of dispute resolution even when information is imperfect?

• The ethical and religious implications of developments in science. When science arguably alters the very nature of humanity, what are the consequences from an ethical or religious viewpoint?

Chapter One of this text is an essay that provides an overview of law and science, with an introduction to the value systems of the two disciplines, and to the role each plays in shaping the other. The remaining chapters contain a wealth of original materials and notes. Chapter Two focuses on the human genome project and concerns the potential of genetics to produce vast benefits as well as harms and inequities. This Chapter ranges from the scientific history of Mendel and the social history of eugenics to modern genomics and proteomics. Chapter Three uses nuclear energy as a lens to explore the modern scientific establishment. It covers basic science through to the control of nuclear energy in the regulatory state, both in terms of its military and civilian uses. This Chapter also includes materials on photovoltaic solar systems and hydrogen-based fuel cells, as a contrast to more centralized energy generation systems. Chapter Four addresses the issue of public control of science, with materials on the control of medicine as well. Government wields significant influence on the practice of science and medicine through the Constitution (e.g., freedom of speech and religion); legal incentives (e.g., patents, trade secrets, copyrights); allocation of funds (federal and state support of science and medicine); direct and indirect regulation of technology at the federal, state, and local levels; and the use of scientific and medical evidence in the courts. Finally, Chapter Five provides a case study at the frontiers of law and science: artificial intelligence. How will increasingly sophisticated computer systems alter our views of privacy, of legal reasoning, and of human values?

We are grateful to the many students at Georgetown and elsewhere whose hard work and ideas have helped to shape this text. We are especially thankful for the efforts of the following fellows, students, and administrators who helped to research and edit this book: Auburn Daily, Joleen Okun, Katrina Pagonis, David Plattner, Abigail Scaffe, and Lesley Stone. We would like to offer a special thanks to Lance Gable, who coordinated the research for the book, and Stephen Barbour, who handled the often voluminous administrative responsibilities. Finally, we would like to again thank our families for their support during this process.

STEVEN GOLDBERG
LAWRENCE O. GOSTIN

Washington, D.C.
September 2005

NOTE ON EDITING

Deletions from materials are indicated by ellipses except when the omitted material consists only of citations or footnotes. All footnotes in the excerpted sections are numbered according to the original source except when noted. All footnotes added by the authors are indicated with ascending lower-case letters.

*

ACKNOWLEDGMENTS

Law & Science

Source

Aden B. Meinel and Marjorie P. Meinel, *Soft Path Leads to a New Dark Age* IN THE ENERGY CONTROVERSY. 225, 226-28, 232-33 (Hugh Nash ed., 1979).

ALLEN BUCHANAN ET AL., TWO MODELS FOR GENETIC INTERVENTIO IN FROM CHANCE TO CHOICE 11-14, 55-60 (2000).

Allen D. Roses, *Pharmacogenetics and the Practice of Medicine* 405 NATURE 857 (2000).

Amory Lovins, *Energy Strategy: The Road Not Taken?* 55 FOREIGN AFF. 55, 77-81 (1976).

Amory Lovins, *Prepared Testimony in* THE ENERGY CONTROVERSY 28-31 (Hugh Nash ed., 1979).

Anita L. Allen, *Genetic Privacy: Emerging Concepts and Values in Genetic Secrets in* PROTECTING PRIVACY AND CONFIDENTIALITY IN THE GENETIC ERA 33-34 (Mark A. Rothstein ed., 1997).

BANESH HOFFMANN, ALBERT EINSTEIN 69-82 (1972).

Bartha Maria Knoppers et al., *Commercialization of Genetic Research and Public Policy* 286 Sci. 2277-2278 (1999).

BARTON J. BERNSTEIN, THE ATOMIC BOMB VII (1976).

BENJAMIN N. CARDOZO, THE PARADOXES OF LEGAL SCIENCE 1-4 (1956).

Bruce L. R. Smith et al., *Technical Advice for Congress: Past Trends and Present Obstacles in Science and Technology Advice for Congress,* (M. Granger Morgan & Jon M. Peha eds., 2003): 25-29, 32-40

Bruce Mazlish, *The Fourth Discontinuity* 8 Tech. & Culture 1, 1-8 (1967).

C.P. SNOW, THE TWO CULTURES 4-7, 10-11 (1964).

Curtis A. Kin, *Coming Soon to the "Genetic Supermarket" Near You* 48 STAN. L. REV. 1573 (1996).

Decision-Making Dilemmas Concerning Testing and Management 55 OBSTETRICAL & GYNECOLOGICAL SURVEY 373-384 (2000)

E.F. SCHUMACHER, SMALL IS BEAUTIFUL 147, 156-58 (1973).

Edward H. Levi, AN INTRODUCTION TO LEGAL REASONING 1, 3-5 (1949).

Edwina L. Rissland, *Artificial Intelligence and Law: Stepping Stones to a Model of Legal Reasoning* 99 Yale L.J. 1957, 1957-61, 1963-64, 1971-73, 1980-81 (1990).

Elizabeth Pennisi, *Human Genome: Reaching Their Goal Early, Sequencing Labs Celebrate*

Francis S. Collins et al., *New Goals for the U.S. Human Genome Project: 1998-2003*

Herman Kahn, THINKING ABOUT THE UNTHINKABLE 18-19, 22-24 (1962).

J.D. Watson & F.H.C. Crick, *A Structure for Deoxyribose Nucleic Acid.* 171 Nature 737 (1953)

Jimmy Carter, Solar Energy. President's Message to Congress, 15 Weekly Comp. of Pres. Doc. 1098 (1979).

Jocelyn Kaiser, *Public-Private Group Maps Out Initiatives.* 296 Sci. 827 (2002).

Jon W. Gordon, *Genetic Enhancement in Humans* 283 *Sci.* 2023-2024 (1999).

Kennedy Institute of Ethics, *Genetic Testing and Genetic Screening* KIEJ (Updated 2004).

Kennedy Institute of Ethics, *Scope Note 24: Human Gene Therapy* KIEJ. (Updated 2004).

Kenneth Offit et al., *The "Duty to Warn" a Patient's Family Members About Hereditary Disease Risks* 292 JAMA 1469 (2004)

Lori Andrews & Dorothy Nelkin, *Body Bazaar: The Market for Human Tissue in the Biotechnology Age* 60-62 (2001).

Louis Beres, APOCALYPSE 123-26 (1980).

Mark A. Rothstein & Phyllis Griffin Epps, *Ethical and Legal Implications of Pharmacogenomics* 2 Nature Reviews Genetics 228-231 (2001).

Michael J. Green & Jeffrey R. Botkin, *Genetic Exceptionalism in Medicine: Clarifying the Differences between Genetic and Nongenetic Tests* 138 ANNALS INTERNAL MED. 571-575 (2003).

Michael Polanyi, *The Republic of Science* 1 MINERVA 54, 62 (1962).

Nuel Pharr Davis, LAWRENCE AND OPPENHEIMER 240-42 (1968).

Philip M. Stern, THE OPPENHEIMER CASE: SECURITY ON TRIAL 181-82, 242-44, 273-74, 281-82, 377, 506-07 (1969).

Richard Delgado et al., *God, Galileo, and Government: Toward Constitutional Protection for Scientific Inquiry* 53 Wash. L. Rev. 349, 354-55, 358-61 (1978).

Richard S. Cooper et al., *Race and Genomics* 348 NEW ENG. J. MED. 1166 (2003).

Robert Jungk, BRIGHTER THAN A THOUSAND SUNS 131-32 (1958).

Robert K. Merton, SOCIAL THEORY AND SOCIAL STRUCTURE 607-14 (1968).

Sandy F. Kraemer, SOLAR LAW 130-32 (1978).

Steven Goldberg, *The Changing Face of Death: Computers, Consciousness, and Nancy Cruzan 43* Stan. L. Rev. 659, 680-83 (1991).

Steven Goldberg, *The Reluctant Embrace: Law and Science in America* 75 GEO. L.J. 1341, 1365-68, 1380-81, 1386-87 (1987).

The President's Council on Bioethics, *Screening and Selection for Genetic Conditions and Traits in* REPRODUCTION AND RESPONSIBILITY: THE REGULATION OF NEW BIOTECHNOLOGIES 89, 89-93 (2004).

Thomas S. Kuhn, THE STRUCTURE OF SCIENTIFIC REVOLUTIONS 10-11, 52, 84-85, 165-67, 172 (1962).

Tom Clarke, *DNA's Family Tree*. 422 NATURE 791 (2003).

United States Bishops, Pastoral Letter on War and Peace, the Challenge of Peace: God's Promise and Our Response. May 19, 1983. *Reprinted in* 13 ORIGINS 1, 9-10, 13-14, 18, 29.

Vicki Brower, *Proteomics: Biology in the Post-Genomic Era*. 2 EMBO REPORTS 558-9 (2001).

Xavier Bosch, Researchers *Try to Unlock Human Genome Potential*. 360 THE LANCET 1481 (2002).

*

SUMMARY OF CONTENTS

DETAILED TABLE OF CONTENTS

*

TABLE OF CASES

Principal cases are in bold type. Non-principal cases are in roman type. References are to Pages.

*

LAW AND SCIENCE

*

CHAPTER 1

AN OVERVIEW OF LAW AND SCIENCE

Law and science are two of the most important features of modern American life. We look to the law to assure that fairness and freedom are preserved, and we look to science to fuel the progress that makes our lives easier and more enjoyable. But neither of these pillars of American culture is uncontroversial. In particular, they sometimes appear to be in conflict: the law is seen as hampering progress, and science can pose risks to equality and to privacy.

This introductory chapter provides an overview of the basic relationship between law and science in America. We will consider the value systems of science and law, the role of law in supporting and regulating science, and the impact of science in the legal system.[a]

I. THE VALUE SYSTEMS OF SCIENCE AND LAW

Scientists and lawyers approach the world differently because the goals of their professions are different. While science values *progress*, the law puts tremendous stress on *process*.

Philosophers, sociologists, and other scholars debate the nature of scientific inquiry. How, if at all, can we apprehend the world outside of ourselves? How does human culture shape the questions we ask about that world? There is no agreed upon set of answers to these or to countless other questions about the nature of science. But most working scientists are not philosophers, and they do not concern themselves with these questions on a daily basis. Most scientists believe they are seeking testable knowledge about the natural world. They want to advance our understanding of nature. The usual process is to have a hypothesis, and then to test it under controlled conditions. If the test falsifies the hypothesis, the hypothesis should be modified or abandoned. If the test supports the hypothesis and others reproduce the test and get the same result, we begin to believe that the hypothesis may be true.

This description obviously oversimplifies all of the ambiguities involved in framing and testing hypotheses, as well as the more fundamental upheavals that occur when revolutions in scientific thinking change the way scientists think about the very questions they should be asking.

---

a. Many of the themes in this Chapter are set forth in STEVEN GOLDBERG, CULTURE CLASH: LAW AND SCIENCE IN AMERICA (1994).

1

Moreover, this description puts to one side the real pressures that shape the professional choices of scientists who are seeking grants or tenure or other recognition.

But the fact remains that scientists believe they are increasing our knowledge of the natural world, and most of us agree. Scientific knowledge is thus cumulative: we know more now than we did before. A young physics professor just starting her career knows more about physics than Isaac Newton. And this increasing knowledge of nature has helped us develop increasing mastery over the physical world. We look to science to fuel the applied discoveries that bring us more energy, better medicines, and much more.

The net result is that the touchstone of science is progress. The professional norm of priority furthers this goal. The scientist who makes the breakthrough wins the Nobel Prize; the one who independently makes the same discovery one day later remains obscure.

The goal of our legal system is different. Legal controversies may involve disputed facts that perhaps could be examined in a scientific or quasi-scientific way. But they involve as well questions of fundamental values, where people of good faith differ and controlled experiments will not help. The law is not trying to describe empirical reality. It is trying to resolve social disputes in a peaceful manner. So the law is concerned fundamentally with questions of process: every side must be heard, every consideration must be aired, so that even those who lose will accept the verdict.

Consider a man who is charged with the murder of his father. There may be some factual inquiries that would help us determine whether he in fact committed the act that killed the victim. Fingerprint evidence, for example, might help, and we would want that evidence to be presented and understood in an accurate manner. But even the pure factual question of whether the accused committed the fateful act is unlikely to yield entirely to science. It is not possible to do controlled experiments with human subjects that will reveal unfailingly what happened, in private, months ago.

Far more importantly, the central questions in a legal case are often not factual. Suppose the man did kill his father, but he did so because his father was ninety years old, in intractable pain, and was begging to die. And suppose the cause of the father's death was an omission: the son declined to give his father the medicine that was keeping the older man alive. And suppose the son stood to inherit a modest sum of money when the father died. Should the son be punished? This question implicates fundamental political and philosophical values, ranging from the proper role of government to the ethical status of euthanasia. Our society is divided on these questions, and no experiment will change that. The goal of the legal system is to resolve these matters in a socially acceptable way, which includes leaving open the possibility that society could reach a different decision in a similar case decades down the road. So the law is concerned with fundamentally procedural questions: should decisions be made by legislatures or courts, by judges or juries, at the state or federal level. And rather than the progressive march of cumulative knowledge, legal decisions may move back and forth over the years as society's values and judgments change.

One vital feature of the task facing the legal system is that, unlike science, the law cannot wait indefinitely to resolve problems. In the world of social disputes, not deciding is a decision. Suppose the son denies that he was in the room the day his father died, while it is central to the prosecutor's case to prove he was there. Imagine that current forensic methods cannot resolve the matter, but future research might yield a new form of highly sensitive testing that will reveal whether the son's shoes were on the room's carpet on the precise day in question. A scientist might say, "we do not presently know whether the son was there that day. We have to wait until we have a new testing method before we can definitively resolve the issue." But what happens in the interim? If the son is out on bail and living his life, waiting is fine with him. If the son is being held in jail without bail, waiting decades to resolve the matter is not fine with him. There is no place to hide here: the real question is what do you do in the face of imperfect knowledge, a problem the law faces every day. So the law asks questions like who bears the burden of proof in cases of conflicting evidence, and the answers may differ depending upon whether you are deciding whether someone should be held in jail, or whether a new drug should be allowed on the market.

II. THE ROLE OF LAW IN SUPPORTING AND REGULATING SCIENCE

We have been looking at a classic criminal case, but our legal system also shapes broader questions of governance. Through our Constitution and laws, we decide what programs to fund, what health and safety restrictions to impose on our activities, and countless other matters of social importance. In particular, the legal system has a strong impact on how science is done in the United States.

The United States is one of the world's leaders in scientific research. This is not in spite of our legal system; it is because of that system. Our federal and state governments have the authority to fund scientific research, and they do so, providing much of the money that supports pure research. Our laws generally create a system of peer review, under which scientists themselves play a key role in deciding which applicants for government research funding are successful. The patent and copyright provisions in the Constitution underpin a statutory system of intellectual property protection that spurs research. And our constitutional guarantee of free speech prevents the government from having a monopoly on all scientific debate. If a scientist believes that the predominant assumptions underlying a field of research are mistaken, he can openly argue the point and try to change attitudes in the scientific community.

Our legal system, of course, must balance a host of interests. Thus scientists, like every other group, do not always get their way. While a physicist has a constitutional right to advocate more research on nuclear materials, he does not have a constitutional right to do such research in his basement. Just as the right to free speech does not mean you can punch someone in the nose to express your views, the right to free scientific expression must give way to health and safety concerns when you actually begin to do experiments. More broadly, when society considers the implementation of technology, the judgments of the scientific community on technical issues are important, but they often are less important than social attitudes toward the issues raised by the technology.

Consider the following situation. Suppose a utility proposes to open a new electricity-generating plant in a rural area but they cannot do so until regulators give their approval. The plant uses a novel technology that will probably make electricity available at cheaper than normal rates. The scientific and engineering community overwhelmingly believe that the risk of a dangerous accident at this plant is less than the risk associated with current coal and nuclear plants, although a few technical people believe the risk is greater. Another decade or so of testing with prototypes and the like might help clarify the issue. Citizens in the state are divided over whether the plant should be opened. How should the relevant regulatory authority rule? First, as noted above, not to decide is a decision. If the regulators conclude that they cannot decide the issue until additional decades of research provide better data, than the citizens who oppose the plant will hold a celebration. In the real world, they have won an important victory, although from a scientific point of view the safety of the plant remains unresolved.

More fundamentally, even if a decision is made now, that decision, whichever way it goes, will not be based on technical input alone. Even if the regulators assume that the risk of an accident is low, the question of whether that risk justifies the likely benefits is not a scientific question. How safe is safe enough is a question of human values and preferences, not subject to controlled experiments.

Often social issues that involve science involve even more fundamental questions. Consider proposals to do research with stem cells. Scientists may be able to provide useful information on whether such research is likely to lead to health benefits. But science alone cannot resolve the question of what weight should be given to the views of those who believe that stem cell research is inconsistent with their moral and religious views on the sanctity of embryonic life. The process-oriented legal system will have to wrestle with all of the relevant interests and values, and it will often conclude that the answer to whether research will be permitted will turn on matters such as federal versus state regulation, public versus private funding, and the like.

So the law may, in the end, limit stem cell research or the deployment of new energy sources, not because the law is anti-science, but because it must consider a host of values, of which science is only one. The legal system tends to be supportive of the scientific community when pure research is at stake, but when applications of that research affect the public, the scientific community is just one interest group among many.

III.   The Impact of Science in the Legal System

None of this is meant to suggest that science is irrelevant to broad social and legal disputes. Accurate and honest technical information is often vital to the sensible resolution of those disputes. How much risk is too much cannot be sensibly addressed without knowing, to the extent possible, how much risk we are talking about. And getting sound scientific data is quite a challenge when many people (including many scientists) have such strong personal views on an issue that they are likely, consciously or not, to distort the underlying science.

Thus the legal system tries to include good technical inputs in a variety of ways. Legislative hearings with scientists, temporary and permanent advisory committees, and administrative agencies staffed with technical experts are all important techniques. Many believe that new techniques are needed to make the system work better.

Perhaps the most dramatic clashes over the inclusion of science in the legal system come in the courtroom. A plaintiff wants to establish that her cancer was caused by toxins in the cleaning materials her employer used. She has a scientific expert prepared to testify that these materials can indeed cause cancer. But the employer, backed by an overwhelming majority of the mainstream scientific community, believes that the expert is nothing more than a gun for hire: there is little reputable evidence that the cleaning materials are dangerous. The plaintiff responds that little evidence is different than none, and mainstream science sometimes turns out to be mistaken. Should the plaintiff's expert be allowed to testify before the jury, with the defendant bringing in experts of his own? The law calls on the trial judge to make a preliminary assessment of reliability before letting an expert appear before a jury. As you can imagine, the depth and nature of that assessment is a matter of lively dispute.

In American society today, few institutions are more central than the legal and scientific communities. In the pages that follow, we will see how those institutions interact, and how that interaction should be shaped in the years ahead.

CHAPTER 2

The Human Genome: Pathways to Health

Law and Science is about pathways to health. How do scientific pursuits evolve from the laboratory to the physician's office and hospital through to interventions to safeguard the public's health? Law can facilitate that process by, for example, incentivizing scientific innovation and efficient delivery of vaccines and pharmaceuticals to the market. Science and medicine pose deeply complex ethical and social issues, and policy makers often turn to law as a means to regulate research, the professions, and private activities. There is no subject that better illustrates the difficult problems that inhere in law and science, than the human genome.

I. Scientific Discovery and Advancement

A. Mendel and How Genetics Began

Gregor Mendel is considered the father of genetics, although he did not enjoy such recognition during his lifetime. Modern genetics had its humble beginning in Mendel's garden, where he examined and quantified the physical traits in pea plants to predict future generations' traits and explain familial resemblances. Charting seven traits (plant height, flower color and position, seed color and shape, and pod color and shape), Mendel concluded that certain particles or "factors" were being transmitted intergenerationally and that these factors were directly responsible for physical traits.

Hereditary traits, he concluded, are determined by cellular elements, now called genes, which exist in pairs, and are responsible for all heritable characteristics. Mendel's law of segregation found that each genetic trait is produced by a pair of alleles that separate (segregate) during reproduction and persist unchanged through successive generations of hereditary transmission. Under his law of independent assortment, genes are distributed randomly and independently of genes for other characteristics. When different alleles for a certain characteristic are inherited, only the dominant trait will be expressed; they do not blend, as previously thought. *See* Daniel L. Hartl & Orel Vitezslav, *What did Gregor Mendel Think he Discovered?*, 131 Genetics 245 (1992).

After initial rejection at peer review, Mendel's paper, "Experiments on Plant Hybridization" was published in 1865. Initially, his paper received little attention, and it was rarely cited by botanists or biologists over the next 35 years. The rationale for Mendel's lack of recognition has been thought to exemplify everything from the failure of traditional modes of scientific communication to the phenomenon of "premature scientific discovery." *See* Vannevar Bush, *As We May Think*, in FROM MEMEX TO HYPERTEXT: VANNEVAR BUSH AND THE MIND'S MACHINE (James M. Nyce et al., eds. 1991); GUNTHER S. STENT, *Prematurity and Uniqueness in Scientific Discovery*, in PARADOXES OF PROGRESS 94–114 (1978). Despite inaccurate interpretations of what Mendel had shown, he gained recognition in 1900 when several European botanists verified his work.

In the decade that followed, Mendel's paper and the contemporary description of his findings stimulated an enormous amount of work in the newly formed field of genetics, particularly in England and the United States. For the generation of scientists who came to think of themselves as "Mendelians," the paper of 1865, and its author, became an inspirational symbol of the revolutionary findings that awaited biologists in the study of heredity. In 1900, shortly after the "rediscovery," the geneticist William Bateson began an article in the *Journal of the Royal Horticultural Society* with the claim that, "An exact determination of the laws of heredity will probably work more change in man's outlook on the world, and in his power over nature, than any other advance in natural knowledge that can be clearly foreseen." WILLIAM BATESON, Mendel's Principles of Heredity (1913).

With this recognition of genetics' importance, scientists began to associate inheritance with chromosomes and to find models—in fruit flies, predominantly—that would help build upon that initial foundation. Two decades later, researchers determined DNA, rather than protein, was the carrier of inheritance. In addition, DNA polymerase was discovered and biochemical regulating units of inheritance were identified, laying the foundation for the future biotechnology revolution. Scientists knew that the DNA molecule was made of a few relatively simple chemicals. However, no one was sure how these simple chemicals combined to carry the huge amount of information required to recreate a living thing. A young American geneticist named James Watson was one of the few researchers who realized that the only way to determine whether nucleic acids carried genes was to understand their structure.

B. MORE THAN 50 YEARS AFTER WATSON AND CRICK

James Watson and Francis Crick provided the foundation for modern genetic research by proposing that the structure of DNA was a double-stranded helix of complementary nucleic acids.[1] On the death of Francis Crick in July 2004, *The Times of London* wrote:

> The beauty of the double helix was that it immediately suggested a way in which the genetic instructions of the cell could be passed on when it divided, to produce a perfect copy. One helix unfurled from the other and then built its own matching helix before curling up again.... It also suggested that the order of the base pairs along the helix was a kind of

---

1. The breakthrough by Watson and Crick led to lasting bitterness over their use of X-ray photographs taken by Rosalind Franklin at Kings College London, whose crucial role they never fully acknowledged. *See* Brenda Maddox, *The Double Helix and the "Wronged Heroine"*, 421 NATURE 407 (2003).

code, containing the instructions used by genes to make proteins. Crick played a major role in working out this code—the key to life itself, shared by every living organism on Earth.

Nigel Hawkes, *Crick: He Revealed the Beauty and Code of Biology*, THE TIMES (London), July 30, 2004, at 2.

Watson and Crick received the Nobel Prize for Medicine in 1962 "for their discoveries concerning the molecular structure of nucleic acids and its significance for information transfer in living material."

J.D. Watson & F.H.C. Crick, *A Structure for Deoxyribose Nucleic Acid*

171 NATURE 737 (1953).

We wish to put forward a radically different structure for the salt of deoxyribose nucleic acid. This structure has two helical chains each coiled round the same axis. We have made the usual chemical assumptions, namely, that each chain consists of phosphate diester groups joining ï-D-deoxyribofuranose residues with 3',5' linkages. The two chains (but not their bases) are related by a dyad perpendicular to the fibre axis. Both chains follow right-handed helices, but owing to the dyad the sequences of the atoms in the two chains run in opposite directions.

The structure is an open one, and its water content is rather high. At lower water contents we would expect the bases to tilt so that the structure could become more compact.

The novel feature of the structure is the manner in which the two chains are held together by the purine and pyrimidine bases. The planes of the bases are perpendicular to the fibre axis. They are joined together in pairs, a single base from the other chain, so that the two lie side by side with identical z-co-ordinates. One of the pair must be a purine and the other a pyrimidine for bonding to occur. The hydrogen bonds are made as follows: purine position 1 to pyrimidine position 1; purine position 6 to pyrimidine position 6.

If it is assumed that the bases only occur in the structure in the most plausible tautomeric forms (that is, with the keto rather than the enol configurations) it is found that only specific pairs of bases can bond together. These pairs are: adenine (purine) with thymine (pyrimidine), and guanine (purine) with cytosine (pyrimidine).

In other words, if an adenine forms one member of a pair, on either chain, then on these assumptions the other member must be thymine; similarly for guanine and cytosine. The sequence of bases on a single chain does not appear to be restricted in any way. However, if only specific pairs of bases can be formed, it follows that if the sequence of bases on one chain is given, then the sequence on the other chain is automatically determined.

———

More than fifty years later, the legacy of Watson and Crick's findings continues to flourish, as they provided the impetus to scrutinize DNA, the genetic material of life, more fully. The structure defined by Watson and Crick gave scientists a critical tool for revealing how DNA encodes the genetic information that is passed from adults to offspring. Now, the DNA of any organism can be represented as a letter code, loaded into a computer database, and shared internationally among scientists. DNA technology has become essential to understanding the fundamental processes of life and the causes of health and disease.

Tom Clarke, *DNA's Family Tree*

422 Nature 791 (2003).

The structure made it obvious that the molecule encodes information. Almost as important, however, "it explained how all that information could be compacted into a cell," says Robert Olby, a science historian at the University of Pittsburgh in Pennsylvania. DNA's tight spiral showed how genetic information can be packed into chromosomes.

. . .

Through the 1950s, researchers put flesh on the bones of Watson and Crick's structure. In 1955, geneticist Seymour Benzer of Purdue University, Indiana, showed that genes in bacteria consist of long stretches of DNA letters, and that just one error could render them useless.

And once researchers discovered how cells boss their genetic information about, they could really start making use of DNA. In 1956, biochemist Arthur Kornberg found the enzyme used to copy DNA, a finding that earned him a Nobel Prize. In 1957 Crick cracked the genetic code, showing how genetic information is translated into the protein molecules that do the work in cells.

In the late 1950s and '60s, researchers discovered enzymes that could split the two strands of DNA apart, stick them back together again, and even bite into DNA strands at the sites of specific sequences. These molecular tools made it possible to cut out lengths of DNA from one organism and paste them into another—genetic engineering was born.

The other major step was figuring out how to read genetic sentences. DNA sequencing, as it became known, was pioneered by the British biochemist Frederick Sanger.

Sanger developed a way of marking the bases of DNA with radioactive tags that could be read using X-rays. Using this technique, he produced the first complete list of the DNA letters needed to code for the structure of a complete protein, insulin, a feat that netted him his second Nobel Prize in 1980.

Sanger's invention gave birth to the science of genomics. With it, we gained the power to compare genes—allowing us to analyze patterns of disease, the evolution of species, and the history of human groups and individuals.

C. DECODING THE STRUCTURE OF LIFE: MAPPING THE HUMAN GENOME

1. TIMELINE AND ACCOMPLISHMENTS

Building upon the seminal work of Mendel and Watson and Crick, researchers involved in the Human Genome Project sequenced the human genome, providing the order of base pairs (adenine, thymine, guanine, and cytosine) in human DNA. Prior to the completion of this 15–year project, the largest genome, or complete set of an organism's DNA, to be sequenced belonged to the fruit fly.[2] Scientists' ability to replicate these findings with the human genome, which is 25 times as large and infinitely more complex, shows the recent rapid advancements in genetic research. The Human Genome Project, which originated when Congress funded the National Institutes of Health's (NIH) and Department of Energy's (DOE) efforts to sequence DNA, has given scientists a more systematic understanding of the human genome.

Francis S. Collins et al., *New Goals for the U.S. Human Genome Project: 1998–2003*

282 SCI. 682 (1998).

The Human Genome Project (HGP) is fulfilling its promise as the single most important project in biology and the biomedical sciences—one that will permanently change biology and medicine. With the recent completion of the genome sequences of several microorganisms.... the door has opened wide on the era of whole genome science. The ability to analyze entire genomes is accelerating gene discovery and revolutionizing the breadth and depth of biological questions that can be addressed in model organisms. These exciting successes confirm the view that acquisition of a comprehensive, high-quality human genome sequence will have unprecedented impact and long-lasting value for basic biology, biomedical research, biotechnology, and health care. The transition to sequence-based biology will spur continued progress in understanding gene-environment interactions and in development of highly accurate DNA-based medical diagnostics and therapeutics.

Human DNA sequencing, the flagship endeavor of the HGP, is entering its decisive phase. It will be the project's central focus during the next 5 years. While partial subsets of the DNA sequence ... have proven enormously valuable, experience with simpler organisms confirms that there can be no substitute for the complete genome sequence....

Availability of the human genome sequence presents unique scientific opportunities, chief among them the study of natural genetic variation in humans. Genetic or DNA sequence variation is the fundamental raw material for evolution. Importantly, it is also the basis for variations in risk among individuals for numerous medically important, genetically complex human diseases. An understanding of the relationship between genetic variation and disease risk promises to change significantly the future

---

2. The fruit fly genome was not completed until March 2000.

prevention and treatment of illness. The new focus on genetic variation, as well as other applications of the human genome sequence, raises additional ethical, legal, and social issues that need to be anticipated, considered, and resolved.

NOTES AND QUESTIONS

The ultimate goal of the Human Genome Project was to develop effective approaches for disease prevention, diagnosis, and treatment through a better understanding of the contribution of genes to the development and functioning of the human body. It was designed to expand our knowledge and grasp of the interactions among genes and between genes and environmental influences. Researchers' specific goals—many of which are still ongoing—were to: locate and map all human genes; discover the entire DNA sequence of the human genome; store this information in databases accessible to researchers and the public; create resources for data analysis; map and sequence the genomes of other living organisms; and study the impact that genetic information and technologies may have on society, including ethical and legal ramifications.

The culmination of these efforts was the publication of the draft sequence in 2001, which provided insight into 90% of the human genome's three billion base pairs. International Human Genome Sequencing Consortium, *Initial Sequencing and Analysis of the Human Genome*, 409 NATURE 860–921 (2001). In April 2003, the International Human Genome Sequencing Consortium announced its task was complete and published a final product in which nearly all bases were identified in the correct order.

Elizabeth Pennisi, *Human Genome: Reaching Their Goal Early, Sequencing Labs Celebrate*

300 SCI. 409 (2003).

It may sound like science by press release, as no formal report has been published, but the news is spectacular all the same: The International Human Genome Sequencing Consortium announced on 14 April that it has completed its work. In a note of rare unanimity, the leaders of the United States, Britain, China, France, Germany, and Japan issued a joint proclamation honoring their scientists who worked on the project.

Twice before—in 2000 and 2001—researchers celebrated draft sequences of the human genome. But the new product is much more complete and of higher quality: 99% of what can be done with current technology is now done, sequencers say. And virtually all the bases are now identified in their proper order, which was not true of the draft versions.

. . .

Completing this labor-intensive phase will come as a big relief for many involved. They were spurred to a faster pace in 1998, when sequencer J. Craig Venter boasted that his new company, Celera Genomics in Rockville, Maryland, would sequence the human genome first. The consortium scrambled to prevent that from happening. Both Celera and the public groups completed drafts in June 2000 and published reports on them simultaneously in February 2001.

Once that milestone had been reached, [questions remained as to whether the public project would finish first]. But the public consortium hunkered down and delivered on the promise 2 years ahead of schedule, says Francis Collins, director of the National Human Genome Research Institute (NHGRI). The U.S. share amounted to about 53% of the 2.9 billion bases, costing $2.7 billion over the project's 15–year duration.

The consortium set out to meet a standard of one error in 10,000 bases; the just-finished version is 10 times better than that. Now only the most difficult regions remain to be done, including about 400 stretches of repetitive DNA and centromeres, which divide the chromosomes. "This is a reference sequence," says Collins, one that will be used by biologists for many years to come.

Even so, sequencers have not yet determined the number of human genes. Three years ago they were so confident that they would have the answer by now that many made bets on their predictions, planning to declare the winner this spring. That's not going to happen, says Collins; there is no clear answer from computer programs that are trained to identify genes. Two years ago, the two drafts indicated there were 35,000 to 45,000 genes. Now the rough estimate "stands a little under 30,000," says Collins.

As the genome community inches toward an accurate gene count, it's also endorsing new, even grander research schemes. . . .

If sequencing the genome was akin to landing a human on the moon, then this new vision calls for landing more humans on the moon, says Edward Rubin, director of the Department of Energy (DOE) Joint Genome Institute. DOE intends to focus on sequencing nonmammalian genomes, including microbes important as potential energy sources. But NHGRI's [broad agenda, unveiled last week,] has many elements, such as extending the haplotype map, a five-nation effort to describe individual and group DNA variations. A project called ENCODE will determine the functions of the genes. And Collins hopes to launch a resource to enable researchers to screen new proteins for interactions with any of about a million small molecules, potentially to find drug candidates. . . .

Nevertheless, the completed genome is already making biologists' work easier, Pollard says—not just by identifying genes but also by revealing what regulates gene expression. He predicts that biology will continue to reap broad benefits: For that reason, it's the right time for Collins and his collaborators "to set off a few fireworks."

NOTES AND QUESTIONS

The sequencing of the human genome is a scientific milestone, opening the door to breathtaking possibilities in medicine and public health. As we will see, the human genome project offers the possibility of developing better prevention and treatment, not only for genetic diseases, but also for complex chronic diseases, such as cancers and cardiovascular disease, that affect large populations.

Despite the undoubted prospective benefits, the potential for harm is apparent. Genetic information can deeply affect personal privacy, stigmatize individuals and groups, and even result in discrimination in employment and insurance. To address these issues, Congress devoted 5% of human genome funding to the exploration of the ethical, legal, and social issues (ELSI). *See* Robert Cook–Deegan, *The Human Genome Project: The Formation of Federal Policies in the United States, 1986–1990, in* Biomedical Politics 99–175 (Kathi E. Hanna ed., 1991). The ELSI program placed science and ethics on a parallel track—both forms of exploration could go ahead simultaneously. Was this a reasoned method to ensure safe and ethical practice in science and medicine? Could some of the legal and ethical issues have been foreseen, thereby providing boundaries for the scientific enterprise? Is it possible that the science will progress so quickly that sober ethical reflection may be too late? For further discussion of the ELSI project, *see* Sec. IV, *infra*.

2. THE HAPMAP PROJECT

A primary goal of the Public Consortium was to make a complete sequence of the human genome widely available for scientists and researchers to stimulate research that would improve human health and serve the greatest public good. In furtherance of this objective, scientists and funding groups from six countries launched a three-year project called the International Haplotype Map (HapMap) Project in 2002. The HapMap will make the knowledge gained about the human genome easier to use by describing the human genome in terms of haplotypes. The HapMap project is based on the premise that genes tend to be inherited in blocks of closely associated genes. In these genes, single nucleotide polymorphisms (SNPs) are the points where individuals differ in their genetic sequences. On a given block, the pattern of SNPs is known as a haplotype. The value of the HapMap project lies in allowing scientists to examine the approximately 500,000 tag SNPs from the haplotype blocks instead of the 10 million SNPs in the human genome.

Xavier Bosch, *Researchers Try to Unlock Human Genome Potential*

360 The Lancet 1481 (2002).

An international consortium of researchers has launched a US$100 million, 3–year project to create a new map of the human genome, which aims to understand how common patterns of variation among genes are related to disease. The International Haplotype Map (HapMap) Project is a collaborative effort between the US National Institutes of Health, Canada, Japan, China, the SNP consortium, and the Wellcome Trust Sanger Institute in the UK.

This project is "indeed groundbreaking and exciting", Francis Collins, director of the National Human Genome Research Institute, Bethesda, USA, told *The Lancet*. The HapMap will be a "powerful tool to help us take the next quantum leap toward understanding the fundamental contribution that genes make to common illnesses like cancer, diabetes, and mental illness." The theory behind the project is that the variation in genetic code from person to person may not be a disordered, random scattering of single base variation but probably exists as ordered blocks of sequence variation or haplotypes.

"The benefit of being able to address gene mapping from the perspective of blocks or haplotypes, rather than single SNPs, is greatly diminished cost and time required to identify genes involved in common genetic diseases", says Peter Doris, Center for Human Genetics, University of Texas Health Science Center. But he notes that "such economies derive from facts that are not yet in evidence."

Furthermore, "while the common disease/common variant hypothesis is reasonable and supported by some existing knowledge, whether it is correct or not is presently unknowable." If it is not correct, he argues, the investment of money, talent, and time may be a costly error. Collins says, "I suspect it [the hypothesis] will not be correct for all disease genes . . . but if it is even correct for a modest fraction it will be fantastically useful."

To create the HapMap, DNA will be taken from blood samples from 200 to 400 people in widely distributed geographic regions. Samples will be collected from people in Nigeria, Japan, China and US residents with ancestry from northern and western Europe. The sampling strategy has been designed to ensure that participants can give full, informed consent without giving away any identifying medical or personal information.

The samples will be processed and stored at the Coriell Institute for Medical Research, Camden, NJ. Then researchers from academic centres, non-profit research groups, and private companies in Japan, UK, Canada, China, and USA will analyse the samples to generate the HapMap, the results of which will be freely available on the internet.

NOTES AND QUESTIONS

1. *What do HapMap Data Reveal About the Human Experience?* The entire human population shares 99.9% of their DNA sequences. What do these data tell us about the sameness or differences among groups of different race and origin? The remaining 0.1% of DNA sequences contains the genetic variants that influence how people differ in their risk of disease and in their response to environmental stressors or pharmaceuticals. Because common haplotypes occur with varying frequency among different populations, data for the HapMap will be gathered from four native populations and the SNP and haplotype frequencies for each population will be calculated. Could the comparisons among these groups and the wider population result in stigmatization or discrimination of persons within the group? If a variant associated with a certain disease has a higher frequency among one population and the risks associated with that variant are over generalized to members of that population, what are the likely social implications? Could the HapMap project's categorization of an individuals' genetic data on the basis of a population's ancestral geography result in labels such as "race," which is largely socially constructed, being incorrectly viewed as a precise and highly meaningful biological construct? Greater understanding of the genetic basis of race could lead to health improvements or new kinds of stereotypes. *See* Robin Marantz Henig, *The Genome in Black and White (and Gray)*, N.Y. TIMES MAG., Oct. 10, 2004, p. 46. What might scientists or policy makers do to prevent the misuse of genomic information for the purposes of stigma or discrimination? *See* further, Sec. IV, *infra.*

2. *Indigenous Groups and Genetics Research.* Should scientists be concerned about their choice of vulnerable native populations? Some geneticists have attempted to gather genetic information from indigenous groups facing extinction. Is genetic research on vulnerable populations appropriate?

Indigenous peoples' organizations now question the purpose behind research that is done on indigenous population groups. In certain parts of the world, indigenous peoples are facing cultural extinction. Where there is mass logging of tropical rain forests, for example, indigenous people who live there are depleted of food and water resources, and driven from their homes. They eventually join the ranks of waged laborers in logging camps and cash crop plantations. As their social fabric breaks up, they are in danger of losing their identity and culture. The struggle to survive as a people is a pressing concern of many groups. In this context, the call for researchers to collect genetic materials from indigenous populations, before they disappear as distinctive genetic groups, may appear to some as grossly insensitive and callous.

Chee Heng Leng et al., International Bioethics Committee, Bioethics and Human Population Genetics Research 16, United Nations Educational, Scientific and Cultural Organization, CIP/BIO/95/CONF.002/5 (Nov. 15, 1995).

3. *Is Public Access Consistent with Private Innovation?* The HapMap policy of openness has led to concerns about what Francis Collins called "parasitic intellectual property claims." Carina Dennis, *The Rough Guide to the Genome*, 425 NATURE 758 (2003). Scientists could combine public data with their own, and then patent the findings in a way that restricts others' ability to work freely with the HapMap data. Is it likely that scientists will use freely available information from the HapMap for personal gain? For a more complete discussion of intellectual property issues in genetics, *see* Marco Segre & Edna Sadayo Miazato Iwamura, *Bioethics, Intellectual Property, and Genomics*, 56 REV. HOSP. CLIN. FAC. MED. S. PAULO 97 (2001). *See also* Sec. III, *infra.*

D.   FROM GENOMICS TO PROTEOMICS

Upon completion of the Human Genome Project, the proteomics era began. To researchers' surprise, the Human Genome Project showed that humans possess only 10,000–20,000 more genes than the fruit fly or the roundworm. It became clear that proteins, rather than genes, are responsible for an organism's complexity. Therefore, the key to understanding health and disease within an organism is to understand how its proteins function.

Vicki Brower, *Proteomics: Biology in the Post–Genomic Era*

2 EMBO REPORTS 558–9 (2001).

In June 2001, when the Human Genome Project and Celera completed the first maps of the human genome, Francis Collins, head of the government-sponsored HGP, warned that only then would the real race begin. This was a prophetic insight indeed. No sooner was the human genome decoded than we found ourselves in the "post-genomic era"—where the name of the game is proteomics. Proteomics is not only the systematic separation, cataloguing and study of all of the proteins produced in an organism, it is also the study of how proteins change structure, interact with other proteins, and ultimately give rise to disease or health in an organism. Since its application in drug discovery promises huge economic returns, it comes as no surprise that biotechnology, computer and software companies around the world are rushing to pour capital and resources into this new research field.

Proteomics is more complex by several orders of magnitude than genomics, with no one company, laboratory or consortium remotely able to run the race alone. Moreover, no one technology will be able to fulfill proteomics' numerous tasks, and new developments are sorely needed.

With the publication of the draft of the human genome in the February 16, 2001 issues of *Science* and *Nature* came what many had already suspected: instead of the earlier estimate of about 100,000 human genes, the actual count reduced this figure by 75%. If humans have only 10,000–20,000 more genes than the fruitfly and the roundworm, then the big question is how do we manage to be so complex? The answer: proteins—not genes—are responsible for an organism's complexity. The interaction of proteins in a complex network adds up to how an organism functions. The key to understanding health and disease within an organism is, therefore, to understand how its proteins function. In a multicellular organism, one needs to be able to look at the entire system in an integrated way. Proteomics is the study of where each protein is located in a cell, when the protein is present and for how long, and with which other proteins it is interacting. Proteomics means looking at many events at the same time and connecting them. New tools are necessary to enable the study of this web of events—to create a movie, rather than a static snapshot of the activities taking place.

A further dimension was added to this complex picture when scientists from the University of Pennsylvania School of Medicine reported this May in *Nature* that proteins are more active and dynamic than they had imagined. The interior of a protein is much more liquid-like than scientists originally anticipated. Everything is moving, and it's moving all the time, very fast.... [Proteins] move so much that it dramatically influences how they work. This is the beginning of a long new story that will have a lot to do with understanding protein function. The concept of proteins as dynamic entities may ultimately help scientists target more accessible sites for drug development.

Currently, drug developers are working with only about 400–500 targets, many of which are receptors. With the shift from genomics to proteomics and the concomitant evolution of technology, many scientists expect the number of potential "druggable" targets to expand many hundred-fold to between 10,000 and 20,000. With such numbers, it will become necessary to winnow through targets rapidly and accurately to determine which should be pursued. The marriage of business and science within the proteomics field indeed promises to achieve this.

A formidable task for proteomics is to develop new tools that can help scientists analyze cellular function with speed and accuracy. Proteins are too numerous, diverse and interactive to be studied by a single method. Proteomics, therefore, is comprised of a number of interrelated, overlapping disciplines: functional and structural genomics, functional and structural proteomics, and bioinformatics—a convergence of "wet" and "dry" laboratories.

Jocelyn Kaiser, *Public–Private Group Maps Out Initiatives*

296 Sci. 827 (2002).

A new group hoping to spur a global effort to determine the structure and function of all proteins made by the human body kicked into gear last week. The Human Proteome Organization (HUPO), an international alliance of industry, academic, and government members, laid out its first set of initiatives and has begun knocking on industry doors for funding.

HUPO was formed about a year ago by a group of scientists who wanted to make sure that companies don't lock up basic proteomics data under trade secrecy. The founders also wanted to include more countries than participated in the Human Genome Project. . . .

[HUPO's initial list of projects] is a mix of technology, tools, and research. For example, HUPO's bioinformatics plan would develop community-wide standards for presenting mass spectrometry and protein-protein interaction data. Another initiative would create a collection of antibodies for the primary proteins made by the 30,000 or more human genes. HUPO also wants to identify thousands of new proteins present in small amounts in blood, which would be very valuable to companies developing diagnostic tests. All the data would be freely available through public databases. . . .

. . .

While HUPO is forging ahead with its first projects, the U.S. National Institutes of Health (NIH) is still mapping out its own proteomics strategy. At a meeting last week in Bethesda, Maryland, proteomics experts went back and forth over possible recommendations on the best way for NIH to encourage the field's development. . . .

NOTES AND QUESTIONS

Proteomics is the study of where each protein is located in a cell, when and for how long the protein is present, and with which other proteins it interacts. Unlike the genome, which is relatively static, the proteome changes constantly in response to tens of thousands of intra-and extra-cellular environmental signals. The proteome varies with health or disease, the nature of each tissue, the stages of cell development, and effects of drug treatments. As such, the proteome is defined as the proteins present in a sample (a tissue, organism, or cell culture) at a certain point in time. Because proteins are too numerous, diverse, and interactive to be studied through a single method, proteomics is comprised of numerous interrelated disciplines including functional and structural genomics, functional and structural proteomics, and bioinformatics. These disciplines require the simultaneous monitoring of different cellular activity so researchers can comprehend the connection between these activities. Technology currently lags behind these demands, and a primary task of these growing disciplines is to develop new tools that can help scientists analyze cellular function quickly and accurately.

The promise that proteomics holds for drug discovery has peaked the interest of biotechnology and computer and software companies which are pouring capital and resources into this growing field. Most pharmaceuticals are directed against proteins and the more that is known about them, the more effective drugs may be. This source of funding is crucial to a field that demands large-scale, costly projects.

However, important questions remain. Will the biotechnology industry make sufficient investments in the program and will their investments be targeted toward the most important health problems? Will the private sector insist on exercising control of the direction of research and hold the results as proprietary information? Will the role of the private sector, therefore, impede certain important discoveries? Some researchers have suggested that a dedicated funding pool and collaborative effort similar to that established for the Human Genome Project are needed to ensure that proteomics attains its projected status as "a watershed in biology and medicine." Mike Tyers & Matthias Mann, *From Genomics to Proteomics*, 422 NATURE 196 (2003). Do you agree and, if so, how much public funding should be devoted to such efforts?

As with genomics, proteomics raises the crucial questions of the nature and scope of private investment, the interaction between private and public access to information, and the best ways to regulate the emerging field. The goal is to spur innovation, pool scarce resources, make advances publicly accessible, and do all of this in an ethically acceptable manner. Needless to say, these are not easy goals to achieve and, in many cases, the objectives are in tension with one another.

II.   THE ROLE OF GENOMICS IN UNDERSTANDING HEALTH AND DISEASE

Some scholars use the terms genetics and genomics interchangeable, but there is a difference. Genetics is the study of "single genes and their effects," while genomics is the study of the "functions and interactions of all the genes in the genome." *See* Alan E. Guttmacher & Francis S. Collins, *Genomic Medicine: A Primer*, 347 NEW ENG. J. MED. 1512 (2002). Muin Khoury reflects on the meaning and importance of genomics:

> This definition implies a quantitative difference between the two fields (the study of multiple genes vs. one gene, which could make genetics part of genomics). In addition, there is a qualitative shift between genetics and genomics in medical and public health applications, ranging from the concept of disease in genetics to the concept of information in genomics. Perhaps more accurately, this shift may be best viewed as a continuum with no clear breakpoint, from single gene disorders with high penetrance to genetic information obtained from multiple loci in somatic cells.
>
> The practice of medical genetics has traditionally focused on those conditions that are known to be due to mutations in single genes (e.g., Huntington disease), whole chromosomes (e.g., trisomy 21 in Down syndrome[3]), or associated with birth defects and developmental disabilities. For these conditions, a traditional genetic services model applies with its accompanying medical processes (genetic counseling/testing/management) and public health processes (assuring delivery of genetic services and newborn screening). On the other hand, the practice of genomics in medicine and public health will center on information resulting from variation at one or multiple loci and strong interactions with environmental factors (broadly defined to include diet, drugs, infectious agents, chemicals, physical agents, and behavioral factors). As will be illustrated, genetic information can come from inherited variation in germ cells or acquired variation in somatic

---

3. Down syndrome is caused by trisomy 21—the inheritance of an extra copy of chro-   mosome 21.

cells[4] (such as in cancer) or could be associated with gene products and expression. Such information can be used in diagnosis, treatment, prediction, and prevention of all diseases, not only genetic disorders. For traditional single-gene disorders, when genetic information is obtained on patients and their relatives, it is used for diagnosing or predicting a genetic disease state. For most human diseases, however, genetic information at one locus is modified by information from many other loci and their interaction with nongenetic risk factors, so much so, that the sum of such genetic information cannot be thought of as disease state but more as biological markers or disease risk factors.

Muin J. Khoury, *Genetics and Genomics in Practice: The Continuum from Genetic Disease to Genetic Information in Health and Disease*, 5 GENETICS IN MED. 261 (2003).

The following section explores the role of genomics in health and health care. The discussion ranges from current applications of genetic knowledge to future uses. We begin with the most frequently used genetic methods—testing and screening. The section goes on to "imagine the future." There are multiple potential applications of genetic knowledge including pharmacogenomics, gene therapy, and genetic enhancement that may revolutionize (for good or bad) health care and public health.

A.   GENETIC TESTING AND SCREENING

Kennedy Institute of Ethics, *Genetic Testing and Genetic Screening*

KIEJ (Updated 2004).

The completion of the mapping of the human genome . . . shifts the spotlight of ethical inquiry from general questions about genetic research to specific issues with such topics as genetic screening. Ethical dilemmas with genetic testing and screening were foreseen over three decades ago by bioethicists who asked whether questionable applications could stop "legitimate pursuits" and whether genetic disease might come to be viewed as "transmissible" in the sense of being contagious.

. . .

In 1983, the report of the U.S. President's Commission for the Study of Ethical Problems in Medicine and Biomedical and Behavioral Research predicted that before the end of the century genetic screening and counseling would become major components of both public health and individual medical care. Following the identification of a gene linked to breast cancer, *BRCA1*, Dr. Francis Sellers Collins, director of the National Center for Human Genome Research, said that "it is not inconceivable that every woman in America may want to be screened for this gene. The economic, ethical, and counseling issues will be very daunting." While genetic testing for *BRCA* mutations has been available commercially since 1996, the results of an evaluation done by the Centers for Disease Control and

---

4. Germ cells are sperm, ovum, and their developmental precursors; somatic cells are all cells other than germ cells.

Prevention (CDC) indicated that population-based screening "... is not recommended because of the complexity of test interpretation and limited data on clinical validity and utility." Educational materials about gene tests and international directories of clinics and laboratories providing genetic testing services can be found on the Web.

As a greater proportion of the U.S. population lives beyond 85 years of age, interest in genetic testing for end-of-life conditions such as Alzheimer Disease (AD) continues to grow. Stephen G. Post observes that the "too-hopeful" general public has assigned a degree of scientific certainty to the as yet preliminary genetic findings for AD, and that teaching critical thinking skills about genetic testing to the general public is of the highest priority.

The [US Congress' Office of Technology Assessment (OTA)] defines genetic testing as "the use of specific assays to determine the genetic status of individuals already suspected to be at high risk for a particular inherited condition. The terms genetic test, genetic assay, and genetic analysis are used interchangeably to mean the actual laboratory examination of samples." In contrast, genetic screening usually uses the same assays employed for genetic testing but is distinguished from genetic testing by its target population. The National Academy of Sciences (NAS) defines screening as the systematic search of populations for persons with latent, early, or asymptomatic disease.

Philip Boyle points out that the language used to describe genetic variation is important and asks what words should be used: *"Defects, flaws, deleterious genes, disorders,* or the more neutral *conditions*? Using words such as *normal*—and its corollary, *abnormal*—is likely to foster stigmatization and discrimination."

Areas of focus in genetic testing include: prenatal diagnosis, newborn screening, carrier screening, forensic screening, and susceptibility screening.

Prenatal diagnosis discerns whether a fetus is at risk for various identifiable genetic diseases or traits. Prenatal diagnosis is made using amniotic fluid, fetal cells, and fetal or maternal blood cells obtained during amniocentesis testing; alpha fetoprotein assays or chorionic villus sampling; or ultrasound tomography, which creates fetal images on a screen. Another method, known as fetoscopy, uses a camera on a needle inserted in the uterus to view the fetus. Since prenatal screening began in 1966, the number of metabolic defects and genetic disorders that can be diagnosed prenatally has expanded greatly. There is also discussion of requiring testing for parents who are participating in an in vitro fertilization program and are at genetic risk. Preimplantation testing of embryos might ensure that only embryos free of genetic disease or problem traits would be placed in the uterus.[5]

Newborn screening involves the analysis of blood or tissue samples taken in early infancy in order to detect genetic diseases for which early intervention can avert serious health problems or death. Newborn screen-

---

5. [Eds.—Prenatal screening will be discussed further in terms of genetic enhancement, *infra*.

ing first came into use in the early 1960s with the ability to test newborns for a rare metabolic disease, phenylketonuria (PKU), which causes mental retardation and can be prevented by following a special diet. Two other examples of newborn screening, in place since the 1970s, are the testing of African–American infants for sickle cell anemia and Ashkenazic Jews for Tay–Sachs disease.

Carrier screening identifies individuals with a gene or a chromosome abnormality that may cause problems either for offspring or the person screened. The testing of blood or tissue samples can indicate the existence of a particular genetic trait, changes in chromosomes, or changes in DNA that are associated with inherited diseases in asymptomatic individuals. Groups tested include persons at risk or a cross-section of the general public for occurrence statistics. Examples of carrier screening include the previously mentioned tests for sickle cell anemia and for Tay–Sachs disease. In the last few years, screening tests have also been developed for cystic fibrosis, Duchenne muscular dystrophy, hemophilia, Huntington's disease, and neurofibromatosis. Recently it also has become possible to identify certain cancer prone individuals through genetic testing.

Forensic testing, which is the newest area to use information obtained from genetic testing, seeks to discover a genetic linkage between suspects and evidence discovered in criminal investigations. Test results have been presented as proof of innocence or guilt in court cases, and jury verdicts have been based on this type of genetic evidence. Critics note that forensic laboratories often test just once, unlike research laboratories, which test many times, and that mistakes can be made. Concern is expressed, too, about the confidentiality of DNA profiles obtained from criminal investigations and stored in national police databanks. Debate now centers on standards and quality control, but it is accepted that the technologies accurately detect genetic differences between humans and are "new, powerful tools to clear the innocent and convict the guilty." Since DNA is unique, many people are reluctant to see such information become part of any national database, which might include information not only about identity but also about proclivity toward disease or behavior.

Finally, **susceptibility screening** is used to identify workers who may be susceptible to toxic substances that are found in their workplace and may cause future disabilities. In 1986, Morton Hunt wrote in the *New York Times Magazine* that 390,000 workers become disabled by occupational illness each year; he thinks these illnesses are precipitated by genetic hypersusceptibility since co-workers are unaffected.

In an early classic work, the National Academy of Sciences says screening can be used for medical intervention and research; for reproductive information; for enumeration, monitoring, and surveillance; and for registries of genetic disease and disability. Many factors affect the use of any routine screening: customs of care (including both professional guidelines and possible malpractice); education of the public about the results and limitations of genetic testing; availability, training, and education of personnel to perform testing; financing of such screening (particularly third-party payor responsibilities); stigmatization and discrimination issues; quality assurance of laboratories and DNA test kits; and costs and cost effectiveness.

.   .   .

Not everyone thinks that the growing field of genetic testing and screening is beneficial. The potential problems raised both by those who favor testing and screening and those who oppose it are similar, but one faction thinks that regulatory or legislative solutions to the problems can be found while concerned opponents find the knowledge itself less valuable and the problems unsolvable. Opponents of widespread genetic testing and screening regard the acceptance of eugenic theories and scientists' inability to control outcomes of their genetic research as dangerous. They foresee a need to outlaw technologies that threaten privacy or civil rights and a need to protect against genetic discrimination. "We need to engage in active debates about the practical consequences of genetic forecasts for our self-image, our health, our work lives, our social relationships, and our privacy." Disability advocates and feminists have criticized genetic screening because they think it fosters intolerance for less than perfect people.

Another possible negative effect is the pressure that might be placed on individuals, as a result of cost-benefit analysis, to test or to be tested. Individuals might thereby be forced to know their genetic predispositions, to tell others, or to act to save society long-term costs resulting in a "new eugenics based, not on undesirable characteristics, but rather on cost-saving." Now that British insurers have government approval to use the results of screening for Huntington's disease to assess insurance premiums, consumer groups say that individuals will be reluctant to have such tests and risk denial of coverage. On the other hand, Lowe points out that genetic testing will not create more illness than presently exists, and it could lead to a reduction in costs due to early treatment.[3] Lippman suggests that control over genetics would create an elite who could control the general populace, particularly if mandatory testing or intervention were viewed as a community good.[4] Other potential adverse effects of such screening include the development of prejudice against those tested and found at risk and the feeling of tested persons that they are predetermined victims of fate or are being branded as "abnormal."

.   .   .

Issues of confidentiality loom large in discussions of genetic testing and screening. According to the Privacy Commission of Canada, genetic privacy has two dimensions: protection from the intrusions of others and protection from one's own secrets. . . .

The President's Commission, in a 1983 study, concluded that genetic information "should not be given to unrelated third parties, such as insurers or employers, without the explicit and informed consent of the person screened or a surrogate for that person." The Commission recom-

---

3. Robert Lowe, *Genetic Testing and Insurance: Apocalypse Now?* 40 DRAKE LAW REVIEW 507–532 (1991).

4. Abby Lippman, *Mother Matters: A Fresh Look at Prenatal Genetic Testing*, 5 ISSUES IN REPRODUCTIVE AND GENETIC ENGINEERING 141–154 (1992).

mended that information stored in computers should be coded and that compulsory genetic screening cannot be justified to create a health gene pool or to reduce health costs. More recently, the NIH/DOE Working Group on the Ethical, Legal and Social Implications of Human Genome Research recommended that health insurers should consider a moratorium on the use of genetic tests in underwriting.

In the area of data protection and professional secrecy, genetic information for health care, the diagnosis or prevention of disease, and for research should be stored separately from other personal records. In addition, those handling the information should be bound by professional rules of confidentiality and legislative rules, and any unexpected findings should be given only to the person tested.

The literature on genetic discrimination suggests several areas of sensitivity: the workplace, where employers may choose to test job applicants, or those already employed, for susceptibility to toxic substances or for genetic variations that could lead to future disabilities, thereby raising health or workmen's compensation costs; the insurers (either life or health insurance companies) who might use genetic information or tests as criteria for denying coverage or require reproductive testing to be done for cost containment purposes; and law enforcement officials, who may test and/or use information without informed consent. Thomas H. Murray thinks that "genetic testing in the workplace was a putative public health measure in its old form and now is used as a means of saving money or promoting health." He opines that access to genetic testing involves considerations of justice since genetic testing competes with other scarce resources and it may emphasize racial and ethnic differences.

. . .

As early as the 1970s, the National Academy of Sciences looked at legal principles and raised questions about the extent of disclosure of test results to the person screened, the extent of disclosure to others without the consent of the person screened, the constitutional barriers to mandatory screening by states, and the constitutional difficulties encountered if screening is done by racial or ethnic group. In a 1992 report, OTA offers six areas for possible action by Congress: genetics education for the public; genetics training and education of health care professionals; discrimination (access to health care coverage); laboratory and other regulation; means of automating diagnostics; and facilitating use of genetic assays in clinical practice.

In an article aimed at family physicians, Howard Stein writes of the physician-patient relationship and reminds his fellow physicians that "[g]enetic knowledge does not occur in a social vacuum. The scientific account is neither the only story, nor the entire story. Decisions to know or not to know, to have children or not to have children, to label as diseased or not, are part of wider life histories, language, and group fantasies." Legal challenges, government regulation, extensive education, and collective bargaining will all be part of the ongoing process needed to solve the complex dilemmas that result from widespread genetic testing and genetic screening.

NOTES AND QUESTIONS

1. *The Future of Genetic Testing.* There are currently some 1,000 genetic tests, 90% of which are related to single-gene disorders. Gene tests (also called DNA-based tests) are the newest and most sophisticated techniques to test for genetic disorders and involve direct examination of the DNA molecule itself. Other genetic tests include biochemical tests for gene products such as enzymes and other proteins and for microscopic examination of stained or fluorescent chromosomes. Currently, testing can cost hundreds or thousands of dollars, depending on the number of mutations tested. However, with advancing technology, scientists are confident that genetic testing will become far less expensive and therefore more accessible to the larger population. In the near future it may be possible for a physician to order a battery of genetic tests from a single drop of blood at a reasonable cost. This may dramatically improve lives by clarifying diagnoses and directing physicians toward appropriate interventions. Interventions can include genetic therapy, changes in diet or environmental exposures, or reproductive counseling. Despite the benefits, widespread availability of genetic tests raises difficult social, ethical, and legal questions.

2. *Would Widespread Use of Genetic Testing Lead to Breaches of Privacy, Stigmatization, and Discrimination?* Much of the early literature on genetics focused on the potential for invasion of privacy, stigma, and discrimination. Advocacy groups feared that genetic information was deeply private, revealing something quite intimate about individual lives. If this information were disclosed to family and friends it could cause stigmatization; if it were disclosed to employers it could cause discrimination in the workplace; and if it were disclosed to insurers it could result in exclusion from coverage. As a result, much legislative activity has been devoted toward genetic privacy and anti-discrimination at the federal and state level. *See* Lawrence O. Gostin et al., GENETICS POLICY AND LAW: A REPORT FOR POLICYMAKERS (National Conference of State Legislatures, 2001); discussion Sec. III, *infra.* Some fear that genetic discrimination may extend beyond the health care system. What if genetic tests revealed a likelihood of adverse personality traits such as anti-social behavior or dangerousness? Could this information be used by, say, immigration, criminal justice, or homeland security officials?

3. *What Benefits Does Genetic Testing Offer for Patients and Populations?* Almost everyone supports genetic testing that is reliable and which leads to cost effective interventions. The health care system can improve lives by accurately identifying those with genetic disorders and providing beneficial counseling or treatment. For example, all newborns in the United States are screened for phenylketonuria (PKU) and changes in diet for those found positive have proved highly effective in preventing the mental retardation that PKU can cause. Consider briefly the capacity of genetic testing and screening to move health care from a palliative endeavor to a more preventative undertaking:

> It is likely that the major genetic factors involved in susceptibility to common diseases like diabetes, heart disease, Alzheimer's disease, cancer and mental illness will be uncovered in the course of the next 5 to 7 years. For many of these conditions, altering diet, lifestyle, or medical surveillance could be beneficial for high-risk individuals. That will open the door to wider availability of genetic tests to identify individual predispositions to future illness, potentially for virtually anyone. If applied properly, this could usher in a new era of individualized preventive medicine that could have considerable health benefits.

Francis S. Collins, A Brief Primer on Genetic Testing, Address at the World Economic Forum (January 24, 2003).

4. *Should Genetic Testing be Encouraged if it has Insufficient Predictive Value or if There are no Effective Interventions?* Genetic testing becomes far more controversial if it is insufficiently reliable and there are no clear medical interventions. This is true for predictive genetic tests such as for breast cancer or Huntington's disease. Patients may have unrealistic expectations for these kinds of tests, believing that they are highly scientific. In fact, there is a great deal of variability in genetic conditions. A positive test result does not mean that a person will necessarily develop clinical disease, but rather provides a *range* of probability. Even if an individual does develop clinical disease, the test cannot predict when symptoms will appear or how serious they will be. Just as important, a positive test may not yield unequivocal benefits. Certainly, the individual may choose to use the information for life planning (e.g., Huntington's disease) or attempt extreme forms of prophylaxis (radical mastectomy for a positive *BRCA* test). Beyond these measures, medicine can offer very little in terms of interventions. Consider this sobering assessment of genetic determinism:

> People tend to see genetic information as more definitive and predictive than other types of data, in the sense that "you cannot change your genes" and that "genes tell all about your future." This notion of genetic determinism, however, includes an unwarranted sense of inevitability, because it reflects a fundamental failure to understand the nature of biologic systems. The DNA sequence is not the Book of Life. Human characteristics are the product of complex interactions over time between genes—both a person's own and those of other organisms—and the environment. Both germ-line and somatic cells undergo mutations, the latter being a primary way in which cancer develops. Moreover, a pathogenic mutation does not doom one to ill health; many diseases can be treated. As is true for so many conditions in medicine, clinicians have a variable but usually limited ability to predict when, how severely, and even whether a person with a genetic predisposition to a certain illness is going to become ill.

Ellen Wright Clayton, *Ethical, Legal, and Social Implications of Genomic Medicine*, 349 New Eng. J. Med. 562–569 (2003).

5. *Is Reproductive Counseling following Genetic Testing Socially Acceptable?* Sometimes the only clear intervention is counseling to allow couples to reproductively plan. Women may choose to avoid or terminate pregnancies armed with the information that their children have a probability of a genetic impairment such as Down Syndrome, Cystic Fibrosis, or Tay Sachs disease. Needless to say, reproductive counseling is highly controversial, partly because of the infamous history of eugenics and partly because of contemporary political battles over abortion. There is also the voice of the disability movement arguing that a decision not to have a child because it will be less-than-perfect sends precisely the wrong message. Those who believe that a woman has the right to terminate a pregnancy for *any* reason may still pause if the reason given is that the infant will not live up to certain expectations for health, intelligence, and/or attractiveness. *See* Adrienne Asche, et al., *Respecting Persons with Disabilities and Preventing Disability: Is There a Conflict?*, *in* The Human Rights of Persons with Intellectual Disabilities: Different But Equal (Stanley S. Herr et al. eds., 2003); discussion of eugenics and genetics, *infra* Sec. IV.

Sozos J. Fasouliotis & Joseph G. Schenker, *BRCA1 and BRCA2 Gene Mutations: Decision–Making Dilemmas Concerning Testing and Management*

55 Obstetrical & Gynecological Survey 373–384 (2000).

Familial clustering of breast and ovarian cancer cases has drawn the attention of scientists for years, but it was not until 1971 that the breast-ovarian cancer syndrome was defined. Since then, several population-based epidemiologic studies also suggested that heredity contributes to the development of some breast and ovarian cancers.

At the same time, other groups initiated studies that sought to elucidate the genetic basis of this form of cancer, culminating in the discovery that many cases of early-onset familial breast and ovarian cancer were caused by a gene on the long arm of chromosome 17. An intense gene-hunting effort resulted in the identification of the *BRCA1* gene in the fall of 1994; and, in 1995, a second gene, named *BRCA2*, was also detected. These two genes are probably responsible for the vast majority of inherited breast and ovarian cancers (75–90 percent), and their discovery ushered in the era of genetic susceptibility testing for cancer.

The identification ... of genes resulting in an inherited predisposition for breast and ovarian cancer offers potential for novel therapeutic intervention. The opportunity to answer questions about the population genetics of cancers that previously had been confounded by epidemiological complexities. The genetic epidemiology of breast and ovarian cancer attributable to *BRCA* gene mutations has become increasingly well characterized. These technological advances encompass an equally significant body of scientific, ethical, legal, and psychological questions and issues pertaining to the most appropriate and effective use of this technology. Although most published consensus opinions have generally urged caution to one degree or another in the widespread implementation of genetic screening for cancer predisposition, it is evident that tests for mutations recently have become commercially available and that commercial availability will become more widespread in the very near future

. . .

BRCA1 and *BRCA2* Testing: Ethical and Social Implications

Genetic testing, as a means of identifying members of families who encompass a high risk of developing cancer, has been considered as one of the most important medical advances. However, uncontrolled access to genetic testing raised a dilemma, especially when preliminary reports indicated that there was a strong interest both in the general population and in high-risk families for performing the test. The complexities and, for the time being, also uncertainties of giving or receiving genetic counseling about the results of such tests in addition to complex medical, scientific, and technical matters such as the reliability of genetic screening tests, the interpretability and predictive value of positive test results, and the clinical ability to prevent cancers in presymptomatic individuals who test positive, prompted medical and scientific organizations to develop criteria for appropriate population testing.

The vast majority of persons who currently seek genetic screening and counseling are usually women with a family history of breast and/or ovarian cancer. The detection of a *BRCA* mutation in a woman may initiate a search for that particular mutation in other female members of that family. In addition, male family members are also encouraged to consider testing because *BRCA1* mutations are found to be associated with an increased risk of colon and prostate cancer and *BRCA2* mutations with an increased risk of breast cancer.

However, from experience to date, serious concerns are raised about our ability to identify appropriate patients for genetic testing when considering the relationship between family history and mutation status in families with breast and/or ovarian cancer patients. Patients from high-penetrance families can be identified easily, but testing only these patients will miss many mutation carriers. On the other hand, testing all women from families with suggestive family histories will produce a very low yield of positive results and will still miss those mutation carriers with negative family histories

. . .

Despite the biologic uncertainties and the potential discrimination and other social and personal problems, biotechnology companies have developed and marketed tests for the detection of *BRCA* gene mutations. The risk of a possible financial and psychological exploitation of the public are obvious. Test providers explain the commercialization of such tests as a result of the increasing public demand and that the incompleteness of our knowledge and the problems involved in the incorporation of testing into clinical practice do not provide sufficient grounds for withholding information. The well-known principle in cancer diagnosis and treatment that states that "prevention is better than treatment, and that early diagnosis is better than late diagnosis" is often used as an argument by these companies that propose that genetic predisposition testing will aid in both prevention and testing. They conclude that insisting on additional research before recommending widespread screening or suggesting that it should not be a decision for the patient alone is seen as unduly cautious or paternalistic.

Although the patient's right to information is one that should greatly be respected, several other issues, mainly those related to the ethical, legal, and psychosocial implications of test results, should in no way be ignored. Misuse of genetic information potentially could have disastrous implications for the psychological well being, family relationships, future marital status, employment, and life or health insurance issues.

Because the fear of genetic discrimination exists, the issues of disclosure of information and confidentiality prove to be essential. Healthcare professionals should actively advocate that genetic testing for *BRCA1* and *BRCA2* and other mutations be used constructively to modify rather than to stigmatize individuals or deprive them of appropriate care

. . .

Although genetic testing on the children of *BRCA* carriers may be of interest, currently there is a debate as to whether parents have the authority to verify the gene status of their child for such genetic diseases as hereditary breast-ovarian cancer or Huntington disease or for any other late-onset gene that does not manifest until adulthood without that child's consent. Because the results of such a study may "stigmatize" an otherwise "normal" child for the rest of his life, a limit on parental authority may be justified. On the other hand, the serious health implications of these genetic mutations suggests that intervention, including the early application of preventive measures or even gene correction, may make it desirable to know the individual's genetic status at a young age. However, because interventional strategies are currently limited, the ethical opinion widely accepted is that parents should not be free to have their children screened for late-onset genetic diseases until the children are able to give their consents

. . .

Conclusion

Physicians need to recognize the limitations and complexities of the new information, and the implementations that this might have on their patients, including the risks to patients of being stigmatized as susceptible by insurers or employers, and the psychological and social risks that may revolve with the application of this new technology. Nevertheless, genetic testing for inherited cancer susceptibility is a reality, and thus physicians are called to prepare and help their patients to face these new and challenging opportunities. Despite the current recognized difficulties and uncertainties, in the future, the ultimate goal should be the development of new and more effective management strategies so that in cases of identification of *BRCA1* and *BRCA2* or other cancer-susceptibility genes, physicians cannot only predict future risks, but also reduce those risks or prevent the disease entirely before it can occur.

NOTES AND QUESTIONS

1. *The Psychological Impact of Genetic Testing.* Fasouliotis and Schenker note the psychological stress associated with genetic testing. After all, a woman informed that she is at high risk of breast or ovarian cancer is deeply affected. How should the potential for psychological harm impact the availability and use of genetic testing in general? If there are few, if any, effective medical interventions for a disease, should the potential for psychological harm militate against genetic testing?

2. *Would Patients be Placed under too Much Pressure to use Genetic Technologies?* Despite the limited utility, patients may be under considerable pressure to use available testing technology. Businesses may aggressively market the tests (e.g., direct-to-consumer advertisements); managed care companies and physicians may feel obliged to make them available due to patient demand or liability concerns; and family members may be keenly interested in the results. This might lead to difficult ethical dilemmas such as whether individuals would seek tests for the benefit of family members. Would patients have an expectation of confidentiality or would they feel obliged to disclose the test result to interested family members? *See* further, Sec. IV, *infra*.

3. *What Forms of Regulation, if any, are Necessary for Genetic Testing?* Some scholars and practitioners have expressed concern because few regulations exist to evaluate the accuracy and reliability of genetic testing. Most tests are categorized as services, which the Food and Drug Administration (FDA) does not regulate, and only a few states have established regulatory guidelines. Given that a handful of companies have started marketing test kits directly to the public, is this lack of government oversight troubling or will existing market forces adequately protect users' well being? Some of these companies make dubious claims about how the kits not only test for disease but also serve as tools for customizing medicine, vitamins, and foods to each individual's genetic makeup. Is it likely that individuals who purchase such kits will seek out genetic counseling to help them interpret results and make the best possible decisions regarding their personal welfare?

Katskee v. Blue Cross/Blue Shield

Supreme Court of Nebraska, 1994.
245 Neb. 808, 515 N.W.2d 645.

■ White, J.

In January 1990, upon the recommendation of her gynecologist, Dr. Larry E. Roffman, appellant consulted with Dr. Henry T. Lynch regarding her family's history of breast and ovarian cancer, and particularly her health in relation to such a history. After examining appellant and investigating her family's medical history, Dr. Lynch diagnosed her as suffering from a genetic condition known as breast-ovarian carcinoma syndrome. Dr. Lynch then recommended that appellant have a total abdominal hysterectomy and bilateral salpingo-oophorectomy, which involves the removal of the uterus, the ovaries, and the fallopian tubes. Dr. Roffman concurred in Dr. Lynch's diagnosis and agreed that the recommended surgery was the most medically appropriate treatment available.

After considering the diagnosis and recommended treatment, appellant decided to have the surgery. In preparation for the surgery, appellant filed a claim with Blue Cross/Blue Shield. Both Drs. Lynch and Roffman wrote to Blue Cross/Blue Shield and explained the diagnosis and their basis for recommending the surgery. Initially, Blue Cross/Blue Shield sent a letter to appellant and indicated that it might pay for the surgery. Two weeks before the surgery, Dr. Roger Mason, the chief medical officer for Blue Cross/Blue Shield, wrote to appellant and stated that Blue Cross/Blue Shield would not cover the cost of the surgery. Nonetheless, appellant had the surgery in November 1990.

Appellant filed this action for breach of contract, seeking to recover $6,022.57 in costs associated with the surgery.... [The District Court granted a motion for summary judgment filed by Blue Cross/Blue Shield].

. . .

Blue Cross/Blue Shield contends that appellant's costs are not covered by the insurance policy. The policy provides coverage for services which are medically necessary. The policy defines "medically necessary" as follows:

> The services, procedures, drugs, supplies or Durable Medical Equipment provided by the Physician, Hospital or other health care provider, in the diagnosis or *treatment of the Covered Person's Illness,* Injury, or Pregnancy, which are:

> *Appropriate for the symptoms and diagnosis of the patient's Illness,* Injury *or* Pregnancy

. . .

> We shall determine whether services provided are Medically Necessary. Services will not automatically be considered Medically Necessary because they have been ordered or provided by a Physician.

(Emphasis supplied.) Blue Cross/Blue Shield denied coverage because it concluded that appellant's condition does not constitute an illness, and thus the treatment she received was not medically necessary. . . .

An insurance policy is to be construed as any other contract to give effect to the parties' intentions at the time the contract was made. When the terms of the contract are clear, a court may not resort to rules of construction, and the terms are to be accorded their plain and ordinary meaning as the ordinary or reasonable person would understand them. In such a case, a court shall seek to ascertain the intention of the parties from the plain language of the policy.

When interpreting the plain meaning of the terms of an insurance policy, we have stated that the "natural and obvious meaning of the provisions in a policy is to be adopted in preference to a fanciful, curious, or hidden meaning." . . .

Applying these principles, our interpretation of the language of the terms employed in the policy is guided by definitions found in dictionaries, and additionally by judicial opinions rendered by other courts which have considered the meaning of these terms. . . .

[Dorland's Illustrated Medical Dictionary (27th ed. 1988) defines disease as:]

> [A]ny deviation from or interruption of the normal structure or function of any part, organ, or system . . . of the body that is manifested by a characteristic set of symptoms and signs and whose etiology [theory of origin or cause], pathology [origin or cause], and prognosis may be known or unknown. . . .

The Iowa Supreme Court considered the meaning of the terms "disease" and "illness" as these terms are used in insurance policies. In *Witcraft v. Sundstrand Health & Dis. Gr.,* 420 N.W.2d 785 (Iowa 1988), the Iowa Supreme Court stated that the terms "illness," "sickness," and "disease" are ordinarily synonymous in the context of an insurance policy and that these terms are defined as a " 'morbid condition of the body, a deviation from the healthy or normal condition of any of the functions or tissues of the body.' " *Id.* at 788 (quoting 45 C.J.S. *Insurance* § 893 (1946)). . . .

. . .

We find that the language used in the policy at issue in the present case is not reasonably susceptible of differing interpretations and thus not ambiguous. The plain and ordinary meaning of the terms "bodily disorder" and "disease," as they are used in the policy to define illness, encompasses any abnormal condition of the body or its components of such a degree that in its natural progression would be expected to be problematic; a deviation from the healthy or normal state affecting the functions or tissues of the body; an inherent defect of the body; or a morbid physical or mental state which deviates from or interrupts the normal structure or function of any part, organ, or system of the body and which is manifested by a characteristic set of symptoms and signs.

The issue then becomes whether appellant's condition—breast-ovarian carcinoma syndrome—constitutes an illness.

Blue Cross/Blue Shield argues that appellant did not suffer from an illness because she did not have cancer. Blue Cross/Blue Shield characterizes appellant's condition only as a "predisposition to an illness (cancer)" and fails to address whether the condition itself constitutes an illness. Brief for appellee at 13. This failure is traceable to Dr. Mason's denial of appellant's claim. Despite acknowledging his inexperience and lack of knowledge about this specialized area of cancer research, Dr. Mason denied appellant's claim without consulting any medical literature or research regarding breast-ovarian carcinoma syndrome. Moreover, Dr. Mason made the decision without submitting appellant's claim for consideration to a claim review committee. . . .

Appellant's condition was diagnosed as breast-ovarian carcinoma syndrome. To adequately determine whether the syndrome constitutes an illness, we must first understand the nature of the syndrome.

. . .

According to Dr. Lynch, some forms of cancer occur on a hereditary basis. Breast and ovarian cancer are such forms of cancer which may occur on a hereditary basis. It is our understanding that the hereditary occurrence of this form of cancer is related to the genetic makeup of the woman. In this regard, the genetic deviation has conferred changes which are manifest in the individual's body and at some time become capable of being diagnosed.

. . .

Women diagnosed with the syndrome have at least a 50–percent chance of developing breast and/or ovarian cancer, whereas unaffected women have only a 1.4–percent risk of developing breast or ovarian cancer. In addition to the genetic deviation, the family history, and the significant risks associated with this condition, the diagnosis also may encompass symptoms of anxiety and stress, which some women experience because of their knowledge of the substantial likelihood of developing cancer.

The procedures for detecting the onset of ovarian cancer are ineffective. Generally, by the time ovarian cancer is capable of being detected, it has already developed to a very advanced stage, making treatment relatively unsuccessful. Drs. Lynch and Roffman agreed that the standard of care for treating women with breast carcinoma syndrome ordinarily involves surveillance methods. However, for women at an inordinately high risk for ovarian cancer, such as appellant, the standard of care may require radical surgery which involves the removal of the uterus, ovaries, and fallopian tubes.

Dr. Lynch explained that the surgery is labeled "prophylactic" and that the surgery is prophylactic as to the prevention of the onset of cancer. Dr. Lynch also stated that appellant's condition itself is the result of a genetic deviation from the normal, healthy state and that the recommended surgery treats that condition by eliminating or significantly reducing the presence of the condition and its likely development.

. . .

In light of the plain and ordinary meaning of the terms "illness," "bodily disorder," and "disease," we find that appellant's condition constitutes an illness within the meaning of the policy. . . .

Although appellant's condition was not detectable by physical evidence or a physical examination, it does not necessarily follow that appellant does not suffer from an illness. The record establishes that a woman who suffers from breast-ovarian carcinoma syndrome does have a physical state which significantly deviates from the physical state of a normal, healthy woman. Specifically, appellant suffered from a different or abnormal genetic constitution which, when combined with a particular family history of hereditary cancer, significantly increases the risk of a devastating outcome.

We are mindful that not every condition which itself constitutes a predisposition to another illness is necessarily an illness within the meaning of an insurance policy. . . .

. . .

In the present case, the medical evidence regarding the nature of breast-ovarian carcinoma syndrome persuades us that appellant suffered from a bodily disorder or disease and, thus, suffered from an illness as defined by the insurance policy. Blue Cross/Blue Shield, therefore, is not entitled to judgment as a matter of law. Moreover, we find that appellant's condition did constitute an illness within the meaning of the policy. We reverse the decision of the district court and remand the cause for further proceedings.

NOTES AND QUESTIONS

1. In *Katskee*, the court found that a genetic makeup entailing a fifty percent likelihood of contracting ovarian cancer, which is difficult to detect and progresses swiftly toward a terminal stage, constitutes a disease. What about a 25 percent disposition to ovarian cancer? What about a 50 percent disposition to a treatable illness? Should a patient be financially forced by her insurance company to run the risk of contracting a treatable illness and enduring the associated pain and suffering when effective prophylactic treatment is available?

2. *Who Should Pay for the Costs of Prophylactic Treatment?* The opinion of the Supreme Court of Nebraska in *Katskee* is important not only for defining the terms "illness," "sickness," and "disease," but for considering the extent to which health insurance contracts cover prophylactic medical procedures. As genetic screening enables modern medicine to predict future disease, patients increasingly may seek prophylactic interventions. Who should decide whether such preventive treatments are medically necessary: the treating physician, the patient, or the third party payer? To what extent should cost effectiveness be determinative and, in the cost benefit calculation, what weight should be given to the anxiety of patients and their families?

B. Pharmacogenomics

Due to the complexity and needed research, another application of genetic knowledge, pharmacogenomics, has only been used to a limited extent. Pharmacogenomics, literally the intersection of pharmaceuticals and genetics, is the study of how an individual's genetic inheritance affects the body's response to drugs. It holds the promise that drugs might one day be tailor-made for individuals and adapted to each person's genetic make-up. Environment, diet, age, lifestyle, and state-of-health all can influence a person's response to medicines, but understanding an individual's genetic makeup is thought to be the key to creating personalized drugs with greater efficacy and safety.

Allen D. Roses, *Pharmacogenetics and the Practice of Medicine*

405 Nature 857 (2000).

"If it were not for the great variability among individuals medicine might as well be a science and not an art." The thoughts of Sir William Osler in 1892 reflect the view of medicine over the past 100 years. The role of physicians in making the necessary judgments about the medicines that they prescribe is often referred to as an art, reflecting the lack of objective data available to make decisions that are tailored to individual patients. Just over a hundred years later we are on the verge of being able to identify inherited differences between individuals which can predict each patient's response to a medicine. This ability will have far-reaching benefits in the discovery, development and delivery of medicines. Sir William Osler, if he were alive today, would be re-considering his view of medicine as an art not a science.

Every individual is a product of the interaction of their genes and the environment. Pharmacogenetics is the study of how genetic differences influence the variability in patients' responses to drugs. Through the use of pharmacogenetics, we will soon be able to profile variations between individuals' DNA to predict responses to a particular medicine. The medical significance and economic value of a simple, predictive medicine response profile, which will provide information on the likelihood of efficacy and safety of a drug for an individual patient, will change the practice and economics of medicine. The ability to rapidly profile patients who are likely to benefit from a particular medicine will also streamline drug development and provide opportunities to develop discrete medicines concurrently for different patients with similar disease phenotypes. Other than relatively rare and highly penetrant diseases related to mutations of a single gene inherited in families, science has never before had the tools to characterize the nuances of inherited metabolic variations that interact over time and lead to common diseases. Powerful pharmacogenetic research tools are now becoming available to classify the heterogeneity of disease as well as individual responses to medicines.

An ongoing ethical debate concerning potential genetic applications and the impact on individuals and families accompanies scientific advances.

Clearly defined terminology should form the basis for informative discussions so that the word "genetics" is not demonized. For example, tests that are specific to disease genes can help diagnose disease, determine the carrier status of an individual or predict the occurrence of disease. These are quite distinct from profiles that, for example, are specific for genes involved in drug metabolism, which provide information on how a medicine will be metabolized in an individual. In the near future (1–3 years) there will be non-disease-and non-gene-specific pharmacogenetic profiles developed to determine whether an individual is likely to respond to a medicine and/or to not experience serious side effects. Language needs to be more precise so that there can be clarity, especially for public policy debates. Pharmacogenetics is not gene therapy, not genetically modified foods, not genetic engineering, and not cloning of humans or their organs. Ethical, legal and social implications for "genetic tests" of single-gene mutational diseases should not automatically be assumed for other non-disease-specific applications simply because they are labeled imprecisely as "genetic tests." Use of inaccurate terminology may hinder and delay the significant health-care benefits that will accrue from pharmacogenetics.

It is important to discuss how the benefits of pharmacogenetics can be applied to drug development and the provision of better health care today—3–5 years before the widespread application of pharmacogenetics. This will enable the maximum benefits for patients to be obtained as rapidly as possible.

Mark A. Rothstein & Phyllis Griffin Epps, *Ethical and Legal Implications of Pharmacogenomics*

2 NATURE REVIEWS GENETICS 228–231 (2001).

A new model of clinical trials

Pharmacogenomics promises to reduce the time and money required to develop a drug. The ability to predict drug efficacy by genotyping participants during the early stages of clinical trials for a drug would enable researchers to recruit for later trials only those patients who, according to their genotype, are likely to benefit from the drug. As a result, clinical trials could become smaller, cheaper and faster to run.

. . .

As in other areas of genetic research that involve human subjects, the likely effect of pharmacogenomics on clinical trials raises important questions regarding informed consent, which might include considerations of privacy and confidentiality. Current ideas regarding patient autonomy and informed consent require that patients agree to enter into research on the basis of adequate information regarding the risks and consequences of participation. Genotyping that is appropriate to pharmacogenomic research might not produce information regarding susceptibility to disease or early death, but it might reveal evidence of genetic variation that could lead to individuals being classified as "difficult to treat", "less profitable to treat", or "more expensive to treat." The fear of being so classified could act as a barrier to the recruitment of research participants.

Fear of stigmatization might prove to be a significant barrier to participation in clinical trials among members of population subgroups. Genetic variations of pharmacological significance are known to occur in varying frequency in groups categorized by their ethnicity. For example, isoniazid is an anti-tuberculosis drug that is inactivated by acetylation; its impaired metabolism by slow acetylation causes it to accumulate to toxic levels. Variation in the N-acetyl transferase 2 (NAT2) gene accounts for whether individuals are rapid or slow acetylators of isoniazid, as well as of other therapeutic and carcinogenic compounds. About 50% of individuals in many Caucasian populations are genotypically slow acetylators of isoniazid, but more than 80% of individuals in certain Middle Eastern populations and fewer than 20% in the Japanese population have the slow acetylator phenotype.

The significance of data that imply a role for ethnicity in research has been a source of considerable debate among the research ethics community. One issue is how to advise potential research participants about the possibility of social harms from group-based findings even where the research is conducted without using the names of participants. Another matter of considerable debate in the literature is whether it is necessary or feasible to engage in community consultation when genetic research focuses on socially or politically distinct population subgroups.

Cost as a barrier to access

Pharmacogenomic drugs will be expensive, cheaper clinical trials notwithstanding. Collectively, the pharmaceutical industry is investing huge amounts of time and money in the development of new technologies that will yield drugs that are more effective than those already available. Without the opportunity to recoup their investment, drug companies will not continue their efforts. At the same time, insurance systems and consumers are struggling to absorb the rising costs of pharmaceutical products.

. . .

Those groups characterized by less-profitable genotypes are at risk of becoming therapeutic "orphans." At present, pharmaceuticals for rare diseases are termed "orphan drugs." The United States and Japan have enacted legislation to stimulate research and the development of orphan drugs through market mechanisms, such as tax-based cost incentives and time-limited monopolies, with varying degrees of governmental intervention. Canada, Sweden, France, the United Kingdom and other countries rely on broader national drug policies based on more substantial governmental intervention. As clinical trials increasingly consist of genetically non-diverse groups, policy makers will need to consider whether to expand the concepts underlying orphan drug policies to stimulate research into and the development of drugs for populations who, by virtue of their genetic make-up, face inequities in drug development efforts.

Cost might act as a barrier to access to pharmacogenomics in that the cost of participating in clinical trials or of the resulting drug therapy might be excluded from insurance coverage. Particularly in the United States, where managed care systems attempt to contain costs by rationing medical services, public and private third-party payers have refused or been reluctant to pay for treatments that they deem "experimental" or not "medically necessary." If consumers must absorb rising pharmaceutical costs, pharmacogenomics will not introduce new questions so much as it will intensify existing ones about equitable access to medical care.

Professional standards of care

.   .   .

As pharmacogenomic-based drugs increase in prevalence over the next several years, the use of genotyping or genetic testing as a diagnostic tool and the prescription of medications based on genotypic information will become the standard of care for physicians. Pharmacogenomics might provide greater information about the likelihood of a drug being effective or causing adverse reactions in persons possessing a particular genetic characteristic, and will certainly yield drugs that are more likely to be suitable for smaller, specific groups of individuals. By increasing the information available for consideration in drug therapy and the importance of matching the right drug to the right person, pharmacogenomics will raise the standard of care applicable to all involved in the safe prescription and distribution of pharmaceuticals.

As information regarding the genotype of an individual becomes increasingly important to safe prescription and dosage, pharmacists might be charged with greater knowledge of their customers' genetic information than they now require. The increased amount of genetic information in pharmacies raises privacy and confidentiality concerns, especially where pharmacists belong to large pharmacy chains or corporations with widely accessible, centralized records. For physicians and pharmacists, the issue of continuing professional education and record maintenance will become more important, not only for improving competence but also for preventing liability.

Pharmacogenomics is likely to increase the burden shared by the pharmaceutical industry to provide adequate warnings of the limitations and dangers of their products. In the United States, for example, pharmaceutical manufacturers have a duty to warn physicians about any known or knowable risks, or dangers, of the use of a manufactured drug. Many states in the US will impose strict liability on a drug company for harm caused by the failure to adequately warn against the dangerous propensities of a drug that it has manufactured.

.   .   .

In June 2000, four individuals filed a class action lawsuit against SmithKline Beecham, alleging that the manufacturer of a vaccine for Lyme disease knew that some individuals would be susceptible to arthritis on exposure to the vaccine because of their genotype, but failed to warn about this by labelling. Similar cases involve malpractice actions by the patient against the prescribing physician, who in turn seeks to recover against the manufacturer for failure to provide adequate information. Put simply, pharmacogenomics will raise the legal stakes for all involved whenever a patient suffers adverse reactions from the use of a drug that might have been contraindicated based on his or her genotype.

Conclusion

By lessening the uncertainty associated with the selection of drug targets and the design of human clinical studies in the development of new drugs, pharmacogenomics will result in the production of safer, more effective drugs for use in therapeutic medicine. The integration of pharma-cogenomic technology into the drug development process and the practice of medicine will require consideration of ethical, social and legal questions. Answers to these questions might well determine the level of social accep-tance and realization of the benefits of pharmacogenomic technology.

NOTES AND QUESTIONS

There are an estimated 100,000 deaths and 2 million hospitalizations that occur each year in the United States as a result of adverse drug response. Pharmacoge-nomics could materially reduce this high burden of morbidity and premature mortality, thus providing powerful benefits to society. Certainly, pharmacogenetics is not as socially and politically charged as gene therapy, genetic engineering, or cloning. Yet, as Mark Rothstein explains, there are important legal and ethical questions that remain unanswered. These questions apply at each stage of the research, development, and marketing processes. Would the requirements of in-formed consent and confidentiality change for human subjects and patients? How would the FDA approval procedures accommodate designer drugs and what could the agency do to ensure that physicians and patients receive full information about appropriate clinical uses? Would drug companies selectively develop and market drugs to more profitable sectors, thereby excluding certain races or classes from full access to the technology? Would the new medications be affordable to the popula-tion, particularly the poor or uninsured? Would pharmacogenomics fuel even higher drug costs with all the repercussions for employers, insurers, and government programs such as Medicaid and Medicare? Alternatively, might pharmacogenomics reduce costs by better tailoring drugs to patients' individual needs? If a pharmaceu-tical that is currently marketed to a large cross-section of the population is shown to be effective only in a small sub-group of that population, what disincentives might this create for industry to engage in expensive research and development? Finally, would individuals and groups be subjected to stigma due a label of "hard to treat?" These issues require society to formulate a careful response. Could the market ensure full and equitable access to the technology in a socially acceptable way? If not, what legal, regulatory, or liability reforms might be necessary? The choices are not easy.

C. Gene Therapy: Germline v. Somatic Cell Interventions

Kennedy Institute of Ethics, *Scope Note 24: Human Gene Therapy*
KIEJ (Updated 2004).

On September 14, 1990 researchers at the U.S. National Institutes of Health performed the first (approved) gene therapy procedure on four-year old Ashanti DeSilva. Born with a rare genetic disease called severe com-bined immune deficiency (SCID), she lacked a healthy immune system, and was vulnerable to every passing germ. Children with this illness usually develop overwhelming infections and rarely survive to adulthood; a common childhood illness like chickenpox is life-threatening. Ashanti led a cloistered existence—avoiding contact with people outside her family, remaining in the sterile environment of her home, and battling frequent illnesses with massive amounts of antibiotics.

In Ashanti's gene therapy procedure, doctors removed white blood cells from the child's body, let the cells grow in the lab, inserted the missing gene into the cells, and then infused the genetically modified blood cells back into the patient's bloodstream. Laboratory tests have shown that the therapy strengthened Ashanti's immune system; she no longer has recurrent colds, she has been allowed to attend school, and she was immunized against whooping cough. This procedure was not a cure; the white blood cells treated genetically only work for a few months, and the process must be repeated every few months.

Although this simplified explanation of a gene therapy procedure sounds like a happy ending, it is little more than an optimistic first chapter in a long story; the road to the first approved gene therapy procedure was rocky and fraught with controversy. The biology of human gene therapy is very complex, and there are many techniques that still need to be developed and diseases that need to be understood more fully before gene therapy can be used appropriately. The public policy debate surrounding the possible use of genetically engineered material in human subjects has been equally complex. Major participants in the debate have come from the fields of biology, government, law, medicine, philosophy, politics, and religion, each bringing different views to the discussion.

In studying the ethics of gene therapy, one should make a distinction between therapy on the somatic (non reproductive) cells and the germ (reproductive) cells of an individual. Only the germ cells carry the genes that will be passed on to the next generation. Some commentators on gene therapy have objected to any form of genetic manipulation, no matter how well-intentioned. Many others approve of the use of somatic cell therapy, but hesitate to allow the use of germ-line gene therapy that could have an unforeseeable effect on future generations. Still others have argued that with proper regulation and safeguards, germ-line gene therapy is a logical extension of the progress made to date, and an ethically acceptable procedure.

Techniques

The first somatic cell gene therapy procedure inserted a normal gene into the DNA of cells in order to compensate for the nonfunctioning defective gene. This technique involves obtaining blood cells from a person afflicted with a genetic disease and then introducing a normal gene into the defective cell. [This can be done by directly introducing the new DNA into the cells or by using domesticated viruses. It is important that the DNA be inserted in the correct cell and at the correct place in the cell's genome.]

. . .

Germ-line gene therapy is technically more difficult, and as noted, raises more ethical challenges. The two main methods of performing germ-line gene therapy would be: 1) to treat a pre-embryo that carries a serious genetic defect before implantation in the mother (this necessitates the use of in vitro fertilization techniques); or 2) to treat the germ cells (sperm or egg cells) of afflicted adults so that their genetic defects would not be passed on to their offspring. This approach requires the technical expertise to delete the defective gene and insert a properly functioning replacement.

Candidate Diseases for Gene Therapy

Gene therapy is likely to have the greatest success with diseases that are cause by single gene defects. By the end of 1993, gene therapy had been approved for use on such diseases as severe combined immune deficiency, familial hypercholesterolemia, cystic fibrosis, and Gaucher's disease. Most protocols to date are aimed toward the treatment of cancer; a few are also targeted toward AIDS. Numerous disorders are discussed as candidates for gene therapy: Parkinson's and Alzheimer's diseases, arthritis, and heart disease. The Human Genome Project, an ongoing effort to identify the location of all the genes in the human genome, continues to identify genetic diseases.

Eve Nichols describes the criteria for selection of disease candidates for human gene therapy: 1) the disease is an incurable, life-threatening disease; 2) organ, tissue and cell types affected by the disease have been identified; 3) the normal counterpart of the defective gene has been isolated and cloned; 4) the normal gene can be introduced into a substantial sub-fraction of the cells from the affected tissue; or that introduction of the gene into the available target tissue, such as bone marrow, will somehow alter the disease process in the tissue affected by the disease; 5) the gene can be expressed adequately (it will direct the production of enough normal protein to make a difference); and 6) techniques are available to verify the safety of the procedure.

Brief History of Gene Therapy in the United States

The first attempt at human gene therapy was performed under questionable circumstances by University of California at Los Angeles (UCLA) researcher, Dr. Martin Cline. Without the approval of his UCLA IRB, Cline performed a recombinant DNA transfer into cells of the bone marrow of two patients with hereditary blood disorders in Italy and Israel. At the time, Italy did not have IRBs, and Dr. Cline did not disclose fully to the Israeli IRB the exact nature of the gene transfers he proposed. In October 1980, the *Los Angeles Times* published details of Dr. Cline's activities. Dr. Cline suffered grave consequences for his over exuberance. He was forced to resign his department chairmanship at UCLA, he lost some grants, and for a period of three years, all of his applications for grant support were accompanied by a report of the investigations into his activities in 1979–1980.

In light of Dr. Cline's experiment, and at the prompting of the National Council of Churches, the Synagogue Council of America and the United States Catholic Conference, the President's Commission for the

Study of Ethical Problems in Medicine and Biomedical and Behavioral Research became involved with the issue of gene therapy and released a landmark study called *Splicing Life* in 1982. The President's Commission vigorously defended the continuation of [gene therapy] research. *Splicing Life* responded to the concern that scientists were playing God, concluding that we can distinguish between acceptable and unacceptable consequences of gene therapy research. The Commission suggested the [Recombinant DNA Advisory Committee (RAC)] broaden the scope of its review to include the ethical and social implications of gene therapy.

In 1984 the RAC created a new group, called the Human Gene Therapy Working Group (later called the Human Gene Therapy Subcommittee (HGTS)) specifically to review gene therapy protocols. The first task of the Working Group was to produce the "Points to Consider for Protocols for the Transfer of Recombinant DNA into the Genome of Human Subjects" document as a guide for those applying for RAC approval of gene therapy protocols.

Another outcome of the hearing was the 1984 U.S. Office of Technology Assessment (OTA) background paper *Human Gene Therapy*, which stressed the difference between somatic and germ-line gene therapy. The OTA also issued an important survey on public opinion regarding genetic technologies

. . .

In October 1999, the death of Jesse Gelsinger, the first fatality in a gene therapy experiment, was reported in *Nature*. Subsequent investigations revealed that the deaths of six gene therapy patients had not received the usual public disclosure that has characterized gene therapy research. Gelsinger's death also raised questions about researcher entrepreneurial activities and conflict-of-interest, and about government oversight procedures. The United States Senate held hearings on this topic on February 2, 2000, and the heightened scrutiny has resulted in increased reporting of adverse effects and renewed oversight by both NIH and FDA.

The success of a multi-center trial for treating children with SCID held from 2000 and 2002 was questioned when two of the ten children treated at the trial's Paris center developed a leukemia-like condition. Clinical trials were halted temporarily, but resumed after regulatory review of the protocol in the United States, the United Kingdom, France, Italy, and Germany.

Arguments in Favor of Gene Therapy

The central argument in favor of gene therapy is that it can be used to treat desperately ill patients, or to prevent the onset of horrible illnesses. Conventional treatment has failed for the candidate diseases for gene therapy, and for these patients, gene therapy is the only hope for a future. Many commentators liken somatic cell gene therapy to other new medical technologies, and argue that we have an obligation to treat patients if we can. . . .

Eric Juengst summarized the arguments in favor of and against human germ-line gene therapy in 1991:[22] 1) germ-line gene therapy offers a true cure, and not simply palliative or symptomatic treatment; 2) germ-line gene therapy may be the only effective way of addressing some genetic diseases; 3) by preventing the transmission of disease genes, the expense and risk of somatic cell therapy for multiple generations is avoided; 4) medicine should respond to the reproductive health needs of prospective parents at risk for transmitting serious genetic diseases; and 5) the scientific community has a right to free inquiry, within the bounds of acceptable human research.

While the development of germ-line gene therapy techniques will undoubtedly place some embryos at risk in the laboratory, once the successful techniques are developed, the therapy could help parents and researchers avoid the moral dilemma of disposing of "defective" embryos in the lab if the embryos could be repaired.

Arguments Against Gene Therapy

Many persons who voice concerns about somatic cell gene therapy use a "slippery slope" argument against it. They wonder whether it is possible to distinguish between "good" and "bad" uses of the gene modification techniques, and whether the potential for harmful abuse of the technology should keep us from developing more techniques. Other commentators have pointed to the difficulty of following up with patients in long-term clinical research. Gene therapy patients would need to be under surveillance for decades to monitor long-term effects of the therapy on future generations. Some are troubled that many gene therapy candidates are children too young to understand the ramifications of gene therapy treatment.

Others have pointed to potential conflict of interest problems pitting an individual's reproductive liberties and privacy interests against the interests of insurance companies, or society not to bear the financial burden of caring for a child with serious genetic defects. Issues of justice and resource allocation have also been raised: in a time of strain on our health care system, can we afford such expensive therapy? Who should receive gene therapy? If it is made available only to those who can afford it, "the distribution of desirable biological traits among different socioeconomic and ethnic groups would become badly skewed."

Arguments specifically against the development of germ-line gene therapy techniques include: 1) germ-line gene therapy experiments would involve too much scientific uncertainty and clinical risks, and the long term effects of such therapy are unknown; 2) such gene therapy would open the door to attempts at altering human traits not associated with disease, which could exacerbate problems of social discrimination; 3) as germ-line gene therapy involves research on early embryos and effects their offspring, such research essentially creates generations of unconsenting research subjects; 4) gene therapy is very expensive, and will never be cost effective enough to merit high social priority; 5) germ-line gene therapy would

22. Eric T. Juengst, *Human Germline Engineering*, 16 J. MED. & PHIL. 587–694 (1991).

violate the rights of subsequent generations to inherit a genetic endowment that has not been intentionally modified.

NOTES AND QUESTIONS

1. *Government Oversight of Gene Therapy.* A very limited number of patients now receive gene therapy through clinical trials, but the Food and Drug Administration (FDA) has not approved any form of gene therapy for use in the general population. Clinical trials involving gene therapy have a unique oversight process that is conducted by the National Institutes of Health (NIH) and FDA. The NIH oversight process is undertaken through the Recombinant DNA Advisory Committee (RAC) and is informed by the NIH Guidelines for Research Involving Recombinant DNA Molecules. The FDA operates through regulation including scientific review, research, testing, and compliance activities. FDA regulations apply to all clinical gene therapy research, while NIH governs gene therapy research that is either supported with NIH funds or conducted at or sponsored by institutions that receive funding for recombinant DNA research. Currently, the majority of somatic cell gene therapy research is subject to the NIH Guidelines. The RAC, however, will not currently consider or approve research protocols using germline gene therapy. National Human Genome Research Institute, National Institutes of Health, *Germline Gene Transfer*, at http://www.genome.gov/10004764.

2. In Utero *Genetic Therapy.* Due to heightened concern after Jesse Gelsinger's death, NIH added the following statement to its guidelines:

> The RAC continues to explore the issues raised by the potential of *in utero* gene transfer clinical research. However, the RAC concludes that, at present, it is premature to undertake any *in utero* gene transfer clinical trial. Significant additional preclinical and clinical studies addressing vector transduction efficacy, biodistribution, and toxicity are required before a human in utero gene transfer protocol can proceed. In addition, a more thorough understanding of the development of human organ systems, such as the immune and nervous systems, is needed to better define the potential efficacy and risks of human *in utero* gene transfer. Prerequisites for considering any specific human *in utero* gene transfer procedure include an understanding of the pathophysiology of the candidate disease and a demonstrable advantage to the *in utero* approach. Once the above criteria are met, the RAC would be willing to consider well rationalized human *in utero* gene transfer clinical trials.

Notice of Action Under the NIH Guidelines for Research Involving Recombinant DNA Molecules 66 Fed. Reg. 1146–47 (Jan. 5, 2001).

3. *Gene Therapy on Somatic Cells.* Given the high risks of somatic gene therapy and the (as yet) unproven value, should this research continue? Are the oversight arrangements instituted by the federal government sufficient to prevent harms or abuses? If research is warranted, should children or other incompetent persons be allowed to participate? What about institutionalized populations such as prisoners or mental patients? Gene therapy is a promising treatment that can help seriously ill patients or prevent the onset of horrible illnesses, but research risks are considerable. Does this suggest that market freedoms should be curtailed by state regulation?

4. *Germline Gene Therapy.* Germline therapy is more scientifically and ethically complex than somatic cell gene therapy and, therefore, more controversial. Could germline therapy have unintended consequences on future generations, and should it therefore be viewed with extreme caution? Germline therapy may serve to

"repair" defective embryos rather than leave parents with the hard choice of terminating a pregnancy or having a child with a severe genetic condition.

5. *Liberty, Privacy, and Distributive Justice.* Gene therapy, both somatic and germline, raises additional questions. There are conflict of interest problems that might pit an individual's reproductive liberties and privacy interests against the interests of insurance companies or society not to bear the financial burden of caring for a child with serious genetic defects. Consider also the problems of distributive justice. Who should receive gene therapy? If it is made available only to those who can afford it, desirable biological traits may be distributed unevenly among different socioeconomic and ethnic groups.

D.   GENETIC ENHANCEMENT: SELECTION OF DESIRED TRAITS

Underlying many people's concerns regarding genetic testing and gene therapy are concerns over genetic enhancement. The application of genetic technology in the reproductive setting allows parents to exercise greater choice in determining various characteristics of their offspring. Genetic technology allows parents to screen embryos and select for embryos on the basis of their genetic makeup. In addition, gene transfer technology would allow even greater parental control as parents could insert genes of interest, rather than simply screening for a certain genotype.

The President's Council on Bioethics, *Screening and Selection for Genetic Conditions and Traits*

in REPRODUCTION AND RESPONSIBILITY: THE REGULATION OF NEW BIOTECHNOLOGIES 89, 89–93 (2004).

The ability to screen developing human life for chromosomal abnormalities and genetic disorders has been ours for some time. Individuals and doctors have for many years been able to test fetuses in utero, either through the genetic analysis of cells obtained from amniotic fluid by amniocentesis (in the second trimester) or through genetic analysis of chorionic villus samples obtained from the placenta by biopsy (in the first trimester). The "selection" that follows such testing is achieved by means of abortion; it amounts to "selecting against" a developing fetus with a diagnosed genetic disease or other unwanted trait (for example, maleness or femaleness).

More recently, however, innovations in assisted reproduction and molecular genetics have yielded new ways to test early-stage embryos in vitro for genetic markers and characteristics. After such testing only those embryos with the desired genetic characteristics are transferred to initiate a pregnancy. By comparison with the older form of screening, this approach is more "positively" selective; it amounts more to "choosing in" rather than merely "weeding out." Methods to test or screen eggs and sperm before fertilization are also being developed, and at least one type of sperm sorting—sorting by the presence of X or Y chromosomes—is already in use in several clinical trials. These two new techniques for testing early-stage embryos—preimplantation genetic diagnosis (PGD) and sperm sorting—are the subjects of the following discussion.

. . .

A.   Preimplantation Genetic Diagnosis of Embryos

PGD is a technique that permits clinicians to analyze embryos in vitro for certain genetic (or chromosomal) traits or markers and to select accordingly for purposes of transfer. The early embryo (six to eight cells) is biopsied by removal of one or two cells, and the sample cell(s) is then examined for the presence or absence of the markers of interest. PGD is practiced in approximately fifty clinics worldwide, the majority of them located in the United States. PGD was first used in 1989 as an adjunct to in vitro fertilization (IVF) for treating infertility. Official statistics do not tell us how many children have been conceived following PGD. Estimates vary widely; one recent report suggested that "more than 1,000 babies have been born worldwide."

PGD was initially used for sex identification to avoid transfer of embryos with X-linked genetic diseases, such as Lesch Nyhan syndrome, hemophilia, and X-linked mental retardation. PGD is now most commonly used to detect aneuploidies (that is, an abnormal number of chromosomes). Some aneuploidies prevent the embryo from implanting, whereas others are associated with disorders such as Down syndrome and Turner syndrome. PGD is used also to detect monogenic diseases such as cystic fibrosis and Tay Sachs disease. More recently PGD has been used to select embryos that would be compatible tissue donors for older siblings in need of transplants. In still other cases PGD has been used for elective (non-medical) sex selection. Today at least one-third of individuals who use PGD are otherwise fertile, and this number may increase as the potential uses of PGD expand.

At present, PGD can identify genetic markers that correlate with (or suggest a predisposition for) more than one hundred diseases, including illnesses that become manifest much later in life, such as early-onset Alzheimer disease. As genomic knowledge increases and more genes that correlate with diseases are identified, the applications for PGD will likely increase. In principle any known gene and its variants can be tested for, and with improved methods for amplifying genetic screening on small samples, it may some day be possible to test the single cell removed from the embryo for hundreds of genetic markers. Dr. Francis Collins, director of the National Human Genome Research Institute, recently speculated that within five to seven years the major contributing genes for diabetes, heart disease, cancer, mental illness, Parkinson disease, stroke, and asthma will be identified. Many couples with family histories of these diseases may be drawn to PGD, even in the absence of infertility. Moreover, if genetic associations with other, non-medical conditions are identified, PGD might one day be used to screen for positive traits and characteristics such as height, leanness, or temperament.

PGD is a multi-step process requiring considerable technical skill and expertise in the fields of genetics and reproductive medicine. Because the testing is performed on early embryos in vitro, individuals electing to use PGD must undergo in vitro fertilization. Typically, embryo biopsy is performed three days after fertilization when the embryo is at the six-to eight-cell stage. The researcher makes a small hole in the zona pellucida (using a sharp pipette, acidic solution, or laser), and then inserts a suction pipette into the opening and removes one or two cells ("blastomeres"). Some researchers wait until the embryo reaches the blastocyst stage (approximately five to six days after fertilization, when the given embryo has grown to approximately one hundred cells) to undertake this biopsy. The procedure is technically less demanding at this stage and more cells can be removed and analyzed.

Once collected, the blastomeres or trophectoderm cells can be analyzed by a variety of means depending on the purpose of the test. PGD for detection of monogenic diseases is performed using a technique called "polymerase chain reaction" (PCR). Sex identity and chromosomal abnormalities are detected using a technique called fluorescence in situ hybridization (FISH). PCR allows clinicians to amplify sections of the DNA sequence, providing them with enough DNA to detect specific gene mutations. In FISH, labeled markers bind to chromosomes, permitting the researcher to observe and enumerate such chromosomes.

In all these procedures, timing is critical. The clinician must complete the analysis before the embryo develops beyond the stage at which it can be successfully transferred. If the biopsy is performed on Day 3, the practitioner has approximately forty-eight hours in which to complete the analysis, verify results, and discuss options with the patient or patients.

The error rate for PGD has been estimated between 1 and 10 percent, depending on the assay used. Several technical difficulties may compromise accuracy. Working with so few cells—in many cases only one or two—leaves little room for technical error. PCR can be problematic. In some instances, for example, one allele fails to amplify to a detectable level. This phenomenon, called "allele dropout," can lead to misdiagnosis. Contamination of the PGD sample can also lead to misdiagnosis. Technical difficulties associated with FISH may also affect accuracy of diagnosis. Following the transfer of the selected embryos and the initiation of pregnancy, clinicians routinely follow up with chorionic villus sampling and amniocentesis to confirm the results of PGD.

B.   Genetic Analysis of Gametes

As well as testing early embryos, researchers are also trying to test and screen gametes (ova and sperm) before fertilization.

1. Preimplantation Genetic Diagnosis of Ova.

As an alternative to embryonic PGD, clinicians can now perform a similar analysis on the developing oocyte, by testing DNA from the polar bodies—nucleus-containing protrusions that are ultimately shed from the maturing oocyte. As with cells obtained from embryo biopsy, PCR or FISH can be used to test for, respectively, monogenic diseases or chromosomal abnormalities (most aneuploidies are maternally derived). The utility of polar body analysis is limited, however, in that it reveals only the maternal contribution to the child's genotype.

2. Sperm Selection.

Another form of gamete screening is sperm sorting. A number of techniques are now under study, all of them aimed at controlling the sexes of the children ultimately conceived from these gametes. Most techniques to sort sperm have proven unreliable. These have included albumin gradients, percoll gradients, sephadex columns, and modified swim-up techniques. One technique currently in clinical trials—commercially called Microsort—has proven more successful. It exploits the difference in total DNA content between X-chromosome (female-producing) sperm and Y-chromosome (male-producing) sperm. The researcher collects the sperm sample and stains it with a fluorescent dye, bisbenzimide, which binds to the DNA in each sperm. A female-producing sperm shines brighter because it has 2.8 percent more DNA than the androgenic sperm, owing to the larger size of the X-chromosome. Using fluorescence-based separating equipment, the researcher sorts the sperm into X-bearing and Y-bearing preparations. The appropriate preparation is selected according to the couple's preference and used to inseminate the woman. The latest statistics report a 90 percent success rate for conceiving female children and 72 percent success for conceiving male children.

Jon W. Gordon, *Genetic Enhancement in Humans*

283 Sci. 2023–2024 (1999).

Dramatic advances in gene transfer technology since the early 1980s have prompted consideration of its use in humans to enhance phenotypic traits. The notion that genetic modification could confer special advantages on an individual has generated excitement. Controversial issues surround this prospect, however. A practical concern is determining how to ensure equal access to such advanced medical technologies. There has also been speculation that genetic enhancement might affect human evolution, and philosophical objections have been raised, based on the belief that to intervene in such fundamental biological processes is to "play God." Although such philosophical questions cannot be resolved through data analysis, we nevertheless have the tools in hand to objectively assess our state of progress.

. . .

Defining genetic enhancement

Some experts have argued that "enhancement" can have different meanings depending on the circumstances. For example, when a disease is common, the risk for developing the disorder may be considered the norm, and genetic alleviation of that risk might be regarded as a form of enhancement. This kind of semantic gamesmanship is misleading. The obvious public concern does not relate to improvement of traits for alleviation of deficiencies or reduction of disease risk, but to augmentation of functions that without intervention would be considered entirely normal. To raise the athletic capabilities of a schoolyard basketball player to those of a professional or to confer the talents of Chopin on a typical college music professor is the sort of genetic enhancement that many find troublesome. The experts in the gene transfer field should acknowledge the distinction in order to avoid causing public distrust and undermining the deliberative process.

Another important distinction is that between genetic changes that are heritable and those that cannot be genetically transmitted. At the present time, gene transfer approaches that involve the early embryo are far more effective than somatic cell gene therapy methodologies. Embryo gene transfer affords the opportunity to transform most or all cells of the organism and thus overcomes the inefficient transformation that plagues somatic cell gene transfer protocols. Moreover, the commonly used approaches to embryo gene insertion—pronuclear microinjection and transfection of embryonic stem cells—are associated with stable, high expression of donor DNA. Typically, however, genetic changes introduced into the embryo extend to the gametes and are heritable.

Scenarios can be constructed wherein introduced genes could be deleted from germ cells or early embryos derived from the treated individual.... Germline gene transfer has already succeeded in several animal species. Because of this and the general belief that voluntary abstention from germline modification in humans is unlikely, a candid discussion of genetic enhancement must include the possibility that changes introduced will be transmitted to offspring.

The state of the art

Animal experiments thus far have attempted to improve what are intuitively regarded as "simple" traits such as growth rate or muscle mass. Efforts to genetically improve the growth of swine have involved insertion of transgenes encoding growth hormone. Nevertheless, despite the fact that growth hormone transgenes are expressed well in swine, increased growth does not occur. Although the transgenic animals fortuitously have less body fat, these unexpected benefits cannot be extrapolated to human clinical protocols. Before a human embryo is treated with recombinant DNA, we must know exactly what we are doing.

Another spectacular failed attempt at enhancement resulted from efforts to increase muscle mass in cattle.... When gene transfer was accomplished, the transgenic calf initially exhibited muscle hypertrophy, but muscle degeneration and wasting soon followed. Unable to stand, the debilitated animal was killed.

.   .   .

Given the inherent limitations of the gene transfer approach to enhancement, discussion of extending such procedures to humans is scientifically unjustified. We clearly do not yet understand how to accomplish controlled genetic modification of even simple phenotypes.

... The genome only provides a blueprint for formation of the brain; the finer details of assembly and intellectual development are beyond direct genetic control and must perforce be subject to innumerable stochastic and environmental influences.

Genetic engineering and human evolution

Some have suggested that genetic enhancement and related reproductive technologies now give us the power to control human evolution. This solemn pronouncement is totally without scientific foundation. The evolution of the human species may be understood as a nonrandom change in allelic frequencies resulting from selective pressure. The change progresses over generations because individuals with specific patterns of alleles are favored reproductively. If new alleles were introduced by gene transfer, the impact on the species would be negligible. Every month worldwide approximately 11 million babies are born. The addition of one genetically modified individual could not significantly affect gene frequencies. Moreover, if the "enhanced" individual had his or her first child at the age of 20, then 2,640,000,000 unengineered children would be born during the interval between the birth and procreation of the gene recipient. Even if 1,000 successful gene transfers were performed per year, a number not likely to be achieved in the foreseeable future, those newborns would constitute only 1/132,000 of all live births. Thus, any effort to enhance the human species experimentally would be swamped by the random attempts of Mother Nature.

Finally, there is no certainty that genetically enhanced individuals would have greater biological fitness, as measured by reproductive success. A genius or great athlete who has no children has no biological fitness as defined in evolutionary theory. For these reasons, neither gene transfer nor any of the other emerging reproductive technologies will ever have a significant impact on human evolution.

Developing policy

If we accept the notion that genetic enhancement is not practicable in the near future, what policies should we develop concerning the use of such technology? The decision to undertake any form of invasive medical intervention immediately renders the treatment subject a patient who has a right to informed consent as well as to protection from unjustifiably dangerous medical manipulation. Our inability to predict the consequences of an attempt at genetic enhancement makes informed consent impossible, and current knowledge from animal experiments tells us that embryo gene transfer is unsafe ... The risks are so high and the documented efficacy is so low for gene transfer that it could not compare favorably to straightforward prenatal diagnosis even when a compelling need for therapy exists, as in cases of genetic disease. The use of gene transfer for elective purposes such as enhancement would stray far beyond the limits of acceptable medical intervention.

To attempt genetic enhancement with extant methods would clearly be medically unacceptable, but attempts to ban gene transfer legally could be a cumbersome approach to limiting its clinical use. Verification of compliance would be difficult. The diverse resources required for gene transfer necessitate that the procedure be carried out in facilities equipped for in vitro fertilization. Direct inspection would be required to uncover gene transfer procedures in such facilities. This would impose on the privacy of patients undergoing accepted assisted reproduction procedures such as sperm injection. Moreover, gene transfer can be easily concealed; in the case of pronuclear microinjection, only a few seconds are needed to complete the process. Legal restrictions can also be easily avoided by performing the procedure outside the area of jurisdiction.

. . .

Fear of genetic manipulation may encourage proposals to limit basic investigations that might ultimately lead to effective human gene transfer. History has shown that effort is far better spent in preparing society to cope with scientific advances than in attempting to restrict basic research. Gene transfer studies may never lead to successful genetic enhancement, but they are certain to provide new treatment and prevention strategies for a variety of devastating diseases. No less significant is the potential for this research to improve our understanding of the most complex and compelling phenomenon ever observed—the life process. We cannot be expected to deny ourselves this knowledge.

NOTES AND QUESTIONS

1. *Is Genetic Enhancement Unethical?* For many years, in utero genetic testing has allowed parents to select against a developing fetus that has been diagnosed with a genetic disease or found to possess unwanted traits. Couples who undergo in vitro fertilization may now have their embryos screened for genetic disease before they are even implanted. Innovations in assisted reproduction and molecular genetics have resulted in new ways to test early-stage embryos in vitro for genetic markers and characteristics. In thinking about the ethics of selection, does it matter what the parent is selecting for? Would it matter, for example, if the selection were for simple sex preference or to choose an infant who would be a desirable organ donor for a sibling? Many people probably would approve selection against a discrete genetic disease such as Tay Sachs or Down syndrome. What if the selection were for one or more late onset chronic conditions such as diabetes, schizophrenia, or Alzheimer's disease? Recent advancements in genetic knowledge may someday allow parents to positively select certain traits rather than merely weed them out. If a parent chooses a positive trait such as beauty, strength, intelligence, or the ability to function on less sleep, is that morally wrong? *See* Leroy Walters, et al., THE ETHICS OF HUMAN GENE THERAPY (1996).

2. *How Can Ethical Arguments for or Against Genetic Enhancement be Appropriately Formulated?* If ethical questions do arise with genetic enhancement, how would they be articulated? Some people might object because they define an embryo or fetus as human life. Once this definition is accepted, any destruction of a life form becomes ethically troublesome. Others have an aversion to too much manipulation of natural biological processes. How valid is the argument that fetal selection is "unnatural," perhaps even bordering on eugenics? Is the fact that a scientific method is "aberrant" or against "God's plan" ethically relevant? (Putting it more starkly, does the "yuck factor" have any moral relevance?). Still others might be troubled by the diminution of the child's autonomy if he or she were "bred" to be, say, an athlete, musician, or scientist. Is genetic enhancement inconsistent with the child's interest in autonomy? If so, why? Couldn't children choose to ignore their inherited traits and follow their own path (e.g., foreswearing sports or music in favor of some other pursuit)?

3. *How Important are Considerations of Distributive Justice in Genetic Enhancement?* Some may claim that a parent seeking a healthy and vigorous child is a social good and highly consistent with the conventional parental role. After all, parents may marry based, in part, on their mate's perceived virtues such as beauty or intelligence. However, what if the higher socioeconomic classes began to aggressively pursue positive traits for their offspring and the same goal was out-of-reach for poorer communities? Would this be fair? Would it increase socioeconomic and health disparities among difference races and classes? Does it matter if disparities are widened and, if so, why?

4. *Does it Matter if Enhancement is for a Single Generation only or for Future Generations?* People may choose to enhance physical or mental attributes for themselves or their children. However, does it matter if those enhancements will carry on indefinitely to future generations? After all, if an attribute is truly positive, why object to carrying it forward to future generations? Does this somehow adversely affect the evolutionary process? Does it pose unnecessary and irremediable risks? Does it exacerbate the problems of distributive justice?

III.   SCIENCE POLICY AND REGULATION: COMPETITION OR CONTROL?

The rapid progress that characterized the end of the Human Genome Project resulted largely from the competition that existed between private and public researchers. Once J. Craig Venter announced that his company, Celera, would complete the sequence first, his public counterparts were spurred to action. As a result, both initiatives finished at the same time, and completed the project ahead of schedule. Does this vignette suggest that competition may spur innovation and efficiency in genomic research?

Competition in science can be a powerful driver; for over a decade, genetic research has been consistently financed by more private than public monies. *See* John Burris et al., *The Human Genome Project After a Decade: Policy Issues*, 20 NATURE GENETICS 333–335 (1998). Genetic information is being used, in many cases, as an investment that will generate revenue for private companies. Although market activity could provide a significant incentive for innovation, will it skew priorities and impede rapid public dissemination of discoveries? For example, some experts worry that patent filings are beginning to replace journal articles as the primary outlet for public disclosure. Sharing information in this way, they contend, has reduced the body of literature available on genomics. Could this shift threaten the shared knowledge that is so crucial to rapid progress? Additionally, entrepreneurs pursue profits in the most lucrative markets, but do not always focus on social goals or the needs of the poor. Is public financing and regulation warranted to help ensure a balance between private innovation and public goods? Furthermore, when public funds are used in genetic research, should the pricing of the resulting product be regulated to reflect the taxpayer contribution to the product's development? How would such a policy impact the pace of research and the ability of the government to encourage research in the public interest?

Lori Andrews & Dorothy Nelkin, BODY BAZAAR: THE MARKET FOR HUMAN TISSUE IN THE BIOTECHNOLOGY AGE
60–62 (2001).

People increasingly feel they are paying twice for research—once to the government to fund the research, and then again to the biotech companies who sell them products developed from taxpayer-funded research. In the pharmaceutical field, patents are generally thought to be necessary in order to encourage the discovery of drugs, and to fund the testing of these drugs in animals and humans. But genetic discoveries are very different from drug development. The public pays for the research that yields discoveries of genetic associations with disease. Genetic testing can be applied to humans as soon as the gene is accurately identified, without costly clinical trials. Financial compensation is thus less warranted.

The high costs of genetic tests and treatments seems ludicrous, given that taxpayers have provided much of the funding for their discovery. The NIH paid $4.6 million toward discovery of gene predisposing women to breast cancer.

This situation—in which private companies such as Myriad, which holds the patent on *BRCA1* gene predisposing to cancer and charges $2,400 per screening, get a boost from taxpayer-funded research—occurs daily. Sixty-three percent of gene patents are based on research funded with federal money. The same thing occurs with funding for drug research. A Boston Globe investigative report revealed "a billion-dollar taxpayers' subsidy for pharmaceutical companies already awash in profits." Of the 50 top-selling drugs, 48 benefited from federal research money in their development or testing phases. A kidney cancer drug, Proleukin, benefited from $46 million in research funds. Patients nevertheless pay up to $20,000 per treatment.

A. The Problem of Patenting: Who Owns DNA?

Over three million genome-related patent applications were filed by 2004. Patent priority is determined on the "first to invent" principle: whoever can demonstrate that he or she made the invention first receives property rights for 20 years and has a one-year grace period after publishing the discovery. Inventors must (1) identify novel genetic sequences; (2) specify the sequence's product; (3) specify how the product functions in nature or is used; and (4) enable one skilled in the field to use the sequence for its stated purpose. Guidelines enacted in January 2001 require that patent applicants demonstrate "specific and substantial utility that is credible" before their genetic discoveries are patentable.[6]

However, some argue that these requirements are too lenient. This rubric permits multiple patents on different parts of gene sequence—for instance, the gene *and* the protein—which creates an undue monetary burden on researchers working with that sequence. In addition to these extra costs, it also allows patents for gene fragments, or expressed sequence tags (ESTs) that represent less than 5% of a single gene, to play a gate-keeping role that may stultify the speed and production of the commercial

6. In *Diamond v. Chakrabarty*, genetically engineered (modified) bacteria could be patented because they did not occur naturally in nature. 447 U.S. 303, 100 S.Ct. 2204, 65 L.Ed.2d 144 (1980). In this case, Chakrabarty had modified a bacteria to create an oil-dissolving bioengineered microbe. The patent examiner rejected the claim because the microorganisms were living things that could not be patented under 35 U.S.C. § 101. The Court ruled that Chakrabarty had produced a new bacterium that was not naturally occurring and was thus patentable under § 101.

fruits of more comprehensive genomic research. The degree to which products are substantially different is determined by the courts. In *Festo Corp. v. Shoketsu Kinzoku Kogyo Kabushiki Co.*, the Supreme Court entered the controversy, seeking to protect patent holders while affording researchers some flexibility when working with previously patented technology. As you read *Festo*, consider its application to genome-related patents.

Festo Corp. v. Shoketsu Kinzoku Kogyo Kabushiki Co.

Supreme Court of the United States, 2002.
535 U.S. 722, 122 S.Ct. 1831, 152 L.Ed.2d 944.

■ JUSTICE KENNEDY delivered the opinion of the Court.

This case requires us to address once again the relation between two patent law concepts, the doctrine of equivalents and the rule of prosecution history estoppel. The Court considered the same concepts in *Warner-Jenkinson Co. v. Hilton Davis Chemical Co.*, 520 U.S. 17 (1997), and reaffirmed that a patent protects its holder against efforts of copyists to evade liability for infringement by making only insubstantial changes to a patented invention. At the same time, we appreciated that by extending protection beyond the literal terms in a patent the doctrine of equivalents can create substantial uncertainty about where the patent monopoly ends. *Id.*, at 29. If the range of equivalents is unclear, competitors may be unable to determine what is a permitted alternative to a patented invention and what is an infringing equivalent.

To reduce the uncertainty, *Warner-Jenkinson* acknowledged that competitors may rely on the prosecution history, the public record of the patent proceedings. In some cases the Patent and Trademark Office (PTO) may have rejected an earlier version of the patent application on the ground that a claim does not meet a statutory requirement for patentability. 35 U.S.C. § 132 (1994 ed., Supp. V). When the patentee responds to the rejection by narrowing his claims, this prosecution history estops him from later arguing that the subject matter covered by the original, broader claim was nothing more than an equivalent. Competitors may rely on the estoppel to ensure that their own devices will not be found to infringe by equivalence.

In the decision now under review the Court of Appeals for the Federal Circuit held that by narrowing a claim to obtain a patent, the patentee surrenders all equivalents to the amended claim element. Petitioner asserts this holding departs from past precedent in two respects. First, it applies estoppel to every amendment made to satisfy the requirements of the Patent Act and not just to amendments made to avoid pre-emption by an earlier invention, *i.e.*, the prior art. Second, it holds that when estoppel arises, it bars suit against every equivalent to the amended claim element. The Court of Appeals acknowledged that this holding departed from its own cases, which applied a flexible bar when considering what claims of equivalence were estopped by the prosecution history. Petitioner argues that by replacing the flexible bar with a complete bar the Court of Appeals cast doubt on many existing patents that were amended during the application process when the law, as it then stood, did not apply so rigorous a standard.

We granted certiorari to consider these questions.

.   .   .

Petitioner Festo Corporation owns two patents for an improved magnetic rodless cylinder, a piston-driven device that relies on magnets to move objects in a conveying system. The device has many industrial uses and has been employed in machinery as diverse as sewing equipment and the Thunder Mountain ride at Disney World. Petitioner's patent applications, as often occurs, were amended during the prosecution proceedings. The application for the first patent, the Stoll Patent (U.S. Patent No. 4,354,-125), was amended after the patent examiner rejected the initial application because the exact method of operation was unclear and some claims were made in an impermissible way. (They were multiply dependent.) 35 U.S.C. § 112 (1994 ed.). The inventor, Dr. Stoll, submitted a new application designed to meet the examiner's objections and also added certain references to prior art. 37 CFR § 1.56 (2000). The second patent, the Carroll Patent (U.S. Patent No. 3,779,401), was also amended during a reexamination proceeding. The prior art references were added to this amended application as well. Both amended patents added a new limitation—that the inventions contain a pair of sealing rings, each having a lip on one side, which would prevent impurities from getting on the piston assembly. The amended Stoll Patent added the further limitation that the outer shell of the device, the sleeve, be made of a magnetizable material.

After Festo began selling its rodless cylinder, respondents (whom we refer to as SMC) entered the market with a device similar, but not identical, to the ones disclosed by Festo's patents. SMC's cylinder, rather than using two one-way sealing rings, employs a single sealing ring with a two-way lip. Furthermore, SMC's sleeve is made of a nonmagnetizable alloy. SMC's device does not fall within the literal claims of either patent, but petitioner contends that it is so similar that it infringes under the doctrine of equivalents.

SMC contends that Festo is estopped from making this argument because of the prosecution history of its patents. The sealing rings and the magnetized alloy in the Festo product were both disclosed for the first time in the amended applications. In SMC's view, these amendments narrowed the earlier applications, surrendering alternatives that are the very points of difference in the competing devices—the sealing rings and the type of alloy used to make the sleeve. As Festo narrowed its claims in these ways in order to obtain the patents, says SMC, Festo is now estopped from saying that these features are immaterial and that SMC's device is an equivalent of its own.

.   .   .

The patentee, as the author of the claim language, may be expected to draft claims encompassing readily known equivalents. A patentee's decision to narrow his claims through amendment may be presumed to be a general disclaimer of the territory between the original claim and the amended claim. *Exhibit Supply,* 315 U.S., at 136–137 ("By the amendment [the patentee] recognized and emphasized the difference between the two phrases and proclaimed his abandonment of all that is embraced in that difference"). There are some cases, however, where the amendment cannot reasonably be viewed as surrendering a particular equivalent. The equivalent may have been unforeseeable at the time of the application; the rationale underlying the amendment may bear no more than a tangential relation to the equivalent in question; or there may be some other reason suggesting that the patentee could not reasonably be expected to have described the insubstantial substitute in question. In those cases the patentee can overcome the presumption that prosecution history estoppel bars a finding of equivalence.

. . .

On the record before us, we cannot say petitioner has rebutted the presumptions that estoppel applies and that the equivalents at issue have been surrendered. Petitioner concedes that the limitations at issue—the sealing rings and the composition of the sleeve—were made in response to a rejection for reasons under § 112, if not also because of the prior art references. As the amendments were made for a reason relating to patentability, the question is not whether estoppel applies but what territory the amendments surrendered. While estoppel does not effect a complete bar, the question remains whether petitioner can demonstrate that the narrowing amendments did not surrender the particular equivalents at issue. On these questions, SMC may well prevail, for the sealing rings and the composition of the sleeve both were noted expressly in the prosecution history. These matters, however, should be determined in the first instance by further proceedings in the Court of Appeals or the District Court.

The judgment of the Federal Circuit is vacated, and the case is remanded for further proceedings consistent with this opinion.

NOTES AND QUESTIONS

1. *Intellectual Property Protections: Incentives or Barriers to Future Research?* Did the Supreme Court strike the right balance in *Festo*? There are strong arguments both for and against patenting genes and creating private databases. Protection of intellectual property provides industry with strong incentives to pursue new discoveries essential to progress in medicine and science. *See* John Burris et al., *The Human Genome Project After a Decade: Policy Issues,* 20 NATURE GENETICS 333–335 (1998). One study even suggested that without the incentives that patents and privatization offer, 60% of pharmaceutical products would not have been able to reach the market. *See* Simone Ayme, *Bridging the Gap Between Molecular Genetics and Metabolic Medicine: Access to Genetic Information,* 159 EUR. J. PEDIATRICS 183–185 (2000). With patenting, researchers are rewarded for their findings and may use revenue gained from patenting to further their research. Efforts are not wastefully duplicated and all researchers are assured access to new inventions.

Despite the undoubted stimulus to innovation, some commentators oppose strong intellectual property protection. They claim that biotechnology patents are inappropriately awarded at the easiest step of research and should be reserved for those who determine biological function or application. Because patents remain secret until they are granted, companies may develop a product only to discover that they have infringed on another's newly granted patent. Could patent stacking, the awarding of separate patents for an EST, a gene, and its protein, discourage product development due to the high royalty costs that all patent holders in the sequence would collect? Even if patents are not stacked, critics argue that the costs associated with patented research data will impede the development of serviceable diagnostics and therapeutics. Of those that are developed, private companies who own certain patents will enjoy a monopoly over certain genetic markets. More fundamentally, some opponents argue that patent holders are being permitted to inappropriately own part of a basic constituent of life. Is this a valid critique? In a 5–4 holding in *Diamond v. Chakrabarty*, 447 U.S. 303, 100 S.Ct. 2204, 65 L.Ed.2d 144 (1980), the Supreme Court allowed patenting on life forms for the first time when it ruled that a human-made, genetically engineered bacterium capable of breaking down components of crude oil constituted a new and useful "manufacture" or "composition of matter" that could be patented under 35 U.S.C. § 101. The Universal Declaration on the Human Genome and Human Rights states that the human genome "is the heritage of humanity." *See* Sec. III, *infra*. Does this militate against "ownership" of genetic discoveries?

2.   *Public Access to Mapping Data*. There is a conflict between intellectual property protection and open dissemination of mapping data to the public. *See* Paul L. Pearson, *Genome Mapping Databases: Data Acquisition, Storage and Access*, 1 Current Sci. 119 (1991). Ready access to genetic information through programs such as the Human Genome Organization (HUGO) and HapMap currently allow anyone with internet access to obtain information on genetic diseases, genes and their locations, and mutations that have been found on cloned genes. Merck Research Laboratories has solidified these efforts by sponsoring a university-based effort to place comparable information to that found in private databases in the public domain. *See* Robert Cook–Deegan et al., *Intellectual Property: Patents, Secrecy and DNA*. 293 Sci. 217 (2001). Is this endeavor by Merck and other companies motivated by a public spirit or self-interest? Further research must be done before genetic information is commercially viable. By making current findings readily available to scientists, can these companies expedite the process of moving innovation from the bench to the market? Is a desire to expedite the process the only incentive for companies to sponsor such efforts?

3.   *Patenting and the Public Interest*. Should policy makers reduce intellectual property protection for the public good? Congress has prohibited patents in a few cases, such as patenting nuclear weapons, where it believed the issuance of a patent was contrary to the public interest. The American Medical Association has made a similar request for Congress to prohibit patenting of medical and surgical procedures. With regard to human gene patenting, Rep. Lynn Rivers introduced two bills (H.R. 3967 and H.R. 3966) to the 107th Congress to address some of the problems surrounding gene patenting, but no action was taken.

B.   The Problem of Commercialization: Mining and Harvesting DNA

Some commentators lament that we have entered an age of *"homo economicus"* in which human genetic material is increasingly becoming an object of trade: tissues, cell lines, and DNA will become commodities in a way that "violates body integrity, exploits powerless people, intrudes on human values, distorts research agendas, and weakens public trust in scientists and clinicians." Dorothy Nelkin et al., *Homo Economicus: Commercialization of Body Tissue in the Age of Biotechnology*, 28 Hastings Cent. Rep. 30, 31 (Sept./Oct. 1998). A legislative approach to these issues could control unbridled commercialization by defining genetic materials as personal attributes rather than property, but no such standard currently exists. Instead, administrative guidelines include a plethora of conflicting DNA "banking" standards with little or no guidance regarding commercialization. Meanwhile, tissue can be extracted from people during routine care or research trials, stored indefinitely, and plumbed for information that could reveal information about entire groups of people. Furthermore, the individuals potentially subject to these measures need not be notified of possible commercial uses or allowed the opportunity to reject such applications. *See* National Bioethics Advisory Committee, RESEARCH INVOLVING HUMAN BIOLOGICAL MATERIALS: ETHICAL ISSUES AND POLICY GUIDANCE (1999). The NBAC report does not recommend any action regarding commercialization, but states that the topic deserves further consideration. Is government inactivity in this area a form of benign neglect or a purposeful laissez-faire approach allowing the market to drive genetic commercialization?

Consider the following statement:

> It is hypocritical to pretend that a free market in genetic information can exist when the very individuals whose privacy rights are being violated are not empowered to participate in that market. Far from promoting a free market in genetic information, the lack of government regulation merely sanctions a forced expropriation of information from those individuals least capable of protecting their own interests.

Richard S. Fedder, *To Know or Not to Know*, 21 J. LEG. MED. 557 (2000).

Bartha Maria Knoppers et al., *Commercialization of Genetic Research and Public Policy*

286 SCI. 2277–2278 (1999).

We are in the age of *"Homo economicus."* Human genetic material is increasingly an object of commerce. For organs at least, there is some international consensus against commercial trade. However, an overview of the issues raised by human genetics reveals confusion and concern among policy-makers and the general public about the appropriateness of commercialization. For society to deal with these new technologies, it is crucial to evaluate four emerging approaches to policy-making and to look at possible strategies in dealing with specific issues.

Human Rights Approach

Through the filter of human rights codes, constitutions, and international conventions, this approach relies on the courts. It circumscribes the applications of new technologies that otherwise might encourage discriminatory or stigmatizing practices. Policy-oriented decisions of high-ranking courts are strengthened by the fact that public interest groups can obtain standing to participate and help case law reflect public values. Such cases clarify issues and set far-reaching precedents in the interpretation of, for example, the right to privacy, or discrimination resulting from application of new technologies in the areas of employment or insurance. Yet, on the whole, they are ad hoc in nature and achieved after the technology has already been integrated into research and health care. Furthermore, like all litigation, the process is a costly and lengthy one. Finally, if the court is timorous and refuses to go beyond the facts or issues, it is a limited recourse.

Statutory Approach

In this method, specific legislation crafted in response to new technologies addresses the implications of scientific advances through prohibitions, constraints, or moratoria. This method has the advantage of immediate certainty, clarification, and precision, as well as being an expression of political consensus. Furthermore, such legislation can also prospectively foreclose avenues of research by prohibiting techniques such as the creation of human chimeras. The danger of this approach is that such legislation is limited to the current issues and tends to close the public debate. Moreover, if such statutes are adopted in rapid succession, there is a risk of contradictory positions and of inadequate definitions. The latter is particularly true when terms such as "embryo" or "cloning" are defined, for example, only to find that new knowledge or different techniques escape the statutory definition. Finally, if hastily adopted because of public outcry, they will be lacking a proper foundation based on scientific risk assessment.

Administrative Approach

A third possibility is an administrative approach through governmental or professional bodies. Such an approach allows for the gradual development of self-regulatory professional codes of conduct and, where necessary, licensing, monitoring, and quality assurance. Professionally and procedurally oriented, it ensures a "buy-in" by those involved, resulting in greater effectiveness and integration into practice. These professional codes, ethical guidelines, and standards of practice, however, can be seen as self-serving and as a way to avoid either lawsuits or restrictive legislation. Furthermore, the public does not participate in the drafting of these codes. Another drawback of this incremental approach is that it "administers" technologies through codes or standards and usually fails to explicitly enunciate the value-choices underlying their acceptance or to explain why certain constraints have been instituted.

Market–Driven Approach

Finally, a liberal, market-driven approach maintains that proper, professional practices will ultimately "win-out" in an unfettered marketplace. This approach seems to be the most flexible and supportive of scientific research. Technological development is dependent on investment and support, either public or private. The market, however, is also subject to lobbying by special interest groups, including those who stand to gain financially from public investment or lack of public control, and those who, for a variety of reasons, see certain technologies as potentially harmful or in conflict with their particular values. The difficulty these advocacy groups have in compromising inhibits the consensus necessary for successful, albeit limited, government-initiated oversight. This leaves the development of any given technology to the vagaries of the market, the chilling effect of litigation, and consumer choice. This is evident in the proliferation of private, unregulated infertility clinics and of mail-order genetic tests.

Particular Issues and Recommendations

Status of genetic material as it relates to commercialization. The current commercialization of the genomics revolution has led to concern that turning tissue, cell lines, and DNA into commodities "violates body integrity, exploits powerless people, intrudes on human values, distorts research agendas, and weakens public trust in scientists and clinicians." Respect for genetic material as part of the person and of humanity is consistent with the domestic positions of most countries. For example, in UNESCO's 1997 *Universal Declaration on the Human Genome and Human Rights*, the genome is considered to be the common heritage of humanity. The Declaration takes no position on the issue of the status of individual human genetic material except to maintain that "in its natural state [it] should not give rise to financial gains." Likewise regional instruments such as the European *Directive on the Legal Protection of Biotechnological Inventions* and the *Convention on Human Rights and Biomedicine* adopt this broad approach and consider human genetic material as part of the person and not as property.

. . .

Policy-makers should be sensitive to specific social, legal, and policy implications. Government inactivity could be perceived as endorsing a laissez-faire and market-driven approach. This would violate important societal values in most countries. Yet, in the face of the current trend toward commercialization of genetic research, extensive legislative interference could dry up the largely private sponsorship of genetic research.

Furthermore, the increasingly multicentered and international nature of human genetic research and pharmacogenomics suggests that the time is ripe for international harmonization. Although the Human Genome Organization (HUGO) has begun this effort, regional and international bodies such as the Council of Europe and the World Health Organization (WHO) would do well to develop a model professional code of DNA banking practices. The continued absence of common international, professional standards on the basic choices to be offered research participants will result in the continuation of contradictory approaches and undermine the possibility of procuring fundamental population data necessary to good science and so, good ethics.

Patents. Two approaches have appeared with regard to the issue of the patentability of human genetic material. The first, largely confined to Europe, and exemplified by the 1998 European Directive maintains that the human body or the simple discovery of some component (including gene sequences or partial sequences) are not patentable inventions [article 5(a)]. The second is market driven and leads to a situation of fragmentary and overlapping patents. This occurs whether the patent rights granted are broad or limited to partial sequences. According to HUGO, this has resulted in problems because, whether broad or narrow, these rights, preclude patenting of innovative disease gene discoveries, act as obstacles to investment, and are deterrents to deposition of information into databases

. . .

In the long run, it remains for national patent offices to take leadership in a way that inhibits a totally market-driven approach from impeding international, scientific collaboration. Failure to do so will eventually lead to costly litigation and loss of potential therapeutic advances.

Conflicts of interest. During the past 15 years, universities and healthcare institutions have looked increasingly at private sources to pay expenses associated with research. Academic health-care centers conduct some kinds of research that may generate special concerns. Principal among these is the development or evaluation of products intended for clinical application that could have great commercial value. Concern grows as the boundary is increasingly blurred between the basic research conducted in the academic health center laboratories and the derivative product development that is often in the commercial sector.

Commercial partnerships represent unfamiliar terrain for many university and health research institutions. They increase institutional obligations to minimize or even eliminate the potential for conflicts of interest that arise when private financial gain becomes part of the research equation. Universities and health-care institutions require strong and clear policies to deal with conflicts of interest, as well as effective ethics review bodies to evaluate human subjects research. Because research institutions themselves face potential conflicts of interest, policy-making is best handled by legislative action that would establish standards and require local institutions, both public and private, to adopt appropriate policies and review mechanisms. It should also ensure that those responsible for conflict of interest and research ethics review have adequate funding as well as sufficient autonomy.

Conclusion

Each approach has advantages and disadvantages. The choice between them, or a mix thereof, depends on the degree of public trust in their credibility and effectiveness and on the state of the particular debate. Policy-makers should frame their decisions according to the values and needs of the persons and populations who contributed to genetic research and have legitimate expectations of participating in the benefits thereof.

C. Regulating Science and Medicine

1. INTERNATIONAL GUIDELINES

Due to the cooperative and international nature of genetic development, is it appropriate for guidelines to be adopted across nations to ensure that countries do not create multilayered barriers to advancement and application? The Human Genome Organization (HUGO) has begun this effort, and the Hereditary Diseases Program of the WHO has proposed guidelines, but no formal adoption has resulted. The only firm outline of international guidelines was created by the General Conference of the United Nations Educational, Scientific and Cultural Organization (UNESCO) in 1997.

UNESCO, which is comprised of 190 member states, adopted the Universal Declaration on the Human Genome and Human Rights to address the unresolved ethical issues of the rapid advancements in science and technology. UNESCO Gen. Conf. Res. 29 C/Res.16, *reprinted in* Records of the General Conference, UNESCO, 29th Sess., 29 C/Resolution 19, at 41 (1997) (adopted by the UN General Assembly, G.A. res. 152, U.N. GAOR, 53rd Sess., U.N. Doc. A/RES/53/152 (1999)) (1997). This document, which identified the genome as the common heritage of humanity, obliges member states to "take appropriate measures to promote the principles set out in the Declaration and encourage their implementation." Namely, it is an effort to place the dignity and privacy of individuals above the push for genetic knowledge and advancement. With regard to commercialization, it takes no specific position, but identifies human genetic material as a part of people rather than property and states that "in its natural state [the human genome] should not give rise to financial gains" (Article 4).

Universal Declaration on the Human Genome and Human Rights

UNESCO Gen. Conf. Res. 29 C/Res.16, *reprinted in* Records of the General Conference, UNESCO, 29th Sess., 29 C/Resolution 19, at 41 (1997) (adopted by the UN General Assembly, G.A. res. 152, U.N. GAOR, 53rd Sess., U.N. Doc. A/RES/53/152 (1999)) (1997).

Introduction

The Universal Declaration on the Human Genome and Human Rights, which was adopted unanimously and by acclamation by the General Conference of UNESCO at its 29th session on 11 November 1997, is the first universal instrument in the field of biology. The uncontested merit of this text resides in the balance it strikes between safeguarding respect for human rights and fundamental freedoms and the need to ensure freedom of research.

Together with the Declaration, UNESCO's General Conference adopted a resolution for its implementation, which commits States to taking appropriate measures to promote the principles set out in the Declaration and encourage their implementation.

The moral commitment entered into by States in adopting the Universal Declaration on the Human Genome and Human Rights is a starting point, the beginning of international awareness of the need for ethical issues to be addressed in science and technology. It is now up to States, through the measures they decide to adopt, to put the Declaration into practice and thus ensure its continued existence.

A. *Human dignity and the human genome*

Article 1

The human genome underlies the fundamental unity of all members of the human family, as well as the recognition of their inherent dignity and diversity. In a symbolic sense, it is the heritage of humanity.

Article 2

(a) Everyone has a right to respect for their dignity and for their rights regardless of their genetic characteristics.

(b) That dignity makes it imperative not to reduce individuals to their genetic characteristics and to respect their uniqueness and diversity.

Article 3

The human genome, which by its nature evolves, is subject to mutations. It contains potentialities that are expressed differently according to each individual's natural and social environment including the individual's state of health, living conditions, nutrition and education.

Article 4

The human genome in its natural state shall not give rise to financial gains.

B. Rights of the persons concerned

Article 5

(a) Research, treatment or diagnosis affecting an individual's genome shall be undertaken only after rigorous and prior assessment of the potential risks and benefits pertaining thereto and in accordance with any other requirement of national law.

(b) In all cases, the prior, free and informed consent of the person concerned shall be obtained. If the latter is not in a position to consent, consent or authorization shall be obtained in the manner prescribed by law, guided by the person's best interest.

(c) The right of each individual to decide whether or not to be informed of the results of genetic examination and the resulting consequences should be respected.

(d) In the case of research, protocols shall, in addition, be submitted for prior review in accordance with relevant national and international research standards or guidelines.

(e) If according to the law a person does not have the capacity to consent, research affecting his or her genome may only be carried out for his or her direct health benefit, subject to the authorization and the protective conditions prescribed by law. Research which does not have an expected direct health benefit may only be undertaken by way of exception, with the utmost restraint, exposing the person only to a minimal risk and minimal burden and if the research is intended to contribute to the health benefit of other persons in the same age category or with the same genetic condition, subject to the conditions prescribed by law, and provided such research is compatible with the protection of the individual's human rights.

Article 6

No one shall be subjected to discrimination based on genetic characteristics that is intended to infringe or has the effect of infringing human rights, fundamental freedoms and human dignity.

Article 7

Genetic data associated with an identifiable person and stored or processed for the purposes of research or any other purpose must be held confidential in the conditions set by law.

Article 8

Every individual shall have the right, according to international and national law, to just reparation for any damage sustained as a direct and determining result of an intervention affecting his or her genome.

Article 9

In order to protect human rights and fundamental freedoms, limitations to the principles of consent and confidentiality may only be prescribed by law, for compelling reasons within the bounds of public international law and the international law of human rights.

C.   Research on the human genome

Article 10

No research or research applications concerning the human genome, in particular in the fields of biology, genetics and medicine, should prevail over respect for the human rights, fundamental freedoms and human dignity of individuals or, where applicable, of groups of people.

Article 11

Practices which are contrary to human dignity, such as reproductive cloning of human beings, shall not be permitted. States and competent international organizations are invited to co-operate in identifying such practices and in taking, at national or international level, the measures necessary to ensure that the principles set out in this Declaration are respected.

Article 12

(a) Benefits from advances in biology, genetics and medicine, concerning the human genome, shall be made available to all, with due regard for the dignity and human rights of each individual.

(b) Freedom of research, which is necessary for the progress of knowledge, is part of freedom of thought. The applications of research, including applications in biology, genetics and medicine, concerning the human genome, shall seek to offer relief from suffering and improve the health of individuals and humankind as a whole.

D.   Conditions for the exercise of scientific activity

Article 13

The responsibilities inherent in the activities of researchers, including meticulousness, caution, intellectual honesty and integrity in carrying out their research as well as in the presentation and utilization of their findings, should be the subject of particular attention in the framework of research on the human genome, because of its ethical and social implications. Public and private science policy-makers also have particular responsibilities in this respect.

Article 14

States should take appropriate measures to foster the intellectual and material conditions favourable to freedom in the conduct of research on the human genome and to consider the ethical, legal, social and economic implications of such research, on the basis of the principles set out in this Declaration.

Article 15

States should take appropriate steps to provide the framework for the free exercise of research on the human genome with due regard for the principles set out in this Declaration, in order to safeguard respect for human rights, fundamental freedoms and human dignity and to protect public health. They should seek to ensure that research results are not used for non-peaceful purposes.

Article 16

States should recognize the value of promoting, at various levels, as appropriate, the establishment of independent, multidisciplinary and pluralist ethics committees to assess the ethical, legal and social issues raised by research on the human genome and its application.

E.   Solidarity and international co-operation

Article 17

States should respect and promote the practice of solidarity towards individuals, families and population groups who are particularly vulnerable to or affected by disease or disability of a genetic character. They should foster, *inter alia,* research on the identification, prevention and treatment of genetically-based and genetically-influenced diseases, in particular rare as well as endemic diseases which affect large numbers of the world's population.

Article 18

States should make every effort, with due and appropriate regard for the principles set out in this Declaration, to continue fostering the international dissemination of scientific knowledge concerning the human genome, human diversity and genetic research and, in that regard, to foster scientific and cultural co-operation, particularly between industrialized and developing countries.

Article 19

(a) In the framework of international co-operation with developing countries, States should seek to encourage measures enabling:

- **(i)** assessment of the risks and benefits pertaining to research on the human genome to be carried out and abuse to be prevented;

- **(ii)** genetics, taking into consideration their specific problems, to be developed and strengthened;

    (iii) developing countries to benefit from the achievements of scientific and technological research so that their use in favour of economic and social progress can be to the benefit of all;

    (iv) the free exchange of scientific knowledge and information in the areas of biology, genetics and medicine to be promoted.

(b) Relevant international organizations should support and promote the initiatives taken by States for the above-mentioned purposes.

F. Promotion of the principles set out in the Declaration

Article 20

States should take appropriate measures to promote the principles set out in the Declaration, through education and relevant means, *inter alia* through the conduct of research and training in interdisciplinary fields and through the promotion of education in bioethics, at all levels, in particular for those responsible for science policies.

Article 21

States should take appropriate measures to encourage other forms of research, training and information dissemination conducive to raising the awareness of society and all of its members of their responsibilities regarding the fundamental issues relating to the defense of human dignity which may be raised by research in biology, in genetics and in medicine, and its applications. They should also undertake to facilitate on this subject an open international discussion, ensuring the free expression of various socio-cultural, religious and philosophical opinions.

NOTES AND QUESTIONS

The Declaration takes a human rights approach to regulating genetic research, contextualizing rights and duties of researchers, practitioners, and individuals in terms of international human rights norms. Note, however, the Declaration's relatively weak expression of states' obligations under Articles 20 and 21. These provisions focus on the state's role as educator rather than as regulator. If a state does no more than educate, and declines to regulate, is it implicitly endorsing a market-driven approach?

2. REGULATORY INITIATIVES IN THE UNITED STATES

Inaction at the international level has been mirrored by lack of progress on the national stage as well. With the completion of the Human Genome Project and the first wave of genetic tests for chronic diseases entering the commercial marketplace, there is intense interest in informed public policy to manage genetic commercialization. Legislators have expressed interest in genetic privacy and anti-discrimination, the appropriate use of genetic services and technologies, and the integration of genetics in health, environmental, and social policy. While nearly twelve bills were read and referred to Congressional committees between 2002 and 2004, no federal legislative action has been taken.

In February 2000, President Clinton signed an executive order that prohibits federal departments and agencies from using genetic information in any hiring or promotion action. As a result of this action, federal employers cannot request or require employees to undergo genetic tests in order to evaluate an employee's ability to perform his or her job; use protected genetic information to classify employees in a manner that deprives them of advancement opportunities; or obtain or disclose genetic information about employees or potential employees, except when it is necessary to provide medical treatment to employees, ensure workplace health and safety, or provide occupational and health researchers access to data. *See* Exec. Order 13145, 65 Fed. Reg. 6,877 (Feb. 10, 2000).

In 1999, the Secretary's Advisory Committee on Genetic Testing (SACGT) was established to advise the Department of Health and Human Services on the medical, scientific, ethical, legal, and social issues raised by genetic testing. SACGT, *About SACGT, at* http://www4.od.nih.gov /oba/sacgt.htm. Muin Khoury and colleagues described SACGT's recommendations:

> There was an overwhelming concern on the part of the public regarding discrimination in employment and insurance. The advisory committee recommended the support of legislation preventing discrimination on the basis of genetic information and increased oversight of genetic testing. The Food and Drug Administration was charged as the lead agency and was urged to take an innovative approach and consult experts outside the agency. The goal is to generate specific language for the labeling of genetic tests, much as drugs are described in the *Physicians' Desk Reference.* Such labeling would provide persons considering, and health professionals recommending, genetic tests with information about the clinical validity and value of the test—what information the test will provide, what choices will be available to people after they know their test results, and the limits of the test.

Muin J. Khoury et al., *Population Screening in the Age of Genomic Medicine,* 348 New Eng. J. Med. 50, 56 (2003). In July 2004, the SACGT was allowed to expire and the Secretary's Advisory Committee on Genetics, Health, and Society (SACGHS) was formed to replace it. Secretary's Advisory Committee on Genetics, Health, and Society, *at* http:// www4.od.nih.gov/oba/SACGHS.htm (last visited Oct. 12, 2004).

Secretary's Advisory Committee on Genetic Testing, Enhancing the Oversight of Genetic Tests: Recommendations of the SACGT

8–14 (2000).

CURRENT SYSTEM OF OVERSIGHT OF GENETIC TESTS

As part of its charge, SACGT reviewed the provisions for oversight of genetic tests already in place. Currently, government agencies accord genetic and nongenetic tests the same level of oversight. Genetic tests are regulated at the federal level through three mechanisms:

  1) the Clinical Laboratory Improvement Amendments (CLIA) (42 CFR 493);

2) the Federal Food, Drug, and Cosmetic Act (21 USC 301 et seq.); and

3) during investigational phases, the Federal Policy for the Protection of Human Subjects (45 CFR 46, 21 CFR 50, and 21 CFR 56).

Four Department of Health and Human Services (DHHS) organizations have roles in the oversight of genetic tests: the Centers for Disease Control and Prevention (CDC), the Food and Drug Administration (FDA), the Health Care Financing Administration (HCFA), and the Office for Human Research Protection (OHRP). Although they do not have regulatory functions, NIH, the Health Resources and Services Administration (HRSA), and the Agency for Healthcare Research and Quality (AHRQ) support research activities and demonstration projects that generate knowledge about and experience with genetics and genetic testing. In addition, some states regulate genetic tests, and some professional organizations have issued relevant guidelines for professional practice.

The Roles of CDC and HCFA

All laboratory tests performed for the purpose of providing information about the health of an individual must be conducted in laboratories certified under CLIA. The CLIA program provides oversight of laboratories through on-site inspections conducted every two years by HCFA, using its own scientific surveyors or surveyors of deemed organizations or state-operated CLIA programs approved for this purpose. This oversight includes a comprehensive evaluation of the laboratory's operating environment, personnel, proficiency testing, quality control, and quality assurance. Although laboratories under CLIA are responsible for all aspects of the testing process (from specimen collection through analysis and reporting of the results), CLIA oversight has emphasized intra-laboratory processes as opposed to the clinical uses of test results. HCFA and CDC are taking steps to develop more specific laboratory requirements for genetic testing under CLIA, including provisions for the pre-and post-analytical phases of the testing process, and CDC issued a Notice of Intent in the *Federal Register* to gather public comment on the proposed changes. Currently, CLIA does not address additional aspects of oversight that are critical to the appropriate use of genetic tests, such as clinical validity including clinical sensitivity and clinical specificity, clinical utility, and issues related to informed consent and genetic counseling.

Through its Office of Genetics and Disease Prevention, CDC also has a role in addressing the public health impact of advances in genetic research; furthering the collection, analysis, dissemination, and use of peer-reviewed epidemiologic information on human genes; and coordinating the translation of genetic information into public health research, policy, and practice. CDC is also leading an interagency effort to explore how voluntary, public/private partnerships might help encourage and facilitate the gathering, review, and dissemination of data on the clinical validity of genetic tests. Two pilot data collection efforts, one for cystic fibrosis and one for hereditary hemochromatosis, are in the preliminary stages.

The Role of FDA

All laboratory tests and their components are subject to FDA oversight under the Federal Food, Drug, and Cosmetic Act. Under this law, laboratory tests are considered to be diagnostic devices, and tests that are packaged and sold as kits to multiple laboratories require pre-market approval or clearance by FDA. This pre-market review involves an analysis of the device's accuracy as well as its analytical sensitivity and analytical specificity. Pre-market review is performed based on data submitted by sponsors to scientific reviewers in the Division of Clinical Laboratory Devices in FDA's Office of Device Evaluation. . . .

Most new genetic tests are being developed by laboratories and are being provided as clinical laboratory services. These tests are referred to as in-house tests or "home brews." FDA has stated that it has authority, by law, to regulate such tests, but the agency has elected as a matter of enforcement discretion to not exercise that authority, in part because the number of such tests is estimated to exceed the agency's current review capacity.

However, FDA has taken steps to establish a measure of regulation of home brew tests by instituting controls over the active ingredients (analyte-specific reagents) used by laboratories to perform genetic tests. This regulation subjects reagent manufacturers to certain general controls, such as good manufacturing practices.

With few exceptions, however, the current regulatory process does not require a pre-market review of the reagents. (The exceptions involve certain reagents that are used to ensure the safety of the blood supply and to test for high-risk public health problems such as HIV and tuberculosis.) The regulation restricts the sale of reagents to laboratories performing high-complexity tests and requires that certain information accompany both the reagents and the test results. The labels for the reagents must, among other things, state that "analytical and performance characteristics are not established." Also, the test results must identify the laboratory that developed the test and its performance characteristics and must include a statement that the test "has not been cleared or approved by the U.S. FDA." In addition, the regulation prohibits direct marketing of most home brew tests to consumers. In 1999, FDA established the Molecular and Clinical Genetics Panel of the Medical Devices Advisory Committee to serve as a source of independent advice in the area of DNA-based diagnostics.

The Role of Regulations Protecting Human Subjects

Additional oversight is provided during the research phase of genetic testing if the research involves human subjects or identifiable samples of their DNA. OHRP and FDA administer regulations governing the protection of human research subjects. OHRP oversees the protection of human research subjects in DHHS-funded research. FDA oversees the protection of human research subjects in trials of investigational (not yet approved) devices, drugs, or biologics being developed for eventual commercial use.

Fundamental requirements of these regulations are that experimental protocols involving human subjects must be reviewed by an organization's Institutional Review Board (IRB) to assure the safety of the subjects, to review and approve the informed consent process, and to evaluate whether risks outweigh potential benefits. The regulations apply if the trial is funded in whole or in part by a DHHS agency or if the trial is conducted with the intent to develop a test for commercial use. However, FDA regulations do not apply to laboratories developing home brew genetic tests.

.   .   .

The Role of the States

State health agencies, particularly state public health laboratories, have an oversight role in genetic testing, including the licensure of personnel and facilities that perform genetic tests. State public health laboratories and state-operated laboratory licensure programs, which have been deemed equivalent to the federal CLIA program, are responsible for quality assurance activities. A few states, such as New York and California, have promulgated regulations that go beyond the requirements of CLIA. States also administer newborn screening programs and provide other genetic services through maternal and child health programs.

The state newborn screening laboratories must meet the requirements of CLIA's quality control and proficiency testing programs, but in general there is little federal oversight of their programs. State newborn screening laboratories and many commercial laboratories that perform testing for state newborn screening programs have used the National Newborn Screening Quality Assurance Program for verifying test accuracy and for meeting CLIA quality assurance requirements. This is particularly important because of the absence of HCFA-approved proficiency testing programs for newborn screening.

CONCLUSIONS AND RECOMMENDATIONS

Genetic tests offer great promise and provide hope for many people who wish to improve the health of their families and themselves. At the same time, if introduced prematurely or applied inappropriately, the outcomes of genetic testing could place some individuals and groups at risk. Thus, an important balance must be struck between the need to encourage the development and dissemination of new tests and the need to ensure that their introduction yields more benefit than harm.

SACGT is aware of the risks of genetic tests and the unique ability of these risks to extend beyond the individual being tested to the family and population. Although many citizens believe that the risks and potential benefits of genetic tests are no different than those posed by any other type of medical test, there is a widespread perception that these tests *are* different and that people experience genetic testing in a way that is dissimilar to the experience of other forms of medical testing. In light of public concerns as well as the potential revolutionary and widespread impact of genetic tests and other genetic technologies on the practice of medicine and health care, society should be assured that genetic tests meet the highest standards available and that information obtained through genetic testing is protected from abuse.

.   .   .

Current oversight does not specifically address whether genetic education and qualified counseling should be made available for all genetic tests. Genetic test results may be difficult to interpret and present in an understandable manner, raise important questions related to disclosure of test results to family members, and sometimes involve difficult treatment decisions. Because of these intricate issues, some have suggested that those who offer genetic tests should be encouraged or required to make genetic education or counseling available to those considering genetic testing and their family members.

Even after a test has been accepted into clinical practice, some observers have suggested that because of the predictive power of some genetic tests and the impact that test results may have on individuals and their families, tests should not be administered unless the individual has been fully informed of the test's risks and benefits and documentation of written informed consent has been obtained. There is currently no requirement for such an informed consent.

NOTES AND QUESTIONS

What are the implications of the relative paucity of regulation in the development and use of genetic technology? In such an environment, can the public be assured that genetic testing will not be "introduced prematurely or applied inappropriately?" Some argue that genetic tests are not materially different from other kinds of clinical tests and, therefore, should not be subject to more intense regulation. Are predictive genetic tests sufficiently different to warrant more rigorous governmental oversight? Suppose the FDA were to require genetic tests to be "safe and effective" before being approved for use. What would it take to prove that a genetic test is "effective?" Would it only require that the test be sufficiently sensitive and specific? Alternatively, would manufacturers have to prove that there were clinically useful interventions to prevent or ameliorate the disease in question? Finally, should the federal government or the states require that genetic counseling be made available to patients who undergo testing?

Curtis A. Kin, *Coming Soon to the "Genetic Supermarket" Near You*

48 Stan. L. Rev. 1573 (1996).

In general, the federal government has not enacted any blanket prohibitions on experimentation with or applications of biotechnology and gene therapy for human subjects. Researchers need only meet the regulatory guidelines and agency policies of the Coordinated Framework on Biotechnology. A federal inter-agency working group proposed the Coordinated Framework in 1984 to address health and environmental concerns triggered by emerging biotechnology and genetic experiments. The Coordinated Framework, however, does not explicitly address the cosmetic enhancement or alteration capabilities of biotechnology and gene therapy because, at the time of its conception, such applications were just coming to fruition. To this day, the Coordinated Framework and other regulatory policies for biotechnology and gene therapy have not properly addressed those capabilities, despite the dawning reality of effective genetic manipulation technologies.

. . .

The old fears and criticisms of eugenics do not apply to the new eugenics movement, which is neither state-sponsored nor an experiment imposed on unwilling participants. Rather, the new eugenics respects individual autonomy in what Robert Nozick has termed the "genetic supermarket," where individuals freely shop and choose the features and traits they desire for themselves and their children. Supporters of the new eugenics argue that the "genetic supermarket" poses no significant problems because there exists no centralized control over the future of human development.

Although the "genetic supermarket" may preserve autonomy by permitting individuals to choose or to refuse biotech and genetic enhancement, unregulated and unrestricted enhancement applications may nevertheless lead to disastrous results. Eugenics should be scrutinized in terms of its consequences, not simply in terms of the motives of its actors. Even if individual actors do not intend their choices to cause larger population effects, the collective results of individual actions may create devastating societal consequences. Thus, in order to protect society from the net effects of individual choices, the government must regulate enhancement applications of emerging genetics. The threat "isn't that the government will get involved in reproductive [and genetic] choices, but that it won't."

.   .   .

In a market economy in which individuals seek to gain competitive advantage over one another, it seems inevitable that the availability of new enhancement applications would trigger a "race to perfection" among individual actors.

IV.   GENETICS AND SOCIETY: ETHICAL, LEGAL, AND SOCIAL IMPLICATIONS

As mentioned earlier, Congress devoted 5% of human genome funding to the ethical, legal, and social issues (ELSI). Congress thus recognized the powerful effects of genetics on individuals and communities as well as the need to consider ethics and law as guideposts for scientific progress. This section discusses important social issues such as privacy, discrimination, and distributive justice. An overarching question is whether genetic data are fundamentally the same as, or different from, other health data. Put another way, should genetics policies be specially designed to take account of the important and unique attributes of the human genome?

A.   GENETICS EXCEPTIONALISM

Thus far, this chapter has demonstrated the vast potential for genetic information to transform our understanding of health and disease. Some scholars see genetic information as so scientifically crucial and so personally intimate that it should attain an "exceptional" status. Exceptionalists view genetic information as distinct from, and more sensitive than, other personal health information. This perspective maintains that genetic information is so closely associated with personal, family, and group identity that its misuse could severely affect people's life opportunities. Policies based on exceptionalism give genetic information special status and protection especially in privacy and anti-discrimination laws. This heightened status is analogous to the decision by many states to treat HIV/AIDS status differently than information about other sexually transmitted diseases such as syphilis, gonorrhea, and hepatitis B.

Michael J. Green & Jeffrey R. Botkin, *Genetic Exceptionalism in Medicine: Clarifying the Differences between Genetic and Nongenetic Tests*

138 ANNALS INTERNAL MED. 571–575 (2003).

The identification of disease-conferring genes and the development of tests to confirm or predict genetic predisposition to disease have been greeted with enthusiasm by the scientific community, but numerous ethical problems related to testing have been identified. Some suggest that genetic testing for susceptibility to diseases such as breast cancer is like any other evaluation of asymptomatic persons and should be handled no differently from cholesterol testing. This point of view is not widely held, however. Others have recommended treating genetic tests as "special" by requiring rules to protect privacy, by providing elaborate pretest education and psychological counseling, and by obtaining meaningful informed consent before genetic testing is performed. Some have argued that certain genetic tests should be offered only in experimental protocols. Legislators have passed laws to limit or prohibit discriminatory uses of genetic information, and an advisory committee to the U.S. Surgeon General has recommended that governmental agencies oversee all genetic testing.

. . .

In this paper, we discuss predictive genetic testing, that is, testing of asymptomatic persons for future health problems. Sometimes known as *susceptibility testing*, this practice often raises particularly troubling ethical concerns. In predictive genetic testing, genetic material is analyzed to identify particular mutations or polymorphisms that increase the probability of disease development. Predictive testing differs from diagnostic testing in that the former is generally used to identify risks in those without symptoms, whereas the latter is used to confirm diagnoses in those who are ill.

Common Factors among Genetic and Nongenetic Predictive Tests

Predictive genetic tests have at least three features in common with nongenetic predictive tests. First, each has a similar main purpose: to identify those at increased risk for developing a health-related disorder later in life (for example, *BRCA1/BRCA2* testing to identify risk for breast cancer or cholesterol evaluation to identify risk for heart attack or stoke). Second, the clinical process for obtaining genetic and nongenetic predictive information is often similar. A patient and physician address health maintenance or discuss a health concern, and a history and physical examination are conducted. Ideally, the physician determines whether additional information is needed, mentions the availability of a test to the patient, and discusses the risks and benefits of testing. If the patient decides to be tested, there is little physical risk other than that involved in a simple blood draw or cheek swab. Third, storage and retrieval of results of genetic and nongenetic tests are the same, in the written or computerized medical record. All of the advantages and disadvantages of medical record keeping, including lapses of privacy, apply equally to genetic and nongenetic information. Thus, genetic and nongenetic tests have several features in common. To understand the rationale for approaching genetic information with special care, it is necessary to examine arguments about the purportedly unique features of this information.

Do Genetic Tests Warrant Exceptional Treatment?

The claim that genetic information is unique and deserves special consideration is known as "genetic exceptionalism." There are several reasons why one might be tempted to treat genetic information, particularly that gathered through predictive genetic tests, as exceptional: 1) It can help predict a person's medical future, 2) it divulges information about family members, 3) it has been used to discriminate and stigmatize, and 4) it may result in serious psychological harm. Such reasons have not been universally persuasive, however and a more detailed evaluation shows that there are few, if any, morally relevant differences between genetic and nongenetic tests. We examine each of the preceding four claims in turn.

Claim 1: Genetic Information Can Predict a Person's Medical Future

One defining characteristic of genetic testing is that it uses molecular information to draw conclusions about a person's past, present, and future health. Susan Vance, whose mother, aunt, two cousins, and two sisters had breast cancer, learned, just before surgery to remove both breasts, that she did not carry the mutated gene that ran in her family. Knowledge of her genetic makeup led to cancellation of surgery, a life-altering event. However, the ability to alter lives by predicting future health is not unique to genetic testing. A positive result on an HIV test portends the development of AIDS, a positive result on a tuberculin skin test may foretell the development of active tuberculosis, and high blood pressure or cholesterol measurements may indicate an increased risk for heart disease. Each of these revelations can be life altering. As such, the mere fact that genetic information is predictive does not distinguish it from nongenetic information.

There are, however, two important differences between the predictive capabilities of genetic and nongenetic tests. First, although both can identify risk factors for future illness, detection of highly penetrant genetic mutations may indicate a substantially higher risk than abnormalities discovered by nongenetic tests. For instance, persons with genetic mutations for Huntington disease or familial adenomatous polyposis are nearly certain to develop Huntington disease or colon cancer. So, while the type of information delivered by both genetic and nongenetic tests may be similar, for some positive genetic test results the risks detected are greater and disease is inevitable.

The second difference is one of perception. Our society views genetic information as somehow more central to our core being than other types of biological information. Right or wrong, genetic information is believed to reveal who we "really" are, so information from genetic testing is often seen as more consequential than that from other sources.

Claim 2:   Genetic Test Results Divulge Information about Family Members

Another feature of predictive genetic testing is that results can affect a patient's family. If a woman inherits a mutation in a *BRCA1/BRCA2* gene, her risk for breast or ovarian cancer is markedly increased, as is that of her female siblings and children. Likewise, a gene mutation for susceptibility to colon cancer has implications for relatives: Should they be tested? Is there an obligation to disclose test results to relatives who may be affected?

. . .

What is different between genetic and nongenetic predictive tests is that genetic tests identify predispositions that are exclusively transmitted vertically (from parent to child), while nongenetic tests identify predispositions transmitted in a variety of ways (exposure to common environmental risk factors or person-to-person contact). Thus, through genetic information, a definitive diagnosis can sometimes be made even in a patient who declines to be tested. For example, if a grandparent and grandchild carry the relevant mutation for Huntington's disease, the parent between these generations also carries the faulty gene and will almost certainly develop the disease.

Claim 3:   Genetic Information Can Be Used To Discriminate against and Stigmatize Individuals

Historically, genetic information has been used to discriminate against individuals and groups, particularly Jewish persons and other minorities. In the early 1900s, bolstered by a popular eugenics movement supported by prominent intellectuals, politicians, and scientists, such discriminatory practices were common in the United States. There is considerable concern that the proliferation of new genetic tests could once more lead to unfair or restrictive practices. Several studies have documented discrimination by insurers and employers, although a recent review concluded that actual discrimination by health insurers is rare. Despite state and federal legislation to limit or prohibit genetic discrimination in the United States, recent rulings in the United Kingdom permit insurers to consider genetic test results when issuing policies, and fear of genetic discrimination in the United States has been cited as one of the greatest barriers to the integration of genetic tests into clinical practice.

However disturbing such reports of discrimination may be, genetic information is not the only medical information used for stigmatization or discrimination. Insurance underwriters routinely rely on such information as HIV status, serum cholesterol levels, alcohol or narcotic addiction, and even blood pressure to determine eligibility and rates for life or disability insurance. For years, patients with AIDS and leprosy have been stigmatized. In addition, as Susan Sontag ably illustrated by citing tuberculosis and cancer as examples, people often use vilifying metaphors to describe patients who are ill, particularly if their disease is poorly understood. If it is wrong to use genetic information to discriminate, stigmatize, or limit access to employment or insurance, it is no less wrong to employ nongenetic information for the same purposes.

Claim 4:   Genetic Testing Can Cause Serious Psychological Harm

A final argument for genetic exceptionalism is that the results of genetic tests may have substantial psychological consequences, such as depression, anxiety, and persistent fear. However, psychological risks to patients are not unique to those who undergo predictive genetic testing, nor are the risks more severe. Patients who learn they may have diseases ranging from HIV infection to hypertension also experience distress, and research on "labeling" shows that simply telling a person he or she has any type of medical disorder can adversely affect that person's life.

. . .

Discussion

The introduction of genetic tests into medical practice raises numerous ethical and policy issues. These tests can help predict the future, have implications for kin, may be used to stigmatize, and often lead to psychological distress. Because of these concerns, some people claim that predictive genetic testing requires special handling. However, as we have shown, little about genetic tests themselves is exceptional, since such problems also occur with nongenetic tests.

We suggest that genetic information is simply one of several types of medical data that have the potential to help or to harm people. Like nongenetic information, genetic data can be used to help guide decisions about lifestyle choices, reproductive behavior, and medical interventions. Like nongenetic information, genetic data can, when misused, cause damage. If genetic information is not exceptional, then, which if any predictive tests of asymptomatic persons should be handled with special care and caution? One way to answer this question is to consider a test's effect on the patient in relation to four domains: 1) the degree to which information learned from the test can be stigmatizing, 2) the effect of the test results on others, 3) the availability of effective interventions to alter the natural course predicted by the information, and 4) the complexity involved in interpreting test results.

. . .

Tests for conditions that are less stigmatizing, have few serious implications for others, can be effectively treated, and yield results clinicians are trained to interpret require no additional consent and privacy precautions beyond standard, accepted procedures. Examples include glucose or cholesterol testing, tests of thyroid-stimulating hormone for hypothyroidism, and perhaps testing for suspected hereditary hemochromatosis. In effect, the justification for applying extra scrutiny to a test has little to do with the biological underpinnings of the disease or the method by which the information is obtained. Rather, the way a test is treated should depend on the consequences of its use in clinical practice. Whether the test is "genetic" is only marginally relevant.

In conclusion, the introduction of predictive genetic testing into medical practice does not fundamentally alter the obligations of physicians to their patients, nor does it introduce novel ethical dilemmas. Physicians must remain committed to avoiding unnecessary harm. However, because both genetic and nongenetic information can result in net benefit or harm, practitioners and patients must consider the consequences of any predictive testing *before* an asymptomatic person learns what he or she might not want to know. If a test could identify a risk for a stigmatizing disease, negatively affect others, identify a disease with no acceptable and effective treatment, and yield complex results difficult for practicing clinicians to interpret, the need for that test (whether genetic or nongenetic) should be carefully assessed.

NOTES AND QUESTIONS

Does genetic information deserve a special status in health policy formulation? If so, what kinds of data should be afforded this status? Is genetic information so integral to health that it cannot realistically be separated from other health information? A growing body of research shows that nearly all health conditions may have a genetic basis. If this is the case, then would segregating genetic information from other health information be practical and effectual? Likewise, because diseases result from the interaction between genes and environment, genetic advances will likely extend and expand current medical practices rather than supplant such efforts. Besides the entanglement problems, would limiting the free use of genetic information hinder the development of beneficial genetic services and technologies? *See generally*, Lawrence O. Gostin & James G. Hodge, Jr., *Genetics Privacy and the Law: An End to Genetics Exceptionalism*, 40 Jurimetrics J. 21 (1999).

Should persons with genetic disorders receive greater legal protection than those with equally serious diseases that are attributable to other causes? Might genetics exceptionalism inadvertently stigmatize individuals with genetic diseases? Which would be the preferable approach to problems of discrimination: a generic antidiscrimination statute that applies to a broad range of diseases and disabilities such as the Americans with Disabilities Act or a genetic-specific antidiscrimination law?

B. Genetic Privacy and the Disclosure of Genetic Information

The rapid increase in genetic testing and the use of family history data have resulted in the substantial collection and use of genetic data in the health care and public health systems. These genetic data reveal important information about an individual's current and future health, as well as the health of family members. Profound ethical questions are posed by the collection and use of genetic data.

1. GENETIC PRIVACY

Anita L. Allen, *Genetic Privacy: Emerging Concepts and Values in Genetic Secrets*

in Protecting Privacy and Confidentiality in the Genetic Era 33–34 (Mark A. Rothstein ed., 1997).

The Four Dimensions of Genetic Privacy

The word *privacy* has a wide range of meanings. It is used ambiguously in law and morals to describe and prescribe, denote and connote, praise and blame. "Genetic privacy" is no less rich in ambiguity than "privacy." Although the expression "genetic privacy" is a product of recent developments in science, it does not stand for a wholly new concept. "Genetic privacy" signifies applications of the familiar concept of privacy to genetic-related phenomena.

When used to label issues that arise in contemporary bioethics and public policy, "privacy" generally refers to one of four categories of concern. They are: (1) informational privacy concerns about access to personal information; (2) physical privacy concerns about access to persons and personal spaces; (3) decisional privacy concerns about governmental and other third-party interference with personal choices; and (4) proprietary privacy concerns about the appropriation and ownership of interests in human personality. "Genetic privacy" typically refers to one of these same four general categories.

"Genetic privacy" often denotes informational privacy, including the confidentiality, anonymity, or secrecy of the data that result from genetic testing and screening. Substantial limits on third-party access to confidential, anonymous, or secret genetic information are requirements of respect for informational privacy. However, family members may possess moral rights to undisclosed genetic data that patients and the professionals who serve them legitimately withhold from other third parties.

George Annas had informational privacy in mind when he warned that "control of and access to the information contained in an individual's genome gives others potential power over the personal life of the individual by providing a basis not only for counseling, but also for stigmatizing and discrimination." Likewise, Alan Westin was thinking of informational privacy when he defined "genetic privacy" by reference to what he called the "core concept of privacy"—namely, "the claim of an individual to determine what information about himself or herself should by known by others." Westin's definition captures well much of the informational dimension of genetic privacy and its connection to ideals of self-determination. Although it is adequate for purposes of a discussion of informational privacy, Westin's definition leaves important physical, decisional, and proprietary dimensions of genetic privacy in the shadows.

The genetic privacy concerns heard today range far beyond informational privacy to concerns about physical, decisional, and proprietary privacy. Briefly, issues of physical privacy underlie concerns about genetic testing, screening, or treatment without voluntary and informed consent. In the absence of consent, these practices constitute unwanted physical contact, compromising interests in bodily integrity and security. Decisional privacy concerns are heard in calls for autonomous decision making by individuals, couples, or families who use genetic services. A degree of choice with regard to genetic counseling, testing, and abortion are requirements of respect for decisional privacy. The fourth category of privacy concern, proprietary privacy, encompasses issues relating to the appropriation of individuals' possessory and economic interest in their genes and other putative bodily repositories of personality.

. . .

The human genome contains many mysteries that await scientific discovery. The air of mystery that shrouds gene science often shrouds discourse about genetic privacy, too. Yet genetic privacy is only an expansive concept, not an unfathomable one.

NOTES AND QUESTIONS

Informational privacy may be defined as the right of an individual to control access to personal genetic information. Scholars such as Anita Allen have explained why society should respect a patient's interest in informational privacy. There is the normative claim that patients' autonomy demands a certain control over personal information. There is also the pragmatic claim that protection of privacy will encourage patients to come forward for testing and treatment. It is for these reasons that policy makers and the public often assert that genetic data should be kept private, and released only with the patient's informed consent.

This assertion raises a number of questions: Should patients have a more robust right to control access to genetic information than they have to control access to other kinds of health information—a form of genetics exceptionalism? What are the implications of a strong, perhaps near-absolute, right to control personal genetic information? Should society grant such control to individuals in the face of competing demands for use of genetic information for the common good? A certain tension exists between individual privacy and collective interests in research, health care, and public health. When faced with a choice between maintaining patient privacy and furthering important societal goals, which should prevail and why?

The same kinds of conflicts arise with some of the other dimensions of genetic privacy offered by Allen. Consider the dimension of proprietary privacy. If individuals have unfettered possessory and economic interests in their genes, would this impede genetic research and scientific innovation?

2. THE "DUTY TO WARN" AND THE "RIGHT TO KNOW"

Kenneth Offit et al., *The "Duty to Warn" a Patient's Family Members About Hereditary Disease Risks*

292 JAMA 1469 (2004).

Genetic tests for specific adult-onset disorders (eg, breast and colon cancer) are now commercially available, and results of research studies for genetic polymorphisms that predict drug effects, for example, response to statin therapy, have recently been published. The failure to warn family members about their hereditary disease risks has resulted in malpractice suits against physicians in the United States. [Pate v. Threlkel, 661 So.2d 278 (Fla. 1995); Safer v. Estate of Pack, 677 A.2d 1188 (N.J. App. 1996), appeal denied, 683 A.2d 1163 (N.J. 1996); Molloy v. Meier, 679 N.W.2d 711 (Minn. 2004) reproduced in Sec. IV, *infra*.] This past year, the obligation, if any, to warn family members of identification of a cancer gene mutation was the topic of discussion among professional societies and advocacy groups. Concerns have been raised regarding the conflict between the physician's ethical obligations to respect the privacy of genetic information vs the potential legal liabilities resulting from the physician's failure to notify at-risk relatives. In many cases, state and federal statutes that bear on the issue of "duty to warn" of inherited health risk are also in conflict. This article discusses these issues and suggests that health care professionals have a responsibility to encourage but not to coerce the sharing of genetic information in families, while respecting the boundaries imposed by the law and by the ethical practice of medicine.

CASE EXAMPLE

A 40–year-old woman presents for a follow-up consultation. She has a family history of breast cancer, heart disease, and Alzheimer disease. At her first visit, the physician had counseled her and provided genetic testing and now tells the patient that she was found to have an inherited BRCA2 mutation that markedly increases her risk for developing breast cancer and/or ovarian cancer. The testing laboratory has also suggested a "genomic profile" that will predict risk for Alzheimer disease as well as sensitivity to a variety of drugs. The patient's sister, who is sitting in the waiting room, has a 50% chance of inheriting this same BRCA2 mutation. Although the physician had discussed the importance of familial risk notification before testing, the patient declines the strong recommendation that she share the results of her genetic tests with her sister and asks that this information be kept completely confidential.

Does this physician have an obligation to tell the patient's sister that she, too, may have inherited these genetic predispositions? If this sister later develops advanced breast cancer, or has a "preventive surgery" unnecessarily, can she take legal action, claiming that the physician had an obligation to contact her about her genetic risk?

ETHICAL AND LEGAL BACKDROP: THE PRACTITIONER'S DUTY TO WARN OF GENETIC RISK

Respect for patients' autonomous choice lies at the heart of bioethical theory. When a physician's notion of "beneficence" (an act done for the benefit of others) and the patient's autonomy come into conflict, an ethical imperative may compel the physician to override the patient's autonomy. A key assumption underlying the ethical justification for a "duty to warn" is the availability of medical interventions to reduce the risk of developing a disease or to lessen the ensuing harm. For some hereditary disorders, such as Huntington disease and Alzheimer disease, effective medical interventions are either minimal or just emerging. For other inherited diseases, there are proven means of prevention, as is the case for dietary modification to prevent the development of mental retardation from phenylketonuria. Presymptomatic interventions can significantly reduce the future harm caused by some common malignancies. For example, surgical removal of the ovaries and fallopian tubes after childbearing in women with BRCA mutations reduces the subsequent risk of developing breast or ovarian cancer by 75%. Other studies have demonstrated the efficacy of screening and prevention in hereditary breast, colon, thyroid, and other cancers. However, for some cancer syndromes, genetic risks may be incompletely defined and interventions may be ineffective, and the impact of failing to warn relatives of their hereditary risk for cancer is less clear. Fewer than 1% of clinicians surveyed believed that a breach of patient confidentiality would be warranted to warn at-risk relatives about a disease for which no medical interventions exist.

CASE LAW IN STATE APPELLATE COURTS

The precedent-setting test of the "duty to warn" in a medical setting stems from a 1976 decision, Tarasoff v. the Regents of the University of California, [551 P.2d 334 (Cal. 1976),] which dealt with a psychotherapist's failure to warn the plaintiffs' deceased daughter of his patient's stated intention to kill her. The California Supreme Court ruled that a physician is required to breach patient confidentiality and take reasonable actions to warn an identifiable third party in instances where the patient poses a serious and imminent threat to that party. Three subsequent lawsuits against physicians have focused attention on the specific question of the duty to warn relatives regarding their hereditary risk for cancer. In Pate v. Threlkel, [661 So. 2d 278 (Fla. 1995),] appellant Heidi Pate filed suit against her mother's physician because he failed to warn her of the risks of hereditary thyroid cancer. In this syndrome, medullary thyroid cancer, and possibly pheochromocytoma and parathyroid hyperplasia, are inherited in an autosomal dominant fashion. Recognition of this syndrome can enable prophylactic removal of the thyroid gland before cancers are clinically detected, followed by thyroid hormone administration. Three years after her mother's diagnosis, Ms Pate was found to have advanced stage thyroid cancer. She claimed that if she had been warned earlier, her cancer could have been detected at a curable stage.

The Supreme Court of Florida agreed with Ms Pate's claim that Dr Threlkel was obliged by accepted medical practice to warn her mother of the need to share the cancer risks with her children. The court concluded that because the standard of care was developed with the specific purpose of benefiting the patient's children, the issue of privity was irrelevant. The court did recognize the logistical challenges posed by having to contact at-risk relatives but noted that, "in any circumstances in which the physician has a duty to warn of a genetically transferable disease, that duty will be satisfied by warning the patient." [Id. at 282.]

In Safer v. Estate of Pack, [677 A.2d 1188,] the court espoused a much more expansive "duty to warn." In this case, Donna Safer sued the estate of the late Dr George Pack, claiming that more than 30 years earlier, when Dr Pack treated her father for multiple polyposis, Dr Pack failed to fulfill his professional duty to warn those at risk for the hereditary disease. In familial adenomatous polyposis, the presence of hundreds or thousands of polyps in childhood leads inevitably to colon cancer by 40 years of age. Prophylactic colectomy in the late teen years remains the intervention of choice for these patients, although recent studies have shown that anti-inflammatory drugs, such as sulindac or celecoxib, may also play a role in management. Thirty years after her father's diagnosis, Donna Safer presented with both polyposis and advanced colorectal cancer. Ms Safer contended that, if she had been told of her elevated risk as a child, she could have benefited from early detection and avoided metastatic colorectal cancer.

Contrary to the Pate ruling, the New Jersey court asserted that a physician's duty to warn at-risk relatives is not, in all cases, met by simply informing the patient of the hereditary nature of the disease. The New Jersey ruling proffered that physicians must take "reasonable steps" to guarantee that immediate family members are warned. The jury in this case ultimately decided in favor of Dr Pack, based on evidence that Safer had indeed undergone rectal screening at the age of 10 years, indicating that she (through her mother) had been sufficiently warned of her elevated risk. However, this favorable decision for the defendant did not obviate the appellate court ruling defining a duty to warn family members of hereditary disease risk in a manner that is comprehensive in scope and may not be feasible for most practitioners.

In May 2004, in Molloy v. Meier, [679 N.W.2d 711,] the Minnesota Supreme Court allowed a parent to proceed with a lawsuit against the physicians who had treated her daughter more than 10 years earlier. In this case, Kimberly Molloy claimed that the physicians failed to inform her and her second husband about future risks due to a hereditary form of mental retardation, fragile X syndrome, present in her first daughter. The court held that "a physician's duty regarding genetic testing and diagnosis extends beyond the patient to biological parents who foreseeably may be harmed by a breach of that duty." In this case, which stems more from an alleged failure to perform a diagnostic test than from a failure to breach confidentiality to warn of a genetic disease, the mother and her second husband stated they would not have conceived another child if they had known of the diagnosis of fragile X syndrome in the mother's first child.

FEDERAL STATUTES AND OTHER CASE LAW

The Pack case notwithstanding, disclosures without patient consent are regulated by a stringent health information privacy rule known as the Standards for Privacy of Individually Identifiable Health Information (Privacy Rule), promulgated under the Health Insurance Portability and Accountability Act of 1996 (HIPAA). Noncompliance with the Privacy Rule may result in civil or criminal penalties.

Included in these regulations are certain "public interest" exceptions to the strict nondisclosure policy that otherwise protects "individually identifiable health information" (including genetic information). These exceptions comprise instances in which the public interest is at risk, ie, there is a "serious and imminent threat to the health or safety of a person or the public"; the threat constitutes an imminent, serious threat to an identifiable third party and the physician has the capacity to avert significant harm. Examples of circumstances requiring a breach of patient confidentiality include the apprehension of an individual by law enforcement and to curtail certain infectious disease.

It is questionable whether the uncertain probability of a future genetic disease constitutes an imminent harm or a threat to the public interest. It has been argued that infectious diseases meet such a criterion. In Tenuto v Lederle Laboratories, [90 N.Y.2d 606 (N.Y. 1997),] the New York Court of Appeals extended a physician's duty to third parties "when the service performed on behalf of the patient necessarily implicated protection of . . .

other identified persons forseeably at risk because of the relationship with the patient, whom the doctor knows or should know may suffer harm by relying on prudent performance of the medical service." The court found that the pediatrician had a duty to warn his patient's father, who had not been vaccinated against polio, about the risk of contracting polio from his son after the child was vaccinated.

. . .

THE POSITION OF PROFESSIONAL SOCIETIES

A Presidential Commission and subsequent reports have defined conditions under which it would be ethically acceptable for physicians to breach confidentiality and disclose information to relatives. These conditions include (1) the high likelihood of harm if the relative were not warned, (2) the identifiability of the relative, and (3) the notion that the harm resulting from failure to disclose would outweigh the harm resulting from disclosure. In the absence of a federally defined general legal "duty to rescue," which exists in certain parts of Canada, the health care professional's duty to warn is generally viewed as discretionary and not compulsory, ie, legally excusable and not legally mandated.

. . .

COMMENT

Against this background of ethical and legal "directives that are in conflict," some lawyers have concluded that considering the legal liabilities, "physicians might understandably conclude that warning relatives is the least risk[y] option." These scholars claim that none of the contested legal constraints and salient social policies serve as legitimate barriers to the requirement to warn of genetic risk for disease. Such an argument would be supported by the Safer malpractice case, as well as the Molloy case in progress in Minnesota. Questioning the notion of genetic information as "property" in the legal sense and casting doubt on the claim of an undue burden on physicians, health care professionals could be held liable for a failure to warn relatives at increased risk of an inheritable genetic disease.

How then is a physician to resolve the competing ethical mandates of autonomy (respect for genetic privacy) and beneficence (duty to warn) while under threat of litigation following either course of action? . . .

The cornerstone of the patient-physician relationship is the assurance of confidentiality. This assurance is especially relevant to genetic information. A universal "duty to warn" would make the patient-physician relationship subservient to a more diffuse public health obligation, benefiting an unspecified number of nonpatient relatives. In the pretesting "negotiation" represented by the "genetic Miranda warning," patients who decline to share their genetic information with relatives could be subject to the coercive, threatened withdrawal of their physicians' care. Consumer and advocacy groups have expressed concern about such scenarios. . . . Indeed, it seems reasonable to question the propriety of coercive threats, whether before genetic testing or afterward. The pretest discussion of duty to warn obligations could be represented in the form of a "contract" between the patient and the physician. Such an a priori understanding of the patient's responsibility regarding notification of family members may provide the physician with some measure of legal protection, but does not address the ultimate liability should the patient later opt to withdraw from the "contract."

In considering the "duty to warn" of genetic risk, a clinical distinction must be made between high penetrance (100% risk) cancer susceptibility syndromes with proven means of intervention, syndromes of variable penetrance with less well-established interventions (such as Alzheimer disease), and low penetrance syndromes in which risk for outcome or toxicity may be only mildly elevated. In each of these circumstances, the potential implications of a failure to warn will be very different.

From a practical standpoint, physicians are in no position to undertake the primary responsibility for identifying and communicating with an untold number of their patients' relatives who might be at some unspecified risk from genetic predispositions. Even if all the patient's affected relatives could be reached, each would require counseling and education that would impose completely unrealistic burdens on the physician. The imposition of such burdens (and the attendant threat of liability should those burdens be unassumed) would discourage physician involvement in the emerging subspecialty of genetic medicine.

. . .

Moreover, the arguments for institutionalizing a "duty to warn" are contrary to the regulations that govern medical records privacy under HIPAA. In addition, certain states have enacted statutes that prohibit the disclosure of genetic information without the prior written consent of the individual tested (eg, New York civil rights law and public health law amendments).

Thus, in considering whether to breach patient confidentiality to warn of risks of a genetic disease, clinicians need to balance the actual risk of that disease, the efficacy of potential preventive interventions, as well as emerging legal considerations and potential liabilities. Overriding patient confidentiality and genetic privacy might very well mean violation of HIPAA and certain state regulations, with attendant civil or criminal liability. At the same time, in one state appellate court decision that has not been overturned, the estate of a physician was held liable for his failure to warn relatives of hereditary disease risk. . . .

An expanded national discussion of the ethical and legal implications of genetic risk notification is required to guide practitioners of "molecular medicine." Fear of loss of privacy among susceptible populations could discourage families from seeking access to potentially life-saving genetic testing. In the genomic era, clinical testing will be offered to predict disease occurrence, as well as sensitivities to drugs or environmental exposures. Because the laws of Mendel will continue to apply to these new markers of genetic risk, the issues surrounding familial notification will loom even larger. The increasing availability of DNA testing will require greater emphasis on informed consent as a process of communication and education, so as to better facilitate the translation of genomic medicine to clinical practice.

NOTES AND QUESTIONS

1. *A Physician's Duty?* Offit and colleagues focus on the obligations of a medical practitioner when confronted with a patient who has a genetic predisposition to a disease that might be shared by close relatives. Physicians owe a duty principally to the patient who surely is entitled to receive any relevant health information. Should the physician's duty extend beyond the patient to biological family members who may be harmed by the failure to disclose genetic information?

2. *A Patient's Duty?* What about the duty of patients who have learned that their genetic makeup predisposes them to an illness? What are the patient's duties, if any, to warn his or her siblings, children, and other relatives? Should a patient ever have a duty to disclose this information? Hook and colleagues discuss varying perspectives on the obligations of patients with regard to genetic testing:

> One of the fundamental principles of the ELSI project is the idea of the right not to know—that patients should be able to remain in ignorance, particularly about late-onset disorders, if they so desire. The right not to know may appear to make sense if there is no remedy for a disease associated with a specific genotype. However, what if the lack of information could prove detrimental to other family members, especially the children of the affected individual? Both sides of the issue have been discussed; some experts have taken a more extreme position: "Knowingly, capriciously, or negligently transmitting a defective gene that causes pain and suffering and an agonizing death to an offspring is certainly a moral wrong if not a legal harm." Taking this claim to its full conclusion, it is further argued that parental obligations are paramount, and if reproduction is contemplated, there is an ethical obligation to prevent harm to the offspring, requiring that one's genotype should be determined so that appropriate steps can be taken to avert disease in future generations.

> However, the aforementioned extreme view disregards the potential harm of both psychological stress and societal repercussions to the would-be parent. Because the chance of passing along the defect is often a statistical risk, rather than an absolute certainty, the following question is important: What calculus should be performed to clearly establish when the risk is sufficient to demand that procreation not be pursued? Furthermore, on practical grounds, each and every one of us has the potential to pass on genetic liabilities, which in turn may cause suffering and pain to our offspring. How much pain and suffering are required to necessitate pursuit of adoption or gene therapy (if and when available)?

C. Christopher Hook et al., *Primer on Medical Genomics Part XIII: Ethical and Regulatory Issues*, 79 Mayo Clin. Proc. 645, 646 (2004). Hook, like Offit, concludes that educating and counseling patients is preferred over the imposition of a duty to warn. When, if ever, is more direct action by a doctor required? When, if ever, should a patient be compelled to divulge genetic information to family members?

3. *Public interest exceptions to privacy and genetics exceptionalism.* Offit and colleagues mention the "public interest" exceptions to medical privacy laws and its application in the context of infectious diseases. Is reluctance amongst the medical community to apply the "public interest" exception to genetic information an example of genetics exceptionalism? Is it appropriate? Note that in some cases, the status of patients with TB who fail to comply with their drug regimen can be reported to the public health officials to protect the public interest, and the patient might be confined as a result. Is it more or less intrusive to inform a patient's close family relatives of the results of a patient's genetic test and counsel them as to their potential risks?

Molloy v. Meier

Supreme Court of Minnesota, 2004.
679 N.W.2d 711.

■ MEYER, J.

This case arises out of the medical treatment of S.F., the daughter of Kimberly Molloy and her ex-husband, Robert Flomer. As a young girl, S.F. was treated by appellant Dr. Diane M. Meier . . . When S.F. was three years old, Dr. Meier noted during a check-up that S.F. was developmentally delayed.

In her notes from the May 18 visit, Dr. Meier wrote "? chromosomes + fragile X," which meant she intended to order chromosomal testing and testing for Fragile X syndrome. In May of 1992, a Fragile X chromosomal test capable of diagnosing the disorder with 70 to 80 percent accuracy was in widespread use. Dr. Meier conceded that "it was appropriate to test [S.F.] for Fragile X in keeping with accepted standards of pediatric practice on May 18, 1992" . . .

. . . Dr. Meier received the [chromosome] test results, telephoned the Flomers and informed them that the test results were negative; i.e., normal. However, Dr. Meier failed to mention that Fragile X testing had not been performed. The Flomers then informed Molloy that the test results were "normal." Based on the fact that Dr. Meier had mentioned Fragile X in her discussion of chromosomal testing, Molloy assumed that the negative test results included a negative result for Fragile X.

Meanwhile, on June 23, 1992, S.F. was referred . . . [to] Dr. Reno Backus . . . Molloy inquired about her chances of conceiving another child with S.F.'s defect. According to Molloy, Dr. Backus responded that S.F.'s problems were not genetic in origin and the risk that Molloy might give birth to another child like S.F. was extremely remote, especially with a father other than Robert Flomer. Dr. Backus was aware that chromosomal testing had been done but he made his assessment before the test results were known.

Several years later S.F. was referred to Dr. Kathryn Green. . . . There were no Fragile X testing results in the chart because the testing had never been done.

In the meantime, Molloy remarried and gave birth to M.M. on June 30, 1998. M.M. showed signs of the same developmental difficulties as S.F., so his pediatrician, Dr. David Tilstra, ordered Fragile X testing for him. The Fragile X test results were positive; i.e., M.M. carried the Fragile X genetic disorder. When Dr. Tilstra received the positive results, he counseled Kimberly and Glenn Molloy about Fragile X syndrome and recommended that they and other potentially affected family members receive testing. Based on Dr. Tilstra's recommendation, S.F. and Kimberly Molloy were tested for Fragile X, and it was discovered that they both carried the genetic disorder.

Molloy commenced this lawsuit on August 23, 2001, alleging that Drs. Meier, Backus, and Green and their employers were negligent in the care and treatment rendered to S.F., Kimberly Molloy, and Glenn Molloy by failing to order Fragile X testing on S.F., failing to properly read those lab tests that were performed, mistakenly reporting that S.F. had been tested for Fragile X, and failing to provide counseling to Kimberly and Glenn Molloy regarding the risk of passing an inheritable genetic abnormality to future children. Molloy claimed she would not have conceived M.M. if Drs. Meier, Backus, and Green had correctly diagnosed S.F. with Fragile X and informed Molloy of the diagnosis.

. . . Molloy presented expert testimony of a pediatrician and a pediatric neurologist who described the prevailing standard of care in the medical community with respect to testing and counseling for genetic disorders. The experts indicated that a patient who exhibits the symptoms of this disorder with a family history of mental retardation should be tested for Fragile X. Further, a physician who identifies the possibility of Fragile X has a responsibility to follow up to confirm that the tests are performed. Finally, the physician of a child with Fragile X has an obligation to provide genetic counseling to the child's family.

. . .

Molloy advances two legal theories. She first argues that a physician-patient relationship existed between her and the appellants that gave rise to a legal duty to warn her about the risks of becoming pregnant as a carrier of Fragile X. Additionally, Molloy urges this court to hold that even if a physician-patient relationship cannot be established, a physician's duty to warn others of a patient's genetic disorder arises from the foreseeability of injury.

The appellants argue that their duty is owed only to S.F., the person with whom they had a physician-patient relationship. The appellants claim that they met with S.F. solely for S.F.'s own benefit and not for the benefit of her family. If any duty extended beyond the minor patient, the appellants argue that it should reach only those parties who have a contractual relationship with the physician, in this case the Flomers, S.F.'s custodial parents.

. . .

Our decision today is informed by the practical reality of the field of genetic testing and counseling; genetic testing and diagnosis does not affect only the patient. Both the patient and her family can benefit from accurate testing and diagnosis. And conversely, both the patient and her family can be harmed by negligent testing and diagnosis. Molloy's experts indicate that a physician would have a duty to inform the parents of a child diagnosed with Fragile X disorder. The appellants admit that their practice is to inform parents in such a case. The standard of care thus acknowledges that families rely on physicians to communicate a diagnosis of the genetic disorder to the patient's family. It is foreseeable that a negligent diagnosis of Fragile X will cause harm not only to the patient, but to the family of the patient as well. This is particularly true regarding parents who have consulted the physicians concerning the patient's condition and have been advised of the need for genetic testing.

We therefore hold that a physician's duty regarding genetic testing and diagnosis extends beyond the patient to biological parents who foreseeably may be harmed by a breach of that duty. In this case, the patient suffered from a serious disorder that had a high probability of being genetically transmitted and for which a reliable and accepted test was widely available. The appellants should have foreseen that parents of childbearing years might conceive another child in the absence of knowledge of the genetic disorder. The appellants owed a duty of care regarding genetic testing and diagnosis, and the resulting medical advice, not only to S.F. but also to her parents. In recognizing this duty, we ... conclude that the duty arises where it is reasonably foreseeable that the parents would be injured if the advice is negligently given.

Appellants suggest that recognizing a duty to Molloy would extend a physician's duty to an unreasonable extent, requiring the physician to seek out and inform distant relatives.... [W]e need not, and do not, address whether the duty recognized here extends beyond biological parents who foreseeably will rely on genetic testing and diagnosis and therefore foreseeably may be injured by negligence in discharging the duty of care.

NOTES AND QUESTIONS

1. Ellen Wright Clayton uses the case of a man who died of colon cancer in the 1960s to illustrate the complexities of the so-called "right to know" genetic information:

> When the same disease developed in his daughter approximately 25 years later, she obtained her father's pathology slides, discovered that he had had diffuse adenomatous polyposis coli, and sued the estate of her father's surgeon, alleging that the physician should have warned her about her 50 percent risk of having the disorder. An intermediate appellate court in New Jersey ruled that the physician had a duty to warn the daughter directly (she would have been a child at the time of her father's death), perhaps even over her father's objections.

> This is only one court's view in one case, but given how much attention it received, it is important to ask whether this was a good result. Two central tenets of Western medicine are that physicians should focus on the interests of their patients and that they should protect the confidentiality of their patients' medical information. Yet the tools of genomic medicine often reveal information about health risks faced not only by patients but also by their relatives. What should clinicians do? It seems clear that they should tell their patients about the risks faced by family members. The harder questions are whether physicians are ethically permitted to contact the relatives themselves, in contravention of traditional patient-centered norms, and whether they should be legally required to do so.

> This issue must be viewed in the light of the fact that the duty to protect confidentiality is not absolute. Physicians are required to report numerous infectious diseases, and they have been held liable for failing to warn people whom their patients have specifically threatened with violence. The question then becomes more complex: are genetic risks sufficiently similar to these existing exceptions to the requirement of confidentiality that they warrant an exception as well? Over the years, numerous prominent advisory bodies have said no, opining that physicians should be permitted to breach confidentiality in

order to warn third parties of genetic risks only as a last resort to avert serious harm.

These learned opinions, however, are not the end of the matter, in part because they lack the force of law. In fact, as the case above illustrates, relatives have sued the primary patients' physicians for failing to warn them of their own genetic risks—and won limited victories, although none have been awarded monetary damages. The decisions in the colon-cancer case and a similar one in Florida have been criticized for both their legal reasoning and their deviation from ethical guidelines, but they have not been overturned and, in the tradition of the common law, may be persuasive to other courts. Physicians who breach their patients' confidentiality and warn family members are not likely to incur substantial liability, even under HIPAA. As a result, physicians might understandably conclude that warning relatives is the least risky option.

The existing directives are thus in conflict: "expert consensus," ethical analysis, and the HIPAA regulations argue for honoring confidentiality, whereas at least one legal opinion holds that physicians fail to warn a patient's relatives at their peril. Given the press of other business, legislators are not likely to resolve this conflict soon. In this setting, clinicians should inform their patients about the risks their relatives face, discuss the appropriateness of sharing this information and offer assistance, trust—usually realistically—that patients will in turn tell their relatives who are at risk, and hope that the courts will get it right in the future.

Ellen Wright Clayton, *Ethical, Legal, and Social Implications of Genomic Medicine*, 349 NEW ENG. J. MED. 562, 566–567 (2003).

2. Patients may be keenly interested in genetic information for the purposes of treatment, reproductive decisionmaking, or life planning. If no beneficial intervention exists, patients are faced with the hard choice about whether they want to know their future health status such as the probability of developing Huntington's or Alzheimer's disease. This is an agonizing decision. How can society ensure that patients receive sound genetic counseling to assist them in such a momentous decision?

3.   HUMAN GENETIC RESEARCH DATABASES: THE PROMISE OF TRANS–NATIONAL BIOBANKS

Before the advent of the Human Genome Project and ensuing research, scientists could collect genetic data from a relatively small number of people and address rare, single-gene diseases. More common diseases are now viewed through a genomic lens. To understand complex diseases such as cancer, diabetes or schizophrenia, it is necessary to collect genetic information from a broader group of people. Human Genetic Research Databases (HGRDs) have amassed thousands of people's genetic material so that it may be stored for research purposes. HGRDs involve the collection, storage, and analysis of genetic samples in the form of blood or tissue. The genetic information is linked with clinical, genealogical, and/or lifestyle information from a specific population, and the data are stored in searchable databases for the use of researchers. *See* Bartha Maria Knoppers, *International Lessons: Biobanks, in* INSTITUTE OF MEDICINE, GENOMICS AND THE PUBLIC'S HEALTH IN THE 21ST CENTURY: WORKSHOP REPORT (Forthcoming 2005); Melissa A. Austin, et al., *Monitoring Ethical, legal, and Social Issues in Developing Population Genetic Databases*, 5 GENETICS IN MED. 451 (2003). HGRDs are sometimes referred to as biobanks, cohorts, gene banks, population studies, or genome databases. HGRDs offer great promise for understanding gene/gene and gene/environment interactions in human diseases. At the same time they hold the potential to embarrass or harm individuals or groups. Can these important social experiments be conducted in an ethically acceptable manner?

To date, a number of HGRDs have been established or proposed, including Iceland DeCode Biobank; United Kingdom Biobank; Estonian Genome Project; CARTaGENE in Québec, Canada; UmanGenomics in Vasterbotten, Sweden; Genome Institute of Singapore; and Personalized Medicine Research Project (PMRP) in Wisconsin. *See* Melissa A. Austin, et al., *Genebanks: A Comparison of Eight Proposed International Genetic Databases*, 6 Community Genetics 37–45 (2003). Perhaps the most publicly discussed HGRD is the Iceland DeCode Biobank:

> Modern information technology . . . offers the possibility of mining large data sets for knowledge, without a priori hypotheses, by systematically juxtaposing various data in the search for the best fit. This kind of pure combinatorial analysis may be particularly powerful in the case of the common diseases, most of which are complex and have remained beyond the reach of the classic hypothesis-driven approach to biomedical research. However, to take full advantage of the new techniques, it is important to have access to large amounts of primary data in one place. This calls for large data bases on health care that can be mined for knowledge, either alone or in combination with other data on disease and health, such as variations in the human genome.
>
> . . . .
>
> According to the law, the data in the IHD [Icelandic Healthcare Database] will be collected under the assumption of "presumed consent." Presumed consent is a nebulous concept, but in the context of this project, we regard it as the consent of society to the use of health care information according to the norms of society. These norms may vary from one society to another and may change with time. It is important that the data in the IHD will be only data from medical records that are produced in the process of delivering health care. Some argue that presumed consent is inconsistent with the right of individuals to decide for themselves and actually amounts to no consent at all. However, presumed consent is the standard used for research on health care data that is produced in the process of delivering medical services. It is not certain that we would have health care as we know it today if explicit consent had been a prerequisite for the use of medical data.
>
> . . . .
>
> The majority of the international bioethics community has supported the use of broad consent. . . . Some members of this community, however, remain skeptical of the wisdom of broad consent because of the difficulties in making certain that consent is informed. Informed consent was devised to protect the autonomy of individual subjects against overzealous scientists. Nobody should participate in biomedical research unless he or she makes an informed decision to do so, and nobody should be coerced or tricked into making such a decision. The goal is to protect the autonomy of the individual; the tool is informed consent.
>
> . . . .

Why should Icelanders trust a private company to protect their personal health care information? It is probably better for a private company to hold this information than for the state to do so, since governments can violate the privacy of individuals to advance the interests of society as a whole. Moreover, if a health care data base managed by a private company violates privacy, the company can be closed down. According to the Icelandic law, deCODE will lose the license to develop and use the data base if the conditions of the license, including the stipulations regarding the protection of privacy, are not met. Violations of the data-base law are also punishable by monetary fines and imprisonment.

. . .

Since the data that are entered into the IHD are simply copies of data that will remain within health care institutions, it is not easy to see how the data base could restrict the freedom of science. There is, however, some concern that the commercial mission of private enterprise will influence the way research on the data base is performed and how the results are distributed and used.

It is important to ensure that research based on the IHD meets international ethical standards. Therefore, the IHD will be subject to the oversight of four government regulatory bodies: the Data Protection Commission of Iceland (appointed by the ministry of justice), an interdisciplinary bioethics committee, the National Bioethics Committee, and an operational oversight committee (the last three appointed by the minister of health).

Jeffrey R. Gulcher & Kári Stefánsson, *The Icelandic Healthcare Database and Informed Consent*, 342 NEW ENG. J. MED. 1827, 1827–1830 (2000).

NOTES AND QUESTIONS

1. *Informed Consent for Participation in HGRDs.* The establishment of genetic databases raises formidable ethical issues. Will each individual be permitted to give or withhold consent before collection of tissue is permitted? If so, would this undermine the scientific integrity of the data by introducing a sampling bias? Do traditional notions of informed consent, when applied to the vast scale of biobanks, unduly inhibit progress? What further consent may be necessary to authorize future or secondary uses of the data? Are notions such as "presumed consent," "broad consent," "generalized consent," "community consent," or "community consultation" helpful or do they distort the true meaning of informed consent?

2. *Protection of Privacy.* How will personal genetic information stored in HGRDs be kept private? Persons whose data are stored on HGRDs express concern about the privacy of their genetic information. Large scale databases may not be able to provide the degree of privacy traditionally expected in the health care system. If personally identifiable data are disclosed to family members, employers or insurers, patients may be embarrassed or harmed. How can researchers protect against stigma and discrimination? These are important questions that have thus far thwarted the development of systematic genetic databases in the United States. Many scholars believe that privacy rules should attach to personally identifiable data, but not anonymous or aggregate data. Given that genetic information is, by definition, associated with a specific individual, does it make sense to think of genetic data as unidentifiable? Would it be reasonable to think of genetic data as anonymous if it would be extraordinarily difficult to identify the source of a single individual in a large database? Other scholars suggest that privacy rules could be relaxed if the data are "linkable" or "double-coded." Linkable data systems make it very difficult for the researchers themselves to identify individuals from their databases because linking data with individuals requires a "key" that is held by a third (neutral) party. Provided that the researcher cannot gain access to the "key," should these data be regarded as effectively anonymous?

3. *Personal Feedback: The "Right to Know."* If data are identifiable or linkable, should individuals have a right to know if their genetic material reveals something important for their health and life? Suppose the data reveal that an individual has a predisposition to a disease that could be prevented or ameliorated? Should the holders of the data have a duty to inform the individual? What about feedback of data that are not wholly reliable or clinically useful to the individual? How practical would it be to assure personal feedback with very large data systems?

4. *Privately Operated Biobanks.* While some biobanks are state-run or non-profit, others are privately organized commercial ventures that will sell their findings to drug companies. Does private data banking pose special ethical concerns? Is it likely that private companies would sufficiently respect patient interests? Would private ventures aggressively and adequately pursue the public interest?

5. *Global Aspects of Biobanks.* As mentioned above, biobanks have been established in many parts of the world. However, they are subject to different national laws[7] and policies,[8] and have highly disparate forms of organization. Is there a case for harmonization of data sets held by biobanks to make them more interchangeable and useful to researchers around the globe? At present, there is a lack of internationally agreed upon rules and common taxonomy, making databases incompatible. There is also a proliferation of international guidelines relating to biobanks.[9]

7. *The Governance of Biobanks.* Biobanks raise important questions about the commercial exchange of human tissue, financial incentives for participation in research, fairness to donors, public access to research materials, and incentives for scientific innovation. Given the novel and large-scale implications of biobanks, there has been a great deal of discussion regarding how they should be governed. Neither government nor private control has provided a comprehensive model for addressing the complexities and potential risks that biobanks involve. David and Richard Winickoff have proposed an innovative solution to this quandary:

> The consent forms that private biobanks use often include clauses that waive donors' rights to their blood and tissue samples. These clauses result from the increasing private investment in research and recent claims by tissue donors for a share of the profits derived from their samples. These clauses are legally and ethically problematic. First, hospital consent forms that transfer property rights to institutional biobanks may be legally unenforceable as contractual promises owing to "power asymmetry" and "undue influence." Second, the

7. *See, e.g.*, Human Gene Research Act, Dec. 13, 2000 (Est.); Biobanks [Health Care] Act, May 23, 2002 (Swed.); Act on Biobanks, May 13, 2000 (Ice.); Act on Biobanks, Feb. 21, 2003 (Nor.).

8. *See, e.g.*, Canadian Biotechnology Advisory Committee, Genetic Research and Privacy (2004); German National Ethics Council, Biobanks for Research (2004); France: CCNE Opinion 77, Ethical Issues Raised by Collections of Biological Material and Associated Information Data: "Biobanks" (2003); Australia law reform Commission, Essentially Yours, Part E: Human Genetic Databases (2003).

9. *See, e.g.*, Human Genome Organization (HUGO), Statement on Human Genomic Databases (Dec. 2002); World Health Organization, Genetic Databases: Assessing the Benefits and the Impact on Human Rights and Patient Rights (2003); UNESCO, International Declaration on Human Genetic Data (2003). *See also*, Melissa A. Austin, et al., *Applying International Guidelines on Ethical, Legal and Social Issues to New International Genebanks*, JURIMETRICS (Forthcoming 2005).

legal transfer of property might signal to the donors that they have given up any control of the samples, which would undermine their right to withdrawal. Soliciting and obtaining gifts of tissue by informed consent overextends its traditional role and threatens the trust between the donor and the institution. Despite some debate about private-sector collaborations with medical institutions, private biobanks are amassing millions of samples, and health centers seem ready to supply them. More creative thinking is needed to solve the problems in the governance of biobanks.

When a person agrees to donate tissue, the recipient has a responsibility to serve as a trustee, or steward, of the tissue in order to ensure protection of the contribution. The National Research Council has suggested that for a worldwide collection of DNA, "a more sophisticated and complicated approach would be to form an international organization to serve as a trustee and fund-holder for all the sampled populations." The charitable trust is a promising legal structure for handling such a set of obligations, for promoting donor participation in research governance, and for stimulating research that will benefit the public.

Under a trust agreement, the tissue donor, or settlor, formally expresses a wish to transfer his or her property interest in the tissue to the trust. The permission form could be used for this purpose. The settlor appoints a trustee of the property, who has legal fiduciary duties to keep or use the property for the benefit of a specified party, the beneficiary. In a charitable trust, the general public acts as the beneficiary.

A charitable trust is an elegant and flexible legal model that has a number of advantages over private biobanks. First, charitable trusts accord well with the altruism that characterizes gifts of tissue. If altruistic donations are solicited by hospitals for research, then the hospitals should act as stewards rather than as brokers. Second, the architect of the trust can provide the donor group with an advisory role in the governance of the trust. We believe that the patient population of a medical center, with appropriate leadership from the institution, would have the necessary sense of community to make the advisory role meaningful. Finally, private biobanks may be forced to sell off their inventory in the event of bankruptcy, but charitable trusts have the advantage of longevity. This feature is important not only for donors but also for researchers who perform longitudinal studies.

The Charitable Trust as a Model for Genomic Biobanks, 349 NEW ENG. J. MED. 1180–1184 (2003).

C.   STRATIFICATION, JUSTICE, AND OPPORTUNITY

The field of genetics is deeply complex, not only because of the science but also, as we have seen, because of the difficult ethical, legal, and social problems which inhere in the field. Genetics research, almost by definition, stratifies the population according to the genetic predisposition for sickness and premature death. It is only by singling out individuals and groups at high genetic risk that it is possible to offer counseling, preventive strategies, or treatment. In this sense, genetic stratification offers great opportunity. If researchers did not, for example, identify people at risk of genetic disease (e.g., sickle cell among African Americans or Tay Sachs among Ashkenazi Jews), they could not offer beneficial services. Indeed, questions of fairness would arise if minorities were excluded from research or needed services. Thus, stratification is essential for fulfilling the promise of genetics to individuals and groups of all religions, races, and cultures.

Stratification, of course, is also the *sine qua non* of stigma and discrimination. Unfair treatment is based on difference and genetics can underscore the differences (as well as the similarities) among people. Just as singling out individuals or groups for genetic risk can bring benefits, so too can it bring harm. People who are labeled as genetically different can suffer embarrassment, stigma, and discrimination. Still worse, these individuals can suffer the humiliation of policies designed to limit their reproductive opportunities. There are shameful historical precedents for just these kinds of harm, which helps explain the public's distrust of overly ambitious projects in the field of genetics. Stratification affects groups as well as individuals. A finding that certain ethnic, religious, or racial groups have adverse genetic traits can be hurtful.

Stratification raises squarely the problem of distributive justice. The benefits and burdens of genetic discovery should be distributed fairly. Those in need should have fair opportunities of receiving services irrespective of race, social class, or other status. Those who are vulnerable should not have to bear disproportionate hardships in research, practice, or policies. Most people would agree that genetic fairness is a worthy goal. Where people disagree, however, is how to determine fair allocations of benefits and burdens.

1.   THE HISTORICAL LESSONS OF EUGENICS

> The core notion of eugenics, that people's lives will probably go better if they have genes conducive to health and other advantageous traits, has lost little of its appeal. Eugenics, in this very limited sense, shines a beacon even as it casts a shadow. Granted, when our society last undertook to improve our genes, the result was mayhem. The task for humanity now is to accomplish what eluded the eugenicists entirely, to square the pursuit of genetic health and enhancement with the requirements of justice

ALLEN BUCHANAN ET AL., FROM CHANCE TO CHOICE: GENETICS AND JUSTICE 56–57 (2000)

The modern-day genetics movement must overcome the sad legacy of eugenics. No matter how noble the intentions of geneticists today, their efforts to improve public health through genetic intervention are likely to elicit haunting memories of a less well-intentioned era. In the first half of the past century, eugenics—the study of hereditary improvement of the human race by controlled selective breeding—became a popular field of inquiry, particularly in Germany. Long before the emergence of Adolf Hitler, Germans were interested in eugenics. Dr. Alfred Ploetz founded the Archives of Race–Theory and Social Biology in 1904 and the German Society of Racial Hygiene in 1905. Under Hitler, the lurking danger of eugenic thought was unleashed in the form of the Holocaust, in which millions who were deemed unfit for life perished at the hands of the Nazis.

The eugenics movement was not limited to Germany. In the United States, as recently as the 1930s, state laws authorized the sterilization of "undesirable" citizens; sterilization statutes remained on the books in many states until the 1960s. Justice Oliver Wendell Holmes approved eugenic policy when, in 1927, he authorized the sterilization of a young woman with mental retardation, commenting, "Three generations of imbeciles are enough." Buck v. Bell, 274 U.S. 200, 207, 47 S.Ct. 584, 71 L.Ed. 1000 (1927).

While modern genetics rejects the policies of eugenics and seeks health improvement, there is still, as the following reading suggests, pause for concern.

Allen Buchanan et al., *Two Models for Genetic Intervention*

in FROM CHANCE TO CHOICE 11–14, 55–60 (2000).

THE PUBLIC HEALTH MODEL

Our "ethical autopsy" on eugenics identifies two quite different perspectives from which genetic intervention may be viewed. The first is what we call the public health model; the second is the personal choice model.

The public health model stresses the production of benefits and the avoidance of harms for groups. It uncritically assumes that the appropriate mode of evaluating options is some form of cost-benefit (or cost-effectiveness) calculation. To the extent that the public health model even recognizes an ethical dimension to decisions about the application of scientific knowledge or technology, it tends to assume that sound ethical reasoning is exclusively consequentialist (or utilitarian) in nature. In other words, it assumes that whether a policy or an action is deemed to be right is thought to depend solely on whether it produces the greatest balance of good over bad outcomes.

More important, consequentialist ethical reasoning—like cost-benefit and cost-effectiveness calculations—assumes that it is not only possible but permissible and even mandatory to aggregate goods and bads (costs and benefits) across individuals. Harms to some can be offset by gains to others; what matters is the sum. Critics of such simple and unqualified consequentialist reasoning, including ourselves, are quick to point out its fundamental flaws: Such reasoning is distributationally insensitive because it fails to take seriously the separateness and inviolability of persons.

.   .   .

THE PERSONAL SERVICE MODEL

Today eugenics is almost universally condemned. Partly in reaction to the tendency of the most extreme eugenicists to discount individual freedom and welfare from the supposed good of society, medical geneticists and genetic counselors since World War II have adopted an almost absolute commitment to "nondirectiveness" in their relations with those seeking genetic services. Recoiling from the public health model that dominated the eugenics movement, and especially from the vertical disease metaphor, they publicly endorse the view that genetic tests and interventions are simply services offered to individuals—goods for private consumption—to be accepted or refused as individuals see fit.

This way of conceiving of genetic interventions takes them out of the public domain, relegating them to the sphere of private choices. Advocates of the personal service model proclaim that the fundamental value on which it rests is individual autonomy. Whether a couple at risk for conceiving a child with a genetic disease takes a genetic test and how they use the knowledge thus obtained is their business, not society's, even if the decision to vaccinate a child for common childhood infectious diseases is a matter of public health and as such justifies restricting parental choice.

The personal service model serves as a formidable bulwark against the excesses of the crude consequentialist ethical reasoning that tainted the application of the public health model in the era of eugenics. But it does so at a prohibitive price: It ignores the obligation to prevent harm as well as some of the most basic requirements of justice. By elevating autonomy to the exclusion of all other values, the personal service model offers a myopic view of the moral landscape.

. . .

In addition, if genetic services are treated as goods for private consumption, the cumulative effects of many individual choices in the "genetic marketplace" may limit the autonomy of many people, and perhaps of all people. Economic pressures, including requirements for insurability and employment, as well as social stigma directed toward those who produce children with "defects" that could have been avoided, may narrow rather than expand meaningful choice. Finally, treating genetic interventions as personal services may exacerbate inequalities in opportunities if the prevention of genetic diseases or genetic enhancements are available only to the rich. It would be more accurate to say, then, that the personal service model gives free reign to some dimensions of the autonomy of some people, often at the expense of others.

NOTES AND QUESTIONS

1. *The Personal Service Model and Eugenics.* Buchanan and colleagues seem to imply that the use of the personal service model ensures that genetic interventions will not amount to eugenics. Other authors, however, claim that there is a new eugenics movement based on the personal service model. Recall Curtis A. Kin's description of the new eugenics movement:

> The old fears and criticisms of eugenics do not apply to the new eugenics movement, which is neither state-sponsored nor an experiment imposed on unwilling participants. Rather, the new eugenics respects individual autonomy in what Robert Nozick has termed the "genetic supermarket," where individuals freely shop and choose the features and traits they desire for themselves and their children. Supporters of the new eugenics argue that the "genetic supermarket" poses no significant problems because there exists no centralized control over the future of human development.

Curtis A. Kin, *Coming Soon to the "Genetic Supermarket" Near You*, 48 STAN. L. REV. 1573 (1996), *reproduced in* Sec. III, *supra*. Does the lack of state action make the personal service model any less threatening? The International Bioethics Committee talks about eugenics in terms of attitudes, rather than state action:

[T]here is an underlying assumption [amongst eugenicists] that genetic differ- ences between individuals constitute a rational basis for labels of "superior" and "inferior." The point is that eugenics is built upon an *attitude* that seeks its justification in science. . . . These are habits of mind and ways of thinking philosophically that are hostile to the key notion of the inherent dignity of the human individual and the inviolable and inalienable human rights that arise from the international consensus about the value of human beings.

Chee Heng Leng et al., Bioethics and Human Population Genetics Research 16, United Nations Educational, Scientific and Cultural Organization, CIP/ BIO/95/CONF.002/5 (Nov. 15, 1995). Under this conception of eugenics, the actor is less relevant. Can eugenics be carried about by individual consumers of genetic interventions? If so, what are the state's obligations in upholding human rights and the inherent dignity of human beings? To what extent should the "genetic super- market" be regulated?

2.   *The Public Health Model of Genetic Intervention.* While the public health model of genetic intervention has been largely supplanted by the personal service model, the "crude consequentialist ethical reasoning that tainted the application of the public health model in the era of eugenics" is not solely a thing of the past. The International Bioethics Committee gives the example of the Singapore Government, whose populations policies are "guided by eugenics—women who graduate from universities are encouraged to bear more children in the belief that their children have higher 'intelligence', while less-educated women are offered disincentives to have more than two children." Chee Heng Leng et al., Bioethics and Human Population Genetics Research 16, United Nations Educational, Scientific and Cul- tural Organization, CIP/BIO/95/CONF.002/5 (Nov. 15, 1995).

2.   GENETIC STRATIFICATION BASED ON RACE AND ETHNICITY

Recent genetic studies have been interpreted in significantly different ways, with some observers arguing that new genetic information is under- mining traditional notions of race by proving that race is nothing more than a social construct and is not biologically based. Other observers reach very different conclusions, arguing that genetic studies confirm that race is biologically rooted. This controversy may have far-reaching effects on public policy.

Richard S. Cooper et al., *Race and Genomics*
348 NEW ENG. J. MED. 1166 (2003).

Race is a thoroughly contentious topic, as one might expect of an idea that intrudes on the everyday life of so many people. The modern concept of race grew out of the experience of Europeans in naming and organizing the populations encountered in the rapid expansion of their empires. As a way to categorize humans, race has since come to take on a wide range of meanings, mixing social and biologic ingredients in varied proportions. This plasticity has made it a tool that fits equally well in the hands of dema- gogues who want to justify genocide and eugenics and of health scientists who want to improve surveillance for disease. It is not surprising, there- fore, that diametrically opposing views have been voiced about its scientific and social value. Indeed, few other concepts used in the conduct of ordinary science are the subject of a passionate debate about whether they actually exist.

Into this storm of controversy rides genomics. With the acknowledgment that race is the product of a marriage of social and biologic influences, it has been proposed that genomics now at least offers the opportunity to put its biologic claims to an objective test. If those claims are validated, race will become a way to choose drug therapy for patients, categorize persons for genetic research, and understand the causes of disease. Genomics, with its technological innovations and authority as "big science," might thereby solve the conundrum of race and bring peace to the warring factions.

Promotion of a drug for a race-specific "niche market" could distract physicians from therapies for which unequivocal evidence of benefit already exists. Race-specific therapy draws its rationale from the presumption that the frequencies of genetic variants influencing the efficacy of the drug are substantially different among races. This result is hard to demonstrate for any class of drugs, including those used to treat heart failure. Although a study of polymorphisms in drug-metabolizing enzymes did, in fact, show statistically significant variation in allele frequencies according to race, neither racial categories nor genetic clusters were sufficiently precise to make them clinically useful in guiding the choice of drugs. What is lost in these arguments is the difficulty of translating differences among groups into a test that has adequate predictive value to help with clinical decisions. Race can help to target screening for a disease-associated mutation that is present at a high frequency in one population and is virtually absent in another, but it is impossible for race as we recognize it clinically to provide both perfect sensitivity and specificity for the presence of a DNA-sequence variant. For this reason, race has never been shown to be an adequate proxy for use in choosing a drug; if you really need to know whether a patient has a particular genotype, you will have to do the test to find out.

The availability of high-throughput genotyping creates the opportunity for increasingly sophisticated analyses of the extent to which continental populations vary genetically. Analysis of a large set of multiallelic microsatellite loci has shown that it is possible to cluster persons into population groups with high statistical accuracy. Although clustering persons according to geographic origin has been accomplished most effectively with the use of highly informative, rapidly mutating, microsatellite loci, the use of single-nucleotide polymorphisms (SNPs) or their corresponding haplotypes also results in some degree of classification according to continent.

However, the public health relevance of these data remains controversial. One view holds that the ability to categorize persons according to continental "race" validates the clinical and epidemiologic use of self-reported racial ancestry in terms of the categories of white, black, Asian, Pacific Islander, and Native American used by the U.S. Census. We disagree. The success of microsatellite loci in classifying persons according to continental group depends in part on the cumulative effect of minor differences in the frequencies of common alleles and in part on the effect of population-specific alleles. In neither case is it apparent that such differences have relevance for traits that are important to health. Most population-specific microsatellite alleles are unlikely to be functional; rather, like a last name, they merely help to verify the geographic origin of a person's ancestry. Accumulated small differences in common alleles will yield differences in population risk only if a disease is caused primarily by interactions among multiple loci, and this is both mathematically and biologically implausible

The real effect of the biologic concept of race has always been its implications for common quantitative traits. Marked differences in the rates of cardiovascular diseases, for example, have been held up as examples of how race matters. Reframed in genomic terms, it is argued that if "biological is defined by susceptibility to, and natural history of, a chronic disease, then ... numerous studies ... have documented biological differences among the races." However, there is no body of evidence to support these broad claims about chronic diseases. Although it is obvious that many genetic diseases vary markedly among populations, those conditions are generally rare. Tay Sachs disease, cystic fibrosis, and hemoglobinopathies, for example, are absent in many populations but present in others. But for these conditions, continental populations are not the categories of interest: persons of Jewish descent, not "whites," share a risk of Tay Sachs disease; the frequency of cystic fibrosis varies widely within Europe; and thalassemia occurs in a variety of populations distributed from Italy to Thailand.

Many single-gene disorders have now been defined at the molecular level, and the emerging challenge faced by geneticists is to "make the genome relevant to public health." Defining the molecular underpinnings of common chronic diseases has therefore become the central focus of genetic epidemiology. By extension, some investigators have turned with renewed enthusiasm to race as a tool for categorizing population risk. This approach draws on the practice, of long standing in the public health field in the United States, of granting priority to race or ethnic background as a demographic category—a surveillance practice, it is worth noting, that is virtually unique in the world. At the present time, however, very little is known about the genetic component of diseases of complex causation. Few, if any, well-characterized susceptibility genes have been identified for any of the degenerative conditions that kill at least 5 percent of the population, and we do not even know whether the individual variants are common or rare or whether they affect a protein's structure or its level of expression.

Since we do not know about the genetic variants that predispose persons to common chronic diseases, one might assume that arguments for the existence of genetic predispositions would be made for all population groups equally. The reality is very different. Minority groups, particularly blacks in the United States, are assumed to be genetically predisposed to virtually all common chronic diseases. Genes are regularly proposed as the cause when no genetic data have been obtained, and the social and biologic factors remain hopelessly confounded. Even when molecular data are collected, causal arguments are based on nonsignificant findings or genetic variation that does not have an established association with the disease being studied. Coincidence is not a plausible explanation of the widespread occurrence of this practice over time and across subdisciplines. The correlation between the use of unsupported genetic inferences and the social standing of a group is glaring evidence of bias and demonstrates how race is used both to categorize and to rank order subpopulations.

Not only are the relevant genetic data absent, but the distribution of polygenic phenotypes does not suggest that race is a useful category. Consider as an example height, a continuous trait that is highly heritable in all populations. Does continental race tell us something useful about average height? People who attain both the tallest stature (the Masai) and the shortest (the Biaka) are found in sub-Saharan Africa; Swedish people have traditionally been much taller than Sicilians; and although Japanese people used to be short, the current generation of children in Japan cannot fit in the desks in schools. The concept of race does not summarize this information effectively. If that complexity is multiplied by thousands of traits, which are randomly distributed among groups within continents, one gets an idea of the limitations of race as a classification scheme.

Although the rapid pace of change in genomics makes today's conclusions obsolete tomorrow, some predictions are in order. We can expect genomics increasingly to negate the old-fashioned concept that differences in genetic susceptibility to common diseases are racially distributed. In any common disease, many genes are likely to be involved, and each gene will have many variants. All the current data indicate that susceptibility alleles tend to be old, have moderate-to-small effects, and are shared among many populations. The *APOE 4* allele, a well-studied example that contributes to a small extent to individual and potential risk for traits such as heart disease and dementia, is found in virtually all populations, albeit at varying rates.

Recent genomic surveys have also shown that as few as three to five common haplotypes capture the bulk of segregating variation at any specific locus throughout the genome, and those haplotypes are generally represented in the populations of all continents. Therefore, if susceptibility alleles for chronic diseases are located on common haplotypes, those alleles must be shared by members of all populations. Measuring the net effect of these genetic influences in a given population will require summing the frequencies of these susceptibility alleles in all genomic regions, while taking into account the environmental factors that are either difficult to measure or wholly unknown. Given these daunting epidemiologic challenges, it will be very difficult to calculate the "genetic susceptibility score" for any particular racial category.

This point requires further attention. There is no doubt that there are some important biologic differences among populations, and molecular techniques can help to define what those differences are. Some traits, such as skin color, vary in a strikingly systematic pattern. The inference does not follow, however, that genetic variation among human populations falls into racial categories or that race, as we currently define it, provides an effective system for summarizing that variation. The confused nature of this debate is apparent when we recognize that although everyone, from geneticists to laypersons, tends to use "race" as if it were a scientific category; with rare exceptions, no one offers a quantifiable definition of what a race is in genetic terms. The free-floating debate that results, while entertaining, has little chance of advancing this field.

What is at stake is a more practical question—namely, has genomics provided evidence that race can act as a surrogate for genetic constitution in medicine or public health? Our answer is no. Race, at the continental level, has not been shown to provide a useful categorization of genetic information about the response to drugs, diagnosis, or causes of disease.

But in the United States, there is substantial variation in health status among major population subgroups. This self-evident truth has been the driving force behind the use of racial or ethnic categories in surveillance for disease. Among persons who are less convinced by the genetic data, variation in environmental exposure is seen as the cause of this phenomenon, and it follows that differences in health occur because privilege and power are unequal in racially stratified societies. The globalization of complex chronic diseases seems to confirm the view that all populations are susceptible and that variation in rates can be understood as the result of differential exposure to environmental causes.

Although we acknowledge the salience of these arguments, the value of continental race as a classification scheme must be questioned in this context much as it was in the context of genetics. For example, persons who could be classified as having "African ancestry" have wide variation in rates of hypertension and diabetes, as do all large continental populations. Without the context provided by such variables as the level of education, occupation, type of diet, and place of residence, race as a social category is not a useful predictor of health outcomes. Just as most genetic heterogeneity occurs within populations, there is enormous variation in the patterns of culture-derived behavioral and risk factors. An unintended result of categorizing people according to race can be to foreclose the question of why they have ill health, leaving us blind to the meaning of the more relevant local and individual context.

Race, in the metaphor introduced above, is the product of an arranged marriage between the social and biologic worlds. Although it often seems to travel back and forth between these parallel universes, it maintains a home in both. From the social sphere, race has inherited certain attributes that cannot be alienated from its meaning, no matter how hard we might try. The concept of race has currency in everyday discourse and is an epistemological category independent of the action of geneticists. From the beginning, it has been used not just to organize populations, but to create a classification scheme that explains the meaning inherent in the social order, according to which some groups dominate others. There is a tendency for scientists to ignore the messy social implications of what they do. At the extreme, the argument is made that "we just tell the truth about nature," and its negative consequences are political problems that do not concern us. Whether or not such a position is defensible from an ethical point of view, the debate over race cannot be sidestepped so easily. Race already has a meaning. To invoke the authority of genomic science in the debate over the value of race as a category of nature is to accept the social meaning as well.

In the 20th century, physics promised us knowledge of how the universe works, space travel, and the ability to harness the atom as an infinite source of energy. Although vast amounts of knowledge did flow from research in those areas, the consequences in practice were not always benign. The accumulated record of peaceful and nonpeaceful atomic energy subsequently led many physicists to understand more fully that science is a part of society. In this century, biology—especially genomics—has emerged as the beacon of science leading us into the future, where data on the genetic sequence will unlock the secret of life. For genomics to fall in lock step with the socially defined use of race is not a propitious beginning to that journey. The ability to catalogue molecular variants in persons and populations has thrust genetics into a new relationship with society. Interpreting that catalogue within the existing framework of race, as was done in the case of eugenics, violates the principles that give science its unique status as a force outside the social hierarchy, one that does not take sides in factional contests. Racial affiliation draws on deep emotions about group identity and the importance of belonging. The discovery that races exist is not an advance of genomic science into uncharted territory; it is an extension of the atavistic belief that human populations are not just organized, but ordered.

NOTES AND QUESTIONS

1. *The Methodological Problem of Using Race in Genetic Studies.* Many researchers use self-identified race in genetic studies. However, self-identification may be methodologically flawed because people do not accurately report their biological race to researchers. The reason may be that race is, in substantial part, socially constructed and individuals feel a cultural attachment to certain groups.

2. *The Responsibility of Researchers in Interpreting Biological Differences in Race.* What are the responsibilities of geneticists, ethicists, and policy makers when interpreting studies on genetics and race? Some geneticists will interpret findings to reinforce a biological basis for race, while others will interpret findings to disprove any biological basis. The International Bioethics Committee suggests that it may not be wise to leave the responsibility of fighting racism to scientific debate. "[W]hat science finds is what science finds, and these findings should be put in support of fundamental human rights which derive from the universal belief in the inherent dignity of the human individual. Such values cannot be 'proved' by science, and neither can they be 'disproved' by science." Chee Heng Leng et al., Bioethics and Human Population Genetics Research 16, United Nations Educational, Scientific and Cultural Organization, CIP/BIO/95/CONF.002/5 (Nov. 15, 1995).

3. *The Future of Race in Genetics Research.* Will research on genetic variation enable people to be grouped in new, positive ways to better tailor prevention and treatment or reinforce existing patterns of racial, ethnic or socioeconomic stratification?

4. *Genomics and Distributive Justice.* The poor are over-represented among low-literacy patients, making it less likely that they would be sufficiently informed to seek genetic benefits. They are also more likely to be served in settings with less skilled personnel and lower quality of care. Finally, the poor have less access to health services due to their lack of health insurance coverage. Does all this mean that the genomics revolution will increase, rather than decrease, socioeconomic and health disparities?

3. THE RISKS OF STRATIFICATION: GENETIC DISCRIMINATION

Recall Articles 1 & 2 Universal Declaration on the Human Genome and Human Rights:

The human genome underlies the fundamental unity of all members of the human family as well as the recognition of their inherent dignity and diversity. In a symbolic sense, it is the heritage of humanity. Everyone has a right of respect for his or her dignity and his or her human rights regardless of their genetic characteristics. That dignity makes it imperative not to reduce individuals to their genetic characteristics and to respect their uniqueness and diversity.

Second Workshop on International Cooperation for the Human Genome Project: Ethics, *Valencia Declaration on Ethics and the Human Genome Project*, 2 J. Int. Bioethique 94–95 (1991).

Despite these promising sentiments, the public continues to express concern about genetic discrimination in employment, health or life insurance, education, and even loans. There are no systematic studies on the frequency of genetic discrimination but data suggest that it does occur. *See* Lawrence Low, et al., *Genetic Discrimination in Life Insurance: Empirical Evidence from a Cross Sectional Survey of Genetic Support Groups in the United Kingdom*, 317 BMJ 1632–1635 (1998) (13% of surveyed population had experienced genetic discrimination). As Ellen Wright Clayton notes, the problem of genetic discrimination is more complex than it first appears:

> The question of whether genetic information should ever be used to affect one's access to health and other forms of insurance has been a dominant issue of public concern in the past decade. People cite fear of losing insurance as a major reason to avoid genetic testing. Others argue that discrimination by insurance companies is not a problem, often pointing out that few of these cases, which are difficult for employees to win, have been filed. Insurers assert that they do not perform tests to obtain genetic information but argue that they should be free to use such information if it is available, citing the need to avoid "moral hazard"—the risk that people who know they will become ill or die soon will try to obtain insurance at regular rates. In response to consumer pressure, many states have passed laws in this area.

Ellen Wright Clayton, *Ethical, Legal, and Social Implications of Genomic Medicine*, 349 New Eng. J. Med. 562, 563 (2003).

[Clayton goes on to illustrate the complexity of genetic discrimination by examining a case involving Burlington Northern Santa Fe Railroad (BNSF):]

> ... Allegedly relying on the advice of its company physician, who in turn had apparently relied on the representations of a diagnostic company, BNSF began obtaining blood for DNA testing from employees who were seeking disability compensation as a result of carpal tunnel syndrome that occurred on the job. The employees were reportedly not told the purpose of the tests, which was to detect a mutation associated with hereditary neuropathy with liability to pressure palsies. The company's motive for pursuing testing was never made clear, but it seems reasonable to suspect that BNSF would have tried to deny disability benefits to any employee who had such a mutation, arguing that the mutation, and not the job, caused the carpal tunnel syndrome. When the company's practice came to light, it was almost immediately stopped by the federal Equal Employment Opportunity Commission, and shortly thereafter, the company settled claims brought by its employees for an undisclosed amount of money.

What lessons can be learned here? One is that the company's effort to find mutations for hereditary neuropathy with liability to pressure palsies made little sense. This disorder is very rare, affecting about 3 to 10 persons per 100,000, and more important, although carpal tunnel syndrome can be a part of hereditary neuropathy with liability to pressure palsies, it has not been reported as the sole symptom. The injuries these employees sustained were not the result of an epidemic of hereditary neuropathy with liability to pressure palsies. Getting the biologic process correct is a critical step in making decisions about genetic testing.

Another important lesson is that identifying a genetic predisposition to carpal tunnel syndrome would not have been the end of the discussion in the eyes of the law. The company got in trouble because its practice violated numerous laws forbidding discrimination in the workplace. In particular, the Americans with Disabilities Act permits employers to require a medical evaluation only under clearly specified circumstances. Testing employees after they were disabled without their informed consent clearly fell outside the bounds of this and other antidiscrimination laws.

The actions of BNSF led to widespread criticism and, not surprisingly, to calls to ban genetic discrimination in the workplace. Although some states have enacted laws, the need for federal action has grown as the Supreme Court has progressively narrowed the protection provided under the Americans with Disabilities Act. The answer, however, is not simply to forbid employers to use genetic information or to require genetic testing.

Id., at 563–64.

Clayton goes on to consider the most appropriate response to discrimination, beginning with how genetic information fits within the broader framework of antidiscrimination laws, which "were passed to create a certain kind of society, one in which people must be included regardless of race, sex, or disability, even at some cost to employers":

... Biology alone does not determine the social outcome. To use an analogy, an employer cannot exclude women from the workplace, even if he or she believes, with some justification, that women are more likely than men to take time off to care for family members. At the same time, employers are not required to bear unlimited costs to promote these social goals—the employee, male or female, who misses months of work at a time to care for sick relatives can still be fired.

A similar debate about social goals and the limits of our pursuit of them must occur with regard to genetic discrimination. The Equal Employment Opportunity Commission recently awarded damages to Terri Sergeant, who was fired from her job as an office manager for an insurance broker because she required extremely expensive medication to treat her at-worst mildly symptomatic alpha$_1$-antitrypsin deficiency. A person's need for expensive health care is not sufficient reason to fire that person or to refuse to hire him or her in the first place. The fact that the costs may cause the employer to go under or to decide not to provide health insurance simply underlines the inherent weakness of employment-based health insurance.

At the same time, one can imagine a genetic condition that might affect a person's ability to perform a job in ways that could not be accommodated with reasonable efforts. Suppose a person with a recurrent and untreatable cardiac arrhythmia that leads to loss of consciousness, owing to an inherited ion-channel defect, is seeking employment as a long-distance truck driver. Because of the risk to third parties, such a person would not even be able to get a driver's license in many jurisdictions. The more difficult question—and the one posed particularly with respect to genetics—would arise if an asymptomatic person had a predisposing, but incompletely penetrant, mutation for the same disorder. Deciding what to do about such predispositions will require close attention both to the true, as opposed to the feared, likelihood that symptoms will develop and to the complex weighing of the interests of the individual, the employer, and society.

A similar calculus must be applied to every question regarding who can obtain and use genetic information to distinguish, or discriminate, among people in ways that affect their ability to obtain social goods, such as health insurance and education. If, as is likely, some uses are deemed to be appropriate, the challenge for clinicians will be to discuss with their patients the potential adverse social consequences of testing so that the patients can make informed choices about whether or not to proceed with testing.

Id., at 565–66.

NOTES AND QUESTIONS

1. *Genetic Antidiscrimination Statutes.* In order to safeguard against discriminatory practices, over 75% of states had, by 2004, enacted genetic discrimination legislation pertaining to employment, health insurance, or both. However, these measures contain loopholes, define genetic information in varying ways, and offer disparate degrees of protection. Definitions vary from state to state, such that one state may protect only DNA and RNA while another may extend protection to family history data and other medical information that could offer genetic information. State laws are also hampered by federal preemption under ERISA, which prevents states from regulating employer risk retention plans. *See* James M. Jeffords & Tom Daschle, *Political Issues in the Genome Era*, 291 SCI. 1249–1251 (2001).

At the federal level, the Health Insurance Portability and Accountability Act of 1996 (HIPAA) does not allow group health plans or those who insure group health plans to use genetic information as a basis for implementing rules for eligibility for the plan. However, HIPAA does not protect people who buy insurance as individuals, nor limit insurers' ability to collect or disclose people's genetic information. Title I of the Americans with Disabilities Act (ADA), enforced by the Equal Employment Opportunity Commission (EEOC), and similar disability-based antidiscrimination laws such as the Rehabilitation Act of 1973 also fail to offer complete employment protection. The ADA protects against discrimination based on a clinically manifest genetic disease amounting to a disability, but, as of yet, no federal court has ruled that pre-symptomatic testing for a predisposition to a disease is protected under the ADA. Jennifer Chorpening, *Genetic Disability: A Modest Proposal to Modify the ADA to Protect Against Some Forms of Genetic Discrimination*, 82 N.C.L. Rev. 1441, 1452 (2004).

2. *What are the Values Underlying Genetic Antidiscrimination Legislation?* There is, of course, the deep intuition that people should not be adversely treated because of a genetic condition over which they have no control. In addition to the issue of justice, does discrimination legislation have an instrumental value? Would people be more likely to come forward for testing, counseling, and treatment if they did not fear discrimination? Does genetic discrimination, therefore, warrant a definitive legislative solution?

3. *The Complexity of Genetic Discrimination.* "Discrimination" literally means treating people differently. However, treating people differently is not always wrong. Is it possible that in some cases there are ethically appropriate reasons for genetic discrimination? Suppose that an employer uses genetic information to exclude a person from a job based on that individual's hyper-susceptibility to a workplace toxin. Would that be unethical? What if the employer used genetic information to fire a person whose genes show that he or she is not (either currently or in the future) able to perform the functions of the job? Finally, what if an employer fired an individual at high risk of a chronic costly disease? Should the employer be compelled to provide health insurance for a person likely to develop an expensive health condition? What if an individual knew she was *BRCA1* positive, placing her for high risk for breast or ovarian cancer? Should she be permitted to hide this information from her employer or insurer? Would this be a form of moral hazard?

4. *Discrimination and Genetics Exceptionalism.* Do persons with genetic disease have a better case for protection against discrimination than those with diseases of non-genetic origin? Consider two women with breast cancer—one with a positive *BRCA* test and the other with a negative test. Both are fired from their job or excluded from health insurance based on their illness. What is the appropriate policy response?

V.   CONCLUSION

The human genome project demonstrates the capacity for remarkable scientific innovation. If science is nurtured and incentivized, it can lead to a future of better health for individuals and populations. At the same time, the human genome raises novel questions of ethics and law. Must scientific progress inevitably pose a cost to society, or can ethical problems be effectively addressed by timely, thoughtful foresight? As the science, and its implications for the medical and public health communities, become increasingly clear, the law must be prepared to untangle the questions that enhanced diagnosis and treatment will evoke. While science will give physicians and public health officials the tools to improve human life, the legal system must provide boundaries that maximize the beneficial implications while curtailing discrimination and invasions of privacy. Above all, there is the question of social justice, which demands that the benefits and burdens of genomics be distributed fairly, irrespective of race or socioeconomic status.

CHAPTER 3

THE FORMATION OF THE MODERN SCIENTIFIC ESTABLISHMENT: THE ROLE OF NUCLEAR ENERGY

I. THE SCIENTIFIC BASIS AND HISTORIC IMPACT OF NUCLEAR WEAPONS

A. THE SCIENTIFIC BASIS OF NUCLEAR ENERGY

BANESH HOFFMANN, ALBERT EINSTEIN
69–82 (1972).

Let us now look at the content of [Einstein's] paper of 1905 on what came to be called the special theory of relativity....

[H]e begins by noting a conflict that goes to the heart of the matter: Maxwell's theory[a] makes unwarranted distinctions between rest and motion. Einstein gives an example. When a magnet and a loop of wire move past one another, an electric current appears in the wire. Suppose we think of the magnet as moving and the loop as at rest. Then Maxwell's theory gives an excellent explanation. Suppose we now switch and think of the coil as moving and the magnet at rest. Then Maxwell's theory again gives an excellent explanation; but it is a quite different one physically, and this even though the calculated currents are equal.

Having thus aroused our suspicions about Maxwellian rest and motion, Einstein bolsters them by adducing "the unsuccessful attempts to discover any motion of the earth relative to the [ether]." He therefore makes the impossibility-type postulate that no experiment of any sort can detect absolute rest or uniform motion.... In view of the evidence, this postulate, which he calls the *principle of relativity,* is certainly plausible. Einstein now quickly adds a second principle that seems, if anything, even more plausible; and with these deft strokes he sets the stage for revolution.

His second principle says that in empty space light travels with a definite speed c that does not depend on the motion of its source. Perhaps this startles us. If, for example, we think of light as consisting of particles, we would naturally say that their speeds depend on the way their sources move. But from the point of view of the wave theory of light, Einstein's second principle takes on the aspect of an utter triviality. For, no matter how a light wave is started, once it is on its way it is carried by the ether at

---

a. [Eds.—James Clerk Maxwell's (1831–1879) theory expressed in a unified mathematical form fundamental principles concerning electricity and magnetism.]

the standard speed with which waves are transmitted therein. If this is so obvious, why does Einstein state it as a principle? Because early in his paper he says that the introduction of an ether will prove "superfluous." His second principle extracts from the ether the essential that he needs. Note his audacity. Fresh from his quantum proposal that light must somehow consist of particles, he takes as the second principle of his theory of relativity something inherent in the wave theory of light, even as he declares the idea of an ether superfluous. There is in this a striking indication of the sureness of his physical intuition.

Here, then, we have two simple principles, each plausible, each seemingly innocent, each bordering on the obvious. Where is the harm in them? Where the threat of revolution?

In his paper, Einstein speaks of them as "only apparently irreconcilable." *Irreconcilable?* Where is the conflict? Only *apparently* irreconcilable? What can he possibly have in mind?

Watch closely. It will be worth the effort. But be forewarned. As we follow the gist of Einstein's argument we shall find ourselves nodding in agreement, and later almost nodding in sleep, so obvious and unimportant will it seem. There will come a stage at which we shall barely be able to stifle a yawn. Beware. We shall by then have committed ourselves and it will be too late to avoid the jolt; for the beauty of Einstein's argument lies precisely in its seeming innocence.

Consider, then, two similar, well-equipped vehicles in uniform motion, as shown in the accompanying diagram, and imagine them far out in space so that they are unaffected by external influences. The vehicles, named *A* and *B* after their captains, have a uniform relative motion of, shall we say, 10,000 miles per second, as indicated. At the center of each vehicle is a lamp. When *A* and *B* come abreast, they flash their lamps on for an instant, thus sending out pulses of light to left and right. The diagram shows these pulses and the vehicles a moment later. For convenience, we have drawn it as though *A* were "at rest."

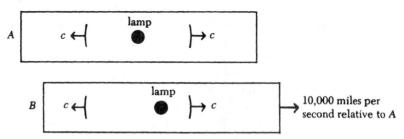

We now set the stage for a question. By Einstein's second principle the speeds of the pulses of light do not depend on the motions of their sources. Therefore—and this is important—the pulses keep abreast as shown. In his vehicle, *A* measures their speeds to the right and the left and finds the value *c* for both. *B* makes corresponding measurements within his own vehicle. He is moving at 10,000 miles per second relative to *A*, while his light pulses keep abreast of *A*'s. Agreed? Then here is the question: What values of the speeds of the pulses relative to himself does *B* obtain?

Because of his motion relative to A, we would expect B to find his leftward-moving light pulse traveling relative to him with a speed of $c + 10,000$, and the other with the vastly different speed of $c - 10,000$.

But if this were the case, we should run afoul of Einstein's first postulate. How so? Because A and B are performing identical internal experiments within their respective vehicles, and since they are in uniform motion they must obtain identical results. Therefore B, like A, must find that the speeds are both c. Indeed, no matter how fast B may travel relative to A in an attempt to overtake the receding light, it will always recede from him with the same speed c. He cannot catch up with the receding light any more than one can reach the horizon on earth. No material object can travel as fast as light. Here in this startling result we see an unexpected answer to the sixteen-year-old Einstein's question about keeping abreast of light waves. [At age sixteen, Einstein had asked himself what a light wave would look like to someone keeping pace with it].

Since the result is so startling, let us look at it differently, if only to convince ourselves that it necessarily follows from Einstein's two principles. Suppose A found the speed in both directions to be c while B found it to be $c + 10,000$ in one direction and $c - 10,000$ in the other. Then A could legitimately conclude that he was at absolute rest and B could legitimately conclude that he was traveling at an absolute speed of 10,000 miles per second. And this would belie the principle of relativity.

A lesser man finding this calamitous consequence of two seemingly innocent postulates would immediately have abandoned one or the other. But Einstein had chosen his two principles precisely because they went to the heart of the matter, and he boldly retained both. Their very plausibility—taken separately—gave his theory a firm foundation. In such treacherous regions of thought he could not afford to build on quicksands.

We have now seen why Einstein used the word "irreconcilable." Yet he had said that his two principles were only "apparently" irreconcilable, and this meant that he was going to reconcile them nevertheless. But how?

Here we enter the crucial stage of the argument. The remedy obviously had to be something drastic. What flashed on Einstein as he sat up in bed that momentous morning was that he would have to give up one of our most cherished notions about time.

To understand Einstein's revolutionary idea about time, we return to the vehicles A and B and give their captains a new task. Four superlatively accurate clocks a_1, a_2, b_1, b_2 are fastened down in the two vehicles as indicated. For convenience let us pretend that the vehicles are millions of miles long so that we can talk of minutes rather than billionths of a second.

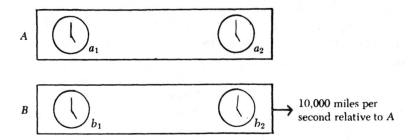

A sends a flash of light from a_1 to a_2, where it is immediately deflected back to a_1. The light leaves a_1 when the hands of a_1 read noon, and reaches a_2 when *its* hands read 3 minutes past noon. We can not be sure from this that the light took 3 minutes to travel from a_1 to a_2: for example, the workmen who installed the clocks may inadvertently have moved the hands. How can we synchronize clock a_2 with clock a_1? Let us consider the double journey. Suppose the light leaves a_1 when the hands of a_1 read noon, reaches a_2 when *its* hands read 3 minutes after noon, and returns to a_1 when a_1's hands read 4 minutes after noon. We immediately suspect that something is wrong. The clocks are alleging that the light took 3 minutes to travel from a_1 to a_2 but only 1 minute to return from a_2 to a_1. We do the obvious thing. We move the minute hand of a_2 back 1 minute. Now, when we perform the experiment, the clocks will indicate that the light took 2 minutes to travel from a_1 to a_2 and 2 minutes to travel back from a_2 to a_1. Since, as we have seen, we want the speed of the light to be c in both directions, we would agree with Einstein that the hands of the clocks a_1 and a_2 are now so set that the clocks are synchronized. And if, a little later, something happens at a_1 when the hands of a_1 read 4:30, and something else happens at a_2 when the hands of a_2 also read 4:30, we would agree with Einstein that the two separated events had occurred simultaneously.

Perhaps all this seems rather pointless—so obvious that we can barely stifle the yawn we spoke about. But, as we have mentioned before, the beauty of Einstein's argument is that it is based on concepts of beguiling acceptability. While politely stifling our yawn, we have unknowingly committed ourselves to a staggering consequence.

As A synchronizes his clocks a_1 and a_2 in the above manner prescribed by Einstein, B observes him in utter amazement. For, relative to B, A is moving to the left at 10,000 miles per second. Thus although A claims that his light is traveling equal distances forward and back like this

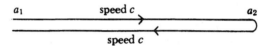

B sees the distances as manifestly unequal, like this

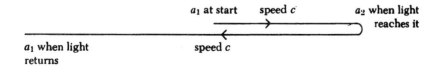

What is B to think? What is he driven to conclude? That since the forward and backward distances are *unequal,* the very fact that the forward and backward journeys of the light take equal times according to a_1 and a_2 is proof to B that clocks a_1 and a_2 are *not* synchronized.

Naturally, when B tells A about this, A is upset. So he asks B to synchronize clocks b_1 and b_2 according to the agreed-upon Einsteinian procedure. B does so, and at once A has his revenge. For, relative to A, B is moving to the right at 10,000 miles per second, and although B claims that his light is traveling equal distances forward and back like this

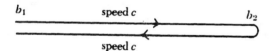

A sees the distances as manifestly unequal, like this

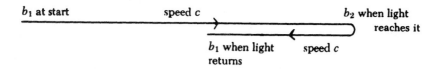

Thus A says that clocks a_1 and a_2 are synchronized, but B says they are not. And B says that clocks b_1 and b_2 are synchronized, but A says they are not. So if A says that events occurring at a_1 and a_2 are simultaneous, B will deny it. And vice versa.

Do we side with A or do we side with B? Einstein's first postulate, the principle of relativity, puts A and B on an equal footing. We must therefore conclude with Einstein that both are right.

Now comes the supreme stroke of genius. Einstein looks on this divergence of views not as a minor squabble but as a characteristic of Time itself. Our common-sense, Newtonian concept of a universal time providing a universal simultaneity has been shattered before our eyes. Time, according to Einstein, is of such a nature that the simultaneity of separated events is relative. Events simultaneous for A are, in general, not simultaneous for B; and events simultaneous for B are, in general, not simultaneous for A. Though this may be shocking, we have to learn to live with it. And to live with further shocks. For time is fundamental, and a drastic change in our conception of it brings the whole structure of theoretical physics tumbling down like a house of cards. Hardly anything remains untouched.

Take length, for instance, that other mainstay of theoretical physics. Imagine a rod moving past A and B. To measure its length as it rushes by, A notes the positions of its ends at a particular instant—which is to say simultaneously. So does B. But since A and B disagree about simultaneity, A will say that B noted the positions of the passing rod at different moments and thus did not measure its true length. B will say the same about A. And in general A and B will find different values for the length thus measured.

We see from this that because simultaneity is relative, so too is distance. And there is obviously no stopping the epidemic. Speed, acceleration, force, energy—all these and more depend on time and distance: the very fabric of physics is changed.

What of the relationship between the measurements of time and space made by A and those made by B? Or by any two observers in vehicles in uniform relative motion? Einstein typically looked for the simplest mathematical relationship deducible from his two principles. In this way he derived from them none other than the Lorentz[b] transformation [that objects contract in the direction of their motion]—a transformation with which, almost certainly, he had not been previously acquainted.

Armed with this transformation, he made further deductions. His two principles may at first have seemed innocent, but their logical consequences are often such as to outrage common sense. For example, as Einstein showed, A finds B's clocks going at a slower rate than his own. After recovering from our surprise—for, were not the clocks all equally reliable?—we expect that B finds A's clocks going at a faster rate than his own. But no. Each finds that the other's clocks go the more slowly.

Again, we recall the proposal ... that objects contract in the directions of their motion through the ether. Einstein obtained precisely the same formula for the amount of the contraction. But in Einstein's theory this is a mutual, relative effect: A finds that B's longitudinal yardsticks are contracted compared with his own, while B finds that A's are the shorter. Nothing could reveal more strikingly the revolutionary boldness of Einstein's ideas compared with those of his elders Lorentz and Poincaré.[c] All three had the Lorentz transformation, in which the startling consequences were implicit. But, when interpreting it, neither Lorentz nor Poincaré

---

b. [Eds.—Hendrik Antoon Lorentz (1853–1928) won the 1902 Nobel Prize for physics for his theory of electromagnetic radiation.]

c. [Eds.—Henri Poincaré (1854–1912) was a prominent mathematician, astronomer, and philosopher of science.]

dared to give the principle of relativity full trust. If A was at rest, as they put it, then B's yardsticks would be contracted. But nothing was said about B finding A's contracted. It was tacitly assumed that B would find A's the longer. As for the rates of actual clocks, no such discussion as Einstein's was given.

Poincaré, one of the greatest mathematicians of his time, was a man of subtle philosophical insight. In his major paper of 1905 he had extraordinary command of the detailed mathematical apparatus of the theory of relativity. For years he had preached the purely conventional nature of physical concepts. He had early sensed the probable validity of a principle of relativity. Yet when he came to the decisive step, his nerve failed him and he clung to old habits of thought and familiar ideas of space and time. If this seems surprising, it is because we underestimate the boldness of Einstein in stating the principle of relativity as an axiom and, by keeping faith with it, changing our notions of time and space.

In making this revolutionary change Einstein was greatly influenced by the ideas of Mach,[d] whose critical book on Newtonian mechanics Besso had brought to Einstein's attention in his student days. Mach will enter our story further, even though Einstein's early enthusiasm for his philosophical ideas did not last. Mach had been profoundly skeptical of concepts like absolute space and absolute time—and atoms. Roughly speaking, he looked on science as a sort of neat cataloguing of data, and he wanted all concepts to be clearly definable in terms of specific procedures. Einstein's treatment of simultaneity in terms of specific synchronizing procedures clearly shows Mach's influence. But others, Poincaré among them, also knew Mach's ideas, yet it was Einstein who made the crucial advance.

The mutual contractions of lengths, like the mutual slowings of clocks, are not self-contradictory. They are closely analogous to effects of perspective. For example, if two people of equal height walk away from one another, stop, and look back, each appears to the other diminished in size; and the reason this particular mutual contraction does not strike us adults as a contradiction is simply that we have grown used to it.

We have told barely enough to give a hint of the revolutionary nature of Einstein's paper of 1905 on relativity. Once the foundations are laid, the paper becomes highly mathematical. Einstein shows how, with the new ideas of time and space, Maxwell's equations conform to the principle of relativity, even as these ideas require a revision of Newtonian mechanics. For example, the faster an object moves relative to an experimenter, the greater will be its mass relative to him. Characteristically, Einstein leads up to a prediction that can be put to experimental test. He gives formulas for the motion of electrons in an electromagnetic field, taking account of the relativistic increases in their masses as their speeds increase relative to the observer. By a different route, Lorentz had made essentially the same prediction in 1904, and had compared it favorably with results already found by an experimenter. The equivalence of the formulas need not

d. [Eds.—Ernst Mach (1838–1916) was a physicist and a philosopher who was among the founders of scientific positivism.]

surprise us, since; as we have said, Lorentz and Einstein had a common Maxwellian heritage. But there is a difference between the men that is worthy of note. In 1906 the same experimenter, publishing new measurements, categorically declared them incompatible with the prediction of Lorentz and Einstein but compatible with certain rival theories. Lorentz was distinctly disheartened. But Einstein was unperturbed. Looking at the rival theories with aesthetic disapproval, he confidently suggested that the experimenter could be in error. And subsequent measurements by others showed that Einstein was correct.

.   .   .

But our chapter cannot stop here. Einstein was not yet done with 1905. In late September, three months after the relativity paper, he sent to *Annalen der Physik* a further paper that was published in November. It occupies three printed pages. Using electromagnetic equations taken from his previous paper, Einstein here shows by calculation that if a body gives off an amount E of energy *in the form of light,* its mass diminishes by an amount E/c 2.

With his instinctive sense of cosmic unity he now tosses off a penetrating and crucially important remark: that the fact that the energy is in the form of light "evidently makes no difference." He therefore announces a general law to the effect that if a body gives off or takes in an amount E of energy *of any sort,* it loses or gains an amount of mass E/c 2.

According to this, because c is so large, if a light bulb emitted 100 watts of light for a hundred years it would give off in that time energy whose total mass was less than a millionth of an ounce. But radium, through its radioactivity, gives off relatively enormous amounts of energy, and Einstein suggested that the theory could thus be tested.

In this paper of 1905 Einstein said that all energy of whatever sort has mass. It took even him two years more to come to the stupendous realization that the reverse must also hold: that all mass, of whatever sort, must have energy. He was led to this by aesthetic reasons. Why should one make a distinction in kind between the mass that an object already has and the mass that it loses in giving off energy? To do so would be to imagine two types of mass for no good reason when one would suffice. The distinction would be inartistic and logically indefensible. Therefore all mass must have energy.

With mass and energy thus wholly equivalent, Einstein was able in 1907, in a long and mainly expository paper published in the *Jahrbuch der Radioaktivität,* to write his famous equation $E = mc^2$. Imagine the audacity of this step: every clod of earth, every feather, every speck of dust becoming a prodigious reservoir of entrapped energy. There was no way of verifying this at the time. Yet in presenting his equation in 1907 Einstein spoke of it as the most important consequence of his theory of relativity. His extraordinary ability to see far ahead is shown by the fact that his equation was not verified quantitatively till some twenty-five years later, and then only in difficult laboratory experiments. He could not foresee the tragic events that were to grow from his artistically motivated $E = mc^2$. . . .

NOTES AND QUESTIONS

1.   Hoffmann's description of Einstein's development of the special theory of relativity provides a glimpse of a great scientific mind at work. Would Einstein's undoubted brilliance have made him a successful judge? Indeed, is brilliance, as contrasted with wisdom or empathy, a necessary characteristic of a good attorney or judge?

When Einstein found two principles in apparent conflict he dared to accept some rather astonishing implications of those principles. Should a judge react similarly when two principles appear to conflict? If judges must resolve value-laden human conflicts, rather than seek timeless truth, should they maintain a greater willingness to reinterpret or refine principles? Consider, in this respect, descriptions of the legal process set forth by Cardozo and Levi in Chapter 2, Sec. I. D., *infra*.

2.   Einstein wrote his paper on special relativity during his spare time while working as a patent examiner in Berne, Switzerland. During this period, the coordination of clocks became a necessity for the efficient operation of modern railroads, shipping, and the like. The historian of science Peter Galison notes that Einstein's office received numerous applications for devices to coordinate clocks, and argues that working on these applications crystallized Einstein's thinking about relativity. PETER GALISON, EINSTEIN'S CLOCKS, POINCARÉ'S MAPS: EMPIRES OF TIME (2003).

The United States Supreme Court has described the work of a patent examiner as "quasi-judicial." Butterworth v. United States *ex rel.* Hoe, 112 U.S. 50, 67, 5 S.Ct. 25, 28 L.Ed. 656 (1884); *see also* Western Elec. Co. v. Piezo Tech., Inc., 860 F.2d 428, 431 (Fed. Cir. 1988). A patent examiner, like a lower court judge, applies reasonably settled legal principles to the facts. Is there an analogy between this activity and the form of Einstein's paper on special relativity? *See* Steven Goldberg, *Albert Einstein, Esq.*, 93 GEO. L.J. (forthcoming 2004).

3.   Whether one sees similarities between legal and scientific reasoning depends in part on whether one views law as a science. Even apart from traditional natural law theories, there have been persistent efforts throughout American history to identify legal reasoning with scientific methods. Thus, for example, Professor G. Edward White has linked the emergence of tort law late in the 19th century, in part, to "an impulse toward 'conceptualization' ... [that] stressed 'scientific methodologies' " and that sought to perfect "the law as a science." Edward White, *The Intellectual Origins of Torts in America*, 86 YALE L.J. 671, 678 (1977). More pointedly, a leader in the field of law and economics has written that "as biology is to living systems, astronomy to the stars, or economics to the price system, so should legal studies be to the legal system: an endeavor to make precise, objective and systematic observations of how the legal system operates in fact and to discover and explain the recurrent patterns in the observations—the 'laws' of the system." Richard Posner, *Volume One of the Journal of Legal Studies—An Afterward*, 1 J. LEGAL STUD. 437 (1972). At the other extreme, Grant Gilmore wrote that "the quest for the laws which will explain the riddle of human behavior leads us not toward truth but toward the illusion of certainty, which is our curse. So far as we have been able to learn, there are no recurrent patterns in the course of human events; it is not possible to make scientific statements about history, sociology, economics—or law." GRANT GILMORE, THE AGES OF AMERICAN LAW 99–100 (1977). Do you agree with Posner that legal studies can be like astronomy? Is the only alternative to that a form of nihilism?

4.   Einstein's historic development of $E = mc^2$ also illustrates the role of aesthetics in science. Recall that aesthetic considerations led him to conclude that there should be no distinction between the mass that an object already has and the mass that it loses in giving off energy. The scientist's search for a beautiful order in nature motivated J.D. Watson, among many others, in his search for the double helix. *See* Chapter 2, Sec. I. A., *supra*. Can lawyers or legal scholars pursue a comparable search for beauty? In analyzing the views of Posner and Gilmore discussed above, Arthur Leff sided with Gilmore's view that law is not a science, yet Leff concluded:

> The truth is, I fear, as Grant Gilmore sees it: all we can understand, and that not very well, are the games we ourselves generate and eventually, but predictably, lose.... But at least there is this: on the way to those final defeats, there are, at least for some, some beautiful innings.

Arthur Leff, *Law And*, 87 YALE L.J. 989, 1011 (1978).

Michael Polanyi, *The Republic of Science*

1 MINERVA 54, 62 (1962).

In January 1945 Lord [Bertrand] Russell and I were together on the BBC Brains Trust. We were asked about the possible technical uses of Einstein's theory of relativity, and neither of us could think of any. This was 40 years after the publication of the theory and 50 years after the inception by Einstein of the work which led to its discovery.... But, actually, the technical application of relativity, which neither Russell nor I could think of, was to be revealed within a few months by the explosion of the first atomic bomb. For the energy of the explosion was released at the expense of mass in accordance with the relativistic equation $E = mc^2$, an equation which was soon to be found splashed over the cover of *Time* magazine, as a token of its supreme practical importance.

Perhaps Russell and I should have done better in foreseeing these applications of relativity in January 1945, but it is obvious that Einstein could not possibly take these future consequences into account when he started on the problem which led to the discovery of relativity at the turn of the century. For one thing, another dozen or more major discoveries had yet to be made before relativity could be combined with them to yield the technical process which opened the atomic age.

Any attempt at guiding scientific research towards a purpose other than its own is an attempt to deflect it from the advancement of science. Emergencies may arise in which all scientists willingly apply their gifts to tasks of public interest. It is conceivable that we may come to abhor the progress of science, and stop all scientific research or at least whole branches of it, as the Soviets stopped research in genetics for 25 years. You can kill or mutilate the advance of science, you cannot shape it. For it can advance only by essentially unpredictable steps, pursuing problems of its own, and the practical benefits of these advances will be incidental and hence doubly unpredictable.

NOTES AND QUESTIONS

When Einstein began his work on the special theory of relativity, he did not have in mind the practical generation of energy, let alone the atomic bomb. As Polanyi indicates, numerous discoveries followed before the bomb became possible. In particular, experimental and theoretical work involving the bombardment of uranium with neutrons led to the discovery of nuclear fission, the "atom-splitting" that liberates energy in accordance with Einstein's equation. *See, e.g.*, SAMUEL GLASSTONE, SOURCEBOOK ON ATOMIC ENERGY 473–504 (1967). One of the central difficulties for the social control of science is finding the point at which unwanted consequences of science can be controlled without harming basic science. A judge considering the environmental implications of the breeder reactor, a nuclear technology described in Sec. II. B., *infra*, put the matter as follows:

> I say this: I say there comes a time, we start out with E equals MC^2, we both agreed you don't have to have the impact statement then. Then there comes a time when there are a thousand of these breeder plants in existence all over the country.
>
> Sometime before that, surely as anything under the present law, there has to be an impact statement, and a long time before that, actually.
>
> But the question is, exactly where in this chain do we have to have an impact statement.

Scientists' Inst. for Pub. Info. v. Atomic Energy Comm'n, 481 F.2d 1079, 1093 (D.C. Cir. 1973).

B.   DEVELOPING AND USING THE ATOMIC BOMB

During World War II, fears that the Germans might develop atomic weapons spurred the United States to undertake a program designed for the same end. The Manhattan Project began in 1942 and led ultimately to the atomic bombing of Hiroshima and Nagasaki in 1945. The Project involved 150,000 people, over $2.2 billion, and a remarkable level of scientific and technological expertise. The scientists' experience with the Manhattan Project, as well as with wartime radar research at the MIT Radiation Laboratory, greatly influenced the post-war relation between science and the state. For decades, most of America's leading spokesmen in science policy, including presidential science advisors such as George Kistiakowsky and Jerome Wiesner, were those who had worked in the wartime labs. *See* DANIEL GREENBERG, THE POLITICS OF PURE SCIENCE 81–96 (1967).

The wartime experience affected American science in a variety of ways. Government assumed a greater role in supporting science and scientists assumed a greater role in policy debates. Scientists also began to question more sharply the morality of their own endeavor. The materials below raise these issues primarily through the eyes of Robert Oppenheimer, a brilliant theoretical physicist who directed the Los Alamos Scientific Laboratory—the heart of the Manhattan Project—and who later lost his security clearance because of his alleged contacts with Communists and his opposition to the post-war construction of the hydrogen bomb.

ROBERT JUNGK, BRIGHTER THAN A THOUSAND SUNS
131–32 (1958).

It seemed as though unsuspected physical resources had come to Oppenheimer's aid in those weeks [when he first took over at Los Alamos]. The first thing he had to do was to travel about the country by air or by rail to persuade other physicists to join him at the new secret laboratory on the edge of the desert. In the course of his recruitment tour he had first to dispose of the prejudices of many of his colleagues against Project S–1 [the Manhattan Project]. During the two years and more it had taken people to make up their minds, while the atomic project stuck fast in a deadlock of overlapping authorities, the opinion had gone round among physicists that nothing good could ever come of the affair. In order to silence such doubts Oppie often went further than he should have gone on security grounds in his descriptions of the new studies and aims.

At that time he believed, in common with the most able of the specialists concerned, for example Hans Bethe, that the bomb could be ready within about a year. It is true that he could give no guarantee that the new weapon would be able to do its job. It might quite possibly turn out to be a dud. Nor did he conceal the fact that those who agreed to go to Los Alamos would have to sign, on security grounds, a more or less binding contract to remain there for the entire duration of the war. He added that they and their families would be cut off, as never before, from the outside world, and would be living in less than comfortable conditions.

In spite of Oppenheimer's frank admission of the many difficulties involved his recruiting campaign had an unexpectedly great success. His remarkable capacity for seeing the other point of view enabled him to find the right answer to the doubts expressed. Some physicists he terrified by the prospect of a German atom bomb. Others he attracted by his descriptions of the beauty of New Mexico. But to all he imparted the feeling of how exciting it would be to participate in the pioneering work to be carried out in this still-quite-novel field of research.

Probably, however, many of those he approached, who were mostly very young, agreed to his request for the reason, above all, that it was Oppenheimer who was to be their chief. His personal magnetism, hitherto only exercised upon his students, both male and female, now proved equally irresistible in wider circles. It was only seldom that one came across such inspiring personalities in the learned world. Oppenheimer bore no resemblance to the dry-as-dust specialist. He could quote Dante and Proust. He could refute objections by citing passages from the works of Indian sages which he had read in the original. And he seemed to be aflame with an inward spiritual passion. It would be extraordinarily stimulating to work in such close and intense association as would never have been possible in times of peace, with this and other outstanding atomic-research experts. Oppenheimer in fact possessed, as one of the victims subsequently put it, in irreverent but striking fashion, "intellectual sex appeal." . . .

––––––––

The following passage describes the reactions of Oppenheimer and of Nobel Prize winner I.I. Rabi to the testing of "Fat Boy"—the first atomic bomb.

NUEL PHARR DAVIS, LAWRENCE AND OPPENHEIMER

240–42 (1968).

While the light faded, not abruptly for him, Oppenheimer became conscious again that he was not alone in the blockhouse. "A few people laughed, a few people cried, most people were silent," he said. "There floated through my mind a line from the *Bhagavad-Gita* in which Krishna is trying to persuade the Prince that he should do his duty: 'I am become death, the shatterer of worlds.' I think we all had this feeling more or less."

By their eyes and eardrums physicists could tell at once that Fat Boy's violence was something new to human capabilities. "We felt the world would never be the same again," said Oppenheimer. While searchlights picked at the faded fireball and re-created it as a huge ghostly cloud in the night sky, preliminary instrument reports indicated blast had far exceeded the official hopeful expectation of five thousand tons. From the blockhouse roof Oppenheimer watched the cloud feint frighteningly north. A little after dawn it turned east in the direction it had been expected to take. He and the other physicists went back to the base camp.

. . .

When the blast came, he [Rabi] was surprised at the response his body made. After a minute he noticed with a scientist's habit of observation that gooseflesh appeared on the backs of his hands. It was not like watching an ordinary explosion scaled up. "The experience was hard to describe," he says. "I haven't got over it yet. It was awful, ominous, personally threatening. I couldn't tell why." Dawn found him still in reverie as he watched the blockhouse party approaching from a long way off across the sand. Oppenheimer parked too far away for Rabi to see his face, but something in his bearing brought Rabi's gooseflesh back again. He moved like a confident stranger, darkly glittering, at ease, in tune with the thing. "I'll never forget his walk," says Rabi. "I'll never forget the way he stepped out of the car."

NOTES AND QUESTIONS

1. When the first nuclear device exploded, Oppenheimer may, as the text indicates, have thought of a line from the Bhagavad–Gita, but, according to his brother Frank, he said, "It worked." Colin Campbell, *Conference Ponders Role of Scientists in Weaponry*, N.Y. TIMES, June 30, 1985, at 27. Oppenheimer's excitement at working on the atomic bomb and his ambivalence after seeing its capabilities are not unusual responses for scientists whose work has social consequences. It is difficult to overestimate the impact on post-war scientists in all disciplines of the Manhattan Project experience; an experience that culminated, in Oppenheimer's phrase, with the realization that "the physicists have known sin." PETER GOODCHILD, J. ROBERT OPPENHEIMER: SHATTERER OF WORLDS 174 (1981). When the cancer researcher Robert Pollack was asked to help organize the first Asilomar Conference on the dangers of recombinant DNA research, he agreed because he felt that inadequate safety standards posed a "pre-Hiroshima condition—It would be a real disaster if one of the agents now being handled in research should in fact be a real human cancer agent." Judith P. Swazey, et al., *Risks and Benefits, Rights and Responsibilities: A History of the Recombinant DNA Research Controversy*, 51 S. CAL. L. REV. 1019, 1022 (1978).

Do scientists have any particular responsibility to control scientific projects that may have undesirable social consequences? On the one hand, scientists are often in the best position to know, early on, what consequences might occur. On the other hand, the value system of scientists makes it particularly difficult for them to slow the progressive growth of knowledge. Shortly after the completion of the Manhattan Project, Oppenheimer, in a speech to Los Alamos scientists, stated:

> But when you come right down to it the reason that we did this job is because it was an organic necessity. If you are a scientist you cannot stop such a thing. If you are a scientist you believe that it is good to find out how the world works; that it is good to find out what the realities are, that it is good to turn over to mankind at large the greatest possible power to control the world and to deal with it according to its lights and values.

J.   ROBERT OPPENHEIMER: LETTERS AND RECOLLECTIONS 317 (Alice Kimball Smith & Charles Weiner eds., 1980).

2.   A final irony surrounding the Manhattan Project is that after the war it became clear that the German nuclear bomb project, headed by Werner Heisenberg, had come nowhere near building a bomb. Whether this was because Heisenberg tried his best but failed or because he deliberately undercut the project so that Hitler would not have the bomb remains the subject of vigorous debate. *See* THOMAS POWERS, HEISENBERG'S WAR: THE SECRET HISTORY OF THE GERMAN BOMB (1993); *see also* DAVID CASSIDY, UNCERTAINTY: THE LIFE AND SCIENCE OF WERNER HEISENBERG (1992). In any event, the Manhattan Project produced the weapon that was ultimately used against Japan.

BARTON J. BERNSTEIN, THE ATOMIC BOMB

vii (1976).

On August 6, 1945, at 8:15 A.M., the *Enola Gay* dropped a uranium bomb ("Little Boy") on Hiroshima, a major Japanese city, killing about 70,000 and injuring 70,000 others—more than half the city's population. On August 9, the day after Russia declared war on Japan, the United States dropped a second bomb (a plutonium weapon, or "Fat Man"), this time at Nagasaki, killing about 40,000 Japanese, injuring 60,000, and also killing some Dutch prisoners of war. President Harry S Truman promised that the United States would "continue . . . until we completely destroy Japan's power to make war. Only a Japanese surrender will stop us." On August 14 Japan surrendered, and on September 2 the nations signed the formal papers. Nearly four years after Japan's attack on Pearl Harbor, the war in the Pacific had finally ended.

Most Americans rejoiced that the costly war was over, and few were troubled by the use of the bomb. For most citizens its justification seemed obvious: the bomb was a legitimate weapon, it speeded victory, and it saved American lives. Policymakers publicly shared these views. In future years, Truman often declared that he never had any doubts about using the bomb, that it saved millions of lives, and that he would do it again. . . .

LOUIS BERES, APOCALYPSE

123–26 (1980).

[Hiroshima] was the site of a genuine nuclear attack by one country upon another, although the bomb itself—a weapon with the mere force of less than 20,000 tons of TNT—was certainly a pygmy by today's standards. The bomb created an area of total destruction which extended about two miles in all directions, destroying 60,000 buildings and killing between 78,000 and 200,000 people. At points close to the hypocenter, all metal and stone were melted, and human beings were completely incinerated. According to Robert Jay Lifton, the distinguished Yale psychiatrist:

> The area was enveloped by fires fanned by a violent "firewind;" these broke out almost immediately within a radius of more than three thousand meters (up to two miles). The inundation with death of the area closest to the hypocenter was such that if a man survived within a thousand meters (.6 miles) and was out of doors (that is, without benefit of shielding from heat or radiation), more than nine tenths of the people around him were fatalities.... Those closest to the hypocenter could usually recall a sudden flash, an intense sensation of heat, being knocked down or thrown some distance, and finding themselves pinned under debris or simply awakening from an indeterminate period of unconsciousness. *The most striking psychological feature of this immediate experience was the sense of a sudden and absolute shift from normal existence to an overwhelming encounter with death.*

After the initial shock, Lifton points out interestingly, the prevailing atmosphere was one of "deathly silence" rather than wild panic. Amidst an aura of weirdness and unreality, the "survivors" described a ghastly stillness in which the normal line between life and death was blurred beyond distinction. In the words of M. Hachiya's classic *Hiroshima Diary:*

> Those who were able walked silently toward the suburbs in the distant hills, their spirits broken, their initiative gone. When asked whence they had come, they pointed to the city and said, "That way:" and when asked where they were going, pointed away from the city and said, "This way." They were so broken and confused that they moved and behaved like automatons. Their reactions had astonished outsiders who reported with amazement the spectacle of long lines of people holding stolidly to a narrow, rough path when close by was a smooth, easy road going in the same direction. The outsiders could not grasp the fact that they were witnessing the exodus of a people who walked in the realm of dreams.

This sort of dreamlike, disoriented behavior was also reportedly characteristic of the Nazi death camp survivors upon their liberation. And in both cases, despite the apparent hopelessness of the situation, numerous survivors—however ineffectually—sought to help others, a factor that probably contributed a great deal to their own survival. This point, that compassion and concern for others in extreme situations is the key to one's own survival, is the main thesis of Terrence Des Pres's account of Hitler's kingdom of death. There are, however, several accounts of the atomic bomb experience which discount this thesis. For example, according to Takashi Nagai, a physician of Nagasaki (the second target of American nuclear attack in August 1945):

> In general, then, those who survived the atom bomb were the people who ignored their friends crying out *in extremis;* or who shook off wounded neighbors who clung to them, pleading to be saved.... In short, those who survived the bomb were, if not merely lucky, in a greater or lesser degree selfish, self-centered, guided by instinct and not civilization ... and we know it, we who have survived. Knowing it is a dull ache without surcease.

This last remark points to the phenomenon of *survivor guilt,* an inevitable and enduring consequence of nuclear attack. Lifton's descriptions of the need of the *hibakusha* (atomic bomb survivors), from the moment of atomic bomb exposure, to justify their own survival in the midst of death for so many others, are paralleled by the death camp accounts of other literary intellectuals.

Survivor guilt, however, is not the only enduring personal consequence of nuclear catastrophe, as the experience of the "Hiroshima Maidens" points out. These twenty-five young women, brought to the United States in 1955 for plastic-surgical treatment of burn scars and hideous accumulations of keloid scar tissue, are still ravaged by their experience of many years ago. Initially tormented by catastrophic injuries that left them with eyes they could not close and mouths that could not speak or eat, they still live in fear that their exposure to radiation might produce deformed children. One of the "maidens," Michiko Sako, expresses her feelings in a poem entitled, "Bring Back My Smile:"

> Though flowers bloom again,
> Even after blossoms have fallen,
> Once injured, the body never heals.

Now that some of the more terrible physical deformities have been corrected or relieved, Mrs. Sako still feels that she will never "be able to erase the nonphysical scars, even in the future."

At the time of their suffering, the survivors of Auschwitz and Hiroshima, of Treblinka and Nagasaki, reacted to the otherworldly grotesqueness of their conditions with what Lifton describes as a profound sense of "death in life." Witnessing, in the one case, the thrusting of newly delivered babies, *alive*, into ovens, and in the other, the appearance of long lines of severely burned, literally melting, ghosts, the survivors found themselves, in Bruno Bettelheim's words, an "anonymous mass," or in the Japanese term, *mugamuchú*, "without self, without a center." Such a total disruption of individual and social order, of one's customary personal and community supports, produced consequences that went far beyond immediate physical and emotional suffering. Indeed, this understanding is incorporated in the Japanese term for atomic bomb survivors, *hibakusha*, which delimits four categories of victims. According to Dr. Lifton, these categories include

> those who at the time of the bomb were within the city limits of Hiroshima as then defined ... those who came into the city within fourteen days and entered a designated area extending to about two thousand meters from the hypocenter; those who came into physical contact with bomb victims, through various forms of aid or disposal of bodies; and those who were *in utero* at the time, and whose mothers fit into any of the first three groups.

The effects of Hiroshima, therefore, are not confined to the immediate or even long-term experiences of those who bore witness, but extend to their rescuers, their progeny, and even to the progeny of their rescuers. Perhaps it would not be unreasonable to expand the category of *habakusha* to include the children of Japanese mothers who do not fit into one of the three above-mentioned groups, as well as several generations of Americans who, willingly or unwillingly, share the burden of national guilt. Perhaps it would not even be unreasonable to include human kind as a whole, since the legacy of Hiroshima is an interloper that can never be fully excluded from our collective destiny.

Herman Kahn, Thinking About the Unthinkable

18–19, 22–24 (1962).

In 1960 I published a book [*On Thermonuclear War*] that attempted to direct attention to the possibility of a thermonuclear war, to ways of reducing the likelihood of such a war, and to methods for coping with the consequences should war occur despite our efforts to avoid it. The book was greeted by a large range of responses—some of them sharply critical. Some of this criticism was substantive, touching on greater or smaller questions of strategy, policy, or research techniques. But much of the criticism was not concerned with the correctness or incorrectness of the views I expressed. It was concerned with whether any book should have been written on this subject at all. It is characteristic of our times that many intelligent and sincere people are willing to argue that it is immoral to think and even more immoral to write in detail about having to fight a thermonuclear war. . . .

The arguments against hard thinking by anyone at all about the realities of thermonuclear war break down into a number of categories: First, it is argued that thinking about the indescribable horror of nuclear war breeds callousness and indifference to the future of civilization in our planners and decision makers. It is true that detailed and dispassionate discussion of such questions is likely to look incredibly hard-hearted. It should also be clear, at least to thoughtful readers, that such questions must be considered. The reality may be so unpleasant that decision makers would prefer not to face it; but to a great extent this reality has been forced on them, or has come uninvited. Thanks to our ever-increasing technology we are living in a terrible and dangerous world; but, unlike the lady in the cartoon we cannot say, "Stop the world, I want to get off." We cannot get off. Even the most utopian of today's visionaries will have to concede that the mere existence of modern technology involves a risk to civilization that would have been unthinkable twenty-five years ago. While we are going to make major attempts to change the nature of this reality, accepting great risks if necessary, most of us are unwilling to choose either a pronounced degree of unilateral disarmament or a preventive war designed to "settle" our problems one way or another. We therefore must face the facts that thermonuclear bombs now exist in the hands of at least four powers; that at least one of these powers has announced it is interested in the destruction of our society, albeit by peaceful means if possible; that the number of thermonuclear powers may grow; that the power most likely to obtain these weapons next, China, stands on the thesis that war with us is inevitable; and, finally, that the possibilities of an immediate solution by negotiation are indeed slim. Unless we are willing to abdicate our responsibilities we are pledged to the maintenance of terrifying weapon systems with known and unknown, calculable and incalculable risks, unless and until better arrangements can be made.

If we are to have an expensive and lethal defense establishment, we must weigh all the risks and benefits. We must at least ask ourselves what are the likely and unlikely results of an inadvertent war, the possibilities of accident, irresponsibility, or unauthorized behavior on the other side as well as on our own.

A variation of the objection to careful consideration of these problems focuses on the personality of the thinker. This argument goes: Better no thought than evil thought; and since only evil and callous people can think about this, better no thought. Alternatively, the thinker's motives are analyzed: This man studies war; he must like war—much like the suspicion that a surgeon is a repressed sadist. Even if the charge were true, which in general it is not, it is not relevant. Like the repressed sadist who can perform a socially useful function by sublimating his urges into surgery, the man who loves war or violence may be able to successfully sublimate his desires into a careful and valuable study of war. It does indeed take an iron will or an unpleasant degree of detachment to go about this task. Ideally it should be possible for the analyst to have a disciplined empathy. In fact, the mind recoils from simultaneously probing deeply and creatively into these problems and being conscious at all times of the human tragedy involved.

This is not new. We do not continually remind the surgeon while he is operating of the humanity of his patient. We do not flash pictures of his patient's wife or children in front of him. We want him to be careful, and we want him to be aware of the importance and frailty of the patient; we do not want him to be distracted or fearful. We do not expect illustrations in a book on surgery to be captioned: "A particularly deplorable tumor," or "Good health is preferable to this kind of cancer." Excessive comments such as, "And now there's a lot of blood," or "This particular cut really hurts," are out of place although these are important things for a surgeon to know. To mention such things may be important. To dwell on them is morbid, and gets in the way of the information. The same tolerance needs be extended to thought on national security.

Some feel that we should consider these problems but view them with such awe and horror that we should not discuss them in normal, neutral, professional everyday language. I tend to disagree, at least so far as technical discussions and research are concerned. One does not do research in a cathedral. Awe is fine for those who come to worship or admire but for those who come to analyze, to tamper, to change, to criticize, a factual and dispassionate, and sometimes even colorful, approach is to be preferred. And if the use of everyday language jars, that is all the more reason for using it. Why would one expect a realistic discussion of thermonuclear war not to be disturbing? . . .

NOTES AND QUESTIONS

1. Kahn supports his view that rigorous cost-benefit analysis should guide our nuclear strategy by arguing that one should not continually remind a surgeon of the humanity of his patient. Do you agree that disinterested physicians provide the best medical care?

2. Are nuclear weapons "the first of mankind's technological innovations which are simply not encompassable within the familiar moral world"? *See* MICHAEL WALZER, JUST AND UNJUST WARS 282 (1977). The Nazis killed millions with conventional means. President Truman justified the bombings of Hiroshima and Nagasaki on the ground that they actually saved lives by shortening the war. *See* Louis Morton, *The Decision to Use the Atomic Bomb, in* ROBERT J. ART & KENNETH WALTZ, THE USE OF FORCE (1993). Analysis of Truman's argument should presumably include the effect of the atomic bombings on the survivors, who suffer from increased rates of leukemia and other diseases, and whose offspring have an increased risk of genetic abnormality. *See* THE COMMITTEE FOR THE COMPILATION OF MATERIALS ON DAMAGE CAUSED BY THE ATOMIC BOMBS IN HIROSHIMA AND NAGASAKI, HIROSHIMA AND NAGASAKI: THE PHYSICAL, MEDICAL, AND SOCIAL EFFECTS OF THE ATOMIC BOMBINGS (1981).

Perhaps nuclear weapons are different in that they would almost inevitably cause extensive civilian casualties as well as a level of destruction that may be disproportionate to the ends of warfare: Would carefully-targeted tactical nuclear weapons be more morally acceptable than large-scale nuclear weapons? Or does nuclear weaponry in any form raise special concerns? Years after the Manhattan Project, Albert Einstein observed that "the unleashed power of the atom has changed everything except our modes of thinking, and thus we drift toward unparalleled catastrophes." Ralph Lapp, *The Einstein Letter That Started It All*, N.Y. TIMES MAG., Aug. 2, 1964.

C.   PROTECTING THE SECRET OF THE HYDROGEN BOMB

After World War II, the United States began efforts to build a hydrogen bomb, a weapon that fuses together hydrogen isotopes to release, in accordance with $E = mc^2$, far more energy than an atomic bomb releases. Robert Oppenheimer, as Chairman of the General Advisory Committee to the Atomic Energy Commission, questioned whether the hydrogen bomb could be built and whether it was necessary. In 1952, the United States conducted the first successful full-scale test of the hydrogen bomb (sometimes then called the "Super"); not much later the Soviet Union developed its own hydrogen bomb.

In 1954, Oppenheimer appeared in a quasi-judicial proceeding before an Atomic Energy Commission security board chaired by an attorney, Gordon Gray. Oppenheimer was charged with having associated with Communists, having been less than frank in naming certain alleged Soviet agents, and of having opposed the development of the hydrogmittee. One of Walker's assignments was to keep tabs on the progress of the AEC's H-bomb work, and as he set about educating himself in the thermonuclear field, he found one name to be ubiquitous, that of J. Robert Oppenheimer—chairman of this, consultant on that, expert witness on the other. Walker became disturbed at the omnipresence of Oppenheimer, but even more at the manner in which Oppenheimer seemed to exploit his role. For example, he found then bomb. The Gray Board ultimately concluded that Oppenheimer, while loyal, should no longer have access to military secrets, since such access would not be "consistent with the security interests of the United States." PETER GOODCHILD, J. ROBERT OPPENHEIMER: SHATTERER OF WORLDS 262 (1981). The excerpt below describes the Gray Board proceeding.

Philip M. Stern, The Oppenheimer Case: Security on Trial

181–82, 242–44, 273–74, 281–82, 377, 506–07 (1969).

That summer John Walker, a Yale Law School [graduate] ... joined the staff of the Atomic Energy Comat Oppenheimer, as a member of a Pentagon policy group, had argued against declaring a military need for the H-bomb since AEC scientists had not yet declared it technically feasible; however, later on the same day, sitting as an AEC adviser, he had discouraged expansion of technical research on the H-bomb, on the ground that the Pentagon had failed to express any military need for such a weapon.

After a nationwide tour of atomic facilities, Walker concluded that Oppenheimer's apparent influence on the H-bomb program was even greater in the scientific community than it was in government councils. As late as October, 1951, even after the unveiling of Edward Teller's promising new approach to the bomb, Walker could find no more than a dozen important scientists who were in favor of the thermonuclear project.

In ensuing months, Walker and his friend William Borden would spend many hours discussing the remarkable Dr. Oppenheimer, whose security file Borden continued to study....

[After deciding to proceed against Oppenheimer,] the AEC's ... problem was how the prodigious amount of evidence in the investigative files should be presented to the hearing board, and by whom. Even before a hearing board was picked, it was decided that an outside attorney should be engaged to handle the case for the Commission.

For aid in finding such a person, Lewis Strauss turned to the Department of Justice. There the matter fell largely to Deputy Attorney General William P. Rogers, who, unlike Attorney General Brownell, had previously practiced law in Washington and was therefore well acquainted with the array of local attorneys. Since the case would clearly call for the presentation of a vast amount of information to the board, Rogers sought a man with considerable trial experience, preferably in the role of prosecutor. Prominent among those who seemed to meet Rogers' prerequisites was a native Washingtonian by the name of Roger Robb, who had had seven years of prosecutorial experience as an Assistant United States Attorney. During that time he had tried twenty-three murder cases, obtaining, according to the local newspaper, "an unusually high percentage of convictions," and had won some local renown for his prosecution of Washington gambling czar Sam Beard. Robb had also been the court-appointed attorney for Communist leader Earl Browder in a contempt-of-Congress case, for which he earned Browder's public praise.[†] William Rogers himself had had occasion to observe Robb's courtroom talents at first hand, since Robb had been his legal adversary in a libel action against Drew Pearson. (Rogers, who represented Pearson, had emerged victorious on that occasion.)

[†] "Despite his pronounced political opinions, which I would call reactionary," Browder wrote in the preface of a book about the trial, Robb provided "substantial, not merely formal, assistance," and displayed a high "pride of profession."

When Chairman Strauss received Rogers' suggested list of Washington attorneys, Roger Robb was the one he selected to approach first. After one preliminary conversation with Robb, and after obtaining the approval of the other Commissioners, Strauss asked Robb to take on the case....

Who would be Roger Robb's adversary in the forthcoming hearing? ...

Early in January, in part at the suggestion of John Lord O'Brian, Oppenheimer called Lloyd K. Garrison [who was to become his counsel], a leading New York attorney whom Oppenheimer had come to know the preceding April, when Garrison joined the board of trustees of the Institute for Advanced Study. Garrison came from a distinguished family. His great-grandfather was abolitionist William Lloyd Garrison, his grandfather literary editor of *The Nation*. Garrison himself had been dean of the Wisconsin Law School and a pioneering expert and activist in government labor relations work. As a private practitioner of the law in New York since the war, and as president of the National Urban League and a leader in the American Civil Liberties Union, Garrison had earned a reputation for unimpeachable integrity and enormous dedication to public causes. Lincolnesque in appearance, mild of manner, Garrison sought weekend respite at a country home where he devoted his sparse leisure time to bird-watching and reading philosophy, Greek literature and books on politics.

[Shortly after the hearing began,] Oppenheimer's account soon reached the crucial 1949 GAC [General Advisory Committee to the AEC] meetings on the H-bomb, and in testifying about the GAC's written reports on those deliberations, he became involved in an apparent conflict of testimony. Had he and the GAC opposed the "Super" *per se?* Or had they merely been against a "crash" development program? Roger Robb had made available to Oppenheimer, not the complete GAC reports, but selected "extracts," and from these the scientist read a statement in the 1949 report to which all eight members of the GAC had agreed:

> We all hope that by one means or another, the development of these weapons [the H-bomb] can be avoided. We are all reluctant to see the United States take the initiative in precipitating this development. We are all agreed that it would be wrong at the present moment to commit ourselves *to an all-out effort towards its development.* [Emphasis added.]

On its face, this passage, which Oppenheimer told the Gray Board was "the crux of it," seemed to argue more against a crash program for the H-bomb than against the bomb itself.

At this time Oppenheimer had before him only those extracts of the 1949 GAC reports that Robb had provided him. Lloyd Garrison, of course, was not allowed to see even the extracts. Neither of them, therefore, could know what Robb knew—namely, that the so-called "majority annex" of the GAC report, which Oppenheimer and five others had signed, contained this passage:

> *We believe a super bomb should never be produced.* Mankind would be far better off not to have a demonstration of the feasibility of such a weapon until the present climate of world opinion changes. [Emphasis added.]

Robb waited until the final days of the four-week hearing to unveil this excerpt—to the complete surprise of both Oppenheimer and Garrison....

Robb quickly established himself as an exacting interrogator. With his very first questions, he sought to manacle Oppenheimer to everything he had said in his lengthy letter of reply to the AEC charges, presumably so that any errors that might later be proven would appear more like deliberate lies than inadvertent mistakes.

Q: Dr. Oppenheimer, did you [with the assistance of counsel] prepare your letter of March 4, 1954, to General Nichols?

A: Yes.

Q: In all events, you were thoroughly familiar with the contents of it?

A: I am.

Q: And have read it over very carefully, I assume?

A: Yes.

Q: Are all the statements which you make in that letter the truth, the whole truth and nothing but the truth?

A: Yes.

Robb then asked about a year-by-year biographical sketch that Lloyd Garrison had given the board. That, said Oppenheimer, had been prepared by his secretary, and he hadn't even read it over very carefully, whereupon Robb, in true prosecutorial style, demanded, "Are you, or are you not prepared to vouch for [its] accuracy?"

Oppenheimer would merely say it was accurate so far as he knew.

Then emerged Roger Robb the bulldog; fiercely tenacious; once set upon a line of questions, impossible to shake off with elliptical answers.

Why, during World War II, had Oppenheimer considered *current* (as distinct from past) Communist Party membership as incompatible with secret war work? Robb inquired. Was it because party members were expected, if so ordered, to commit espionage? "I was never told that," replied Oppenheimer.

Robb was not satisfied. He wanted a direct answer. It required four separate forays, but ultimately he prevailed:

Q: [*First probe*] Doctor, let me ask you a blunt question. Don't you know, and didn't you know certainly by 1943, that the Communist Party was an instrument or a vehicle of espionage in this country?

A: I was not clear about it.

Q: [*Second probe*] Didn't you suspect it?

A: No.

Q: [*Third probe*] Wasn't that the reason why you felt that membership in the party was inconsistent with the work on a secret war project?

A: I think I have stated the reason about right.

Q: [*Fourth probe*] I am asking you now if your fear of espionage wasn't *one of the reasons* why you felt that association with the Communist Party was inconsistent with work on a secret war project. [Emphasis added.]

A: Yes.

Q: [*Success. Now, nail it down*] Your answer is that it was?

A: Yes.

Soon Robb was to catch Oppenheimer in another contradiction. When, he asked, had the physicist been a "fellow traveler"?

A: From late 1936 or early 1937, and then it tapered off, and I would say I traveled much less fellow after 1939 and very much less after 1942.

Then, this exchange:

Q: How long after 1942 did you continue as a fellow traveler?

A: After 1942 I would say not at all.

Q: But you did continue as a fellow traveler until 1942?

A: Well, now, let us be careful.

Q: I want you to be, Doctor.

A: I had no sympathy with the Communist line about [U.S. intervention in] the war between the spring of 1940 and when they changed [from isolationism to interventionism]. . . .

Q: Did you cease to be a fellow traveler at the time of the Nazi–Russian [nonaggression] Pact in 1939?

A: I think I did, yes.

Q: [After one intervening question] Are you now amending your previous answer that you were more or less a fellow traveler until 1942?

A: *Yes, I think I am.* [Emphasis added.] . . .

What must Robert Oppenheimer have felt at these and similar moments during Robb's interrogation? The defendant sits in the witness chair, facing first the prospect and then the reality of being pummeled by skillful, relentless and hostile questions from a tough, adroit trial attorney. The heart pounds; the blood rises into the face. . . .

How much does the prosecutor know? . . . What will he ask? . . . What is he getting at with this question or that? . . . Is he leading me into a trap? . . . Is my memory correct? . . . Can I outguess him? . . . Is he closing in on me? . . . Has he outsmarted me? . . . Emotion rises; and as it does, reason and intellect recede. Common sense flees. The interrogator appears more and more omniscient; the beleaguered witness feels growingly impotent. It is, at best, an intimidating experience; at worst, it is terrifying.

Particularly must this have been true for Robert Oppenheimer. Aware that for eleven years his daily life had been under the Federal Government's most high-powered investigative microscope, he nevertheless must have been appalled, as he testified, to realize the full extent of the government's scrutiny. As the hearing proceeded, it became clear that the secretly made tape recordings of the Pash and Lansdale interrogations were only the beginning of the intimate, mysteriously gathered information that Robb had in his possession. Pitted against Robb's hidden reports, in the struggle to recapture the truth about events, people and places after more than a decade's passage of time, was the naked memory of J. Robert Oppenheimer, prey not only to the toll that time itself exacts, but also to the tendency of all humans to permit their recollections to be cosmetically altered by their wishes. As Oppenheimer himself put it, in the Gray Board hearing, "I don't want to remember more than I do remember." . . .

The Gray Board's finding on the H-bomb charge (presented here with interpolations) went roughly as follows: After the presidential go-ahead was made public on January 31, 1950, Oppenheimer "did not oppose the [H-bomb] project in a positive or open manner" (*as had Hans Bethe, Albert Einstein and other leading scientists*), nor did he decline to cooperate in the project (*as Edward Teller had done at Los Alamo during the height of global war, in refusing to work on the projects assigned him by his superiors*). Oppenheimer's sin lay in the supremacy of his personal influence in the scientific community, and in the fact that he "did not make it known that he had abandoned" his well-known anti-H-bomb views. This, the board concluded, "undoubtedly had an adverse effect on recruitment of scientists" for the H-bomb program. . . .

Why should so debasing a tragedy have befallen so extraordinary a man? Oppenheimer himself took a rather fatalistic view of the matter. Not long after the security case, he said to an interviewer, "I think of this as a major accident—much like a train wreck or the collapse of a building. It has no relation or connection with my life. I just happened to be there."

To some extent, Oppenheimer did just happen to be in the way of external forces that had very little relation to his personal life:

• *The "McCarthy era"*: A wave of postwar anxiety and fear of the unorthodox not dissimilar to that which followed World War I. But in the 1950's popular fears were intensified by the emergence of Russia as a hostile power, the revelations of Soviet espionage against Western powers, and by the rise of a superlative and fearsome demagogue—Senator Joseph McCarthy. . . .

• *The emergence of the scientist-as-policy-maker:* Oppenheimer was both the symbol and the victim of a new and perplexing problem in American Government: the sudden transformation of The Scientist from a rumpled, abstracted, ivory-tower figure into a major force in American policy-making. If technology put new tools in the hands of the statesmen and the military, it also made them increasingly dependent on the technical advice of The Scientist. But how does the nonexpert layman who receives such advice distinguish a scientist-adviser's "technical" views from his political, moral or philosophical predilections? For example, when such an adviser gives counsel as to the "technical" feasibility of a new weapon, might not his judgment be clouded—however unconsciously—by his view that the weapon is, say, morally repugnant or, on the contrary, absolutely essential to the survival of the nation?

Statesmen and politicians have long had to wrestle with their reliance, in military matters, on generals and admirals. But the postwar dependence on scientists and their sudden inclusion in the high councils of government was something far newer; and because it was new it was, to many, perplexing. The concern it caused was often reflected in the Oppenheimer proceeding, nowhere more clearly than in the Gray Board's plea that scientist-advisers rely on their "special competence" and their "soundly-based convictions . . . uncolored and uninfluenced by considerations of an emotional character."

NOTES AND QUESTIONS

1. Do the methods of prosecutor Robb (later a judge of the United States Court of Appeals for the District of Columbia Circuit) and of the Oppenheimer hearing itself bear any resemblance to the methods used by Albert Einstein as described in Chapter 3, Sec. I. A., *supra*? Do not the trial attorney and the scientist both seek the truth? Why then do the approaches seem so different?

2. Lawyers often note with pride the ability of someone like Robb to represent ably disparate clients such as Communist leader Earl Browder and the Atomic Energy Commission. Why do you suppose scientists often feel uncomfortable with this aspect of the legal profession?

3. Oppenheimer arguably used his expertise to attempt to affect United States policy on the hydrogen bomb. Does this constitute a misuse of his expertise? Does Oppenheimer deserve a special role in the hydrogen bomb debate compared with, for example, the engineer who makes the materials used in the bomb? In addition, Oppenheimer's alleged activities raise questions about the personal responsibility of a scientific "insider" who comes to disagree with government or industrial policy. Should we place special obligations or restrictions on the "whistleblower"?

4. The Oppenheimer case also highlights the tension created when scientific research and debate, which rely on the free national and international exchange of ideas, come in conflict with military secrecy. That tension remains a central problem today. *See, e.g.*, Chapter 4, Sec. I. A, *infra*, on the efforts of the *Progressive* magazine to publish material about the hydrogen bomb.

5. In the end, apart from all of the security clearance issues, Oppenheimer's hydrogen bomb experience demonstrates, as did his atomic bomb experience, the deep ambivalence felt by a socially conscious scientist toward progress that might lead to dangerous ends. Oppenheimer based his reluctance about the hydrogen bomb partly on its apparent scientific unfeasibility; part of his opposition was undercut by the scientific attractiveness of the ultimate bomb design developed by Edward Teller:

> Oppenheimer later held that if a weapon of this kind had been suggested initially, he would never have opposed it. He described Teller's new development as "technically so sweet that you could not argue about that" and now he could see only one possible course of action. "You go ahead and do it and you argue about what to do about it only after you have had your technical success."

PETER GOODCHILD, J. ROBERT OPPENHEIMER: SHATTERER OF WORLDS 210 (1981).

6. Consider the view of science implicit in the work of Einstein and Oppenheimer as you evaluate the following classic accounts of scientific change and of the social structure of the scientific community.

D. COMPARING SCIENTIFIC AND LEGAL REASONING

THOMAS S. KUHN, THE STRUCTURE OF SCIENTIFIC REVOLUTIONS
10–11, 52, 84–85, 165–67, 172 (1962).

In this essay, "normal science" means research firmly based upon one or more past scientific achievements, achievements that some particular scientific community acknowledges for a time as supplying the foundation for its further practice. Today such achievements are recounted, though seldom in their original form, by science textbooks, elementary and advanced. These textbooks expound the body of accepted theory, illustrate many or all of its successful applications, and compare these applications with exemplary observations and experiments. Before such books became popular early in the nineteenth century (and until even more recently in the newly matured sciences), many of the famous classics of science fulfilled a similar function. Aristotle's *Physica,* Ptolemy's *Almagest,* Newton's *Principia* and *Opticks,* Franklin's *Electricity,* Lavoisier's *Chemistry,* and Lyell's *Geology*—these and many other works served for a time implicitly to define the legitimate problems and methods of a research field for succeeding generations of practitioners. They were able to do so because they shared two essential characteristics. Their achievement was sufficiently unprecedented to attract an enduring group of adherents away from competing modes of scientific activity. Simultaneously, it was sufficiently open-ended to leave all sorts of problems for the redefined group of practitioners to resolve.

Achievements that share these two characteristics I shall henceforth refer to as "paradigms," a term that relates closely to "normal science." By choosing it, I mean to suggest that some accepted examples of actual scientific practice—examples which include law, theory, application, and instrumentation together—provide models from which spring particular coherent traditions of scientific research. These are the traditions which the historian describes under such rubrics as "Ptolemaic astronomy" (or "Copernican"), "Aristotelian dynamics" (or "Newtonian"), "corpuscular optics" (or "wave optics"), and so on. The study of paradigms, including many that are far more specialized than those named illustratively above, is what mainly prepares the student for membership in the particular scientific community with which he will later practice. Because he there joins men who learned the bases of their field from the same concrete models, his subsequent practice will seldom evoke overt disagreement over fundamentals. Men whose research is based on shared paradigms are committed to the same rules and standards for scientific practice. That commitment and the apparent consensus it produces are prerequisites for normal science, i.e., for the genesis and continuation of a particular research tradition....

Normal science, the puzzle-solving activity we have just examined, is a highly cumulative enterprise, eminently successful in its aim, the steady extension of the scope and precision of scientific knowledge. In all these respects it fits with great precision the most usual image of scientific work. Yet one standard product of the scientific enterprise is missing. Normal science does not aim at novelties of fact or theory and, when successful, finds none. New and unsuspected phenomena are, however, repeatedly uncovered by scientific research, and radical new theories have again and again been invented by scientists. History even suggests that the scientific enterprise has developed a uniquely powerful technique for producing surprises of this sort. If this characteristic of science is to be reconciled with what has already been said, then research under a paradigm must be a particularly effective way of inducing paradigm change. That is what fundamental novelties of fact and theory do. Produced inadvertently by a game played under one set of rules, their assimilation requires the elaboration of another set. After they have become parts of science, the enterprise, at least of those specialists in whose particular field the novelties lie, is never quite the same again....

The transition from a paradigm in crisis to a new one from which a new tradition of normal science can emerge is far from a cumulative process, one achieved by an articulation or extension of the old paradigm. Rather it is a reconstruction of the field from new fundamentals, a reconstruction that changes some of the field's most elementary theoretical generalizations as well as many of its paradigm methods and applications. During the transition period there will be a large but never complete overlap between the problems that can be solved by the old and by the new paradigm. But there will also be a decisive difference in the modes of solution. When the transition is complete, the profession will have changed its view of the field, its methods, and its goals. One perceptive historian, viewing a classic case of a science's reorientation by paradigm change, recently described it as "picking up the other end of the stick," a process that involves "handling the same bundle of data as before, but placing them in a new system of relations with one another by giving them a different framework." Others who have noted this aspect of scientific advance have emphasized its similarity to a change in visual gestalt: the marks on paper that were first seen as a bird are now seen as an antelope, or vice versa. . . .

In its normal state, then, a scientific community is an immensely efficient instrument for solving the problems or puzzles that its paradigms define. Furthermore, the result of solving those problems must inevitably be progress. There is no problem here. Seeing that much, however, only highlights the second main part of the problem of progress in the sciences. Let us therefore turn to it and ask about progress through extraordinary science. Why should progress also be the apparently universal concomitant of scientific revolutions? . . . If authority alone, and particularly if nonprofessional authority, were the arbiter of paradigm debates, the outcome of those debates might still be revolution, but it would not be *scientific* revolution. The very existence of science depends upon vesting the power to choose between paradigms in the members of a special kind of community. Just how special that community must be if science is to survive and grow may be indicated by the very tenuousness of humanity's hold on the scientific enterprise. Every civilization of which we have records has possessed a technology, an art, a religion, a political system, laws, and so on. In many cases those facets of civilization have been as developed as our own. But only the civilizations that descend from Hellenic Greece have possessed more than the most rudimentary science. The bulk of scientific knowledge is a product of Europe in the last four centuries. No other place and time has supported the very special communities from which scientific productivity comes.

What are the essential characteristics of these communities? Obviously, they need vastly more study. In this area only the most tentative generalizations are possible. Nevertheless, a number of requisites for membership in a professional scientific group must already be strikingly clear. The scientist must, for example, be concerned to solve problems about the behavior of nature. In addition, though his concern with nature may be global in its extent, the problems on which he works must be problems of detail. More important, the solutions that satisfy him may not be merely personal but must instead be accepted as solutions by many. The group that shares them may not, however, be drawn at random from society as a whole, but is rather the well-defined community of the scientist's professional compeers. One of the strongest, if still unwritten, rules of scientific life is the prohibition of appeals to heads of state or to the populace at large in matters scientific. Recognition of the existence of a uniquely competent professional group and acceptance of its role as the exclusive arbiter of professional achievement has further implications. The group's members, as individuals and by virtue of their shared training and experience, must be seen as the sole possessors of the rules of the game or of some equivalent basis for unequivocal judgments. To doubt that they shared some such basis for evaluations would be to admit the existence of incompatible standards of scientific achievement. That admission would inevitably raise the question whether truth in the sciences can be one. . . .

Anyone who has followed the argument this far will nevertheless feel the need to ask why the evolutionary process should work. What must nature, including man, be like in order that science be possible at all? Why should scientific communities be able to reach a firm consensus unattainable in other fields? Why should consensus endure across one paradigm change after another? And why should paradigm change invariably produce an instrument more perfect in any sense than those known before? From one point of view those questions, excepting the first, have already been answered. But from another they are as open as they were when this essay began. It is not only the scientific community that must be special. The world of which that community is a part must also possess quite special characteristics, and we are no closer than we were at the start to knowing what these must be. That problem—What must the world be like in order that man may know it?—was not, however, created by this essay. On the contrary, it is as old as science itself, and it remains unanswered. But it need not be answered in this place. Any conception of nature compatible with the growth of science by proof is compatible with the evolutionary view of science developed here. Since this view is also compatible with close observation of scientific life, there are strong arguments for employing it in attempts to solve the host of problems that still remain.

ROBERT K. MERTON, SOCIAL THEORY AND SOCIAL STRUCTURE
607–14 (1968).

Four sets of institutional imperatives—universalism, communism, disinterestedness, organized skepticism—comprise the ethos of modern science.

Universalism finds immediate expression in the canon that truth claims, whatever their source, are to be subjected to *preestablished impersonal criteria:* consonant with observation and with previously confirmed knowledge. The acceptance or rejection of claims entering the lists of science is not to depend on the personal or social attributes of their protagonist; his race, nationality, religion, class and personal qualities are as such irrelevant. Objectivity precludes particularism. The circumstance that scientifically verified formulations refer to objective sequences and correlations militates against all efforts to impose particularistic criteria of validity. The Haber process cannot be invalidated by a Nuremberg decree nor can an Anglophobe repeal the law of gravitation. The chauvinist may expunge the names of alien scientists from historical textbooks but their formulations remain indispensable to science and technology. However *echtdeutsch* or hundred-per-cent American the final increment, some aliens are accessories before the fact of every new technical advance. The imperative of universalism is rooted deep in the impersonal character of science. . . .

"Communism," in the non-technical and extended sense of common ownership of goods, is a second integral element of the scientific ethos. The substantive findings of science are a product of social collaboration and are assigned to the community. They constitute a common heritage in which the equity of the individual producer is severely limited. An eponymous law or theory does not enter into the exclusive possession of the discoverer and his heirs, nor do the mores bestow upon them special rights of use and disposition. Property rights in science are whittled down to a bare minimum by the rationale of the scientific ethic. The scientist's claim to "his" intellectual "property" is limited to that of recognition and esteem which, if the institution functions with a modicum of efficiency, is roughly commensurate with the significance of the increments brought to the common fund of knowledge. Eponymy—e.g., the Copernican system, Boyle's law—is thus at once a mnemonic and a commemorative device.

Given such institutional emphasis upon recognition and esteem as the sole property right of the scientist in his discoveries, the concern with scientific priority becomes a "normal" response. Those controversies over priority which punctuate the history of modern science are generated by the institutional accent on originality. There issues a competitive cooperation. The products of competition are communized, and esteem accrues to the producer. Nations take up claims to priority, and fresh entries into the commonwealth of science are tagged with the names of nationals: witness the controversy raging over the rival claims of Newton and Leibniz to the differential calculus. But all this does not challenge the status of scientific knowledge as common property.

The institutional conception of science as part of the public domain is linked with the imperative for communication of findings. Secrecy is the antithesis of this norm; full and open communication its enactment. The pressure for diffusion of results is reenforced by the institutional goal of advancing the boundaries of knowledge and by the incentive of recognition which is, of course, contingent upon publication. A scientist who does not communicate his important discoveries to the scientific fraternity—thus, a Henry Cavendish—becomes the target for ambivalent responses. He is esteemed for his talent and, perhaps, for his modesty. But, institutionally considered, his modesty is seriously misplaced, in view of the moral compulsive for sharing the wealth of science. Layman though he is, Aldous Huxley's comment on Cavendish is illuminating in this connection: "Our admiration of his genius is tempered by a certain disapproval; we feel that such a man is selfish and anti-social." The epithets are particularly instructive for they imply the violation of a definite institutional imperative. Even though it serves no ulterior motive, the suppression of scientific discovery is condemned.

The communal character of science is further reflected in the recognition by scientists of their dependence upon a cultural heritage to which they lay no differential claims. Newton's remark—"If I have seen farther it is by standing on the shoulders of giants"—expresses at once a sense of indebtedness to the common heritage and a recognition of the essentially cooperative and cumulative quality of scientific achievement. The humility of scientific genius is not simply culturally appropriate but results from the realization that scientific advance involves the collaboration of past and present generations. . . .

Science, as is the case with the professions in general, includes disinterestedness as a basic institutional element. Disinterestedness is not to be equated with altruism nor interested action with egoism. Such equivalences confuse institutional and motivational levels of analysis. A passion for knowledge, idle curiosity, altruistic concern with the benefit to humanity and a host of other special motives have been attributed to the scientist. The quest for distinctive motives appears to have been misdirected. *It is rather a distinctive pattern of institutional control of a wide range of motives which characterizes the behavior of scientists.* For once the institution enjoins disinterested activity, it is to the interest of the scientists to conform on pain of sanctions and, in so far as the norm has been internalized, on pain of psychological conflict. . . .

Organized scepticism is variously interrelated with the other elements of the scientific ethos. It is both a methodologic and an institutional mandate. The suspension of judgment until "the facts are at hand" and the detached scrutiny of beliefs in terms of empirical and logical criteria have periodically involved science in conflict with other institutions. Science which asks questions of fact, including potentialities, concerning every aspect of nature and society may come into conflict with other attitudes toward these same data which have been crystallized and often ritualized by other institutions. . . .

NOTES AND QUESTIONS

The scientific process involves the construction and testing of hypotheses. In a famous discussion of "the task of the logic of scientific discovery, or the logic of knowledge," Karl Popper argued that it is "not the *verifiability* but the *falsifiability* of a system" that is a criterion of its being empirical or scientific:

> Various objections might be raised against the criterion of demarcation here proposed. In the first place, it may well seem somewhat wrong-headed to suggest that science, which is supposed to give us positive information, should be characterized as satisfying a negative requirement such as refutability. However, . . . this objection has little weight, since the amount of positive information about the world which is conveyed by a scientific statement is the greater the more likely it is to clash, because of its logical character, with possible singular statements. (Not for nothing do we call the laws of nature "laws": the more they prohibit the more they say.) . . .

KARL POPPER, THE LOGIC OF SCIENTIFIC DISCOVERY 27, 41 (1968).

The point is that a scientific assertion is one that can be tested and, if the results of the test so indicate, be rejected as false. This is why the vast majority of scientists do not regard astrology as science:

> Astrologers can so hedge their predictions that they are devoid of genuine content. We may be told that a person will "tend to be creative" or "tend to be outgoing," where the evasiveness of a verb and the fuzziness of adjectives serve to insulate the claim from repudiation. But even if a prediction should be regarded as a failure, astrological devotees can go on believing that the stars rule our destinies; for there is always some item of information, perhaps as to a planet's location at a long gone time, that may be alleged to have been overlooked....

W.V. Quine & J.S. Ullian, *Hypothesis, in* W.V. Quine & J.S. Ullian, The Web of Belief 64, 80 (1978).

Of course, falsifiability is not an adequate measure of all things. Indeed, is the statement "only falsifiable assertions are of interest" itself falsifiable? Clearly in areas other than science different standards are used. Even in the scientific traditions of other cultures the "either-or" approach of falsifiability has not dominated. *See* Joseph Needham, *History and Human Values: A Chinese Perspective for World Science and Technology*, 20 Centennial Rev. 1, 27–30 (1976).

Moreover, as Kuhn suggests, in times of change in Western science, when rival theories are contending for support, there may be situations when the rival approaches are comparable in their ability to accurately predict the outcome of experiments. Until that situation changes, how do scientists choose which approach to favor? We have already noted the role of aesthetics—the beauty of a theory—in explaining the work of scientists such as J.D. Watson and Albert Einstein. This consideration may account for the frequent statement that scientists favor "simplicity" in their theories, although of course "simplicity" can depend on one's point of view; as Quine and Ullian put it, simplicity introduces a "nagging subjectivity" into the decision as to what counts in favor of a hypothesis. Quine & Ullian, *supra* at 71. Nor do accuracy and simplicity exhaust the standards that are used for evaluating ideas in Western science—Kuhn, for example, has suggested that a theory is also judged by whether it is fruitful in the sense of setting forth a new research agenda. Thomas S. Kuhn, *Objectivity, Value Judgment, and Theory Choice, in* Thomas S. Kuhn, The Essential Tension 320 (1977). Factors like these tend to put pressure on the norms of the scientific community identified by Merton, in particular the norms of universalism and organized skepticism. *See, e.g.,* Robert Hollinger, *From Weber to Habermas, in* E.D. Klemke, et al., Introductory Readings in the Philosophy of Science 416 (1988). *See generally* Karin D. Knorr, et al., The Social Process of Scientific Investigation (1981).

Kuhn's work has been enormously influential. Nonetheless, his emphasis on the importance of conceptual ideas in scientific progress may need to be balanced by a careful analysis of the actual tools and equipment scientists use in their work. *See, e.g.,* Peter Galison, Image and Logic: A Material Culture of Microphysics (1997); Freeman Dyson, *Clockwork Science*, N.Y. Rev. of Books, Nov. 6, 2003, at 42.

C.P. Snow, The Two Cultures

4–7, 10–11 (1964).

Literary intellectuals at one pole—at the other scientists, and as the most representative, the physical scientists. Between the two a gulf of mutual incomprehension—sometimes (particularly among the young) hostility and dislike, but most of all lack of understanding. They have a curious distorted image of each other. Their attitudes are so different that, even on the level of emotion, they can't find much common ground. Non-scientists tend to think of scientists as brash and boastful. They hear Mr. T.S. Eliot, who just for these illustrations we can take as an archetypal figure, saying about his attempts to revive verse-drama that we can hope for very little, but that he would feel content if he and his co-workers could prepare the ground for a new Kyd or a new Greene. That is the tone, restricted and constrained, with which literary intellectuals are at home: it is the subdued voice of their culture. Then they hear a much louder voice, that of another archetypal figure, Rutherford, trumpeting: "This is the heroic age of science! This is the Elizabethan age!" Many of us heard that, and a good many other statements beside which that was mild; and we weren't left in any doubt whom Rutherford was casting for the role of Shakespeare. What is hard for the literary intellectuals to understand, imaginatively or intellectually, is that he was absolutely right.

And compare "this is the way the world ends, not with a bang but a whimper"—incidentally, one of the least likely scientific prophecies ever made—compare that with Rutherford's famous repartee, "Lucky fellow, Rutherford, always on the crest of the wave." "Well, I made the wave, didn't I?"

The non-scientists have a rooted impression that the scientists are shallowly optimistic, unaware of man's condition. On the other hand, the scientists believe that the literary intellectuals are totally lacking in foresight, peculiarly unconcerned with their brother men, in a deep sense antiintellectual, anxious to restrict both art and thought to the existential moment. And so on. Anyone with a mild talent for invective could produce plenty of this kind of subterranean back-chat. On each side there is some of it which is not entirely baseless. It is all destructive. Much of it rests on misinterpretations which are dangerous. . . .

First, about the scientists' optimism. This is an accusation which has been made so often that it has become a platitude. It has been made by some of the acutest non-scientific minds of the day. But it depends upon a confusion between the individual experience and the social experience, between the individual condition of man and his social condition. Most of the scientists I have known well have felt—just as deeply as the nonscientists I have known well—that the individual condition of each of us is tragic. Each of us is alone: sometimes we escape from solitariness, through love or affection or perhaps creative moments, but those triumphs of life are pools of light we make for ourselves while the edge of the road is black: each of us dies alone. Some scientists I have known have had faith in revealed religion. Perhaps with them the sense of the tragic condition is not so strong. I don't know. With most people of deep feeling, however highspirited and happy they are, sometimes most with those who are happiest and most high-spirited, it seems to be right in the fibres, part of the weight of life. That is as true of the scientists I have known best as of anyone at all.

But nearly all of them—and this is where the colour of hope genuinely comes in—would see no reason why, just because the individual condition is tragic, so must the social condition be. Each of us is solitary: each of us dies alone: all right, that's a fate against which we can't struggle—but there is plenty in our condition which is not fate, and against which we are less than human unless we do struggle.

Most of our fellow human beings, for instance, are underfed and die before their time. In the crudest terms, *that* is the social condition. There is a moral trap which comes through the insight into man's loneliness: it tempts one to sit back, complacent in one's unique tragedy, and let the others go without a meal.

As a group, the scientists fall into that trap less than others. They are inclined to be impatient to see if something can be done: and inclined to think that it can be done, until it's proved otherwise. That is their real optimism, and it's an optimism that the rest of us badly need. . . . If I were to risk a piece of shorthand, I should say that naturally they had the future in their bones. . . .

Edward H. Levi, An Introduction to Legal Reasoning
1, 3–5 (1949).

It is important that the mechanism of legal reasoning should not be concealed by its pretense. The pretense is that the law is a system of known rules applied by a judge; the pretense has long been under attack.[1] In an important sense legal rules are never clear, and, if a rule had to be clear before it could be imposed, society would be impossible. The mechanism accepts the differences of view and ambiguities of words. It provides for the participation of the community in resolving the ambiguity by providing a forum for the discussion of policy in the gap of ambiguity. On serious controversial questions, it makes it possible to take the first step in the direction of what otherwise would be forbidden ends. The mechanism is indispensable to peace in a community. . . .

Therefore it appears that the kind of reasoning involved in the legal process is one in which the classification changes as the classification is made. The rules change as the rules are applied. More important, the rules arise out of a process which, while comparing fact situations, creates the rules and then applies them. But this kind of reasoning is open to the charge that it is classifying things as equal when they are somewhat different, justifying the classification by rules made up as the reasoning or classification proceeds. In a sense all reasoning is of this type, but there is an additional requirement which compels the legal process to be this way. Not only do new situations arise, but in addition peoples' wants change. The categories used in the legal process must be left ambiguous in order to permit the infusion of new ideas. And this is true even where legislation or a constitution is involved. The words used by the legislature or the constitutional convention must come to have new meanings. Furthermore, agreement on any other basis would be impossible. In this manner the laws come to express the ideas of the community and even when written in general terms, in statute or constitution, are molded for the specific case.

1. The controlling book is Frank, Law and the Modern Mind (1936).

But attention must be paid to the process. A controversy as to whether the law is certain, unchanging, and expressed in rules, or uncertain, changing, and only a technique for deciding specific cases misses the point. It is both. Nor is it helpful to dispose of the process as a wonderful mystery possibly reflecting a higher law, by which the law can remain the same and yet change. The law forum is the most explicit demonstration of the mechanism required for a moving classification system. The folklore of law may choose to ignore the imperfections in legal reasoning, but the law forum itself has taken care of them.

What does the law forum require? It requires the presentation of competing examples. The forum protects the parties and the community by making sure that the competing analogies are before the court. The rule which will be created arises out of a process in which if different things are to be treated as similar, at least the differences have been urged. In this sense the parties as well as the court participate in the law-making. In this sense, also, lawyers represent more than the litigants.

Reasoning by example in the law is a key to many things. It indicates in part the hold which the law process has over the litigants. They have participated in the law-making. They are bound by something they helped to make. Moreover, the examples or analogies urged by the parties bring into the law the common ideas of the society. The ideas have their day in court, and they will have their day again. This is what makes the hearing fair, rather than any idea that the judge is completely impartial, for of course he cannot be completely so. Moreover, the hearing in a sense compels at least vicarious participation by all the citizens, for the rule which is made, even though ambiguous, will be law as to them.

BENJAMIN N. CARDOZO, THE PARADOXES OF LEGAL SCIENCE
1–4 (1956).

"They do things better with logarithms." The wail escapes me now and again when after putting forth the best that is in me, I look upon the finished product, and cannot say that it is good. In these moments of disquietude, I figure to myself the peace of mind that must come, let us say, to the designer of a mighty bridge. The finished product of his work is there before his eyes with all the beauty and simplicity and inevitableness of truth. He is not harrowed by misgivings whether the towers and piers and cables will stand the stress and strain. His business is to know. If his bridge were to fall, he would go down with it in disgrace and ruin. Yet withal, he has never a fear. No mere experiment has he wrought, but a highway to carry men and women from shore to shore, to carry them secure and unafraid, though the floods rage and boil below.

So I cry out at times in rebellion, "why cannot I do as much, or at least something measurably as much to bridge with my rules of law the torrents of life?" I have given my years to the task, and behind me are untold generations, the judges and lawgivers of old, who strove with a passion as burning. Code and commentary, manor-roll and year-book, treatise and law-report, reveal the processes of trial and error by which they struggled to attain the truth, enshrine their blunders and their triumphs for warning and example. All these memorials are mine; yet unwritten is my table of logarithms, the index of the power to which a precedent must be raised to produce the formula of justice. My bridges are experiments. I cannot span the tiniest stream in a region unexplored by judges or lawgivers before me, and go to rest in the secure belief that the span is wisely laid.

Let me not seem to cavil at the difficulties that learning can subdue. They are trying enough in all conscience, yet what industry can master, it would be weakness to lament. I am not thinking of the multitude of precedents and the labor of making them our own. The pangs that convulse are born of other trials. Diligence and memory and normal powers of reasoning may suffice to guide us truly in those fields where the judicial function is imitative or static, where known rules are to be applied to combinations of facts identical with present patterns, or, at worst, but slightly different. The travail comes when the judicial function is dynamic or creative. The rule must be announced for a novel situation where competitive analogies supply a hint or clue, but where precedents are lacking with authoritative commands.

I know the common answer to these and like laments. The law is not an exact science, we are told, and there the matter ends, if we are willing there to end it. One does not appease the rebellion of the intellect by the reaffirmance of the evil against which intellect rebels. Exactness may be impossible, but this is not enough to cause the mind to acquiesce in a predestined incoherence. Jurisprudence will be the gainer in the long run by fanning the fires of mental insurrection instead of smothering them with platitudes. "If science," says Whitehead, "is not to degenerate into a medley of *ad hoc* hypotheses, it must become philosophical and must enter upon a thorough criticism of its own foundations." We may say the like of law.

So I keep reaching out and groping for a pathway to the light. The outlet may not be found. At least there may be glimmerings that will deny themselves to a craven *non possumus,* the sterility of ignoble ease. Somewhere beneath the welter, there may be a rationalizing principle revealing system and harmony in what passes for discord and disorder. Modern science is tending to revolutionize our ideas of motion within the atom, and so of motion generally. We had thought of radiation as continuous and flowing. We are told that in truth it is discrete and irregular.... Is it possible that in rationalizing the development of law, in measuring the radiating energy of principle and precedent, we have been hampered by a like illusion? We have sought for a formula consistent with steady advance through a continuum. The continuum does not exist. Instead there are leaps from point to point. We have been beguiled by the ideal of an harmonious progression. Centres of energy exist, of attraction and repulsion. A landing-place is found between them. We make these landing places for ourselves through the methods of the judicial process. How shall they be wrought? Where shall they be found? ...

NOTES AND QUESTIONS

1. What are the main contrasts between science and the law? Consider in particular their approaches to the universality of knowledge, the nature of "truth," and the role of (and means for resolving) disputes. For an analysis that stresses the contrast between the scientist's emphasis on progress with the lawyer's reliance on process, see STEVEN GOLDBERG, CULTURE CLASH: LAW AND SCIENCE IN AMERICA (1994). Other perspectives are provided in articles in two valuable symposia: *Science in the Regulatory Process*, 66 LAW & CONTEMP. PROBS, No. 4 (Autumn 2003), and *The Interpretation Symposium*, 58 S. CAL. L. REV, Nos. 1, 2 (1985). *See also* Nancy Levit, *Listening to Tribal Legends: An Essay on Law and the Scientific Method*, 58 FORDHAM L. REV. 263 (1989). For centuries, science has provided a powerful metaphor for those analyzing the law. *See, e.g.*, John Veilleux, *The Scientific Model in Law*, 75 GEO. L. J. 1967 (1987); Laurence H. Tribe, *The Curvature of Constitutional Space: What Lawyers Can Learn From Modern Physics*, 103 HARV. L. REV. 1 (1989). See Robert P. Merges, *The Nature and Necessity of Law and Science, 39 J. LEGAL EDUC. 315 (1988); Steven Goldberg,* The Central Dogmas of Law and Science, 36 J. LEGAL EDUC. 371 (1986) (exploring the role of science in the law school curriculum).

2. Does traditional scientific reasoning represent a particularly "masculine" approach to understanding the world? *See* SANDRA HARDING, WHOSE SCIENCE? WHOSE KNOWLEDGE? THINKING FROM WOMEN'S LIVES 19–50 (1991); EVELYN F. KELLER, REFLECTIONS ON GENDER AND SCIENCE, 177–79 (1985). Does legal reasoning represent such an approach? *See* Carrie Menkel–Meadow, *Portia in a Different Voice: Speculations on a Women's Lawyering Process*, 1 BERKELEY WOMEN'S L.J. 39 (1985).

3. Are lawyers likely to be particularly pessimistic (or cynical) compared with what Snow says some view as scientists' "shallow optimism?" The subject matter of law—human relations—is certainly capable of giving rise to pessimism. Yet Snow argues further that scientists are rightly optimistic about improving social conditions. What, if anything, does science tell us, for example, about whether poverty can be eliminated?

4. Are there "paradigms" in law in the sense that Kuhn uses the term? Levi's image of a "moving classification system" responding to changing desires could be seen as presenting law as an evolutionary process somewhat similar to science. But law rarely appears as cumulative and progressive as science. Is it inevitable that legal rules seem to swing back and forth rather than moving forward? Cardozo holds out hope that someday judges may discover a rationalizing principle that will bring order out of chaos. Would the results be permanent or would they change as quickly as society changes?

E. NUCLEAR WEAPONS AFTER THE COLD WAR

In the years following the development of the hydrogen bomb, nuclear weapons played a major role in American military planning. During the Cold War, the United States and the former Soviet Union trained these weapons on each other. One result of this situation was the Reagan administration's controversial Strategic Defense Initiative (SDI) designed to create a largely spaced-based defensive system to thwart nuclear attack. Legal controversy centered on whether SDI was consistent with the ABM Treaty, *see, e.g.*, Frances V. Harbour, *The ABM Treaty, New Technology and the Strategic Defense Initiative*, 15 J. LEGIS. 119 (1989), while technical debate over the so-called "Star Wars" plan focused on whether it was feasible, *see, e.g.*, Harold Brown, *Is SDI Technically Feasible?* 64 FOREIGN AFF. 435 (1986). The feasibility debate was marked by strident charges of political opportunism on both sides. Opponents of SDI maintained that those scientists who argued it was a workable plan were simply "cheerleaders" for the Administration, while proponents of the system accused experts in opposition of being "politically motivated demagogues." Daniel Greenberg, *Keyworth Draws Fire for Star Wars Cheerleading*, 15 SCI. & GOV'T REP. 8, Dec. 1, 1985. What issues other than technical efficacy were at work here? Even if SDI had functioned perfectly, would there have been grounds for opposing it? *See, e.g.*, Thomas Schelling, *What Went Wrong with Arms Control?*, 64 FOREIGN AFF. 219, 231–33 (1985).

The collapse of the Soviet Union did not end the importance of nuclear weapons, but it did shift the focus of American planning. The greatest concern became the possibility that regional powers such as Iraq or North Korea might develop and use such weapons against American allies such as Israel or South Korea. As a result, the SDI program evolved into the Ballistic Missile Defense program with a new focus on ground-based weapons that can shoot down enemy missiles whether those missiles are armed with conventional or nuclear warheads, although in the latter case the consequences of missing are obviously greater. Marc Dean Millot, *Facing the Emerging Reality of Regional Nuclear Adversaries*, 17 WASH. Q., No. 3 (Summer 1994), at 41.

In late 2004, the administration of President George W. Bush began to deploy in Delta Junction, Alaska, the first operating portion of its ballistic missile defense system. This ground-based set of rockets was hailed by the Administration as "a bulwark against the ultimate calamity, a nuclear attack," and criticized by skeptics as "a defense that will not work against a threat that does not exist." James Glanz, *Star Wars: The Next Version*, N.Y. TIMES, May 4, 2004, at F1. These opposing views are spelled out in the following excerpts from speeches by Secretary of Defense Donald H. Rumsfeld and Congresswoman Jane Harman (D–California), the ranking member of the House Permanent Select Committee on Intelligence.

Speech by Secretary of Defense Donald H. Rumsfeld at the AUSA Air, Space, and Missile Defense Symposium

December 10, 2003.
Transcript available at http://www.defenselink.mil/speeches/2003/sp20031210–secdef0782.html (last visited July 16, 2004).

Today, more than 20 countries including a number of terrorist states either possess ballistic missiles or have established programs to develop or to acquire them. And a number of terrorist regimes either have or are working to acquire chemical, biological, and in some cases nuclear weapons.

For example, North Korea is the world's most aggressive proliferator of ballistic missiles and related technologies. And the North Koreans have publicly said that they're willing to sell those technologies to the highest bidders. . . .

To defend the American people against these threats we need to find new ways to stop the growth in trade of weapons of mass destruction related materials, technologies, and delivery capabilities among rogue states. That's why we're working with friends and allies to find new approaches such as the Proliferation Security Initiative. . . .

We also need to continue the transformation of our forces and capabilities for the challenges of the 21st Century, including ballistic missile defenses to protect our people, to help protect our friends and allies, and certainly to protect our deployed forces. . . . I'm told that in Operation Iraqi Freedom, Patriot batteries successfully engaged nine short-range ballistic missiles that were heading towards concentrations of Coalition military equipment and personnel. . . .

. . .

When President Bush announced his decision to begin deploying a missile defense system in 2004 for the United States he called missile defense "an essential element" of our new defense strategy. "The new strategic challenges of the 21st Century require us to think differently," he said, "but they also require us to act." . . .

Floor Debate on Consideration of H.R. 4200, National Defense Authorization Act for Fiscal Year 2005

150 Cong. Rec. H3248–49 (May 19, 2004).

Ms. HARMAN. Mr. Speaker, I thank the gentleman for yielding me this time, and I rise in strong support of the defense authorization bill, but strong opposition to this rule.

Let me point out, Mr. Speaker, that the rule we are considering leaves out many important amendments which many on our side had hoped to offer. I had one which would have postponed additional expenditures for a ground-based missile system in Alaska which has not met operational testing requirements, and would have put those funds into port security. My amendment reflects the views of 49 Admirals and Generals whose letter to the President is dated March 26.

In my view, as ranking member of the House Permanent Select Committee on Intelligence, the potential damage from a radiological device coming in through our ports is a much greater risk than the risk of a missile attack from North Korea.

. . .

Mr. Speaker, I submit herewith for the Record the March 26, 2004 letter to President Bush from 49 Admirals and Generals:

. . .

Dear Mr. President: In December 2002, you ordered the deployment of a ground-based strategic mid-course ballistic missile defense (GMD) capability, now scheduled to become operational before the end of September 2004. . . .

To meet this deployment deadline, the Pentagon has waived the operational testing requirements that are essential to determining whether or not this highly complex system of systems is effective and suitable. . . .

Another important consideration is balancing the high costs of missile defense with funding allocated to other national security programs. Since President Reagan's strategic defense initiative speech in March 1983, a conservative estimate of about $130 billion, not adjusted upward for inflation, has been spent on missile defense, much of it on GMD. . . .

. . .

As you have said, Mr. President, our highest priority is to prevent terrorists from acquiring and employing weapons of mass destruction. We agree. We therefore recommend, as the militarily responsible course of action, that you postpone operational deployment of the expensive and untested GMD system and transfer the associated funding to accelerated programs to secure the multitude of facilities containing nuclear weapons and materials and to protect our ports and borders against terrorists who may attempt to smuggle weapons of mass destruction into the United States. . . .

NOTES AND QUESTIONS

1. This sort of debate involves careful calculations of deterrence, missile accuracy, and the like. Yet, as the Hiroshima materials in Sec. I. B., *supra*, suggest, the prospect of nuclear war makes the use of cost benefit analysis particularly problematic. Given this tension, how do you view the following observation by Senator Howard Baker during an arms treaty debate in 1979?

> There is a young man who flies for me in Tennessee. He lets me sit in the right seat of that small plane from time to time. The other day we were flying through a thunderstorm, and I was watching the radar screen intently for weather and severe turbulence. I had had my head in the radar-scope. He touched me on the shoulder and said, "Senator, why don't we turn that thing off before we scare ourselves."

> You know, I sort of get the feeling that every time we conjure up the idea and the image of nuclear holocaust, if we are not careful, we are going to scare ourselves. We are not here to decide whether the world is going to be faced with nuclear holocaust. We are here to determine whether this treaty better serves the purpose of diminishing that prospect.

The SALT II Treaty: Hearings Before the Senate Committee on Foreign Relations, 96th Cong., 1st Sess. (July 9, 1979).

2. The moral issues raised by warfare are often felt acutely by scientists whose work contributes to weapons development. There have always been, for example, physicists in the nuclear weapons field who have pushed for arms control. *See, e.g.*, WASH. POST, Feb. 9, 1983, at A15, col. 5. After the Persian Gulf war brought public attention to the use of computer controlled "smart bombs," a group called Computer Professionals for Social Responsibility announced that "[w]e are not proud that the fruit of our labor—computer technology—has been used for such deadly ends. . . . We call . . . for computer technology to advance public well-being rather than wage armed conflict. . . ." N.Y. TIMES, June 18, 1991, at B7. Can the issues raised by nuclear deterrence and by participation in military affairs be illuminated by traditional religious perspectives? Consider in this light the following passage.

United States Bishops, Pastoral Letter on War and Peace, the Challenge of Peace: God's Promise and Our Response

May 19, 1983
Reprinted in 13 ORIGINS 1, 9–10, 13–14, 18, 29.

The moral theory of the "just-war" or "limited-war" doctrine begins with the presumption which binds all Christians: We should do no harm to our neighbors; how we treat our enemy is the key test of whether we love our neighbor; and the possibility of taking even one human life is a prospect we should consider in fear and trembling. How is it possible to move from these presumptions to the idea of a justifiable use of lethal force?

Historically and theologically the clearest answer to the question is found in St. Augustine. Augustine was impressed by the fact and the consequences of sin in history—the "not yet" dimension of the kingdom. In his view war was both the result of sin and a tragic remedy for sin in the life of political societies. War arose from disordered ambitions, but it could also be used in some cases at least to restrain evil and protect the innocent. The classic case which illustrated his view was the use of lethal force to prevent aggression against innocent victims. Faced with the fact of attack on the innocent, the presumption that we do no harm even to our enemy yielded to the command of love understood as the need to restrain an enemy who would injure the innocent.

The just-war argument has taken several forms in the history of Catholic theology, but this Augustinian insight is its central premise. In the 20th century, papal teaching has used the logic of Augustine and Aquinas to articulate a right of self-defense for states in a decentralized international order and to state the criteria for exercising that right. The essential position was stated by Vatican II: "As long as the danger of war persists and there is no international authority with the necessary competence and power, governments cannot be denied the right of lawful self-defense, once all peace efforts have failed." We have already indicated the centrality of this principle for understanding Catholic teaching about the state and its duties.

Just-war teaching has evolved, however, as an effort to prevent war; only if war cannot be rationally avoided does the teaching then seek to restrict and reduce its horrors. It does this by establishing a set of rigorous conditions which must be met if the decision to go to war is to be morally permissible. Such a decision, especially today, requires extraordinarily strong reasons for overriding the presumption *in favor of peace* and *against* war. This is one significant reason why valid just-war teaching makes provision for conscientious dissent. It is presumed that all sane people prefer peace, never *want* to initiate war and accept even the most justifiable defensive war only as a sad necessity. Only the most powerful reasons may be permitted to override such objection.

.   .   .

[T]he just-war teaching . . . [is] confronted with a unique challenge by nuclear warfare. This must be the starting point of any further moral reflection: Nuclear weapons particularly and nuclear warfare as it is planned today raise new moral questions. No previously conceived moral position escapes the fundamental confrontation posed by contemporary nuclear strategy. Many have noted the similarity of the statements made by eminent scientists and Vatican II's observation that we are forced today "to undertake a completely fresh reappraisal of war." The task before us is not simply to repeat what we have said before; it is first to consider anew whether and how our religious-moral tradition can assess, direct, contain and, we hope, help to eliminate the threat posed to the human family by the nuclear arsenals of the world. Pope John Paul II captured the essence of the problem during his pilgrimage to Hiroshima: "In the past it was possible to destroy a village, a town, a region, even a country. Now it is the whole planet that has come under threat."

The Holy Father's observation illustrates why the moral problem is also a religious question of the most profound significance. In the nuclear arsenals of the United States or the Soviet Union alone there exists a capacity to do something no other age could imagine: We can threaten the entire planet. For people of faith this means we read the Book of Genesis with a new awareness; the moral issue at stake in nuclear war involves the meaning of sin in its most graphic dimensions. Every sinful act is a confrontation of the creature and the Creator. Today the destructive potential of the nuclear powers threatens the human person, the civilization we have slowly constructed and even the created order itself.

We live today, therefore, in the midst of a cosmic drama; we possess a power which should never be used, but which might be used if we do not reverse our direction. We live with nuclear weapons knowing we cannot afford to make one serious mistake. This fact dramatizes the precariousness of our position, politically, morally and spiritually.

A prominent "sign of the times" today is a sharply increased awareness of the danger of the nuclear arms race. Such awareness has produced a public discussion about nuclear policy here and in other countries which is unprecedented in its scope and depth. What has been accepted for years with almost no question is now being subjected to the sharpest criticism. What previously had been defined as a safe and stable system of deterrence is today viewed with political and moral skepticism.

. . .

We have had to examine, with the assistance of a broad spectrum of advisers of varying persuasions, the nature of existing and proposed weapons systems, the doctrines which govern their use and the consequences of using them. We have consulted people who engage their lives in protest against the existing nuclear strategy of the United States, and we have consulted others who have held or do hold responsibility for this strategy. It has been a sobering and perplexing experience. In light of the evidence which witnesses presented and in light of our study, reflection and consultation, we must reject nuclear war. But we feel obliged to relate our judgment to the specific elements which comprise the nuclear problem.

Though certain that the dangerous and delicate nuclear relationship the superpowers now maintain should not exist, we understand how it came to exist. In a world of sovereign states devoid of central authority and possessing the knowledge to produce nuclear weapons many choices were made, some clearly objectionable, others well-intended with mixed results, which brought the world to its present dangerous situation.

We see with increasing clarity the political folly of a system which threatens mutual suicide, the psychological damage this does to ordinary people, especially the young, the economic distortion of priorities—billions readily spent for destructive instruments while pitched battles are waged daily in our legislatures over much smaller amounts for the homeless, the hungry and the helpless here and abroad. But it is much less clear how we translate a no to nuclear war into the personal and public choices which can move us in a new direction, toward a national policy and an international system which more adequately reflect the values and vision of the kingdom of God.

.   .   .

[W]e wish now to make some specific evaluations:

1. If nuclear deterrence exists only to prevent the *use* of nuclear weapons by others, then proposals to go beyond this to planning for prolonged periods of repeated nuclear strikes and counterstrikes, or "prevailing" in nuclear war, are not acceptable. They encourage notions that nuclear war can be engaged in with tolerable human and moral consequences. Rather, we must continually say no to the idea of nuclear war.

2. If nuclear deterrence is our goal, "sufficiency" to deter is an adequate strategy; the quest for nuclear superiority must be rejected.

3. Nuclear deterrence should be used as a step on the way toward progressive disarmament. Each proposed addition to our strategic system or change in strategic doctrine must be assessed precisely in light of whether it will render steps toward "progressive disarmament" more or less likely....

.   .   .

To Men and Women in Defense Industries

You also face specific questions because the defense industry is directly involved in the development and production of the weapons of mass destruction which have concerned us in this letter. We do not presume or pretend that clear answers exist to many of the personal, professional and financial choices facing you in your varying responsibilities. In this letter we have ruled out certain uses of nuclear weapons, while also expressing conditional moral acceptance for deterrence. All Catholics, at every level of defense industries, can and should use the moral principles of this letter to form their consciences. We realize that different judgments of conscience will face different people, and we recognize the possibility of diverse concrete judgments being made in this complex area. We seek as moral teachers and pastors to be available to all who confront these questions of personal and vocational choice. Those who in conscience decide that they should no longer be associated with defense activities should find support in the Catholic community. Those who remain in these industries or earn a profit from the weapons industry should find in the church guidance and support for the ongoing evaluation of their work.

To Men and Women of Science

At Hiroshima Pope John Paul said:

"Criticism of science and technology is sometimes so severe that it comes close to condemning science itself. On the contrary, science and technology are a wonderful product of a God-given human creativity, since they have provided us with wonderful possibilities and we all gratefully benefit from them. But we know that this potential is not a neutral one: It can be used either for man's progress or for his degradation."

We appreciate the efforts of scientists, some of whom first unlocked the secret of atomic power and others of whom have developed it in diverse ways, to turn the enormous power of science to the cause of peace.

Modern history is not lacking scientists who have looked back with deep remorse on the development of weapons to which they contributed, sometimes with the highest motivation, even believing that they were creating weapons that would render all other weapons obsolete and convince the world of the unthinkableness of war. Such efforts have ever proved illusory. Surely equivalent dedication of scientific minds to reverse current trends and to pursue concepts as bold and adventuresome in favor of peace as those which in the past have magnified the risks of war could result in dramatic benefits for all of humanity. We particularly note in this regard the extensive efforts of public education undertaken by physicians and scientists on the medical consequences of nuclear war.

We do not, however, wish to limit our remarks to the physical sciences alone. Nor do we limit our remarks to physical scientists. In his address at the United Nations University in Hiroshima, Pope John Paul II warned about misuse of "the social sciences and the human behavioral sciences when they are utilized to manipulate people, to crush their mind, souls, dignity and freedom." The positive role of social science in overcoming the dangers of the nuclear age is evident in this letter. We have been dependent upon the research and analysis of social scientists in our effort to apply the moral principles of the Catholic tradition to the concrete problems of our day. We encourage social scientists to continue this work of relating moral wisdom and political reality. We are in continuing need of your insights.

.   .   .

NOTES AND QUESTIONS

1. The Catholic Bishops' letter has occasioned lively debate in the Catholic community and elsewhere. *See, e.g.,* Monica K. Hellwig, et al., *From the University: American Catholics and the Peace Debate*, WASH. Q. 120 (1982). Does the constitutional separation of church and state bear on the propriety of Catholic Bishops speaking out on nuclear weapons? Are the problems here similar to those raised when religious leaders speak out on evolution? *See* Chapter 4, Sec. I. B., *infra.* On abortion? For a survey of the views of non-Catholic religious groups on nuclear weapons, *see* Bruce van Voorst, *The Churches and Nuclear Deterrence*, 61 FOREIGN AFF. 827 (1983).

2. The Bishops state that they were assisted by "a broad spectrum of advisers of varying persuasions...." What expertise did the Bishops themselves bring to bear on the issue of nuclear deterrence?

3. The Bishops contend that if "scientific minds" turned from developing weapons to the pursuit of "bold and adventuresome" concepts for peace the result would be "dramatic benefits for all of humanity." Do you agree that the scientific approach would be particularly helpful in the quest for peace?

II.   THE SOCIAL CONSEQUENCES OF CIVILIAN NUCLEAR POWER

A.   GOVERNMENT REGULATION OF NUCLEAR REACTORS: OPERATING SAFETY AND WASTE DISPOSAL

Dwight D. Eisenhower, The Atom for Progress and Peace

Address Before the General Assembly of the United Nations.
December 8, 1953.

It is not enough to take this weapon out of the hands of the soldiers. It must be put into the hands of those who will know how to strip its military casing and adapt it to the arts of peace.

The United States knows that if the fearful trend of atomic military buildup can be reversed, this greatest of destructive forces can be developed into a great boon, for the benefit of all mankind.

The United States knows that peaceful power from atomic energy is no dream of the future. That capability, already proved, is here—now—today. Who can doubt, if the entire body of the world's scientists and engineers had adequate amounts of fissionable material with which to test and develop their ideas, that this capability would rapidly be transformed into universal, efficient, and economic usage. . . .

NOTES AND QUESTIONS

In linking the destructive power of the atom to its peaceful potential, President Eisenhower touched on a common theme in the years after World War II. Just as some seem to oppose civilian nuclear power because of the existence of nuclear weapons, others seem to support it because it somehow cleanses the wartime experience.

While President Eisenhower's predictions appear overly optimistic today, nuclear energy did begin to assume a civilian role in the 1950's. Since that time, the United States has used such power primarily to generate electricity. In a reactor, a controlled fission reaction is used to boil water. After that, the process is just like that in a coal or oil-fired plant—the steam drives a turbine that turns a generator to produce electricity.

The materials that follow describe the history and present status of government regulation of civilian fission reactors, as well as some of the issues that have embroiled nuclear power in controversy.

Vermont Yankee Nuclear Power Corp. v. Natural Resources Defense Council, Inc.

Supreme Court of the United States, 1978.
435 U.S. 519, 98 S.Ct. 1197, 55 L.Ed.2d 460.

■ JUSTICE REHNQUIST delivered the opinion of the Court.

. . .

Under the Atomic Energy Act of 1954, 68 Stat. 919, as amended, 42 U.S.C. § 2011 *et seq.,* the Atomic Energy Commission[2] was given broad regulatory authority over the development of nuclear energy. Under the terms of the Act, a utility seeking to construct and operate a nuclear power plant must obtain a separate permit or license at both the construction and the operation stage of the project. *See* 42 U.S.C. §§ 2133, 2232, 2235, 2239. In order to obtain the construction permit, the utility must file a preliminary safety analysis report, an environmental report, and certain information regarding the antitrust implications of the proposed project. *See* 10 CFR §§ 2.101, 50.30(f), 50.33a, 50.34(a) (1977). This application then undergoes exhaustive review by the Commission's staff and by the Advisory Committee on Reactor Safeguards (ACRS), a group of distinguished experts in the field of atomic energy. Both groups submit to the Commission their own evaluations, which then become part of the record of the utility's application. *See* 42 U.S.C. §§ 2039, 2232(b). The Commission staff also undertakes the review required by the National Environmental Policy Act of 1969 (NEPA), 83 Stat. 852, 42 U.S.C. § 4321 *et seq.,* and prepares a draft environmental impact statement, which, after being circulated for comment, 10 CFR §§ 51.22–51.25 (1977), is revised and becomes a final environmental impact statement. § 51.26. Thereupon a three-member Atomic Safety and Licensing Board conducts a public adjudicatory hearing, 42 U.S.C. § 2241, and reaches a decision which can be appealed to the Atomic Safety and Licensing Appeal Board, and currently, in the Commission's discretion, to the Commission itself. 10 CFR §§ 2.714, 2.721, 2.786, 2.787 (1977). The final agency decision may be appealed to the courts of appeals. 42 U.S.C. § 2239; 28 U.S.C. § 2342. The same sort of process occurs when the utility applies for a license to operate the plant, 10 CFR § 50.34(b) (1977), except that a hearing need only be held in contested cases and may be limited to the matters in controversy. *See* 42 U.S.C. § 2239(a); 10 CFR § 2.105 (1977); 10 CFR pt. 2, App. A, V(f) (1977).

. . .

In December 1967, after the mandatory adjudicatory hearing and necessary review, the Commission granted petitioner Vermont Yankee a permit to build a nuclear power plant in Vernon, Vt. *See* 4 A.E.C. 36 (1967). Thereafter, Vermont Yankee applied for an operating license. Respondent Natural Resources Defense Council (NRDC) objected to the granting of a license, however, and therefore a hearing on the application commenced on August 10, 1971. Excluded from consideration at the hearings, over NRDC's objection, was the issue of the environmental effects of operations to reprocess fuel or dispose of wastes resulting from the reprocessing operations.[6] This ruling was affirmed by the Appeal Board in June 1972.

---

2. The licensing and regulatory functions of the Atomic Energy Commission (AEC) were transferred to the Nuclear Regulatory Commission (NRC) by the Energy Reorganization Act of 1974, 42 U.S.C. § 5801 *et seq.* (1970 ed., Supp. V). Hereinafter both the AEC and NRC will be referred to as the Commission.

6. The nuclear fission which takes place in light-water nuclear reactors apparently converts its principal fuel, uranium, into plutonium, which is itself highly radioactive but can be used as reactor fuel if separated from the remaining uranium and radioactive waste products. Fuel reprocessing refers to the process necessary to recapture usable plutonium.

In November 1972, however, the Commission, making specific reference to the Appeal Board's decision with respect to the Vermont Yankee license, instituted rulemaking proceedings "that would specifically deal with the question of consideration of environmental effects associated with the uranium fuel cycle in the individual cost-benefit analyses for light water cooled nuclear power reactors." App. 352. The notice of proposed rulemaking offered two alternatives, both predicated on a report prepared by the Commission's staff entitled Environmental Survey of the Nuclear Fuel Cycle. The first would have required no quantitative evaluation of the environmental hazards of fuel reprocessing or disposal because the Environmental Survey had found them to be slight. The second would have specified numerical values for the environmental impact of this part of the fuel cycle, which values would then be incorporated into a table, along with the other relevant factors, to determine the overall cost-benefit balance for each operating license. *See id.*, at 356–357.

Much of the controversy in this case revolves around the procedures used in the rulemaking hearing which commenced in February 1973. In a supplemental notice of hearing the Commission indicated that while discovery or cross-examination would not be utilized, the Environmental Survey would be available to the public before the hearing along with the extensive background documents cited therein. All participants would be given a reasonable opportunity to present their position and could be represented by counsel if they so desired. Written and, time permitting, oral statements would be received and incorporated into the record. All persons giving oral statements would be subject to questioning by the Commission. At the conclusion of the hearing, a transcript would be made available to the public and the record would remain open for 30 days to allow the filing of supplemental written statements. *See generally id.*, at 361–363. More than 40 individuals and organizations representing a wide variety of interests submitted written comments. On January 17, 1973, the Licensing Board held a planning session to schedule the appearance of witnesses and to discuss methods for compiling a record. The hearing was held on February 1 and 2, with participation by a number of groups, including the Commission's staff, the United States Environmental Protection Agency, a manufacturer of reactor equipment, a trade association from the nuclear industry, a group of electric utility companies, and a group called Consolidated National Intervenors which represented 79 groups and individuals including respondent NRDC.

After the hearing, the Commission's staff filed a supplemental document for the purpose of clarifying and revising the Environmental Survey. Then the Licensing Board forwarded its report to the Commission without rendering any decision. The Licensing Board identified as the principal procedural question the propriety of declining to use full formal adjudicatory procedures. The major substantive issue was the technical adequacy of the Environmental Survey.

Waste disposal, at the present stage of technological development, refers to the storage of the very long lived and highly radioactive waste products until they detoxify sufficiently that they no longer present an environmental hazard. There are presently no physical or chemical steps which render this waste less toxic, other than simply the passage of time.

In April 1974, the Commission issued a rule which adopted the second of the two proposed alternatives described above. The Commission also approved the procedures used at the hearing, and indicated that the record, including the Environmental Survey, provided an "adequate data base for the regulation adopted." *Id.*, at 392. Finally, the Commission ruled that to the extent the rule differed from the Appeal Board decisions in Vermont Yankee "those decisions have no further precedential significance," *id.*, at 386, but that since "the environmental effects of the uranium fuel cycle have been shown to be relatively insignificant, . . . it is unnecessary to apply the amendment to applicant's environmental reports submitted prior to its effective date or to Final Environmental Statements for which Draft Environmental Statements have been circulated for comment prior to the effective date," id., at 395.

Respondents appealed from both the Commission's adoption of the rule and its decision to grant Vermont Yankee's license to the Court of Appeals for the District of Columbia Circuit.

. . .

With respect to the challenge of Vermont Yankee's license, the court first ruled that in the absence of effective rulemaking proceedings,[13] the Commission must deal with the environmental impact of fuel reprocessing and disposal in individual licensing proceedings. Aeschliman v. NRC, 547 F.2d 622, 641 (D.C. Cir. 1976). The court then examined the rulemaking proceedings and, despite the fact that it appeared that the agency employed all the procedures required by 5 U.S.C. § 553 (1976 ed.)[e] and more, the court determined the proceedings to be inadequate and overturned the rule. Accordingly, the Commission's determination with respect to Vermont Yankee's license was also remanded for further proceedings. 547 F.2d, at 655.

Petitioner Vermont Yankee first argues that the Commission may grant a license to operate a nuclear reactor without any consideration of waste disposal and fuel reprocessing. We find, however, that this issue is no longer presented by the record in this case. The Commission does not contend that it is not required to consider the environmental impact of the spent fuel processes when licensing nuclear power plants. Indeed, the Commission has publicly stated subsequent to the Court of Appeals' decision in the instant case that consideration of the environmental impact of the back end of the fuel cycle in "the environmental impact statements for individual LWR's [light-water power reactors] would represent a full and

13. In the Court of Appeals no one questioned the Commission's authority to deal with fuel cycle issues by informal rulemaking as opposed to adjudication. 547 F.2d, at 642–643. Neither does anyone seriously question before this Court the Commission's authority in this respect.

e. [Eds.—This section of the Administrative Procedure Act covers so-called "notice-and-comment" or "informal" rulemaking. The section provides that the agency shall publish notice of a proposed rule in the Federal Register and shall then give interested persons an opportunity to submit written statements concerning the rule. Oral presentations may or may not be allowed, at the agency's discretion. All relevant material presented to the agency is to be considered before promulgation of the final rule. *See generally* B. Schwartz, ADMINISTRATIVE LAW 165–175 (1976).]

candid assessment of costs and benefits consistent with the legal requirements and spirit of NEPA." 41 Fed.Reg. 45849 (1976). Even prior to the
Court of Appeals' decision the Commission implicitly agreed that it would
consider the back end of the fuel cycle in all licensing proceedings: It
indicated that it was not necessary to reopen prior licensing proceedings
because "the environmental effects of the uranium fuel cycle have been
shown to be relatively insignificant," and thus incorporation of those
effects into the cost-benefit analysis would not change the results of such
licensing proceedings. App. 395. Thus, at this stage of the proceedings the
only question presented for review in this regard is whether the Commission may consider the environmental impact of the fuel processes when
licensing nuclear reactors. In addition to the weight which normally attaches to the agency's determination of such a question, other reasons
support the Commission's conclusion.

Vermont Yankee will produce annually well over 100 pounds of radioactive wastes, some of which will be highly toxic. The Commission itself, in
a pamphlet published by its information office, clearly recognizes that these
wastes "pose the most severe potential health hazard...." U.S. Atomic
Energy Commission, Radioactive Wastes 12 (1965). Many of these substances must be isolated for anywhere from 600 to hundreds of thousands
of years. It is hard to argue that these wastes do not constitute "adverse
environmental effects which cannot be avoided should the proposal be
implemented," or that by operating nuclear power plants we are not
making "irreversible and irretrievable commitments of resources." 42
U.S.C. §§ 4332(2)(C)(ii), (v). As the Court of Appeals recognized, the
environmental impact of the radioactive wastes produced by a nuclear
power plant is analytically indistinguishable from the environmental effects
of "the stack gases produced by a coal-burning power plant." 547 F.2d, at
638. For these reasons we hold that the Commission acted well within its
statutory authority when it considered the back end of the fuel cycle in
individual licensing proceedings.

We next turn to the invalidation of the fuel cycle rule.... [T]he
majority of the Court of Appeals struck down the rule because of the
perceived inadequacies of the procedures employed in the rulemaking
proceedings. The court first determined the intervenors' primary argument
to be "that the decision to preclude 'discovery or cross-examination' denied
them a meaningful opportunity to participate in the proceedings as guaranteed by due process." 547 F.2d, at 643. The court then went on to frame
the issue for decision thus:

"Thus, we are called upon to decide whether the procedures provided
by the agency were sufficient to ventilate the issues." [ ] 547 F.2d, at 643.

The court conceded that absent extraordinary circumstances it is
improper for a reviewing court to prescribe the procedural format an
agency must follow, but it likewise clearly thought it entirely appropriate to
"scrutinize the record as a whole to insure that genuine opportunities to
participate in a meaningful way were provided...." 547 F.2d, at 644. The
court also refrained from actually ordering the agency to follow any specific
procedures, 547 F.2d at 653–654, but there is little doubt in our minds that
the ineluctable mandate of the court's decision is that the procedures

afforded during the hearings were inadequate. This conclusion is particularly buttressed by the fact that after the court examined the record, particularly the testimony of Dr. Pittman [Director of the AEC's Division of Waste Management and Transportation], and declared it insufficient, the court proceeded to discuss at some length the necessity for further procedural devices or a more "sensitive" application of those devices employed during the proceedings. *Ibid.* The exploration of the record and the statement regarding its insufficiency might initially lead one to conclude that the court was only examining the sufficiency of the evidence, but the remaining portions of the opinion dispel any doubt that this was certainly not the sole or even the principal basis of the decision. Accordingly, we feel compelled to address the opinion on its own terms, and we conclude that it was wrong.

In prior opinions we have intimated that even in a rulemaking proceeding when an agency is making a " 'quasi-judicial' " determination by which a very small number of persons are " 'exceptionally affected, in each case upon individual grounds,' " in some circumstances additional procedures may be required in order to afford the aggrieved individuals due process.[16] United States v. Florida East Coast R. Co., 410 U.S., at 242, 245, *quoting from* Bi–Metallic Investment Co. v. State Board of Equalization, 239 U.S. 441, 446 (1915). It might also be true, although we do not think the issue is presented in this case and accordingly do not decide it, that a totally unjustified departure from well-settled agency procedures of long standing might require judicial correction.

But this much is absolutely clear. Absent constitutional constraints or extremely compelling circumstances the "administrative agencies 'should be free to fashion their own rules of procedure and to pursue methods of inquiry capable of permitting them to discharge their multitudinous duties.' " FCC v. Schreiber, 381 U.S., at 290, *quoting from* FCC v. Pottsville Broadcasting Co., 309 U.S., at 143. Indeed, our cases could hardly be more explicit in this regard.

Respondent NRDC argues that § 4 of the Administrative Procedure Act, 5 U.S.C. § 553 (1976 ed.), merely establishes lower procedural bounds and that a court may routinely require more than the minimum when an agency's proposed rule addresses complex or technical factual issues or "Issues of Great Public Import." Brief for Respondents in No. 76–419, p. 49. We have, however, previously shown that our decisions reject this view. *Supra*, at 542 to this page. We also think the legislative history, even the part which it cites, does not bear out its contention. The Senate Report explains what eventually became § 4 thus:

> [ ]This subsection states ... the minimum requirements of public rule making procedure short of statutory hearing. Under it agencies might in addition confer with industry advisory committees, consult organizations, hold informal "hearings," and the like. Considerations of practicality,

16. Respondent NRDC does not now argue that additional procedural devices were required under the Constitution. Since this was clearly a rulemaking proceeding in its purest form, we see nothing to support such a view. *See* United States v. Florida East Coast R. Co., 410 U.S. 224, 244–245 (1973); Bowles v. Willingham, 321 U.S. 503 (1944); Bi–Metallic Investment Co. v. State Board of Equalization, 239 U.S. 441 (1915).

necessity, and public interest ... will naturally govern the agency's determination of the extent to which public proceedings should go. Matters of
great import, or those where the public submission of facts will be either
useful to the agency or a protection to the public, should naturally be
accorded more elaborate public procedures.[ ] S.Rep. No. 752, 79th Cong.,
1st Sess., 14–15 (1945).

The House Report is in complete accord:

[ ]"[U]niformity has been found possible and desirable for all classes of
both equity and law actions in the courts.... It would seem to require no
argument to demonstrate that the administrative agencies, exercising but a
fraction of the judicial power may likewise operate under uniform rules of
practice and procedure and that they may be required to remain within the
terms of the law as to the exercise of both quasi-legislative and quasi-
judicial power."

. . .

[ ]The bill is an outline of minimum essential rights and procedures.... It
affords private parties a means of knowing what their rights are and how
they may protect them....

. . .

[ ] ... [The bill contains] the essentials of the different forms of administrative proceedings....[ ] H.R.Rep. No. 1980, 79th Cong., 2d Sess., 9, 16–
17 (1946).

And the Attorney General's Manual on the Administrative Procedure Act
31, 35 (1947), a contemporaneous interpretation previously given some
deference by this Court because of the role played by the Department of
Justice in drafting the legislation, further confirms that view. In short, all
of this leaves little doubt that Congress intended that the discretion of the
agencies and not that of the courts be exercised in determining when extra
procedural devices should be employed.

There are compelling reasons for construing § 4 in this manner. In the
first place, if courts continually review agency proceedings to determine
whether the agency employed procedures which were, in the court's opinion, perfectly tailored to reach what the court perceives to be the "best" or
"correct" result, judicial review would be totally unpredictable. And the
agencies, operating under this vague injunction to employ the "best"
procedures and facing the threat of reversal if they did not, would undoubtedly adopt full adjudicatory procedures in every instance. Not only would
this totally disrupt the statutory scheme, through which Congress enacted
"a formula upon which opposing social and political forces have come to
rest," Wong Yang Sung v. McGrath, 339 U.S., at 40, but all the inherent
advantages of informal rulemaking would be totally lost.

Secondly, it is obvious that the court in these cases reviewed the
agency's choice of procedures on the basis of the record actually produced
at the hearing, 547 F.2d., at 644, and not on the basis of the information
available to the agency when it made the decision to structure the proceedings in a certain way. This sort of Monday morning quarterbacking not
only encourages but almost compels the agency to conduct all rulemaking

proceedings with the full panoply of procedural devices normally associated only with adjudicatory hearings.

Finally, and perhaps most importantly, this sort of review fundamentally misconceives the nature of the standard for judicial review of an agency rule. The court below uncritically assumed that additional procedures will automatically result in a more adequate record because it will give interested parties more of an opportunity to participate in and contribute to the proceedings. But informal rulemaking need not be based solely on the transcript of a hearing held before an agency. Indeed, the agency need not even hold a formal hearing. *See* 5 U.S.C. § 553(c) (1976 ed.). Thus, the adequacy of the "record" in this type of proceeding is not correlated directly to the type of procedural devices employed, but rather turns on whether the agency has followed the statutory mandate of the Administrative Procedure Act or other relevant statutes. If the agency is compelled to support the rule which it ultimately adopts with the type of record produced only after a full adjudicatory hearing, it simply will have no choice but to conduct a full adjudicatory hearing prior to promulgating every rule. In sum, this sort of unwarranted judicial examination of perceived procedural shortcomings of a rulemaking proceeding can do nothing but seriously interfere with that process prescribed by Congress.

Respondent NRDC also argues that the fact that the Commission's inquiry was undertaken in the context of NEPA somehow permits a court to require procedures beyond those specified in § 4 of the APA when investigating factual issues through rulemaking. The Court of Appeals was apparently also of this view, indicating that agencies may be required to "develop new procedures to accomplish the innovative task of implementing NEPA through rulemaking." 547 F.2d, at 653. But we search in vain for something in NEPA which would mandate such a result. We have before observed that "NEPA does not repeal by implication any other statute." Aberdeen & Rockfish R. Co. v. SCRAP, 422 U.S. 289, 319 (1975). *See also* United States v. SCRAP, 412 U.S. 669, 694 (1973). In fact, just two Terms ago, we emphasized that the only procedural requirements imposed by NEPA are those stated in the plain language of the Act. Kleppe v. Sierra Club, 427 U.S. 390, 405–406 (1976). Thus, it is clear NEPA cannot serve as the basis for a substantial revision of the carefully constructed procedural specifications of the APA.

In short, nothing in the APA, NEPA, the circumstances of this case, the nature of the issues being considered, past agency practice, or the statutory mandate under which the Commission operates permitted the court to review and overturn the rulemaking proceeding on the basis of the procedural devices employed (or not employed) by the Commission so long as the Commission employed at least the statutory *minima,* a matter about which there is no doubt in this case.

There remains, of course, the question of whether the challenged rule finds sufficient justification in the administrative proceedings that it should be upheld by the reviewing court. Judge Tamm, concurring in the result reached by the majority of the Court of Appeals, thought that it did not. There are also intimations in the majority opinion which suggest that the judges who joined it likewise may have thought the administrative proceedings an insufficient basis upon which to predicate the rule in question. We accordingly remand so that the Court of Appeals may review the rule as the Administrative Procedure Act provides. We have made it abundantly clear before that when there is a contemporaneous explanation of the agency decision, the validity of that action must "stand or fall on the propriety of that finding, judged, of course, by the appropriate standard of review. If that finding is not sustainable on the administrative record made, then the Comptroller's decision must be vacated and the matter remanded to him for further consideration." Camp v. Pitts, 411 U.S. 138 (1973). *See also* SEC v. Chenery Corp., 318 U.S. 80 (1943). The court should engage in this kind of review and not stray beyond the judicial province to explore the procedural format or to impose upon the agency its own notion of which procedures are "best" or most likely to further some vague, undefined public good. . . .

NOTES AND QUESTIONS

1. As *Vermont Yankee* indicates, the regulation of civilian nuclear power follows a rather traditional administrative law framework. Legislative-style rulemaking proceedings are used to frame general standards, while trial-type adjudications are used for the resolution of specific cases, such as whether a given reactor complies with the general standards. Do issues involving conflicting scientific expertise fit comfortably into this framework? *See* Chapter 4, Sec. III. A, *infra*.

2. Both rulemaking and adjudicatory decisions of the Nuclear Regulatory Commission are, of course, typically subject to judicial review, as *Vermont Yankee* assumes. At the time of that decision, reactor licensing was a two-step process in which separate adjudications were held prior to both construction and operation, but today a single hearing may be adequate. *See* Energy Policy Act of 1992, Pub. L. No. 102–486. But in one important area, not mentioned in *Vermont Yankee,* Commission decisions are unreviewable. In *Heckler v. Chaney*, 470 U.S. 821, 105 S.Ct. 1649, 84 L.Ed.2d 714 (1985), a case involving the Food and Drug Administration, the Supreme Court held that refusal by an agency to take enforcement action is presumptively unreviewable. The presumption can be overcome if the agency's governing statute contains guidelines concerning when the agency must take enforcement action. *Id*. at 832–33. In applying this case to nuclear regulation, the courts have held that the relevant statutes and regulations do not provide meaningful guidance as to when the Nuclear Regulatory Commission should initiate enforcement action. Thus the decision not to take such action is committed to agency discretion and is unreviewable in court. Accordingly, if the Commission finds baseless a citizen petition alleging that a plant should be shut down because of safety deficiencies there is no judicial review. *See, e.g.*, Massachusetts Pub. Interest Research Group, Inc. v. United States Nuclear Regulatory Comm'n, 852 F.2d 9 (1st Cir. 1988).

3. Perhaps the most controversial part of *Vermont Yankee* was its holding that legislative-style rulemaking is all that is required to set standards for issues like nuclear waste storage, unless Congress explicitly requires more. In reaching this decision, the court relied heavily on the intent of the framers of the 1946 Administrative Procedure Act, a statute that predates the civilian uses of nuclear energy. Is the legislature the only appropriate institution to say whether new procedures are needed? For a diverse set of views on whether *Vermont Yankee* unwisely limits the judicial role, *see* Richard B. Stewart, Vermont Yankee *and the Evolution of Administrative Procedure*, 91 HARV. L. REV. 1805 (1978); Clark Byse, Vermont Yankee *and* *the Evolution of Administrative Procedure: A Somewhat Different View*, 91 HARV. L. REV. 1823 (1978); Stephen G. Breyer, Vermont Yankee *and the Court's Role in the Nuclear Power Controversy*, 91 HARV. L. REV. 1833 (1978).

4. Although *Vermont Yankee* held that the procedures used in developing the nuclear waste rule were adequate, it remanded the case to the Court of Appeals for a determination of whether the agency had provided adequate substantive justification for the rule. In 1982, the Court of Appeals held that the agency had not provided adequate justification because it had not allowed for proper consideration of the uncertainties involved in long-term waste storage. Natural Res. Def. Council v. United States Nuclear Regulatory Comm'n, 685 F.2d 459 (D.C. Cir. 1982). The Court of Appeals noted that nuclear waste contains materials that remain radioactive for periods ranging from hundreds of years for the bulk of fission products to millions of years for certain portions of those products. *Id.* at 467, n. 14. The Supreme Court granted review of this decision and rendered the following opinion.

Baltimore Gas and Electric Co. v. Natural Resources Defense Council, Inc.

Supreme Court of the United States, 1983.
462 U.S. 87, 103 S.Ct. 2246, 76 L.Ed.2d 437.

■ JUSTICE O'CONNOR delivered the opinion of the Court.

Section 102(2)(C) of the National Environmental Policy Act, 42 U.S.C. § 4332(2)(C) (NEPA), requires federal agencies to consider the environmental impact of any major federal action.[1] As part of its generic rulemaking proceedings to evaluate the environmental effects of the nuclear fuel cycle for nuclear power plants, the Nuclear Regulatory Commission (Commission)[2] decided that licensing boards should assume, for purposes of NEPA, that the permanent storage of certain nuclear wastes would have no significant environmental impact and thus should not affect the decision whether to license a particular nuclear power plant. We conclude that the Commission complied with NEPA and that its decision is not arbitrary or capricious within the meaning of § 10(e) of the Administrative Procedure Act (APA), 5 U.S.C. § 706.[3]

. . .

1. Section 102(2)(C) provides:

"The Congress authorizes and directs that, to the fullest extent possible . . . all agencies of the Federal Government shall . . . include in every recommendation or report on proposals for legislation and other major Federal actions significantly affecting the quality of the human environment, a detailed statement by the responsible official on—

(i) the environmental impact of the proposed action,

(ii) any adverse environmental effects which cannot be avoided should the proposal be implemented, . . . , and

(v) any irreversible and irretrievable commitments of resources which would

be involved in the proposed action should it be implemented."

2. The original Table S–3 rule was promulgated by the Atomic Energy Commission (AEC). Congress abolished the Atomic Energy Commission in the Energy Reorganization Act of 1974, 42 U.S.C. § 5801 et seq., and transferred its licensing and regulatory functions to the Nuclear Regulatory Commission (NRC). The interim and final rules were promulgated by the NRC. This opinion will use the term "Commission" to refer to both the NRC and the predecessor AEC.

3. 5 U.S.C. § 706 states in part:

"The reviewing court shall—

The environmental impact of operating a light-water nuclear power plant includes the effects of offsite activities necessary to provide fuel for the plant ("front end" activities), and of offsite activities necessary to dispose of the highly toxic and long-lived nuclear wastes generated by the plant ("back end" activities). The dispute in these cases concerns the Commission's adoption of a series of generic rules to evaluate the environmental effects of a nuclear power plant's fuel cycle. At the heart of each rule is Table S–3, a numerical compilation of the estimated resources used and effluents released by fuel cycle activities supporting a year's operation of a typical light-water reactor....

. . .

The Commission first adopted Table S–3 in 1974, after extensive informal rulemaking proceedings. 39 Fed.Reg. 14188 et seq. (1974). This "original" rule, as it later came to be described, declared that in environmental reports and impact statements for individual licensing proceedings the environmental costs of the fuel cycle "shall be as set forth" in Table S–3 and that "[n]o further discussion of such environmental effects shall be required." Id. at 14191. The original Table S–3 contained no numerical entry for the long-term environmental effects of storing solidified transuranic and high-level wastes, because the Commission staff believed that technology would be developed to isolate the wastes from the environment. The Commission and the parties have later termed this assumption of complete repository integrity as the "zero-release" assumption: the reasonableness of this assumption is at the core of the present controversy....

. . .

In 1979, following further hearings, the Commission adopted the "final" Table S–3 rule. 44 Fed.Reg. 45362 *et seq.* (1979).... The Commission ... continued to adhere to the zero-release assumption that the solidified waste would not escape and harm the environment once the repository was sealed. It acknowledged that this assumption was uncertain because of the remote possibility that water might enter the repository, dissolve the radioactive materials, and transport them to the biosphere. Nevertheless, the Commission predicted that a bedded-salt repository would maintain its integrity, and found the evidence "tentative but favorable" that an appropriate site would be found. *Id.* at 45368. The Commission ultimately determined that any undue optimism in the assumption of appropriate selection and perfect performance of the repository is offset by the cautious assumption, reflected in other parts of the Table, that *all* radioactive gases in the spent fuel would escape during the initial 6 to 20 year period that the repository remained open, ibid, and thus did not significantly reduce the overall conservatism of the S–3 Table. *Id.*, at 45369.

The Commission rejected the option of expressing the uncertainties in Table S–3 or permitting licensing boards, in performing the NEPA analysis

(2) hold unlawful and set aside agency action, findings, and conclusions found to be—

(A) arbitrary, capricious, an abuse of discretion, or otherwise not in accordance with law."

for individual nuclear plants, to consider those uncertainties. It saw no advantage in reassessing the significance of the uncertainties in individual licensing proceedings:

> [ ]In view of the uncertainties noted regarding waste disposal, the question then arises whether these uncertainties can or should be reflected explicitly in the fuel cycle rule. The Commission has concluded that the rule should not be so modified. On the individual reactor licensing level, where the proceedings deal with fuel cycle issues only peripherally, the Commission sees no advantage in having licensing boards repeatedly weigh for themselves the effect of uncertainties on the selection of fuel cycle impacts for use in cost-benefit balancing. This is a generic question properly dealt with in the rulemaking as part of choosing what impact values should go into the fuel cycle rule. The Commission concludes, having noted that uncertainties exist, that for the limited purpose of the fuel cycle rule it is reasonable to base impacts on the assumption which the Commission believes the probabilities favor, i.e., that bedded-salt repository sites can be found which will provide effective isolation of radioactive waste from the biosphere.[ ] 44 Fed.Reg. 45362, 45369 (1979). . . .

. . .

We are acutely aware that the extent to which this Nation should rely on nuclear power as a source of energy is an important and sensitive issue. Much of the debate focuses on whether development of nuclear generation facilities should proceed in the face of uncertainties about their long-term effects on the environment. Resolution of these fundamental policy questions lies, however, with Congress and the agencies to which Congress has delegated authority, as well as with state legislatures and, ultimately, the populace as a whole. Congress has assigned the courts only the limited, albeit important, task of reviewing agency action to determine whether the agency conformed with controlling statutes. As we emphasized in our earlier encounter with these very proceedings, "[a]dministrative decisions should be set aside in this context, as in every other, only for substantial procedural or substantive reasons as mandated by statute . . ., not simply because the court is unhappy with the result reached." *Vermont Yankee,* 435 U.S., at 558.

The controlling statute at issue here is the National Environmental Policy Act. NEPA has twin aims. First, it "places upon an agency the obligation to consider every significant aspect of the environmental impact of a proposed action." *Vermont Yankee, supra,* at 553. Second, it ensures that the agency will inform the public that it has indeed considered environmental concerns in its decisionmaking process. Weinberger v. Catholic Action of Hawaii, 454 U.S. 139, 143 (1981). Congress in enacting NEPA, however, did not require agencies to elevate environmental concerns over other appropriate considerations. *See* Strycker's Bay Neighborhood Council v. Karlen, 444 U.S. 223, 227 (1980) (per curiam). Rather, it required only that the agency take a "hard look" at the environmental consequences before taking a major action. *See* Kleppe v. Sierra Club, 427 U.S. 390, 410, n. 21 (1976). The role of the courts is simply to ensure that the agency has adequately considered and disclosed the environmental impact of its actions and that its decision is not arbitrary or capricious. *See generally* Citizens to Preserve Overton Park v. Volpe, 401 U.S. 402, 415–417 (1971).

In its Table S–3 Rule here, the Commission has determined that the probabilities favor the zero-release assumption, because the Nation is likely to develop methods to store the wastes with no leakage to the environment. The NRDC did not challenge and the Court of Appeals did not decide the reasonableness of this determination, 685 F.2d, at 478, n. 96, and no party seriously challenges it here. The Commission recognized, however, that the geological, chemical, physical and other data it relied on in making this prediction were based, in part, on assumptions which involve substantial uncertainties. Again, no one suggests that the uncertainties are trivial or the potential effects insignificant if time proves the zero-release assumption to have been seriously wrong. After confronting the issue, though, the Commission has determined that the uncertainties concerning the development of nuclear waste storage facilities are not sufficient to affect the outcome of any individual licensing decision.

It is clear that the Commission, in making this determination, has made the careful consideration and disclosure required by NEPA. The sheer volume of proceedings before the Commission is impressive. Of far greater importance, the Commission's Statement of Consideration announcing the final Table S–3 Rule shows that it has digested this mass of material and disclosed all substantial risks. 44 Fed.Reg. 45362, 45367–45369 (1979). The Statement summarizes the major uncertainty of long-term storage in bedded-salt repositories, which is that water could infiltrate the repository as a result of such diverse factors as geologic faulting, a meteor strike, or accidental or deliberate intrusion by man. The Commission noted that the probability of intrusion was small, and that the plasticity of salt would tend to heal some types of intrusions. The Commission also found the evidence "tentative but favorable" that an appropriate site could be found. Table S–3 refers interested persons to staff studies that discuss the uncertainties in greater detail. Given this record and the Commission's statement, it simply cannot be said that the Commission ignored or failed to disclose the uncertainties surrounding its zero-release assumption.

Congress did not enact NEPA, of course, so that an agency would contemplate the environmental impact of an action as an abstract exercise. Rather, Congress intended that the "hard look" be incorporated as part of the agency's process of deciding whether to pursue a particular federal action. It was on this ground that the Court of Appeals faulted the Commission's action, for failing to allow the uncertainties potentially to "tip the balance" in a particular licensing decision. As a general proposition, we can agree with the Court of Appeals' determination that an agency must allow all significant environmental risks to be factored into the decision whether to undertake a proposed action. We think, however, that the Court of Appeals erred in concluding the Commission had not complied with this standard.

As *Vermont Yankee* made clear, NEPA does not require agencies to adopt any particular internal decisionmaking structure. Here, the agency has chosen to evaluate generically the environmental impact of the fuel cycle and inform individual licensing boards, through the Table S–3 rule, of its evaluation. The generic method chosen by the agency is clearly an appropriate method of conducting the hard look required by NEPA. *See Vermont Yankee, supra*, 435 U.S., at 535, n. 13. The environmental effects of much of the fuel cycle are not plant specific, for any plant, regardless of its particular attributes, will create additional wastes that must be stored in a common long-term repository. Administrative efficiency and consistency of decision are both furthered by a generic determination of these effects without needless repetition of the litigation in individual proceedings, which are subject to review by the Commission in any event. *See generally* Ecology Action v. AEC, 492 F.2d 998, 1002, n. 5 (CA2 1974) (Friendly, J.) (quoting Administrative Conference Proposed Recommendation 73–6).

The Court of Appeals recognized that the Commission has discretion to evaluate generically the environmental effects of the fuel cycle and require that these values be "plugged into" individual licensing decisions. The court concluded that the Commission nevertheless violated NEPA by failing to factor the uncertainty surrounding long-term storage into Table S–3 and precluding individual licensing decisionmakers from considering it.

The Commission's decision to affix a zero value to the environmental impact of long-term storage would violate NEPA, however, only if the Commission acted arbitrarily and capriciously in deciding generically that the uncertainty was insufficient to affect any individual licensing decision. In assessing whether the Commission's decision is arbitrary and capricious, it is crucial to place the zero-release assumption in context. Three factors are particularly important. First is the Commission's repeated emphasis that the zero-risk assumption—and, indeed, all of the Table S–3 rule—was made for a limited purpose. The Commission expressly noted its intention to supplement the rule with an explanatory narrative. It also emphasized that the purpose of the rule was not to evaluate or select the most effective long-term waste disposal technology or develop site selection criteria. A separate and comprehensive series of programs has been undertaken to serve these broader purposes. In the proceedings before us, the Commission's staff did not attempt to evaluate the environmental effects of all possible methods of disposing of waste. Rather, it chose to analyze intensively the most probable long-term waste disposal method—burial in a bedded-salt repository several hundred meters below ground—and then "estimate its impact conservatively, based on the best available information and analysis." 44 Fed.Reg. 45362, 45363 (1979). The zero-release assumption cannot be evaluated in isolation. Rather, it must be assessed in relation to the limited purpose for which the Commission made the assumption.

Second, the Commission emphasized that the zero-release assumption is but a single figure in an entire Table, which the Commission expressly designed as a risk-averse estimate of the environmental impact of the fuel cycle. It noted that Table S–3 assumed that the fuel storage canisters and the fuel rod cladding would be corroded before a repository is closed and that all volatile materials in the fuel would escape to the environment. Given that assumption, and the improbability that materials would escape after sealing, the Commission determined that the overall Table represented a conservative (i.e., inflated) statement of environmental impacts. It is not unreasonable for the Commission to counteract the uncertainties in post-sealing releases by balancing them with an overestimate of presealing releases. A reviewing court should not magnify a single line item beyond its significance as only part of a larger Table.

Third, a reviewing court must remember that the Commission is making predictions, within its area of special expertise, at the frontiers of science. When examining this kind of scientific determination, as opposed to simple findings of fact, a reviewing court must generally be at its most deferential. *See, e.g.,* Industrial Union Department v. American Petroleum Institute, 448 U.S. 607, 656 (1980) (plurality opinion); *id.,* at 705–706 (Marshall, J., dissenting).

With these three guides in mind, we find the Commission's zero-release assumption to be within the bounds of reasoned decisionmaking required by the APA. We have already noted that the Commission's Statement of Consideration detailed several areas of uncertainty and discussed why they were insubstantial for purposes of an individual licensing decision. The Table S–3 Rule also refers to the staff reports, public documents that contain a more expanded discussion of the uncertainties involved in concluding that long-term storage will have no environmental effects. These staff reports recognize that rigorous verification of long-term risks for waste repositories is not possible, but suggest that data and extrapolation of past experience allow the Commission to identify events that could produce repository failure, estimate the probability of those events, and calculate the resulting consequences. NUREG–0116, at 4–86. The Commission staff also modelled the consequences of repository failure by tracing the flow of contaminated water, and found them to be insignificant. *Id.,* at 4–89 through 4–94. Ultimately, the staff concluded that

> [t]he radiotoxic hazard index analyses and the modeling studies that have been done indicate that consequences of all but the most improbable events will be small. Risks (probabilities times consequences) inherent in the long term for geological disposal will therefore also be small.[ ] NUREG–0116, at 2–11.

We also find significant the separate views of Commissioners Bradford and Gilinsky. These Commissioners expressed dissatisfaction with the zero-release assumption and yet emphasized the limited purpose of the assumption and the overall conservatism of Table S–3. Commissioner Bradford characterized the bedded-salt repository as a responsible working assumption for NEPA purposes and concurred in the zero-release figure because it does not appear to affect Table S–3's overall conservatism. 44 Fed.Reg. 45362, 45372 (1979). Commissioner Gilinsky was more critical of the entire Table, stating that the Commission should confront directly whether it should license any nuclear reactors in light of the problems of waste disposal, rather than hide an affirmative conclusion to this issue behind a table of numbers. He emphasized that the "waste confidence proceeding", *see* note 14, *supra,* should provide the Commission an appropriate vehicle for a thorough evaluation of the problems involved in the Government's commitment to a waste disposal solution. For the limited purpose of individual licensing proceedings, however, Commissioner Gilinsky found it "virtually inconceivable" that the Table should affect the decision whether to license, and characterized as "naive" the notion that the fuel cycle effluents could tip the balance in some cases and not in others. *Id.*, at 45374 (1979).

In sum, we think that the zero-release assumption—a policy judgment concerning one line in a conservative Table designed for the limited purpose of individual licensing decisions—is within the bounds of reasoned decisionmaking. It is not our task to determine what decision we, as Commissioners, would have reached. Our only task is to determine whether the Commission has considered the relevant factors and articulated a rational connection between the facts found and the choice made. Bowman Transportation, Inc. v. Arkansas–Best Freight System, Inc., 419 U.S. 281, 285–286 (1974); Citizens to Preserve Overton Park v. Volpe, *supra.* Under this standard, we think the Commission's zero-release assumption, within the context of Table S–3 as a whole, was not arbitrary and capricious. . . .

NOTES AND QUESTIONS

1. Why should a court give particular deference to an agency which acts "at the frontiers of science"? When uncertainties pervade a policy area, technical expertise often includes implicit policy judgments. On the respective role of agencies and the courts in science policy, *see* Chapter 4, Sec. III A. *See also* Peter Huber, *Safety and the Second Best: The Hazards of Public Risk Management in the Courts*, 85 Colum. L. Rev. 277 (1985).

2. In addition to emphasizing the role of the agency, the Supreme Court decision above stresses that Congress and the state legislatures must make the fundamental policy decisions about nuclear power. In recent years a number of legislative steps have been taken in an effort to deal with nuclear waste issues. As to the so-called low-level wastes from civilian sources, which include contaminated materials from hospitals, industrial sites, and the like, Congress created a system designed to encourage states to form regional disposal compacts, in part by allowing states to exclude waste from other states and in part by requiring states that did not provide for the disposal of low-level waste by a certain date to "take title" to it. *See* Low–Level Radioactive Waste Policy Act of 1980, Pub. L. No. 96–573, 94 Stat. 3347; Low–Level Radioactive Waste Policy Amendments Act of 1985, Pub. L. No. 99–240, 99 Stat. 1842. In 1992, the United States Supreme Court upheld the bulk of these provisions, but struck down the "take title" portion on federalism grounds. New York v. United States, 505 U.S. 144, 112 S.Ct. 2408, 120 L.Ed.2d 120 (1992). The remaining provisions of the statute "have not been entirely successful in encouraging states to take responsibility for their waste." Emma Garrison, Note, *Entergy Arkansas, Inc. v. Nebraska, Does a Radioactive Waste Compact Nuke Sovereign Immunity?*, 30 Ecology L.Q. 449, 454 (2003).

3. There has been somewhat more progress in the disposal of low-level waste from the nation's nuclear weapons program. In 1999, the Waste Isolation Pilot Project (WIPP), located in deep salt beds near Carlsbad, New Mexico, began receiving shipments from sites such as Los Alamos, New Mexico and Rocky Flats, Colorado. Richard A. Kerr, *For Radioactive Waste From Weapons, A Home at Last*, 283 Sci. 1626 (1999). Although disagreements have arisen concerning the consequences if there is leakage, WIPP has now received and stored substantial shipments for many years. John Fleck, *WIPP Waste Leaks May Top Estimates*, Albuquerque J., May 28, 2003.

4. But the biggest area of public concern remains the high-level waste from civilian reactors discussed in *Vermont Yankee* and *Baltimore Gas*—waste that can remain dangerous for centuries. The issue is particularly acute for those who support nuclear power, not only because of the environmental dangers involved, but because states are free to limit reactor licensing on economic grounds so long as there is no federally approved waste disposal program. *See* Pacific Gas & Elec. Co. v. State Energy Resources Comm'n, 461 U.S. 190, 103 S.Ct. 1713, 75 L.Ed.2d 752 (1983). At present, the waste remains at the reactor sites waiting to be shipped to a long-term repository.

The federal effort to solve this problem began in earnest when President Reagan signed the Nuclear Waste Policy Act of 1982, Pub. L. No. 97–425, 96 Stat. 2201, which established a schedule "for the siting, construction and operation of repositories that will provide a reasonable assurance that the public and the environment will be adequately protected from the hazards of high-level radioactive waste." Sec. 111(b)(1). Of course, one of the difficulties in waste storage—a difficulty not limited to the nuclear field—is that while many localities are happy to receive the electricity generated by nuclear energy, few are eager to host waste-storage sites. The Nuclear Waste Policy Act created an elaborate scheme under which potential sites chosen by the Secretary of Energy and President could be disapproved by the state involved, but Congress could overturn the disapproval. Secs. 115, 116.

On May 27, 1986, the President, pursuant to the Act, approved three potential high-level waste storage sites that had been recommended by the Secretary of Energy. The sites were located at Yucca Mountain, Nevada, Deaf Smith County, Texas, and Hanford, Washington. Under the Act, the Department of Energy was supposed to recommend one site to the President for construction of the first repository; the President was then to recommend one site to Congress. However, after the three potential sites were announced, an outburst of public protests and litigation threatened to delay the process indefinitely. On December 22, 1987, Congress stepped in dramatically by passing legislation that altered the process set up by the 1982 Act. In the Omnibus Budget Reconciliation Act of 1987, Pub. L. No. 100–203, 101 Stat. 1330, Congress directed the Department of Energy to study only the Yucca Mountain site. That site would become the waste storage site unless Department of Energy officials found it unsuitable within the next seven years. One congressional aide was quoted a saying, "It's a roll of the dice with Yucca Mountain. We have reason to believe it will work out, but if it doesn't ... man, we're in trouble." Eliot Marshall, *Nevada Wins the Nuclear Waste Lottery*, 239 SCI. 15 (1988).

In 2002, the Department of Energy recommended the Yucca Mountain site, President Bush adopted the recommendation, Nevada Governor Kenny Guinn vetoed the measure, and Congress overrode his veto, thus carrying out the provisions of the original 1982 statute. As far as the federal government is concerned, the Department of Energy is now free to apply to the U.S. Nuclear Regulatory Commission to build and operate a high-level waste repository at Yucca Mountain. Robert Schlesinger, *A Nuclear Waste Site in Nevada Gets Senate Nod,* BOSTON GLOBE, July 10, 2002, at A1. When such an application is made, the Commission is likely to take four years to review it. Steve Tetreault, *Agency Chairman Predicts Four–Year Review of Yucca*, LAS VEGAS REV.-J., May 28, 2004, at A1. In the meantime, on July 9, 2004, the United States Court of Appeals for the District of Columbia Circuit ruled on 13 consolidated lawsuits filed by Nevada and environmental groups against the United States challenging the choice of Yucca Mountain on numerous statutory and constitutional grounds. While the Court upheld the basic statutory mechanism Congress had created for selecting the site, it said that the government's standards for protecting the public from radioactivity leaking from Yucca were inadequate. The government had relied on evidence that Yucca would remain safe for 10,000 years, but the Court said that Congress had required the government to defer to advice from the National Academy of Sciences on this issue, and the Academy had called for assurances that the site would remain safe for a much longer period. Nuclear Energy Inst. v. Environmental Protection Agency, 373 F.3d 1251 (D.C. Cir. 2004). This decision left open the possibility of further action by Congress, the courts, and the relevant agencies, with the Department of Energy's ability to seek a license for Yucca from the U.S. Nuclear Energy Commission likely to be, at a minimum, delayed. *See* Mathew L. Wald, *Nuclear Waste Repository in Nevada Suffers Setback*, N.Y. Times, July 10, 2004, at A12.

Thus the ultimate outcome of the "roll of the dice" with Yucca Mountain will not be known for many years. Meanwhile, the federal government may owe money to the utilities because it did not live up to its promise, made in the original 1982 Act, that it would take over the waste by 1998. *See, e.g.*, Riley Snow, *Recent Development: Federal Court of Claims Further Defines Nuclear Power Companies Ability to Collect Damages*, 24 J. Land Resources & Envtl. L. 151 (2004).

Up to this point, we have discussed government regulation of civilian nuclear power. The government has also encouraged the development of nuclear energy in various ways, as the following case demonstrates.

Duke Power Co. v. Carolina Environmental Study Group, Inc.

Supreme Court of the United States, 1978.
438 U.S. 59, 98 S.Ct. 2620, 57 L.Ed.2d 595.

■ Chief Justice Burger delivered the opinion of the Court.

These appeals present the question of whether Congress may, consistent with the Constitution, impose a limitation on liability for nuclear accidents resulting from the operation of private nuclear power plants licensed by the Federal Government.

When Congress passed the Atomic Energy Act of 1946, it contemplated that the development of nuclear power would be a Government monopoly. *See* Act of Aug. 1, 1946, ch. 724, 60 Stat. 755. Within a decade, however, Congress concluded that the national interest would be best served if the Government encouraged the private sector to become involved in the development of atomic energy for peaceful purposes under a program of federal regulation and licensing. *See* H.R.Rep. No. 2181, 83d Cong., 2d Sess., 1–11 (1954). The Atomic Energy Act of 1954, Act of Aug. 30, 1954, ch. 1073, 68 Stat. 919, as amended, 42 U.S.C. §§ 2011–2281 (1970 ed. and Supp. V), implemented this policy decision, providing for licensing of private construction, ownership, and operation of commercial nuclear power reactors for energy production under strict supervision by the Atomic Energy Commission (AEC).[1] *See* Power Reactor Development Co. v. Electrical Workers, 367 U.S. 396 (1961), *rev'g and remanding* 280 F.2d 645 (1960).

---

1. Under the terms of the Energy Reorganization Act of 1974, 42 U.S.C. § 5801 *et seq.* (1970 ed., Supp. V), the Nuclear Regulatory Commission (NRC) has now replaced the AEC as the licensing and regulatory authority.

Private industry responded to the Atomic Energy Act of 1954 with the development of an experimental power plant constructed under the auspices of a consortium of interested companies. It soon became apparent that profits from the private exploitation of atomic energy were uncertain and the accompanying risks substantial. *See* Green, *Nuclear Power: Risk, Liability, and Indemnity*, 71 Mich.L.Rev. 479–481 (1973) (Green). Although the AEC offered incentives to encourage investment, there remained in the path of the private nuclear power industry various problems—the risk of potentially vast liability in the event of a nuclear accident of a sizable magnitude being the major obstacle. Notwithstanding comprehensive testing and study, the uniqueness of this form of energy production made it impossible totally to rule out the risk of a major nuclear accident resulting in extensive damage. Private industry and the AEC were confident that such a disaster would not occur, but the very uniqueness of nuclear power meant that the possibility remained, and the potential liability dwarfed the ability of the industry and private insurance companies to absorb the risk. *See* Hearings before the Joint Committee on Atomic Energy on Government Indemnity for Private Licensees and AEC Contractors Against Reactor Hazards, 84th Cong., 2d Sess., 122–124 (1956). Thus, while repeatedly stressing that the risk of a major nuclear accident was extremely remote, spokesmen for the private sector informed Congress that they would be forced to withdraw from the field if their liability were not limited by appropriate legislation. *Id.*, at 9, 109–110, 115, 120, 136–137, 148, 181, 195, and 240.

Congress responded in 1957 by passing the Price–Anderson Act, 71 Stat. 576, 42 U.S.C. § 2210 (1970 ed. and Supp. V). The Act had the dual purpose of "protect[ing] the public and ... encourag[ing] the development of the atomic energy industry." 42 U.S.C. § 2012(i). In its original form, the Act limited the aggregate liability for a single nuclear incident to $500 million plus the amount of liability insurance available on the private market—some $60 million in 1957. The nuclear industry was required to purchase the maximum available amount of privately underwritten public liability insurance, and the Act provided that if damages from a nuclear disaster exceeded the amount of that private insurance coverage, the Federal Government would indemnify the licensee and other "persons indemnified" in an amount not to exceed $500 million. Thus, the actual ceiling on liability was the amount of private insurance coverage plus the Government's indemnification obligation which totaled $560 million.

Since its enactment, the Act has been twice amended, the first occasion being on the eve of its expiration in 1966. These amendments extended the basic liability-limitation provisions for another 10 years, and added a provision which had the effect of requiring those indemnified under the Act to waive all legal defenses in the event of a substantial nuclear accident. This provision was based on a congressional concern that state tort law dealing with liability for nuclear incidents was generally unsettled and that some way of insuring a common standard of responsibility for all jurisdictions—strict liability—was needed. A waiver of defenses was thought to be the preferable approach since it entailed less interference with state tort law than would the enactment of a federal statute prescribing strict liability. *See* S.Rep. No. 1605, 89th Cong., 2d Sess., 6–10 (1966).

In 1975, Congress again extended the Act's coverage until 1987, and continued the $560 million limitation on liability. However a new provision was added requiring, in the event of a nuclear incident, each of the 60 or more reactor owners to contribute between $2 and $5 million toward the cost of compensating victims. 42 U.S.C. § 2210(b) (1970 ed., Supp. V). Since the liability ceiling remained at the same level, the effect of the "deferred premium" provision was to reduce the Federal Government's contribution to the liability pool. In its amendments to the Act in 1975, Congress also explicitly provided that "in the event of a nuclear incident involving damages in excess of [the] amount of aggregate liability, the Congress will thoroughly review the particular incident and will take whatever action is deemed necessary and appropriate to protect the public from the consequences of a disaster of such magnitude...." 42 U.S.C. § 2210(e) (1970 ed., Supp. V).

Under the Price–Anderson Act as it presently stands, liability in the event of a nuclear incident causing damages of $560 million or more would be spread as follows: $315 million would be paid from contributions by the licensees of the 63 private operating nuclear power plants; $140 million would come from private insurance (the maximum now available); the remainder of $105 million would be borne by the Federal Government.

Appellant in No. 77–262, Duke Power Co., is an investor-owned public utility which is constructing one nuclear power plant in North Carolina and one in South Carolina. Duke Power, along with the NRC, was sued by appellees, two organizations—Carolina Environmental Study Group and the Catawba Central Labor Union—and 40 individuals who live within close proximity to the planned facilities. The action was commenced in 1973, and sought, among other relief, a declaration that the Price–Anderson Act is unconstitutional....

Specifically, as we read the complaint, appellees are making two basic challenges to the Act—both of which find their moorings in the Fifth Amendment. First, appellees contend that the Due Process Clause protects them against arbitrary governmental action adversely affecting their property rights and that the Price–Anderson Act—which both creates the source of the underlying injury and limits the recovery therefore—constitutes such arbitrary action. And second, they are contending that in the event of a nuclear accident their property would be "taken" without any assurance of just compensation. The Price–Anderson Act is the instrument of the taking since on this record, without it, there would be no power plants and no possibility of an accident....

The District Court held that the Price–Anderson Act contravened the Due Process Clause because "[t]he amount of recovery is not rationally related to the potential losses"; because "[t]he Act tends to encourage irresponsibility in matters of safety and environmental protection...."; and finally because "[t]here is no *quid pro quo* for the liability" limitations. 431 F.Supp., at 222–223. An equal protection violation was also found because the Act "places the cost of [nuclear power] on an arbitrarily chosen segment of society, those injured by nuclear catastrophe." *Id.*, at 225. Application of the relevant constitutional principles forces the conclusion that these holdings of the District Court cannot be sustained.

Our due process analysis properly begins with a discussion of the appropriate standard of review. Appellants, portraying the liability-limitation provision as a legislative balancing of economic interests, urge that the Price–Anderson Act be accorded the traditional presumption of constitutionality generally accorded economic regulations and that it be upheld absent proof of arbitrariness or irrationality on the part of Congress. *See* Ferguson v. Skrupa, 372 U.S. 726, 731–732 (1963); Usery v. Turner Elkhorn Mining Co., 428 U.S. 1, 15 (1976). Appellees, however, urge a more elevated standard of review on the ground that the interests jeopardized by the Price–Anderson Act "are far more important than those in the economic due process and business-oriented cases" where the traditional rationality standard has been invoked. Brief for Appellees 36. An intermediate standard like that applied in cases such as *Craig v. Boren*, 429 U.S. 190 (1976) (equal protection challenge to statute requiring that males be older than females in order to purchase beer) or *United States Trust Co. of New York v. New Jersey*, 431 U.S. 1 (1977) (Contract Clause challenge to repeal of statutory covenant providing security for bondholders) is thus recommended for our use here.

As we read the Act and its legislative history, it is clear that Congress' purpose was to remove the economic impediments in order to stimulate the private development of electric energy by nuclear power while simultaneously providing the public compensation in the event of a catastrophic nuclear incident. *See, e.g.*, S.Rep. No. 296, 85th Cong., 1st Sess., 15 (1957). The liability-limitation provision thus emerges as a classic example of an economic regulation—a legislative effort to structure and accommodate "the burdens and benefits of economic life." Usery v. Turner Elkhorn Mining Co., [ ] 428 U.S. at 15. "It is by now well established that [such] legislative Acts ... come to the Court with a presumption of constitutionality, and that the burden is on one complaining of a due process violation to establish that the legislature has acted in an arbitrary and irrational way." *Ibid*. That the accommodation struck may have profound and far-reaching consequences, contrary to appellees' suggestion, provides all the more reason for this Court to defer to the congressional judgment unless it is demonstrably arbitrary or irrational.

When examined in light of this standard of review, the Price–Anderson Act, in our view, passes constitutional muster. The record before us fully supports the need for the imposition of a statutory limit on liability to encourage private industry participation and hence bears a rational relationship to Congress' concern for stimulating the involvement of private enterprise in the production of electric energy through the use of atomic power; nor do we understand appellees or the District Court to be of a different view. Rather their challenge is to the alleged arbitrariness of the *particular figure* of $560 million, which is the statutory ceiling on liability. The District Court aptly summarized its position:

> [ ]The amount of recovery is not rationally related to the potential losses. Abundant evidence in the record shows that although major catastrophe in any particular place is not certain and may not be extremely likely, nevertheless, in the territory where these plants are located, damage to life and property for this and future generations could well be many, many times the limit which the law places on liability.[ ] 431 F.Supp., at 222.

Assuming, *arguendo,* that the $560 million fund would not insure full recovery in all conceivable circumstances[28] and the hard truth is that no one can ever know—it does not by any means follow that the liability limitation is therefore irrational and violative of due process. The legislative history clearly indicates that the $560 million figure was not arrived at on the supposition that it alone would necessarily be sufficient to guarantee full compensation in the event of a nuclear incident. Instead, it was conceived of as a "starting point" or a working hypothesis.[29] The reasonableness of the statute's assumed ceiling on liability was predicated on two corollary considerations—expert appraisals of the exceedingly small risk of a nuclear incident involving claims in excess of $560 million, and the recognition that in the event of such an incident, Congress would likely enact extraordinary relief provisions to provide additional relief, in accord with prior practice.

> [T]his limitation does not, as a practical matter, detract from the public protection afforded by this legislation. In the first place, the likelihood of an accident occurring which would result in claims exceeding the sum of the financial protection required and the governmental indemnity is exceedingly remote, albeit theoretically possible. Perhaps more important, in the event of a national disaster of this magnitude, it is obvious that Congress would have to review the problem and take appropriate action. The history of other natural or man-made disasters, such as the Texas City incident, bears this out. The limitation of liability serves primarily as a device for facilitating further congressional review of such a situation, rather than as an ultimate bar to further relief of the public.[ ] H.R.Rep. No. 883, 89th Cong., 1st Sess., 6–7 (1965).

See also S.Rep. No. 296, *supra,* at 21; H.R.Rep. No. 94–648, pp. 12, 15 (1975).

Given our conclusion that, in general, limiting liability is an acceptable method for Congress to utilize in encouraging the private development of electric energy by atomic power, candor requires acknowledgment that whatever ceiling figure is selected will, of necessity, be arbitrary in the sense that any choice of a figure based on imponderables like those at issue here can always be so characterized. This is not, however, the kind of

---

28. As the various studies considered by the District Court indicate, there is considerable uncertainty as to the amount of damages which would result from a catastrophic nuclear accident. *See* 431 F.Supp., at 210–214. The Reactor Safety Study published by the NRC in 1975 suggested that there was a 1 in 20,000 chance (per reactor year) of an accident causing property damage approaching $100 million and having only minor health effects. By contrast, when the odds were reduced to the range of 1 in 1 billion (per reactor year), the level of damages approached $14 billion; and 3,300 early fatalities and 45,000 early illnesses were predicted. NRC, Reactor Safety Study, An Assessment of Accident Risks in U.S. Commercial Nuclear Power Plants 83–85 (Wash–1400, Oct. 1975). For a thorough criticism of the Reac-

tor Safety Study, *see* EPA, Reactor Safety Study (Wash–1400): A Review of the Final Report (June 1976).

29. "What we were thinking about was the magnitude of protection and we set an arbitrary figure because it seemed to be practical at that time and because we didn't think an accident would happen ... but yet we recognize that it could happen. *We wanted to have a base to work from.*" Hearings before the Joint Committee on Atomic Energy on Possible Modification or Extension of the Price–Anderson Insurance And Indemnity Act of 1957 In Order for Proper Planning of Nuclear Power Plants to Continue Without Delay, 93d Cong., 2d Sess., 68 (1974) (remarks of Rep. Holifield) (emphasis added).

arbitrariness which flaws otherwise constitutional action. When appraised in terms of both the extremely remote possibility of an accident where liability would exceed the limitation[30] and Congress' now statutory commitment to "take whatever action is deemed necessary and appropriate to protect the public from the consequences of" any such disaster, 42 U.S.C. § 2210(e) (1970 ed., Supp. V),[31] we hold the congressional decision to fix a $560 million ceiling, at this stage in the private development and production of electric energy by nuclear power, to be within permissible limits and not violative of due process.

This District Court's further conclusion that the Price–Anderson Act "tends to encourage irresponsibility ... on the part of builders and owners" of the nuclear power plants, 431 F.Supp., at 222, simply cannot withstand careful scrutiny. We recently outlined the multitude of detailed steps involved in the review of any application for a license to construct or to operate a nuclear power plant, Vermont Yankee Nuclear Power Corp. v. NRDC, 435 U.S. 519, 526–527, and n. 5 (1978); nothing in the liability-limitation provision undermines or alters in any respect the rigor and integrity of that process. Moreover, in the event of a nuclear accident the utility itself would suffer perhaps the largest damages. While obviously not to be compared with the loss of human life and injury to health, the risk of financial loss and possible bankruptcy to the utility is in itself no small incentive to avoid the kind of irresponsible and cavalier conduct implicitly attributed to licensees by the District Court.

The remaining due process objection to the liability-limitation provision is that it fails to provide those injured by a nuclear accident with a satisfactory *quid pro quo* for the common-law rights of recovery which the Act abrogates. Initially, it is not at all clear that the Due Process Clause in fact requires that a legislatively enacted compensation scheme either duplicate the recovery at common law or provide a reasonable substitute remedy. However, we need not resolve this question here since the Price–Anderson Act does, in our view, provide a reasonably just substitute for the common-law or state tort law remedies it replaces. *Cf.* New York Central R. Co. v. White, 243 U.S. 188 (1917); Crowell v. Benson, 285 U.S. 22 (1932).

---

30. Congress' conclusion that "the probabilities of a nuclear incident are much lower and the likely consequences much less severe than has been thought previously," was a key factor in the decision not to increase the $560 million liability ceiling in 1975. S.Rep. No. 94–454, p. 12 (1975).

31. In the past Congress has provided emergency assistance for victims of catastrophic accidents even in the absence of a prior statutory commitment to do so. For example, in 1955, Congress passed the Texas City Explosion Relief Act, 69 Stat. 707, to provide relief for victims of the explosion of ammonium nitrate fertilizer in 1947. Congress took this action despite the decision in *Dalehite v. United States*, 346 U.S. 15 (1953), holding the United States free from any liability under the Federal Tort Claims Act for

the damages incurred and injuries suffered. More recently Congress enacted legislation to provide relief for victims of the flood resulting from the collapse of the Teton Dam in Idaho. Pub.L. 94–400, 90 Stat. 1211. Under the Act, the Secretary of the Interior was authorized to provide full compensation for any deaths, personal injuries, or property damage caused by the failure of the dam. Ibid.

The Price–Anderson Act is, of course, a significant improvement on these prior relief efforts because it provides an advance guarantee of recovery up to $560 million plus an express commitment by Congress to take whatever further steps are necessary to aid the victims of a nuclear incident.

The legislative history of the liability-limitation provisions and the accompanying compensation mechanism reflects Congress' determination that reliance on state tort law remedies and state-court procedures was an unsatisfactory approach to assuring public compensation for nuclear accidents, while at the same time providing the necessary incentives for private development of nuclear-produced energy. The remarks of Chairman Anders of the NRC before the Joint Committee on Atomic Energy during the 1975 hearings on the need for renewal of the Price–Anderson Act are illustrative of this concern and of the expectation that the Act would provide a more efficient and certain vehicle for assuring compensation in the unlikely event of a nuclear incident:

> [ ]The primary defect of this alternative [nonrenewal of the Act], however, is its failure to afford the public either a secure source of funds or a firm basis for legal liability with respect to new plants. While in theory no legal limit would be placed on liability, as a practical matter the public would be less assured of obtaining compensation than under Price–Anderson. Establishing liability would depend in each case on state tort law and procedures, and these might or might not provide for no-fault liability, let alone the multiple other protections now embodied in Price–Anderson. The present assurance of prompt and equitable compensation under a pre-structured and nationally applicable protective system would give way to uncertainties, variations and potentially lengthy delays in recovery. It should be emphasized, moreover, that it is collecting a judgment, not filing a lawsuit, that counts. Even if defenses are waived under state law, a defendant with theoretically "unlimited" liability may be unable to pay a judgment once obtained. When the defendant's assets are exhausted by earlier judgments, subsequent claimants would be left with uncollectable awards. The prospect of inequitable distribution would produce a race to the courthouse door in contrast to the present system of assured orderly and equitable compensation.[ ] Hearings on H.R. 8631 before Joint Committee on Atomic Energy, 94th Cong., 1st Sess., 69 (1975).

Appellees, like the District Court, differ with this appraisal on several grounds. They argue, *inter alia,* that recovery under the Act would not be greater than without it, that the waiver of defenses required by the Act, 42 U.S.C. § 2210(n) (1970 ed., Supp. V), is an idle gesture since those involved in the development of nuclear energy would likely be held strictly liable under common-law principles; that the claim-administration procedure under the Act delays rather than expedites individual recovery; and finally that recovery of even limited compensation is uncertain since the liability ceiling does not vary with the number of persons injured or amount of property damaged. The extension of short state statutes of limitations and the provision of omnibus coverage do not save the Act, in their view, since such provisions could equally well be included in a fairer plan which would assure greater compensation.

We disagree. We view the congressional *assurance* of a $560 million fund for recovery, accompanied by an express statutory commitment, to "take whatever action is deemed necessary and appropriate to protect the public from the consequences of" a nuclear accident, 42 U.S.C. § 2210(e) (1970 ed., Supp. V), to be a fair and reasonable substitute for the uncertain recovery of damages of this magnitude from a utility or component manufacturer, whose resources might well be exhausted at an early stage. The record in this case raises serious questions about the ability of a utility or component manufacturer to satisfy a judgment approaching $560 million—the amount guaranteed under the Price–Anderson Act. Nor are we persuaded that the mandatory waiver of defenses required by the Act is of no benefit to potential claimants. Since there has never been, to our knowledge, a case arising out of a nuclear incident like those covered by the Price–Anderson Act, any discussion of the standard of liability that state courts will apply is necessarily speculative. At the minimum, the statutorily mandated waiver of defenses establishes at the threshold the right of injured parties to compensation without proof of fault and eliminates the burden of delay and uncertainty which would follow from the need to litigate the question of liability after an accident. Further, even if strict liability were routinely applied, the common-law doctrine is subject to exceptions for acts of God or of third parties—two of the very factors which appellees emphasized in the District Court in the course of arguing that the risks of a nuclear accident are greater than generally admitted. All of these considerations belie the suggestion that the Act leaves the potential victims of a nuclear disaster in a more disadvantageous position than they would be in if left to their common law remedies—not known in modern times for either their speed or economy.

Appellees' remaining objections can be briefly treated. The claim-administration procedures under the Act provide that in the event of an accident with potential liability exceeding the $560 million ceiling, no more than 15% of the limit can be distributed pending court approval of a plan of distribution taking into account the need to assure compensation for "possible latent injury claims which may not be discovered until a later time." 42 U.S.C. § 2210(o)(3) (1970 ed., Supp. V). Although some delay might follow from compliance with this statutory procedure, we doubt that it would approach that resulting from routine litigation of the large number of claims caused by a catastrophic accident. Moreover, the statutory scheme insures the equitable distribution of benefits to all who suffer injury—both immediate and latent; under the common-law route, the proverbial race to the courthouse would instead determine who had "first crack" at the diminishing resources of the tortfeasor, and fairness could well be sacrificed in the process. The remaining contention that recovery is uncertain because of the aggregate rather than individualized nature of the liability ceiling is but a thinly disguised version of the contention that the $560 million figure is inadequate, which we have already rejected.

In the course of adjudicating a similar challenge to the Workmen's Compensation Act in *New York Central R. Co. v. White*, 243 U.S., at 201, the Court observed that the Due Process Clause of the Fourteenth Amendment was not violated simply because an injured party would not be able to recover as much under the Act as before its enactment. "[H]e is entitled to moderate compensation in all cases of injury, and has a certain and speedy remedy without the difficulty and expense of establishing negligence or proving the amount of the damages." The logic of *New York Central* would seem to apply with renewed force in the context of this challenge to the Price–Anderson Act. The Price–Anderson Act not only provides a reasonable, prompt, and equitable mechanism for compensating victims of a catastrophic nuclear incident, it also guarantees a level of net compensation generally exceeding that recoverable in private litigation. Moreover, the Act contains an explicit congressional commitment to take further action to aid victims of a nuclear accident in the event that the $560 million ceiling on liability is exceeded. This panoply of remedies and guarantees is at the least a reasonably just substitute for the common-law rights replaced by the Price–Anderson Act. Nothing more is required by the Due Process Clause.

Although the District Court also found the Price–Anderson Act to contravene the "equal protection provision that is included within the Due Process Clause of the Fifth Amendment," 431 F.Supp., at 224–225, appellees have not relied on this ground since the equal protection arguments largely track and duplicate those made in support of the due process claim. In any event, we conclude that there is no equal protection violation. The general rationality of the Price–Anderson Act liability limitations—particularly with reference to the important congressional purpose of encouraging private participation in the exploitation of nuclear energy—is ample justification for the difference in treatment between those injured in nuclear accidents and those whose injuries are derived from other causes. Speculation regarding other arrangements that might be used to spread the risk of liability in ways different from the Price–Anderson Act is, of course, not pertinent to the equal protection analysis. *See* Mourning v. Family Publications Service, Inc., 411 U.S. 356, 378 (1973).

Accordingly, the decision of the District Court is reversed, and the cases are remanded for proceedings consistent with this opinion.

Reversed and remanded.

NOTES AND QUESTIONS

1. *Duke Power* involves a form of subsidy—government liability limits—for nuclear power. Do subsidies for research and development differ in principle from the subsidy implicit in a liability limit? As the decision notes, the government has for many years encouraged the development of nuclear power. Should nuclear energy compete in the market place without subsidies? Should solar energy? Scientific research and development is not generally left to the private market place since science is a public good with distant and uncertain payoffs. *See* Chapter 4, Sec. II. B, *infra*. On the other hand, once science has given birth to a commercially feasible technology, the case for government subsidies weakens. Id. Is nuclear power now at that stage where the government should leave it on its own or are there national security considerations involved in assuring certain forms of energy supply?

2. The court upheld the liability limit in *Duke Power* in part because it found an analogy to traditional worker's compensation. Do you believe there are differences of constitutional significance between the two situations? Does the traditional judicial technique of looking decades back for precedent, even in cases involving a new technology, trouble you?

3. The availability of punitive damages under the Price–Anderson Act liability framework is discussed in *Silkwood v. Kerr–McGee Corp.*, 464 U.S. 238, 104 S.Ct. 615, 78 L.Ed.2d 443 (1984).

In 1988, Congress passed a 15–year extension of Price–Anderson that retained the liability limit, although that limit—now to be funded entirely by the nuclear industry through private insurance and direct payments in case of an accident—was raised to roughly $7 billion. *See* Price–Anderson Amendments Act of 1988, 42

U.S.C. § 2210, et seq. This Act authorized federal district courts to hear claims that might arise from a nuclear accident, a provision found constitutional in *In re TMI Litigation Cases Consolidated II*, 940 F.2d 832 (3d Cir. 1991), *cert. denied*, 503 U.S. 906, 112 S.Ct. 1262, 117 L.Ed.2d 491 (1992). In the case of an accident that causes damages exceeding the $7 billion limit, the Price–Anderson extension contains a number of promises: Congress "will ... provide full and prompt compensation," 42 U.S.C. § 2210(e)(2), apparently by passing on a compensation plan which "the President shall submit to Congress...." 42 U.S.C. § 2210(i)(2). The utility of these promises remains highly uncertain. President Reagan, in signing the extension, said of the last provision cited above: "Under the Constitution the President enjoys plenary and exclusive authority to determine whether and when he should propose legislation to Congress.... In order to avoid constitutional difficulties, I will construe [Sec. 2210(i)(2)] as recommendatory rather than obligatory." 1988 U.S.C.C.A.N. 1502–03. The Price–Anderson Act extension did create a Presidential Commission designed to make recommendations on how victims might be compensated if an accident leads to damages that exceed the liability limit, and that Commission has issued a report outlining a "judicial process containing administrative features designed to speed the resolution of cases." 1 REPORT TO THE CONGRESS FROM THE PRESIDENTIAL COMMISSION ON CATASTROPHIC NUCLEAR ACCIDENTS 5 (1990).

In 2004, Congress began again to debate the extension of Price–Anderson, although all civilian nuclear plants licensed before January 1, 2004 are covered indefinitely by the earlier versions of the Act. *Nuclear Energy Liability and Incentives: Hearing Before the Senate Energy and Natural Res. Comm.*, 107th Cong., 1st Sess. 144 (2001) (statement of John Bradburne, President and CEO, Fluor Fernald, Inc.). Price–Anderson has taken on renewed importance in light of the possibility of a terrorist attack on a nuclear power plant. *See* Jason Zorn, *Compensation in the Event of a Terrorist Attack on a Nuclear Power Plant: Will Victims Be Adequately Protected?*, 38 NEW ENG. L. REV. 1087 (2004).

Despite all of the controversy that surrounds it, Price–Anderson has at times served as a model for efforts to balance tort liability with the need for technology. The National Childhood Vaccine Injury Act of 1986, for example, uses a fund financed by an excise tax on each dose of vaccine administered to provide no-fault compensation for children injured by the vaccine. While not free of controversy of its own, this Act responded to a concern that vaccine manufacturing was becoming too risky, and it has provided compensation to a number of individuals. *See* Robert L. Rabin, *Some Thoughts on the Efficacy of a Mass Toxics Administrative Compensation Scheme*, 52 MD. L. REV. 951 (1993); Peter H. Schuck, *Mass Torts: An Institutional Evolutionist Perspective*, 80 CORNELL L. REV. 941 (1995). More recently, Price–Anderson has been discussed as a model for proposed legislation designed to spur the biotechnology industry, an industry that has arguably been hampered by tort liability fears. *See* Dan L. Burk & Barbara A. Boczar, *Biotechnology and Tort Liability: A Strategic Industry at Risk*, 55 U. PITT. L. REV. 791 (1994). From this perspective, is it useful to think of the 1957 passage of Price–Anderson as a legal "invention" on a par with the invention of the smoke detector or the microwave oven?

Report of the President's Commission on the Accident at Three Mile Island

2, 8–9, 12–14, 28 (October 1979).

At 4:00 a.m. on March 28, 1979, a serious accident occurred at the Three Mile Island 2 nuclear power plant near Middletown, Pennsylvania. The accident was initiated by mechanical malfunctions in the plant and made much worse by a combination of human errors in responding to it.... During the next 4 days, the extent and gravity of the accident was unclear to the managers of the plant, to federal and state officials, and to the general public. What is quite clear is that its impact, nationally and internationally, has raised serious concerns about the safety of nuclear power. This Commission was established in response to those concerns.

. . .

[The accident began when] [t]he pilot-operated relief valve (PORV) at the top of the pressurizer opened as expected when pressure rose but failed to close when pressure decreased, thereby creating an opening in the primary coolant system—a small-break loss-of-coolant accident (LOCA).[f] The PORV indicator light in the control room showed only that the signal had been sent to close the PORV rather than the fact that the PORV remained open. The operators, relying on the indicator light and believing that the PORV had closed, did not need other indications and were unaware of the PORV failure; the LOCA continued for over 2 hours. The TMI–2 emergency procedure for a stuck-open PORV did not state that unless the PORV block valve was closed, a LOCA would exist. Prior to TMI, the NRC had paid insufficient attention to LOCAs of this size and the probability of their occurrence in licensing reviews. Instead, the NRC focused most of its attention on large-break LOCAs.

The high pressure injection system (HPI)—a major design safety system—came on automatically. However, the operators were conditioned to maintain the specified water level in the pressurizer and were concerned that the plant was "going solid," that is, filled with water. Therefore, they cut back HPI from 1,000 gallons per minute to less than 100 gallons per minute. For extended periods on March 28, HPI was either not operating or operating at an insufficient rate. This led to much of the core being uncovered for extended periods on March 28 and resulted in severe damage to the core. If the HPI had not been throttled, core damage would have been prevented in spite of a stuck-open PORV.

. . .

Just how serious was the accident? Based on our investigation of the health effects of the accident, we conclude that in spite of serious damage to the plant, most of the radiation was contained and the actual release will have a negligible effect on the physical health of individuals. The major health effect of the accident was found to be mental stress.

The amount of radiation received by any one individual outside the plant was very low. However, even low levels of radiation may result in the later development of cancer, genetic defects, or birth defects among children who are exposed in the womb. Since there is no direct way of measuring the danger of low-level radiation to health, the degree of danger must be estimated indirectly. Different scientists make different assumptions about how this estimate should be made and, therefore, estimates

f. [Eds.—Loss-of-coolant accident (LOCA) is an accident involving a broken pipe, stuck-open valve, or other leak in the reactor coolant system that results in a loss of the water cooling the reactor core.]

vary. Fortunately, in this case the radiation doses were so low that we conclude that the overall health effects will be minimal. There will either be no case of cancer or the number of cases will be so small that it will never be possible to detect them. The same conclusion applies to the other possible health effects. The reasons for these conclusions are as follows.

An example of a projection derived for the total number of radiation-induced cancers among the population affected by the accident at TMI was 0.7. This number is an estimate of an average, such as the one that appears in the statement: "The average American family has 2.3 children."

In the case of TMI, what it really means is that each of some 2 million individuals living within 50 miles has a miniscule additional chance of dying of cancer, and when all of these minute probabilities are added up, they total 0.7. In such a situation, a mathematical law known as a Poisson distribution (named after a famous French mathematician) applies. If the estimated average is 0.7, then the actual probabilities for cancer deaths due to the accident work out as follows: There is a roughly 50 percent chance that there will be no additional cancer deaths, a 35 percent chance that one individual will die of cancer, a 12 percent chance that 2 people will die of cancer, and it is practically certain that there will not be as many as five cancer deaths.

Similar probabilities can be calculated for our various estimates. All of them have in common the following: It is entirely possible that not a single extra cancer death will result. And for all our estimates, it is practically certain that the additional number of cancer deaths will be less than 10.

Since a cancer caused by nuclear radiation is no different from any other cancer, additional cancers can only be determined statistically. We know from statistics on cancer deaths that among the more than 2 million people living within 50 miles of TMI, eventually some 325,000 people will die of cancer, for reasons having nothing to do with the nuclear power plant. Again, this number is only an estimate, and the actual figure could be as much as 1,000 higher or 1,000 lower. Therefore, there is no conceivable statistical method by which fewer than 10 additional deaths would ever be detected. Therefore, the accident may result in no additional cancer deaths or, if there were any, they would be so few that they could not be detected.

We found that the mental stress to which those living within the vicinity of Three Mile Island were subjected was quite severe. There were several factors that contributed to this stress. Throughout the first week of the accident, there was extensive speculation of just how serious the accident might turn out to be. At various times, senior officials of the NRC and the state government were considering the possibility of a major evacuation. There were a number of advisories recommending steps short of a full evacuation. Some significant fraction of the population in the immediate vicinity voluntarily left the region. NRC officials contributed to the raising of anxiety in the period from Friday to Sunday (March 30–April 1). On Friday, a mistaken interpretation of the release of a burst of radiation led some NRC officials to recommend immediate evacuation. And on Friday Governor Thornburgh advised pregnant women and preschool aged children within 5 miles of TMI to leave the area. On Saturday and

Sunday, other NRC officials mistakenly believed that there was an imminent danger of an explosion of a hydrogen bubble within the reactor vessel, and evacuation was again a major subject of discussion.

We conclude that the most serious health effect of the accident was severe mental stress, which was short-lived. The highest levels of distress were found among those living within 5 miles of TMI and in families with preschool children.

There was very extensive damage to the plant. While the reactor itself has been brought to a "cold shutdown," there are vast amounts of radioactive material trapped within the containment and auxiliary buildings. The utility is therefore faced with a massive cleanup process that carries its own potential dangers to public health. The ongoing cleanup operation at TMI demonstrates that the plant was inadequately designed to cope with the cleanup of a damaged plant. The direct financial cost of the accident is enormous. Our best estimate puts it in a range of $1 to $2 billion, even if TMI–2 can be put back into operation. (The largest portion of this is for replacement power estimated for the next few years.) And since it may not be possible to put it back into operation, the cost could even be much larger.

The accident raised concerns all over the world and led to a lowering of public confidence in the nuclear industry and in the NRC.

From the beginning, we felt it important to determine not only how serious the actual impact of the accident was on public health, but whether we came close to a catastrophic accident in which a large number of people would have died. Issues that had to be examined were whether a chemical (hydrogen) or steam explosion could have ruptured the reactor vessel and containment building, and whether extremely hot molten fuel could have caused severe damage to the containment. The danger was never—and could *not* have been—that of a *nuclear* explosion (bomb).

We have made a conscientious effort to get an answer to this difficult question. Since the accident was due to a complex combination of minor equipment failures and major inappropriate human actions, we have asked the question: "What if one more thing had gone wrong?"

We explored each of several different scenarios representing a change in the sequence of events that actually took place. The greatest concern during the accident was that significant amounts of radioactive material (especially radioactive iodine) trapped within the plant might be released. Therefore, in each case, we asked whether the amount released would have been smaller or greater, and whether large amounts could have been released.

Some of these scenarios lead to a more favorable outcome than what actually happened. Several other scenarios lead to increases in the amount of radioactive iodine released, but still at levels that would not have presented a danger to public health. But we have also explored two or three scenarios whose precise consequences are much more difficult to calculate. They lead to more severe damage to the core, with additional melting of fuel in the hottest regions. These consequences are, surprisingly, independent of the age of the fuel.

Because of the uncertain physical condition of the fuel, cladding, and core, we have explored certain special and severe conditions that would, unequivocally, lead to a fuel-melting accident. In this sequence of events fuel melts, falls to the bottom of the vessel, melts through the steel reactor vessel, and finally, some fuel reaches the floor of the containment building below the reactor vessel where there is enough water to cover the molten fuel and remove some of the decay heat. To contain such an accident, it is necessary to continue removing decay heat for a period of many months.

At this stage we approach the limits of our engineering knowledge of the interactions of molten fuel, concrete, steel, and water, and even the best available calculations have a degree of uncertainty associated with them. Our calculations show that even if a meltdown occurred, there is a high probability that the containment building and the hard rock on which the TMI-2 containment building is built would have been able to prevent the escape of a large amount of radioactivity. These results derive from very careful calculations, which hold only insofar as our assumptions are valid. We cannot be absolutely certain of these results. . . .

NOTES AND QUESTIONS

1.   In assessing the costs and benefits of nuclear energy, how would you weigh the probability of cancer deaths found by the President's Commission on Three Mile Island? How did the Commission determine that mental stress was a greater health effect of the accident than the potential deaths from cancer? Almost three years after the Commission's report, a federal court held that the National Environmental Protection Act required that environmental impact statements prepared in connection with the resumption of operations of a reactor at Three Mile Island must include an analysis of the psychological health of the residents living near the reactor. *See* People Against Nuclear Energy v. United States Nuclear Regulatory Comm'n, 678 F.2d 222 (D.C. Cir. 1982). The Supreme Court reversed, stating that, "NEPA does not require the agency to assess *every* impact or effect of its proposed action, but only the impact or effect on the environment." 460 U.S. 766, 772, 103 S.Ct. 1556, 75 L.Ed.2d 534 (1983). Should Congress amend NEPA to require agencies to consider psychological impacts such as those involved at Three Mile Island? *See also* Robert A. Bohrer, *Fear and Trembling in the Twentieth Century: Technological Risk, Uncertainty and Emotional Distress*, 1984 WIS. L. REV. 83 (1984).

2.   Given the relatively small direct physical impact of the accident at Three Mile Island, what explains the enormous level of public concern caused by the accident? Is it the fear that a much larger number of deaths was possible? Is it a subconscious association of civilian nuclear power with the bomb? Does it reflect a broader concern with modern science generally?

3.   The accident at the Soviet reactor at Chernobyl in April of 1986 caused 31 deaths, as well as potential health effects for thousands. Nonetheless, as with Three Mile Island, the most dramatic impact of the accident may have been psychological. It appeared, for example, that the immediate international concern was sharper for the Chernobyl accident than it had been for the chemical plant tragedy at Bhopal, India that killed 2,200 while posing long-term health threats for many more. Some of the concern caused by the Chernobyl accident may have been increased by widely-varying estimates of the number killed as Soviet officials remained silent and westerners speculated in the early days after the accident took place. *See, e.g.*, Eliot Marshall, *Reactor Explodes Amid Soviet Silence*, 232 SCI. 814 (1986).

It was prior to Chernobyl, but with feelings still running high about the Three Mile Island accident, that the Metropolitan Edison Co. sought permission to restart the undamaged reactor No. 1 at Three Mile Island. The ensuing dispute led to the following decision.

In re Three Mile Island Alert, Inc., et al.

United States Court of Appeals for the Third Circuit, 1985.
771 F.2d 720, *cert. denied* 475 U.S. 1082, 106 S.Ct. 1460, 89 L.Ed.2d 717.

■ STAPLETON, J.

Three Mile Island Nuclear Station has two units, TMI–1 and TMI–2. On March 28, 1979, an accident severely damaged TMI–2. Prior to the accident, TMI–1 had been shut down for normal refueling and maintenance. On July 2, 1979, the Nuclear Regulatory Commission ("NRC") issued an immediately effective order requiring that TMI–1 remain shut down until the Commission, after a public hearing, determined that there was reasonable assurance that the licensee could restart and operate the unit without endangering the health and safety of the public. 44 Fed.Reg. 40,461 (July 10, 1979). On August 9, 1979, the NRC issued a further order specifying the procedural and substantive format for the hearing. *Metropolitan Edison Co.* (Three Mile Island Nuclear Station, Unit No. 1), CLI–79–8, 10 NRC 141 (1979).

The petitioners in this review proceeding are the Commonwealth of Pennsylvania (the "Commonwealth"), Three Mile Island Alert, Inc. ("TMIA"), the Union of Concerned Scientists ("UCS"), and Norman and Marjorie Aamodt (the "Aamodts"). These petitioners intervened before the Commission and participated actively and effectively in the extensive hearings conducted pursuant to the August 9, 1979 order. While the issues addressed in these hearings remained under advisement at various levels of the administrative process, several motions were filed asking that the hearing record be reopened. While the record was reopened to receive some additional evidence, the Commission denied motions of these petitioners.

On May 29, 1985, the Commission decided that TMI–1 could be safely restarted under certain stipulated conditions and ordered that the 1979 immediately effective suspension of the TMI–1 operating license be lifted. Petitioners insist that the Commission could not legally take this action without holding an adjudicatory hearing on the issues raised in their motions to reopen the administrative record. Some of the petitioners also contend that the decision reflected in the Commission's May 29th Order is arbitrary and capricious. We conclude that the May 29th Order is not arbitrary, capricious, or contrary to law and that, accordingly, the petitions for review should be denied. . . .

The comprehensiveness of the NRC proceeding can be measured in part by the enormity of its record. The administrative record currently consists of more than 100,000 pages, including approximately 33,000 transcribed pages of testimony and argument and thousands of additional pages of exhibits and written testimony. The Licensing and Appeal Boards and the Commission have published opinions filling 1,500 pages in the NRC's official reports. The Commission itself has heard oral presentations from the parties on five different occasions, has held a meeting in Harrisburg, Pennsylvania, to hear from members of the public, and has issued more than 26 substantive orders.

At the hearings themselves, all parties had the opportunity to cross-examine witnesses and offer rebuttal evidence. The Licensing Board conducted an extensive inquiry regarding the management competence issues. . . .

With respect to petitioners' procedural arguments, this Court has noted that the NRC regulatory scheme is "virtually unique in the degree to which broad responsibility is reposed in the administering agency, free of close prescription in its charter as to how it shall proceed in achieving the statutory objectives." Westinghouse Electric Corp. v. Nuclear Regulatory Commission, 598 F.2d 759, 771 (3d Cir. 1979), *quoting* Siegel v. Atomic Energy Commission, 400 F.2d 778, 783 (D.C. Cir. 1968). *See also* San Luis Obispo Mothers for Peace v. Nuclear Regulatory Commission, 751 F.2d 1287, 1294 (D.C. Cir. 1984); Carstens v. Nuclear Regulatory Commission, 742 F.2d 1546, 1551 (D.C. Cir. 1984). A narrow standard is particularly appropriate in reviewing petitioners' central challenge, an attack on the Commission's refusal to reopen the record of the Restart Proceedings to hear further evidence on certain issues. As the United States Court of Appeals for the District of Columbia recently held, "[w]here as here the agency has taken final action on a matter that is peculiarly within its realm of expertise, we will not require the agency to reopen its proceedings except upon a clear showing of abuse of discretion or of extraordinary circumstances." *San Luis Obispo, supra*, at 1317–18, *quoting* Mobil Oil Corp. v. Interstate Commerce Commission, 685 F.2d 624, 632 (D.C. Cir. 1982).

With regard to the claim raised by petitioners Aamodts that the TMI–2 accident caused greater amounts of radiation to be released than the NRC believes, deference must be accorded to the Commission's expertise. "When examining this kind of scientific determination, as opposed to simple findings of fact, a reviewing court must generally be at its most deferential." Baltimore Gas & Electric Co. v. Natural Resources Defense Council, Inc., 462 U.S. 87, 103 (1983).

Our "limited, albeit important, task" is to review "agency action to determine whether the agency conformed with controlling statutes." *Id.* at 97. In undertaking this task, we must be mindful both of the Congressional policy choice favoring the development of nuclear power and of the Congressional mandate that the Commission be charged with the responsibility of protecting the public health and safety while overseeing the activities of the nuclear power industry. Our words in *Westinghouse Electric Corp. v. Nuclear Regulatory Commission* are equally appropriate here:

> Congress has delegated authority in the delicate area of nuclear energy to a number of agencies, among them the NRC. The NRC is charged with the responsibility of protecting the common defense and security as well as the public health and safety, while overseeing the licensing of nuclear facilities. Some of the decisions it makes to further its statutory mandate may be unpopular in the nuclear industry, among environmentalists, or with other groups of citizens. But Congress has decreed that the agency be independent from outside control, and it would subvert this design were we to

invalidate the challenged NRC action when it appears to be consonant with statutory dictates and not an unreasonable exercise of its discretion.

Westinghouse Electric Corp., supra, 598 F.2d at 779. . . .

As we have noted, the parties extensively litigated the management competence issues before the Licensing Board closed the hearing record and issued its August 27, 1981 decision favorable to the licensee. L–P–81–32, 14 NRC 381 (1981). After the record closed, however, there were several potentially significant developments. The most important of these was Met Ed's guilty plea to federal criminal charges of leak rate falsification at TMI–2. Petitioners moved to reopen the record on management competence, and the Appeal Board granted their motions on four issues. ALA— 738, 18 NRC 177 (1983); ALA—772, 19 NRC 1193 (1984). After receiving briefs from the parties, the Commission decided, on February 25, 1985, that the hearing record need not be reopened prior to restart: CLI–85–2, 21 NRC 282 (1985). Petitioners insist that the Commission's refusal to hold hearings on post-record developments renders the May 29, 1985 decision arbitrary and capricious.

In refusing to reopen the record, the Commission engaged in its traditional tripartite inquiry for determining if new evidence is of sufficient importance to outweigh the general policy against permitting reopenings. The Commission asked:

> (1) Is the motion timely; (2) does it address significant safety . . . issues; and (3) might a different result have been reached had the newly proffered material been considered initially.

21 NRC at 285, n. 3. This test has been judicially sanctioned, San Luis Obispo Mothers for Peace v. N.R.C., 751 F.2d 1287, 1316–18 (D.C. Cir. 1984). . . .

By far the most important of the reopening issues is whether the record on management competence should be reopened for hearings on the pre-accident falsification of leak rate data by TMI–2 operators in violation of NRC regulations. Harold Hartman, a TMI–2 control room operator prior to the accident, alleged that plant operators, with the knowledge of shift supervisors, had falsified tests that measured whether primary system leakage surpassed technical specifications in the TMI–2 license. In April, 1980 the NRC referred the matter to the Department of Justice for criminal investigation. This investigation culminated in the February 28, 1984 guilty plea of Met Ed.

Although we recognize the importance of the issue, we are unable to say that the Commission acted arbitrarily or capriciously in refusing to reopen the record on the leak rate tests. It is undisputable that leak rate falsification had been a serious problem at TMI–2 prior to the accident and further investigation of that problem was clearly called for. The issue was whether to pursue that potentially lengthy process in a new proceeding or whether to reopen the proceeding that had already resulted in TMI–1 being closed down for five and a half years. If the leak rate issue was safety significant to the current operation of TMI–1, the additional delay and attendant expense would, of course, be justified. If that issue was not safety significant to the current operation of TMI–1, further delay and expense would be difficult to justify. In this context, the Commission framed the issues for decision as follows:

> To determine whether the Hartman allegations still raise a significant safety issue, the Commission must first consider whether the personnel likely responsible for the falsifications under Met Ed are now in responsible management positions at GPU Nuclear or directly associated with the operation of TMI–1. If the personnel are still the same, then there is merit to the argument that there has been a change only in name, not in substance, and the integrity concerns raised by the Hartman allegations remain significant. However, if the persons likely responsible for or involved in the TMI–2 leak rate falsifications are not assigned to responsible management or operational positions at TMI–1, then the Hartman allegations no longer raise concerns about the integrity of those who will operate TMI–1. In that event, however, the Commission further should consider whether the new personnel, organizational structure, and procedures provide reasonable assurance that similar procedural violations will not recur.

21 NRC at 297.

The Commission concluded that no one assigned to a responsible management or operational position at TMI–1 was responsible in any way for leak rate falsification at TMI–2 and that new personnel, organizational structure and procedures provided reasonable assurance that similar violations would not recur.

The Commission, as a result of the lengthy proceedings before it and the investigation of its staff, was intimately familiar with the events leading up to the accident at TMI–2, with the operating and managerial personnel of the licensee prior to the accident and with the operating and managerial personnel of the licensee prepared to restart TMI–1. The Commission was also intimately familiar with the extensive changes in everything from hardware to training which had been effected at TMI–1 after the accident and with the 153 conditions that had already been imposed. In addition, the Commission was aware that the investigation which had uncovered the leak rate falsification problem had indicated that current GPUN management personnel were unaware of that activity and that current operating and supervisory personnel at TMI–1, with one possible exception, had had no connection with pre-accident TMI–2. Finally, the Commission realized that it could assure a continuing absence of taint in the operating personnel at TMI–1 simply by imposing an additional condition, and it did so. Under these circumstances, we conclude that the Commission could reasonably find, as it did, that altered conditions rendered the fact of TMI–2 leak rate falsifications no longer safety significant to TMI–1's operation.

Petitioners' argument that the Commission acted arbitrarily or capriciously necessarily focuses on the three individuals who will have some responsibility with respect to TMI–1 who also had some pre-accident involvement with TMI–2: Michael Ross, William Kuhns, and Herman Dieckamp. The Commission recognized this fact and set forth the reasons it believed the continued presence of these men did not detract from the assurance provided by the changed conditions at TMI–1.

Michael Ross, as current Manager of Operations at TMI–1, is the only one of the three to hold a safety significant "operational position" at the plant. 21 NRC at 298. Because of the position he would hold, as earlier noted, Ross was one of the focal points of the hearings and extensive findings were made about his competence, including his integrity in the context of alleged operator cheating on tests. Nevertheless, in response to petitioners' motion to reopen, the OI, at the Commission's direction, conducted an investigation to determine whether Ross had in any way participated in or condoned leak rate manipulation. As the Commission noted, the "evidence developed by OI showed that Ross' role at TMI–2 was minimal, that during the period falsifications took place he was present at TMI–2 only the minimum time necessary to maintain his Unit 2 license, and that he was not involved in the falsifications." 21 NRC at 298–9. The Commission, accordingly, determined that Ross posed no risk to the safe operation of TMI–1. The only additional information which petitioners advance in support of their position is that Ross has a reputation for being a "stickler for details." Petitioners infer from this that, despite his minimal contact with TMI–2, Ross must have known that leak rate manipulation was going on there. While this is perhaps a permissible inference, it is not a necessary one, particularly in light of the other information about Ross available to the Commission. Accordingly, we are unable to find that the Commission acted arbitrarily in concluding that the continued presence of Ross at TMI–1 did not require the Commission to reopen the record on TMI–2 leak rate falsifications.

The Commission considered as well the safety significance of the continued presence of Messrs. Kuhns and Dieckamp at GPU. Kuhns has been Chairman of GPU during all relevant periods. Dieckamp remains a member of the Board of GPUN, as well as President, Chief Operating Officer, and a Director of GPU. The Commission found it highly unlikely that corporate officers of their rank would have been aware of the details of normal plant operation such as leak rate testing, and also concluded that Kuhns and Dieckamp were not responsible for the attitude at TMI–2 that permitted the falsifications to occur. 21 NRC at 301. The Commission also relied on the exculpatory statement offered by the United States Attorney in connection with the sentencing hearing of Met Ed:

> [T]he evidence presented to the Grand Jury and developed by the United States Attorney does not indicate that any of the following persons participated in, directed, condoned or was aware of the acts or omissions that are the subject of this indictment. And they are Williams G. Kuhns, Herman M. Dieckamp....

Transcript of Proceedings, Change of Plea and Sentencing, United States v. Metropolitan Edison Co., Crim. No. 83–00188, at 16 (M.D.Pa. Feb. 28–29, 1984). We believe the Commission could reasonably rely on this statement in determining that the presence of Kuhns and Dieckamp at TMI–2 did not make the leak rate falsifications at TMI–2 safety significant to TMI–1 operations.

In summary, the Commission made a policy decision between holding hearings on the TMI–2 pre-accident, leak rate manipulation problem in the TMI–1 restart proceeding or in a separate proceeding. It chose the latter course because it concluded that changed personnel and altered procedures at TMI–1 rendered the pre-accident experience at TMI–2 irrelevant to an assessment of the safety of TMI–1 operations. In making this choice, the Commission analyzed the relevant issues relying on information from reliable sources, reasoned to a logical conclusion, and articulated the reasons for its decision. As a reviewing court, we can ask nothing more of the Commission. . . .

■ ADAMS, J., dissenting.

The extent of public concern surrounding the Three Mile Island nuclear plant is matched only by the gravity of the accident that occurred there on March 28, 1979, an accident widely acknowledged as the worst in the history of commercial nuclear power in the United States. Deep anxiety has been expressed by the Pennsylvania residents who live in the reactor's shadow, as well as by citizens throughout the nation. It is in this setting that we are asked to determine whether the Nuclear Regulatory Commission ("Commission" or "NRC") properly refused to hold further hearings on issues of management integrity arising out of actions taken by the licensee prior to, during, and after the accident. Because I believe that in a case of this consequence full public disclosure of serious charges of management misconduct is required, I respectfully dissent.

The primary ground for my disagreement with the majority is that the Commission has failed to provide a statutorily mandated hearing on charges that operators at TMI–2, with full knowledge and authorization of supervisory personnel, systematically falsified leak rate data in order to avoid shutting down the facility. All parties to the original NRC hearings were aware of the leak rate falsification allegations, and recognized their materiality to the issue of management integrity, a central subject of the hearings. The NRC Staff, however, discouraged the parties from pursuing the matter because of a pending criminal investigation. In effect, hearings on this issue were postponed by the Licensing Board, which issued a favorable determination on management integrity, but reserved judgment on the leak rate falsification issue. The criminal investigation eventually led to an indictment and conviction of Metropolitan Edison, the licensee, for manipulating leak rate data in violation of safety regulations. Despite this criminal conviction, the Commission determined that leak rate falsification no longer needed to be addressed in public hearings. The Commission thus transformed a postponement into a cancellation, and deprived petitioners of their statutory right to a public hearing on the most serious charges of licensee misconduct to emerge since the accident. *See* 42 U.S.C. § 2239(a) (1982) (hereinafter § 189(a)). . . .

As the majority notes, the Commission's treatment of allegations of pre-accident leak rate falsification at TMI–2 constitutes "by far the most important" of the issues to be addressed on appeal. Leak rate tests measure leakage from the reactor coolant system. They are to be conducted every 72 hours, and where they indicate leakage in excess of one gallon per minute (gpm), the reactor must be placed on "Hot Standby" for six hours and "Cold Shutdown" for the next thirty hours. Harold Hartman, a control room operator at TMI–2, alleged that for several months prior to the March 1979 TMI–2 accident it was difficult to obtain leak rate data under the one gpm threshold, yet the facility was never put on standby or shutdown. Hartman explained that instead he and other control room operators, with the knowledge of supervising management, customarily repeated the leakage tests until they obtained a good rate (by covertly adding water or hydrogen to the testing system) and threw out bad test results. *See generally* ALA—738, 18 NRC 177, 185–186 (1983).

The widespread nature of leak rate falsification was brought to light by Hartman in a May 1979 interview with the NRC Staff and in a deposition several months later. It was not until Hartman made his allegations publicly, however, in a television program in March 1980, that the NRC and the licensee began to investigate his charges. The NRC Staff halted its investigation after just one month, when the Department of Justice (DOJ) undertook its own investigation. The DOJ inquiry led to a criminal indictment resolved by a plea agreement; Metropolitan Edison, the licensee, was convicted of manipulation of leak data in violation of safety regulations. At the plea hearing, the United States Attorney outlined the evidence he would have introduced at trial. He stated that the falsification had been carried out with the express knowledge of supervisory personnel; that three supervisors told an operator who showed them a test result revealing excess leakage that "We do not want to see this shit"; and that even after an NRC inspector discovered this practice on October 18, 1978, and warned the licensee, the licensee made no changes in its faulty practice. After the warning, the licensee failed to make required reports to the NRC, and even sent false memoranda to the NRC investigators explaining proper procedures, which were purportedly, but not actually, provided to operators....

Applying the reopening standard, the Commission determined that in view of changes in the management structure of the operating company, a statement by the United States Attorney, and its own internal investigation of Michael Ross, there was no need to hold hearings because those associated with leak rate falsification were no longer in relevant positions of operation or authority at TMI–1....

I would hold that the Commission abused its discretion in refusing to reopen the record on that issue. The extra-record evidence upon which the Commission relied in deciding that a hearing was not required is insufficient in light of the importance of the matter at hand. As the majority observes, Maj. Opinion at 735–736, the Commission reached its decision in reliance on a statement by the United States Attorney at the sentencing hearing, which purportedly exculpated William G. Kuhns, Chairman of the Board of GPU and Herman M. Dieckamp, GPU President. This statement, however, is negative rather than affirmative. The U.S. Attorney stated only that the evidence "does not indicate" that certain persons *were* involved; he did not declare that the evidence indicated that the listed persons were in fact *not* involved. In addition, neither the Court nor the Commission is privy to the basis for the statement, because the grand jury investigation is secret. Perhaps most importantly, the statement was made as part of a guilty plea hearing, and as such may be the compromised result of a plea bargain agreement. It is curious that at the same time that the corporation pleaded guilty, presumably through a decision of its Board of Directors, the United States Attorney issued a statement purportedly exculpating all directors and officers of the defendant's successor, GPU Nuclear Corporation, as well as all directors of the defendant corporation itself, Metropolitan Edison. Given these inconsistencies, and the lack of any evidentiary explanation to support the United States Attorney's conclusory statement, I believe the Commission abused its discretion in relying upon that statement.

The Commission similarly abused its discretion in rejecting without a hearing all charges that Michael Ross, Manager of Operations at TMI–1, may have been implicated in the TMI–2 leak rate falsification. The Commission presumed that *all* TMI–2 operators and supervisors were aware of the falsification, CLI–85–2, 21 NRC at 299 n. 23, but at the same time dismissed as mere speculation the claim that Ross, who attended monthly TMI–2 supervisor's meetings, may also have known. *Id.* at 299, 313. Ross was cross-licensed at TMI–2, exchanged duties with the TMI–2 Manager of Operations, and apparently was in daily contact with the TMI–2 Manager. *Id.* at 295. Leak rate falsification occurred on a daily basis from January 1979 to March 1979, and for a significant period prior to 1979. Several operators testified that Ross, who was a stickler for detail, must have known about the falsification. Investigative Interview of Robert William Flannagan, Jr., TMIA App. p. 843; Investigative Interview of Tex Howard Acker, TMIA App. p. 847, 850; Investigative Interview of Joseph J. Chastwyk, TMIA App. pp. 876–77. Moreover, precisely the same methods of falsification—adding hydrogen and discarding test results—were used, though less frequently, at TMI–1. In light of this evidence, I believe the Commission abused its discretion in refusing to allow Ross to be questioned on this matter in a public hearing. . . .

NOTES AND QUESTIONS

1.   The Supreme Court declined to review the Third Circuit decision and the TMI–1 reactor went back into service. *In re* Three Mile Island Alert, Inc., 771 F.2d 720 (3d Cir. 1985), *cert. denied*, 475 U.S. 1082, 106 S.Ct. 1460, 89 L.Ed.2d 717 (1986).

2.   The respective responses by the United States and Soviet governments to Three Mile Island and Chernobyl present a dramatic contrast. As noted in the case above, a federal grand jury indictment on charges that safety-test results had been falsified before the accident led to a guilty plea by Metropolitan Edison. Under the plea, Met Ed paid a fine of $45,000 and provided $1 million to establish an emergency planning fund for the Three Mile Island area. After Chernobyl a three week trial was held. A Soviet judge, noting "an atmosphere of lack of control and lack of responsibility at the plant," sentenced the power plant's director, top engineer, and engineer's deputy to 10 years each in a labor camp. *Ten Years in Stir for Chernobyl's Scapegoats*, NEWSWEEK, Aug. 10, 1987, at 47.

B.   THE DECLINE OF NUCLEAR ENERGY AND THE PROSPECTS FOR REBIRTH

Kansas Gas and Electric Co. v. State Corporation Commission

Supreme Court of Kansas, 1986.
239 Kan. 483, 720 P.2d 1063, *appeal dismissed*, 481 U.S. 1044, 107 S.Ct. 2171, 95 L.Ed.2d 829.

■ PRAGER, J.

This is a consolidation of three appeals by three electrical utilities from orders of the State Corporation Commission (KCC) granting in part and denying in part the requests of the utilities for rate increases due to the commercial operations of the Wolf Creek Generating Station (Wolf Creek) near Burlington, Kansas. The three utilities are Kansas Gas and Electric Company (KGE), Kansas City Power and Light Company (KCPL), and Kansas Electric Power Cooperative, Inc. (KEPCo). The KCC is the appellee. There are also a number of intervenors, including the Kansas Attorney General and various individuals and organizations representing interested citizens and the public.

Historical Background

The legal issues presented in this case are not peculiar to Kansas but are the natural result of the national controversy over the construction of nuclear power plants which has developed over the past thirty years. On December 8, 1953, in his address to the United Nations, President Dwight D. Eisenhower announced his "Atoms for Peace" program. Among other subjects, he spoke of using the atom "to serve the peaceful pursuits of mankind." He spoke of providing abundant electrical energy in the power-starved areas of the world and envisioned the cooperation of the nations of the world to serve the needs rather than the fears of mankind. The possibility that nuclear energy could be used to improve rather than to destroy the world excited most Americans. Today, three decades later, the future of nuclear power is uncertain and the national debate has not been resolved.

In 1953, the Atomic Energy Commission, an agency created by Congress to supervise atomic energy and its development, allocated funds for a demonstration nuclear plant at Shippingport, Pennsylvania. The reactor used in that plant was very small and, by modern standards, its output of electricity was very modest. During the 1960s, several private companies developed nuclear reactors and marketed them to utilities at prices competitive with conventional generators. Between 1965 and 1975, the nuclear industry was perhaps the fastest growing major industry in the United States.

During the 1960s, KGE used natural gas to generate its electricity. Some time during the late 1960s, KGE was notified by its natural gas supplier that the utility's access to natural gas eventually would end. At that time, KGE was experiencing a growth in demand for electricity of approximately seven percent per year. KCPL, an electrical utility in northeast Kansas, was experiencing the same growth in demand. Both utilities, like many others around the country, faced the decision of whether to generate electricity from coal or from natural gas or from nuclear power. Studies were commissioned which suggested that nuclear power rather than coal or natural gas was the most cost efficient and environmentally sound alternative for expansion of electrical capacity. As a result, KGE and KCPL, and later KEPCo, decided to take the nuclear route. KGE and KCPL each took 47% shares in the project, and KEPCo took a 6% share.

In January of 1977, the Nuclear Regulatory Commission (NRC), the successor to the Atomic Energy Commission, issued a temporary work authorization permit for the construction of a nuclear facility on Wolf Creek in Coffey County. In May of 1977, major construction work began. It was estimated in February of 1973 that the cost of constructing the nuclear plant at Wolf Creek would be in the neighborhood of $525,000,000. The ultimate cost of construction amounted to about $3,000,000,000, almost a six-fold increase.

It is clear that three unforeseen events occurred during the mid–1970s which affected the relative attractiveness of the nuclear option and brought about a tremendous increase in the cost of construction. After several nuclear power plants were constructed, a series of accidents occurred which intensified the debate over the use of nuclear energy. At the Three Mile Island accident in March 1979, a mechanical malfunction, compounded with human errors, brought the Three Mile Island nuclear reactor close to a meltdown. This required the utilities to increase their efforts to improve plant safety. New safety equipment, which the NRC required, added millions of dollars to the costs of nuclear plant construction at Wolf Creek and elsewhere.

Another important factor was the change in "energy economics" that occurred during the 1970s. When OPEC in 1973–74 raised the price of oil, making nuclear power even more attractive, orders for nuclear reactors increased. A second oil shock occurred in 1979 when, following the overthrow of the Shah of Iran, the price of oil reached $40 per barrel. The American people responded to the oil crisis and an unexpected and dramatic decline in the demand for oil followed. The demand for energy also diminished. Electrical utilities, which had already implemented plans to substantially increase their supply of electricity, now discovered that the supply greatly exceeded the demand for electricity. Some utilities responded to this new economic environment by canceling plans for additional generating facilities including scheduled nuclear plants, some of which were then under construction.

A third unforeseen development which the utilities faced in the construction of nuclear plants was the increased inflation of the 1970s, the effect of which was to increase substantially the cost of building a nuclear plant. By adding millions to interest costs, cost overruns strained the cash flow positions of some utilities and thus impeded the ability of some utilities to raise capital to complete these projects. All of these unforeseen changes affected the Wolf Creek project. The project was delayed both by the post-Three Mile Island safety standards and construction problems which developed at the site. Although the original plans called for the Wolf Creek plant to start producing electricity in April 1981, production did not commence until September 1985. There is an excellent discussion of this historical background in an article by Professor Robert H. Jerry, II, entitled *Introduction to Wolf Creek Symposium,* 33 KAN. L. REV. 419 (1985).

As the time for commencement of operations at the Wolf Creek plant approached, the three utilities involved in this case filed petitions with the KCC requesting the granting of appropriate electrical rates for the electricity to be produced. At this same time, regulatory agencies in other states were faced with the same or similar problems. In some states, state regulatory agencies had to determine whether the costs of an abandoned nuclear plant should be included in an electrical utility's rate base. Where a nuclear plant had been completed and placed in operation, the state regulatory agency had the problem of determining whether the inflated construction costs of a nuclear facility had to be included in the rate base in a manner which would financially hurt the ratepayers, the consumers, and the general public. It is this same basic problem which was faced by the KCC in the case now before us.

. . .

The overall effect of the KCC orders may be summarized as follows:

(1) The utilities received virtually all they requested as expenses to operate and maintain the plant and to decommission it at the end of its life.

(2) The KCC determined that a total of $183 million, or about 10% of the costs of construction of the Wolf Creek plant, was inefficiently and imprudently incurred. The utilities were denied both a recovery of and a return on that portion of the costs of the construction.

(3) The KCC allowed all of the remaining 90% of the Wolf Creek construction costs to be recovered through annual depreciation expenses over the expected life of the plant.

. . .

At the hearing before the KCC, a great deal of expert testimony was presented by the utilities showing that great efficiency and prudence was used by the contractor in the construction of the Wolf Creek plant. To the contrary, the staff of the KCC presented other competent experts who testified that a substantial portion of the construction costs was inefficiently and imprudently incurred. The findings of the KCC set forth this testimony in great detail. It would serve no useful purpose to restate the testimony of the various expert witnesses who testified on behalf of the parties. As noted heretofore, the KCC disallowed a total of approximately $183,000,000 or about 10% of the total cost of construction as costs which were imprudently incurred.

The KCC's disallowance for imprudent construction costs consisted of three distinct quantifications:

(1) $37,961,400 of direct and associated indirect costs attributable to disallowed man-hour overruns;

(2) $244,561,400 of indirect and overhead costs attributable to disallowed schedule delays; and

(3) $450,000 of the fees paid to the primary contractor, Daniel International Corporation, for work which was not performed and which was performed by other contractors.

There is substantial, competent evidence in the record to support the disallowances in each of these categories. There was evidence from which the KCC could reasonably find that KGE and KCPL, as owners of the plant, were imprudent and inefficient in the manner in which they supervised the construction of the plant. We recognize, of course, that there was expert testimony to support findings of both imprudence on the one hand and prudent management control on the other. Perhaps if this court had the obligation and authority to determine this issue, it might have decided it differently. However, because there is substantial, competent evidence in the record to support the findings of the KCC as to imprudent construction costs, we are bound by those findings and cannot substitute our judgment for that of the Commission. . . .

NOTES AND QUESTIONS

The court in *Kansas Gas & Elec.* identifies a number of factors that played a role in the decline of nuclear power—new safety requirements imposed in part because of the Three Mile Island accident, decreasing demand for electricity, and inflation. After the attacks of September 11, 2001, there were also increased fears of a terrorist strike against a nuclear plant. Paul Gaukler, D. Sean Barnett & Douglas J. Rosinski, *Nuclear Energy and Terrorism*, 16 NAT. RESOURCES & ENV'T 165 (2002). Even before September 11, other factors contributing to nuclear's decline included the failure to resolve the waste storage issue, poor management by utilities, and the presence of a strong anti-nuclear movement. *See generally* JOHN L. CAMPBELL, COLLAPSE OF AN INDUSTRY: NUCLEAR POWER AND THE CONTRADICTIONS OF U.S. POLICY (1988); PETER STOLER, DECLINE AND FAIL: THE AILING NUCLEAR POWER INDUSTRY (1985). Finally, an additional factor—the need to safeguard certain nuclear materials so they cannot be misused—helped cause the demise of the breeder reactor, a nuclear technology that never got off the ground in the United States because it utilized plutonium, which can be converted into weapons. *See* Helen Dewar, *Seemingly Fatal Blow Dealt Breeder Reactor by Senate*, WASH. POST, Oct. 27, 1983, at A2.

The net effect of all this has been to leave the United States with a large but static nuclear industry. About 100 reactors produce roughly twenty per cent of the nation's electricity, but no new reactor has been ordered by a utility since 1978. Julie Deardorff, *Nuclear Power May Get New Life*, CHI. TRIB., July 20, 2003, at C1.

Accordingly, there has been an enormous amount of litigation concerning who pays the bill for plants that cost more than budgeted, were never completed at all, or were decommissioned after their forty-year licenses had run out. Utilities often want to pass these costs on to ratepayers, while ratepayers believe that shareholders in the utility or bondholders who lent the money for a particular project should bear the losses. As *Kansas Gas & Elec.* suggests, these issues are typically matters of state law, involving an initial decision by a public service commission that is reviewed by the state courts. *See, e.g.*, Commonwealth Edison Co. v. Illinois Commerce Comm'n, 332 Ill.App.3d 1038, 266 Ill.Dec. 551, 775 N.E.2d 113 (2002) (utility can charge ratepayers for decommissioning costs); Citizens Action Coalition v. Northern Indiana Pub. Serv. Co., 485 N.E.2d 610 (Ind. 1985), *cert. denied*, 476 U.S. 1137, 106 S.Ct. 2239, 90 L.Ed.2d 687 (1986) (ratepayers not liable for cost of cancelled nuclear plant); People's Org. for Wash. Energy Resources v. Washington Util. & Transp. Comm'n, 104 Wash.2d 798, 711 P.2d 319 (1985) (en banc) (ratepayers are liable for cost of cancelled nuclear plant). In some settings federal agencies play a role. When, for example, cost overruns occur in multistate nuclear projects, the Federal Energy Regulatory Commission sets wholesale rates and the states may not bar utilities from passing those through to retail consumers. Mississippi Power & Light Co. v. Mississippi, 487 U.S. 354, 108 S.Ct. 2428, 101 L.Ed.2d 322 (1988).

Yet precisely at this time, with utilities still reluctant to order new nuclear plants, there is a rebirth of interest in nuclear's virtues. Most of our electricity is generated by the burning of coal, oil, and natural gas, which has disadvantages of its own. In particular, nuclear energy, unlike the burning of these fossil fuels, does not contribute to global warming. *See Profile: James Lovelock*, THE SUNDAY TELE-GRAPH (LONDON), May 30, 2004. Moreover, new reactor designs have been proposed that may enhance efficiency and safety. *See* Glenn Garelik, *Beyond Oil*, Audubon Mag., Sept.-Oct. 2001. About forty of the nation's 100 nuclear plants have applied to the Nuclear Regulatory Commission to extend the forty-year life of their operating licenses by twenty years, and most have received extensions, while the rest are pending. Jim McKay, *Still Circling the Globe at "Circle W,"* Pittsburgh Post-Gazette, June 16, 2004, at C10.

Should nuclear power play an enhanced role in the future? One crucial question is that of alternatives. Are there places other than traditional fossil fuels and nuclear to look for electricity generation?

III.   Alternative Means of Electricity Generation: The Question of Scale

The materials that follow examine two alternative means of electricity generation—photovoltaic solar systems and hydrogen-based fuel cells—that are novel in large part because they can be used on a very small scale. Fossil fuel, nuclear, and hydroelectric systems all generate electricity at central plants that feed power into a grid which utilities bring to your home or office. Some solar and hydrogen systems could operate the same way. But photovoltaics and fuel cells have the special feature that they are typically envisioned as working on a very different scale. You could use these systems to provide electricity for just one house, either on a stand-alone basis or with a connection to the traditional utility grid available as a back up. Such possibilities may become increasingly relevant as deregulation increases in the electricity industry.

At present, photovoltaic and fuel cell systems exist, but the electricity they provide costs roughly five times as much as the electricity available from the traditional grid. *See, e.g.*, Seth Dunn, *Micropower: The Next Electrical Era (Worldwatch Paper #151)* 22–24 (2000). But research, including government-funded research, may bring these costs down. In the long run, the most fundamental question they raise is whether small-scale electricity production is desirable.

A.   Photovoltaic Energy Systems

Photovoltaic solar cells are used to generate electricity, but, as with nuclear energy, they began with advances in basic science not aimed at power production.

Long before Einstein developed what would become the theoretical basis for nuclear power, the first instance of photovoltaic activity was observed. In 1839, Edmund Becquerel, a French scientist, noted that when light fell on one side of a certain type of battery cell an electric current was produced. Neither Becquerel nor anyone else could explain this "photoelectric effect." In this century scientists came to understand the process in terms of atomic structure—when a photon of light strikes an atom, it can be absorbed by electrons with the added energy driving off one of the atom's outer electrons. The stream of electrons set free in this fashion creates an electric current. Scientists using this knowledge built simple photovoltaic cells made of selenium, but they were so costly and inefficient that they had no practical use. In 1954, researchers at Bell Laboratories accidentally discovered that certain silicon devices produced electricity when exposed to sunlight. Bell Labs pursued the matter because it was interested in finding a way to generate electricity for telephone systems in remote areas not connected to power grids. It turned out that silicon solar cells were much more efficient than selenium. Still the cost of generating electricity with silicon cells was quite high, and research slowed. *See generally* PAUL D. MAYCOCK & EDWARD N. STIREWALT, PHOTOVOLTAICS: SUNLIGHT TO ELECTRICITY IN ONE STEP 169–71 (1981).

At this point, the federal government began to play a major role because scientists working on the space program needed a power source for satellites. Silicon solar cells filled the bill, particularly because 24–hour sunlight is available in space while power lines are not. By the late 1950's, satellites had solar cells and the National Aeronautics and Space Administration had begun funding research into photovoltaics generally. *See generally* CHRISTOPHER FLAVIN, ELECTRICITY FROM SUNLIGHT: THE FUTURE OF PHOTOVOLTAICS (1982). By the 1970's, the Department of Energy had taken the lead in funding photovoltaic research.

Jimmy Carter, Solar Energy

President's Message to Congress, 15 WEEKLY COMP. OF PRES. DOC. 1098 (1979).

Energy from the sun is clean and safe. It will not pollute the air we breathe or the water we drink. It does not run the risk of an accident which may threaten the health or life of our citizens. There are no toxic wastes to cause disposal problems. . . .

Hearing on the Administration's Views on the Role That Renewable Energy Technologies Can Play in Sustainable Electricity Generation, Before the Senate Committee on Energy and Natural Resources

108th Cong., 2d Sess. (April 27, 2004).
Testimony of David K. Garman, Assistant Secretary for Energy Efficiency and Renewable Energy, U.S. Department of Energy.

Mr. Chairman, Members of the Committee, I appreciate the opportunity to discuss the Administration's views on the role that renewable energy technologies can play in sustainable electricity generation.

As stated in the President's National Energy Policy, the Administration believes that renewable sources of energy can help provide for our future energy needs by harnessing abundant, naturally occurring sources of energy with less impact on the environment than conventional sources. We are committed to a research, development, demonstration and deployment program that supports that role. The Department of Energy (DOE) FY 2005 budget request for renewable technologies totals $374.8 million, a $17.3 million increase over the FY 2004 appropriation. This year's budget proposes increases in our programs for wind, hydropower, geothermal, hydrogen, and (when the impact of Congressional earmarks is taken into account), solar and biomass as well. Over the past three years we have invested nearly a billion dollars in renewable energy technologies, not including substantial cost-sharing from our private sector partners.

Advances in technology over the past 25 years have brought us great strides in lower costs, improved performance and competitiveness of renewable energy technologies. Today, electricity is being produced from the wind, the sun, the earth's heat and biomass in a variety of applications across the Nation.

. . .

Solar Energy Technology

Fifty years ago scientists at Bell Laboratories developed the first silicon solar cell. With efficiencies of less than six percent, these solar cells offered, for the first time, the ability to power a wide range of electrical equipment. Photovoltaic (PV) arrays convert sunlight to electricity without moving parts and without fuel wastes, air pollution, or greenhouse gasses. PV systems can be installed as either grid supply technologies or as residential or commercial scale customer-sited alternatives to retail electricity.

Today solar energy accounts for one percent of non-hydroelectric renewable electricity generation and 0.02 percent of total U.S. electricity supply. But PV technology has progressed remarkably in terms of both performance and cost in recent decades. The cost of PV-generated electricity has dropped 15 to 20 fold over the past 25 years and such systems are highly reliable. Thousands of systems are successfully operating today, serving applications that range from water pumping to residential power to remote utility power applications.

Crystalline silicon wafer technology dominates today's PV market. Direct manufacturing costs (labor and materials) for crystalline silicon module power in the United States are around $1.95/watt. This corresponds to an installed system vendor price for grid-tied PV energy of about $0.22 per kWh over a 25–year lifetime. Crystalline silicon module reliability has greatly improved to the point where modules are now warranted for 25 years, and many will probably have a functional lifetime much longer than this.

DOE's photovoltaic program is focused on the next-generation technologies such as thin-film photovoltaic cells, leap-frog technologies such as polymers and nanostructures, and technologies to improve interconnections with the electric grid. Our research and development seeks primarily to reduce the manufacturing cost of highly reliable photovoltaic modules. DOE's research goal is to achieve grid-tied systems with lifetime energy costs around $0.06/kWh and 30 years lifetime by 2020.

Even though some thin-film modules are now commercially available, their real impact is expected to become significant during the next decade. Thin films using amorphous silicon, a growing segment of the U.S. market, have several potential advantages over crystalline silicon. They can be manufactured at lower cost, are more responsive to indoor light, and can be manufactured on flexible or low-cost substrates. Other thin film materials are expected to become increasingly important in the future.

In addition to improvements in crystalline silicon technology, other notable technical accomplishments achieved over the past decade through our research and development programs include:

- The price of inverters (for changing direct current of the PV modules into alternating current suitable for the commercial power grid) is decreasing, and their reliability is steadily increasing. DOE seeks at least ten year warranted reliability.

- Production of thin film modules is expected to increase sharply in CY 2004 and 2005. The environmental issues of safely retiring these modules have been successfully resolved by DOE researchers at Brookhaven National Laboratories.

- The development of super-high efficiency cells, with efficiencies now nearing 38 percent under concentrated sunlight, has progressed faster than expected ten years ago, in part due to the major investment in this technology by the space PV industry in collaboration with NREL researchers.

- DOE made extensive contributions to Article 690 of the National Electric Code which deals with PV safety issues. This is a major development because it helps to remove a serious impediment to wide-scale PV grid-tied deployment—the reluctance of commercial power companies to allow PV systems to be interfaced to their power lines.

NOTES AND QUESTIONS

1. Federal, state, and local governments support photovoltaic research through research grants and a variety of subsidies and tax incentives, although some contend that more should be done. *See* Mark Detsky, *The Global Light: An Analysis of International and Local Developments in the Solar Electric Industry and Their Lessons for United States Energy Policy*, 14 COLO. J. INT'L ENVTL. L. & POL'Y 301 (2003).

2. Compare President Carter's optimistic assessment of solar energy's environmental impact with President Eisenhower's statements about nuclear power in Chapter 3, Sec. II. A., *supra*. The latest scientific advances often look perfectly safe and inexpensive at first. But photovoltaics are not only costly, they raise environmental concerns as well. The manufacture of silicon cells, for example, can bring about exposure to silicon particulates that cause the scarring of lung tissues known as silicosis, while the fabrication of finished photovoltaic arrays involves the use of toxic substances including known and suspected carcinogens. *SEE* Thomas L. Neff, The Social Costs of Solar Energy: A Study of Photovoltaic Energy Systems 9–10 (1981).

3. Advocates of solar energy, or of any new power source, disserve their cause by arguing that the new approach is utterly free of costs or risks. A clear focus today on the possible environmental impact of solar energy can lead to planning that will reduce environmental hazards in the future. Inattention to matters such as waste disposal in the early years of nuclear energy led to enormous problems. *See, e.g.*, IRVIN BUPP & JEAN-CLAUDE DERIAN, LIGHT WATER: HOW THE NUCLEAR DREAM DISSOLVED 124 (1978). For a useful early study of the risks associated with the manufacture of silicon photovoltaic cells, *see* I. Wilenitz, V.M. Fthenakis & P.O. Moskowitz, *Costs of Controlling Environmental Emissions from the Manufacture of Silicon Dendritic Web Photovoltaic Cells,* 15 SOLAR CELLS 247 (1985). Non-silicon based photovoltaic cells present other hazards. *See* P.O. Moskowitz, V.M. Fthenakis & J.C. Lee, *Potential Health and Safety Hazards Associated with the Production of Cadmium*

Telluride, Copper Indium Diselenide, and Zinc Phosphide Photovoltaic Cells, Brookhaven Nat'l Lab. 51832 (Apr. 1985). The difficult problem is to assess a new technology's social impact without unduly hampering research that may lead in unexpected and desirable directions. *See* Chapter 3, Sec. I. A., *supra.*

4. There is one crucial respect in which solar energy raises a distinctive social issue. Photovoltaic arrays must be exposed to sunlight, but what happens if your neighbor builds an addition to his house that shades your property? As the following cases illustrate, the common law has grappled with this type of problem for quite some time.

Fontainebleau Hotel Corp. v. Forty–Five Twenty–Five, Inc.

District Court of Appeals of Florida, Third District, 1959.
114 So.2d 357.

■ PER CURIAM.

This is an interlocutory appeal from an order temporarily enjoining the appellants from continuing with the construction of a fourteen-story addition to the Fontainebleau Hotel, owned and operated by the appellants. Appellee, plaintiff below, owns the Eden Roc Hotel, which was constructed in 1955, about a year after the Fontainebleau, and adjoins the Fontainebleau on the north. Both are luxury hotels, facing the Atlantic Ocean. The proposed addition to the Fontainebleau is being constructed twenty feet from its north property line, 130 feet from the mean high water mark of the Atlantic Ocean, and 76 feet 8 inches from the ocean bulkhead line. The 14–story tower will extend 160 feet above grade in height and is 416 feet long from east to west. During the winter months, from around two o'clock in the afternoon for the remainder of the day, the shadow of the addition will extend over the cabana, swimming pool, and sunbathing areas of the Eden Roc, which are located in the southern portion of its property.

In this action, plaintiff-appellee sought to enjoin the defendants-appellants from proceeding with the construction of the addition to the Fontainebleau (it appears to have been roughly eight stories high at the time suit was filed), alleging that the construction would interfere with the light and air on the beach in front of the Eden Roc and cast a shadow of such size as to render the beach wholly unfitted for the use and enjoyment of its guests, to the irreparable injury of the plaintiff; further, that the construction of such addition on the north side of defendants' property, rather than the south side, was actuated by malice and ill will on the part of the defendants' president toward the plaintiff's president; and that the construction was in violation of a building ordinance requiring a 100–foot setback from the ocean. It was also alleged that the construction would interfere with the easements of light and air enjoyed by plaintiff and its predecessors in title for more than twenty years and "impliedly granted by virtue of the acts of the plaintiff's predecessors in title, as well as under the common law and the express recognition of such rights by virtue of Chapter 9837, Laws of Florida 1923...." Some attempt was also made to allege an easement by implication in favor of the plaintiff's property, as the dominant, and against the defendants' property as the servient, tenement.

The defendants' answer denied the material allegations of the complaint, pleaded laches and estoppel by judgment.

The chancellor heard considerable testimony on the issues made by the complaint and the answer and, as noted, entered a temporary injunction restraining the defendants from continuing with the construction of the addition. His reason for so doing was stated by him, in a memorandum opinion, as follows:

> [ ]In granting the temporary injunction in this case the Court wishes to make several things very clear. The ruling is not based on any alleged presumptive title nor prescriptive right of the plaintiff to light and air nor is it based on any deed restrictions nor recorded plats in the title of the plaintiff nor of the defendant nor of any plat of record. It is not based on any zoning ordinance nor on any provision of the building code of the City of Miami Beach nor on the decision of any court, nisi prius or appellate. It is based solely on the proposition that no one has a right to use his property to the injury of another. In this case it is clear from the evidence that the proposed use by the Fontainebleau will materially damage the Eden Roc. There is evidence indicating that the construction of the proposed annex by the Fontainebleau is malicious or deliberate for the purpose of injuring the Eden Roc, but it is scarcely sufficient, standing alone, to afford a basis for equitable relief.[ ]

This is indeed a novel application of the maxim *sic utere tuo ut alienum nou laedas*. This maxim does not mean that one must never use his own property in such a way as to do any injury to his neighbor. Beckman v. Marshall, Fla.1956, 85 So.2d 552. It means only that one must use his property so as not to injure the lawful *rights* of another. Cason v. Florida Power Co., 74 Fla. 1, 76 So. 535. In *Reaver v. Martin Theatres*, Fla.1951, 52 So.2d 682, 683, under this maxim, it was stated that "it is well settled that a property owner may put his own property to any reasonable and lawful use, so long as he does not thereby deprive the adjoining landowner of any right of enjoyment of his property *which is recognized and protected by law, and so long as his use is not such a one as the law will pronounce a nuisance*." [Emphasis supplied.]

No American decision has been cited, and independent research has revealed none, in which it has been held that—in the absence of some contractual or statutory obligation—a landowner has a legal right to the free flow of light and air across the adjoining land of his neighbor. Even at common law, the landowner had no legal right, in the absence of an easement or uninterrupted use and enjoyment for a period of 20 years, to unobstructed light and air from the adjoining land. Blumberg v. Weiss, 1941, 129 N.J.Eq. 34, 17 A.2d 823; 1 Am.Jur., Adjoining Landowners, § 51. And the English doctrine of "ancient lights" has been unanimously repudiated in this country. 1 Am.Jur., Adjoining Landowners, § 49, p. 533; Lynch v. Hill, 1939, 24 Del.Ch. 86, 6 A.2d 614, overruling Clawson v. Primrose, 4 Del.Ch. 643.

There being, then, no legal right to the free flow of light and air from the adjoining land, it is universally held that where a structure serves a useful and beneficial purpose, it does not give rise to a cause of action, either for damages or for an injunction under the maxim *sic utere tuo ut alienum non laedas,* even though it causes injury to another by cutting off the light and air and interfering with the view that would otherwise be available over adjoining land in its natural state, regardless of the fact that the structure may have been erected partly for spite. See the cases collected in the annotation in 133 A.L.R. at pp. 701 et seq.; 1 Am.Jur., Adjoining Landowners, § 54, p. 536; Taliaferro v. Salyer, 1958, 162 Cal.App.2d 685, 328 P.2d 799; Musumeci v. Leonardo, 1950, 77 R.I. 255, 75 A.2d 175; Harrison v. Langlinais, Tex.Civ.App.1958, 312 S.W.2d 286; Granberry v. Jones, 1949, 188 Tenn. 51, 216 S.W.2d 721; Letts v. Kessler, 1896, 54 Ohio St. 73, 42 N.E. 765; Kulbitsky v. Zimnoch, 1950, 196 Md. 504, 77 A.2d 14; Southern Advertising Co. v. Sherman, Tenn.App.1957, 308 S.W.2d 491.

We see no reason for departing from this universal rule. If, as contended on behalf of plaintiff, public policy demands that a landowner in the Miami Beach area refrain from constructing buildings on his premises that will cast a shadow on the adjoining premises, an amendment of its comprehensive planning and zoning ordinance, applicable to the public as a whole, is the means by which such purpose should be achieved. (No opinion is expressed here as to the validity of such an ordinance, if one should be enacted pursuant to the requirements of law. *Cf.* City of Miami Beach v. State *ex rel.* Fontainebleau Hotel Corp., Fla.App.1959, 108 So.2d 614, 619; *certiorari denied*, Fla.1959, 111 So.2d 437.) But to change the universal rule—and the custom followed in this state since its inception—that adjoining landowners have an equal right under the law to build to the line of their respective tracts and to such a height as is desired by them (in the absence, of course, of building restrictions or regulations) amounts, in our opinion, to judicial legislation. As stated in *Musumeci v. Leonardo*, supra [77 R.I. 255, 75 A.2d 177], "So use your own as not to injure another's property is, indeed, a sound and salutary principle for the promotion of justice, but it may not and should not be applied so as gratuitously to confer upon an adjacent property owner incorporeal rights incidental to his ownership of land which the law does not sanction."

Since it affirmatively appears that the plaintiff has not established a cause of action against the defendants by reason of the structure here in question, the order granting a temporary injunction should be and it is hereby reversed with directions to dismiss the complaint.

Reversed with directions.

■ Horton, C.J., Carroll, J., and Cabot, J. concur.

Sandy F. Kraemer, Solar Law

130–32 (1978).

These rulings [like *Fontainebleau*] find their genesis in the repudiation of the English doctrine of "ancient lights" under which a landowner acquired by uninterrupted use an easement over adjoining property for the passage of light and air. The doctrine of ancient lights has been disavowed repeatedly in the United States.

The doctrine of ancient lights provides that if a landowner has received light from across his neighbor's land for a certain time, he has the right to continue enjoying it. The length of time necessary to establish this right in

England is now twenty-seven years. The British devised an ingenious aid for determining the light entitlement, called the "grumble line." The "grumble line" is the position in a room at which an ordinary person reading ordinary print grumbles and turns on the artificial light. The rule of thumb seems to be that if at least one-half of the room is between the "grumble line" and the window, there is a reasonable amount of light entering it. Engineers have developed an empirical standard for the position of the "grumble line" that is equivalent to one foot-candle on the top of a desk 33 inches (84 cm.) high. In conjunction with the 50–50 rule, if over one-half of the room at 33 inches above the floor receives one foot-candle, the room is considered to receive an adequate amount of light from the window to satisfy the doctrine of ancient light. A problem exists, of course, in that architectural styles change, as does the concept of reasonableness, causing all sorts of conflicts, not to mention that a solar collector requires a great deal more light than that required to make a man refrain from a "grumble." This treatment of solar energy rights has been associated by commentators with the claims that the sun is rarely seen in England.

The major reason [American] courts have rejected this doctrine is that it conflicts with the goal of full development of property. The classic American high-rise metropolitan core areas of our greatest cities could not have been built under the Ancient Lights Doctrine. While full development is being questioned today, it was a useful and important policy for a young nation with expanding frontiers. The doctrine of ancient lights, if accepted, would have restricted full development under some circumstances. Some courts apparently fear that recognition of a cause of action for creating a shadow will prevent any use of adjoining land. In residential areas normal use of the property should not cause shadows on a collector unless trees are planted too near to the lot line. In other areas, only those buildings tall enough and close enough to the collector will blot out the sun's rays.

NOTES AND QUESTIONS

As Kraemer indicates, the American rejection of the doctrine of ancient lights poses a problem for residential solar energy. When, for example, a homeowner in Hawaii with solar collectors on her house sought to prevent construction of an adjoining building that would shade her collectors, the court granted summary judgment for the defendant. Siu v. McCully Citron Co., No. 56405 Civ. 105–106 (Haw., Jan. 9, 1979), *reported in* 1 SOLAR L. REP. 542 (1979), *discussed in* John Gergacz, *Legal Aspects of Solar Energy: Statutory Approaches for Access to Sunlight*, 10 B.C. ENVTL. AFF. L. REV. 1, 2 (1982). Does the following case persuade you that American courts should support the ancient lights idea in cases involving solar energy?

Prah v. Maretti

Supreme Court of Wisconsin, 1982.
108 Wis.2d 223, 321 N.W.2d 182.

■ SHIRLEY S. ABRAHAMSON, J.

This appeal from a judgment of the circuit court for Waukesha county, Max Raskin, circuit judge, was certified to this court by the court of appeals, sec. (Rule) 809.61, Stats.1979–80, as presenting an issue of first impression, namely, whether an owner of a solar-heated residence states a claim upon which relief can be granted when he asserts that his neighbor's proposed construction of a residence (which conforms to existing deed restrictions and local ordinances) interferes with his access to an unobstructed path for sunlight across the neighbor's property. This case thus involves a conflict between one landowner (Glenn Prah, the plaintiff) interested in unobstructed access to sunlight across adjoining property as a natural source of energy and an adjoining landowner (Richard D. Maretti, the defendant) interested in the development of his land.

The circuit court concluded that the plaintiff presented no claim upon which relief could be granted and granted summary judgment for the defendant. We reverse the judgment of the circuit court and remand the cause to the circuit court for further proceedings.

I.

According to the complaint, the plaintiff is the owner of a residence which was constructed during the years 1978–1979. The complaint alleges that the residence has a solar system which includes collectors on the roof to supply energy for heat and hot water and that after the plaintiff built his solar-heated house, the defendant purchased the lot adjacent to and immediately to the south of the plaintiff's lot and commenced planning construction of a home. The complaint further states that when the plaintiff learned of defendant's plans to build the house he advised the defendant that if the house were built at the proposed location, defendant's house would substantially and adversely affect the integrity of plaintiff's solar system and could cause plaintiff other damage. Nevertheless, the defendant began construction. The complaint further alleges that the plaintiff is entitled to "unrestricted use of the sun and its solar power" and demands judgment for injunctive relief and damages.

After filing his complaint, the plaintiff moved for a temporary injunction to restrain and enjoin construction by the defendant. In ruling on that motion the circuit court heard testimony, received affidavits and viewed the site.

The record made on the motion reveals the following additional facts: Plaintiff's home was the first residence built in the subdivision, and although plaintiff did not build his house in the center of the lot it was built in accordance with applicable restrictions. Plaintiff advised defendant that if the defendant's home were built at the proposed site it would cause a shadowing effect on the solar collectors which would reduce the efficiency of the system and possibly damage the system. To avoid these adverse effects, plaintiff requested defendant to locate his home an additional several feet away from the plaintiff's lot line, the exact number being disputed. Plaintiff and defendant failed to reach an agreement on the location of defendant's home before defendant started construction. The Architectural Control Committee and the Planning Commission of the City of Muskego approved the defendant's plans for his home, including its location on the lot. After such approval, the defendant apparently changed the grade of the property without prior notice to the Architectural Control

Committee. The problem with defendant's proposed construction, as far as the plaintiff's interests are concerned, arises from a combination of the grade and the distance of defendant's home from the defendant's lot line.

The circuit court denied plaintiff's motion for injunctive relief, declared it would entertain a motion for summary judgment and thereafter entered judgment in favor of the defendant.

. . .

We consider first whether the complaint states a claim for relief based on common law private nuisance. This state has long recognized that an owner of land does not have an absolute or unlimited right to use the land in a way which injures the rights of others. The rights of neighboring landowners are relative; the uses by one must not unreasonably impair the uses or enjoyment of the other. VI–A *American Law of Property* sec. 28.22, pp. 64–65 (1954). When one landowner's use of his or her property unreasonably interferes with another's enjoyment of his or her property, that use is said to be a private nuisance. Hoene v. Milwaukee, 17 Wis.2d 209, 214, 116 N.W.2d 112 (1962); Metzger v. Hochrein, 107 Wis. 267, 269, 83 N.W. 308 (1900). *See also* Prosser, *Law of Torts*, sec. 89, p. 591 (2d ed. 1971).

The private nuisance doctrine has traditionally been employed in this state to balance the rights of landowners, and this court has recently adopted the analysis of private nuisance set forth in the Restatement (Second) of Torts. CEW Mgmt. Corp. v. First Federal Savings & Loan Association, 88 Wis.2d 631, 633, 277 N.W.2d 766 (1979). The Restatement defines private nuisance as "a nontrespassory invasion of another's interest in the private use and enjoyment of land." Restatement (Second) of Torts, Sec. 821D (1977). The phrase "interest in the private use and enjoyment of land" as used in sec. 821D is broadly defined to include any disturbance of the enjoyment of property. The comment in the Restatement describes the landowner's interest protected by private nuisance law as follows:

> [ ]The phrase "interest in the use and enjoyment of land" is used in this Restatement in a broad sense. It comprehends not only the interests that a person may have in the actual present use of land for residential, agricultural, commercial, industrial and other purposes, but also his interests in having the present use value of the land unimpaired by changes in its physical condition. Thus the destruction of trees on vacant land is as much an invasion of the owner's interest in its use and enjoyment as is the destruction of crops or flowers that he is growing on the land for his present use. "Interest in use and enjoyment" also comprehends the pleasure, comfort and enjoyment that a person normally derives from the occupancy of land. Freedom from discomfort and annoyance while using land is often as important to a person as freedom from physical interruption with his use or freedom from detrimental change in the physical condition of the land itself.[ ] Restatement (Second) of Torts, Sec. 821D, Comment b, p. 101 (1977)

Although the defendant's obstruction of the plaintiff's access to sunlight appears to fall within the Restatement's broad concept of a private nuisance as a nontrespassory invasion of another's interest in the private use and enjoyment of land, the defendant asserts that he has a right to develop his property in compliance with statutes, ordinances and private covenants without regard to the effect of such development upon the plaintiff's access to sunlight. In essence, the defendant is asking this court to hold that the private nuisance doctrine is not applicable in the instant case and that his right to develop his land is a right which is per se superior to his neighbor's interest in access to sunlight. This position is expressed in the maxim "cujus est solum, ejus est usque ad coelum et ad infernos," that is, the owner of land owns up to the sky and down to the center of the earth. The rights of the surface owner are, however, not unlimited. U.S. v. Causby, 328 U.S. 256, 260–61 (1946). *See also* 114.03, Stats.1979–80.

The defendant is not completely correct in asserting that the common law did not protect a landowner's access to sunlight across adjoining property. At English common law a landowner could acquire a right to receive sunlight across adjoining land by both express agreement and under the judge-made doctrine of "ancient lights." Under the doctrine of ancient lights if the landowner had received sunlight across adjoining property for a specified period of time, the landowner was entitled to continue to receive unobstructed access to sunlight across the adjoining property. Under the doctrine the landowner acquired a negative prescriptive easement and could prevent the adjoining landowner from obstructing access to light.

Although American courts have not been as receptive to protecting a landowner's access to sunlight as the English courts, American courts have afforded some protection to a landowner's interest in access to sunlight. American courts honor express easements to sunlight. American courts initially enforced the English common law doctrine of ancient lights, but later every state which considered the doctrine repudiated it as inconsistent with the needs of a developing country. Indeed, for just that reason this court concluded that an easement to light and air over adjacent property could not be created or acquired by prescription and has been unwilling to recognize such an easement by implication. Depner v. United States National Bank, 202 Wis. 405, 408, 232 N.W. 851 (1930); Miller v. Hoeschler, 126 Wis. 263, 268–69, 105 N.W. 790 (1905).

Many jurisdictions in this country have protected a landowner from malicious obstruction of access to light (the spite fence cases) under the common law private nuisance doctrine. If an activity is motivated by malice it lacks utility and the harm it causes others outweighs any social values. VI–A *Law of Property* sec. 28.28, p. 79 (1954). This court was reluctant to protect a landowner's interest in sunlight even against a spite fence, only to be overruled by the legislature. Shortly after this court upheld a landowner's right to erect a useless and unsightly sixteen-foot spite fence four feet from his neighbor's windows, Metzger v. Hochrein, 83 N.W. 308 (Wis. 1900), the legislature enacted a law specifically defining a spite fence as an actionable private nuisance. Thus a landowner's interest in sunlight has been protected in this country by common law private nuisance law at least in the narrow context of the modern American rule invalidating spite fences. *See, e.g.,* Sundowner, Inc. v. King, 509 P.2d 785 (Idaho 1973); Restatement (Second) of Torts, sec. 829 (1977).

This court's reluctance in the nineteenth and early part of the twentieth century to provide broader protection for a landowner's access to sunlight was premised on three policy considerations. First, the right of landowners to use their property as they wished, as long as they did not cause physical damage to a neighbor, was jealously guarded. Metzger v. Hochrein, 107 Wis. 267, 272, 83 N.W. 308 (1900).

Second, sunlight was valued only for aesthetic enjoyment or as illumination. Since artificial light could be used for illumination, loss of sunlight was at most a personal annoyance which was given little, if any, weight by society.

Third, society had a significant interest in not restricting or impeding land development. Dillman v. Hoffman, 38 Wis. 559, 574 (1875). This court repeatedly emphasized that in the growth period of the nineteenth and early twentieth centuries change is to be expected and is essential to property and that recognition of a right to sunlight would hinder property development. The court expressed this concept as follows:

> [ ]As the city grows, large grounds appurtenant to residences must be cut up to supply more residences. . . . The cistern, the outhouse, the cesspool, and the private drain must disappear in deference to the public waterworks and sewer; the terrace and the garden, to the need for more complete occupancy. . . . Strict limitation [on the recognition of easements of light and air over adjacent premises is] in accord with the popular conception upon which real estate has been and is daily being conveyed in Wisconsin and to be essential to easy and rapid development at least of our municipalities.[ ] Miller v. Hoeschler, *supra*, 126 Wis. at 268, 270, 105 N.W. 790; *quoted with approval in Depner, supra*, 202 Wis. at 409, 232 N.W. 851.

Considering these three policies, this court concluded that in the absence of an express agreement granting access to sunlight, a landowner's obstruction of another's access to sunlight was not actionable. Miller v. Hoeschler, *supra*, 126 Wis. at 271, 105 N.W. 790; Depner v. United States National Bank*, supra*, 202 Wis. at 410, 232 N.W. 851. These three policies are no longer fully accepted or applicable. They reflect factual circumstances and social priorities that are now obsolete.

First, society has increasingly regulated the use of land by the landowner for the general welfare. Euclid v. Ambler Realty Co., 272 U.S. 365 (1926); Just v. Marinette, 201 N.W.2d 761 (Wis. 1972).

Second, access to sunlight has taken on a new significance in recent years. In this case the plaintiff seeks to protect access to sunlight, not for aesthetic reasons or as a source of illumination but as a source of energy. Access to sunlight as an energy source is of significance both to the landowner who invests in solar collectors and to a society which has an interest in developing alternative sources of energy.

Third, the policy of favoring unhindered private development in an expanding economy is no longer in harmony with the realities of our society. State v. Deetz, 224 N.W.2d 407 (Wis. 1974). The need for easy and rapid development is not as great today as it once was, while our perception of the value of sunlight as a source of energy has increased significantly.

Courts should not implement obsolete policies that have lost their vigor over the course of the years. The law of private nuisance is better suited to resolve landowners' disputes about property development in the 1980's than is a rigid rule which does not recognize a landowner's interest in access to sunlight. As we said in *Ballstadt v. Pagel*, 202 Wis. 484, 489, 232 N.W. 862 (1930), "What is regarded in law as constituting a nuisance in modern times would no doubt have been tolerated without question in former times." We read *State v. Deetz*, 66 Wis.2d 1, 224 N.W.2d 407 (1974), as an endorsement of the application of common law nuisance to situations involving the conflicting interests of landowners and as rejecting *per se* exclusions to the nuisance law reasonable use doctrine.

In *Deetz* the court abandoned the rigid common law common enemy rule with respect to surface water and adopted the private nuisance reasonable use rule, namely that the landowner is subject to liability if his or her interference with the flow of surface waters unreasonably invades a neighbor's interest in the use and enjoyment of land. Restatement (Second) of Torts, sec. 822, 826, 829 (1977). This court concluded that the common enemy rule which served society "well in the days of burgeoning national expansion of the mid-nineteenth and early-twentieth centuries" should be abandoned because it was no longer "in harmony with the realities of our society." *Deetz, supra,* 66 Wis.2d at 14–15. We recognized in *Deetz* that common law rules adapt to changing social values and conditions.

Yet the defendant would have us ignore the flexible private nuisance law as a means of resolving the dispute between the landowners in this case and would have us adopt an approach, already abandoned in *Deetz,* of favoring the unrestricted development of land and of applying a rigid and inflexible rule protecting his right to build on his land and disregarding any interest of the plaintiff in the use and enjoyment of his land. This we refuse to do.

Private nuisance law, the law traditionally used to adjudicate conflicts between private landowners, has the flexibility to protect both a landowner's right of access to sunlight and another landowner's right to develop land. Private nuisance law is better suited to regulate access to sunlight in modern society and is more in harmony with legislative policy and the prior decisions of this court than is an inflexible doctrine of non-recognition of any interest in access to sunlight across adjoining land.

We therefore hold that private nuisance law, that is, the reasonable use doctrine as set forth in the Restatement, is applicable to the instant case. Recognition of a nuisance claim for unreasonable obstruction of access to sunlight will not prevent land development or unduly hinder the use of adjoining land. It will promote the reasonable use and enjoyment of land in a manner suitable to the 1980's. That obstruction of access to light might be found to constitute a nuisance in certain circumstances does not mean that it will be or must be found to constitute a nuisance under all circumstances. The result in each case depends on whether the conduct complained of is unreasonable.

Accordingly we hold that the plaintiff in this case has stated a claim under which relief can be granted. Nonetheless we do not determine whether the plaintiff in this case is entitled to relief. In order to be entitled to relief the plaintiff must prove the elements required to establish actionable nuisance, and the conduct of the defendant herein must be judged by the reasonable use doctrine.

IV.

The defendant asserts that even if we hold that the private nuisance doctrine applies to obstruction of access to sunlight across adjoining land, the circuit court's granting of summary judgment should be affirmed.

Although the memorandum decision of the circuit court in the instant case is unclear, it appears that the circuit court recognized that the common law private nuisance doctrine was applicable but concluded that defendant's conduct was not unreasonable. The circuit court apparently attempted to balance the utility of the defendant's conduct with the gravity of the harm. Sec. 826, Restatement (Second) of Torts (1977). The defendant urges us to accept the circuit court's balance as adequate. We decline to do so.

The circuit court concluded that because the defendant's proposed house was in conformity with zoning regulations, building codes and deed restrictions, the defendant's use of the land was reasonable. This court has concluded that a landowner's compliance with zoning laws does not automatically bar a nuisance claim. Compliance with the law "is not the controlling factor, though it is, of course, entitled to some weight." Bie v. Ingersoll, 27 Wis.2d 490, 495, 135 N.W.2d 250 (1965). The circuit court also concluded that the plaintiff could have avoided any harm by locating his own house in a better place. Again, plaintiff's ability to avoid the harm is a relevant but not a conclusive factor. *See* secs. 826, 827, 828, Restatement (Second) of Torts (1977).

Furthermore, our examination of the record leads us to conclude that the record does not furnish an adequate basis for the circuit court to apply the proper legal principles on summary judgment. The application of the reasonable use standard in nuisance cases normally requires a full exposition of all underlying facts and circumstances. Too little is known in this case of such matters as the extent of the harm to the plaintiff, the suitability of solar heat in that neighborhood, the availability of remedies to the plaintiff, and the costs to the defendant of avoiding the harm. Summary judgment is not an appropriate procedural vehicle in this case when the circuit court must weigh evidence which has not been presented at trial. 6 (Pt. 2) Moore's *Federal Practice*, 56.15[7], pp. 56–638 (1982); 10 Wright and Miller, *Federal Practice and Procedure—Civil*, secs. 2729, 2731 (1973).

Because the plaintiff has stated a claim of common law private nuisance upon which relief can be granted, the judgment of the circuit court must be reversed. We need not, and do not, reach the question of whether the complaint states a claim under sec. 844.01, Stats.1979–80, or under the doctrine of prior appropriation. Attoe v. Madison Professional Policemen's Assoc., 79 Wis.2d 199, 205, 255 N.W.2d 489 (1977).

For the reasons set forth, we reverse the judgment of the circuit court dismissing the complaint and remand the matter to circuit court for further proceedings not inconsistent with this opinion.

By the Court. The judgment of the circuit court is reversed and the cause remanded for proceedings not inconsistent with this opinion.

■ WILLIAM G. CALLOW, J., dissenting.

The majority has adopted the Restatement's reasonable use doctrine to grant an owner of a solar heated home a cause of action against his neighbor who, in acting entirely within the applicable ordinances and statutes, seeks to design and build his home in such a location that it may, at various times during the day, shade the plaintiff's solar collector, thereby impeding the efficiency of his heating system during several months of the year. Because I believe the facts of this case clearly reveal that a cause of action for private nuisance will not lie, I dissent.

I would submit that any policy decisions in this area are best left for the legislature. "What is 'desirable' or 'advisable' or 'ought to be' is a question of policy, not a question of fact. What is 'necessary' or what is 'in the best interest' is not a fact and its determination by the judiciary is an exercise of legislative power when each involves political considerations." *In re* City of Beloit, 37 Wis.2d 637, 644, 155 N.W.2d 633 (1968). *See generally* Holifield v. Setco Industries, Inc., 42 Wis.2d 750, 758, 160 N.W.2d 177 (1969); Comment, *Solar Rights: Guaranteeing a Place in the Sun*, 57 Or.L.Rev. 94, 126–27 (1977) (litigation is a slow, costly, and uncertain method of reform). I would concur with these observations of the trial judge: "While temptation lingers for the court to declare by judicial fiat what is right and what should be done, under the facts in this case, such action under our form of constitutional government where the three branches each have their defined jurisdiction and power, would be an intrusion of judicial egoism over legislative passivity."

The legislature has recently acted in this area. Chapter 354, Laws of 1981 (effective May 7, 1982 [after the dispute in this case arose]), was enacted to provide the underlying legislation enabling local governments to enact ordinances establishing procedures for guaranteeing access to sunlight. This court's intrusion into an area where legislative action is being taken is unwarranted, and it may undermine a legislative scheme for orderly development not yet fully operational.

Chapter 354, Laws of 1981, sec. 66.032, provides specific conditions for solar access permits. In part that section provides for impermissible interference with solar collectors within specific limitations:

"66.032   Solar access permits. . . .

"(f) 'Impermissible interference' means the blockage of solar energy from a collector surface or proposed collector surface for which a permit has been granted under this section during a collector use period if such blockage is by any structure or vegetation on property, an owner of which was notified under sub. (3)(b). *"Impermissible interference" does not include:*

"1. Blockage by a narrow protrusion, including but not limited to a pole or wire, which does not substantially interfere with absorption of solar energy by a solar collector.

"2. *Blockage by any structure constructed, under construction or for which a building permit has been applied for before the date the last notice is mailed or delivered under sub. (3)(b).*

"3. Blockage by any vegetation planted before the date the last notice is mailed or delivered under sub. (3)(b) unless a municipality by ordinance under sub. (2) defines impermissible interference to include such vegetation." (Emphasis added.)

Sec. 66.032(3)(b) provides for notice:

"(3) Permit applications.

"(b) An agency shall determine if an application is satisfactorily completed and shall notify the applicant of its determination. If an applicant receives notice that an application has been satisfactorily completed, *the applicant shall deliver by certified mail or by hand a notice to the owner of any property which the applicant proposes to be restricted by the permit under* sub. (7). The applicant shall submit to the agency a copy of a signed receipt for every notice delivered under this paragraph. The agency shall supply the notice form. The information on the form may include, without limitation because of enumeration:

"1. The name and address of the applicant, and the address of the land upon which the solar collector is or will be located.

"2. That an application has been filed by the applicant.

"3. That the permit, if granted, may affect the rights of the notified owner to develop his or her property and to plant vegetation.

"4. The telephone number, address and office hours of the agency.

"5. That *any person may request a hearing* under sub. (4) within 30 days after receipt of the notice, and the address and procedure for filing the request." (Emphasis added.)

This legislative scheme would deal with the type of problem presented in the present case and precludes the need for judicial activism in this area. . . .

Tenn v. 889 Associates, Ltd.

Supreme Court of New Hampshire, 1985.
127 N.H. 321, 500 A.2d 366.

■ SOUTER, J.

The plaintiff appeals the superior court's dismissal of a bill in equity, by which she sought an injunction against construction of a building and an award of damages. We affirm.

The plaintiff, Sylvia Tenn, owns a six-story office building constructed in 1891 at 907–913 Elm Street in Manchester, known as the Pickering Building. Its south wall is built to the southerly line of its lot. A neighboring building formerly located to the south of the plaintiff's property was built to the same lot line and to a height of nearly four stories, so that up to that height, the south wall of the Pickering Building had no windows. Above the fourth story, a total of twelve windows faced south, as did the glazed south wall of a light shaft, capped with a skylight, which provided light for the offices and halls. Several of the south windows held room air conditioners.

The defendant, 889 Associates, Ltd., now owns the lot south of the Pickering Building. In November, 1983, the defendant's president and treasurer, Michael Ingram, wrote to a representative of the plaintiff, Dr. James Tenn, informing him of the defendant's plans to demolish the existing four-story structure and to replace it with a new one. The letter indicated that the defendant intended to construct the new building, like the old one, to abut the south wall of the Pickering Building, but to a full height of six stories, so that the Pickering Building's room air conditioners would have to be removed. Mr. Ingram offered to meet with Dr. Tenn to describe the plans in more detail.

When they met in December, 1983, Dr. Tenn objected to the plans to block the Pickering Building's south windows and asked Mr. Ingram to redesign the new building with an accommodating set-back of several feet. Mr. Ingram declined to do so and proceeded to seek the requisite zoning variances and building permits.

One such requested variance was on the agenda of the Manchester Board of Adjustment for March 19, 1984. Although the written notice of that meeting did not reach the plaintiff, because of an improperly addressed envelope, the plaintiff had actual notice of the meeting, which Dr. Tenn attended with legal counsel. When Mr. Ingram explained to Dr. Tenn that the variance at issue would affect only a back alley, Dr. Tenn and his counsel left the meeting before the board discussed Mr. Ingram's application.

On April 19, 1984, nearly five months after learning of the defendant's plans, and after demolition of the existing building had already begun, the plaintiff filed the present bill in equity. To the extent that the new building would block the windows and the wall of the light shaft, the plaintiff claimed that it would be a private nuisance. She also claimed a prescriptive easement to occupy air space with the air conditioners. She sought an injunction against the construction, plus ancillary damages.

. . .

[T]he court made findings that the defendant's building would not be a private nuisance. The court specifically found that the construction would not result in an unreasonable or substantial interference with the plaintiff's use and enjoyment of her property; it specifically found that no easement for the air conditioners had arisen by prescription; and it ruled that there could be no prescriptive right to light, air or view. Accordingly, the court dismissed the petition, and this appeal followed.

. . .

We thus reach the substantial issues in this appeal, whether the law of private nuisance is broad enough to comprehend a claim of interference with light and air, whether the court correctly applied that law in this case and whether there was a prescriptive right to maintain the air conditioners. In considering the applicability of nuisance law to the interests at stake, it will be helpful to start by canvassing the alternative possibilities that the parties have discussed.

At one extreme there is the English common law doctrine of ancient lights, under which the owner of a window that has enjoyed unobstructed access to sunlight for a sufficient period of time can acquire a prescriptive easement entitling him to prevent an adjoining landowner from obstructing the accustomed light. Comment, *Solar Rights: Guaranteeing a Place in the Sun*, 57 Or.L.Rev. 94, 108–09 (1977); *see also* R. Megarry and H. Wade, The Law of Real Property 831 (2d ed. 1959). While in the early days some American courts adopted a similar rule, it fell into disfavor during the nineteenth century. By 1977 "no American common-law jurisdiction affirmatively recognize[d] an ability to acquire an easement of light by prescription," Comment, *supra* at 112 (footnotes omitted), and "very few, if any, American courts today would uphold a prescriptive right to light," Pfeiffer, *Ancient Lights: Legal Protection of Access to Solar Energy*, 68 A.B.A.J. 288, 289 (1982).

Historically, there have been three principal reasons for the unpopularity of the doctrine of ancient lights: a desire to foster unimpeded development of real estate, a belief that in an age of artificial illumination light should be classed as an aesthetic rather than a property interest, and a suspicion that the enjoyment of light was so far from a characteristically adverse use that it could not fall within the basic concept of prescriptive use. *See* Comment, *supra* at 110–11; Prah v. Maretti, 321 N.W.2d 182, 189 (Wis. 1982).

While time has not weakened the third of these historical reasons, the first and second have definitely begun to wane. The desire to encourage unrestricted development has receded as zoning and planning regulations have become more comprehensive, and access to natural light can be expected to justify an increasing degree of protection as the technology of solar energy develops. It does not follow, however, that we should turn to the doctrine of ancient lights to accomplish this purpose. Because the law of zoning is itself one means to recognize an interest in access to light and air, and because, as we will discuss below, the law of nuisance is another, we reject the argument that a prescriptive right to light or air should be recognized at this time. *Cf.* Morton v. State, 181 A.2d 831, 835 (N.H. 1962) (assuming possibility of conveyance of rights to light, air, etc.).

At the other extreme among the positions taken in this litigation is the rule customarily identified with *Fontainebleau H. Corp. v. Forty–Five Twenty-Five, Inc.*, 114 So.2d 357 (Fla.App.1959), *cert. denied*, 117 So.2d 842 (Fla.1960). In that case the court dissolved a trial court's preliminary injunction against construction of a building that would have cast a shadow over the cabana, pool and sunbathing areas of a neighboring hotel. The court ruled out the possibility of proving a nuisance on the facts before it by affirming Florida's traditional rule, that in the absence of a zoning restriction, a property owner could build up to his property line and as high as he chose. The rule in *Fontainebleau* thus stands at the furthest remove from the doctrine of ancient lights. Where the latter would limit the neighbor's right to build, the former never would.

The present defendant urges us to adopt the *Fontainebleau* rule and thereby to refuse any common law recognition to interests in light and air, but we decline to do so. If we were so to limit the ability of the common law to grow, we would in effect be rejecting one of the wise assumptions underlying the traditional law of nuisance: that we cannot anticipate at any one time the variety of predicaments in which protection of property interests or redress for their violation will be justifiable. For it is just this recognition that has led the courts to avoid rigid formulations for determining when an interference with the use of property will be actionable, and to rest instead on the flexible rule that actionable, private nuisance consists of an unreasonable as well as a substantial interference with another person's use and enjoyment of his property. *See* Robie v. Lillis, 299 A.2d 155, 158 (N.H. 1972). That is, because we have to anticipate that the uses of property will change over time, we have developed a law of nuisance that protects the use and enjoyment of property when a threatened harm to the plaintiff owner can be said to outweigh the utility of the defendant owner's conduct to himself and to the community. *Id*. at 159.

Viewing the elements and concept of private nuisance as thus formulated in *Robie*, there is no reason in principle why the law of nuisance should not be applied to claims for the protection of a property owner's interests in light and air, and for reasons already given we believe that considerations of policy support just such an application of nuisance concepts. We therefore hold that the law of private nuisance as expressed in *Robie* provides the appropriate standard for passing on a property owner's claims of interference with interests in light and air. *See* Prah v. Maretti, 321 N.W.2d 182, 191 (Wis. 1982).

Since this is the course that the trial court followed, the [question] is whether the evidence supported the court's finding that the defendant's building would not be a private nuisance. . . .

The court found, first, that the threatened interference would not be unreasonable. It based this conclusion on findings that nearly all the affected office windows had previously been covered with translucent but not transparent plastic sheets or were blocked by heavy drapes. The southerly openings to the light shaft were covered by translucent but not transparent glass, which admitted substantially less light than the clear skylight above it. It was uncontested that virtually every affected office would continue to receive light from the shaft or from the east or west windows of the building.

The court addressed both the issues of reasonableness and of substantiality when it further found that such interference as there would be would not exceed what was normal under the circumstances. The sites were in the downtown commercial area of Manchester, where buildings commonly buttress and block the sides of adjacent structures. Moreover, the defendant proposed to do no more than the plaintiff's own predecessor had done, by building right to the lot line and to a height of six stories. If, as the plaintiff claimed, this would require expenditures for additional artificial lighting and ventilation systems, she failed to present any evidence that the costs would exceed what was customarily necessary for such buildings.

The court again alluded to the element of substantiality of the threatened interference when it expressly found that little weight should be accorded to the evidence that the Pickering Building would drop in value. This finding was warranted both by the plaintiff's unconvincing evidence on the point, and by this court's holding in *Robie* that evidence of depreciation in value is to be given little weight in the law of nuisance, since "the law cannot generally protect landowners from fluctuating land values which is a risk necessarily inherent in all land ownership." Robie v. Lillis, 299 A.2d at 160.

Thus on the issues of unreasonableness and substantiality the evidence supported the findings. The evidence also supported the court in its more general conclusion under *Robie*, that the utility to the defendant and to the public of a new office building would outweigh the burden to the plaintiff of installing additional lighting and ventilating equipment. The court therefore was warranted in finding that the building as planned would not be a private nuisance.

. . .

The trial court did not err in dismissing the bill in equity.

Affirmed.

■ JOHNSON, J., did not sit; the others concurred.

NOTES AND QUESTIONS

1. Does *Tenn* create the same standard as *Prah*?

2. Many states and localities have enacted statutes providing access to sunlight for solar energy devices under certain conditions. *See*, John Gergacz, *Legal Aspects of Solar Energy: Statutory Approaches for Access to Sunlight*, 10 B.C. ENVTL. AFF. L. REV. 1 (1982). These statutes embody numerous choices and compromises; some, for example, distinguish between shading caused by vegetation as opposed to that caused by buildings; some distinguish between various types of solar devices. Id. Should the courts or the legislature make these kinds of choices? Do you agree with the assertion in *Prah* that development of an expanding economy is less significant today than it was earlier in American history and thus restrictions on development to provide access to sunlight make more sense today than in the past?

The creation of solar access rights through litigation has remained rare, as several courts have rejected the *Prah* rationale. *See* SANDY F. KRAEMER, SOLAR L. 63–67 (Supp. 1991). Moreover, the private nuisance approach, used in *Prah*, can result in highly uncertain outcomes. Recall that in *Prah* itself the court remanded to determine if the elements of an actionable nuisance had been established. That decision was never made since the trial court in *Prah* ultimately dismissed the suit without reaching the nuisance issue. Kenneth James, Note, *Potis, Solar Access Rights in Florida: Is There a Right to Sunlight in the Sunshine State?*, 10 NOVA L.J. 125, 133 (1985). As noted above, the establishment of solar access rights through legislation has proven to be the more common approach. Id. at 135–46; *see also* Adrian Bradbrook, *Future Directions in Solar Access Protection*, 9 ENVTL. L. 167 (1988).

The evolution of legal rules that balance development and access to sunlight is similar to changes in other areas of the law. Many American jurisdictions, for example, enacted in the 19th century "fencing out" statutes that limited strict liability to cases in which a defendant's cattle broke through a plaintiff's fence and caused property damage; when the country became more settled, however, legislatures switched to "fencing in" statutes that imposed strict liability on owners of cattle unless they fenced in their livestock. WILLIAM PROSSER, JOHN WADE & VICTOR SCHWARTZ, TORTS 706–07 (7th ed. 1982).

The practical impact of changing the legal rule for access to sunlight may be less obvious than first appears. Under the traditional rule, when you wished to put up a solar collector, you could buy from your neighbor an express easement to light. *See, e.g.*, Richard Powell & Patrick Rohan, Powell on Real Property & 34.11[5] (1994). When the traditional rule is changed—whether by a decision like *Prah* or by statute—the process is reversed: your neighbor who wishes to shade your house now has to buy from you your right to sunlight. It is possible, depending on such factors as the cost of bargaining, that two neighbors will, through bargaining with each other, reach the same outcome regardless of which rule governs. A considerable amount of literature in law and economics has developed around problems of this type. Seminal pieces include Ronald Coase, *The Problem of Social Cost*, 3 J.Law & Econ. 1 (1960); Guido Calabresi, *Transaction Costs, Resource Allocation and Liability Rules—A Comment*, 11 J.Law & Econ. 67 (1968).

B. Hydrogen Fuel Cells and the Soft Path Debate

In his January 28, 2003 State of the Union Address, President George W. Bush called for a new commitment to the use of hydrogen as a fuel "to make our air significantly cleaner, and our country much less dependent on foreign sources of energy." About a year later the President's Assistant Secretary of Energy testified before a House of Representatives Committee on the President's plan "to transform the Nation's energy future from one dependent on foreign petroleum to one that utilizes the most abundant element in the universe—hydrogen. This solution holds the potential to provide virtually limitless clean, safe, secure, affordable, and reliable energy from domestic resources." *Hydrogen Fuel and FreedomCAR Initiatives: Hearing Before the House Comm. on Science*, 108th Cong., 2d Sess. (March 3, 2004) (testimony of David K. Garman, Assistant Secretary for Energy Efficiency & Renewable Energy, U.S. Department of Energy).

This enthusiasm recalls that of President Eisenhower for nuclear energy, Sec. II. A., *supra*, and President Carter for solar energy, Sec. III. A., *supra*. As with nuclear and solar energy, a note of caution is a precondition to a sensible policy. Producing hydrogen at low cost involves the use of polluting fuels like coal, while producing it through alternative means like wind energy may be quite costly for many years. In addition, hydrogen is difficult to store and ship safely. *See, e.g.*, Matthew L. Wald, *Report Questions Bush Plan for Hydrogen–Fueled Cars*, N.Y. Times, Feb. 6, 2004, at A20. Sustained research funding for many years as well as a variety of other incentives may be necessary to determine if hydrogen can become an important fuel source.

The primary focus today is on the use of hydrogen to generate electricity through the use of a device known as the fuel cell. The history of the fuel cell illustrates the indirect path from basic science to application that we have seen with nuclear energy and photovoltaics. In 1839, the same year that Becquerel noted the photoelectric effect that eventually lead to photovoltaics, the British physicist William Grove created the first example of what was later called the fuel cell. Grove knew that sending an electric current through water split the water into its component parts of hydrogen and oxygen. He reversed the reaction and combined hydrogen and oxygen to create electricity and water. Grove, like Einstein and Becquerel, was interested in scientific knowledge, not practical applications. Fuel cells found their first use in the 1960's when they were employed as power sources for U.S. space missions. While fuel cells still remain expensive, they are an attractive source of electricity because if you use pure hydrogen as the fuel, you get electricity without the production of greenhouse gases. As noted above, obtaining usable hydrogen at a reasonable cost without producing pollution remains a challenge, but the promise is there that fuel cells could be used to provide electricity to power automobiles, homes, laptop computers, and the like. *See* Seth Dunn, *Hydrogen Futures: Toward a Sustainable Energy System (Worldwatch Paper #157)* 39–54 (2001).

As with photovoltaics, the most significant impact of fuel cells may someday derive from their small scale. A home, for example, could draw its electricity from a photovoltaic array on the roof or a fuel cell in the basement without connecting to the central power grid. Some commentators see "micropower" technologies like these as someday revolutionizing the energy system "toward a more small-scale decentralized model ... [like] the computer industry, which has been completely realigned by the rapid shift from mainframes to personal computers." Seth Dunn, *Micropower: The Next Electrical Era (Worldwatch Paper #151)* 226–27 (2000). The excerpts that follow explore the implications of that vision.

Amory Lovins, *Energy Strategy: The Road Not Taken?*

55 FOREIGN AFF. 55, 77–81 (1976).

There exists today a body of energy technologies that have certain specific features in common and that offer great technical, economic and political attractions, yet for which there is no generic term. For lack of a more satisfactory term, I shall call them "soft" technologies: a textural description, intended to mean not vague, mushy, speculative or ephemeral, but rather flexible, resilient, sustainable and benign. Energy paths dependent on soft technologies ... will be called "soft" energy paths, as the "hard" technologies ... constitute a "hard" path (in both senses). The distinction between hard and soft energy paths rests not on how much energy is used, but on the technical and sociopolitical *structure* of the energy system, thus focusing our attention on consequent and crucial political differences.

[T]he social structure is significantly shaped by the rapid deployment of soft technologies. These are defined by five characteristics:

— They rely on renewable energy flows that are always there whether we use them or not, such as sun and wind and vegetation: on energy income, not on depletable energy capital.

— They are diverse, so that energy supply is an aggregate of very many individually modest contributions, each designed for maximum effectiveness in particular circumstances.

— They are flexible and relatively low-technology—which does not mean unsophisticated, but rather, easy to understand and use without esoteric skills, accessible rather than arcane.

— They are matched in *scale* and in geographic distribution to end-use needs, taking advantage of the free distribution of most natural energy flows.

— They are matched in *energy quality* to end-use needs: a key feature that deserves immediate explanation. . . .

A feature of soft technologies as essential as their fitting end-use needs (for a different reason) is their appropriate scale, which can achieve important types of economies not available to larger, more centralized systems. This is done in five ways, of which the first is reducing and sharing overheads. Roughly half your electricity bill is fixed distribution costs to pay the overheads of a sprawling energy system: transmission lines, transformers, cables, meters and people to read them, planners, headquarters, billing computers, interoffice memos, advertising agencies. For electrical and some fossil-fuel systems, distribution accounts for more than half of total capital cost, and administration for a significant fraction of total operating cost. Local or domestic energy systems can reduce or even eliminate these infrastructure costs. The resulting savings can far outweigh the extra costs of the dispersed maintenance infrastructure that the small systems require, particularly where that infrastructure already exists or can be shared (e.g., plumbers fixing solar heaters as well as sinks).

Small scale brings further savings by virtually eliminating distribution losses, which are cumulative and pervasive in centralized energy systems (particularly those using high-quality energy). Small systems also avoid direct diseconomies of scale, such as the frequent unreliability of large units and the related need to provide instant "spinning reserve" capacity on electrical grids to replace large stations that suddenly fail. Small systems with short lead times greatly reduce exposure to interest escalation and mistimed demand forecasts—major indirect diseconomies of large scale.

The fifth type of economy available to small systems arises from mass production. Consider, as Henrik Harboe suggests, the 100–odd million cars in this country. In round numbers, each car probably has an average cost of less than $4,000 and a shaft power over 100 kilowatts (134 horsepower). Presumably a good engineer could build a generator and upgrade an automobile engine to a reliable, 35–percent-efficient diesel at no greater total cost, yielding a mass-produced diesel generator unit costing less than $40 per kW. In contrast, the motive capacity in our central power stations—currently totaling about 1/40 as much as in our cars—costs perhaps ten times more per kW, partly because it is not mass-produced. It is not surprising that at least one foreign car maker hopes to go into the wind-machine and heat-pump business. Such a market can be entered incrementally, without the billions of dollars' investment required for, say, liquefying natural gas or gasifying coal. It may require a production philosophy oriented toward technical simplicity, low replacement cost, slow obsolescence, high reliability, high volume and low markup; but these are familiar concepts in mass production. Industrial resistance would presumably melt when—as with pollution-abatement equipment—the scope for profit was perceived.

This is not to say that all energy systems need be at domestic scale. For example, the medium scale of urban neighborhoods and rural villages offers fine prospects for solar collectors—especially for adding collectors to existing buildings of which some (perhaps with large flat roofs) can take excess collector area while others cannot take any. They could be joined via communal heat storage systems, saving on labor cost and on heat losses. The costly craftwork of remodeling existing systems—"backfitting" idiosyncratic houses with individual collectors—could thereby be greatly reduced. Despite these advantages, medium-scale solar technologies are currently receiving little attention apart from a condominium-village project in Vermont sponsored by the Department of Housing and Urban Development and the 100–dwelling-unit Mejannes-le-Clap project in France.

The schemes that dominate ERDA's [the predecessor of the Department of Energy] solar research budget—such as making electricity from huge collectors in the desert, or from temperature differences in the oceans, or from Brooklyn Bridge-like satellites in outer space—do not satisfy our criteria, for they are ingenious high-technology ways to supply energy in a form and at a scale inappropriate to most end-use needs. Not all solar technologies are soft. Nor, for the same reason, is nuclear fusion a soft technology. But many genuine soft technologies are now available and are now economic. What are some of them?

Solar heating and, imminently, cooling head the list. They are incrementally cheaper than electric heating, and far more inflation-proof, practically anywhere in the world. In the United States (with fairly high average sunlight levels), they are cheaper than present electric heating virtually anywhere, cheaper than oil heat in many parts, and cheaper than gas and coal in some. Even in the least favorable parts of the continental United States, far more sunlight falls on a typical building than is required to heat and cool it without supplement; whether this is considered economic depends on how the accounts are done. The difference in solar input between the most and least favorable parts of the lower 49 states is generally less than two-fold, and in cold regions, the long heating season can improve solar economics.

Ingenious ways of backfitting existing urban and rural buildings (even large commercial ones) or their neighborhoods with efficient and exceedingly reliable solar collectors are being rapidly developed in both the private and public sectors. . . .

Amory Lovins, *Prepared Testimony*

in THE ENERGY CONTROVERSY 28–31 (Hugh Nash ed., 1979).

Hard and soft technologies have very different implications for technologists. Hard technologies are demanding and frustrating. They are not much fun to do and are therefore unlikely to be done well. While they strain technology to (and beyond) its limits, the scope they offer for innovation is of a rather narrow, routine sort, and is buried within huge, anonymous research teams. The systems are beyond the developmental reach of all but a few giant corporations, liberally aided by public subsidies, subventions, and bailouts. The disproportionate talent and money devoted to hard technologies gives their proponents disproportionate influence, reinforcing the trend and discouraging good technologists from devoting their careers to soft technologies—which then cannot absorb funds effectively for lack of good people. And once hard technologies are developed, the enormous investments required to tool up to make them effectively exclude small business from the market, thus sacrificing rapid and sustained returns in money, energy, and jobs for all but a small segment of society.

Soft technologies have a completely different character. They are best developed by innovative small businesses and even individuals, for they offer immense scope for basically new ideas. Their challenge lies not in complexity but in simplicity. They permit but do not require mass production, thus encouraging local manufacture, by capital-saving and labor-intensive methods, of equipment adapted to local needs, materials, and skills. Soft technologies are multi-purpose and can be integrated with buildings and with transport and food systems, saving on infrastructure. Their diversity matches our own pluralism: there is a soft energy system to match any settlement pattern. Soft technologies do not distort political structures or priorities; they improve the quality of work by emphasizing personal ingenuity, responsibility, and craftsmanship; they are inherently non-violent, and are therefore a livelihood that technologists can have good dreams about. . . .

The choice between the soft and hard paths is urgent. Though each path is only illustrative and embraces an infinite spectrum of variations on a theme, there is a deep structural and conceptual dichotomy between them. Soft and hard *technologies* are not *technically* incompatible: in principle, nuclear power stations and solar collectors can coexist. But soft and hard *paths* are *culturally* incompatible: each path entails a certain evolution of social values and perceptions that makes the other kind of world harder to imagine. The two paths are *institutionally* antagonistic: the policy actions, institutions, and political commitments required for each (especially for the hard path) would seriously inhibit the other. And they are *logistically* competitive: every dollar, every bit of sweat and technical talent, every barrel of irreplaceable oil, every year that we devote to the very demanding high technologies is a resource that we cannot use to pursue the elements of a soft path urgently enough to make them work together properly. In this sense, technologies like nuclear power are not only unnecessary but a positive encumbrance, for their resource commitments foreclose other and more attractive options, delaying soft technologies until the fossil-fuel bridge has been burned. Thus we must, with due deliberate speed, choose one path or the other, before one has foreclosed the other or before nuclear proliferation has foreclosed both. We should use fossil fuels—thriftily—to capitalize a transition as nearly as possible straight to our ultimate energy-income sources, because we won't have another chance to get there. . . .

Aden B. Meinel and Marjorie P. Meinel, *Soft Path Leads to a New Dark Age*

in The Energy Controversy 225, 226–28, 232–33 (Hugh Nash ed., 1979).

When Lovins discusses solar and other exotic options, he is naive, accepting only what pleases him and ignoring very fundamental problems as though they did not exist. There are problems for both high technology and low technology solar options. We have traced the discouraging history of attempts to inject new low-level solar technology into developing countries and know that the facts of capital and economics are as inexorable in these societies as in advanced societies. To like only simple technology and eschew any technology that appears beyond the comprehension of the average individual is an illusion.

Our work has taken us to much of the world, and we have seen that Lovins' type of simple society does exist in some developing countries. His proposals greatly resemble Mahatma Gandhi's "cottage industries," held by many educated Indians to have been a diversion from the effort to improve the lot of the masses. One of the greatest improvements in the welfare of the village inhabitants in India has been, contrary to Lovins' hypothesis, the electrification of the villages. This step parallels the dramatic changes caused by the Rural Electrification Agency in the United States in the '30's, a period before the personal knowledge of most of the population today. His proposal also has echoes of Mao's "great leap forward," wherein technology was forced toward backyard industries, including even steel smelting! It, too, was a notable failure of an enticing dream. For the industrialized world to toy with such a set of ideas could be the beginning of a irreversible process leading downward, one from which recovery might be denied as problem piles upon problem and acrimony upon acrimony.... [T]he alternative which we prefer, and which Mr. Lovins would dismiss as a "hard" technology, is the production of electric power or hydrogen on large-scale solar farms located in the arid southwest on land not now in use.

Our advocacy of large-scale solar power farms is contrary to the stream of popular enthusiasm. Small-scale individual applications are the center of attention today. We feel this is contrary to the way society has gone for centuries, in fact, ever since the isolated castle of the Middle Ages gave way slowly before renewed commerce and order. There is no reason why each of us could not have our own gasoline, or diesel, powered generator and water well today—as Mr. Lovins advocates—except that it would be inconvenient, unreliable and costly. We have lived in a solar-heated house with a solar-heated swimming pool. We do not think many other persons, other than avid do-it-yourselfers, would enjoy it after the novelty wore off.

Solar energy may first come into use on people's rooftops, but we are certain that, as soon as possible, they will prefer to have it delivered as electrical energy and transportable fuels. People already use electrical energy for a vast array of needs and luxuries. Public and private utilities provide it for us and take care that the system supplies it with high reliability. American industry is geared to produce electricity-consuming devices. Solar electric power therefore meets the requirement of minimum perturbation of the socio-economic system we live in, a requirement that must be met for change to be socially acceptable.

We think that the utilities have a long future of delivering energy and water to consumers at the lowest possible cost and maximum convenience, whether the energy be fossil, nuclear, geothermal, wind or solar. For everyone to abandon the utility and get his own energy system seems like a step back toward the Dark Ages, or like a person abandoning the ship to cling to his personal life jacket. We have confidence in the viability of the ship....

E.F. Schumacher, Small Is Beautiful

147, 156–58 (1973).

Suddenly, if not altogether surprisingly, the modern world, shaped by modern technology, finds itself involved in three crises simultaneously. First, human nature revolts against inhuman technological, organisational, and political patterns, which it experiences as suffocating and debilitating; second, the living environment which supports human life aches and groans and gives signs of partial breakdown; and, third, it is clear to anyone fully knowledgeable in the subject matter that the inroads being made into the world's non-renewable resources, particularly those of fossil fuels, are such that serious bottlenecks and virtual exhaustion loom ahead in the quite foreseeable future.... Strange to say, the Sermon on the Mount gives pretty precise instructions on how to construct an outlook that could lead to an Economics of Survival.

— How blessed are those who know that they are poor:

the Kingdom of Heaven is theirs.

— How blessed are the sorrowful;

they shall find consolation.

— How blessed are those of a gentle spirit;

they shall have the earth for their possession.

— How blessed are those who hunger and thirst to see right prevail;

they shall be satisfied;

— How blessed are the peacemakers;

God shall call them his sons.

It may seem daring to connect these beatitudes with matters of technology and economics. But may it not be that we are in trouble precisely because we have failed for so long to make this connection? It is not difficult to discern what these beatitudes may mean for us today:

— We are poor, not demigods.

— We have plenty to be sorrowful about, and are not emerging into a golden age.

— We need a gentle approach, a non-violent spirit, and small is beautiful.

— We must concern ourselves with justice and see right prevail.

— And all this, only this, can enable us to become peacemakers.

The home-comers base themselves upon a different picture of man from that which motivates the people of the forward stampede. It would be very superficial to say that the latter believe in "growth" while the former do not. In a sense, everybody believes in growth, and rightly so, because growth is an essential feature of life. The whole point, however, is to give the idea of growth a qualitative determination; for there are always many things that ought to be growing and many things that ought to be diminishing.

Equally, it would be very superficial to say that the home-comers do not believe in progress, which also can be said to be an essential feature of all life. The whole point is to determine what constitutes progress. And the home-comers believe that the direction which modern technology has taken and is continuing to pursue—towards ever-greater size, ever-higher speeds, and ever-increased violence, in defiance of all laws of natural harmony—is the opposite of progress. Hence the call for taking stock and finding a new orientation. The stocktaking indicates that we are destroying our very basis of existence, and the reorientation is based on remembering what human life is really about.

In one way or another everybody will have to take sides in this great conflict. To "leave it to the experts" means to side with the people of the forward stampede. It is widely accepted that politics is too important a matter to be left to experts. Today, the main content of politics is economics, and the main content of economics is technology. If politics cannot be left to the experts, neither can economics and technology....

NOTES AND QUESTIONS

1. Would Lovins or Schumacher accept "hard" technologies if those technologies were controlled by "the people"? Would the Meinels accept "soft" technologies if they believed those technologies to be consistent with increasing wealth and economic growth?

2. Is the laptop computer a "hard" or a "soft" technology? What difference does it make?

3. Lovins' views have sparked much debate, particularly on the issue of whether his approach could actually satisfy world energy needs at reasonable cost. *See, e.g., Alternative Long Range Energy Strategies: Joint Hearing Before the House Select Committee on Small Business and the House Committee on Interior and Insular Affairs,* 94th Cong., 2d Sess. (1976).

4. As Lovins notes, not all solar devices are "soft." "Hard" solar technologies, such as central power stations fueled by heat from mirrors, would fit in with current utility systems. "Soft" decentralized solar energy systems, such as rooftop collectors, may in part or in whole supplant those systems. Utility pricing structures could arguably encourage the use of collectors combined with traditional sources of electricity for those times when collectors are inadequate. *See, e.g.,* William H. Lawrence & John Minan, *Solar Energy and Public Utility Rate Regulation,* 26 UCLA L.REV. 550 (1979). If you had a choice, and costs were equal, would you prefer electricity from a central source or from a rooftop collector? Does it matter which system gives you more personal control and responsibility in areas such as system repair?

5. The hard vs. soft path debate indicates how scientific and technological developments can alter the very structure of a society. In deciding whether or not to encourage a particular area of science, does cost benefit analysis adequately consider this type of impact?

6. In the long run, can following the hard or soft path do any more than postpone the painful process of accommodating population growth to a world of finite resources? *See* Garrett Hardin, *The Tragedy of the Commons,* 162 SCI. 1243 (1968).

CHAPTER 4

PUBLIC CONTROL OF SCIENCE AND MEDICINE

I. LIMITS ON GOVERNMENT CONTROL OF SCIENCE AND MEDICINE: THE FIRST AMENDMENT FRAMEWORK

A. FREE SPEECH

United States v. The Progressive, Inc.

United States District Court for the Western District of Wisconsin, 1979.
467 F.Supp. 990.

MEMORANDUM AND ORDER

■ WARREN, J.

On March 9, 1979, this Court, at the request of the government, but after hearing from both parties, issued a temporary restraining order enjoining defendants, their employees, and agents from publishing or otherwise communicating or disclosing in any manner any restricted data contained in the article: "The H–Bomb Secret: How We Got It, Why We're Telling It."

In keeping with the Court's order that the temporary restraining order should be in effect for the shortest time possible, a preliminary injunction hearing was scheduled for one week later, on March 16, 1979. At the request of the parties and with the Court's acquiescence, the preliminary injunction hearing was rescheduled for 10:00 A.M. today in order that both sides might have additional time to file affidavits and arguments. The Court continued the temporary restraining order until 5:00 P.M. today.

In order to grant a preliminary injunction, the Court must find that plaintiff has a reasonable likelihood of success on the merits, and that the plaintiff will suffer irreparable harm if the injunction does not issue. In addition, the Court must consider the interest of the public and the balance of the potential harm to plaintiff and defendants.

Jurisdiction in this action is grounded on 42 U.S.C. § 2280, the Atomic Energy Act and 28 U.S.C. § 1345.

Under the facts here alleged, the question before this Court involves a clash between allegedly vital security interests of the United States and the competing constitutional doctrine against prior restraint in publication.

In its argument and briefs, plaintiff relies on national security, as enunciated by Congress in The Atomic Energy Act of 1954, as the basis for classification of certain documents. Plaintiff contends that, in certain areas, national preservation and self-interest permit the retention and classification of government secrets. The government argues that its national security interest also permits it to impress classification and censorship upon information originating in the public domain, if when drawn together, synthesized and collated, such information acquires the character of presenting immediate, direct and irreparable harm to the interests of the United States.

Defendants argue that freedom of expression as embodied in the First Amendment is so central to the heart of liberty that prior restraint in any form becomes anathema. They contend that this is particularly true when a nation is not at war and where the prior restraint is based on surmise or conjecture. While acknowledging that freedom of the press is not absolute, they maintain that the publication of the projected article does not rise to the level of immediate, direct and irreparable harm which could justify incursion into First Amendment freedoms.

Hence, although embodying deep and fundamental principles of democratic philosophy, the issue also requires a factual determination by a federal court sitting in equity. At the level of a temporary restraining order, or a preliminary injunction, such matters are customarily dealt with through affidavits.

Thus far the affidavits filed are numerous and complex. They come from individuals of learning and renown. They deal with how the information at issue was assembled, what it means, and how injurious the affiant believes it to be.

The Court notes the *amici curiae* briefs filed by the American Civil Liberties Union, the Wisconsin Civil Liberties Union, the Federation of American Scientists and the Fund for Open Information and Accountability, Inc., and expresses thanks for them. The Court gave consideration to the suggestion that a panel of experts be appointed to serve as witnesses for the Court to assist it in determining whether the dangers of publication are as great as the government asserts or as inconsequential as *The Progressive* states. However, the Court concluded that such a procedure really would merely proliferate the opinions of experts arrayed on both sides of the issue.

. . .

From the founding days of this nation, the rights to freedom of speech and of the press have held an honored place in our constitutional scheme. The establishment and nurturing of these rights is one of the true achievements of our form of government.

Because of the importance of these rights, any prior restraint on publication comes into court under a heavy presumption against its constitutional validity. New York Times v. United States, 403 U.S. 713 (1971).

However, First Amendment rights are not absolute. They are not boundless.

Justice Frankfurter dissenting in *Bridges v. California*, 314 U.S. 252, 282 (1941), stated it in this fashion: "Free speech is not so absolute or irrational a conception as to imply paralysis of the means for effective protection of all the freedoms secured by the Bill of Rights." In the *Schenck* case, Justice Holmes recognized: "The character of every act depends upon the circumstances in which it is done." Schenck v. United States, 249 U.S. 47, 52 (1919).

In *Near v. Minnesota*, 283 U.S. 697 (1931), the Supreme Court specifically recognized an extremely narrow area, involving national security, in which interference with First Amendment rights might be tolerated and a prior restraint on publication might be appropriate. The Court stated:

> "When a nation is at war many things that might be said in time of peace are such a hindrance to its effort that their utterance will not be endured so long as men fight and that no Court could regard them as protected by any constitutional right." No one would question but that a government might prevent actual obstruction to its recruiting service or the publication of the sailing dates of transports or the number and location of troops. *Id.* at 716, (citation omitted).

Thus, it is clear that few things, save grave national security concerns, are sufficient to override First Amendment interests. A court is well admonished to approach any requested prior restraint with a great deal of skepticism.

Juxtaposed against the right to freedom of expression is the government's contention that the national security of this country could be jeopardized by publication of the article.

The Court is convinced that the government has a right to classify certain sensitive documents to protect its national security. The problem is with the scope of the classification system.

Defendants contend that the projected article merely contains data already in the public domain and readily available to any diligent seeker. They say other nations already have the same information or the opportunity to obtain it. How then, they argue, can they be in violation of 42 U.S.C. §§ 2274(b) and 2280 which purport to authorize injunctive relief against one who would disclose restricted data "with reason to believe such data will be utilized to injure the United States or to secure an advantage to any foreign nation ...?"

Although the government states that some of the information is in the public domain, it contends that much of the data is not, and that the Morland article contains a core of information that has never before been published.

Furthermore, the government's position is that whether or not specific information is "in the public domain" or has been "declassified" at some point is not determinative. The government states that a court must look at the nature and context of prior disclosures and analyze what the practical impact of the prior disclosures are as contrasted to that of the present revelation.

The government feels that the mere fact that the author, Howard Morland, could prepare an article explaining the technical processes of thermonuclear weapons does not mean that those processes are available to everyone. They lay heavy emphasis on the argument that the danger lies in the exposition of certain concepts never heretofore disclosed in conjunction with one another.

In an impressive affidavit, Dr. Hans A. Bethe, whose affidavit was introduced by the government and whose article, *The Hydrogen Bomb: II,* was a source document for Theodore Postol's affidavit I filed by the defendants states that sizeable portions of the Morland text should be classified as restricted data because the processes outlined in the manuscript describe the essential design and operation of thermonuclear weapons. He later concludes, "that the design and operational concepts described in the manuscript are not expressed or revealed in the public literature nor do I believe they are known to scientists not associated with the government weapons programs."

The Court has grappled with this difficult problem and has read and studied the affidavits and other documents on file. After all this, the Court finds concepts within the article that it does not find in the public realm— concepts that are vital to the operation of the hydrogen bomb.

Even if some of the information is in the public domain, due recognition must be given to the human skills and expertise involved in writing this article. The author needed sufficient expertise to recognize relevant, as opposed to irrelevant, information and to assimilate the information obtained. The right questions had to be asked or the correct educated guesses had to be made.

The ability of G.I. Taylor to calculate the yield of the first nuclear explosion from a *Life* magazine photo demonstrates that certain individuals with some knowledge, ability to reason and extraordinary perseverance may acquire additional knowledge without access to classified information, even though the information thus acquired may not be obvious to others not so equipped or motivated. All of this must be considered in resolving the issues before the Court.

Does the article provide a "do-it yourself" guide for the hydrogen bomb? Probably not. A number of affidavits make quite clear that a *sine qua non* to thermonuclear capability is a large, sophisticated industrial capability coupled with a coterie of imaginative, resourceful scientists and technicians. One does not build a hydrogen bomb in the basement. However, the article could possibly provide sufficient information to allow a medium size nation to move faster in developing a hydrogen weapon. It could provide a ticket to by-pass blind alleys.

The Morland piece could accelerate the membership of a candidate nation in the thermonuclear club. Pursuit of blind alleys or failure to grasp seemingly basic concepts have been the cause of many inventive failures.

For example, in one of the articles submitted to the Court, the author described how, in the late 1930's physicists in various countries were simultaneously, but independently, working on the idea of a nuclear chain reaction. The French physicists in their equation neglected to take full account of the fact that the neutrons produced by fission could go on to provoke further fissions in a many-step process—which is the essence of a chain reaction. Even though this idea seems so elementary, the concept of neutron multiplication was so novel that no nuclear physicists saw through the French team's oversight for about a year.

Thus, once basic concepts are learned, the remainder of the process may easily follow.

Although the defendants state that the information contained in the article is relatively easy to obtain, only five countries now have a hydrogen bomb. Yet the United States first successfully exploded the hydrogen bomb some twenty-six years ago.

The point has also been made that it is only a question of time before other countries will have the hydrogen bomb. That may be true. However, there are times in the course of human history when time itself may be very important. This time factor becomes critical when considering mass annihilation weaponry—witness the failure of Hitler to get his V–1 and V–2 bombs operational quickly enough to materially affect the outcome of World War II.

Defendants have stated that publication of the article will alert the people of this country to the false illusion of security created by the government's futile efforts at secrecy. They believe publication will provide the people with needed information to make informed decisions on an urgent issue of public concern.

However, this Court can find no plausible reason why the public needs to know the technical details about hydrogen bomb construction to carry on an informed debate on this issue. Furthermore, the Court believes that the defendants' position in favor of nuclear non-proliferation would be harmed, not aided, by the publication of this article.

The defendants have also relied on the decision in the *New York Times* case. In that case, the Supreme Court refused to enjoin the *New York Times* and the *Washington Post* from publishing the contents of a classified historical study of United States decision-making in Viet Nam, the so-called "Pentagon Papers."

This case is different in several important respects. In the first place, the study involved in the *New York Times* case contained historical data relating to events that occurred some three to twenty years previously. Secondly, the Supreme Court agreed with the lower court that no cogent reasons were advanced by the government as to why the article affected national security except that publication might cause some embarrassment to the United States.

A final and most vital difference between these two cases is the fact that a specific statute is involved here. Section 2274 of The Atomic Energy Act prohibits anyone from communicating, transmitting or disclosing any restricted data to any person "with reason to believe such data will be utilized to injure the United States or to secure an advantage to any foreign nation."

Section 2014 of the Act defines restricted data. " 'Restricted Data' means all data concerning 1) design, manufacture, or utilization of atomic weapons; 2) the production of special nuclear material; or 3) the use of special nuclear material in the production of energy, but shall not include data declassified or removed from the Restricted Data category pursuant to section 2162 of this title."

As applied to this case, the Court finds that the statute in question is not vague or overbroad. The Court is convinced that the terms used in the statute—"communicates, transmits or discloses"—include publishing in a magazine.

The Court is of the opinion that the government has shown that the defendants had reason to believe that the data in the article, if published, would injure the United States or give an advantage to a foreign nation. Extensive reading and studying of the documents on file lead to the conclusion that not all the data is available in the public realm in the same fashion, if it is available at all.

What is involved here is information dealing with the most destructive weapon in the history of mankind, information of sufficient destructive potential to nullify the right to free speech and to endanger the right to life itself.

Stripped to its essence then, the question before the Court is a basic confrontation between the First Amendment right to freedom of the press and national security.

Our Founding Fathers believed, as we do, that one is born with certain inalienable rights, which, as the Declaration of Independence intones, include the right to life, liberty and the pursuit of happiness. The Constitution, including the Bill of Rights, was enacted to make those rights operable in everyday life.

The Court believes that each of us is born seized of a panoply of basic rights, that we institute governments to secure these rights and that there is a hierarchy of values attached to these rights which is helpful in deciding the clash now before us.

Certain of these rights have an aspect of imperativeness or centrality that make them transcend other rights. Somehow it does not seem that the right to life and the right to not have soldiers quartered in your home can be of equal import in the grand scheme of things. While it may be true in the long-run, as Patrick Henry instructs us, that one would prefer death to life without liberty, nonetheless, in the short-run, one cannot enjoy freedom of speech, freedom to worship or freedom of the press unless one first enjoys the freedom to live.

Faced with a stark choice between upholding the right to continued life and the right to freedom of the press, most jurists would have no difficulty in opting for the chance to continue to breathe and function as they work to achieve perfect freedom of expression.

Is the choice here so stark? Only time can give us a definitive answer. But considering another aspect of this panoply of rights we all have is helpful in answering the question now before us. This aspect is the disparity of the risk involved.

The destruction of various human rights can come about in differing ways and at varying speeds. Freedom of the press can be obliterated overnight by some dictator's imposition of censorship or by the slow nibbling away at a free press through successive bits of repressive legislation enacted by a nation's lawmakers. Yet, even in the most drastic of such situations, it is always possible for a dictator to be overthrown, for a bad law to be repealed or for a judge's error to be subsequently rectified. Only when human life is at stake are such corrections impossible.

The case at bar is so difficult precisely because the consequences of error involve human life itself and on such an awesome scale.

The Secretary of State states that publication will increase thermonuclear proliferation and that this would "irreparably impair the national security of the United States." The Secretary of Defense says that dissemination of the Morland paper will mean a substantial increase in the risk of thermonuclear proliferation and lead to use or threats that would "adversely affect the national security of the United States."

Howard Morland asserts that "if the information in my article were not in the public domain, it should be put there ... so that ordinary citizens may have informed opinions about nuclear weapons."

Erwin Knoll, the editor of *The Progressive,* states he is "totally convinced that publication of the article will be of substantial benefit to the United States because it will demonstrate that this country's security does not lie in an oppressive and ineffective system of secrecy and classification but in open, honest, and informed public debate about issues which the people must decide."

The Court is faced with the difficult task of weighing and resolving these divergent views.

A mistake in ruling against *The Progressive* will seriously infringe cherished First Amendment rights. If a preliminary injunction is issued, it will constitute the first instance of prior restraint against a publication in this fashion in the history of this country, to this Court's knowledge. Such notoriety is not to be sought. It will curtail defendants' First Amendment rights in a drastic and substantial fashion. It will infringe upon our right to know and to be informed as well.

A mistake in ruling against the United States could pave the way for thermonuclear annihilation for us all. In that event, our right to life is extinguished and the right to publish becomes moot.

In the *Near* case, the Supreme Court recognized that publication of troop movements in time of war would threaten national security and could therefore be restrained. Times have changed significantly since 1931 when *Near* was decided. Now war by foot soldiers has been replaced in large part by war by machines and bombs. No longer need there be any advance warning or any preparation time before a nuclear war could be commenced.

In light of these factors, this Court concludes that publication of the technical information on the hydrogen bomb contained in the article is analogous to publication of troop movements or locations in time of war and falls within the extremely narrow exception to the rule against prior restraint.

Because of this "disparity of risk," because the government has met its heavy burden of showing justification for the imposition of a prior restraint on publication of the objected-to technical portions of the Morland article, and because the Court is unconvinced that suppression of the objected-to technical portions of the Morland article would in any plausible fashion impede the defendants in their laudable crusade to stimulate public knowledge of nuclear armament and bring about enlightened debate on national policy questions, the Court finds that the objected-to portions of the article fall within the narrow area recognized by the Court in *Near v. Minnesota* in which a prior restraint on publication is appropriate.

The government has met its burden under section 2274 of The Atomic Energy Act. In the Court's opinion, it has also met the test enunciated by two Justices in the *New York Times* case, namely grave, direct, immediate and irreparable harm to the United States.

The Court has just determined that if necessary it will at this time assume the awesome responsibility of issuing a preliminary injunction against *The Progressive's* use of the Morland article in its current form. . . .

NOTES AND QUESTIONS

1. After the district court handed down the above decision, another journal obtained and published the Morland article. The 7th Circuit therefore viewed the case as moot and dismissed *The Progressive*'s appeal. United States v. The Progressive, Inc., 610 F.2d 819 (7th Cir. 1979).

2. As Chapter 3 indicates, the government's concern over hydrogen bomb secrets dates back to the immediate post-World War II period and, in particular, to the Oppenheimer affair. The protection of military secrets often hampers scientific progress as well as public debate on science policy issues. Did the district court properly strike this extraordinarily difficult balance in *The Progressive?*

3. As the district court decision assumes, the First Amendment protects scientific speech, including the publication of articles. Thus, for example, in its obscenity decisions, the United States Supreme Court has carefully noted that the "First Amendment protects works, which taken as a whole, have serious . . . scientific value." Miller v. California, 413 U.S. 15, 34, 93 S.Ct. 2607, 37 L.Ed.2d 419 (1973). As the opinion in *The Progressive* makes clear, the First Amendment does not afford absolute protection to scientific speech, but does provide a substantial barrier to government regulation.

4. Most commentators agree that the First Amendment protection for the actual conduct of scientific or medical experiments, as opposed to the writing of papers, is reduced since experiments involve action as well as speech. On this view, the approach set forth in United States v. O'Brien, 391 U.S. 367, 88 S.Ct. 1673, 20 L.Ed.2d 672 (1968), applies to the regulation of experiments. *O'Brien* upheld the conviction of a draft card burner on grounds that "when 'speech' and 'nonspeech' elements are combined in the same course of conduct, a sufficiently important governmental interest in regulating the nonspeech element can justify incidental limitations on First Amendment freedoms." Id. at 376. Thus, for example, the state can regulate a scientific experiment involving poisons so as to protect the public health and safety. *See, e.g.*, John A. Robertson, *The Scientists' Right to Research: A Constitutional Analysis*, 51 S. CAL. L. REV. 1203, 1254–56 (1978); Richard Delgado & David R. Millen, *God, Galileo and Government: Toward Constitutional Protection for Scientific Inquiry*, 53 WASH. L. REV. 349, 390–92 (1978); James R. Ferguson, *Scientific Inquiry and the First Amendment*, 64 CORNELL L. REV. 639, 655 (1979). Other scholars suggest that scientific experimentation is entitled to even less First Amendment protection than that provided by *O'Brien*. *See* Gary L. Francione,

Experimentation and the Marketplace Theory of the First Amendment, 136 U. Pa. L. Rev. 417 (1987); *see also* Stephen L. Carter, *The Bellman, The Snark, and the Biohazard Debate*, 3 Yale L. & Pol'y Rev. 358 (1985). Under either view, should the federal government be allowed to restrict experiments involving human cloning on the ground that such experiments will lead to decreased respect for such values as individuality and human freedom?

5. In recent years, the First Amendment status of software has raised particular problems. Is software a form of speech entitled to robust First Amendment protection, a kind of device entitled to little such protection, or some combination of the two? The issue becomes particularly acute when the government seeks to impose export restrictions on encryption software. *See, e.g.*, Robert Plotkin, *Fighting Keywords: Translating the First Amendment to Protect Software Speech*, 2003 U. Ill. J.L. Tech. & Pol'y 329 (2003). On the general question of applying export controls to emerging technologies, *see, e.g.*, Christopher F. Corr, *The Wall Still Stands! Complying With Export Controls on Technology Transfers in the Post–Cold War, Post–9/11 Era*, 25 Hous. J. Int'l L. 441 (2003). On the domestic front, the growing judicial protection of commercial speech has affected the regulation of science, as when the Second Circuit held that Vermont could not mandate that milk producers be required to disclose on their labels that they had used recombinant bovine growth hormone. *See* International Dairy Foods Ass'n v. Amestoy, 92 F.3d 67 (2d Cir. 1996); *see generally* Jonathan Adler, *Food Biotechnology: A Legal Perspective: Regulating Genetically Modified Foods: Is Mandatory Labeling the Right Answer?*, 10 Rich. J.L. & Tech. 14 (2004).

6. But by far the most pervasive issues at the intersection of free speech and modern science and technology have involved government efforts to regulate the Internet. The Supreme Court has struggled for decades with applying the First Amendment to modern communications technology. In 1969, the Court held that, because of the scarcity of broadcast channels, the Federal Communications Commission could require television broadcasters to present public issues and to give fair coverage to each side of those issues, Red Lion Broad. Co. v. Federal Communications Comm'n, 395 U.S. 367, 89 S.Ct. 1794, 23 L.Ed.2d 371 (1969), an imposition that cannot be applied to newspapers. Miami Herald Publ'g Co. v. Tornillo, 418 U.S. 241, 94 S.Ct. 2831, 41 L.Ed.2d 730 (1974). But as the scarcity rationale waned, the Commission abandoned these restrictions on broadcasters. *See* John Hayes, *The Right to Reply: A Conflict of Fundamental Rights*, 37 Colum. J.L. & Soc. Probs. 551, 564–66 (2004). With cable television, the Court has upheld only those government regulations that are content-neutral. *Cf.* Turner Broad. Sys. v. Federal Communications Comm'n, 520 U.S. 180, 117 S.Ct. 1174, 137 L.Ed.2d 369 (1997) (cable systems can be required to carry local broadcast stations), *with* United States v. Playboy Entm't Group, 529 U.S. 803, 120 S.Ct. 1878, 146 L.Ed.2d 865 (2000) (cable systems cannot be required to scramble sexually explicit channels). But the largest controversies have involved government efforts to regulate indecent speech on the Internet, as the following landmark decision demonstrates.

Reno v. American Civil Liberties Union

Supreme Court of the United States, 1997.
521 U.S. 844, 117 S.Ct. 2329, 138 L.Ed.2d 874.

■ Justice Stevens delivered the opinion of the Court.

At issue is the constitutionality of two statutory provisions enacted to protect minors from "indecent" and "patently offensive" communications on the Internet. Notwithstanding the legitimacy and importance of the congressional goal of protecting children from harmful materials, we agree with the three-judge District Court that the statute abridges "the freedom of speech" protected by the First Amendment.

I.

The District Court made extensive findings of fact, most of which were based on a detailed stipulation prepared by the parties. *See* 929 F.Supp. 824, 830–49 (E.D.Pa. 1996). The findings describe the character and the dimensions of the Internet, the availability of sexually explicit material in that medium, and the problems confronting age verification for recipients of Internet communications. Because those findings provide the underpinnings for the legal issues, we begin with a summary of the undisputed facts.

The Internet

The Internet is an international network of interconnected computers. It is the outgrowth of what began in 1969 as a military program called "ARPANET," which was designed to enable computers operated by the military, defense contractors, and universities conducting defense-related research to communicate with one another by redundant channels even if some portions of the network were damaged in a war. While the ARPANET no longer exists, it provided an example for the development of a number of civilian networks that, eventually linking with each other, now enable tens of millions of people to communicate with one another and to access vast amounts of information from around the world. The Internet is "a unique and wholly new medium of worldwide human communication."

The Internet has experienced "extraordinary growth." The number of "host" computers—those that store information and relay communications—increased from about 300 in 1981 to approximately 9,400,000 by the time of the trial in 1996. Roughly 60% of these hosts are located in the United States. About 40 million people used the Internet at the time of trial, a number that is expected to mushroom to 200 million by 1999.

Individuals can obtain access to the Internet from many different sources, generally hosts themselves or entities with a host affiliation. Most colleges and universities provide access for their students and faculty; many corporations provide their employees with access through an office network; many communities and local libraries provide free access; and an increasing number of storefront "computer coffee shops" provide access for a small hourly fee. Several major national "online services" such as America Online, CompuServe, the Microsoft Network, and Prodigy offer access to their own extensive proprietary networks as well as a link to the much larger resources of the Internet. These commercial online services had almost 12 million individual subscribers at the time of trial.

Anyone with access to the Internet may take advantage of a wide variety of communication and information retrieval methods. These methods are constantly evolving and difficult to categorize precisely. But, as presently constituted, those most relevant to this case are electronic mail (e-mail), automatic mailing list services ("mail exploders," sometimes referred to as "listservs"), "newsgroups," "chat rooms," and the "World Wide Web." All of these methods can be used to transmit text; most can transmit sound, pictures, and moving video images. Taken together, these tools constitute a unique medium—known to its users as "cyberspace"—located in no particular geographical location but available to anyone, anywhere in the world, with access to the Internet.

. . .

Sexually Explicit Material

Sexually explicit material on the Internet includes text, pictures, and chat and "extends from the modestly titillating to the hardest-core." These files are created, named, and posted in the same manner as material that is not sexually explicit, and may be accessed either deliberately or unintentionally during the course of an imprecise search. "Once a provider posts its content on the Internet, it cannot prevent that content from entering any community." Thus, for example,

> when the UCR/California Museum of Photography posts to its Web site nudes by Edward Weston and Robert Mapplethorpe to announce that its new exhibit will travel to Baltimore and New York City, those images are available not only in Los Angeles, Baltimore, and New York City, but also in Cincinnati, Mobile, or Beijing—wherever Internet users live. Similarly, the safer sex instructions that Critical Path posts to its Web site, written in street language so that the teenage receiver can understand them, are available not just in Philadelphia, but also in Provo and Prague.

Some of the communications over the Internet that originate in foreign countries are also sexually explicit.

Though such material is widely available, users seldom encounter such content accidentally. "A document's title or a description of the document will usually appear before the document itself ... and in many cases the user will receive detailed information about a site's content before he or she need take the step to access the document. Almost all sexually explicit images are preceded by warnings as to the content." For that reason, the "odds are slim" that a user would enter a sexually explicit site by accident. Unlike communications received by radio or television, "the receipt of information on the Internet requires a series of affirmative steps more deliberate and directed than merely turning a dial. A child requires some sophistication and some ability to read to retrieve material and thereby to use the Internet unattended."

Systems have been developed to help parents control the material that may be available on a home computer with Internet access. A system may either limit a computer's access to an approved list of sources that have been identified as containing no adult material, it may block designated inappropriate sites, or it may attempt to block messages containing identifiable objectionable features. "Although parental control software currently can screen for certain suggestive words or for known sexually explicit sites, it cannot now screen for sexually explicit images." Nevertheless, the evidence indicates that, "a reasonably effective method by which parents can prevent their children from accessing sexually explicit and other material which parents may believe is inappropriate for their children will soon be widely available."

Age Verification

The problem of age verification differs for different uses of the Internet. The District Court categorically determined that there "is no effective way to determine the identity or the age of a user who is accessing material through e-mail, mail exploders, newsgroups or chat rooms." The Government offered no evidence that there was a reliable way to screen recipients and participants in such forums for age. Moreover, even if it were technologically feasible to block minors' access to newsgroups and chat rooms containing discussions of art, politics, or other subjects that potentially elicit "indecent" or "patently offensive" contributions, it would not be possible to block their access to that material and "still allow them access to the remaining content, even if the overwhelming majority of that content was not indecent."

Technology exists by which an operator of a Web site may condition access on the verification of requested information such as a credit card number or an adult password. Credit card verification is only feasible, however, either in connection with a commercial transaction in which the card is used, or by payment to a verification agency. Using credit card possession as a surrogate for proof of age would impose costs on noncommercial Web sites that would require many of them to shut down. For that reason, at the time of the trial, credit card verification was "effectively unavailable to a substantial number of Internet content providers." 929 F.Supp. at 846 (finding 102). Moreover, the imposition of such a requirement "would completely bar adults who do not have a credit card and lack the resources to obtain one from accessing any blocked material."

Commercial pornographic sites that charge their users for access have assigned them passwords as a method of age verification. The record does not contain any evidence concerning the reliability of these technologies. Even if passwords are effective for commercial purveyors of indecent material, the District Court found that an adult password requirement would impose significant burdens on noncommercial sites, both because they would discourage users from accessing their sites and because the cost of creating and maintaining such screening systems would be "beyond their reach."

In sum, the District Court found:

> Even if credit card verification or adult password verification were implemented, the Government presented no testimony as to how such systems could ensure that the user of the password or credit card is in fact over 18. The burdens imposed by credit card verification and adult password verification systems make them effectively unavailable to a substantial number of Internet content providers. *Ibid.* (finding 107).

II.

The Telecommunications Act of 1996, Pub.L. 104–104, 110 Stat. 56, was an unusually important legislative enactment. As stated on the first of its 103 pages, its primary purpose was to reduce regulation and encourage "the rapid deployment of new telecommunications technologies." The major components of the statute have nothing to do with the Internet; they were designed to promote competition in the local telephone service market, the multi-channel video market, and the market for over-the-air broadcasting. The Act includes seven Titles, six of which are the product of extensive committee hearings and the subject of discussion in Reports prepared by Committees of the Senate and the House of Representatives. By contrast, Title V—known as the "Communications Decency Act of 1996" (CDA)—contains provisions that were either added in executive committee after the hearings were concluded or as amendments offered during floor debate on the legislation. An amendment offered in the Senate was the source of the two statutory provisions challenged in this case. They are informally described as the "indecent transmission" provision and the "patently offensive display" provision.

The first, 47 U.S.C. § 223(a) (1994 ed., Supp. II), prohibits the knowing transmission of obscene or indecent messages to any recipient under 18 years of age. It provides in pertinent part:

(a) Whoever—

(1) in interstate or foreign communications—...

(B) by means of a telecommunications device knowingly—

(i) makes, creates, or solicits, and

(ii) initiates the transmission of, "any comment, request, suggestion, proposal, image, or other communication which is obscene or indecent, knowing that the recipient of the communication is under 18 years of age, regardless of whether the maker of such communication placed the call or initiated the communication;" ...

(2) knowingly permits any telecommunications facility under his control to be used for any activity prohibited by paragraph (1) with the intent that it be used for such activity, shall be fined under Title 18, or imprisoned not more than two years, or both.

The second provision, § 223(d), prohibits the knowing sending or displaying of patently offensive messages in a manner that is available to a person under 18 years of age. It provides:

(d) Whoever—

(1) in interstate or foreign communications knowingly—

(A) uses an interactive computer service to send to a specific person or persons under 18 years of age, or

(B) uses any interactive computer service to display in a manner available to a person under 18 years of age, "any comment, request, suggestion, proposal, image, or other communication that, in context, depicts or describes, in terms patently offensive as measured by contemporary community standards, gailsexual or excretory activities or organs, regardless of whether the user of such service placed the call or initiated the communication; or"

(2) knowingly permits any telecommunications facility under such person's control to be used for an activity prohibited by paragraph (1) with the intent that it be used for such activity, "shall be fined under Title 18, or imprisoned not more than two years, or both."

The breadth of these prohibitions is qualified by two affirmative defenses. See § 223(e)(5). One covers those who take "good faith, reasonable, effective, and appropriate actions" to restrict access by minors to the prohibited communications. § 223(e)(5)(A). The other covers those who restrict access to covered material by requiring certain designated forms of age proof, such as a verified credit card or an adult identification number or code. § 223(e)(5)(B).

. . .

IV.

In arguing for reversal, the Government contends that the CDA is plainly constitutional under three of our prior decisions: (1) Ginsberg v. New York, 390 U.S. 629 (1968); (2) FCC v. Pacifica Foundation, 438 U.S. 726 (1978); and (3) Renton v. Playtime Theatres, Inc., 475 U.S. 41 (1986). A close look at these cases, however, raises—rather than relieves—doubts concerning the constitutionality of the CDA.

In *Ginsberg* we upheld the constitutionality of a New York statute that prohibited selling to minors under 17 years of age material that was considered obscene as to them even if not obscene as to adults. We rejected the defendant's broad submission that "the scope of the constitutional freedom of expression secured to a citizen to read or see material concerned with sex cannot be made to depend on whether the citizen is an adult or a minor." 390 U.S., at 636. In rejecting that contention, we relied not only on the State's independent interest in the well-being of its youth, but also on our consistent recognition of the principle that "the parents' claim to authority in their own household to direct the rearing of their children is basic in the structure of our society."

In four important respects, the statute upheld in *Ginsberg* was narrower than the CDA. First, we noted in *Ginsberg* that, "the prohibition against sales to minors does not bar parents who so desire from purchasing the magazines for their children." *Id.*, at 639. Under the CDA, by contrast, neither the parents' consent—nor even their participation—in the communication would avoid the application of the statute.[32] Second, the New York statute applied only to commercial transactions, *id.*, at 647, whereas the CDA contains no such limitation. Third, the New York statute cabined its definition of material that is harmful to minors with the requirement that it be "utterly without redeeming social importance for minors." *Id.*, at 646. The CDA fails to provide us with any definition of the term "indecent" as used in § 223(a)(1) and, importantly, omits any requirement that the "patently offensive" material covered by § 223(d) lack serious literary, artistic, political, or scientific value. Fourth, the New York statute defined a minor as a person under the age of 17, whereas the CDA, in applying to all those under 18 years, includes an additional year of those nearest majority.

In *Pacifica* we upheld a declaratory order of the Federal Communications Commission, holding that the broadcast of a recording of a 12–minute monologue entitled "Filthy Words" that had previously been delivered to a live audience "could have been the subject of administrative sanctions."

32. Given the likelihood that many e-mail transmissions from an adult to a minor are conversations between family members, it is therefore incorrect for the partial dissent to suggest that the provisions of the CDA, even in this narrow area, "are no different from the law we sustained in *Ginsberg*." *Post,* at 2355.

438 U.S., at 730 (internal quotation marks omitted). The Commission had found that the repetitive use of certain words referring to excretory or sexual activities or organs "in an afternoon broadcast when children are in the audience was patently offensive" and concluded that the monologue was indecent "as broadcast." *Id.*, at 735. The respondent did not quarrel with the finding that the afternoon broadcast was patently offensive, but contended that it was not "indecent" within the meaning of the relevant statutes because it contained no prurient appeal. After rejecting respondent's statutory arguments, we confronted its two constitutional arguments: (1) that the Commission's construction of its authority to ban indecent speech was so broad that its order had to be set aside even if the broadcast at issue was unprotected; and (2) that since the recording was not obscene, the First Amendment forbade any abridgment of the right to broadcast it on the radio.

In the portion of the lead opinion not joined by Justices Powell and Blackmun, the plurality stated that the First Amendment does not prohibit all governmental regulation that depends on the content of speech. *Id.*, at 742–43. Accordingly, the availability of constitutional protection for a vulgar and offensive monologue that was not obscene depended on the context of the broadcast. *Id.*, at 744–48. Relying on the premise that "of all forms of communication" broadcasting had received the most limited First Amendment protection, *id.*, at 748–49, the Court concluded that the ease with which children may obtain access to broadcasts, "coupled with the concerns recognized in *Ginsberg*" justified special treatment of indecent broadcasting. Id., at 749–50.

As with the New York statute at issue in *Ginsberg* there are significant differences between the order upheld in *Pacifica* and the CDA. First, the order in *Pacifica* issued by an agency that had been regulating radio stations for decades, targeted a specific broadcast that represented a rather dramatic departure from traditional program content in order to designate when—rather than whether—it would be permissible to air such a program in that particular medium. The CDA's broad categorical prohibitions are not limited to particular times and are not dependent on any evaluation by an agency familiar with the unique characteristics of the Internet. Second, unlike the CDA, the Commission's declaratory order was not punitive; we expressly refused to decide whether the indecent broadcast "would justify a criminal prosecution." 438 U.S., at 750. Finally, the Commission's order applied to a medium which as a matter of history had "received the most limited First Amendment protection," *id.*, at 748, in large part because warnings could not adequately protect the listener from unexpected program content. The Internet, however, has no comparable history. Moreover, the District Court found that the risk of encountering indecent material by accident is remote because a series of affirmative steps is required to access specific material.

In *Renton* we upheld a zoning ordinance that kept adult movie theaters out of residential neighborhoods. The ordinance was aimed, not at the content of the films shown in the theaters, but rather at the "secondary effects"—such as crime and deteriorating property values—that these theaters fostered: " 'It is th[e] secondary effect which these zoning ordinances attempt to avoid, not the dissemination of "offensive" speech.' " 475 U.S., at 49 (*quoting* Young v. American Mini Theatres, Inc., 427 U.S. 50, 71 (1976)). According to the Government, the CDA is constitutional because it constitutes a sort of "cyberzoning" on the Internet. But the CDA applies broadly to the entire universe of cyberspace. And the purpose of the CDA is to protect children from the primary effects of "indecent" and "patently offensive" speech, rather than any "secondary" effect of such speech. Thus, the CDA is a content-based blanket restriction on speech, and, as such, cannot be "properly analyzed as a form of time, place, and manner regulation." 475 U.S., at 46. *See also* Boos v. Barry, 485 U.S. 312 (1988) ("Regulations that focus on the direct impact of speech on its audience" are not properly analyzed under Renton); Forsyth County v. Nationalist Movement, 505 U.S. 123, 134 (1992) ("Listeners' reaction to speech is not a content-neutral basis for regulation").

These precedents, then, surely do not require us to uphold the CDA and are fully consistent with the application of the most stringent review of its provisions.

V.

In *Southeastern Promotions, Ltd. v. Conrad*, 420 U.S. 546, 557 (1975), we observed that "[e]ach medium of expression . . . may present its own problems." Thus, some of our cases have recognized special justifications for regulation of the broadcast media that are not applicable to other speakers, *see* Red Lion Broadcasting Co. v. FCC, 395 U.S. 367 (1969); FCC v. Pacifica Foundation, 438 U.S. 726 (1978). In these cases, the Court relied on the history of extensive Government regulation of the broadcast medium, *see, e.g., Red Lion*, 395 U.S., at 399–400; the scarcity of available frequencies at its inception, *see, e.g.*, Turner Broadcasting System, Inc. v. FCC, 512 U.S. 622, 637–38 (1994); and its "invasive" nature, *see* Sable Communications of Cal., Inc. v. FCC, 492 U.S. 115, 128 (1989). Those factors are not present in cyberspace. Neither before nor after the enactment of the CDA have the vast democratic forums of the Internet been subject to the type of government supervision and regulation that has attended the broadcast industry. Moreover, the Internet is not as "invasive" as radio or television. The District Court specifically found that "[c]ommunications over the Internet do not 'invade' an individual's home or appear on one's computer screen unbidden. Users seldom encounter content 'by accident.' " 929 F.Supp., at 844 (finding 88). It also found that "[a]lmost all sexually explicit images are preceded by warnings as to the content," and cited testimony that " 'odds are slim' that a user would come across a sexually explicit sight by accident." *Ibid.*

We distinguished *Pacifica* in *Sable*, 492 U.S., at 128, on just this basis. In *Sable*, a company engaged in the business of offering sexually oriented prerecorded telephone messages (popularly known as "dial-a-porn") challenged the constitutionality of an amendment to the Communications Act of 1934 that imposed a blanket prohibition on indecent as well as obscene interstate commercial telephone messages. We held that the statute was constitutional insofar as it applied to obscene messages but invalid as applied to indecent messages. In attempting to justify the complete ban and criminalization of indecent commercial telephone messages, the Government relied on Pacifica, arguing that the ban was necessary to prevent children from gaining access to such messages. We agreed that "there is a compelling interest in protecting the physical and psychological well-being of minors" which extended to shielding them from indecent messages that are not obscene by adult standards, 492 U.S., at 126, but distinguished our "emphatically narrow holding" in Pacifica because it did not involve a complete ban and because it involved a different medium of communication, *id.*, at 127. We explained that, "the dial-it medium requires the listener to take affirmative steps to receive the communication." *Id.*, at 127–28. "Placing a telephone call," we continued, "is not the same as turning on a radio and being taken by surprise by an indecent message." *Id.*, at 128.

Finally, unlike the conditions that prevailed when Congress first authorized regulation of the broadcast spectrum, the Internet can hardly be considered a "scarce" expressive commodity. It provides relatively unlimited, low-cost capacity for communication of all kinds. The Government estimates that "[a]s many as 40 million people use the Internet today, and that figure is expected to grow to 200 million by 1999." This dynamic, multifaceted category of communication includes, not only traditional print and news services, but also audio, video, and still images, as well as interactive, real-time dialogue. Through the use of chat rooms, any person with a phone line can become a town crier with a voice that resonates farther than it could from any soapbox. Through the use of Web pages, mail exploders, and newsgroups, the same individual can become a pamphleteer. As the District Court found, "the content on the Internet is as diverse as human thought." 929 F.Supp., at 842 (finding 74). We agree with its conclusion that our cases provide no basis for qualifying the level of First Amendment scrutiny that should be applied to this medium.

VI.

Regardless of whether the CDA is so vague that it violates the Fifth Amendment, the many ambiguities concerning the scope of its coverage render it problematic for purposes of the First Amendment. For instance, each of the two parts of the CDA uses a different linguistic form. The first uses the word "indecent," 47 U.S.C. § 223(a) (1994 ed., Supp. II), while the second speaks of material that "in context, depicts or describes, in terms patently offensive as measured by contemporary community standards, sexual or excretory activities or organs," § 223(d). Given the absence of a definition of either term, this difference in language will provoke uncertainty among speakers about how the two standards relate to each other and just what they mean. Could a speaker confidently assume that a serious discussion about birth control practices, homosexuality, the First Amendment issues raised by the Appendix to our *Pacifica* opinion, or the consequences of prison rape would not violate the CDA? This uncertainty undermines the likelihood that the CDA has been carefully tailored to the congressional goal of protecting minors from potentially harmful materials.

The vagueness of the CDA is a matter of special concern for two reasons. First, the CDA is a content-based regulation of speech. The vagueness of such a regulation raises special First Amendment concerns because of its obvious chilling effect on free speech. *See, e.g.,* Gentile v. State Bar of Nev., 501 U.S. 1030, 1048–51 (1991). Second, the CDA is a criminal statute. In addition to the opprobrium and stigma of a criminal conviction, the CDA threatens violators with penalties including up to two years in prison for each act of violation. The severity of criminal sanctions may well cause speakers to remain silent rather than communicate even arguably unlawful words, ideas, and images. *See, e.g.,* Dombrowski v. Pfister, 380 U.S. 479, 494. As a practical matter, this increased deterrent effect, coupled with the "risk of discriminatory enforcement" of vague regulations, poses greater First Amendment concerns than those implicated by the civil regulation reviewed in *Denver Area Ed. Telecommunications Consortium, Inc. v. FCC*, 518 U.S. 727 (1996).

The Government argues that the statute is no more vague than the obscenity standard this Court established in *Miller v. California*, 413 U.S. 15 (1973). But that is not so. In *Miller*, this Court reviewed a criminal conviction against a commercial vendor who mailed brochures containing pictures of sexually explicit activities to individuals who had not requested such materials. *Id.,* at 18. Having struggled for some time to establish a definition of obscenity, we set forth in *Miller* the test for obscenity that controls to this day:

> (a) whether the average person, applying contemporary community standards would find that the work, taken as a whole, appeals to the prurient interest; (b) whether the work depicts or describes, in a patently offensive way, sexual conduct specifically defined by the applicable state law; and (c) whether the work, taken as a whole, lacks serious literary, artistic, political, or scientific value. *Id.,* at 24 (internal quotation marks and citations omitted).

Because the CDA's "patently offensive" standard (and, we assume, arguendo, its synonymous "indecent" standard) is one part of the three-prong *Miller* test, the Government reasons, it cannot be unconstitutionally vague.

The Government's assertion is incorrect as a matter of fact. The second prong of the *Miller* test—the purportedly analogous standard—contains a critical requirement that is omitted from the CDA: that the proscribed material be "specifically defined by the applicable state law." This requirement reduces the vagueness inherent in the open-ended term "patently offensive" as used in the CDA. Moreover, the *Miller* definition is limited to "sexual conduct," whereas the CDA extends also to include (1) "excretory activities" as well as (2) "organs" of both a sexual and excretory nature.

The Government's reasoning is also flawed. Just because a definition including three limitations is not vague, it does not follow that one of those limitations, standing by itself, is not vague.38 Each of *Miller*'s additional two prongs—(1) that, taken as a whole, the material appeal to the "prurient" interest, and (2) that it "lac[k] serious literary, artistic, political, or scientific value"—critically limits the uncertain sweep of the obscenity definition. The second requirement is particularly important because, unlike the "patently offensive" and "prurient interest" criteria, it is not judged by contemporary community standards. *See* Pope v. Illinois, 481 U.S. 497, 500 (1987). This "societal value" requirement, absent in the CDA, allows appellate courts to impose some limitations and regularity on the definition by setting, as a matter of law, a national floor for socially redeeming value. The Government's contention that courts will be able to give such legal limitations to the CDA's standards is belied by *Miller*'s own rationale for having juries determine whether material is "patently offensive" according to community standards: that such questions are essentially ones of fact.

In contrast to *Miller* and our other previous cases, the CDA thus presents a greater threat of censoring speech that, in fact, falls outside the statute's scope. Given the vague contours of the coverage of the statute, it unquestionably silences some speakers whose messages would be entitled to constitutional protection. That danger provides further reason for insisting that the statute not be overly broad. The CDA's burden on protected speech cannot be justified if it could be avoided by a more carefully drafted statute.

VII.

We are persuaded that the CDA lacks the precision that the First Amendment requires when a statute regulates the content of speech. In order to deny minors access to potentially harmful speech, the CDA effectively suppresses a large amount of speech that adults have a constitutional right to receive and to address to one another. That burden on adult speech is unacceptable if less restrictive alternatives would be at least as effective in achieving the legitimate purpose that the statute was enacted to serve.

In evaluating the free speech rights of adults, we have made it perfectly clear that "[s]exual expression which is indecent but not obscene is protected by the First Amendment." *Sable*, 492 U.S., at 126. *See also* Carey v. Population Services Int'l, 431 U.S. 678, 701 (1977) ("[W]here obscenity is not involved, we have consistently held that the fact that protected speech may be offensive to some does not justify its suppression"). Indeed, *Pacifica* itself admonished that "the fact that society may find speech offensive is not a sufficient reason for suppressing it." 438 U.S., at 745.

It is true that we have repeatedly recognized the governmental interest in protecting children from harmful materials. *See Ginsberg*, 390 U.S., at 639; *Pacifica*, 438 U.S., at 749. But that interest does not justify an unnecessarily broad suppression of speech addressed to adults. As we have explained, the Government may not "reduc[e] the adult population ... to ... only what is fit for children." *Denver*, 518 U.S., at 759 (internal quotation marks omitted) (*quoting Sable*, 492 U.S., at 128). "[R]egardless of the strength of the government's interest" in protecting children, "[t]he level of discourse reaching a mailbox simply cannot be limited to that which would be suitable for a sandbox." Bolger v. Youngs Drug Products Corps., 463 U.S. 60, 74–75 (1983).

The District Court was correct to conclude that the CDA effectively resembles the ban on "dial-a-porn" invalidated in *Sable*. 929 F.Supp., at

854. In *Sable*, 492 U.S., at 129, this Court rejected the argument that we should defer to the congressional judgment that nothing less than a total ban would be effective in preventing enterprising youngsters from gaining access to indecent communications. Sable thus made clear that the mere fact that a statutory regulation of speech was enacted for the important purpose of protecting children from exposure to sexually explicit material does not foreclose inquiry into its validity. As we pointed out last Term, that inquiry embodies an "overarching commitment" to make sure that Congress has designed its statute to accomplish its purpose "without imposing an unnecessarily great restriction on speech." *Denver*, 518 U.S., at 741.

In arguing that the CDA does not so diminish adult communication, the Government relies on the incorrect factual premise that prohibiting a transmission whenever it is known that one of its recipients is a minor would not interfere with adult-to-adult communication. The findings of the District Court make clear that this premise is untenable. Given the size of the potential audience for most messages, in the absence of a viable age verification process, the sender must be charged with knowing that one or more minors will likely view it. Knowledge that, for instance, one or more members of a 100–person chat group will be a minor—and therefore that it would be a crime to send the group an indecent message—would surely burden communication among adults.

The District Court found that at the time of trial existing technology did not include any effective method for a sender to prevent minors from obtaining access to its communications on the Internet without also denying access to adults. The Court found no effective way to determine the age of a user who is accessing material through e-mail, mail exploders, newsgroups, or chat rooms. 929 F.Supp., at 845 (findings 90–94). As a practical matter, the Court also found that it would be prohibitively expensive for noncommercial—as well as some commercial—speakers who have Web sites to verify that their users are adults. *Id.*, at 845–48 (findings 95–116). These limitations must inevitably curtail a significant amount of adult communication on the Internet. By contrast, the District Court found that "[d]espite its limitations, currently available user-based software suggests that a reasonably effective method by which parents can prevent their children from accessing sexually explicit and other material which parents may believe is inappropriate for their children will soon be widely available." *Id.*, at 842 (finding 73) (emphases added).

The breadth of the CDA's coverage is wholly unprecedented. Unlike the regulations upheld in *Ginsberg* and *Pacifica,* the scope of the CDA is not limited to commercial speech or commercial entities. Its open-ended prohibitions embrace all nonprofit entities and individuals posting indecent messages or displaying them on their own computers in the presence of minors. The general, undefined terms "indecent" and "patently offensive" cover large amounts of non-pornographic material with serious educational or other value. Moreover, the "community standards" criterion as applied to the Internet means that any communication available to a nation wide audience will be judged by the standards of the community most likely to be offended by the message. The regulated subject matter includes any of the seven "dirty words" used in the *Pacifica* monologue, the use of which the Government's expert acknowledged could constitute a felony. *See* Olsen Testimony, Tr. Vol. V, 53:16–54:10. It may also extend to discussions about prison rape or safe sexual practices, artistic images that include nude subjects, and arguably the card catalog of the Carnegie Library.

For the purposes of our decision, we need neither accept nor reject the Government's submission that the First Amendment does not forbid a blanket prohibition on all "indecent" and "patently offensive" messages communicated to a 17–year-old—no matter how much value the message may contain and regardless of parental approval. It is at least clear that the strength of the Government's interest in protecting minors is not equally strong throughout the coverage of this broad statute. Under the CDA, a parent allowing her 17–year-old to use the family computer to obtain information on the Internet that she, in her parental judgment, deems appropriate could face a lengthy prison term. *See* 47 U.S.C. § 223(a)(2) (1994 ed., Supp. II). Similarly, a parent who sent his 17–year-old college freshman information on birth control via e-mail could be incarcerated even though neither he, his child, nor anyone in their home community found the material "indecent" or "patently offensive," if the college town's community thought otherwise.

The breadth of this content-based restriction of speech imposes an especially heavy burden on the Government to explain why a less restrictive provision would not be as effective as the CDA. It has not done so. The arguments in this Court have referred to possible alternatives such as requiring that indecent material be "tagged" in a way that facilitates parental control of material coming into their homes, making exceptions for messages with artistic or educational value, providing some tolerance for parental choice, and regulating some portions of the Internet—such as commercial Web sites—differently from others, such as chat rooms. Particularly in the light of the absence of any detailed findings by the Congress, or even hearings addressing the special problems of the CDA, we are persuaded that the CDA is not narrowly tailored if that requirement has any meaning at all.

VIII.

In an attempt to curtail the CDA's facial overbreadth, the Government advances three additional arguments for sustaining the Act's affirmative prohibitions: (1) that the CDA is constitutional because it leaves open ample "alternative channels" of communication; (2) that the plain meaning of the CDA's "knowledge" and "specific person" requirement significantly restricts its permissible applications; and (3) that the CDA's prohibitions are "almost always" limited to material lacking redeeming social value.

The Government first contends that, even though the CDA effectively censors discourse on many of the Internet's modalities—such as chat groups, newsgroups, and mail exploders—it is nonetheless constitutional because it provides a "reasonable opportunity" for speakers to engage in the restricted speech on the World Wide Web. Brief for Appellants 39. This argument is unpersuasive because the CDA regulates speech on the basis of its content. A "time, place, and manner" analysis is therefore inapplicable.

See Consolidated Edison Co. of N.Y. v. Public Serv. Comm'n of N.Y., 447 U.S. 530, 536 (1980). It is thus immaterial whether such speech would be feasible on the Web (which, as the Government's own expert acknowledged, would cost up to $10,000 if the speaker's interests were not accommodated by an existing Web site, not including costs for data base management and age verification). The Government's position is equivalent to arguing that a statute could ban leaflets on certain subjects as long as individuals are free to publish books. In invalidating a number of laws that banned leaf-letting on the streets *regardless of* their content, we explained that "one is not to have the exercise of his liberty of expression in appropriate places abridged on the plea that it may be exercised in some other place." Schneider v. State of N.J. (Town of Irvington), 308 U.S. 147, 163 (1939).

The Government also asserts that the "knowledge" requirement of both §§ 223(a) and (d), especially when coupled with the "specific child" element found in § 223(d), saves the CDA from overbreadth. Because both sections prohibit the dissemination of indecent messages only to persons known to be under 18, the Government argues, it does not require transmitters to "refrain from communicating indecent material to adults; they need only refrain from disseminating such materials to persons they know to be under 18." Brief for Appellants 24.

This argument ignores the fact that most Internet forums—including chat rooms, newsgroups, mail exploders, and the Web—are open to all comers. The Government's assertion that the knowledge requirement somehow protects the communications of adults is therefore untenable. Even the strongest reading of the "specific person" requirement of § 223(d) cannot save the statute. It would confer broad powers of censorship, in the form of a "heckler's veto," upon any opponent of indecent speech who might simply log on and inform the would-be discoursers that his 17–year-old child—a "specific person ... under 18 years of age," 47 U.S.C.A. § 223(d)(1)(A) (Supp.1997)—would be present.

Finally, we find no textual support for the Government's submission that material having scientific, educational, or other redeeming social value will necessarily fall outside the CDA's "patently offensive" and "indecent" prohibitions. *See also* n. 37, *supra*.

IX.

The Government's three remaining arguments focus on the defenses provided in § 223(e)(5). First, relying on the "good faith, reasonable, effective, and appropriate actions" provision, the Government suggests that "tagging" provides a defense that saves the constitutionality of the CDA. The suggestion assumes that transmitters may encode their indecent communications in a way that would indicate their contents, thus permitting recipients to block their reception with appropriate software. It is the requirement that the good-faith action must be "effective" that makes this defense illusory. The Government recognizes that its proposed screening software does not currently exist. Even if it did, there is no way to know whether a potential recipient will actually block the encoded material. Without the impossible knowledge that every guardian in America is screening for the "tag," the transmitter could not reasonably rely on its action to be "effective."

For its second and third arguments concerning defenses—which we can consider together—the Government relies on the latter half of § 223(e)(5), which applies when the transmitter has restricted access by requiring use of a verified credit card or adult identification. Such verification is not only technologically available but actually is used by commercial providers of sexually explicit material. These providers, therefore, would be protected by the defense. Under the findings of the District Court, however, it is not economically feasible for most noncommercial speakers to employ such verification. Accordingly, this defense would not significantly narrow the statute's burden on noncommercial speech. Even with respect to the commercial pornographers that would be protected by the defense, the Government failed to adduce any evidence that these verification techniques actually preclude minors from posing as adults. Given that the risk of criminal sanctions "hovers over each content provider, like the proverbial sword of Damocles," the District Court correctly refused to rely on unproven future technology to save the statute. The Government thus failed to prove that the proffered defense would significantly reduce the heavy burden on adult speech produced by the prohibition on offensive displays.

We agree with the District Court's conclusion that the CDA places an unacceptably heavy burden on protected speech, and that the defenses do not constitute the sort of "narrow tailoring" that will save an otherwise patently invalid unconstitutional provision. In *Sable*, 492 U.S., at 127, we remarked that the speech restriction at issue there amounted to " 'burn[ing] the house to roast the pig.' " The CDA, casting a far darker shadow over free speech, threatens to torch a large segment of the Internet community.

. . .

XI.

In this Court, though not in the District Court, the Government asserts that—in addition to its interest in protecting children—its "[e]qually significant" interest in fostering the growth of the Internet provides an independent basis for upholding the constitutionality of the CDA. Brief for Appellants 19. The Government apparently assumes that the unregulated availability of "indecent" and "patently offensive" material on the Internet is driving countless citizens away from the medium because of the risk of exposing themselves or their children to harmful material.

We find this argument singularly unpersuasive. The dramatic expansion of this new marketplace of ideas contradicts the factual basis of this contention. The record demonstrates that the growth of the Internet has been and continues to be phenomenal. As a matter of constitutional tradition, in the absence of evidence to the contrary, we presume that governmental regulation of the content of speech is more likely to interfere with the free exchange of ideas than to encourage it. The interest in encouraging freedom of expression in a democratic society outweighs any theoretical but unproven benefit of censorship.

For the foregoing reasons, the judgment of the District Court is affirmed.

It is so ordered.

■ JUSTICE O'CONNOR, with whom the CHIEF JUSTICE joins, concurring in the judgment in part and dissenting in part.

I write separately to explain why I view the Communications Decency Act of 1996 (CDA) as little more than an attempt by Congress to create "adult zones" on the Internet. Our precedent indicates that the creation of such zones can be constitutionally sound. Despite the soundness of its purpose, however, portions of the CDA are unconstitutional because they stray from the blueprint our prior cases have developed for constructing a "zoning law" that passes constitutional muster.

Appellees bring a facial challenge to three provisions of the CDA. The first, which the Court describes as the "indecency transmission" provision, makes it a crime to knowingly transmit an obscene or indecent message or image to a person the sender knows is under 18 years old. 47 U.S.C. § 223(a)(1)(B) (1994 ed., Supp. II). What the Court classifies as a single " 'patently offensive display' " provision, *see ante,* at 2338, is in reality two separate provisions. The first of these makes it a crime to knowingly send a patently offensive message or image to a specific person under the age of 18 ("specific person" provision). § 223(d)(1)(A). The second criminalizes the display of patently offensive messages or images "in a[ny] manner available" to minors ("display" provision). § 223(d)(1)(B). None of these provisions purports to keep indecent (or patently offensive) material away from adults, who have a First Amendment right to obtain this speech. Sable Communications of Cal., Inc. v. FCC, 492 U.S. 115, 126 (1989) ("Sexual expression which is indecent but not obscene is protected by the First Amendment"). Thus, the undeniable purpose of the CDA is to segregate indecent material on the Internet into certain areas that minors cannot access. *See* S. Conf. Rep. No. 104–230, p. 189 (1996) (CDA imposes "access restrictions . . . to protect minors from exposure to indecent material").

The creation of "adult zones" is by no means a novel concept. States have long denied minors access to certain establishments frequented by adults. States have also denied minors access to speech deemed to be "harmful to minors." The Court has previously sustained such zoning laws, but only if they respect the First Amendment rights of adults and minors. That is to say, a zoning law is valid if (i) it does not unduly restrict adult access to the material; and (ii) minors have no First Amendment right to read or view the banned material. As applied to the Internet as it exists in 1997, the "display" provision and some applications of the "indecency transmission" and "specific person" provisions fail to adhere to the first of these limiting principles by restricting adults' access to protected materials in certain circumstances. Unlike the Court, however, I would invalidate the provisions only in those circumstances.

I.

Our cases make clear that a "zoning" law is valid only if adults are still able to obtain the regulated speech. If they cannot, the law does more than simply keep children away from speech they have no right to obtain—it interferes with the rights of adults to obtain constitutionally protected speech and effectively "reduce[s] the adult population . . . to reading only what is fit for children." Butler v. Michigan, 352 U.S. 380, 383 (1957). The First Amendment does not tolerate such interference. *Ibid.* (striking down a Michigan criminal law banning sale of books—to minors or adults—that contained words or pictures that " 'tende[d] to . . . corrup[t] the morals of youth' "); *Sable Communications, supra* (invalidating federal law that made it a crime to transmit indecent, but nonobscene, commercial telephone messages to minors and adults); Bolger v. Youngs Drug Products Corps., 463 U.S. 60, 74 (1983) (striking down a federal law prohibiting the mailing of unsolicited advertisements for contraceptives). If the law does not unduly restrict adults' access to constitutionally protected speech, however, it may be valid. In Ginsberg v. New York, 390 U.S. 629, 634 (1968), for example, the Court sustained a New York law that barred store owners from selling pornographic magazines to minors in part because adults could still buy those magazines.

The Court in *Ginsberg* concluded that the New York law created a constitutionally adequate adult zone simply because, on its face, it denied access only to minors. The Court did not question—and therefore necessarily assumed—that an adult zone, once created, would succeed in preserving adults' access while denying minors' access to the regulated speech. Before today, there was no reason to question this assumption, for the Court has previously only considered laws that operated in the physical world, a world that with two characteristics that make it possible to create "adult zones": geography and identity. *See* Lessig, *Reading the Constitution in Cyberspace*, 45 Emory L.J. 869, 886 (1996). A minor can see an adult dance show only if he enters an establishment that provides such entertainment. And should he attempt to do so, the minor will not be able to conceal completely his identity (or, consequently, his age). Thus, the twin characteristics of geography and identity enable the establishment's proprietor to prevent children from entering the establishment, but to let adults inside.

The electronic world is fundamentally different. Because it is no more than the interconnection of electronic pathways, cyberspace allows speakers and listeners to mask their identities. Cyberspace undeniably reflects some form of geography; chat rooms and Web sites, for example, exist at fixed "locations" on the Internet. Since users can transmit and receive messages on the Internet without revealing anything about their identities or ages, *see id.,* at 901, however, it is not currently possible to exclude persons from accessing certain messages on the basis of their identity.

Cyberspace differs from the physical world in another basic way: Cyberspace is malleable. Thus, it is possible to construct barriers in cyberspace and use them to screen for identity, making cyberspace more like the physical world and, consequently, more amenable to zoning laws. This transformation of cyberspace is already underway. *Id.,* at 888–89; *id.,* at 887 (cyberspace "is moving . . . from a relatively unzoned place to a universe that is extraordinarily well zoned"). Internet speakers (users who post material on the Internet) have begun to zone cyberspace itself through the use of "gateway" technology. Such technology requires Internet users to enter information about themselves—perhaps an adult identification number or a credit card number—before they can access certain areas of cyberspace, 929 F. Supp. 824, 845 (E.D.Pa.1996), much like a bouncer checks a person's driver's license before admitting him to a nightclub. Internet users who access information have not attempted to zone cyberspace itself, but have tried to limit their own power to access information in cyberspace, much as a parent controls what her children watch on television by installing a lock box. This user-based zoning is accomplished through the use of screening software (such as Cyber Patrol or SurfWatch) or browsers with screening capabilities, both of which search addresses and text for keywords that are associated with "adult" sites and, if the user wishes, blocks access to such sites. *Id.,* at 839–42. The Platform for Internet Content Selection project is designed to facilitate user-based zoning by encouraging Internet speakers to rate the content of their speech using codes recognized by all screening programs. *Id.,* at 838–39.

Despite this progress, the transformation of cyberspace is not complete. Although gateway technology has been available on the World Wide Web for some time now, *id.,* at 845; Shea v. Reno, 930 F.Supp. 916, 933–34 (S.D.N.Y.1996), it is not available to all Web speakers, 929 F.Supp., at 845–46, and is just now becoming technologically feasible for chat rooms and USENET newsgroups, Brief for Appellants 37–38. Gateway technology is not ubiquitous in cyberspace, and because without it "there is no means of age verification," cyberspace still remains largely unzoned—and unzoneable. 929 F.Supp., at 846; *Shea, supra,* at 934. User-based zoning is also in its infancy. For it to be effective, (i) an agreed-upon code (or "tag") would have to exist; (ii) screening software or browsers with screening capabilities would have to be able to recognize the "tag"; and (iii) those programs would have to be widely available—and widely used—by Internet users. At present, none of these conditions is true. Screening software "is not in wide use today" and "only a handful of browsers have screening capabilities." *Shea, supra,* at 945–46. There is, moreover, no agreed-upon "tag" for those programs to recognize. 929 F.Supp., at 848; *Shea, supra,* at 945.

Although the prospects for the eventual zoning of the Internet appear promising, I agree with the Court that we must evaluate the constitutionality of the CDA as it applies to the Internet as it exists today. Given the present state of cyberspace, I agree with the Court that the "display" provision cannot pass muster. Until gateway technology is available throughout cyberspace, and it is not in 1997, a speaker cannot be reasonably assured that the speech he displays will reach only adults because it is impossible to confine speech to an "adult zone." Thus, the only way for a speaker to avoid liability under the CDA is to refrain completely from using indecent speech. But this forced silence impinges on the First Amendment right of adults to make and obtain this speech and, for all intents and purposes, "reduce[s] the adult population [on the Internet] to reading only what is fit for children." *Butler,* 352 U.S., at 383. As a result, the "display" provision cannot withstand scrutiny. *Accord Sable Communications,* 492 U.S., at 126–31; Bolger v. Youngs Drug Products Corps., 463 U.S., at 73–75.

The "indecency transmission" and "specific person" provisions present a closer issue, for they are not unconstitutional in all of their applications.

As discussed above, the "indecency transmission" provision makes it a crime to transmit knowingly an indecent message to a person the sender knows is under 18 years of age. 47 U.S.C.A. § 223(a)(1)(B) (May 1996 Supp.). The "specific person" provision proscribes the same conduct, although it does not as explicitly require the sender to know that the intended recipient of his indecent message is a minor. § 223(d)(1)(A). The Government urges the Court to construe the provision to impose such a knowledge requirement, see Brief for Appellants 25–27, and I would do so. *See* Edward J. DeBartolo Corp. v. Florida Gulf Coast Bldg. & Constr. Trades Council, 485 U.S. 568, 575 (1988) ("[W]here an otherwise acceptable construction of a statute would raise serious constitutional problems, the Court will construe the statute to avoid such problems unless such construction is plainly contrary to the intent of Congress").

So construed, both provisions are constitutional as applied to a conversation involving only an adult and one or more minors—*e.g.,* when an adult speaker sends an e-mail knowing the addressee is a minor, or when an adult and minor converse by themselves or with other minors in a chat room. In this context, these provisions are no different from the law we sustained in *Ginsberg*. Restricting what the adult may say to the minors in no way restricts the adult's ability to communicate with other adults. He is not prevented from speaking indecently to other adults in a chat room (because there are no other adults participating in the conversation) and he remains free to send indecent e-mails to other adults. The relevant universe contains only one adult, and the adult in that universe has the power to refrain from using indecent speech and consequently to keep all such speech within the room in an "adult" zone.

The analogy to *Ginsberg* breaks down, however, when more than one adult is a party to the conversation. If a minor enters a chat room otherwise occupied by adults, the CDA effectively requires the adults in the room to stop using indecent speech. If they did not, they could be prosecuted under the "indecency transmission" and "specific person" provisions for any indecent statements they make to the group, since they would be transmitting an indecent message to specific persons, one of whom is a minor. *Bolger* 463 U.S. at 75. The CDA is therefore akin to a law that makes it a crime for a bookstore owner to sell pornographic magazines to anyone once a minor enters his store. Even assuming such a law might be constitutional in the physical world as a reasonable alternative to excluding minors completely from the store, the absence of any means of excluding minors from chat rooms in cyberspace restricts the rights of adults to engage in indecent speech in those rooms. The "indecency transmission" and "specific person" provisions share this defect.

But these two provisions do not infringe on adults' speech in *all* situations. And as discussed below, I do not find that the provisions are overbroad in the sense that they restrict minors' access to a substantial amount of speech that minors have the right to read and view. Accordingly, the CDA can be applied constitutionally in some situations. Normally, this fact would require the Court to reject a direct facial challenge. United States v. Salerno, 481 U.S. 739, 745 (1987) ("A facial challenge to a legislative Act [succeeds only if] the challenger . . . establish[es] that no set of circumstances exists under which the Act would be valid"). Appellees' claim arises under the First Amendment, however, and they argue that the CDA is facially invalid because it is "substantially overbroad"—that is, it "sweeps too broadly ... [and] penaliz[es] a substantial amount of speech that is constitutionally protected," Forsyth County v. Nationalist Movement, 505 U.S. 123, 130 (1992). *See* Brief for Appellees American Library Association et al. 48; Brief for Appellees American Civil Liberties Union et al. 39–41. I agree with the Court that the provisions are overbroad in that they cover any and all communications between adults and minors, regardless of how many adults might be part of the audience to the communication.

This conclusion does not end the matter, however. Where, as here, "the parties challenging the statute are those who desire to engage in protected speech that the overbroad statute purports to punish, ... [t]he statute may forthwith be declared invalid to the extent that it reaches too far, but otherwise left intact." Brockett v. Spokane Arcades, Inc., 472 U.S. 491, 504 (1985). There is no question that Congress intended to prohibit certain communications between one adult and one or more minors. *See* 47 U.S.C. § 223(a)(1)(B) (1994 ed., Supp. II) (punishing "[w]hoever ... initiates the transmission of [any indecent communication] knowing that the recipient of the communication is under 18 years of age"); § 223(d)(1)(A) (punishing "[w]hoever ... send[s] to a specific person or persons under 18 years of age [a patently offensive message]"). There is also no question that Congress would have enacted a narrower version of these provisions had it known a broader version would be declared unconstitutional. 47 U.S.C. § 608 ("If ... the application [of any provision of the CDA] to any person or circumstance is held invalid, ... the application of such provision to other persons or circumstances shall not be affected thereby"). I would therefore sustain the "indecency transmission" and "specific person" provisions to the extent they apply to the transmission of Internet communications where the party initiating the communication knows that all of the recipients are minors.

II.

Whether the CDA substantially interferes with the First Amendment rights of minors, and thereby runs afoul of the second characteristic of valid zoning laws, presents a closer question. In *Ginsberg*, the New York law we sustained prohibited the sale to minors of magazines that were "harmful to minors." Under that law, a magazine was "harmful to minors" only if it was obscene as to minors. 390 U.S., at 632–33. Noting that obscene speech is not protected by the First Amendment, Roth v. United States, 354 U.S. 476, 485 (1957), and that New York was constitutionally free to adjust the definition of obscenity for minors, 390 U.S., at 638, the Court concluded that the law did not "invad[e] the area of freedom of expression constitutionally secured to minors," *id.*, at 637. New York therefore did not infringe upon the First Amendment rights of minors. *Cf.* Erznoznik v. Jacksonville, 422 U.S. 205, 213 (1975) (striking down city ordinance that banned nudity that was not "obscene even as to minors").

The Court neither "accept[s] nor reject[s]" the argument that the CDA is facially overbroad because it substantially interferes with the First

Amendment rights of minors. I would reject it. *Ginsberg* established that minors may constitutionally be denied access to material that is obscene as to minors. As *Ginsberg* explained, material is obscene as to minors if it (i) is "patently offensive to prevailing standards in the adult community as a whole with respect to what is suitable . . . for minors"; (ii) appeals to the prurient interest of minors; and (iii) is "utterly without redeeming social importance for minors." 390 U.S., at 633. Because the CDA denies minors the right to obtain material that is "patently offensive"—even if it has some redeeming value for minors and even if it does not appeal to their prurient interests—Congress' rejection of the *Ginsberg* "harmful to minors" standard means that the CDA could ban some speech that is "indecent" (*i.e.,* "patently offensive") but that is not obscene as to minors.

I do not deny this possibility, but to prevail in a facial challenge, it is not enough for a plaintiff to show "some" overbreadth. Our cases require a proof of "real" and "substantial" overbreadth, Broadrick v. Oklahoma, 413 U.S. 601, 615 (1973), and appellees have not carried their burden in this case. In my view, the universe of speech constitutionally protected as to minors but banned by the CDA—*i.e.,* the universe of material that is "patently offensive," but which nonetheless has some redeeming value for minors or does not appeal to their prurient interest—is a very small one. Appellees cite no examples of speech falling within this universe and do not attempt to explain why that universe is substantial "in relation to the statute's plainly legitimate sweep." *Ibid.* That the CDA might deny minors the right to obtain material that has some "value," is largely beside the point. While discussions about prison rape or nude art, *see ibid.,* may have some redeeming educational value for *adults,* they do not necessarily have any such value *for minors,* and under *Ginsberg,* minors only have a First Amendment right to obtain patently offensive material that has "redeeming social importance *for minors,"* 390 U.S., at 633 (emphasis added). There is also no evidence in the record to support the contention that "many e-mail transmissions from an adult to a minor are conversations between family members," and no support for the legal proposition that such speech is absolutely immune from regulation. Accordingly, in my view, the CDA does not burden a substantial amount of minors' constitutionally protected speech.

Thus, the constitutionality of the CDA as a zoning law hinges on the extent to which it substantially interferes with the First Amendment rights of adults. Because the rights of adults are infringed only by the "display" provision and by the "indecency transmission" and "specific person" provisions as applied to communications involving more than one adult, I would invalidate the CDA only to that extent. Insofar as the "indecency transmission" and "specific person" provisions prohibit the use of indecent speech in communications between an adult and one or more minors, however, they can and should be sustained. The Court reaches a contrary conclusion, and from that holding that I respectfully dissent.

NOTES AND QUESTIONS

1. Do you agree with Justice O'Connor that cyberspace can be zoned? Is it useful or misleading to analogize cyberspace to a physical location?

2. Since *Reno* the Supreme Court has continued to provide expansive First Amendment protection to the Internet. *See* Ashcroft v. Free Speech Coalition, 535 U.S. 234, 122 S.Ct. 1389, 152 L.Ed.2d 403 (2002) (ban on virtual child pornography struck down); Ashcroft v. American Civil Liberties Union, 542 U.S. 656, 124 S.Ct. 2783, 159 L.Ed.2d 690 (2004) (challengers likely to prevail on claim that Child Online Protection Act violates First Amendment by burdening adults' access to protected speech); *cf.* United States v. American Library Association, 539 U.S. 194, 123 S.Ct. 2297, 156 L.Ed.2d 221 (2003) (Congress can forbid public libraries from receiving federal funds unless they install software capable of blocking material that is harmful to minors). Is there commercially available filtering software that enables parents to effectively control what their children access on the Internet?

3. Free speech is not, of course, the only constitutional value that is shaped by new technologies. Whether it is government surveillance of electronic communications to fight terrorism or police efforts to use new techniques to search for evidence, the scope of our freedoms cannot be understood apart from the state of modern science. *See, e.g.*, Kyllo v. United States, 533 U.S. 27, 121 S.Ct. 2038, 150 L.Ed.2d 94 (2001) (use of thermal imaging device to explore interior of private home is a Fourth Amendment "search" presumptively requiring a warrant). Can the 18th Century perspective of the Framers of the Constitution contribute meaningfully to these debates?

B.   SCIENCE AND RELIGION: CAN THE GOVERNMENT CHOOSE SIDES?

Edwards v. Aguillard

Supreme Court of the United States, 1987.
482 U.S. 578, 107 S.Ct. 2573, 96 L.Ed.2d 510.

■ JUSTICE BRENNAN delivered the opinion of the Court.

The question for decision is whether Louisiana's "Balanced Treatment for Creation—Science and Evolution—Science in Public School Instruction" Act (Creationism Act), La.Rev.Stat.Ann. §§ 17:286.1–17:286.7 (West 1982), is facially invalid as violative of the Establishment Clause of the First Amendment.

The Creationism Act forbids the teaching of the theory of evolution in public schools unless accompanied by instruction in "creation science." § 17:286.4A. No school is required to teach evolution or creation science. If either is taught, however, the other must also be taught. *Ibid.* The theories of evolution and creation science are statutorily defined as "the scientific evidences for [creation or evolution] and inferences from those scientific evidences." §§ 17.286.3(2) and (3).

Appellees, who include parents of children attending Louisiana public schools, Louisiana teachers, and religious leaders, challenged the constitutionality of the Act in District Court, seeking an injunction and declaratory relief. Appellants, Louisiana officials charged with implementing the Act, defended on the ground that the purpose of the Act is to protect a legitimate secular interest, namely, academic freedom. Appellees attacked the Act as facially invalid because it violated the Establishment Clause and made a motion for summary judgment. The District Court granted the motion. [The Court of Appeals affirmed.]

. . .

The Establishment Clause forbids the enactment of any law "respecting an establishment of religion." The Court has applied a three-pronged test to determine whether legislation comports with the Establishment Clause. First, the legislature must have adopted the law with a secular purpose. Second, the statute's principal or primary effect must be one that neither advances nor inhibits religion. Third, the statute must not result in an excessive entanglement of government with religion. Lemon v. Kurtzman, 403 U.S. 602, 612–13 (1971). State action violates the Establishment Clause if it fails to satisfy any of these prongs. . . .

. . .

Lemon's first prong focuses on the purpose that animated adoption of the Act. "The purpose prong of the *Lemon* test asks whether government's actual purpose is to endorse or disapprove of religion." Lynch v. Donnelly, 465 U.S. 668, 690 (1984) (O'CONNOR, J., concurring). A governmental intention to promote religion is clear when the State enacts a law to serve a religious purpose. This intention may be evidenced by promotion of religion in general, *see* Wallace v. Jaffree, *supra*, 472 U.S., at 52–53 (Establishment Clause protects individual freedom of conscience "to select any religious faith or none at all"), or by advancement of a particular religious belief, *e.g.*, Stone v. Graham, *supra*, 449 U.S., at 41 (invalidating requirement to post Ten Commandments, which are "undeniably a sacred text in the Jewish and Christian faiths") (footnote omitted); Epperson v. Arkansas, *supra*, 393 U.S., at 106 (holding that banning the teaching of evolution in public schools violates the First Amendment since "teaching and learning" must not "be tailored to the principles or prohibitions of any religious sect or dogma"). If the law was enacted for the purpose of endorsing religion, "no consideration of the second or third criteria [of *Lemon*] is necessary." *Wallace* 472 U.S., at 56. In this case, the petitioners have identified no clear secular purpose for the Louisiana Act.

True, the Act's stated purpose is to protect academic freedom. La.Rev. Stat.Ann. § 17:286.2 (West 1982). This phrase might, in common parlance, be understood as referring to enhancing the freedom of teachers to teach what they will. The Court of Appeals, however, correctly concluded that the Act was not designed to further that goal. We find no merit in the State's argument that the "legislature may not [have] use[d] the terms 'academic freedom' in the correct legal sense. They might have [had] in mind, instead, a basic concept of fairness; teaching all of the evidence." Tr. of Oral Arg. 60. Even if "academic freedom" is read to mean "teaching all of the evidence" with respect to the origin of human beings, the Act does not further this purpose. The goal of providing a more comprehensive science curriculum is not furthered either by outlawing the teaching of evolution or by requiring the teaching of creation science.

While the Court is normally deferential to a State's articulation of a secular purpose, it is required that the statement of such purpose be sincere and not a sham. *See* Wallace v. Jaffree, 472 U.S., at 64 (Powell, J., concurring); *id.*, at 75, (O'Connor, J., concurring in judgment); Stone v. Graham, *supra*, 449 U.S., at 41; Abington School District v. Schempp, 374 U.S., at 223–24. As Justice O'Connor stated in *Wallace:* "It is not a trivial matter, however, to require that the legislature manifest a secular purpose and omit all sectarian endorsements from its laws. That requirement is precisely tailored to the Establishment Clause's purpose of assuring that Government not intentionally endorse religion or a religious practice." 472 U.S., at 75 (concurring in judgment).

It is clear from the legislative history that the purpose of the legislative sponsor, Senator Bill Keith, was to narrow the science curriculum. During the legislative hearings, Senator Keith stated: "My preference would be that neither [creationism nor evolution] be taught." 2 App. E621. Such a ban on teaching does not promote—indeed, it undermines—the provision of a comprehensive scientific education.

It is equally clear that requiring schools to teach creation science with evolution does not advance academic freedom. The Act does not grant teachers a flexibility that they did not already possess to supplant the present science curriculum with the presentation of theories, besides evolution, about the origin of life. Indeed, the Court of Appeals found that no law prohibited Louisiana public schoolteachers from teaching any scientific theory. United States v. Ismail, 756 F.2d 1253, 1257 (5th Cir. 1985). As the president of the Louisiana Science Teachers Association testified, "[a]ny scientific concept that's based on established fact can be included in our curriculum already, and no legislation allowing this is necessary." 2 App. E616. The Act provides Louisiana schoolteachers with no new authority. Thus the stated purpose is not furthered by it.

The Alabama statute held unconstitutional in *Wallace*, is analogous. In *Wallace,* the State characterized its new law as one designed to provide a one-minute period for meditation. We rejected that stated purpose as insufficient, because a previously adopted Alabama law already provided for such a one-minute period. Thus, in this case, as in *Wallace,* "[a]ppellants have not identified any secular purpose that was not fully served by [existing state law] before the enactment of [the statute in question]." 472 U.S., at 59.

Furthermore, the goal of basic "fairness" is hardly furthered by the Act's discriminatory preference for the teaching of creation science and against the teaching of evolution. While requiring that curriculum guides be developed for creation science, the Act says nothing of comparable guides for evolution. La.Rev.Stat.Ann. § 17:286.7A (West 1982). Similarly, research services are supplied for creation science but not for evolution. § 17:286.7B. Only "creation scientists" can serve on the panel that supplies the resource services. Ibid. The Act forbids school boards to discriminate against anyone who "chooses to be a creation-scientist" or to teach "creationism," but fails to protect those who choose to teach evolution or any other non-creation science theory, or who refuse to teach creation science. § 27:286.4C.

If the Louisiana legislature's purpose was solely to maximize the comprehensiveness and effectiveness of science instruction, it would have encouraged the teaching of all scientific theories about the origins of humankind. But under the Act's requirements, teachers who were once free to teach any and all facets of this subject are now unable to do so. Moreover, the Act fails even to ensure that creation science will be taught, but instead requires the teaching of this theory only when the theory of evolution is taught. Thus we agree with the Court of Appeals' conclusion that the Act does not serve to protect academic freedom, but has the distinctly different purpose of discrediting "evolution by counterbalancing its teaching at every turn with the teaching of creation science...." 765 F.2d, at 1257.

Stone v. Graham, invalidated the State's requirement that the Ten Commandments be posted in public classrooms. "The Ten Commandments are undeniably a sacred text in the Jewish and Christian faiths, and no legislative recitation of a supposed secular purpose can blind us to that fact." 449 U.S., at 41 (footnote omitted). As a result, the contention that the law was designed to provide instruction on a "fundamental legal code" was "not sufficient to avoid conflict with the First Amendment." *Ibid.* Similarly, *Abington School District v. Schempp* held unconstitutional a statute "requiring the selection and reading at the opening of the school day of verses from the Holy Bible and the recitation of the Lord's Prayer by the students in unison," despite the proffer of such secular purposes as the "promotion of moral values, the contradiction to the materialistic trends of our times, the perpetuation of our institutions and the teaching of literature." 374 U.S., at 223.

As in *Stone* and *Abington*, we need not be blind in this case to the legislature's preeminent religious purpose in enacting this statute. There is a historic and contemporaneous link between the teachings of certain religious denominations and the teaching of evolution. It was this link that concerned the Court in Epperson v. Arkansas, 393 U.S. 97 (1968), which also involved a facial challenge to a statute regulating the teaching of evolution. In that case, the Court reviewed an Arkansas statute that made it unlawful for an instructor to teach evolution or to use a textbook that referred to this scientific theory. Although the Arkansas anti-evolution law did not explicitly state its predominant religious purpose, the Court could not ignore that "[t]he statute was a product of the upsurge of 'fundamentalist' religious fervor" that has long viewed this particular scientific theory as contradicting the literal interpretation of the Bible. *Id.*, 393 U.S., at 98, 106–07. After reviewing the history of anti-evolution statutes, the Court determined that "there can be no doubt that the motivation for the [Arkansas] law was the same [as other anti-evolution statutes]: to suppress the teaching of a theory which, it was thought, 'denied' the divine creation of man." *Id.*, at 109. The Court found that there can be no legitimate state interest in protecting particular religions from scientific views "distasteful to them," *id.*, at 107 (citation omitted), and concluded "that the First Amendment does not permit the State to require that teaching and learning must be tailored to the principles or prohibitions of any religious sect or dogma," *id.*, at 106.

These same historic and contemporaneous antagonisms between the teachings of certain religious denominations and the teaching of evolution are present in this case. The preeminent purpose of the Louisiana legislature was clearly to advance the religious viewpoint that a supernatural being created humankind. The term "creation science" was defined as embracing this particular religious doctrine by those responsible for the passage of the Creationism Act. Senator Keith's leading expert on creation science, Edward Boudreaux, testified at the legislative hearings that the theory of creation science included belief in the existence of a supernatural creator. *See* 1 App. E421–22 (noting that "creation scientists" point to high probability that life was "created by an intelligent mind"). Senator Keith also cited testimony from other experts to support the creation-science view that "a creator [was] responsible for the universe and everything in it." 2 App. E497. The legislative history therefore reveals that the term "creation science," as contemplated by the legislature that adopted this Act, embodies the religious belief that a supernatural creator was responsible for the creation of humankind.

Furthermore, it is not happenstance that the legislature required the teaching of a theory that coincided with this religious view. The legislative history documents that the Act's primary purpose was to change the science curriculum of public schools in order to provide persuasive advantage to a particular religious doctrine that rejects the factual basis of evolution in its entirety. The sponsor of the Creationism Act, Senator Keith, explained during the legislative hearings that his disdain for the theory of evolution resulted from the support that evolution supplied to views contrary to his own religious beliefs. According to Senator Keith, the theory of evolution was consonant with the "cardinal principle[s] of religious humanism, secular humanism, theological liberalism, aetheistism [*sic*]." 1 App. E312–13; *see also* 2 App. E499–500. The state senator repeatedly stated that scientific evidence supporting his religious views should be included in the public school curriculum to redress the fact that the theory of evolution incidentally coincided with what he characterized as religious beliefs antithetical to his own. The legislation therefore sought to alter the science curriculum to reflect endorsement of a religious view that is antagonistic to the theory of evolution.

In this case, the purpose of the Creationism Act was to restructure the science curriculum to conform with a particular religious viewpoint. Out of many possible science subjects taught in the public schools, the legislature chose to affect the teaching of the one scientific theory that historically has been opposed by certain religious sects. As in *Epperson,* the legislature passed the Act to give preference to those religious groups, which have as one of their tenets the creation of humankind by a divine creator. The "overriding fact" that confronted the Court in *Epperson* was "that Arkansas' law selects from the body of knowledge a particular segment which it proscribes for the sole reason that it is deemed to conflict with ... a particular interpretation of the Book of Genesis by a particular religious group." 393 U.S., at 103. Similarly, the Creationism Act is designed *either* to promote the theory of creation science which embodies a particular religious tenet by requiring that creation science be taught whenever evolution is taught *or* to prohibit the teaching of a scientific theory disfavored by certain religious sects by forbidding the teaching of evolution when creation science is not also taught. The Establishment Clause, however, "forbids *alike* the preference of a religious doctrine *or* the prohibition of theory which is deemed antagonistic to a particular dogma." *Id.*, at 106–07 (emphasis added). Because the primary purpose of the Creationism Act is to advance a particular religious belief, the Act endorses religion in violation of the First Amendment.

We do not imply that a legislature could never require that scientific critiques of prevailing scientific theories be taught. Indeed, the Court acknowledged in *Stone* that its decision forbidding the posting of the Ten Commandments did not mean that no use could ever be made of the Ten Commandments, or that the Ten Commandments played an exclusively religious role in the history of Western Civilization. 449 U.S., at 42. In a similar way, teaching a variety of scientific theories about the origins of humankind to schoolchildren might be validly done with the clear secular intent of enhancing the effectiveness of science instruction. But because the primary purpose of the Creationism Act is to endorse a particular religious doctrine, the Act furthers religion in violation of the Establishment Clause.

. . .

■ Justice Scalia, with whom the Chief Justice joins, dissenting.

Even if I agreed with the questionable premise that legislation can be invalidated under the Establishment Clause on the basis of its motivation alone, without regard to its effects, I would still find no justification for today's decision. The Louisiana legislators who passed the "Balanced Treatment for Creation–Science and Evolution–Science Act" (Balanced Treatment Act), La.Rev.Stat.Ann. §§ 17:286.1–17:286.7 (West 1982), each of whom had sworn to support the Constitution, were well aware of the potential Establishment Clause problems and considered that aspect of the legislation with great care. After seven hearings and several months of study, resulting in substantial revision of the original proposal, they approved the Act overwhelmingly and specifically articulated the secular purpose they meant it to serve. Although the record contains abundant evidence of the sincerity of that purpose (the only issue pertinent to this case), the Court today holds, essentially on the basis of "its visceral knowledge regarding what *must* have motivated the legislators," 778 F.2d 225, 227 (5th Cir. 1985) (Gee, J., dissenting) (emphasis added), that the members of the Louisiana Legislature knowingly violated their oaths and then lied about it. I dissent. . . .

. . .

We have relatively little information upon which to judge the motives of those who supported the Act. About the only direct evidence is the statute itself and transcripts of the seven committee hearings at which it was considered. Unfortunately, several of those hearings were sparsely attended, and the legislators who were present revealed little about their motives. We have no committee reports, no floor debates, no remarks inserted into the legislative history, no statement from the Governor, and no post-enactment statements or testimony from the bill's sponsor or any other legislators. *Compare* Wallace v. Jaffree, 472 U.S. 38, 43, 56–57 (1985). Nevertheless, there is ample evidence that the majority is wrong in holding that the Balanced Treatment Act is without secular purpose.

At the outset, it is important to note that the Balanced Treatment Act did not fly through the Louisiana Legislature on wings of fundamentalist religious fervor—which would be unlikely, in any event, since only a small minority of the State's citizens belong to fundamentalist religious denominations. *See* B. Quinn, et al., *Churches and Church Membership in the United States 16* (1982). The Act had its genesis (so to speak) in legislation introduced by Senator Bill Keith in June 1980. After two hearings before the Senate Committee on Education, Senator Keith asked that his bill be referred to a study commission composed of members of both houses of the Louisiana Legislature. He expressed hope that the joint committee would give the bill careful consideration and determine whether his arguments were "legitimate." 1 App. E29–E30. The committee met twice during the interim, heard testimony (both for and against the bill) from several witnesses, and received staff reports. Senator Keith introduced his bill again when the legislature reconvened. The Senate Committee on Education held two more hearings and approved the bill after substantially amending it (in part over Senator Keith's objection). After approval by the full Senate, the bill was referred to the House Committee on Education. That committee conducted a lengthy hearing, adopted further amendments, and sent the bill on to the full House, where it received favorable consideration. The Senate concurred in the House amendments and on July 20, 1981, the Governor signed the bill into law.

. . .

Before summarizing the testimony of Senator Keith and his supporters, I wish to make clear that I by no means intend to endorse its accuracy. But my views (and the views of this Court) about creation science and evolution are (or should be) beside the point. Our task is not to judge the debate about teaching the origins of life, but to ascertain what the members of the Louisiana Legislature believed. The vast majority of them voted to approve a bill which explicitly stated a secular purpose; what is crucial is not their *wisdom* in believing that purpose would be achieved by the bill, but their *sincerity* in believing it would be.

Most of the testimony in support of Senator Keith's bill came from the Senator himself and from scientists and educators he presented, many of whom enjoyed academic credentials that may have been regarded as quite impressive by members of the Louisiana Legislature. To a substantial extent, their testimony was devoted to lengthy, and, to the layman, seemingly expert scientific expositions on the origin of life. These scientific lectures touched upon, *inter alia,* biology, paleontology, genetics, astronomy, astrophysics, probability analysis, and biochemistry. The witnesses repeatedly assured committee members that "hundreds and hundreds" of highly respected, internationally renowned scientists believed in creation science and would support their testimony.

Senator Keith and his witnesses testified essentially as set forth in the following numbered paragraphs:

(1) There are two and only two scientific explanations for the beginning of life—evolution and creation science. Both are bona fide "sciences." Both posit a theory of the origin of life and subject that theory to empirical testing. Evolution posits that life arose out of inanimate chemical com-

pounds and has gradually evolved over millions of years. Creation science posits that all life forms now on earth appeared suddenly and relatively recently and have changed little. Since there are only two possible explanations of the origin of life, any evidence that tends to disprove the theory of evolution necessarily tends to prove the theory of creation science, and vice versa. For example, the abrupt appearance in the fossil record of complex life, and the extreme rarity of transitional life forms in that record, are evidence for creation science.

(2) The body of scientific evidence supporting creation science is as strong as that supporting evolution. In fact, it may be *stronger*. The evidence for evolution is far less compelling than we have been led to believe. Evolution is not a scientific "fact," since it cannot actually be observed in a laboratory. Rather, evolution is merely a scientific theory or "guess." It is a very bad guess at that. The scientific problems with evolution are so serious that it could accurately be termed a "myth."

(3) Creation science is educationally valuable. Students exposed to it better understand the current state of scientific evidence about the origin of life. Those students even have a better understanding of evolution. Creation science can and should be presented to children without any religious content.

(4) Although creation science is educationally valuable and strictly scientific, it is now being censored from or misrepresented in the public schools. Evolution, in turn, is misrepresented as an absolute truth. Teachers have been brainwashed by an entrenched scientific establishment composed almost exclusively of scientists to whom evolution is like a "religion." These scientists discriminate against creation scientists so as to prevent evolution's weaknesses from being exposed.

(5) The censorship of creation science has at least two harmful effects. First, it deprives students of knowledge of one of the two scientific explanations for the origin of life and leads them to believe that evolution is proven fact; thus, their education suffers and they are wrongly taught that science has proven their religious beliefs false. Second, it violates the Establishment Clause. The United States Supreme Court has held that secular humanism is a religion. Belief in evolution is a central tenet of that religion. Thus, by censoring creation science and instructing students that evolution is fact, public school teachers are *now* advancing religion in violation of the Establishment Clause.

Senator Keith repeatedly and vehemently denied that his purpose was to advance a particular religious doctrine. At the outset of the first hearing on the legislation, he testified, "We are not going to say today that you should have some kind of religious instructions in our schools.... We are not talking about religion today.... I am not proposing that we take the Bible in each science class and read the first chapter of Genesis." At a later hearing, Senator Keith stressed that "to ... teach religion and disguise it as creationism ... is not my intent. My intent is to see to it that our textbooks are not censored." He made many similar statements throughout the hearings.

We have no way of knowing, of course, how many legislators believed the testimony of Senator Keith and his witnesses. But in the absence of evidence to the contrary, we have to assume that many of them did. Given that assumption, the Court today plainly errs in holding that the Louisiana

Legislature passed the Balanced Treatment Act for exclusively religious purposes.

.   .   .

The Court seeks to evade the force of this expression of purpose by stubbornly misinterpreting it, and then finding that the provisions of the Act do not advance that misinterpreted purpose, thereby showing it to be a sham. The Court first surmises that "academic freedom" means "enhancing the freedom of teachers to teach what they will,"—even though "academic freedom" in that sense has little scope in the structured elementary and secondary curriculums with which the Act is concerned. Alternatively, the Court suggests that it might mean "maximiz[ing] the comprehensiveness and effectiveness of science instruction,"—though that is an exceeding strange interpretation of the words, and one that is refuted on the very face of the statute. See § 17:286.5. Had the Court devoted to this central question of the meaning of the legislatively expressed purpose a small fraction of the research into legislative history that produced its quotations of religiously motivated statements by individual legislators, it would have discerned quite readily what "academic freedom" meant: *students'* freedom from *indoctrination*. The legislature wanted to ensure that students would be free to decide for themselves how life began, based upon a fair and balanced presentation of the scientific evidence—that is, to protect "the right of each [student] voluntarily to determine what to believe (and what not to believe) free of any coercive pressures from the State." Grand Rapids School District v. Ball, 473 U.S., at 385. The legislature did not care *whether* the topic of origins was taught; it simply wished to ensure that *when* the topic was taught, students would receive " 'all of the evidence.' " (quoting Tr. of Oral Arg. 60).

.   .   .

It is undoubtedly true that what prompted the Legislature to direct its attention to the misrepresentation of evolution in the schools (rather than the inaccurate presentation of other topics) was its awareness of the tension between evolution and the religious beliefs of many children. But even appellees concede that a valid secular purpose is not rendered impermissible simply because its pursuit is prompted by concern for religious sensitivities. Tr. of Oral Arg. 43, 56. If a history teacher falsely told her students that the bones of Jesus Christ had been discovered, or a physics teacher that the Shroud of Turin had been conclusively established to be inexplicable on the basis of natural causes, I cannot believe (despite the majority's implication to the contrary) that legislators or school board members would be constitutionally prohibited from taking corrective action, simply because that action was prompted by concern for the religious beliefs of the misinstructed students.

In sum, even if one concedes, for the sake of argument, that a majority of the Louisiana Legislature voted for the Balanced Treatment Act partly in order to foster (rather than merely eliminate discrimination against) Christian fundamentalist beliefs, our cases establish that that alone would not suffice to invalidate the Act, so long as there was a genuine secular purpose as well. We have, moreover, no adequate basis for disbelieving the secular purpose set forth in the Act itself, or for concluding that it is a sham enacted to conceal the legislators' violation of their oaths of office. I am astonished by the Court's unprecedented readiness to reach such a conclusion, which I can only attribute to an intellectual predisposition created by the facts and the legend of Scopes v. State, 289 S.W. 363 (Tenn. 1927)—an instinctive reaction that any governmentally imposed requirements bearing upon the teaching of evolution must be a manifestation of Christian fundamentalist repression. In this case, however, it seems to me the Court's position is the repressive one. The people of Louisiana, including those who are Christian fundamentalists, are quite entitled, as a secular matter, to have whatever scientific evidence there may be against evolution presented in their schools, just as Mr. Scopes was entitled to present whatever scientific evidence there was for it. Perhaps what the Louisiana Legislature has done is unconstitutional because there is no such evidence, and the scheme they have established will amount to no more than a presentation of the Book of Genesis. But we cannot say that on the evidence before us in this summary judgment context, which includes ample uncontradicted testimony that "creation science" is a body of scientific knowledge rather than revealed belief. Infinitely less can we say (or should we say) that the scientific evidence for evolution is so conclusive that no one could be gullible enough to believe that there is any real scientific evidence to the contrary, so that the legislation's stated purpose must be a lie. Yet that illiberal judgment, that Scopes-in-reverse, is ultimately the basis on which the Court's facile rejection of the Louisiana Legislature's purpose must rest.

.   .   .

NOTES AND QUESTIONS

1. In *Epperson*, discussed in the Court's opinion, and in *Aguillard* itself, the Court said it was rejecting efforts to have religious views shape the teaching of science in the public schools. Is the Court as vigilant when religious views shape public school teaching in other areas? For an argument that the Constitution does in fact provide science with particular protection from religion, see Steven Goldberg, *The Constitutional Status of American Science*, 1979 U. ILL. L. REV. 1, 2–11.

2. Because the Constitution forbids the establishment of religion, the courts are forced to decide whether creationism is science or religion. Mainstream scientists are convinced that it is the latter. *See, e.g.*, NATIONAL ACADEMY OF SCIENCES, SCIENCE AND CREATIONISM (1984). In recent years, related disputes have arisen concerning whether the theory of intelligent design can be taught in the public schools. Intelligent design accepts some elements of evolutionary theory, but argues that the input of an "intelligent designer" is necessary to fully account for the complex forms of life we see around us. *See, e.g.*, Kent Greenawalt, *Establishing Religious Ideas: Evolution, Creationism, and Intelligent Design*, 17 N.D. J.L. ETHICS & PUB. POL'Y 321 (2003).

3. Perhaps the most important aspect of these disputes is the way they reveal the centrality of science in American culture. The attempt to justify Genesis in terms of science can be seen as a victory for those who believe science is the sole or most important truth system in existence. The use of science to validate the Bible is similar in this respect to arguments that prayer is important primarily because it confers medical benefits, or the argument that research in genetics has theological implications because genes are the essence of who we are. For a criticism of this tendency, see STEVEN GOLDBERG, SEDUCED BY SCIENCE: HOW AMERICAN RELIGION HAS LOST ITS WAY (1999).

4. Many, of course, regard the theory of evolution as fully compatible with religious belief and would happily leave religion out of the public schools. Nonetheless, the continued opposition to evolution reflects in part an undeniable tension between a scientific theory that closely links humans with nonhumans and traditional ethical and theological beliefs that humans unlike nonhumans are capable of good and evil. A similar tension may well accompany scientific advances relating to genetic engineering, see Chapter 2, supra, and artificial intelligence, see Chapter 5, infra.

5. After *Epperson* and *Aguillard* what options are available for those parents who cannot afford private school or home schooling for their children but who do not want those children exposed to the theory of evolution? So far, parents in that situation have not had much success in court. In *Mozert v. Hawkins County Bd. of Educ.*, 827 F.2d 1058 (6th Cir. 1987), *cert. denied* 484 U.S. 1066, 108 S.Ct. 1029, 98 L.Ed.2d 993 (1988), for example, parents, citing the free exercise of religion clause, sought to have their children excused from class when certain matters, including the theory of evolution, were being taught. The court rejected their claim. However, as noted above, to suppose that judicial hostility to the doctrine of creation will make the issue disappear is a mistake. As one scholar has concluded, regardless of the outcome of cases like *Aguillard,* "[t]he 60–year old creation-evolution legal controversy [will] continue ... because its impetus comes from social forces lying far beyond the reach of the courts." EDWARD J. LARSON, TRIAL AND ERROR: THE AMERICAN CONTROVERSY OVER CREATION AND EVOLUTION 166 (1985).

II.   GOVERNMENT SUPPORT FOR SCIENCE AND MEDICINE

A.   THE HISTORICAL BACKGROUND: THE FRAMERS AND SCIENCE

Richard Delgado et al., *God, Galileo, and Government: Toward Constitutional Protection for Scientific Inquiry*

53 WASH. L. REV. 349, 354–55, 358–61 (1978).

Several colonial figures were leading exponents of Enlightenment thought, the principal source of the American revolutionary spirit. Central to Enlightenment thought are the notions of toleration and liberalism, and a concept of truth-seeking as a continual process subject to objective verification and correction. Because these are also some of the basic values of science, the development and growing influence of science during the same period reinforced the rationalistic, anti-authoritarian tenor of social and political thought. Political theory borrowed basic values and assumptions from science, while politics contributed such metaphors as the "laws" which all physical bodies were assumed to obey. John Locke believed that natural laws for government could be derived empirically by studying nature. Madison saw the United States Constitution as a gigantic machine for the regulation of interest groups, by means of which the struggles among social classes would be balanced by political structures in much the same manner in which the physical universe remained in equilibrium under the influence of the laws of dynamics discovered by Newton....

. . .

[Thomas Jefferson, who was interested in a variety of scientific pursuits, including natural history] described freedom as "the first-born daughter of science," and equated scientific progress with forward development in government and morals. His beloved University of Virginia was to be based on the "illimitable freedom of the human mind" and was to include a medical school as well as a curriculum rich in mathematics and natural science. He was convinced that nothing was so conducive to intellectual and moral development as the study of science, and in language reminiscent of the account of the education of philosopher kings in Plato's *Republic* he wrote, "When your mind shall be well improved with science, nothing will be necessary to place you in the highest points of view, but to pursue the interests of your country ... with the purest integrity, the most chaste honor." Indeed, Jefferson concluded that the American reaction against "monkish ignorance and superstition" in favor of the natural rights of man was caused by the general spread of the light of science....

[Benjamin] Franklin was one of the leading experimental scientists of his day. His studies embraced electricity, magnetism, light, sound, geology, and human and animal physiology. His papers were read before learned societies in many countries and translated into several foreign languages. He founded, with Jefferson, the American Philosophical Society, whose members included leading colonial scientists and intellectuals. The organization's charter was granted in 1743 by the Pennsylvania General Assembly and signed by clerk Thomas Paine. Like Jefferson, Franklin wrote of the importance of including mathematical and scientific training in the curricula of colonial schools and universities, urging that these studies would help students develop habits of tolerance, practicality, and respect for truth. Although as a careful experimentalist he avoided over-literal importation of Newtonian metaphors into political theory, it is clear that he believed in a physically and politically ordered universe, with science as the method by which this order was to be ascertained....

. . .

A thoroughgoing rationalist and exponent of Enlightenment thought, [James] Madison conceived of the Constitution in Newtonian terms, as a collection of devices to balance and to maintain equilibrium among opposing groups and forces. Among these devices was the first amendment, of which Madison was the principal author. He worked with Thomas Jefferson in planning the University of Virginia, a strictly secular institution, which would serve as a "temple dedicated to science and liberty." Outside politics, his chief interests were science and philosophy. He read widely the work of Pascal, Montesquieu, Locke, and other leading natural scientists and economists. He carried out his own investigations of natural history, and at his death there was found among his papers an unfinished essay titled *The Symmetry of Nature,* in which he described the harmony of the physical and human realms under the universal rule of law. His maxim was "Dare to

Know." He saw the scientific method as offering the only sure guide to progress in both social and physical spheres....

Other leading colonial figures evidenced in either their personal lives or their writings the same respect for science held by Franklin, Jefferson, and Madison. Adams and Taylor corresponded about constitutional arrangements, agreeing that the idea of checks and balances borrowed from physical theory offered the best hope for political stability. Adams was influenced by the work of Montesquieu, whose book applied Cartesian and Newtonian ideas to sociopolitical problems. Rush, an eminent physician and signer of the Declaration of Independence, served as trustee of Princeton University, an early center of scientific education and liberal thought.

Scientific ideas and the scientific spirit were thus central to the thinking of leading colonial figures and integral to the Revolutionary idea. The political thinking of the colonial era was steeped in the heritage of the Enlightenment, including the ideals of liberty, zeal for truth-seeking, humility in the face of error, and hatred of authoritarianism. Many of the Revolution's leaders and theorists were leading scientists in their own right; others borrowed from the prevailing scientific climate metaphors and assumptions which they applied to politics, sometimes almost uncritically....

NOTES AND QUESTIONS

1. The list of colonial figures who combined interests in science and government could be extended considerably. Alexander Hamilton studied medicine and urged his friends to master chemistry to improve their thinking. JAMES T. FLEXNER, THE YOUNG HAMILTON: A BIOGRAPHY 47, 62 (1978); BROADUS MITCHELL, ALEXANDER HAMILTON: YOUTH TO MATURITY 54 (1957). David Rittenhouse, the leading American astronomer of the Revolutionary period, was a member of the Pennsylvania General Assembly and of that state's constitutional convention. *See generally*, BROOKE HINDLE, DAVID RITTENHOUSE (1964). In the 18th century, the word "science"—often used in the excerpts from Delgado and Millen—referred to knowledge generally. WHITFIELD BELL, EARLY AMERICAN SCIENCE: NEEDS AND OPPORTUNITIES FOR STUDY 8 (1955). Many of the Framers believed that areas as disparate as politics and physics would yield to a Newtonian approach. *See generally* I. BERNARD COHEN, SCIENCE AND THE FOUNDING FATHERS (1995). Why is that view less prevalent today? Why are fewer modern presidents and cabinet members scientists?

2. In addition to the protections afforded science by the First Amendment, *see* Sec. I. A, *supra*, the Constitution framed by these 18th century science enthusiasts provided support for science in several ways. The patent clause, discussed in Sec. II. D., *infra*, gave an important incentive for scientific research. The first administrator of the patent law, Thomas Jefferson, personally inspected various inventions soon after passage of the law in 1790. A. HUNTER DUPREE, SCIENCE IN THE FEDERAL GOVERNMENT 12–13 (1957). The federal power over weights and measures led to the creation in 1901 of the National Bureau of Standards, renamed the National Institute of Standards and Technology in 1988. 31 Stat. 1449 (1901) (current version codified at 15 U.S.C. § 271 (1988)). Through its census provision, the Constitution required the federal government to "make the largest collection of social-science data in the world...." DON K. PRICE, GOVERNMENT AND SCIENCE 5 (1962).

3. It cannot be denied, however, that in the early years of the republic, direct federal spending to support scientific research and development was sharply limited. Strict constructionists, including Thomas Jefferson, believed the Constitution left such activities to the states, not to the federal government. *See, e.g.*, A. Hunter Dupree, Science in the Federal Government, at 22. Thus, before the Civil War, federal science spending was generally tied to specific Congressional powers, such as those relating to national defense. The Constitution does not list scientific and medical research among Congress' enumerated powers. The central constitutional question for science was whether Congress' spending power was limited to the powers enumerated in Article 1, or whether Congress could spend for the general welfare, which would undoubtedly include science. The breakthrough for scientists came in 1862 when Congress created the Department of Agriculture pursuant to the power to spend for the general welfare and directed the Department to employ "chemists, botanists, entomologists, and other persons skilled in the natural sciences pertaining to agriculture." 12 Stat. 388 (1862) (current version codified at 7 U.S.C. § 2201 (1977)). The Supreme Court's later decision in United States v. Butler, 297 U.S. 1, 56 S.Ct. 312, 80 L.Ed. 477 (1936), holding that federal spending could be for the general welfare, resolved the constitutional controversy and provided a solid constitutional basis for federal spending for scientific and medical research. *See generally* Steven Goldberg, *The Constitutional Status of American Science*, 1979 U. Ill. L. F. 1 (1979). Such spending has increased throughout this century, particularly after World War II.

Given the existence of free enterprise in America, the government's ability to spend for science does not settle the issue of whether it should. There is, however, remarkable agreement among economists and politicians of all parties that the private marketplace alone will not produce enough basic research. While private industry invests in research and development, it shies away from the kind of basic research that is unlikely to produce immediate returns. *See* Daniel S. Greenberg, Science, Money, and Politics: Political Triumph and Ethical Erosion 465 (2001). Science is a public good; producers of science cannot fully appropriate the benefits of what they have created. *See, e.g.*, Gordon Tullock, Private Wants, Public Means 224–25 (1970). So while the federal government's total research and development spending, basic and applied, is not as great as private spending in this area, the federal government does support the majority of basic research in the United States. National Science Board, Science and Engineering Indicators 2004 4:5, 4:25. How much the federal government should spend on science and how that money should be allocated among various federal agencies is the subject of the materials that follow.

B. Government Spending for Science and Medicine: The Federal Budget Process

1. PRESIDENTIAL CONTROL OF AGENCY BUDGET REQUESTS

The National Science and Technology Policy, Organization, and Priorities Act of 1976

Pub. L. No. 94–282 (1976).
42 U.S.C. §§ 6601, 6611, 6613.

TITLE II—OFFICE OF SCIENCE AND TECHNOLOGY POLICY

Short Title

Sec. 201.   This title may be cited as the "Presidential Science and Technology Advisory Organization Act of 1976."

Establishment

Sec. 202.   There is established in the Executive Office of the President an Office of Science and Technology Policy (hereinafter referred to in this title as the "Office").

Director; Associate Directors

Sec. 203.   There shall be at the head of the Office a Director who shall be appointed by the President, by and with the advice and consent of the Senate, and who shall be compensated at the rate provided for level II of the Executive Schedule in section 5313 of title 5, United States Code. The President is authorized to appoint not more than four Associate Directors, by and with the advice and consent of the Senate, who shall be compensated, at a rate not to exceed that provided for level III of the Executive Schedule in section 5314 of such title. Associate Directors shall perform such functions as the Director may prescribe.

Functions

Sec. 204.   (a) The primary function of the Director is to provide, within the Executive Office of the President, advice on the scientific, engineering, and technological aspects of issues that require attention at the highest levels of Government.

(b) In addition to such other functions and activities as the President may assign, the Director shall—

(1) advise the President of scientific and technological considerations involved in areas of national concern including, but not limited to, the economy, national security, health, foreign relations, the environment, and the technological recovery and use of resources;

(2) evaluate the scale, quality, and effectiveness of the Federal effort in science and technology and advise on appropriate actions;

(3) advise the President on scientific and technological considerations with regard to Federal budgets, assist the Office of Management and Budget with an annual review and analysis of funding proposed for research and development in budgets of all Federal agencies, and aid the Office of Management and Budget and the agencies throughout the budget development process; and

(4) assist the President in providing general leadership and coordination of the research and development programs of the Federal Government.

Excerpts From House Report on Pub. L. No. 94–282

U.S. Code Congressional and Administrative News Vol. 2, 898–900.
94th Congress, 2d Sess. (1976).

TITLE II

Title II would make available to the President a new organizational entity to assist in using science and technology in national decision-making—an Office of Science and Technology Policy, whose Director also serves as science adviser. The basic premise is not to insist upon a particular style of scientific support for the President, but to provide a way of mobilizing expertise in the President's behalf. The President can use the Director of the Office, and such Assistant Directors as are appointed, in whatever manner he chooses. In any case, the Office would speak for the best public use and understanding of science and technology and not as an advocate for science and technology per se.

Numerous witnesses have contended that as the Federal role and support structure for R & D has grown, so has grown the need for better awareness and attention at the highest levels of government. Increasingly complex scientific and technological issues confront the President. Off and on since the beginning of World War II, the nation has been debating the issue of how best to incorporate science and technology into national decision-making.

World War II led to widespread use of science and technology by our allies, our enemies and ourselves. For the first time, a President had what amounted to a "science adviser"—Dr. Vannevar Bush, who marshaled the U.S. scientific and technological effort and worked closely with President Roosevelt.

Dr. John Steelman was designated by President Truman to head a Scientific Research Board in the Executive Office of the President. Close personally to the President, Steelman also acted as the President's liaison with the scientific community.

From 1952 until late 1957, science advice for President Eisenhower was provided by a Science Advisory Committee through the Director of the Office of Defense Mobilization. With the launch of Sputnik in October 1957, science and technology came once again to center stage and President Eisenhower created the position of Special Assistant to the President for Science and Technology. Dr. James R. Killian, Jr. was appointed to the post. Also, ODM's Science Advisory Committee was reconstituted as the President's Science Advisory Committee (PSAC).

In time, Congress became dissatisfied with these steps and pushed for a more formal arrangement. In mid–1962 President Kennedy established an Office of Science and Technology (OST) and his Science Adviser then wore several "hats," including Science Adviser to the President and Director of OST in the Executive Office of the President.

Most agree that the role of presidential science adviser was strong and influential from Roosevelt through Kennedy. Beginning with President Johnson and continuing with President Nixon, it was "downhill" to January 1973.

At that time President Nixon announced Reorganization Plan No. 1 of 1973, which abolished OST and PSAC, and transferred the function of Science Adviser to the Director of the National Science Foundation as an additional duty. Hearings were held by the Government Operations Committees, but the prevailing mood seemed different from that of 1961–1962 when President Kennedy was more or less persuaded to establish OST. The view in 1973 seemed to be, "If the President doesn't want a science advisory capability in the Executive Office, there is no point in making him keep one."

This Committee's inquiries have produced very few outside the Administration (in '73) who really approved the present setup. Virtually all of the Committee's other testimony indicated a conviction that the dual role of the Science Adviser and the Director of the National Science Foundation was not tenable. It is particularly noteworthy that Dr. McElroy, who had preceded Dr. Stever in the post of Director of the Science Foundation, was quite emphatic on this point. Since Dr. McElroy is the only former Director to have held that post during NSF's modern history, his views carried quite a bit of weight. . . .

.   .   .

Hence the substance of Title II. That Title encompasses the duties and functions of the proposed Office of Science and Technology Policy and its Director. The number of statutory Assistants may run from 0 to 4 depending on the President's desire.

Among the important features of this Title are (1) evaluating the quality and effectiveness of the Federal R & D effort; (2) advising the President with regard to scientific and technological considerations in all major fields including national security; (3) advising and assisting in the development of Federal R & D budgets; (4) developing criteria for optimum levels of Federal R & D support in accordance with the principles established in Title I.

It is also important to note the reorganization feature, which would permit the President to reorganize the advisory setup within his own Executive Office, unless vetoed by both houses of Congress. However, the President could not simply abolish the advisory setup and replace it with nothing. He could alter it, but he would be obliged to establish something in the place of whatever advisory arrangements were in existence.

NOTES AND QUESTIONS

1. The President's science advisor, typically a prominent scientist, heads the Office of Science and Technology Policy (OSTP), which provides the President with technical advice independent of the views of other government agencies. The science advisor thus inevitably becomes embroiled in political disputes over matters such as the effectiveness of weapons systems, the environmental impact of pesticides, and the use of surveillance technology to fight terrorism. If you were a leading scientist, would you accept the job of science advisor to the President? What relevance would your scientific knowledge have in such a job?

2. The OSTP is a presidential staff operation with advisory power. Huge mission agencies, such as Defense, Energy and the National Institutes of Health (NIH), actually spend the vast bulk of federal research and development funds. Although there have been various efforts throughout American history to create a centralized science agency, none has succeeded—there is no Department of Science. *See* A. HUNTER DUPREE, SCIENCE IN THE FEDERAL GOVERNMENT 377–79 (1957). The National Academy of Sciences, established by Congress in 1863, is a private group that advises the federal government when it is requested to do so. The National Science Foundation, created by Congress in 1950, funds basic research in a variety of fields but has never become dominant in federal research and development. The leading actors in science spending are the agencies created by Congress over the years to perform particular tasks. In 2004, federal research and development spending totaled over $120 billion, roughly $25 billion of which was allotted for basic research. The leading agencies in spending that $120 billion were Defense, Health and Human Services (which includes the National Institutes of Health), the National Aeronautics and Space Administration, Energy, the National Science Foundation, and Agriculture.

3.   The President, of course, appoints the top officials of these agencies. Needless to say, however, that power alone does not guarantee that agency budget requests will reflect presidential priorities. The agencies are large and the appointees may have priorities of their own. Accordingly, the President, through the OSTP and through another White House agency—the Office of Management and Budget (OMB)— reviews and revises agency budget requests relating to science before those requests go to Congress.

2.   THE CONGRESSIONAL BUDGET PROCESS

After White House review, the budget requests of the agencies, including the components of those budgets that involve science, go to Congress where they are handled by a variety of committees and subcommittees. Because there is no "Department of Science," there is no single "science budget" for Congress to consider. Congress decides on science spending as it acts on the budget requests of the various agencies. Thus, science spending on cancer research, for example, does not compete directly for funds with science spending for solar energy; it competes instead with non-science programs such as anti-cancer publicity campaigns. This system allows for few generalizations about Congressional attitudes toward science. One common reality is that Members of Congress, understandably concerned about their political futures, often prefer programs promising immediate payoffs over those with only long-term prospects. Thus, one study found that over a multi-year period, Congress was harder on budget requests from the National Science Foundation than from the National Institutes of Health, in part because the former requests involved more pure science with its relatively distant and uncertain benefits. *See* Roback, *Congress and the Science Budget*, 160 Sci. 964–71 (1968).

Would consolidating all federal research and development spending in one Department of Science, with a unified annual science budget for Congress to consider, better serve national goals or those of science? Do you think overall science spending would go up or down if there were a Department of Science? The practical chances of such a Department coming about are limited, not only because of doubts about whether it is a good idea, but because huge agencies like Defense and Health and Human Services would not likely give up their science programs without an enormous political fight. Nonetheless, proposals surface from time to time—in 1983, for example, President Reagan's science advisor reportedly began a study of the wisdom of merging some civilian science programs into a new department. Colin Norman, *NSF, Do You Take NBS . . .*, 221 Sci. 1363 (1983). In 1995, some congressional leaders suggested that a Department of Science be created, but their proposal did not include defense or health research. Colleen Cordes, *Proposed "Department of Science" Would Replace Many Agencies*, CHRON. HIGHER EDUC., Apr. 21, 1995, at A40.

At present, however, the story of Congressional treatment of science is largely a story of fragmentation. Budget requests wend their way through various subcommittees, often with overlapping jurisdictions and conflicting points of view, in both the House of Representatives and the Senate.

The excerpt that follows addresses the central question of how Congress receives technical advice. Such advice is relevant not only to budgetary matters, but to policy issues that have a high technical component.

Bruce L. R. Smith et al., *Technical Advice for Congress: Past Trends and Present Obstacles*

in SCIENCE AND TECHNOLOGY ADVICE FOR CONGRESS, (M. Granger Morgan & Jon M. Peha eds., 2003).
25–29, 32–40.

The scientific advice that Congress needs is in principle no different from any other kind of specialized advice—that is, an expert in some subject knows something that the generalist does not know, whether the subject is taxation, archaeology, microbiology, constitutional law, economics, tumor virology, or astronomy. Any subject will admit of virtually limitless division into ever more specialized subfields. The nature of science is to advance by breaking difficult questions down into more manageable questions that can be answered at some point, or in principle, empirically (though what constitutes adequate verification of theory is an issue on which philosophers of science may disagree). Congress, on the other hand, is usually not interested in learning more and more about the specifics of a technical issue; members of Congress want to know enough so that they can integrate various bits of specialized information into a broader context. Members of Congress are not interested in a physics or chemistry lesson; they absorb specialized information to apply it in a broad, value-laden context. Members of Congress may wish to learn from the leading specialists in a field but reserve for themselves the task of synthesizing the various inputs into a framework for decision. More commonly, however, elected representatives will find it convenient to deal with specialized inputs that have already been to some degree screened, synthesized, and packaged into a more manageable form for them. The filtered analyses are more easily digested by the members. The nature of Congress's work—the reverse of scientific endeavor—is to want to assemble parts into a whole, to blur the sharp edges of issues in the hope of achieving consensus and fostering compromise. Members of Congress seek agreement, not truth.

The policy issues facing Congress will usually involve the perspectives of more than one set of experts. Choosing among a multiplicity of views will be important. Indeed, on the more complex policy issues with significant technical content, experts from the same scientific field will often disagree. There are matters involving science and engineering where consensus is eventually reached (as on other matters) and where the affected interest groups, congressional staffs, and executive branch agencies all agree. Cooperation and agreement in many areas mark the normal business of the legislative branch, but cooperation is rarely newsworthy. However, even if contention is less frequent than one might infer from the media coverage of Congress, the issues on which Congress needs advice are generally not those where the constituencies, committee staffs, executive agencies, and the members themselves are in full agreement. The disagreements, moreover, frequently do not arise from ignorance but from tenaciously held, conflicting views, and from opposing priorities and policy preferences.

To consider an example, in the 106th Congress more than 50 bills were introduced to deal with Internet policy, including taxation, privacy, barring children's access to pornography, regulation, intellectual property rights, and many other issues (Smith et al. 2001). Members may or may not have understood the technical aspects of the Internet, but they generally understood what they wanted to achieve. What blocked action was not ignorance of the issues but disagreement over priorities. What was the most important goal: To expand Internet use? To protect the privacy of users? Or should the nation first address the right of state and local governments to tax Internet commerce so as to provide a "level playing field" between e-commerce and more traditional forms of business? Or should one shelter the Internet from all regulation for a time until it has become firmly established? Are we at such a point already? Numerous committees had jurisdiction over some aspect of Internet use, but none had full jurisdiction. Should there be a comprehensive policy toward the Internet, a series of limited and partial measures (which could possibly work at cross-purposes), or no policy at all for the time being other than to keep hands off? Members can readily grasp some Internet policy issues with little or no knowledge of the technical details, while other policy components will require some familiarity with the underlying technical dimensions. A quick briefing can often supply the need. In certain other respects, coming up with a policy framework that is coherent, sensible, and practical may well call for a much deeper technical understanding. However, technical knowledge alone will not guarantee agreement on policy goals, and members may disagree on what constitutes good technical advice.

Advice that is useful to Congress usually meets a number of criteria. First, it must be *relevant* to the policy issue at hand. Members of Congress are not scientists and must quickly move past the purely analytical issues to the broader normative context of policy. One does not need to know how a refrigerator works to use a refrigerator, and one does not need to know all the technical workings of the Internet to formulate policy toward the Internet. A brief explanation of the technical aspects of a problem will frequently suffice for the congressional staffer or member of Congress. On other occasions, the technical details may be an integral part of developing an adequate policy. The Internet policy context, for example, clearly contains complicated side issues. Hence, a clarification of the overlaps and links among the different aspects of the whole problem may demand a deep technical understanding before Congress can formulate sensible policy for any part. The technical advice, whether a brief explanation or a thorough analysis, must come in a form that can be digested by Congress. Congress is a decentralized institution and will tend to absorb information in bits and pieces through its different receptors (i.e., its individual members and numerous committees and subcommittees). Sometimes, however, a case can be made for centralizing some analytic functions, and recommendations for jurisdictional changes may be an eventual product of a policy review (always a difficult task in practice and frequently unwise).

Second, the scientific advice that is most needed at the moment is that which strives to be *disinterested*. This is not an easy concept for a member of Congress to grasp because most politicians have a suspicion—born of a certain healthy realism—that scientists are not altogether immune from disciplinary, institutional, or other forms of self-interest. There are enough *interested* perspectives on the Internet, to return to the example set forth above, including those held by technical experts from cable companies and equipment suppliers and from children's rights and privacy advocacy groups. The scientist adviser will add little value if he or she is merely one more interested party. Our political and judicial systems, however, make effective use of adversarial processes in reaching decisions. So we must be careful not to claim too much for neutral experts who are removed one step from the political battle. Clearly, however, another interested perspective would probably not resolve the current Internet impasse. The most useful advice for Congress in helping it move toward policies for the Internet will likely be disinterested.

A final criterion is that the advice should be credible. This concept includes both the criteria of relevance and disinterestedness, but it adds something more: the notion that the unit, organization, or individuals making a recommendation have done their homework, have proceeded in a fair-minded and thorough manner, have been in touch with all of the parties, and have a back-ground or *gravitas* that makes them worthy of being heard. The idea is partly in conflict with the earlier criteria because, if the decision-makers have a comfort level with the advisers, it usually means that they know where the group is "coming from," that is, what predispositions the advisers have acquired in the process of becoming accepted as credible analysts on an issue. Thus the advisers must have enough weight, familiarity with the issues, and acceptance from the parties to a dispute, without having too much prior standing and too established a niche in the political and institutional landscape. The good advisory group has a hard time working its way into the process and a hard time staying fresh and independent from longstanding institutional and political interests. Congress wants its advisory apparatus to be connected enough to be taken seriously by the interest groups but not so connected as to be merely an ally of one camp or another, and it would not want the advisory mechanism to bias the policy debate or constrain Congress's own freedom of action. Finally, because advising is a two-sided process—giving and receiving credible information—our reform ideas should not be limited to the legislators' side. How the scientific community gives advice and interacts with Congress may be as fruitful an area of reform as how Congress should position itself to receive advice.

.   .   .

The U.S. Congress differs from all other legislative bodies of the world in the extent and depth of its staff resources. The question of congressional staff is significant because staffers are critical to how Congress operates. Adequate staff resources enable Congress to exercise its full constitutional powers to organize hearings, conduct investigations, carry out oversight activities, vote appropriations, draft laws, and otherwise function. Staff members heavily influence how Congress receives and processes technical information. Congressional staff support operates at three levels: the individual member's own staff, committee staffs, and the congressional support agencies. The House member typically employs, on his or her personal staff, 15 to 18 full-time staff members, who are divided between Washington and the home district. The senator's personal staff varies, depending on the size of the state: a senator from a small state might employ 25 staff, and a large-state senator some 45, again divided between Washington and the home state....

The second level is that of committee staff. Most committees have between 45 and 70 staff members; the numbers grew spectacularly in the 1970s and 1980s and declined somewhat after 1994. Committee staffs are organized along party lines, with a larger number of majority party staff members reporting to the chairman of the relevant committee or subcommittee and a smaller number of minority party staffers assigned to the ranking minority member of the full committee or subcommittee....

. . .

Congress has at its disposal a set of staff support agencies, including the Congressional Research Service (CRS) of the Library of Congress, the General Accounting Office (GAO), the Congressional Budget Office (CBO), and—from 1972 to 1995—the Office of Technology Assessment (OTA)....

CRS as a whole continues to enjoy modest respect on the Hill, while the fortunes of the individual divisions wax and wane like those of academic departments. Whereas science policy seems to have disappeared from the agency's organizational chart, many of the major topics previously embraced by that heading continue to be analyzed as part of environment, energy, and health policy research. The American Law Division has retained its organizational identity and remains one of the strongest and most widely respected CRS units; it is regularly called on by committee and individual member staffs. The CRS has largely escaped the budget-cutting axe that has descended on other Congress-wide staff units. CRS's sustained congressional support stems from the fact that the agency has always provided direct support to individual members of Congress (who acquire information for their speeches, to assist in constituent services, and the like), not just to committees and subcommittees.

The General Accounting Office, created by the Budget and Accounting Act of 1921, has provided advice to Congress on a variety of topics over the years....

. . .

The Congressional Budget Office, established by the Congressional Budget and Impoundment Control Act of 1974, fills a specialized niche in the panoply of congressional support agencies. Its functions of cost estimation, "scorekeeping," and projections of budget deficits and surpluses are delineated and mandated steps in the budget reforms enacted by Congress and provide a stable source of funding and core mission for the agency. The

CBO has earned a reputation for professional competence and nonpartisanship; it has remained small, generally having about 130 full-time equivalent positions. Unless Congress were to change its budget process or the agency's performance were to decline sharply, the CBO's future seems assured.

. . .

Congress has also turned to the National Academy of Sciences (NAS; now the National Academies complex) for advice on matters dealing with science and technology from time to time beginning in the 1960s (Stine 1988). Since its inception during the Civil War, the NAS has advised the federal government, but such work had been traditionally oriented toward the executive branch....

The experience of the Office of Technology Assessment, to begin with, can be conveniently addressed by posing three questions:

- What were Congress's original intentions in establishing the office in 1972?
- How did its day-to-day functioning relate to congressional activities?
- What were the causes of OTA's abolition in 1995?

From the outset the OTA suffered from a lack of clarity as to what its role should be. Congress in the 1960s debated the establishment of a Congressional Office of Science and Technology but came to no clear resolution of what need would be served and did not implement the idea. The enthusiasm behind the idea for the OTA in 1972 stemmed originally more from the congressional support agencies and from the outside scientific community than from Congress itself. Only a relatively narrow base of congressional support materialized. The early association of the OTA with Senator Edward Kennedy (Democrat, Massachusetts) created the impression, however unfairly, that political motives were behind the creation of the office. In actuality, the OTA mission was narrowly circumscribed in its charter ... the agency was forbidden to issue recommendations to Congress but was instead directed to make presumably neutral background studies and analyses. The governing Technology Assessment Board of representatives and senators was evenly divided between the two political parties to help lessen the suspicions of partisan motivations. But what, exactly, was the OTA to study? No precise definition of an "assessment" was ever to emerge, but the words "technology" and "assessment" were wisely ignored in favor of a broad definition encompassing any significant issue involving scientific and technological developments with which Congress had to deal. Nonetheless, under its first director, Emilio Q. Daddario, a former Democratic congressman from Connecticut who had been a prominent member of the House Committee on Science and Technology and an early advocate for creating a congressional office of technology assessment, the OTA struggled to avoid being abolished in the face of budgetary stringency. Survival in the early years was an accomplishment attributable to Daddario's political skills. Internal quarreling among members of the staff over its mission and personality clashes also plagued the office in its formative years.

Russell W. Peterson, a former Republican governor of Delaware who held a doctorate in physical chemistry and who had spent his early career working for DuPont, took the reins as OTA's second director. He sought to calm the political turmoil surrounding the agency by launching an elaborate and time-consuming effort to tap the broad scientific community for ideas on the OTA's work plan and appropriate goals. The effort did not result in a clear management or policy orientation for the agency, but Peterson's term did establish the principle of bipartisan leadership for the office. Peterson also reorganized the staff to place program operations in the hands of technically competent directors, and he formalized recruitment practices to stress the hiring of individuals with training in the hard sciences. More than 50% of OTA's permanent staff eventually had doctoral degrees in science, engineering, or medicine, and political party affiliation played no part in hiring. Furthermore, Peterson instituted the practice of requiring the support of the ranking minority member of a community before the OTA would undertake a study. (The OTA responded to requests for studies only from committee chairs, not from individual members, a practice that had the unintended consequence of limiting OTA's contacts with other members of Congress and their staffs.)

Under its third director, John Gibbons, a scientist from Tennessee with extensive national laboratory and science policy experience (and with service on the staff of the last energy office in the Nixon White House), the OTA evolved into a competent applied research organization with high standards, strong ties to the scientific community, a solid professional staff, and a reputation for conducting thorough studies. In some respects, the agency functioned like the NAS in drawing on outside scientists who served on a pro bono basis on committees backing up the work of the OTA staff. OTA studies and procedures, like those of the National Academies, could be highly structured, ponderous, and slow moving. However, the contrasts with the NAS were more notable. OTA volunteer committees were advisory only to the OTA staff who wrote the reports (in contrast, NAS's committees are the authors of Academy reports, the staff their instrument). OTA panels were selected to hear all viewpoints (NAS's panels try to achieve consensus). Reports of the NAS invariably issue recommendations, whereas OTA's reports rarely issued explicit recommendations. The OTA work product, nonetheless, was deemed by critics to be too voluminous (reports were frequently lengthy) and submitted too late to be truly responsive to congressional needs.

The Republicans generally chafed under the long period of Democratic congressional hegemony and felt short-changed on staff requests and the allotment of committee seats by what they saw as an increasingly arrogant majority leadership. They became indignant in the 1980s over a series of OTA studies that seemed to them to advocate a highly partisan set of industrial policy goals and measures. Policies reflecting these ideas were incorporated into the 1988 Trade Act, including the creation of the Advanced Technology Program (ATP) in the Department of Commerce, the renaming of the National Bureau of Standards as the National Institute of Standards and Technology (NIST), and enhanced trade protections. Republicans in Congress strenuously opposed such measures as protectionist in intent and unwise subsidies, or "corporate welfare" measures that pushed the government inappropriately into the marketplace. The Reagan–Bush administration reluctantly accepted the initiatives of the Trade Act as the price of doing business with a Congress controlled by the Democrats. For the OTA the result was a paradox: relevance was achieved by participating in the congressional policymaking process but at the cost of alienating many in the minority party. OTA studies of the Reagan "Star Wars" proposals were perhaps even more significant in shaping critical reactions toward the agency among Republicans.

The criticisms were not always consistent: the OTA was assailed, on the one hand, for irrelevance and, on the other, for being too influential in a partisan direction. Nor were only Republicans irritated by OTA studies. OTA studies of deregulation of the electric power industry, automobile fuel economy standards, and environmental risk assessment angered some Democrats as much as the agency's assessments of Star Wars and ATP angered some Republicans. The OTA in the 104th Congress issued a study critical of its earlier industrial policy enthusiasms, but as the ideological controversies heated up, there was no solid base of support in Congress protecting the agency. The OTA enjoyed only limited backing in Congress, and this support principally came from a small circle in the majority Democratic party and an even smaller group of ranking minority Republican members. The chief Republican supporters were, on the Senate side, Ted Stevens of Alaska (who chaired the Technology Assessment Board when the Republicans controlled the Senate during President Reagan's first term), Orrin Hatch of Utah, and Charles E. (Chuck) Grassley of Iowa, and on the House of Representatives side, Amo Houghton of New York.

When the Republicans swept into control of Congress in the 1994 midterm elections, it soon became evident that the OTA was in trouble. The Republicans had talked during the campaign, which prominently featured Newt Gingrich's *Contract with America*, of reducing congressional staffing, abolishing a number of federal agencies (such as the Department of Energy and the Department of Education), and sharply curtailing or eliminating various programs (including the Advanced Technology Program in the Commerce Department, the Technology Reinvestment Program in Defense, and legal aid). They had also promised not to spare their own congressional prerogatives from critical scrutiny. When they encountered resistance to the more ambitious efforts (or had second thoughts about the wisdom of some of the proposed measures), it was natural to look for a target that could be more readily achieved. The OTA was an ideal candidate: it was a weak opponent with thin support within Congress; its abolition would fulfill a pledge to reduce congressional staff; and no significant outside constituency group would be offended (the almost total lack of reaction to OTA's demise from the scientific community and the various professional societies appeared to be ample confirmation of this judgment). In retrospect, it may be wondered why the agency lasted as long as it did. It was founded in controversy, struggled to find a mission and a secure niche in the congressional scheme of things (and only partially succeeded), and had limited support within Congress even if it was admired by many in the outside scientific community and emulated by several foreign legislatures ..., became a focal point of partisan dispute whether unfairly or not, and tried to function as a kind of internal "think tank" at a time when sharp ideological cross-currents were increasingly buffeting congressional operations.

Could or should an OTA be reestablished to provide timely and relevant technical advice to Congress? In strict terms, the OTA was not abolished since its authorizing statute was never specifically repealed; it was simply defunded in 1995 (and no appropriation has been voted since then, notwithstanding repeated efforts by Representative Rush Holt [Democrat, New Jersey] to appropriate funds to revive the office). A last-ditch compromise proposal by Representative Vic Fazio (Democrat, California) to salvage a pared-down OTA in the 104th Congress by placing it in the Congressional Research Service failed at the time but presumably could be revived if it had any support. Any effort to recreate the agency would have to overcome a built-in resistance to the formation of any new congressional bureaucracy on the part of most Republican and many Democratic members of Congress, and any new mechanism might also have to counter a presumption of past failure that may linger from the OTA's demise.

. . .

NOTES AND QUESTIONS

As this excerpt demonstrates, the problem is not that there is a paucity of technical information available to Congress. The question is whether Congress receives information that is useful to it in performing its Constitutional role. Do you agree that the most valuable criteria for such information are that it be *relevant, disinterested,* and *credible*? Are these realistic goals? Would reviving the Office of Technology Assessment improve Congress' ability to handle technical information? *See* Jim Dawson, *Legislation to Revive OTA Focuses on Science Advice to Congress,* 54 PHYSICS TODAY 24 (2001).

3.   SPENDING THE MONEY: WHO GETS IT AND WHAT STRINGS ARE ATTACHED

Grassetti v. Weinberger

United States District Court for the Northern District of California, 1976.
408 F.Supp. 142.

■ CONTI, J.

Plaintiff Davide R. Grassetti, Director of Research for the Arequipa Foundation, San Francisco, Clinical Associate Professor of Biochemistry, School of Dentistry, University of the Pacific, San Francisco, and holder of a Ph.D. degree in chemistry from the University of Lausanne, Switzerland, brings this action against various individuals associated with the federal government's cancer research program, alleging that at their hands he received unfair treatment in their denial of research grant money to enable him to study and develop a certain chemical compound, CPDS,[1] and a

---

1. "CPDS", or carboxypridine disulphide, according to plaintiff, retards the growth or spread of cancer by reacting with cancer cells in such manner as to form a stable compound on the surface of such cell. In a sense, then, the theory of the anti-family of compounds related thereto, which he discovered, and which he claims "impede the spread of existing cancer."[2] He labels their decisions to disapprove his grant applications arbitrary and capricious and without factual foundation, and as being the product of invidious discrimination practiced against him because, *inter alia,* he held patents covering the series of compounds, and he had made various public statements, some of which were critical of National Cancer Institute funding procedures, and others which tended to disparage an FDA-approved antibiotic known as Rifampicin.[3]

In addition to the challenges brought against the disapprovals of his grant applications, Grassetti alleges that the defendants arbitrarily refused adequately to test CPDS for its alleged anti-metastatic effects,[4] or to provide for its testing by others, in order that it could be considered for possible development by other scientists if the government would not fund plaintiff to do so. Further, he makes general claims that various agencies within the National Institutes of Health (NIH), which are charged by Congress with the responsibility of waging a comprehensive war on cancer, are failing to do so, in contravention of the statutory mandates. The crux of this contention as it relates to the instant controversy seems to be that since the government's cancer research apparatus has "blocked" the development of plaintiff's life-prolonging drug for improper reasons or for no reasons at all, the agencies and individuals responsible are not living up to their statutory duty, as plaintiff states it, "to comprehensively and energetically exploit scientific leads which may aid in the treatment of cancer." One specific violation of this duty is purported to lie in defendants' failure to promulgate regulations, which set forth specific guidelines and standards to be applied in the process by which applications for cancer research grants are reviewed for scientific merit. Had such regulations been in existence, asserts plaintiff, there would have been no opportunity for the kind of arbitrary and discriminatory treatment to which his grant applications allegedly were subjected. Finally, plaintiff challenges the entire administrative scheme, which allocates, as between the NIH and the National Cancer Institute (NCI), decision-making power in the area of scientific review of grant applications. These claims will be dealt with in detail below. . . .

metastatic (or anti-growth or spread) mechanism of CPDS is that it forms a hard wall around cancer cells, which does not admit of further growth.

2. *See* Complaint at p. 1.

3. Some biomedical theorists suggest, Dr. Grassetti among them that Rifampicin actually favors the formation of metastases (or secondary cancer tumors) due to its immunosuppressant properties. *See* Attachments 1 and 2 to Plaintiff's Supplemental Response to Defendants' Motion for Summary Judgment. Plaintiff made several public statements expressing his beliefs in 1972 and 1973 in an attempt to bring them to the

attention of the FDA and National Institutes of Health. National Cancer Institute testing of the drug gave negative results.

4. Metastasis is the growth or spread of cancer cells. Dr. Grassetti claims that the National Cancer Institute's screening of compounds submitted for anti-cancer testing is inadequate in that only toxicity and anti-tumor activity, and not anti-metastatic activity, are measured, and thus that CPDS did not get a fair chance to exhibit positive beneficial results. This matter is taken up in part IV.B. *infra.*

I. *Facts*

Over the past several years, Dr. Grassetti has applied on numerous occasions for grant support in the areas of chemistry, pharmacology, and cancer, and has several times been successful in receiving funds. The last award was made in the amount of $105,850 for the period October 1, 1971, through September 30, 1973, on an application entitled "Prevention of the Spread of Cancer", under which Dr. Grassetti was to study and document the chemical and pharmacological properties of CPDS and related compounds as they affect the growth of cancer. On April 6, 1973, as the above grant was nearing the end of its term, Dr. Grassetti submitted an application (CA 12469–03A1) in order to obtain additional funds in the amount of $538,041 for five years to continue his research and exploration of the same family of compounds, the specific purpose of the new request being "to determine the precise mechanism through which the spread of cancer is prevented by this type of compound." Consistent with the procedure which is followed by NIH upon receipt of grant applications, see infra, plaintiff's application was sent for scientific merit review to a study section chosen for its particular expertise in the technical field concerned—in this case, the Experimental Therapeutics Study Section. This proposal was reviewed during the Section's September, 1973, meeting, and disapproval was unanimously recommended to the National Cancer Advisory Board "because of the lack of meaningful progress in Dr. Grassetti's research and his failure to follow previous Study Section recommendations relative to obtaining data to support the biological and pharmacological aspects of his research." Dr. Grassetti was subsequently advised of the Study Section's recommendation.

Dr. Grassetti submitted another research proposal on October 1, 1973 (CA 16150–01) which the Division of Research Grants (DRG) of the NIH, *see infra*, determined to be not significantly different from the April 6, 1973, proposal (CA 12469–03A1) previously reviewed by the Experimental Therapeutics Study Section. DRG did not, therefore, send this proposal on to that Study Section or to another for review, but rather ruled that further review would be repetitive. Having been advised of this disposition, Dr. Grassetti sent a letter to all members of the NCAB [National Cancer Advisory Board] expressing disappointment; nevertheless, the NCAB at its November, 1973, meeting concurred with the Study Section's recommendations concerning application CA 12469–03A1, and, by necessary implication (assuming the DRG's assessment of CA 16150–01 was correct), the latter application as well.

On March 11, 1974, another application, entitled "Metastasis Prevention by Cell Surface Modification" (CA 16150–01A1), was submitted by plaintiff. In view of Dr. Grassetti's expressed dissatisfaction with the recommendations of the Experimental Therapeutics Study Section concerning the earlier proposal, a Special Study Section was formed, composed of five scientists with expertise in relevant fields, none of whom were members of the Experimental Therapeutics Study Section, who conducted a visit of Dr. Grassetti's laboratory at the University of the Pacific to obtain first-hand information concerning plaintiff's facilities and research support, in the light of which the grant application could be comprehensively evaluated. Following their scientific review of this latest proposal, the Section unanimously recommended that the application be disapproved, which decision was communicated to plaintiff. Plaintiff thereupon requested of the Executive Secretary of the NCAB that he be allowed to make an oral presentation at the next NCAB meeting. While this request was denied, in the exercise of the Board's discretion over the scope and content of its proceedings, plaintiff was informed that he could submit a written statement, which would be circulated to the Board's members. So far as the record shows, plaintiff submitted no such statement.

Upon further requests by Dr. Grassetti for the NCAB to conduct a special review of his latest application (CA 16150–01A1), the Chairman of the Board appointed two members to conduct an independent review of the administrative details of the Special Study Section's actions. These doctors reported to the NCAB that, "the administrative peer review procedures followed by both the Special Study Section and the NCI staff were proper and fair."

On December 27, 1974, plaintiff submitted a further grant application (CA 16150–01A2) entitled "Mechanism of Metastasis Prevention", which was reviewed by the Experimental Therapeutics Study Section during its April, 1975, meeting, and unanimously recommended by that Section for disapproval by the NCAB. That recommendation was followed. Shortly thereafter, plaintiff requested and received a report of the Study Section's reasons for its action, which stated in part that "lack of detail in [the application] was indicative of a lack of appreciation by Dr. Grassetti for biomedical and pharmacological studies."

Concurrent with plaintiff's various submissions of grant proposals, he sent to NCI several compounds for testing, among them CPDS, which were screened for anti-cancer activity, without significant positive results.

II. *The Issues*

While the instant complaint, its prayer for relief and the supporting papers are extremely prolix and wide-ranging, it is the opinion of this court that the issues meritorious of our consideration separate along two major lines of inquiry, the first having several subparts.

First, we must consider whether the various administrative determinations respecting plaintiff's grant applications were made in accordance with law. Resolution of this issue necessarily includes consideration of plaintiff's allegations of (1) conflicts of interest on the part of scientists assigned to evaluate the applications, (2) discrimination against plaintiff because he had patents, (3) discrimination against plaintiff because of his exercise of rights guaranteed by the First Amendment, (4) defendants' failure to promulgate adequate regulations as required by law setting forth standards for scientific review, (5) the NCI's and the NCAB's improper delegation of scientific merit review functions to the Division of Research Grants (DRG) of NIH, and (6) defendants' refusal to make full disclosure to plaintiff of the contents of all reports, documents and files concerning his grant applications, as he claims is required by the Freedom of Information Act.

Second, independent of the relationship between the various agencies and plaintiff as a grant applicant, we must consider whether the federal agencies and individuals charged under the National Cancer Act with various responsibilities in administering the government's war on cancer have lived up to their statutory duties in their handling of the chemical compounds submitted by plaintiff for testing.

Resolution of the important issues raised by the first inquiry necessarily requires a complete understanding of the administrative and scientific schemata pursuant to which a grant application is evaluated and a decision whether or not to fund it is made. This background will be presented first. The court will then pass to the testing issue.

III. *The Grant Application Review Process*

A. *Statutes and Regulations:*

Subchapter III of Title 42 of the U.S. Code provides the statutory framework for the formation of the National Research Institutes, one of which is the National Cancer Institute, created under Part A, 42 U.S.C. §§ 281–286g. The NCI is a division of the National Institutes of Health, which is composed of ten other institutes and various support divisions, all dedicated to research and development activities in the area of public health and welfare. NIH is in turn a component of the Public Health Service, a part of the Department of Health, Education and Welfare (HEW). [Now Health and Human Services (HHS).]

Section 301(c) of the Public Health Service Act, 42 U.S.C. § 241(c), authorizes the Secretary of HEW to:

> Make grants-in-aid to universities, hospitals, laboratories, and other public or private institutions, and to individuals for such research projects as are ... with respect to cancer, recommended by the National Cancer Advisory Board....

The award of research grants under the above provision is governed by 42 C.F.R. Part 52. With respect to evaluation and disposition of research grant applications, 42 C.F.R. § 52.13(a) states:

> (a) Evaluation. All applications filed in accordance with § 52.12 shall be evaluated by the Secretary through such officers and employees and such experts or consultants engaged for this purpose as he determines are specially qualified in the areas of research involved in the project, including review by an appropriate National Advisory Council or other body as may be required by law. The Secretary's evaluation shall take into account among other pertinent factors the scientific merit and significance of the project, the competency of the proposed staff in relation to the type of research involved, the feasibility of the project, the likelihood of its producing meaningful results, the proposed project and the amount of grant funds necessary for completion, and in the case of applications for support of research in emergency medical services, special consideration shall be given to applications for grants for research relating to the delivery of emergency medical services in rural areas.

In the case of cancer research grant applications, the direct costs of which do not exceed $35,000, the Director of NCI, under procedures approved by the Director of NIH, may approve grants after "appropriate

review for scientific merit" without the necessity for review and recommendation by the NCAB. Where direct costs exceed that figure, the NCAB must
review and recommend approval to the Director of NCI. *See* 42 U.S.C.
§ 282(b)(1) and (2). In this manner, requests for small grants can receive
expedited treatment. *See* 1971 U.S.Code Congressional & Administrative
News, pp. 2356–57. When the NCAB recommends approval, it in effect
certifies to the Secretary of HEW that the application "show[s] promise of
making valuable contributions to human knowledge with respect to the
cause, prevention, or methods of diagnosis or treatment of cancer." 42
U.S.C. § 284(c). The NCAB's decision to approve reflects the Board's
assessment of the proposal's technical and scientific merit as well as its
determination that the proposed project fits into the NCI's mission and
research priorities and into the total pattern of research in universities and
other institutions. The determination whether or not to grant funding
must still be made after approval of the Director of NCI, on the basis of
budget and priorities existing within the Institute as a whole, by the
Secretary of HEW, who considers the Institute's own assessment of the
application, in light of Institute policies and program priorities and availability of appropriations. The power to make a final decision is, by operation of the statutory scheme, lodged in the Secretary, HEW.

B.   *Administrative Grant Application Processes within NIH.*

Applications for research grants received at NIH, are sent to the NIH's
Division of Research Grants, which normally assigns them to one of a
number of regularly constituted advisory committees (referred to as "study
sections") responsible for initial scientific review and recommendation. At
the same time, DRG designates the appropriate awarding unit or Institute
(such as NCI), to which the proposed research grant application will be
referred. DRG makes the study section assignments and the awarding unit
designation on the basis of the scientific or technical area into which the
application's subject matter falls. Often, of course, the subject of a given
application reaches across many technical disciplines, in which case an ad
hoc study group may be formed, composed of scientists and biomedical
experts from all relevant areas of technical expertise. In such a case DRG
designates more than one Institute as the appropriate awarding units. It is
presumably in response to the obvious need for coordination of all research
activities within NIH that a central clearing house of grant applications,
namely DRG, is maintained separate from any particular Institute.

The scientist administrators in DRG who assign applications to study
sections are organizationally separate from the Institutes and their programs. Each study section is made up of experts in the biomedical sciences
and other scientific areas relevant to the particular inquiry, who come, with
few exceptions, from universities and other organizations outside the
federal government.

Following the initial study section review a "summary statement" is
prepared by the executive secretary, a DRG staff member, in which the
salient features of the members' deliberations, recommendations, and substantive conclusions relating to the application are documented. Upon

request, the applicant is provided with reasons abstracted from the "summary statement" for the action recommended on the application.

The study section's recommendation on the application represents an assessment of scientific and technical merit only. It is not intended as a competitive review in relation to other applications being reviewed by the same group or other groups. If approval is recommended, the study section is required to assign to the application a rating of its scientific merit, which can aid the appropriate national council (such as the NCAB) in making its decision on relative priorities of approved projects.

Whether the study section advises approval or disapproval, the recommendation as to cancer research proposals goes to the NCAB, which, considering not only technical merit but also the needs of the Institute and NIH as a whole, the need for the initiation of research in new areas, the degree of relevance of the proposed research to the mission of the Institute, and other matters of policy, can make an independent decision on the application. If the study section has recommended disapproval, the NCAB can "remand" for reconsideration, or simply recommend approval in the exercise of its own judgment. Applications, with their attached study section recommendations, are reviewed by the NCAB at three of its four yearly meetings, in March, June and November. The October NCAB meeting is generally reserved for review of ongoing NCI research programs.

As noted, NCAB approval is communicated to the Director, NIH and eventually the Secretary, HEW, who makes the final decision and disburses the funds.

IV. *The Law Governing Plaintiff's Claims*

A. *Denial of Research Funding*

In this aspect of the case, plaintiff is basically alleging that the administrative determinations made by first the study sections and eventually the NCAB, the Director, NIH, and the Secretary, HEW, in disapproving his grant applications were arbitrary, discriminatory, without factual basis, were made as a reprisal for his exercise of his First Amendment rights or because he held patents on his chemical compounds and thus constituted an abuse of administrative discretion.

These charges require the court to inquire into whether it is given jurisdiction to review such an administrative determination, and, if so, the scope of that review. The answer is found in the provisions of the Administrative Procedure Act dealing with judicial review of administrative action, namely, 5 U.S.C. §§ 701 and 702. Section 702 states:

> A person suffering legal wrong because of agency action, or adversely affected or aggrieved by agency action within the meaning of a relevant statute, is entitled to judicial review thereof.

Section 701(a) states, in pertinent part:

> This chapter applies ... except to the extent that—
>
> (1) statutes preclude judicial review; or
>
> (2) agency action is committed to agency discretion by law.

Since neither the Public Health Service Act nor the National Cancer Act contains any provision expressly precluding review, jurisdiction exists here to the extent that the action undertaken ultimately by the Secretary, HEW, is not of a type committed to his agency's or his delegate agency's discretion by law. *See* 4 Davis, Admin. Law, § 28.16.

While we need not go so far as to decide the question, it is probable that the medical merits of agency decisions on research grant applications are committed to the unreviewable discretion of the agency, subject to judicial scrutiny only where it is alleged that the agency has transgressed a constitutional guarantee or violated an express statutory or procedural directive. *See, e.g.,* Apter v. Richardson, 510 F.2d 351 (7th Cir.1975); Kletschka v. Driver, 411 F.2d 436 (2d Cir.1969); Cappadora v. Celebrezze, 356 F.2d 1 (2d Cir.1966); *see generally* Saferstein, Nonreviewability: A Functional Analysis of "Committed to Agency Discretion", 82 Harv.L.Rev. 367 (1968). In cases such as these, and the one at bar here, were a substantial evidence or abuse of discretion standard held to apply, the result would be to place a tremendous burden on the courts to digest masses of technical data before it could be decided that one grant application was so superior that it was an abuse of discretion to reject it in favor of others. A much more important consideration is that, unfortunate as it might be, it is a fact of life that courts are simply not competent to step into the role of a medical research scientist faced with having to evaluate an applicant's technical expertise, the theoretical chemical and pharmacological underpinnings of his study methodology, the statistical validity of his test results and the conclusions drawn therefrom, or just about any other factor of importance to NCI in deciding who should get its research money. But in this court's opinion the preeminent consideration militating against general judicial review of research grant decisions is that such review would place a heavy burden of litigation on an agency with more important matters at hand, would delay the funding process to the detriment of potential grantees, and would perforce place in jeopardy a program designed to combat cancer.

Even assuming, however, that a substantial evidence standard should be applied, it is amply satisfied here. Some of the reasons given for the denial of research funds were that: (1) The application "indicates a lack of appreciation for experiments which should be conducted, and those which have been done have in nearly every respect been inadequately presented both in the application and in the discussion during the site visit. There are serious questions of the significance and reproducibility of the test system, as used here, to detect effects upon metastases and the entire program is dependent upon this;" (2) Proposed experiments to determine, among other things, the interaction of CPDS with the surface of cancer cells, were presented "in a diffuse way with the details either not settled upon or not presented in a manner to permit evaluation;" (3) "There are reservations on the chemical interpretation of what the principal investigator observes in his studies in cellular systems...." Plaintiff's interpretations of the relevant chemical phenomena were in many cases contrary to hard results obtained by other experimenters; (4) "In summary, the results are interesting, however, appropriate design of experiments has not been made and a rather naive chemical view of the reaction of CPDS (or related derivatives) with cells has been adopted. The applicant failed to present well thought out ideas about his short-term goals and did not project the insight to pursue a longer term planned series of experiments to warrant project support. It does not appear that he is familiar with the chemistry of unsymmetrical disulfides nor the principles, which govern their reactions. This proposal did not generate confidence that the applicant could work with chemically modified macromolecules in a careful and meaningful series of experiments." *See particularly,* Attachments O and W to Affidavit of Richard A. Tjalma, Assistant Director for Board and Panel Affairs, NCI, Defendants' Motion for Summary Judgment. The record more than adequately shows that the determination to disapprove the applications was made after careful review by expert medical and scientific professionals, who, in the exercise of their best technical judgment, simply were not satisfied that the proposals had such scientific merit as to justify funding.

The court's only legitimate function in a case such as this is the extremely limited one of insuring that the agency's determination was arrived at through procedures, which were reasonable and fair. After a careful review of the record, the court finds that there was no deviation here from the usual procedures under which grant applications are processed, and those procedures, which have been in existence for a number of years in NCI and NIH, are eminently fair in guaranteeing to the maximum extent possible that the best ideas in the field of cancer research are highlighted for government support, and that notwithstanding plaintiff's allegations to the contrary, the administrative decision here is sufficiently supported by the medical and scientific evidence. This case bears striking similarity to *Kletschka,* supra, in which the court upheld a denial of research funds in affirming the district court's grant of defendants' motion for summary judgment, against plaintiff's charge that the agency action was undertaken in retaliation against him for his having exercised certain of his legal rights. *Id.* at 441–42.

Apart from the reviewability or nonreviewability of the decision not to award plaintiff a grant, however, plaintiff charges that the defendants' action constituted certain violations of law, as to which a reviewing court may take cognizance and in the appropriate case, substitute its own judicial judgment as to what the law is and whether a violation has occurred. *See* 4 Davis, Administrative Law § 30.01 et seq. Specifically, plaintiff has charged (1) that certain individuals who had a part in reviewing his applications were acting with conflicts of interest, violative of 18 U.S.C. § 208, 43 C.F.R. § 73.735–1202, and Executive Order 11222, including Section 302 thereof; (2) that the National Cancer Act, specifically Section 410A thereof, 42 U.S.C. § 286e, requires the Director, NCI, to promulgate certain regulations, which he has not done; and (3) that the delegation by NCI to the Division of Research Grants, NIH, of initial responsibility for review of grant applications is violative of the express provisions of the National Cancer Act where under scientific review is to be accomplished by NCI and not by NIH or its divisions. We now turn to these contentions.

(1) The conflict of interest provisions above require that one with a financial interest in the outcome of a given decision to be made by a government agency not be allowed to contribute in any way to making that

decision. Plaintiff claims that the three members of the study group which initially evaluated application CA 16150–01A1 in May of 1974 were acting with conflicts of interest in that these individuals or the institutions with which they were associated were recipients of NCI funded grants. Suffice to say that this fact in itself does not create a conflict of interest within the meaning of the relevant statutes and regulations. In no way would the individuals involved benefit financially by denying grant money to Dr. Grassetti, unless it be argued that their denial to him would leave more money in the pot for future proposals from themselves, a possibility of conflict of interest which the court deems to be much too remote. As a practical matter, high-level cancer research probably cannot be carried forward with the kind of vigor needed to solve this important and complex problem without government funding on a large scale; and probably in some way every doctor or scientist meeting the extremely high standards of technical competence required to be named to a study group has in the past been or is in the present on the receiving end of government support.

Putting this issue in its correct context, conflicts of interest in the grant review process would arise when a study section or NCAB member contributed to a decision as to whether to award himself or his institution a funding grant. This is assiduously avoided by NIH, NCI and NCAB policies and directives which disqualify such individuals from serving on study groups or being in attendance at NCAB meetings during which the individual's or his institution's proposal is being discussed and reviewed. *See* Release 4506, NIH Manual, "Review of Research Grant Applications" at par. G.1.b. and Attachment E to Affidavit of Dr. Tjalma, Defendants' motion for Summary Judgment.

The court finds the above procedures designed to avoid conflicts of interest in the grant application review process adequate and reasonable, and finds that there was no violation of law in defendants' actions with respect to Dr. Grassetti's applications.

(2) Section 410A of the National Cancer Act, as amended, 42 U.S.C. § 286e(a) states:

> The Director of the National Cancer Institute shall, by regulation, provide for proper scientific review of all research grants and programs over which he has authority (1) by utilizing, to the maximum extent possible, appropriate peer review groups established within the National Institutes of Health and composed principally of non-Federal scientists and other experts in the scientific and disease fields, and (2) when appropriate, by establishing, with the approval of the National Cancer Advisory Board and the Director of the National Institutes of Health, other formal peer review groups as may be required.

Subsection (b) directs the Director, NCI, to prepare annual reports to the President for transmittal to the Congress on the "activities, progress, and accomplishments" under the National Cancer Program.

Citing subsection (a), plaintiff asserts that the Director, NCI, has failed to obey the duty contained therein by virtue of his not having promulgated a regulation providing objective standards and criteria under which applications for research grants can be reviewed for scientific merit.

This contention is without merit. First, as a matter of statutory construction, it is by no means clear that subsection (a) requires such a regulation. The thrust of the provision seems to cover only existing grants and programs, that is to say, those as to which a decision to fund has been made and which at that point actually constitute an element of the National Cancer Program's research activities. This would not include potential grants, those as to which a decision to fund has not been made. Support for this construction is found in subsection (b) in that the duties placed on the Director, NCI, in subsection (a) seem to look to the requirement that that official make an annual comprehensive report on on-going activities and accomplishments to the President and Congress. The Director must have some means of apprising himself of these activities, through the mechanism of scientific review thereof.

It is not necessary to so hold, however, because in the opinion of this court, the Director, NCI, has, in fact, promulgated regulations governing review for scientific merit, through NIH and its grant application review component, DRG. *See* Referral Handbook, NIH, DRG (Attachment A to Tjalma Affidavit, Defendants' Motion for Summary Judgment); Orientation Handbook for New Members of Study Sections, NIH, DRG (Attachment B to Tjalma Affidavit); Releases 4506 and 4507, NIH Manual, "Review of Research Grant Applications" and "Exchange of Information between Initial Review Groups and Awarding Units" (Attachment C to Tjalma Affidavit); Handbook for Executive Secretaries, 3d ed., NIH, DRG (February 1973) (Attachment D to Tjalma Affidavit). The court finds that the guidelines for scientific merit review contained in these publications go just about as far as is practicably possible in setting forth "objective criteria" for evaluations on scientific bases. What the plaintiff seems to request is something much more specific in the way of exact pre-established standards for deciding a proposal has the requisite "scientific merit" to justify funding it. As a scientist, plaintiff surely realizes that a great deal of independent scientific judgment must go into an assessment of a given proposal, and that hard and fast rules against which can be tested "scientific merit" simply do not exist. The only way there can be assurance that those proposals with "scientific merit" are recommended for funding and those without it are not, is to pick the best qualified experts in the relevant technical fields to make the decision on the basis of their well-informed judgment. There is absolutely no indication in the record that NIH is doing other than that, and plaintiff has made no challenge of the credentials of the scientists assigned to evaluate his proposals.

In view of the foregoing, the court holds that defendant Director, NIH, has in Dr. Grassetti's case complied in every respect with the law, particularly section 410A of the National Cancer Act.

(3) Plaintiff also challenges the delegation by NCI of initial review for scientific merit to NIH and its component, DRG. Plaintiff's position basically is that NCI and NCAB should perform the entire review function where research proposals in the cancer area are concerned. Plaintiff cannot reasonably challenge the use of peer groups for initial review purposes, given the strong congressional approbation their use received, as is shown in the legislative history. *See* 1971 U.S. Code Congressional & Administra-

tive News, pp. 2356–57. It is also evident from that history that Congress contemplated the coordination of all health-related research by a group within NIH:

> One of the important concerns of the biomedical research community had to do with preserving the integrity of the peer review system now applied across all biomedical research areas. The concern, expressed by a number of witnesses before the Committee, was that the latitude allowed in the Senate bill for the creation of special cancer review bodies would lead to the development of two peer review systems applying disparate standards; and that, further, a dual system in this area would effectively fragment the biomedical research community.... The hazards of evaluating the scientific merit of research projects are many, but the Committee has received abundant testimony that no system has yet surpassed the study section system of the National Institutes of Health in assuring that high standards of quality and scientific merit—in addition to program relevance—are applied before public funds are expended. The Committee, therefore, has taken steps to assure that these advantages of the NIH study section system will be applied to the effort to find a cure for cancer.... *Id.*

The history also unequivocally indicates that Congress intended the attack on cancer to be undertaken in the "interdisciplinary setting" provided by NIH coordination. *Id.* At 2339. *See also id.* At 2348–49.

In view of these strong indications of Congressional intent that cancer research activities be coordinated by NIH and that the existing peer review or study group systems be utilized, plaintiff's contention is seen to be untenable. The procedure employed by NIH, NCI and the NCAB in evaluating grant applications is exactly what Congress hoped for, indeed, mandated, in the National Cancer Act. The court finds no violation of law in the method by which cancer research grant applications in general, and plaintiff's in particular, are processed through NIH, DRG, NCI and NCAB....

B.   *Testing of CPDS*

As noted, plaintiff claims that defendants failed adequately to test CPDS, which, he asserts, they are legally required to do if they are to obey their statutory command to exploit every available lead showing promise in the treatment or cure of cancer. The contention basically is that CPDS is an anti-metastatic compound, whose beneficial effects are seen only in the retardation or termination of growth or spread of cancer, whereas defendants have tested it only for its toxicity and its anti-tumor effects, which Dr. Grassetti never intimated that it had.

Apart from whatever legal duty may lie on defendants to test compounds submitted to them, the court finds that defendants did in fact perform various standard tests, and the treatment accorded plaintiff's chemical compounds was reasonable and non-arbitrary. Tests are conducted by the Division of Cancer Treatment of NCI in the following manner: Tumor cells are injected into two groups of mice. One group is treated with the subject substance (test group), the other group is left untreated (control group). The prime criterion used to assess potential anti-cancer activity is the effect of the substance on mortality. If there is no difference in survival between the test and control groups, or if there is no shrinking of visible tumor masses, the substance is not tested further unless something unique is known about the compound or class of compounds which would lead to further tests.

NCI does not routinely screen substances *specifically* for their anti-metastatic (prevention of cancer spread) activity. This is because, if anti-cancer effects are observed during regular screening, NCI proceeds with drug development regardless of the anti-cancer mechanism involved. In its screening activity, NCI is interested in the net outcome of the test (i.e., survival rate and tumor shrinkage) and not the precise mechanism involved. Thus, the NCI approach is a "black box" approach; that is, total anti-cancer activity, including one or both of two possible factors, anti-tumor and anti-metastatic effects, is measured, without careful differentiation between the two. Differentiation is not absolutely necessary, since it is the total anti-cancer effect, which is the most significant variable.

The Director of the Division of Cancer Treatment, Vincent T. DeVita, M.D., states:

> Although there are tests which could perhaps be utilized to determine specifically the anti-metastatic effects of drugs, in the judgment of NCI scientists these approaches would be no more reliable for predicting the potential utility of anti-cancer drugs than those currently employed to screen for overall anti-cancer activity. In other words, if no anti-cancer activity is observed for a substance tested, as evidenced by the absence of a reduction in mortality or of tumor shrinkage, there is no scientific purpose served by testing for added results of anti-metastatic activity of hundreds of thousands of compounds, most of which will not be shown to inhibit tumor growth in any site. Furthermore, currently there is no *generally* accepted test that directly measures anti-metastatic effects of drugs, which does not also show an effect on either the primary lesion (shrinkage) or on metastasis (survival).

Affidavit of Dr. DeVita, Exhibit D of Defendants' Reply to Plaintiff's Opposition.

NCI tests approximately 50,000 compounds each year in the fashion described above. The annual cost of this program is five million dollars. In order to test 50,000 compounds each year specifically for anti-metastatic activity, it would cost much more because the tests are apparently more complex. Defendants state "The NCI staff believes the added cost to be prohibitive and not of high enough priority in view of the questionable value of such testing and other scientific opportunities competing for the same funds."

Under the above procedures, Dr. Grassetti's compounds were tested by NCI. According to the defendants, all were found to be inactive by criteria routinely applied to all compounds regardless of their source. In addition, a special test was performed on CPDS, at the repeated requests of Dr. Grassetti. While "slight activity" was shown, it was defendants' judgment that this activity was not of sufficient magnitude to be considered worth pursuing, under normal criteria.

Defendants' determination of which test to use and of how extensive such testing should be is a matter clearly outside the scope of this court's jurisdiction to review. Likewise, defendants' assessment that a test specifically picking up anti-metastatic activity is cost-prohibitive when weighed against the advantages thereof, is not reviewable here. These are matters for the judgment of medical experts, not courts. At the risk of being pedantic, the court reiterates that which was said before. The only role for this court to play on this issue of testing, like the other issues presented here, is to see that normal procedures were followed and that plaintiff received fair treatment. This he clearly did. If anything, defendants have gone to greater lengths than usual to explore any possible beneficial effects of CPDS and its derivatives. They found none.

For this court to order defendants to perform certain tests on CPDS, or any other compound, would not only be ludicrous, but would also constitute interference of a most egregious sort with an administrative agency trying to do an important job. This the court will not do.

Accordingly, it is the order of this court that defendants' motion for summary judgment be, and hereby is, granted.

NOTES AND QUESTIONS

1. As we have seen, agencies begin the science funding process by sending their budget requests to the White House and then to Congress. After Congress appropriates the money, the agency then has the task of deciding which projects get funded within the guidelines established by Congress. As *Grassetti* suggests, when the agency grants money to private applicants, it typically employs a peer review process in which scientists select the applications which have the most merit. As one can see from *Grassetti,* courts are reluctant to second-guess these judgments, unless an applicant can show not a scientific error, but rather a grant decision infected with prejudice involving, for example, race or gender. *See, e.g.,* Apter v. Richardson, 510 F.2d 351 (7th Cir.1975). As a result, the scientific community itself plays a dominant role in determining which individual research projects get funded.

2. The peer review system is not adversarial; it reflects an effort at finding consensus within the scientific community. Beyond that, agencies vary in the way they do peer review. Some, such as the National Science Foundation, tend to use external peer review panels made up of scientists who do not work full-time for the government. Others, such as the National Aeronautics and Space Administration, prefer to use largely in-house agency experts.

3. Peer review is a remarkably durable and ubiquitous feature of American science. *See* Thomas O. McGarity, *Peer Review in Awarding Federal Grants in the Arts and Science*, 9 HIGH TECH. L.J. 1 (1994); *see also* SHEILA JASANOFF, THE FIFTH BRANCH: SCIENCE ADVISERS AS POLICYMAKERS 61–79 (1990). Indeed, to a considerable extent, peer review defines the boundaries of the scientific community. Scientists use peer review not only to decide who gets funded, but also to decide which proposed articles get published in scientific journals. In other words, scientists in a given field make the key publication decisions. Scientists are often astonished to discover that most law reviews follow a different model: students decide which faculty manuscripts are published. How would you explain this difference?

4. Peer review is obviously not without flaws. The reviewers typically know the name and the institutional affiliation of the person seeking a grant, reducing the odds for little-known researchers who may have novel ideas. *See, e.g.,* DANIEL S. GREENBERG, THE POLITICS OF PURE SCIENCE 43–46 (1967). Indeed, true novelty may not appeal to established leaders in a field. On the other hand, scientists sometimes disagree among themselves about the value of a particular line of research. In that case an applicant's chance of approval may turn on the happenstance of who happens to sit on his peer review panel. One National Science Foundation study concluded that, "the fate of a particular grant application is roughly half determined by the characteristics of the proposal and the principal investigator, and about half by apparently random elements which might be characterized as the 'luck of the reviewer draw.'" Stephen Cole et al., *Chance and Consensus in Peer Review*, 214 Sci. 881, 885 (1981).

5. Government support for some science projects at the expense of others also effects the first amendment values discussed in Sec. I. A., *supra*. Under the first amendment, Dr. Grassetti has the right to publish articles claiming that his theories concerning cancer are correct and the government's theories are wrong. This vital right keeps open the possibility that Dr. Grassetti and others like him can persuade Congress or other responsible institutions to change the nation's cancer policy. But Dr. Grassetti's right to free speech hardly puts him on an equal footing with those who share the government's views on cancer and who therefore receive funding. Writing an article is one thing; actually doing research requires money and, for basic scientific research, government money is often the only realistic source. Doesn't the government's choice to fund research in one area rather than another inevitably disrupt the free market place of scientific ideas? We would, after all, be deeply troubled if the government allowed free speech to all political parties, but provided government funding only to Democrats. *See* Steven Goldberg, *The Constitutional Status of American Science*, 1979 U. Ill. L.F. 1 (1979).

6. This distortion may be inevitable since not all conceivable scientific theories can be funded. But the dangers involved here can provide guidelines for government action. Diverse, broad-ranging funding policies can help alleviate the dangers of an inbred, narrow view becoming the dominant scientific approach even though that view may turn out to be mistaken. Indeed, one of the most important current protections in this regard may be America's diverse, even disorganized, set of federal agencies engaged in science. The "Department of Science" idea may be particularly dangerous if it involves an increased centralization of views on what constitutes good science. Moreover, a "Department of Science" may be a vulnerable target in times of budget cutting; at present, a year when one sector, such as defense research, is cut, another sector, such as health research, may be well-funded.

7. Government funding for scientific research raises another set of concerns with constitutional implications. When the government provides money it often attaches conditions on how that money is to be used. *See, e.g.,* John A. Robertson, *The Law of Institutional Review Boards*, 26 UCLA L.Rev. 484 (1979). The courts often uphold this use of the conditional spending power when the conditions relate to the purpose of the spending program and they are not independently unconstitutional. *See* South Dakota v. Dole, 483 U.S. 203, 107 S.Ct. 2793, 97 L.Ed.2d 171 (1987). Thus, the Supreme Court held that it was constitutional for the Department of Health and Human Services to construe the Public Health Act in such a way that recipients of federal family planning funds could not engage in abortion counseling, referral, or advocacy. Rust v. Sullivan, 500 U.S. 173, 111 S.Ct. 1759, 114 L.Ed.2d 233 (1991). On the other hand, shortly after *Rust,* a federal district judge held that the government could not constitutionally require that the recipient of a federal contract to do medical research promise to obtain government approval before disclosing preliminary research results. Leland Stanford Junior Univ. v. Sullivan, 773 F.Supp. 472 (D.D.C. 1991).

8. When we step back from the peer review process that dominates science funding decisions we see a relatively limited role for elected officials. Congress appropriates large sums of money but the recipients of the money are typically chosen by the scientific community itself. Indeed, when Congress specifies that a particular research project be to be undertaken by a particular university, the science community and many others decry "pork barrel politics." Congressional earmarking of this sort is certainly controversial, but it may at times improve research competitiveness. For a thorough study of the matter, see JAMES D. SAVAGE, FUNDING SCIENCE IN AMERICA: CONGRESS, UNIVERSITIES, AND THE POLITICS OF THE ACADEMIC PORK BARREL (1999).

9.   Whether peer review or earmarking is the means, the receipt of federal money is the goal for most scientific researchers. Whether it is "big science" such as the space program, or "little science" such as a small-scale laboratory experiment, money is often indispensable. *See* DEREK J. DE SOLLA PRICE, LITTLE SCIENCE, BIG SCIENCE (1963). Scientists have hardly escaped the political and ethical costs that come with relying on federal largess. *See* DANIEL S. GREENBERG, SCIENCE, MONEY, AND POLITICS: POLITICAL TRIUMPH AND ETHICAL EROSION (2001). But few would go back to the day, if it ever existed, when scientific knowledge could be sought without outside support.

C.   STATE SPENDING FOR SCIENCE AND MEDICINE

State spending on scientific research cannot measure up to the federal effort. While the federal government's yearly expenditure of over $120 billion on research and development, basic and applied, is less than half of national spending in this area, the remainder is almost entirely accounted for by industry, non-profit organizations, and academia. According to the most recent estimate, combined state spending on research and development totals only about $2.5 billion a year. NATIONAL SCIENCE FOUNDATION, WHAT IS THE STATE GOVERNMENT ROLE IN R & D ENTERPRISE? 2 (1999).

Historically, states played an important role in funding agricultural research. *See, e.g.,* Alex F. McCalla, *Politics of the Agricultural Research Establishment, in* THE NEW POLITICS OF FOOD 77 (DON FRANK HADWIGER & WILLIAM PAUL BROWNE EDS., 1978). In recent decades, however, states have become more involved in stimulating high technology and in doing health research, as the following excerpt indicates.

Michael McGreary et al., *State Support for Health Research: An Assessment* for the Mary Woodard Lasker Charitable Trust and Funding First.
October 26, 2001.

State support for R & D, including medical and biotechnology research, began to gain momentum in the late 1970s and early 1980s, when governors of both parties and all regions began to see a changing national, regional, and state economic landscape emerging. Traditional U.S. manufacturing sectors were losing their competitive edge in the global economy. Some states were affected when defense and aerospace companies began downsizing, because military and space programs had a lower priority at the national level. Information technology and the then new recombinant DNA technology were giving rise to new high technology-based companies leading to new jobs and new industries, but these developments tended to concentrate in locations where there was preexisting research excellence in universities and other resources, such as tax credits and venture capital that nurtured technological innovation. A few pioneering states such as New York and North Carolina were aggressively crafting programs to stimulate investments in R & D for economic development, e.g., through New York State Science and Technology Foundation's university-industry technology centers and North Carolina's Research Triangle Park and North Carolina Biotechnology Center.[3]

State-level activities to stimulate R & D and innovation became a regular topic on the agenda of meetings of governors and state legislators beginning in the early 1980s, when a National Governors Association taskforce co-chaired by then-Governors James Hunt of North Carolina and Dick Thornburgh of Pennsylvania issued a report making the case for state-sponsored innovation programs. By the end of the 1980s, state R & D initiatives for economic development had gained significant momentum. Perhaps 30 to 40 states had one or more strategies and programs to invest in R & D and stimulate economic development within the states. The various state programs and state-federal partnerships for university-industry R & D and incubator programs reflected the strengths and needs of the individual states, and thus there was a considerable variation from state to state in the emerging initiatives. Nonetheless, some common patterns began to emerge. States were making use of direct appropriations to their universities, establishing permanent or endowment funds, forming non-profit corporations to guide technology-based enterprise, making use of state R & D tax credits, and so on. Support for information technology, materials, manufacturing, and biotechnology for medicine and agriculture became major themes.

. . .

The most significant recent development in state support for medical research is the dedication of tobacco litigation settlement funds to health research by some states. This substantial infusion of money into state coffers has been studied by several organizations, including the National Conference of State Legislatures (NCSL), General Accounting Office, and Battelle/SSTI. Taken together, these studies indicate that approximately 16–17 states are making some use of tobacco settlement money for research, most or all of it health research. The GAO report of June 2001 did not ask the states to categorize expenditures in a common format, including research, but it included ad hoc examples of trust funds established to provide support for medical and biotechnology research in Michigan, Ohio, Pennsylvania, and Missouri. NCSL issued a report in August 2001. According to the NCSL report, 49 states have allocated $10.44 billion in tobacco settlement revenues for use in fiscal year 2002. Of this, $602 million (5.8 percent) was designated for research, by 17 states. The Battelle/SSTI report on state support of biotechnology described above found that 16 states are using tobacco settlement funds for health research, but did not report the amounts of funding except for a few states (e.g., Ohio is spending more than $400 million over 12 years).

As noted earlier, economists who study innovation became interested in state programs in the early 1990s. They are able to document benefits to

---

3. Research Triangle Park was started in 1953, but evidence of its effect on North Carolina's high-tech industry was not conclusive until the end of the 1970s and early 1980s, illustrating the long time horizons that some of the state investments must have to be successful.

the economy flowing from investments in R & D, including basic research investment. Most recently, Michael Porter and his associates at Harvard have studied state and regional economic benefits flowing from investments in R & D in specific regions of the U.S. The studies show the importance of investments in high technology sectors such as biomedical science and information technology, although they do not disaggregate data in ways that allows state expenditures specifically for health research to be separated.

. . . The states' fiscal outlook for fiscal year 2002 is not encouraging. Well before the fuller implications of the current economic slowdown were known and the economic ramifications of the September 11 terrorist attack could have been anticipated, the fiscal health of many states was shaky. The economic aftershocks of the terrorist attack on state revenues is already being felt, with travel for business and pleasure, state convention business, and other elements of state economies are being way down, at least temporarily. The implications for state support of medical and health research cannot be known for sure at this time. However, press reports indicate that Michigan is rescinding $10 million of the $50 million it budgeted from tobacco settlement funds for biosciences research, and the governor of Ohio, who established the Biomedical Research and Technology Transfer Fund of more than $400 million, is proposing to borrow $100 million of it to offset the deficit in the state's current budget that has developed since it was approved. In contrast, at the federal level, support for medical research through NIH has grown steadily during the post-World War II period. Whatever their enthusiasm for medical and health research, governors and legislators must respond immediately to their state's economic downturns, because they are prohibited by state constitution or law from deficit spending. The impact of the current slowdown, if not recession, in the national economy that is reducing state revenues is likely to have a negative impact on state support for medical and health research, along with other programs. Such shifts in state fiscal conditions resulting from ups and downs in the national economy are thus disruptive in implementing research programs, which depend on long-term stability.

NOTES AND QUESTIONS

The vulnerability of state science spending to difficult economic times is telling. As the excerpt notes, states are often under a legal obligation to balance their budgets. If the federal government operated under a similar constraint, do you think spending on research and development would be at risk, or is the federal commitment to science more robust?

D. INDIRECT SUPPORT FOR RESEARCH AND DEVELOPMENT: PATENT, TRADE SECRET, COPYRIGHT, AND OTHER INCENTIVES

State Street Bank & Trust Co. v. Signature Financial Group, Inc.

United States Court of Appeals for the Federal Circuit, 1998.
149 F.3d 1368, *cert. denied*, 525 U.S. 1093, 119 S.Ct. 851, 142 L.Ed.2d 704 (1999).

■ RICH, J.

Signature Financial Group, Inc. (Signature) appeals from the decision of the United States District Court for the District of Massachusetts granting a motion for summary judgment in favor of State Street Bank & Trust Co. (State Street), finding U.S. Patent No. 5,193,056 (the '056 patent) invalid on the ground that the claimed subject matter is not encompassed by 35 U.S.C. § 101 (1994). *See* State Street Bank & Trust Co. v. Signature Financial Group, Inc., 927 F.Supp. 502 (D.Mass.1996). We reverse and remand because we conclude that the patent claims are directed to statutory subject matter.

BACKGROUND

Signature is the assignee of the '056 patent which is entitled "Data Processing System for Hub and Spoke Financial Services Configuration." The '056 patent issued to Signature on 9 March 1993, naming R. Todd Boes as the inventor. The '056 patent is generally directed to a data processing system (the system) for implementing an investment structure which was developed for use in Signature's business as an administrator and accounting agent for mutual funds. In essence, the system, identified by the proprietary name Hub and Spoke®, facilitates a structure whereby mutual funds (Spokes) pool their assets in an investment portfolio (Hub) organized as a partnership. This investment configuration provides the administrator of a mutual fund with the advantageous combination of economies of scale in administering investments coupled with the tax advantages of a partnership.

State Street and Signature are both in the business of acting as custodians and accounting agents for multi-tiered partnership fund financial services. State Street negotiated with Signature for a license to use its patented data processing system described and claimed in the '056 patent. When negotiations broke down, State Street brought a declaratory judgment action asserting invalidity, unenforceability, and noninfringement in Massachusetts district court, and then filed a motion for partial summary judgment of patent invalidity for failure to claim statutory subject matter under § 101. The motion was granted and this appeal followed.

DISCUSSION

... We hold that declaratory judgment plaintiff State Street was not entitled to the grant of summary judgment of invalidity of the '056 patent under § 101 as a matter of law, because the patent claims are directed to statutory subject matter.

The following facts pertinent to the statutory subject matter issue are either undisputed or represent the version alleged by the nonmovant. *See* Anderson v. Liberty Lobby, Inc., 477 U.S. 242, 255 (1986). The patented invention relates generally to a system that allows an administrator to monitor and record the financial information flow and make all calculations necessary for maintaining a partner fund financial services configuration. As previously mentioned, a partner fund financial services configuration essentially allows several mutual funds, or "Spokes," to pool their investment funds into a single portfolio, or "Hub," allowing for consolidation of, *inter alia*, the costs of administering the fund combined with the tax advantages of a partnership. In particular, this system provides means for a daily allocation of assets for two or more Spokes that are invested in the same Hub. The system determines the percentage share that each Spoke maintains in the Hub, while taking into consideration daily changes both in the value of the Hub's investment securities and in the concomitant amount of each Spoke's assets.

In determining daily changes, the system also allows for the allocation among the Spokes of the Hub's daily income, expenses, and net realized and unrealized gain or loss, calculating each day's total investments based on the concept of a book capital account. This enables the determination of a true asset value of each Spoke and accurate calculation of allocation ratios between or among the Spokes. The system additionally tracks all the relevant data determined on a daily basis for the Hub and each Spoke, so that aggregate year end income, expenses, and capital gain or loss can be determined for accounting and for tax purposes for the Hub and, as a result, for each publicly traded Spoke.

It is essential that these calculations are quickly and accurately performed. In large part this is required because each Spoke sells shares to the public and the price of those shares is substantially based on the Spoke's percentage interest in the portfolio. In some instances, a mutual fund administrator is required to calculate the value of the shares to the nearest penny within as little as an hour and a half after the market closes. Given the complexity of the calculations, a computer or equivalent device is a virtual necessity to perform the task.

The '056 patent application was filed 11 March 1991. It initially contained six "machine" claims, which incorporated means-plus-function clauses, and six method claims. According to Signature, during prosecution the examiner contemplated a § 101 rejection for failure to claim statutory subject matter. However, upon cancellation of the six method claims, the examiner issued a notice of allowance for the remaining present six claims on appeal. Only claim 1 is an independent claim.

The district court began its analysis by construing the claims to be directed to a process, with each "means" clause merely representing a step in that process. However, "machine" claims having "means" clauses may only be reasonably viewed as process claims if there is no supporting structure in the written description that corresponds to the claimed "means" elements. *See In re* Alappat, 33 F.3d 1526, 1540–41 (Fed.Cir.1994) (*en banc*). This is not the case now before us.

When independent claim 1 is properly construed in accordance with § 112, ¶ 6, it is directed to a machine, as demonstrated below, where representative claim 1 is set forth, the subject matter in brackets stating the structure the written description discloses as corresponding to the respective "means" recited in the claims.

> 1.   A data processing system for managing a financial services configuration of a portfolio established as a partnership, each partner being one of a plurality of funds, comprising:
>
> > (a) computer processor means [a personal computer including a CPU] for processing data;
>
> > (b) storage means [a data disk] for storing data on a storage medium;

(c) first means [an arithmetic logic circuit configured to prepare the data disk to magnetically store selected data] for initializing the storage medium;

(d) second means [an arithmetic logic circuit configured to retrieve information from a specific file, calculate incremental increases or decreases based on specific input, allocate the results on a percentage basis, and store the output in a separate file] for processing data regarding assets in the portfolio and each of the funds from a previous day and data regarding increases or decreases in each of the funds, [sic, funds'] assets and for allocating the percentage share that each fund holds in the portfolio;

(e) third means [an arithmetic logic circuit configured to retrieve information from a specific file, calculate incremental increases and decreases based on specific input, allocate the results on a percentage basis and store the output in a separate file] for processing data regarding daily incremental income, expenses, and net realized gain or loss for the portfolio and for allocating such data among each fund;

(f) fourth means [an arithmetic logic circuit configured to retrieve information from a specific file, calculate incremental increases and decreases based on specific input, allocate the results on a percentage basis and store the output in a separate file] for processing data regarding daily net unrealized gain or loss for the portfolio and for allocating such data among each fund; and

(g) fifth means [an arithmetic logic circuit configured to retrieve information from specific files, calculate that information on an aggregate basis and store the output in a separate file] for processing data regarding aggregate year-end income, expenses, and capital gain or loss for the portfolio and each of the funds.

Each claim component, recited as a "means" plus its function, is to be read, of course, pursuant to § 112, ¶ 6, as inclusive of the "equivalents" of the structures disclosed in the written description portion of the specification. Thus, claim 1, properly construed, claims a machine, namely, a data processing system for managing a financial services configuration of a portfolio established as a partnership, which machine is made up of, at the very least, the specific structures disclosed in the written description and corresponding to the means-plus-function elements (a)–(g) recited in the claim. A "machine" is proper statutory subject matter under § 101. We note that, for the purposes of a § 101 analysis, it is of little relevance whether claim 1 is directed to a "machine" or a "process," as long as it falls within at least one of the four enumerated categories of patentable subject matter, "machine" and "process" being such categories.

This does not end our analysis, however, because the court concluded that the claimed subject matter fell into one of two alternative judicially-created exceptions to statutory subject matter. The court refers to the first exception as the "mathematical algorithm" exception and the second exception as the "business method" exception. Section 101 reads:

Whoever invents or discovers any new and useful process, machine, manufacture, or composition of matter, or any new and useful improvement thereof, may obtain a patent therefor, subject to the conditions and requirements of this title.

The plain and unambiguous meaning of § 101 is that any invention falling within one of the four stated categories of statutory subject matter may be patented, provided it meets the other requirements for patentability set forth in Title 35, i.e., those found in §§ 102, 103, and 112, ¶ 2.

The repetitive use of the expansive term "any" in § 101 shows Congress's intent not to place any restrictions on the subject matter for which a patent may be obtained beyond those specifically recited in § 101. Indeed, the Supreme Court has acknowledged that Congress intended § 101 to extend to "anything under the sun that is made by man." *Diamond v. Chakrabarty*, 447 U.S. 303, 309 (1980); *see also Diamond v. Diehr*, 450 U.S. 175, 182 (1981). Thus, it is improper to read limitations into § 101 on the subject matter that may be patented where the legislative history indicates that Congress clearly did not intend such limitations. *See Chakrabarty*, 447 U.S. at 308 ("We have also cautioned that courts 'should not read into the patent laws limitations and conditions which the legislature has not expressed.' " (citations omitted)).

The "Mathematical Algorithm" Exception

The Supreme Court has identified three categories of subject matter that are unpatentable, namely "laws of nature, natural phenomena, and abstract ideas." *Diehr*, 450 U.S. at 185. Of particular relevance to this case, the Court has held that mathematical algorithms are not patentable subject matter to the extent that they are merely abstract ideas. *See Diehr*, 450 U.S. 175, *passim*; Parker v. Flook, 437 U.S. 584 (1978); Gottschalk v. Benson, 409 U.S. 63 (1972). In *Diehr*, the Court explained that certain types of mathematical subject matter, standing alone, represent nothing more than abstract ideas until reduced to some type of practical application, *i.e.*, "a useful, concrete and tangible result." *Alappat*, 33 F.3d at 1544.

Unpatentable mathematical algorithms are identifiable by showing they are merely abstract ideas constituting disembodied concepts or truths that are not "useful." From a practical standpoint, this means that to be patentable an algorithm must be applied in a "useful" way. In *Alappat*, we held that data, transformed by a machine through a series of mathematical calculations to produce a smooth waveform display on a rasterizer monitor, constituted a practical application of an abstract idea (a mathematical algorithm, formula, or calculation), because it produced "a useful, concrete and tangible result"—the smooth waveform.

Similarly, in *Arrhythmia Research Technology Inc. v. Corazonix Corp.*, 958 F.2d 1053 (Fed.Cir.1992), we held that the transformation of electrocardiograph signals from a patient's heartbeat by a machine through a series of mathematical calculations constituted a practical application of an abstract idea (a mathematical algorithm, formula, or calculation), because it corresponded to a useful, concrete or tangible thing—the condition of a patient's heart.

Today, we hold that the transformation of data, representing discrete dollar amounts, by a machine through a series of mathematical calculations into a final share price, constitutes a practical application of a mathematical algorithm, formula, or calculation, because it produces "a useful, concrete and tangible result"—a final share price momentarily fixed for recording and reporting purposes and even accepted and relied upon by regulatory authorities and in subsequent trades.

The district court erred by applying the Freeman–Walter–Abele test to determine whether the claimed subject matter was an unpatentable abstract idea. The Freeman–Walter–Abele test was designed by the Court of Customs and Patent Appeals, and subsequently adopted by this court, to extract and identify unpatentable mathematical algorithms in the aftermath of *Benson* and *Flook*. *See In re* Freeman, 573 F.2d 1237 (CCPA 1978) as modified by In re Walter, 618 F.2d 758 (CCPA 1980). The test has been thus articulated:

> First, the claim is analyzed to determine whether a mathematical algorithm is directly or indirectly recited. Next, if a mathematical algorithm is found, the claim as a whole is further analyzed to determine whether the algorithm is "applied in any manner to physical elements or process steps," and, if it is, it "passes muster under § 101."

In re Pardo, 684 F.2d 912, 915 (CCPA 1982) (*citing In re* Abele, 684 F.2d 902 (CCPA 1982)).

After *Diehr* and *Chakrabarty*, the Freeman–Walter–Abele test has little, if any, applicability to determining the presence of statutory subject matter. As we pointed out in *Alappat*, 33 F.3d at 1543, application of the test could be misleading, because a process, machine, manufacture, or composition of matter employing a law of nature, natural phenomenon, or abstract idea is patentable subject matter even though a law of nature, natural phenomenon, or abstract idea would not, by itself, be entitled to such protection. The test determines the presence of, for example, an algorithm. Under *Benson*, this may have been a sufficient indicium of nonstatutory subject matter. However, after *Diehr* and *Alappat*, the mere fact that a claimed invention involves inputting numbers, calculating numbers, outputting numbers, and storing numbers, in and of itself, would not render it nonstatutory subject matter, unless, of course, its operation does not produce a "useful, concrete and tangible result." *Alappat*, 33 F.3d at 1544. After all, as we have repeatedly stated,

> every step-by-step process, be it electronic or chemical or mechanical, involves an algorithm in the broad sense of the term. Since § 101 expressly includes processes as a category of inventions which may be patented and § 100(b) further defines the word "process" as meaning "process, art or method, and includes a new use of a known process, machine, manufacture, composition of matter, or material," it follows that it is no ground for holding a claim is directed to nonstatutory subject matter to say it includes or is directed to an algorithm. This is why the proscription against patenting has been limited to mathematical algorithms. . . .

In re Iwahashi, 888 F.2d 1370, 1374 (Fed.Cir.1989) (emphasis in the original).

The question of whether a claim encompasses statutory subject matter should not focus on *which* of the four categories of subject matter a claim is directed to—process, machine, manufacture, or composition of matter—but rather on the essential characteristics of the subject matter, in particular, its practical utility. Section 101 specifies that statutory subject matter must also satisfy the other "conditions and requirements" of Title 35, including novelty, nonobviousness, and adequacy of disclosure and notice. *See In re Warmerdam*, 33 F.3d 1354, 1359 (Fed.Cir.1994). For purpose of our analysis, as noted above, claim 1 is directed to a machine programmed with the Hub and Spoke software and admittedly produces a "useful, concrete, and tangible result." *Alappat*, 33 F.3d at 1544. This renders it statutory subject matter, even if the useful result is expressed in numbers, such as price, profit, percentage, cost, or loss.

The Business Method Exception

As an alternative ground for invalidating the '056 patent under § 101, the court relied on the judicially-created, so-called "business method" exception to statutory subject matter. We take this opportunity to lay this ill-conceived exception to rest. Since its inception, the "business method" exception has merely represented the application of some general, but no longer applicable legal principle, perhaps arising out of the "requirement for invention"—which was eliminated by § 103. Since the 1952 Patent Act, business methods have been, and should have been, subject to the same legal requirements for patentability as applied to any other process or method.

. . .

In view of this background, it comes as no surprise that in the most recent edition of the Manual of Patent Examining Procedures (MPEP) (1996), a paragraph of § 706.03(a) was deleted. In past editions it read:

> Though seemingly within the category of process or method, a method of doing business can be rejected as not being within the statutory classes. *See* Hotel Security Checking Co. v. Lorraine Co., 160 F. 467 (2nd Cir.1908) and *In re* Wait, 73 F.2d 982 (CCPA 1934).

MPEP § 706.03(a) (1994). This acknowledgment is buttressed by the U.S. Patent and Trademark 1996 Examination Guidelines for Computer Related Inventions which now read:

> Office personnel have had difficulty in properly treating claims directed to methods of doing business. Claims should not be categorized as methods of doing business. Instead such claims should be treated like any other process claims.

Examination Guidelines, 61 Fed.Reg. 7478, 7479 (1996). We agree that this is precisely the manner in which this type of claim should be treated. Whether the claims are directed to subject matter within § 101 should not turn on whether the claimed subject matter does "business" instead of something else.

CONCLUSION

The appealed decision is reversed and the case is remanded to the district court for further proceedings consistent with this opinion.

REVERSED and *REMANDED.*

NOTES AND QUESTIONS

1. The patent power given to Congress in the United States Constitution and implemented in subsequent statutes is an important incentive for innovation.

Patents give the inventor an exclusive opportunity for 20 years from the filing date to exploit the invention, while simultaneously making the invention public. *State Street Bank* is a leading example of the modern trend to expand the scope of patentable subject matter. The court's approval of software patents resolved a matter that had long been controversial. *See, e.g.*, Pamela Samuelson, *Benson Revisited: The Case Against Patent Protection for Algorithms and Other Computer Program–Related Inventions*, 39 EMORY L.J. 1025 (1990). The court's conclusion remains controversial, particularly in light of its further decision to allow patents for business methods. This combination has particular implications in the Internet business world, see Julia Alpert Gladstone, *Why Patenting Information Technology and Business Methods Is Not Sound Policy: Lessons From History and Prophecies For The Future*, 25 HAMLINE L. REV. 217 (2002), particularly when considered from an international perspective. *See, e.g.*, Note, *Tackling Global Software Piracy Under TRIPS: Insights From Internal Relations Theory*, 116 HARV. L. REV. 1139 (2003).

2. The importance of *State Street Bank* illustrates the importance of the court that issued the decision, the United States Court of Appeals for the Federal Circuit. Created in 1982, the Federal Circuit hears all patent appeals. While the court hears other matters as well, it has provided a measure of uniformity in the patent field. Its decisions are reviewable in the United States Supreme Court, but, as the denial of certiorari in *State Street Bank* suggests, the Supreme Court is often willing to leave the judicial evolution of patent law to the Federal Circuit.

3. *State Street Bank* cites *Diamond v. Chakrabarty*, a 1980 Supreme Court decision which also expanded the universe of patentable subject matter when it allowed a patent for a human-made microorganism. The patenting of living organisms, whether engineered or extracted from the natural world, remains a source of controversy. *See, e.g.*, Carol A. Schneider, Felicia Cohn, & Cynthia Bonner, *Patenting Life: A View from the Constitution and Beyond*, 24 WHITTIER L. REV. 385 (2002). Should Congress play a more active role in deciding whether to allow patents in new areas of science?

4. Patent law is often not the only form of intellectual property protection available to an inventor. In *Kewanee Oil Co. v. Bicron*, 416 U.S. 470, 94 S.Ct. 1879, 40 L.Ed.2d 315 (1974), the Supreme Court held that state trade secret law is not preempted by patent law. Moreover, copyright protection may sometimes be useful for an inventor: it is available, for example, for computer software because software is the expression of how to instruct a computer to do its job. *See* 17 U.S.C. §§ 101–810, 1001–10 (1994).

5. So the developer of software has a choice to make. Patents are relatively difficult to obtain since you must meet the tests of novelty, utility and nonobviousness. On the other hand, the 20–year patent monopoly protects you from people who independently make the same discovery you did. Copyright protects you only from copying, not from independent discovery, but you can obtain a copyright more easily than a patent and it lasts for the life of the author plus 70 years. Trade secret protection lasts as long as you can keep the secret, and unlike patent you do not make your idea public. But secrets are hard to keep and, like copyright, trade secret does not protect you from independent discovery. For discussions of these alternatives, *see, e.g.*, Klaus M. Schmidt & Monika Schnitzer, *Public Subsidies for Open Source? Some Economic Policy Issues of the Software Market*, 16 HARV. J.L. & TECH. 473 (2003); Christopher S. Cantzler, *State Street: Leading the Way to Consistency For Patentability Of Computer Software*, 71 U. COLO. L. REV. 423 (2000).

6. Beyond intellectual property, there are other forms of indirect government support for scientific research. A variety of tax incentives, for example, are available for the research and development activities of private companies. *See* Belinda L. Heath, *The Importance of Research and Development Tax Incentives in the World*

Market, 11 MSU-DCL J. INT'L 351 (2002). One area that brings many techniques to bear is the Orphan Drug Act, where Congress has combined tax policy and the awarding of market exclusivity in an effort to spur the development of drugs for rare ailments. *See, e.g.*, David Duffield Rohde, *The Orphan Drug Act: An Engine of Innovation? At What Cost?*, 55 FOOD DRUG L.J. 125 (2000).

III.   GOVERNMENT REGULATION OF SCIENCE AND MEDICINE

A.   FEDERAL REGULATION: THE CENTRAL ROLE OF THE ADMINISTRATIVE AGENCY

We have already noted the importance of administrative agencies—primarily Cabinet departments such as Defense, Energy and Health and Human Services—in federal science spending. These agencies formulate budget requests and dispense large sums in accordance with their own judgment, often guided only by quite broad legislative language, as to what research projects deserve support. In practice, decisions whether to fund individual research projects are often made by scientists through a peer review process. Judicial review in the funding area is typically quite limited. *See* Sec. II. B., *supra*.

Federal regulation of science and medicine also relies heavily on administrative agencies. Congressional legislation again often provides only broad guidance—"protect the public health and safety"—and then gives the job of implementation to an agency. The agencies involved include the Environmental Protection Agency, the Nuclear Regulatory Commission, the Food and Drug Administration, the Occupational Safety and Health Administration, and many others. In every case the regulatory agency must comply with the statute that defined its mission as well as with the general requirements of administrative law. Courts review regulatory decisions more often than funding matters, although, as we shall see, even in the regulatory arena the courts at times show considerable deference to the agencies.

As we noted in discussing *Vermont Yankee v. Natural Resources Defense Council*, Chapter 3, Sec. II. A., *supra*, agencies use two basic approaches in performing their regulatory mission. Legislative-type rule-making involves publication of a proposed rule, receipt of written and sometimes oral comments, followed by publication of a final rule. Trial-type adjudication involves application of a rule or statutory standard to a specific case. Evidence is introduced, cross-examination is held, and a final opinion is rendered. As you can see, neither approach to regulation is similar to the scientist-dominated peer review used for funding. In regulation, impact on the public is more immediate, and adversarial legal norms become more prominent. Although scientists often act as technical advisers in regulatory matters, they cannot escape the public controversy surrounding those matters. *See* SHEILA JASANOFF, THE FIFTH BRANCH: SCIENCE ADVISERS AS POLICYMAKERS (1990). Indeed, it is often alleged that political considerations play a role in which scientists are chosen to advise policymakers. *See, e.g.*, David Brown, *Panel Debates Role in Scientists' Appointment*, WASH. POST, July 22, 2004, at A19.

There are periodic efforts to import the peer review process into regulatory decision-making. But peer review works for scientific funding and publication decisions because the scientific community enjoys an unusual degree of consensus as to what constitutes good work. With regulatory matters—where it is hard to separate out value questions about how much risk is acceptable and where there is no consensus on how to answer those questions—peer review by experts often becomes embroiled in controversy. *See, e.g.*, Lars Noah, *Scientific "Republicanism": Expert Peer Review and the Quest for Regulatory Deliberation*, 49 Emory L.J. 1033 (2000); Rick Weiss, *OMB Modifies Peer–Review Proposal: Guidelines Partly Retreat From Strict Control of Agencies' Information Process*, Wash. Post, April 16, 2004, at A19.

Once an agency reaches a final decision, judicial review is available. We are now in the world of administrative law, where formal factual findings are upheld unless unsupported by substantial evidence, informal factual findings are measured by the arbitrary and capricious test, and agency interpretations of ambiguous statutory language are affirmed unless found to be unreasonable under the famous *Chevron* approach. *See* Richard J. Pierce, Jr., Sidney A. Shapiro, & Paul R. Verkuil, Administrative Law and Process, 361–80 (3rd ed. 1999). Everyone knows that the formal standards for judicial review do not tell the whole story. While agency decisions apart from purely legal questions are always given deference, judges differ in how willing they are to second-guess administrators in cases involving technical complexity. Perhaps the most interesting exchanges on this matter remains those between D.C. Circuit Judges Bazelon and Leventhal, with the former emphasizing procedural concerns and the latter calling for searching substantive review. *See* International Harvester Co. v. Ruckelshaus, 478 F.2d 615 (D.C.Cir. 1973); *see also* Ethyl Corp. v. Environmental Protection Agency, 541 F.2d 1 (D.C. Cir. 1976).

One of the major reasons for the creation of administrative agencies was to provide organizations with expertise that could study the information available and, on the basis of that information, render fair decisions. Thus it is not surprising that Congress often delegates to agencies issues involving a high level of scientific or technical data. It may have once been hoped that agency decisions would be purely technical, that is, nonpolitical. But because Congress often gives only general guidance and because it is so difficult to separate scientific judgments from policy judgments in areas of uncertainty, it cannot be denied that agencies today often make vital policy decisions, particularly in areas of scientific and medical uncertainty. Moreover, just as there is no single Department of Science making funding decisions, there is no single regulatory agency, and thus a variety of approaches to regulation are used throughout the federal government. *See* National Research Council, Risk Assessment in the Federal Government: Managing the Process (1983). Since agency heads are appointed by the President, not elected, and since agency personnel are often career civil servants, this central role for regulatory agencies poses vital questions about American democracy. To approach these questions in a context involving controversial technical issues, the materials in this section begin with an examination of the Occupational Safety and Health Administration's historic decision on occupational exposure to cotton dust.

Occupational Exposure to Cotton Dust

43 Fed. Reg. 27,350, 27,351–27,355 (1978).

AGENCY: Occupational Safety and Health Administration, Department of Labor.

ACTION: Final Standard.

SUMMARY: This final standard establishes occupational safety and health requirements for occupational exposure to cotton dust. It reflects OSHA's determination, based on evidence that has been placed in the public record in this rulemaking proceeding, that exposure to cotton dust presents a significant health hazard to employees. The standard establishes permissible exposure limit of 200 μg/m^3 for yarn manufacturing, 750 Sg/m^3 for slashing and weaving operations, and 500 μg/m^3 for all other processes in the cotton industry and for non-textile industries where there is exposure to cotton dust. Cotton ginning is the subject of a separate regulation, § 1910.1040, published today also in Part III of this Federal Register. The harvesting of cotton and the manufacture of garments from cotton fabrics are not covered by this standard. The cotton dust standard, which is promulgated as 29 CFR 1910.1043, also provides for employee exposure monitoring, engineering controls and work practices, respirators, employee training, medical surveillance, signs and record-keeping. . . .

B.   History of the Regulation

(1) Early developments. Substantial improvement in working conditions in the cotton textile industry did not occur until well into the twentieth century. The most important early improvements came in England as a result of legislative acts requiring medical inspection of workplaces, compulsory reporting of industrial diseases and compensation of diseased and disabled workers. In 1942 a compensation scheme was introduced in England as a means of implementing the Factory Act of 1937 and associated legislation which for the first time recognized byssinosis as an occupational disease.

In 1934 the American Conference of Governmental Industrial Hygienists (ACGIH) placed cotton dust on its tentative list of threshold limit values (TLV), and in 1966 they adopted a 1000 μg/m^3 of total cotton dust as their recommended value for exposure. This TLV was based upon the work of Roach and Schilling in the Lancashire cotton mills. Exposure to cotton dust was not regulated in the United States until 1968, when the Secretary of Labor under the Walsh–Healey Act (41 U.S.C. 35 et seq.), promulgated the 1968 ACGIH list of Threshold Limit Values which included for "Cotton dust (raw)" the limit of 1000 μg/m^3. This standard was subsequently adopted as an established Federal standard under section 6(a) of the Occupational Safety and Health Act of 1970. In 1972, the British Occupational Hygiene Society (BOHS) published a report, largely based upon Molyneux and Berry's "Correlation of Cotton Dust Exposure with the Prevalence of Respiratory Symptoms," recommending a new standard of 500 μg/m^3 less "fly"; the term fly meaning dust particles removed by a 2–mm wire screen. In addition, in 1972, on the basis of BOHS and others, a revision of the ACGIH TLV was recommended that would measure respirable dust rather than "total dust." In 1974, a TLV of 200 μg/m^3 of cotton dust as measured by the vertical elutriator was adopted by ACGIH.

On September 26, 1974, pursuant to section 20(a)(3) of the Act, the Director of the National Institute for Occupational Safety and Health (NIOSH) submitted to the Secretary of Labor a criteria document which contained NIOSH's recommendations for a new cotton dust standard.

On December 27, 1974, OSHA published an Advance Notice of Proposed Rulemaking (39 FR 44769) requesting that interested persons submit their views on specific issues relating to cotton dust, particularly the NIOSH Criteria Document.

Thereafter, in January 1975, the Textile Worker's Union of America filed a petition with the Secretary urging the Secretary to propose a modified standard for occupational exposure to cotton dust, setting an exposure limit of 100 μg/m^3. They were joined in this petition by the North Carolina Public Interest Research Group.

(2) The Proposal. On December 28, 1976, OSHA published a proposal to revise the existing standard for occupational exposure to cotton dust (41 FR 56498). The proposal called for a permissible exposure limit of 200 ` Sg/m^3 of vertical elutriated cotton dust for all segments of the cotton industry.

The proposal allowed 90 days for interested parties to submit written comments, views, and arguments and announced that an informal public hearing for the submission of oral testimony would begin on April 5, 1977. Additional hearing dates were set by notice published March 15, 1977 (42 FR 14134). There were 263 comments and 109 notices of intent to appear at the hearings.

(3) The Hearing. The OSHA rulemaking hearing was conducted in Washington, D.C. from April 5–8, May 2–6, and 16–17; in Greenville, Mississippi on April 12; and in Lubbock, Texas on May 10–12, 1977.

Numerous persons appeared at the hearings as witnesses. Among the witnesses were large corporate and small business employers, manufacturers, representatives from the affected workforce, experts in every relevant field including physicians, scientists, statisticians, economists, industrial hygienists, representatives from agriculture, and other interested parties. Public participation was representative of virtually the entire "cotton community." The written and oral testimony of all participants was made part of the rulemaking record. The hearing record was originally scheduled to close on July 17, 1977, but at the request of several parties it was kept open until September 2, 1977 (42 FR 39120).

(4) Environmental Impact Statement. In conjunction with the development of the proposed standard, OSHA prepared a draft environmental impact statement. The draft environmental impact statement was published in the Federal Register (41 FR 56498) on December 28, 1976, along with the proposal.

Prior to the promulgation of this final standard, OSHA prepared a final environmental impact statement (FEIS) in accordance with 29 CFR

1999.5. Notice of the availability of the FEIS was published by the Environmental Protection Agency on December 30, 1977 (42 FR 65263).

(5) The Record. This final cotton dust standard is based on careful consideration of the entire record in this proceeding, including materials relied on in the proposal and the record of the informal rulemaking hearing including the transcript, exhibits pre-hearing and post-hearing written comments and briefs. Copies of the official list of hearing exhibits, comments, and notices of intent to appear at the hearing can be obtained from the Docket Office, Docket No. H–052, Room 56212, U.S. Department of Labor, Third Street and Constitution Avenue NW., Washington, D.C. 20210 . . .

III. OCCUPATIONAL HEALTH IMPLICATIONS OF EXPOSURE TO COTTON DUST

A. General

The preamble to the proposed standard for exposure to cotton dust presented detailed scientific evidence demonstrating the health hazard to workers in the various cotton industries and the extent of that risk (41 FR 56498, Ex. 6 #1, 2, 3, 7, 13, 14, 15, 16, 17, 18, 19, 20, 21, 42, 43, 44, 51, 54, 55). The provisions of the proposed standard were based on this evidence. Upon reviewing the complete body of data compiled in the record, including a thorough discussion of the underlying evidence, OSHA has determined that the basic conclusions advanced in the proposed regulations have withstood critical scrutiny by the public, the cotton industry and the scientific community. Accordingly, the evidence set forth in detail in the preamble to the proposal, will not be repeated here.

The overwhelming scientific evidence in the record supports the finding that cotton dust produces adverse health effects among cotton workers (Ex. 1, Ex. 11, Ex. 13, Ex. 19, Ex. 12, Ex. 38, d). The disorders range from an acute reaction manifested by a depression of pulmonary function indicators, or by subjective symptoms such as chest-tightness, shortness of breath, or cough, to a stage characteristic of chronic obstructive pulmonary disease which is often disabling (Ex. 48, p. 1; Ex. 6, #17, 20, 21, 42, 43, 57, 54, 56). The chronic stages of cotton dust induced respiratory disease are, as a clinical entity, similar to chronic bronchitis or emphysema (Ex. 41, p. 5). While gaps exist in the understanding of the etiology of respiratory disease caused by cotton dust and their progression from acute to chronic stages, the evidence in the record supports the fundamental connection between cotton dust and various respiratory disorders in both the textile and the non-textile industries (Ex. 1, Ex. 38d, Ex. 11).

Byssinosis is the specific respiratory disease attributable to the action of cotton dust on the respiratory passages. The essential hallmark of byssinosis is the Monday phenomenon, the cyclic disorder characterized by cough, breathlessness or tightness of the chest experienced on the first day of the work week (Ex. 48, p. 1). The Schilling grading scheme for byssinosis discussed in the proposal inherently reflects the differences in duration and degree of the Monday morning symptoms (41 FR 56498).

In addition to the familiar subjective symptoms, objective measurements sometimes indicate the presence of airways obstruction (Ex. 41, pp. 8–10). Pulmonary function measurements such as Forced Expiratory Volume in one second (FEV $_1$), or Forced Vital Capacity (FVC) are frequently used to indicate deviation from normal breathing. As the NIOSH statement (Ex. 38, a) introduced at the hearing explains:

> Pooled data on groups of workers with byssinosis consistently show a strong association between byssinosis and drops in expiratory flow rates on Monday . . ., both also clearly attributable to cotton dust exposure. Among individuals, however, it has been observed repeatedly that those with Monday chest tightness do not necessarily show a drop in FEV_1, and conversely, individuals with clearcut drops in Monday FEV_1 will not necessarily have a history of byssinosis.

There is further testimony that, if large groups of workers are surveyed for subjective symptoms and for pulmonary function changes, approximately the same proportion exhibit both subjective symptoms and decrements of pulmonary function (Ex. 38d). OSHA also agrees with NIOSH that "characteristic respiratory symptoms and drops in flow rates are useful epidemiologic and clinical tools and are highly associated with cotton dust concentration (Ex. 38d)."

From the description of its manifestations, it is clear that byssinosis represents a constellation of respiratory effects (Ex. 38d, Ex. 11, Ex. 6, Ex. 1, Ex. 12, Ex. 13). These effects range from acute to chronic and from reversible to disabling, and may be described by diverse terminology, such as reactor state or chronic bronchitis, but these respiratory diseases have been conclusively shown to be causally related to exposure to cotton dust (Ex. 1, Ex. 11, Ex. 38a, b, d).

B.   Chronic Obstructive Pulmonary Disease

It was the overwhelming opinion of the medical experts testifying at the hearings that byssinosis can develop into chronic obstructive pulmonary disease which is, in most cases, irreversible and disabling (Ex. 38d, Ex. 11, Ex. 41, Ex. 46). The preamble to the proposal describes Grade 3 byssinosis as follows:

> In this advanced stage the clinical picture often becomes confused, as the chronic disease process is neither well understood nor well defined. Workers frequently manifest symptoms consistent with chronic bronchitis and emphysema. This stage is generally considered to be irreversible, with work in dusty atmospheres becoming extremely difficult or impossible. The rate at which a worker progresses to this stage, if at all, depends upon the amount of the causative agent contained in the dust inhaled, and the susceptibility of the individual.

In human terms, the affected worker frequently loses the ability to function normally on or off the job. Members of the Carolina Brown Lung Association (CBLA) testified at the hearing that the respiratory disease contracted in the textile mills typically resulted in premature retirement often after futile and painful attempts to continue on the job (Ex. 51, Ex. 54).

Testimony pointed out that several terms were being used interchangeably to describe the final clinical stage of cotton dust induced respiratory disease. These include: grade 3 byssinosis, chronic or advanced byssinosis, chronic obstructive lung disease, or the specific names of chronic obstructive pulmonary diseases (i.e. chronic bronchitis and emphysema). Among textile workers "brown lung" appears to be a synonym for disabling respiratory disease. In that sense, Dr. Russell Harley's suggestion that the term chronic obstructive pulmonary disease (COPD) constituted a generally accepted clinical definition of chronic lung disease that described the clinical end product of cotton dust induced lung disease without becoming entangled in definitions of preceding stages of the disease has merit (Ex. 41, p. 2).

The record strongly indicates that chronic bronchitis, one form of COPD, is prevalent among byssinotics (Ex. 6, #8, 17, 19, 20). Data on groups of workers with byssinosis consistently demonstrate a strong association between byssinosis and drops in expiratory flow rates on Monday and chronic cough and phlegm (bronchitis), which are both also clearly related to cotton dust exposure (Ex. 6, #17, Ex. 38d, Ex. 6, #22, 23, 25; Ex. 11). Chronic bronchitis which is not specifically related to cotton dust exposure has also been found to be far more common along cotton textile workers than among workers in mills processing only synthetic fibers (Ex. 6, #17, 21, 22, 23, 24, 32).

Since exposure to environmental pollutants such as cigarette smoke has also been identified as a causative agent of COPD, parties to the hearings representing industry argued that COPD caused by cotton dust was a minor fraction of COPD prevalence among textile workers and that most was caused by smoking (Ex. 41, p. 6; Ex. 47, #18; Ex. 46, p. 1). Dr. Mario Battigelli, testifying on behalf of the American Textile Manufacturers Institute (ATMI), stated that the background level of chronic bronchitis among the general population, estimated by him at between 10 and 40%, easily explained the observed high prevalence of chronic bronchitis, 3–50%, among cotton textile workers (Ex. 48, p. 8). It should be noted that Dr. Battigelli's estimate of background chronic bronchitis, based as it is on autopsy studies, is not comparable with other studies of relatively healthy men and women (Ex. 6, #17).

OSHA recognizes that smoking is an influential variable in the production of COPD among cotton workers (Ex. 6). Indeed, the co-existence of exposure to cotton dust and exposure to cigarette smoke has been shown to result in increased risk of COPD (Ex. 41, p. 6; Ex. 47, Ref. #18; Ex. 46, p. 1; Ex. 38d; Ex. 11). However, persuasive evidence demonstrates that the cigarette smoking variable, rather than overwhelming the cotton dust variable, is merely related to it. Indeed, there are no studies in the literature attributing the high prevalence of respiratory disease found among cotton workers primarily to smoking, or, in other words, there is no documentation for Dr. Battigelli's statement. Conversely, where the relationship between exposure to cotton dust and smoking has been explored scientifically, substantial evidence characterizes the increased risk from smoking to be additive or multiplicative to the risk due to exposure to cotton dust (Ex. 11). Dr. Arend Bouhuys of Yale University, a preeminent authority on pulmonary function, described the relationship as follows (Ex. 11, p. 16):

.... in our statistical analysis of symptom prevalence among large numbers of cotton textile workers and appropriate controls we found that, for all symptoms, work in textile mills was by far the largest factor in determining the prevalence of respiratory symptoms. For shortness of breath, mill work was the only significant variable. For chronic cough, sputum and wheezing, cigarette smoking was an additional important variable, but of lesser degree of significance than work in the mills. In other studies where similar analyses have been performed, cigarette smoking has also emerged as a contributing factor to chronic symptoms. But in these studies no control group was considered at the same time, so that the preponderant effect of exposure to dust in mills (in comparison with the absence of such exposure among persons not employed in textile mills) could not be assessed. It is also important to point out that shortness of breath is an important factor in disability among cotton textile workers, and that this symptom was not significantly affected by smoking. Although it should be considered an additional risk for cotton textile workers, the extent of the risk of smoking is not clearly different for cotton workers and for others not employed in the cotton textile industry. In fact, we found that the effects of cotton dust exposure and of smoking on chronic lung function loss were additive, and there is no indication in our data for any synergism between the two exposures with respect to long-term lung function.

Other evidence is consistent with Dr. Bouhuys' findings. One particularly striking feature is the high prevalence of respiratory disease among women textile workers who have never smoked (Ex. 6, #17, p. 427). Finally, it has generally been found that bronchitis prevalence is proportional to level of dust wherever this parameter has been studied.

Undoubtedly some COPD exists in the cotton worker population which is independent of exposure to cotton dust. Neither Dr. Battigelli's figures nor morbidity data from a study done in a Colorado community appear to shed light on the normal state of employee health. However, Merchant's control population consisting of textile workers in wool and synthetic industries provides a reasonable estimate of the prevalence of bronchitis among textile workers not exposed to cotton dust (Ex. 6, #17). These levels of chronic bronchitis varied from 2–3% to approximately 12% depending upon age, sex and smoking habit (Ex. 6, #17). As Merchant's work made clear, compared to these controls, workers exposed to cotton dust exhibit a significantly greater prevalence of chronic bronchitis, i.e. 24% (Ex. 6, #43, p. 173); in this study, not only cotton dust exposure but also smoking (Ex. 6, #43) and age (Ex. 6, #17, p. 427) were found to be determinants of chronic bronchitis frequency and severity....

IV. PERMISSIBLE EXPOSURE LIMITS

A. General Considerations

OSHA believes that the causal relationship between exposure to cotton dust and the development of byssinosis and other respiratory diseases has been clearly established. It follows, then, that the most important step in reducing the risk of cotton dust induced respiratory disease is to reduce employee exposure to cotton dust (Ex. 6, #1, 19, 30, 51, 55, 57, 58; Ex. 124).

At the same time, OSHA recognizes that cotton dust is a heterogeneous mixture containing an as yet unidentified active agent or agents. Cotton dust is defined in this standard as "dust present during the handling or processing of cotton which may contain a mixture of substances including ground-up plant matter, fiber, bacteria, fungi, soil, pesticides, non-cotton plant matter and other contaminants which may have accumulated during the growing, harvesting and subsequent processing or storage periods." As the preamble to the proposal states, the relative proportion of these substances in "cotton dust" can vary depending upon the type of plant, harvesting and storage methods, and cleaning operations, both at the gin and in subsequent processing (41 FR 56503).

Some parties at the hearings argued that the standard should be delayed until an active agent was isolated (e.g. Ex. 65a). OSHA has concluded that the weight of evidence in the record requires the implementation of a standard based on "cotton dust," as broadly defined, to all the segments within the scope of the cotton industry in order to prevent further and widespread development of acute and chronic respiratory disease including irreversible and disabling chronic obstructive pulmonary disease. The continuing scientific debate over the identity of the specific agent does not detract from the conclusion that "cotton dust," as defined and regulated by this standard, has been shown to cause a constellation of respiratory illnesses (Ex. 11, Ex. 38a, d; Ex. 124; Ex. 6, #1, 30, 17, 31, 32, 33, 34, 51, 55, 57, 58). Protection of employees cannot await resolution of all the points of scientific debate. . . .

NOTES AND QUESTIONS

1. The excerpts above provide only a glimpse at OSHA's cotton dust decision. The Federal Register notice concerning the final cotton dust rule also discussed a host of other matters, including why OSHA selected the specific exposure level over various alternatives, an estimate of compliance costs for industry, an analysis of applicable legal standards, and so on. The entire notice occupies 69 pages of the Federal Register; the record compiled by the agency in the course of the cotton dust proceeding exceeded 100,000 pages. *See* American Textile v. Donovan, 452 U.S. 490, 501, 101 S.Ct. 2478, 69 L.Ed.2d 185 (1981).

2. Does the agency's reasoning in the above excerpt persuade you? Do you think a ban on cigarette smoking would cause the problem to disappear or decrease greatly? How can the agency assert that "the causal relationship between exposure to cotton dust and the development of byssinosis . . . has been clearly established," and yet admit that the "active agent or agents" in cotton dust have not been identified?

3. Judicial review of agency decisions typically takes place in a federal court of appeals. The record—in the cotton dust case, over 100,000 pages long—goes to the court, along with briefs from the opposing parties. No new evidence is submitted to the court. In this case, the United States Court of Appeals for the District of Columbia Circuit upheld the cotton dust rule in all major respects. AFL–CIO v. Marshall, 617 F.2d 636 (D.C. Cir. 1979). The case was then taken by the United States Supreme Court. At this stage, the issues involved covered only a few aspects of the original 69–page Federal Register notice. As is usually the case, a variety of largely factual matters argued at the agency level were not being pursued by the parties in the judicial filings. Accordingly, the Supreme Court's decision focused on a central issue of statutory construction.

American Textile Manufacturers Institute, Inc. v. Donovan

Supreme Court of the United States, 1981.
452 U.S. 490, 101 S.Ct. 2478, 69 L.Ed.2d 185.

■ Justice Brennan delivered the opinion of the Court.

. . .

The principal question presented in these cases is whether the Occupational Safety and Health Act requires the Secretary, in promulgating a standard pursuant to § 6(b)(5) of the Act, 29 U.S.C. § 655(b)(5), to determine that the costs of the standard bear a reasonable relationship to its benefits. Relying on §§ 6(b)(5) and 3(8) of the Act, 29 U.S.C. §§ 655(b)(5) and 652(8), petitioners urge not only that OSHA must show that a standard addresses a significant risk of material health impairment, *see* Industrial Union Dept. v. American Petroleum Institute, 448 U.S., at 639 (plurality opinion), but also that OSHA must demonstrate that the reduction in risk of material health impairment is significant in light of the costs of attaining that reduction. *See* Brief for Petitioners in No. 79–1429, pp. 38–41. Respondents on the other hand contend that the Act requires OSHA to promulgate standards that eliminate or reduce such risks "to the extent such protection is technologically and economically feasible." Brief for Federal Respondent 38; Brief for Union Respondents 26–27. To resolve this debate, we must turn to the language, structure, and legislative history of the Act.

The starting point of our analysis is the language of the statute itself. Steadman v. SEC, 450 U.S. 91, 97 (1981); Reiter v. Sonotone Corp., 442 U.S. 330, 337 (1979). Section 6(b)(5) of the Act, 29 U.S.C. § 655(b)(5) (emphasis added), provides:

> The Secretary, in promulgating standards dealing with toxic materials or harmful physical agents under this subsection, shall set the standard which most adequately assures, *to the extent feasible,* on the basis of the best available evidence, that no employee will suffer material impairment of health or functional capacity even if such employee has regular exposure to the hazard dealt with by such standard for the period of his working life.

Although their interpretations differ, all parties agree that the phrase "to the extent feasible" contains the critical language in § 6(b)(5) for purposes of these cases.

The plain meaning of the word "feasible" supports respondents' interpretation of the statute. According to Webster's Third New International Dictionary of the English Language 831 (1976), "feasible" means "capable of being done, executed, or effected." Accord, the Oxford English Dictionary 116 (1933) ("Capable of being done, accomplished or carried out"); Funk & Wagnalls New "Standard" Dictionary of the English Language 903 (1957) ("That may be done, performed or effected"). Thus, § 6(b)(5) directs the Secretary to issue the standard that "most adequately assures . . . that no employee will suffer material impairment of health," limited only by the extent to which this is "capable of being done." In effect then, as the Court of Appeals held, Congress itself defined the basic relationship between costs and benefits, by placing the "benefit" of worker health above all other considerations save those making attainment of this "benefit" unachievable. Any standard based on a balancing of costs and benefits by the Secretary that strikes a different balance than that struck by Congress would be inconsistent with the command set forth in § 6(b)(5). Thus, cost-benefit analysis by OSHA is not required by the statute because feasibility analysis is. *See* Industrial Union Dept. v. American Petroleum Institute, 448 U.S., at 718–19 (Marshall, J., dissenting).

When Congress has intended that an agency engage in cost-benefit analysis, it has clearly indicated such intent on the face of the statute. One early example is the Flood Control Act of 1936, 33 U.S.C. § 701:

> [T]he Federal Government should improve or participate in the improvement of navigable waters or their tributaries, including watersheds thereof, for flood-control purposes if the *benefits to whomsoever they may accrue are in excess of the estimated costs,* and if the lives and social security of people are otherwise adversely affected. (Emphasis added.)

A more recent example is the Outer Continental Shelf Lands Act Amendments of 1978, 43 U.S.C. § 1347(b) (1976 ed., Supp. III), providing that offshore drilling operations shall use

> the best available and safest technologies which the Secretary determines to be economically *feasible,* wherever failure of equipment would have a significant effect on safety, health, or the environment, except where the Secretary determines that the *incremental benefits are clearly insufficient to justify the incremental costs of using such technologies.*

These and other statutes demonstrate that Congress uses specific language when intending that an agency engage in cost-benefit analysis. *See* Industrial Union Dept. v. American Petroleum Institute, *supra,* at 710, n. 27 (Marshall, J., dissenting). Certainly in light of its ordinary meaning, the word "feasible" cannot be construed to articulate such congressional intent. We therefore reject the argument that Congress required cost-benefit analysis in § 6(b)(5)....

When Congress passed the Occupational Safety and Health Act in 1970, it chose to place pre-eminent value on assuring employees a safe and healthful working environment, limited only by the feasibility of achieving such an environment. We must measure the validity of the Secretary's actions against the requirements of that Act. For "[t]he judicial function does not extend to substantive revision of regulatory policy. That function lies elsewhere—in Congressional and Executive oversight or amendatory legislation." Industrial Union Dept. v. American Petroleum Institute, supra, 448 U.S., at 663 (Burger, C.J., concurring); *see* TVA v. Hill, 437 U.S. 153, 185, 187–88, 194–95 (1978).

. . .

■ JUSTICE REHNQUIST, with whom the CHIEF JUSTICE joins, dissenting.

A year ago I stated my belief that Congress in enacting § 6(b)(5) of the Occupational Safety and Health Act of 1970 unconstitutionally delegated to the Executive Branch the authority to make the "hard policy choices" properly the task of the legislature. Industrial Union Dept. v. American Petroleum Institute, 448 U.S. 607, 671 (1980) (concurring in judgment). Because I continue to believe that the Act exceeds Congress' power to delegate legislative authority to nonelected officials, *see* J.W. Hampton & Co. v. United States, 276 U.S. 394 (1928), and Panama Refining Co. v. Ryan, 293 U.S. 388 (1935), I dissent.

I will repeat only a little of what I said last Term. Section 6(b)(5) provides in pertinent part:

> The Secretary, in promulgating standards dealing with toxic materials or harmful physical agents under this subsection, shall set the standard which most adequately assures, *to the extent feasible,* on the basis of the best available evidence, that no employee will suffer material impairment of health or functional capacity even if such employee has regular exposure to the hazard dealt with by such standard for the period of his working life. (Emphasis added.)

As the Court correctly observes, the phrase "to the extent feasible" contains the critical language for the purpose of these cases. We are presented with a remarkable range of interpretations of that language. Petitioners contend that the statute *requires* the Secretary to demonstrate that the benefits of its "Cotton Dust Standard," in terms of reducing health risks, bear a reasonable relationship to its costs. Brief for Petitioners in No. 79–1429, pp. 38–41. Respondents, including the Secretary of Labor at least until his postargument motion, counter that Congress itself balanced costs and benefits when it enacted the statute, and that the statute *prohibits* the Secretary from engaging in a cost-benefit type balancing. Their view is that the Act merely requires the Secretary to promulgate standards that eliminate or reduce such risks "to the extent . . . technologically or economically feasible." Brief for Federal Respondent 38; Brief for Union Respondents 26–27. As I read the Court's opinion, it takes a different position. It concludes that, at least as to the "Cotton Dust Standard," the Act does not require the Secretary to engage in a cost-benefit analysis, which suggests of course that the Act *permits* the Secretary to undertake such an analysis if he so chooses.

Throughout its opinion, the Court refers to § 6(b)(5) as adopting a "feasibility standard" or a "feasibility requirement." But as I attempted to point out last Term in *Industrial Union Dept. v. American Petroleum Institute, supra,* at 681–85, the "feasibility standard" is no standard at all. Quite the contrary, I argued there that the insertion into § 6(b)(5) of the words "to the extent feasible" rendered what had been a clear, if somewhat unrealistic, statute into one so vague and precatory as to be an unconstitutional delegation of legislative authority to the Executive Branch. Prior to the inclusion of the "feasibility" language, § 6(b)(5) simply required the Secretary to "set the standard which most adequately assures, on the basis of the best available professional evidence, that no employee will suffer any impairment of health. . . ." Legislative History, Occupational Safety and Health Act of 1970, p. 943 (Comm.Print 1971) (hereinafter Leg.Hist.). Had that statute been enacted, it would undoubtedly support the result the Court reaches in these cases, and it would not have created an excessive delegation problem. The Secretary of Labor would quite clearly have been authorized to set exposure standards without regard to any kind of cost-benefit analysis.

But Congress did not enact that statute. The legislative history of the Act reveals that a number of Members of Congress, such as Senators Javits, Saxbe, and Dominick, had difficulty with the proposed statute and engaged Congress in a lengthy debate about the extent to which the Secretary should be authorized to create a risk-free work environment. Congress had at least three choices. It could have required the Secretary to engage in a cost-benefit analysis prior to the setting of exposure levels, it could have prohibited cost-benefit analysis, or it could have permitted the use of such an analysis. Rather than make that choice and resolve that difficult policy issue, however, Congress passed. Congress simply said that the Secretary should set standards "to the extent feasible." Last year, Justice Powell reflected that "one might wish that Congress had spoken with greater clarity." *American Petroleum Institute,* 448 U.S., at 668 (Powell, J., concurring in part and in judgment). I am convinced that the reason that Congress did not speak with greater "clarity" was because it could not. The words "to the extent feasible" were used to mask a fundamental policy disagreement in Congress. I have no doubt that if Congress had been required to choose whether to mandate, permit, or prohibit the Secretary from engaging in a cost-benefit analysis, there would have been no bill for the President to sign.

The Court seems to argue that Congress *did* make a policy choice when it enacted the "feasibility" language. Its view is that Congress required the Secretary to engage in something called "feasibility analysis." But those words mean nothing at all. They are a "legislative mirage, appearing to some Members [of Congress] but not to others, and assuming any form desired by the beholder." *American Petroleum Institute,* supra, at 681. Even the Court does not settle on a meaning. It first suggests that the language requires the Secretary to do what is "capable of being done." But, if that is all the language means, it is merely precatory and "no more than an admonition to the Secretary to do his duty...." Leg.Hist. 367 (remarks of Sen. Dominick). The Court then seems to adopt the Secretary's view that feasibility means "technological and economic feasibility." But there is nothing in the words of § 6(b)(5), or their legislative history, to suggest why they should be so limited. One wonders why the "requirement" of § 6(b)(5) could not include considerations of administrative or even political feasibility. As even the Court recognizes, when Congress has wanted to limit the concept of feasibility to technological and economic feasibility, it has said so. Thus the words "to the extent feasible" provide no meaningful guidance to those who will administer the law.

In believing that § 6(b)(5) amounts to an unconstitutional delegation of legislative authority to the Executive Branch, I do not mean to suggest that Congress, in enacting a statute, must resolve all ambiguities or must "fill in all of the blanks." Even the neophyte student of government realizes that legislation is the art of compromise, and that an important, controversial bill is seldom enacted by Congress in the form in which it is first introduced. It is not unusual for the various factions supporting or opposing a proposal to accept some departure from the language they would prefer and to adopt substitute language agreeable to all. But that sort of compromise is a far cry from this case, where Congress simply abdicated its responsibility for the making of a fundamental and most difficult policy choice—whether and to what extent "the statistical possibility of future deaths should ... be disregarded in light of the economic costs of preventing those deaths." *American Petroleum Institute,* supra, at 672. That is a "quintessential legislative" choice and must be made by the elected representatives of the people, not by nonelected officials in the Executive Branch. As stated last Term:

> In drafting § 6(b)(5), Congress was faced with a clear, if difficult, choice between balancing statistical lives and industrial resources or authorizing the Secretary to elevate human life above all concerns save massive dislocation in an affected industry. That Congress recognized the difficulty of this choice is clear.... That Congress chose, intentionally or unintentionally, to pass the difficult choice on to the Secretary is evident from the spectral quality of the standard it selected. 448 U.S., at 685.

In sum, the Court is quite correct in asserting that the phrase "to the extent feasible" is the critical language for the purposes of these cases. But that language is critical, not because it establishes a general standard by which those charged with administering the statute may be guided, but because it has precisely the opposite effect: in failing to agree on whether the Secretary should be either mandated, permitted, or prohibited from undertaking a cost-benefit analysis, Congress simply left the crucial policy choices in the hands of the Secretary of Labor. As I stated at greater length last Term, I believe that in so doing Congress unconstitutionally delegated its legislative responsibility to the Executive Branch.

NOTES AND QUESTIONS

1. Does Justice Brennan's opinion that Congress meant to place the " 'benefit' of worker health above all other considerations save those making attainment of this 'benefit' unachievable" persuade you? Does this mean that if reducing the exposure level further would improve the health of one worker while throwing hundreds out of work, the agency must reduce the exposure level? Current cotton dust regulations, which are still based in large part on the proceeding described above, may be found at 29 C.F.R. § 1910.1043 (2000).

2. The Supreme Court has not used the non-delegation doctrine invoked by Justice (now Chief Justice) Rehnquist to strike down legislation since the New Deal. In 1999, a panel of the D.C. Circuit found an unconstitutional delegation to the Environmental Protection Agency to set national ambient air quality standards, but the Supreme Court reversed. Whitman v. American Trucking Ass'n, 531 U.S. 457, 121 S.Ct. 903, 149 L.Ed.2d 1 (2001). Of course, agencies cannot regulate outside of the jurisdiction conveyed to them by Congress. *See, e.g.,* Food & Drug Admin. v. Brown & Williamson Tobacco Corp., 529 U.S. 120, 120 S.Ct. 1291, 146 L.Ed.2d 121 (2000) (Congress did not grant the FDA jurisdiction to regulate tobacco products).

3. At present, given the Court's willingness to uphold extensive Congressional delegations of authority, the agencies play the central role in regulatory matters involving technical issues. Indeed, in practice, White House and Congressional figures often find themselves "lobbying" agencies in a striking reversal of the textbook depiction of elected officials as the target of lobbyists. In upholding the

Environmental Protection Agency's authority to receive certain informal contacts while formulating rules for emission standards for coal-fired power plants, the United States Court of Appeals for the District of Columbia Circuit allowed lobbying by then-majority leader Senator Robert Byrd: "[W]e believe it entirely proper for Congressional representatives vigorously to represent the interests of their constituents before administrative agencies engaged in informal, general policy rulemaking. . . ." Sierra Club v. Costle, 657 F.2d 298, 409 (D.C. Cir. 1981). The court also upheld the propriety of certain agency contacts with the executive branch. Does this make you feel better or worse about having agencies perform "general policy rulemaking"?

4.   The agencies at the center of regulation are subject as well to complaints that they are too beholden to special interest groups. The employees of the agencies themselves are often criticized for moving through a "revolving door" between government and the regulated industry. The net effect is continued controversy; it is rare, for example, to find someone who does not think that the Food and Drug Administration has either been too lax or too strict in regulating the drug industry. *See, e.g.,* Alison R. McCabe, *A Precarious Balancing Act—The Role of the FDA As Protector of Public Health and Industry Wealth*, 36 SUFFOLK U. L. REV. 787 (2003). Yet there are very few alternatives; indeed, when the subject turns to the control of a new area of science such as molecular nanotechnology, agency regulation is generally taken as the appropriate model. Jason Wejnert, *Regulatory Mechanisms for Molecular Nanotechnology*, 44 JURIMETRICS J. 323, 338 (2004).

5.   So we are left with a system in which government support for science is largely shaped by the values of the scientific community, while government regulation of the technology that comes out of that science is shaped by the wider community. The following excerpt considers the implications of this "regulatory gap."

Steven Goldberg, *The Reluctant Embrace: Law and Science in America*
75 GEO. L.J. 1341, 1365–68, 1380–81, 1386–87 (1987).

[S]crutiny of new technologies is more intense than scrutiny of funding in several respects. First, the agencies making the initial decisions are less likely to adopt the views of the science community. When the Food and Drug Administration declines to approve a new drug, or when the Nuclear Regulatory Commission defers approval of a new reactor fuel, it is quite possible that most of the scientists in the relevant field would disagree. Regulatory agencies are regularly accused of being "captured" by industry, consumer groups, members of Congress, or bureaucratic inertia. They are never accused, however, of being captured by scientists. The reason is that although scientists work for the agencies, the agencies reflect, to a greater or lesser degree, the whole spectrum of interest groups in American society. They are not dominated by the science community.

Even when regulatory agencies do make decisions consistent with the views of the science community, the courts, in lawsuits brought by citizen groups, competitors, and others, are less likely to uphold the regulators than they are to uphold the decisions of the agencies that fund research. Indeed, in some cases, even Congress and the White House, or elected officials at the state level, get involved in regulatory issues. Of course most regulatory decisions with a high technical component are still made by administrative agencies. Nevertheless, as the decisions to keep saccharin on the market and to keep American supersonic transport planes out of the skies illustrate, elected officials themselves can and do take direct action.

To give examples of legal restrictions on technology is to survey much of modern American law. . . . Major projects, from nuclear power plants to pipelines, have been slowed or stopped by litigation. Food and drug law has become recognized as a discrete area of study that includes cases where new products have been delayed in reaching the market or prevented from doing so altogether. In other areas, ranging from communications to computers, regulation is a fact of modern life. At the state level, statutes and judicial decisions, concerning, for example, malpractice, products liability, and exposure to radioactive materials, have subjected technology to extraordinarily close scrutiny. . . .

[J]udges are acutely aware that the regulatory issues before them combine scientific and policy matters, and they want to be sure that controversial policy decisions are made openly and persuasively, rather than under the guise of scientific neutrality. While the question of how much radiation will escape a given reactor is a technical question, the question of whether that level of radiation poses an unacceptable risk to the public is not. . . . Even when a court declines to resolve a technical issue, it still may cause a regulatory delay. In many cases involving judicial review of agency action, the court, if troubled, will remand the case to the agency to enable the agency to change its mind or provide a better justification for its first decision. Thus, the court does not directly resolve the matter. However, the court in such cases often causes delay, and when the issue is whether to move forward, a delay is a decision. When, for example, a new drug is not available for a certain period of time, those who favor marketing it are losing profits, and potential users of the drug are losing health benefits. In contrast, groups that oppose selling the drug are delighted—the harmful side effects they fear are being avoided, and the market situation may change, making the drug less attractive. That is why, in almost any litigated regulatory dispute, at least one side benefits from delay.

The numerous hurdles confronting new technology are not evidence that America is fundamentally anti-science or anti-technology. The hurdles merely show that when technology enters the marketplace it is not given a free ride. Obviously, legal control of technology is not something new and different from the lawyers' point of view. From the railroad to the automobile to the airplane and beyond, legal doctrines have been shaped by technology and have, in turn, shaped technology itself. The law had to adjust to new issues raised by airplanes passing over property; airplanes had to be built with legal notions of tort liability in mind. The American legal system's adjustment to the industrial revolution suggests that it will adjust to the technological revolutions that lie ahead. It also reveals the contrast between the scientists' sense of a world making progress and the lawyers' sense of a more or less endless process of mediating social disputes. . . .

Thus, the stage is set for the regulatory gap—a gap between research and application that has enormous practical consequences. The gap results because basic research receives unusually little public scrutiny while applications of that research receive an extraordinary dose of public involvement. . . .

[F]or scientists, narrowing the regulatory gap is quite important. Scientists are well aware that the costs of the regulatory gap are so high that eventually regulators, rather than making a careful, painstaking effort to narrow the gap, will lash out with wholesale control of research. The possibility of such a reaction down the road is real. After all, the consequences of the regulatory gap have not been benign. With nuclear fission, years of research and billions of dollars have created a stunted industry with some reactors operating, some abandoned half-built, and many canceled before construction could begin. This halfway policy pleases neither nuclear power's advocates nor its adversaries. With recombinant DNA, we see the beginnings of lawsuits and regulatory inquiries that will shape, or slow, technological development in ways that may render useless large areas of research. If there is no change in the regulatory gap, other areas of development now in embryonic stages, such as nuclear fusion, will be similarly affected.

Scientists will gradually move into this breach. Some have begun to do so; many more will follow. Ordinary scientists doing research will begin to participate more fully in public debate on the applications of research and will even begin to shape research, early on, to increase the likelihood that the resulting commercial product will encounter a relatively calm regulatory climate. Nothing can remove the pinch of regulation entirely. Any new product alters rights in ways that create disputes, but the most wasteful outcomes can often be avoided. Scientific research need not produce a type of product that is least acceptable to society. That outcome follows from the indifference of researchers to commercialization. If research is guided by a socially conscious hand from the outset, choices can be made that improve the product's chances of relatively smooth commercialization. Scientists increasingly realize that taking these steps is in the interests of science. Doing research today without concern for the ultimate legal consequences is like doing a high wire act without the wire. . . .

When . . . scientists . . . routinely shape their research with regulatory consequences foremost in mind, they will become what might be called science counselors. The evolution of the science counselor is a gradual process. Many mission oriented scientists today have some of the characteristics of a science counselor, a few have all of the characteristics. . . .

The danger is that science will be loved to death, smothered in the embrace of social considerations. . . . Indeed [scientists], by engaging in socially directed research, may overlook some of the entirely unexpected developments that spur so much of science. . . . [S]ociety does not want to shut off the flow of science completely; it wants to pick and choose among scientific developments and use or shape those it likes. It is difficult to have it both ways. Because society's efforts to shape science are likely to be clumsy, scientists are forced to temper their own work. In so doing they gradually change the culture of science.

NOTES AND QUESTIONS

1. For a further explication of these views see STEVEN GOLDBERG, CULTURE CLASH: LAW AND SCIENCE IN AMERICA (1994). For a contrasting analysis of the proper relationship between lawyers and scientists in the public policy arena, see Harold Green, *The Law–Science Interface in Public Policy Decisionmaking*, 51 OHIO ST. L.J. 375 (1990). Another perspective on the difficulties new technologies face in the marketplace is presented in Peter Huber, *The Old–New Division in Risk Regulation*, 69 VA. L. REV. 1025 (1983).

2. One recent proposal that commercial considerations play a heightened role in basic research came in the field of superconductivity, where a White House committee concluded:

> We believe the optimal way to proceed is to take advantage of the scientific strength at universities and government laboratories and infuse it with detailed knowledge of applications. This knowledge is resident in industry. This is best done if the three institutions, university, industry and government, work together to develop goals and to jointly support them, manage them, and review them for progress.

THE WHITE HOUSE SCIENCE COUNCIL COMMITTEE TO ADVISE THE PRESIDENT ON HIGH TEMPERATURE SUPERCONDUCTIVITY: PERSEVERANCE AND COOPERATION ON THE ROAD TO COMMERCIALIZATION, 35 (Jan. 1989). For a discussion of the societal issues raised by the potential applications of superconductivity research, see Steven Goldberg, *Narrowing the Regulatory Gap Between Law and Science: The Prospects for Superconductivity*, 1 CTS. HEALTH SCI. & L. 163 (1990).

3. Is it realistic to fear that a concern for social impacts inevitably poses a threat to all pure research? Why can't society fund relatively unfettered inquiry into areas, such as high energy physics, where the intellectual appeal and possible unpredictable payoffs merit it, while shaping research more directly where the social implications are more clear?

B.   STATE AND LOCAL REGULATION

Wisconsin Public Intervenor v. Mortier

Supreme Court of the United States, 1991.
501 U.S. 597, 111 S.Ct. 2476, 115 L.Ed.2d 532.

■ JUSTICE WHITE delivered the opinion of the Court.

This case requires us to consider whether the Federal Insecticide, Fungicide, and Rodenticide Act, (FIFRA), 61 Stat. 163, as amended, 7 U.S.C. § 136 *et seq.* pre-empts the regulation of pesticides by local governments. We hold that it does not.

I.

FIFRA was enacted in 1947 to replace the Federal Government's first effort at pesticide regulation, the Insecticide Act of 1910, 36 Stat. 331. 61 Stat. 163. Like its predecessor, FIFRA as originally adopted "was primarily a licensing and labeling statute." Ruckelshaus v. Monsanto Co., 467 U.S. 986, 991 (1984). In 1972, growing environmental and safety concerns led Congress to undertake a comprehensive revision of FIFRA through the Federal Environmental Pesticide Control Act. 86 Stat. 973. The 1972 amendments significantly strengthened FIFRA's registration and labeling standards. 7 U.S.C. § 136a. To help make certain that pesticides would be applied in accordance with these standards, the revisions further insured that FIFRA "regulated the use, as well as the sale and labeling, of pesticides; regulated pesticides produced and sold in both intrastate and interstate commerce; [and] provided for review, cancellation, and suspension of registration." *Ruckleshaus,* 467 U.S. at 991–92. An additional change was the grant of increased enforcement authority to the Environmental Protection Agency (EPA), which had been charged with federal oversight of pesticides since 1970. *See* Reorganization Plan No. 3 of 1970, 35 Fed.Reg. 15623 (1970), 5 U.S.C.App., 1343. In this fashion, the 1972 amendments "transformed FIFRA from a labeling law into a comprehensive regulatory statute." 467 U.S., at 991.

As amended, FIFRA specifies several roles for state and local authorities. The statute, for example, authorizes the EPA Administrator to enter into cooperative agreements with the States to enforce FIFRA provisions. 7 U.S.C. §§ 136u, 136w–1. As part of the enforcement scheme, FIFRA requires manufacturers to produce records for inspection "upon request of any officer or employee of the Environmental Protection Agency or of any State or political subdivision, duly designated by the Administrator." § 136f(b). FIFRA further directs the EPA Administrator to cooperate with "any appropriate agency of any State or any political subdivision thereof." § 136t(b). Of particular relevance to this case, § 24(a) specifies that States may regulate the sale or use of pesticides so long as the state regulation does not permit a sale or use prohibited by the Act. § 136v(a).

Petitioner, the town of Casey, is a small rural community located in Washburn County, Wisconsin, several miles northwest of Spooner, on the road to Superior. In 1985, the town adopted Ordinance 85–1, which regulates the use of pesticides. The ordinance expressly borrows statutory definitions from both Wisconsin laws and FIFRA, and was enacted under Wis.Stat. §§ 61.34(1), (5) (1989–1990), which accords village boards with general police, health, and taxing powers.

The ordinance requires a permit for the application of any pesticide to public lands, to private lands subject to public use, or for the aerial application of any pesticide to private lands. Ord. § 1.2, 2 App. to Pet. for Cert. 6. A permit applicant must file a form including information about the proposed pesticide use not less than 60 days before the desired use. § 1.3(2), *id.,* at 7. The town board may "deny the permit, grant the permit, or grant the permit with ... any reasonable conditions on a permitted application related to the protection of the health, safety and welfare of the residents of the Town of Casey." § 1.3(3), *id.,* at 11–12. After an initial decision, the applicant or any town resident may obtain a hearing to provide additional information regarding the proposed application. §§ 1.3(4), (5), *id.,* at 12–14. When a permit is granted, or granted with conditions, the ordinance further requires the permittee to post placards giving notice of the pesticide use and of any label information prescribing a safe reentry time. § 1.3(7), *id.,* at 14–16. Persons found guilty of violating the ordinance are subject to fines of up to $5,000 for each violation. § 1.3(7)(c), *id.,* at 16.

Respondent Ralph Mortier applied for a permit for aerial spraying of a portion of his land. The town granted him a permit, but precluded any aerial spraying and restricted the lands on which ground spraying would be allowed. Mortier, in conjunction with respondent Wisconsin Forestry/Rights-of-Way/Turf Coalition, brought a declaratory judgment action in the Circuit Court for Washburn County against the town of Casey and named board members, claiming that the town of Casey's ordinance is pre-empted by state and federal law. The Wisconsin Public Intervenor, an assistant attorney general charged under state law with the protection of environmental public rights, Wis.Stat. §§ 165.07, 165.075 (1989–1990), was admitted without objection as a party defendant. On cross-motions for summary judgment, the Circuit Court ruled in favor of Mortier, holding that the town's ordinance was pre-empted both by FIFRA and by state statute, §§ 94.67–94.71; 2 App. to Pet. for Cert. 14.

The Supreme Court of Wisconsin affirmed in a 4–to–3 decision. Mortier v. Casey, 452 N.W.2d 555 (Wisc. 1990). Declining to address the issue of state-law pre-emption, the court concluded that FIFRA pre-empted the town of Casey's ordinance because the statute's text and legislative history demonstrated a clearly manifest congressional intent to prohibit "any regulation of pesticides by local units of government." Id., at 555, n. 2, 560. . . .

II.

Under the Supremacy Clause, U.S. Const., Art. VI, cl. 2, state laws that "interfere with, or are contrary to the laws of congress, made in pursuance of the constitution" are invalid. Gibbons v. Ogden, 9 Wheat. 1, 211 (1824) (Marshall, C.J.). The ways in which federal law may pre-empt state law are well established and in the first instance turn on congressional intent. Ingersoll–Rand Co. v. McClendon, 498 U.S. 133 (1990). Congress' intent to supplant state authority in a particular field may be expressed in the terms of the statute. Jones v. Rath Packing Co., 430 U.S. 519, 525 (1977). Absent explicit pre-emptive language, Congress' intent to supersede state law in a given area may nonetheless be implicit if a scheme of federal regulation is "so pervasive as to make reasonable the inference that Congress left no room for the States to supplement it," if "the Act of Congress . . . touch[es] a field in which the federal interest is so dominant that the federal system will be assumed to preclude enforcement of state laws on the same subject," or if the goals "sought to be obtained" and the "obligations imposed" reveal a purpose to preclude state authority. Rice v. Santa Fe Elevator Corp., 331 U.S. 218, 230 (1947). See Pacific Gas & Electric Co. v. State Energy Resources Conservation and Development Commission, 461 U.S. 190, 203–04 (1983). When considering pre-emption, "we start with the assumption that the historic police powers of the States were not to be superseded by the Federal Act unless that was the clear and manifest purpose of Congress." Rice, 331 U.S., at 230.

Even when Congress has not chosen to occupy a particular field, pre-emption may occur to the extent that state and federal law actually conflict. Such a conflict arises when "compliance with both federal and state regulations is a physical impossibility," Florida Lime & Avocado Growers, Inc. v. Paul, 373 U.S. 132, 142–43 (1963), or when a state law "stands as an obstacle to the accomplishment and execution of the full purposes and objectives of Congress," Hines v. Davidowitz, 312 U.S. 52 (1941).

It is, finally, axiomatic that "for the purposes of the Supremacy Clause, the constitutionality of local ordinances is analyzed in the same way as that of statewide laws." Hillsborough v. Automated Medical Laboratories, Inc., 471 U.S. 707, 713 (1985). *See, e.g.,* City of Burbank v. Lockheed Air Terminal, Inc., 411 U.S. 624 (1973).

III.

Applying these principles, we conclude that FIFRA does not pre-empt the town's ordinance either explicitly, implicitly, or by virtue of an actual conflict.

As the Wisconsin Supreme Court recognized, FIFRA nowhere expressly supersedes local regulation of pesticide use. The court, however, purported to find statutory language "which is indicative" of pre-emptive intent in the statute's provision delineating the "Authority of States." 7 U.S.C. § 136v. The key portions of that provision state:

> (a) ... A State may regulate the sale or use of any federally registered pesticide or device in the State, but only if and to the extent the regulation does not permit any sale or use prohibited by this subchapter.

> (b) ... Such State shall not impose or continue in effect any requirements for labeling or packaging in addition to or different from those required under this subchapter.

Also significant, in the court's eyes, was FIFRA's failure to specify political subdivisions in defining "State" as "a State, the District of Columbia, the Commonwealth of Puerto Rico, the Virgin Islands, Guam, the Trust Territory of the Pacific Islands, and American Samoa." 7 U.S.C. § 136(aa).

It is not clear to the State Supreme Court, however, "that the statutory language [§§ 136v and 136(aa)] alone evince[d] congress' manifest intent to deprive political subdivisions of authority to regulate pesticides." *Casey,* 452 N.W.2d, at 557–58. It was nevertheless "possible" to infer from the statutory language alone that pesticide regulation by local entities was pre-empted; and when coupled with its legislative history, that language "unmistakably demonstrates the intent of Congress to pre-empt local ordinances such as that adopted by the Town of Casey." *Id.,* at 559. The court's holding thus rested on both §§ 136v and 136(aa) and their legislative history; neither the language nor the legislative history would have sufficed alone. There was no suggestion that absent the two critical sections, FIFRA was a sufficiently comprehensive statute to justify an inference that Congress had occupied the field to the exclusion of the States. Nor have the respondents argued in this Court to that effect. On the other hand, it is sufficiently clear that under the opinion announced by the court below, the State would have been precluded from permitting local authorities to regulate pesticides.

We agree that neither the language of the statute nor its legislative history, standing alone, would suffice to pre-empt local regulation. But it is also our view that even when considered together the language and the legislative materials relied on below are insufficient to demonstrate the necessary congressional intent to pre-empt. As for the statutory language, it is wholly inadequate to convey an express preemptive intent on its own. Section 136v plainly authorizes the "States" to regulate pesticides and just as plainly is silent with reference to local governments. Mere silence, in this context, cannot suffice to establish a "clear and manifest purpose" to pre-empt local authority. *Rice,* 331 U.S. at 230. Even if FIFRA's express grant of regulatory authority to the States could not be read as applying to municipalities, it would not follow that municipalities were left with no regulatory authority. Rather, it would mean that localities could not claim the regulatory authority explicitly conferred upon the States that might otherwise have been pre-empted through actual conflicts with Federal law. At a minimum, localities would still be free to regulate subject to the usual principles of pre-emption. . . .

Mortier, like the court below and other courts that have found pre-emption, attempts to compensate for the statute's textual inadequacies by stressing the legislative history. *Casey,* 452 N.W.2d, at 558–59; *Professional Lawn Care Association,* 909 F.2d, at 933–34. The evidence from this source, which centers on the meaning of what would become § 136v, is at best ambiguous. The House Agriculture Committee Report accompanying the proposed FIFRA amendments stated that it had "rejected a proposal which would have permitted political subdivisions to further regulate pesticides on the grounds that the 50 States and the Federal Government should provide an adequate number of regulatory jurisdictions." H.R.Rep. No. 92–511, 16 (1971). While this statement indicates an unwillingness by Congress to grant political subdivisions regulatory authority, it does not demonstrate an intent to prevent the States from delegating such authority to its subdivisions, and still less does it show a desire to prohibit local regulation altogether. At least one other statement, however, concededly goes further. The Senate Committee on Agriculture and Forestry Report states outright that it "considered the decision of the House Committee to deprive political subdivisions of States and other local authorities of any authority or jurisdiction over pesticides and concurs with the decision of the House of Representatives." S.Rep. No. 92–838, 16 (1972), U.S.Code Cong. & Admin.News 1972, 3993, 4008.

But other Members of Congress clearly disagreed. The Senate Commerce Committee, which also had jurisdiction over the bill, observed that "[w]hile the [Senate] Agriculture Committee bill does not specifically prohibit local governments from regulating pesticides, the report of that committee states explicitly that local governments cannot regulate pesticides in any manner. Many local governments now regulate pesticides to meet their own specific needs which they are often better able to perceive than are State and Federal regulators." S.Rep. No. 92–970, 27 (1972), U.S.Code Cong. & Admin.News 1972, 4111. To counter the language in the Agriculture and Forestry Committee Report, the Commerce Committee proposed an amendment expressly authorizing local regulation among numerous other, unrelated proposals. This amendment was rejected after negotiations between the two Committees. *See* 118 Cong.Rec. 32251 (1972); H.R.Conf.Rep. No. 92–1540, 33 (1972), U.S.Code Cong. & Admin.News 1972, 3993.

As a result, matters were left with the two principal Committees responsible for the bill in disagreement over whether it pre-empted pesticide regulation by political subdivisions. It is important to note, moreover, that even this disagreement was confined to the pre-emptive effect of FIFRA's authorization of regulatory power to the States in § 136v. None of the Committees mentioned asserted that FIFRA pre-empted the field of pesticide regulation. Like FIFRA's text, the legislative history thus falls far short of establishing that pre-emption of local pesticide regulation was the "clear and manifest purpose of Congress." *Rice,* 331 U.S., at 230. We thus agree with the submission in the *amicus* brief of the United States expressing the views of the Environmental Protection Agency, the agency charged with enforcing FIFRA.

Likewise, FIFRA fails to provide any clear and manifest indication that Congress sought to supplant local authority over pesticide regulation impliedly. . . . It certainly does not equate registration and labeling requirements with a general approval to apply pesticides throughout the Nation without regard to regional and local factors like climate, population, geography, and water supply. Whatever else FIFRA may supplant, it does not occupy the field of pesticide regulation in general or the area of local use permitting in particular.

In contrast to other implicitly pre-empted fields, the 1972 enhancement of FIFRA does not mean that the use of pesticides can occur " 'only by federal permission, subject to federal inspection, in the hands of federally certified personnel and under an intricate system of federal commands.' " City of Burbank v. Lockheed Air Terminal, 411 U.S., at 634 (quoting Northwest Airlines v. Minnesota, 322 U.S. 292, 303 (1944) (Jackson, J., concurring)). The specific grant of authority in § 136v(a) consequently does not serve to hand back to the States powers that the statute had impliedly usurped. Rather, it acts to ensure that the States could continue to regulate use and sales even where, such as with regard to the banning of mislabeled products, a narrow pre-emptive overlap might occur. As noted in our discussion of express pre-emption, it is doubtful that Congress intended to exclude localities from the scope of § 136v(a)'s authorization, but however this may be, the type of local regulation at issue here would not fall within any impliedly pre-empted field.

Finally, like the EPA, we discern no actual conflict either between FIFRA and the ordinance before us or between FIFRA and local regulation generally. Mortier does not rely, nor could he, on the theory that compliance with the ordinance and FIFRA is a "physical impossibility." *Florida Lime & Avocado Growers,* 373 U.S., at 142–43. Instead, he urges that the town's ordinance stands as an obstacle to the statute's goals of promoting pesticide regulation that is coordinated solely on the federal and state levels, that rests upon some degree of technical expertise, and that does not unduly burden interstate commerce. Each one of these assertions rests on little more than snippets of legislative history and policy speculations. None of them is convincing.

To begin with, FIFRA does not suggest a goal of regulatory coordination that sweeps either as exclusively or as broadly as Mortier contends. The statute gives no indication that Congress was sufficiently concerned about this goal to require pre-emption of local use ordinances simply because they were enacted locally. Mortier suggests otherwise, quoting legislative history which states that FIFRA establishes "a coordinated Federal–State administrative system to carry out the new program," and raising the specter of gypsy moth hoards safely navigating through thousands of contradictory and ineffective municipal regulations. H.R.Rep. No. 92–511, at 1–2. As we have made plain, the statute does not expressly or impliedly preclude regulatory action by political subdivisions with regard to local use. To the contrary, FIFRA implies a regulatory partnership between federal, state, *and* local governments. Section 136t(b) expressly states that the Administrator "shall cooperate with . . . any appropriate agency of any State or any political subdivision thereof, in carrying out the provisions of this [Act] and in securing uniformity of regulations." Nor does FIFRA suggest that any goal of coordination precludes local use ordinances because they were enacted independent of specific state or federal oversight. As we have also made plain, local use permit regulations—unlike labeling or certification—do not fall within an area that FIFRA's "program" pre-empts or even plainly addresses. There is no indication that any coordination which the statute seeks to promote extends beyond the matters with which it deals, or does so strongly enough to compel the conclusion that an independently enacted ordinance that falls outside the statute's reach frustrates its purpose.

FIFRA provides even less indication that local ordinances must yield to statutory purposes of promoting technical expertise or maintaining unfettered interstate commerce. Once more, isolated passages of legislative history that were themselves insufficient to establish a pre-emptive congressional intent do not by themselves establish legislative goals with pre-emptive effect. *See, e.g.,* S.Rep. No. 92–838, at 16, U.S.Code Cong. & Admin.News 1972, 4007. Mortier nonetheless asserts that local ordinances necessarily rest on insufficient expertise and burden commerce by allowing, among other things, large-scale crop infestation. As with the specter of the gypsy moth, Congress is free to find that local regulation does wreak such havoc and enact legislation with the purpose of preventing it. We are satisfied, however, that Congress has not done so yet.

IV.

We hold that FIFRA does not pre-empt the town of Casey's ordinance regulating the use of pesticides. The judgment of the Wisconsin Supreme Court is reversed, and the case is remanded for proceedings not inconsistent with this opinion.

It is so ordered.

■ Justice Scalia, concurring in the judgment.

[Eds.—Justice Scalia argued that the statute on its face does not preempt local pesticide regulation, and thus he concurred. He contended, however, that if one looked at the legislative history to give meaning to the statutory text—a practice he disfavors—a contrary result would be mandated. On this point, Scalia particularly noted the following:]

The House Agriculture Committee's bill was passed by the full House on November 9, 1971, and upon transmittal to the Senate was referred to the Senate Committee on Agriculture and Forestry, which reported it out on June 7, 1972. The accompanying Committee Report both clearly confirms the foregoing interpretation of the House Committee Report, and clearly endorses the disposition that interpretation produces.

"[We have] considered the decision of the House Committee to deprive political subdivisions of States and other local authorities of any authority or jurisdiction over pesticides and concurs with the decision of the House of Representatives. Clearly, the fifty States and the Federal Government provide sufficient jurisdictions to properly regulate pesticides. Moreover, few, if any, local authorities whether towns, counties, villages, or municipalities have the financial wherewithal to provide necessary expert regulation comparable with that provided by the State and Federal Governments. On this basis and on the basis that permitting such regulation would be an extreme burden on interstate commerce, *it is the intent that section [136v], by not providing any authority to political subdivisions and other local authorities of or in the States, should be understood as depriving such local authorities and political subdivisions of any and all jurisdiction and authority over pesticides and the regulation of pesticides.*" S.Rep. No. 92–838, 16–17 (1972), U.S.Code Cong. & Admin.News 1972, 4008 (emphasis added).

Clearer committee language "directing" the courts how to interpret a statute of Congress could not be found, and if such a direction had any binding effect, the question of interpretation in this case would be no question at all. . . .

NOTES AND QUESTIONS

1. When Congress has the power to regulate, it can, of course, preempt state law. As Mortier indicates, however, Congress can also choose to allow state and local regulation in addition to or in place of federal regulation. The Court determined in Mortier that Congress intended that pesticides could be regulated, for example, by towns such as Casey, Wisconsin, which has a population of under 500. Do you agree with that policy choice?

2. This question is difficult because while state or local control brings decisions closer to home, state boundaries do not confine the costs and benefits of a technology. Thus a complete absence of federal regulation can lead to the state with the lowest safety standards attracting activities that might endanger neighboring states. Where the federal government sets minimum standards that a state can raise, a state may shield its citizens from the costs of research or power generation by setting very high safety standards, yet still draw the ultimate benefits from the activity in question. Everyone would like to have dangerous cancer research done elsewhere, as long as the resulting cure for cancer is available to all. Compare the discussion of siting a nuclear waste repository in Chapter 3, Sec. II. A., *supra*.

3. At present no one approach pervades the federal-state regulation issue in science and medicine. With nuclear energy, the general formulation is that the federal government sets safety standards while the states regulate economic matters, but this formulation conceals many complexities. *See, e.g.*, Pacific Gas & Elec. v. State Energy Res. Conservation Comm'n, 461 U.S. 190, 103 S.Ct. 1713, 75 L.Ed.2d 752 (1983); *see also* Silkwood v. Kerr–McGee Corp., 464 U.S. 238, 104 S.Ct. 615, 78 L.Ed.2d 443 (1984). The Food and Drug Administration has not approved laetrile, see United States v. Rutherford, 442 U.S. 544, 99 S.Ct. 2470, 61 L.Ed.2d 68 (1979), but several states allow its use in the intrastate market. *See, e.g.*, N.J.Rev. Stat. § 24:6F–4 (1990); *see also* Comment, *The Uncertain Application of the Right of Privacy in Personal Medical Decisions: The Laetrile Cases*, 42 OHIO ST. L.J. 523, 530 (1981). In the environmental field, as Mortier suggests, a host of federal and state statutes interact in a variety of ways. With respect to tobacco, the Supreme Court has held that federal law preempts certain state regulations governing cigarette advertising. Lorillard Tobacco Co. v. Reilly, 533 U.S. 525, 121 S.Ct. 2404, 150 L.Ed.2d 532 (2001).

IV. Trial Court Use of Scientific and Medical Evidence

Daubert v. Merrell Dow Pharmaceuticals

Supreme Court of the United States, 1993.
509 U.S. 579, 113 S.Ct. 2786, 125 L.Ed.2d 469.

■ Justice Blackmun delivered the opinion for a unanimous Court with respect to Parts I and II–A, and the opinion of the Court with respect to Parts II–B, II–C, III, and IV, in which Justice White, Justice O'Connor, Justice Scalia, Justice Kennedy, Justice Souter, and Justice Thomas, joined. Chief Justice Rehnquist filed an opinion concurring in part and dissenting in part, in which Justice Stevens, joined.

. . .

■ Justice Blackmun delivered the opinion of the Court.

In this case we are called upon to determine the standard for admitting expert scientific testimony in a federal trial.

I

Petitioners Jason Daubert and Eric Schuller are minor children born with serious birth defects. They and their parents sued respondent in California state court, alleging that the birth defects had been caused by the mothers' ingestion of Bendectin, a prescription anti-nausea drug marketed by respondent. Respondent removed the suits to federal court on diversity grounds.

After extensive discovery, respondent moved for summary judgment, contending that Bendectin does not cause birth defects in humans and that petitioners would be unable to come forward with any admissible evidence that it does. In support of its motion, respondent submitted an affidavit of Steven H. Lamm, physician and epidemiologist, who is a well-credentialed expert on the risks from exposure to various chemical substances.[1] Doctor Lamm stated that he had reviewed all the literature on Bendectin and human birth defects—more than 30 published studies involving over 130,-000 patients. No study had found Bendectin to be a human teratogen (i.e., a substance capable of causing malformations in fetuses). On the basis of this review, Doctor Lamm concluded that maternal use of Bendectin during

---

1. Doctor Lamm received his master's and doctor of medicine degrees from the University of Southern California. He has served as a consultant in birth-defect epidemiology for the National Center for Health Statistics and has published numerous articles on the magnitude of risk from exposure to various chemical and biological substances. App. 34–44.

the first trimester of pregnancy has not been shown to be a risk factor for human birth defects.

Petitioners did not (and do not) contest this characterization of the published record regarding Bendectin. Instead, they responded to respondent's motion with the testimony of eight experts of their own, each of whom also possessed impressive credentials.[2] These experts had concluded that Bendectin can cause birth defects. Their conclusions were based upon "in vitro" (test tube) and "in vivo" (live) animal studies that found a link between Bendectin and malformations; pharmacological studies of the chemical structure of Bendectin that purported to show similarities between the structure of the drug and that of other substances known to cause birth defects; and the "reanalysis" of previously published epidemiological (human statistical) studies.

The District Court granted respondent's motion for summary judgment. The court stated that scientific evidence is admissible only if the principle upon which it is based is " 'sufficiently established to have general acceptance in the field to which it belongs.' " 727 F.Supp. 570, 572 (S.D.Cal.1989) (quoting United States v. Kilgus, 571 F.2d 508, 510 (9th Cir. 1978)). The court concluded that petitioners' evidence did not meet this standard. Given the vast body of epidemiological data concerning Bendectin, the court held, expert opinion which is not based on epidemiological evidence is not admissible to establish causation. 727 F.Supp., at 575. Thus, the animal-cell studies, live-animal studies, and chemical-structure analyses on which petitioners had relied could not raise by themselves a reasonably disputable jury issue regarding causation. *Ibid.* Petitioners' epidemiological analyses, based as they were on recalculations of data in previously published studies that had found no causal link between the drug and birth defects, were ruled to be inadmissible because they had not been published or subjected to peer review. *Ibid.*

The United States Court of Appeals for the Ninth Circuit affirmed. 951 F.2d 1128 (1991). Citing Frye v. United States, 293 F. 1013, 1014 (D.C. Cir. 1923), the court stated that expert opinion based on a scientific technique is inadmissible unless the technique is "generally accepted" as reliable in the relevant scientific community. 951 F.2d, at 1129–1130. The court declared that expert opinion based on a methodology that diverges "significantly from the procedures accepted by recognized authorities in the field ... cannot be shown to be 'generally accepted as a reliable technique.' " *Id.*, at 1130, quoting United States v. Solomon, 753 F.2d 1522, 1526 (9th Cir. 1985).

---

2. For example, Shanna Helen Swan, who received a master's degree in biostatics from Columbia University and a doctorate in statistics from the University of California at Berkeley, is chief of the section of the California Department of Health and Services that determines causes of birth defects, and has served as a consultant to the World Health Organization, the Food and Drug Administration, and the National Institutes of Health. App. 113–14, 131–32. Stewart A. Newman, who received his master's and a doctorate in chemistry from Columbia University and the University of Chicago, respectively, is a professor at New York Medical College and has spent over a decade studying the effect of chemicals on limb development. App. 54–56. The credentials of the others are similarly impressive. *See* App. 61–66, 73–80, 148–53, 187–92, and Attachment to Petitioners' Opposition to Summary Judgment, Tabs 12, 20, 21, 26, 31, 32.

The court emphasized that other Courts of Appeals considering the risks of Bendectin had refused to admit reanalyses of epidemiological studies that had been neither published nor subjected to peer review. 951 F.2d, at 1130–31. Those courts had found unpublished reanalyses "particularly problematic in light of the massive weight of the original published studies supporting [respondent's] position, all of which had undergone full scrutiny from the scientific community." *Id.,* at 1130. Contending that reanalysis is generally accepted by the scientific community only when it is subjected to verification and scrutiny by others in the field, the Court of Appeals rejected petitioners' reanalyses as "unpublished, not subjected to the normal peer review process and generated solely for use in litigation." *Id.,* at 1131. The court concluded that petitioners' evidence provided an insufficient foundation to allow admission of expert testimony that Bendectin caused their injuries and, accordingly, that petitioners could not satisfy their burden of proving causation at trial.

We granted certiorari, 506 U.S. 904 (1992), in light of sharp divisions among the courts regarding the proper standard for the admission of expert testimony. Compare, *e.g.,* United States v. Shorter, 809 F.2d 54, 59–60 (D.C. Cir. 1987) (applying the "general acceptance" standard), *cert. denied,* 484 U.S. 817, with DeLuca v. Merrell Dow Pharmaceuticals, Inc., 911 F.2d 941, 955 (3d Cir. 1990) (rejecting the "general acceptance" standard).

II.

A.

In the 70 years since its formulation in the *Frye* case, the "general acceptance" test has been the dominant standard for determining the admissibility of novel scientific evidence at trial. *See* E. GREEN ET AL., CASES, AND MATERIALS ON EVIDENCE 649 (1983). Although under increasing attack of late, the rule continues to be followed by a majority of courts, including the Ninth Circuit.[3]

The *Frye* test has its origin in a short and citation-free 1923 decision concerning the admissibility of evidence derived from a systolic blood pressure deception test, a crude precursor to the polygraph machine. In what has become a famous (perhaps infamous) passage, the then Court of Appeals for the District of Columbia described the device and its operation and declared:

> Just when a scientific principle or discovery crosses the line between the experimental and demonstrable stages is difficult to define. Somewhere in this twilight zone the evidential force of the principle must be recognized, and while courts will go a long way in admitting expert testimony deduced from a well-recognized scientific principle or discovery, *the thing from which the deduction is made must be sufficiently established to have gained general acceptance in the particular field in which it belongs.* 293 F., at 1014 (emphasis added).

Because the deception test had "not yet gained such standing and scientific recognition among physiological and psychological authorities as would

---

3. For a catalogue of the many cases on either side of this controversy, see P. Gianelli & E. Imwinkelried, Scientific Evidence § 1–5, 10–14 (1986 & Supp.1991).

justify the courts in admitting expert testimony deduced from the discovery, development, and experiments thus far made," evidence of its results was ruled inadmissible. *Ibid.*

The merits of the *Frye* test have been much debated, and scholarship on its proper scope and application is legion.[4] Petitioners' primary attack, however, is not on the content but on the continuing authority of the rule. They contend that the *Frye* test was superseded by the adoption of the Federal Rules of Evidence.[5] We agree.

We interpret the legislatively-enacted Federal Rules of Evidence as we would any statute. Beech Aircraft Corp. v. Rainey, 488 U.S. 153, 163 (1988). Rule 402 provides the baseline:

> All relevant evidence is admissible, except as otherwise provided by the Constitution of the United States, by Act of Congress, by these rules, or by other rules prescribed by the Supreme Court pursuant to statutory authority. Evidence which is not relevant is not admissible.

"Relevant evidence" is defined as that which has "any tendency to make the existence of any fact that is of consequence to the determination of the action more probable or less probable than it would be without the evidence." Rule 401. The Rule's basic standard of relevance thus is a liberal one.

Frye, of course, predated the Rules by half a century. In United States v. Abel, 469 U.S. 45 (1984), we considered the pertinence of background common law in interpreting the Rules of Evidence. We noted that the Rules occupy the field, *id.,* at 49, but, quoting Professor Cleary, the Reporter, explained that the common law nevertheless could serve as an aid to their application:

> In principle, under the Federal Rules no common law of evidence remains. "All relevant evidence is admissible, except as otherwise provided. . . ." In reality, of course, the body of common law knowledge continues to exist,

4. *See, e.g.,* Green, *Expert Witnesses and Sufficiency of Evidence in Toxic Substances Litigation: The Legacy of Agent Orange and Bendectin Litigation,* 86 Nw. U.L.Rev. 643 (1992) (hereinafter Green); Becker & Orenstein, *The Federal Rules of Evidence After Sixteen Years—the Effect of "Plain Meaning" Jurisprudence, the Need for an Advisory Committee on the Rules of Evidence, and Suggestions for Selective Revision of the Rules,* 60 Geo.Wash.L.Rev. 857, 876–85 (1992); Hanson, James *Alphonso Frye is Sixty–Five Years Old; Should He Retire?,* 16 W.St.U.L.Rev. 357 (1989); Black, *A Unified Theory of Scientific Evidence,* 56 Ford.L.Rev. 595 (1988); Imwinkelried, *The "Bases" of Expert Testimony: The Syllogistic Structure of Scientific Testimony,* 67 N.C.L.Rev. 1 (1988); *Proposals for a Model Rule on the Admissibility of Scientific Evidence,* 26 Jurimetrics J. 235 (1986); Gianelli, *The Admissibility of Novel Scientific Evidence: Frye v.*

United States, A Half–Century Later, 80 Colum.L.Rev. 1197 (1980), *The Supreme Court, 1986 Term,* 101 Harv.L.Rev. 7, 119, 125–127 (1987).

5. Like the question of *Frye*'s merit, the dispute over its survival has divided courts and commentators. Compare, *e.g.,* United States v. Williams, 583 F.2d 1194 (2d Cir. 1978), *cert. denied,* 439 U.S. 1117 (1979) (*Frye* is superseded by the Rules of Evidence), with Christopherson v. Allied–Signal Corp., 939 F.2d 1106, 1111, 1115–16 (5th Cir. 1991) (en banc) (*Frye* and the Rules coexist), *cert. denied,* 503 U.S. 912 (1992), 3 J. Weinstein & M. Berger, Weinstein's Evidence, 702–36 to 702–37 (1988) (hereinafter Weinstein & Berger) (*Frye* is dead), and M. Graham, Handbook of Federal Evidence § 703.2 (2d ed. 1991) (*Frye* lives). *See generally* P. Gianelli & E. Imwinkelried, Scientific Evidence § 1–5, 28–29 (1986 & Supp.1991) (citing authorities).

though in the somewhat altered form of a source of guidance in the exercise of delegated powers. *Id., at* 51–52.

We found the common-law precept at issue in the *Abel* case entirely consistent with Rule 402's general requirement of admissibility, and considered it unlikely that the drafters had intended to change the rule. *Id., at* 50–51. In Bourjaily v. United States, 483 U.S. 171 (1987), on the other hand, the Court was unable to find a particular common-law doctrine in the Rules, and so held it superseded.

Here there is a specific Rule that speaks to the contested issue. Rule 702, governing expert testimony, provides:

> If scientific, technical, or other specialized knowledge will assist the trier of fact to understand the evidence or to determine a fact in issue, a witness qualified as an expert by knowledge, skill, experience, training, or education, may testify thereto in the form of an opinion or otherwise.

Nothing in the text of this Rule establishes "general acceptance" as an absolute prerequisite to admissibility. Nor does respondent present any clear indication that Rule 702 or the Rules as a whole were intended to incorporate a "general acceptance" standard. The drafting history makes no mention of *Frye*, and a rigid "general acceptance" requirement would be at odds with the "liberal thrust" of the Federal Rules and their "general approach of relaxing the traditional barriers to 'opinion' testimony." *Beech Aircraft Corp.,* 488 U.S., at 169 (citing Rules 701 to 705). *See also* Weinstein, *Rule 702 of the Federal Rules of Evidence is Sound; It Should Not Be Amended,* 138 F.R.D. 631, 631 (1991) ("The Rules were designed to depend primarily upon lawyer-adversaries and sensible triers of fact to evaluate conflicts"). Given the Rules' permissive backdrop and their inclusion of a specific rule on expert testimony that does not mention "general acceptance," the assertion that the Rules somehow assimilated *Frye* is unconvincing. *Frye* made "general acceptance" the exclusive test for admitting expert scientific testimony. That austere standard, absent from and incompatible with the Federal Rules of Evidence, should not be applied in federal trials.[6]

B.

That the *Frye* test was displaced by the Rules of Evidence does not mean, however, that the Rules themselves place no limits on the admissibility of purportedly scientific evidence.[7] Nor is the trial judge disabled from screening such evidence. To the contrary, under the Rules the trial judge must ensure that any and all scientific testimony or evidence admitted is not only relevant, but reliable.

---

6. Because we hold that *Frye* has been superseded and base the discussion that follows on the content of the congressionally-enacted Federal Rules of Evidence, we do not address petitioners' argument that application of the *Frye* rule in this diversity case, as the application of a judge made rule affecting substantive rights, would violate the doctrine of Erie R. Co. v. Tompkins, 304 U.S. 64 (1938).

7. The CHIEF JUSTICE "do[es] not doubt that Rule 702 confides to the judge some gatekeeping responsibility," *post,* at 2800, but would neither say how it does so, nor explain what that role entails. We believe the better course is to note the nature and source of the duty.

The primary locus of this obligation is Rule 702, which clearly contemplates some degree of regulation of the subjects and theories about which an expert may testify. *"If scientific,* technical, or other specialized *knowledge will assist the trier of fact* to understand the evidence or to determine a fact in issue" an expert "may testify *thereto.*" The subject of an expert's testimony must be "scientific . . . knowledge."[8] The adjective "scientific" implies a grounding in the methods and procedures of science. Similarly, the word "knowledge" connotes more than subjective belief or unsupported speculation. The term "applies to any body of known facts or to any body of ideas inferred from such facts or accepted as truths on good grounds." Webster's Third New International Dictionary 1252 (1986). Of course, it would be unreasonable to conclude that the subject of scientific testimony must be "known" to a certainty; arguably, there are no certainties in science. See, *e.g.,* Brief for Nicolaas Bloembergen et al. as *Amici Curiae* 9 ("Indeed, scientists do not assert that they know what is immutably 'true'—they are committed to searching for new, temporary theories to explain, as best they can, phenomena"); Brief for American Association for the Advancement of Science and the National Academy of Sciences as *Amici Curiae* 7–8 ("Science is not an encyclopedic body of knowledge about the universe. Instead, it represents a *process* for proposing and refining theoretical explanations about the world that are subject to further testing and refinement") (emphasis in original). But, in order to qualify as "scientific knowledge," an inference or assertion must be derived by the scientific method. Proposed testimony must be supported by appropriate validation— *i.e.,* "good grounds," based on what is known. In short, the requirement that an expert's testimony pertain to "scientific knowledge" establishes a standard of evidentiary reliability.[9]

Rule 702 further requires that the evidence or testimony "assist the trier of fact to understand the evidence or to determine a fact in issue." This condition goes primarily to relevance. "Expert testimony which does not relate to any issue in the case is not relevant and, ergo, non-helpful." 3 WEINSTEIN & BERGER, 702–18. *See also* United States v. Downing, 753 F.2d 1224, 1242 (3d Cir. 1985) ("An additional consideration under Rule 702—

---

8. Rule 702 also applies to "technical, or other specialized knowledge." Our discussion is limited to the scientific context because that is the nature of the expertise offered here.

9. We note that scientists typically distinguish between "validity" (does the principle support what it purports to show?) and "reliability" (does application of the principle produce consistent results?). *See* Black, *A Unified Theory of Scientific Evidence,* 56 FORD.L.REV. 595, 599 (1988). Although "the difference between accuracy, validity, and reliability may be such that each is distinct from the other by no more than a hen's kick," Starrs, *Frye v. United States Restructured and Revitalized: A Proposal to Amend Federal Evidence Rule 702,* 26 JURIMETRICS J. 249, 256 (1986), our reference here is to

evidentiary reliability—that is, trustworthiness. Cf., *e.g.,* Advisory Committee's Notes on Fed. Rule Evid. 602 (" '[T]he rule requiring that a witness who testifies to a fact which can be perceived by the senses must have had an opportunity to observe, and must have actually observed the fact' is a 'most pervasive manifestation' of the common law insistence upon 'the most reliable sources of information.' " (citation omitted)); Advisory Committee's Notes on Art. VIII of the Rules of Evidence (hearsay exceptions will be recognized only "under circumstances supposed to furnish guarantees of trustworthiness"). In a case involving scientific evidence, *evidentiary reliability* will be based upon *scientific validity.*

and another aspect of relevancy—is whether expert testimony proffered in the case is sufficiently tied to the facts of the case that it will aid the jury in resolving a factual dispute"). The consideration has been aptly described by Judge Becker as one of "fit." *Ibid.* "Fit" is not always obvious, and scientific validity for one purpose is not necessarily scientific validity for other, unrelated purposes. *See* Starrs, *Frye v. United States Restructured and Revitalized: A Proposal to Amend Federal Evidence Rule 702,* 26 JURIMETRICS J. 249, 258 (1986). The study of the phases of the moon, for example, may provide valid scientific "knowledge" about whether a certain night was dark, and if darkness is a fact in issue, the knowledge will assist the trier of fact. However (absent creatable grounds supporting such a link), evidence that the moon was full on a certain night will not assist the trier of fact in determining whether an individual was unusually likely to have behaved irrationally on that night. Rule 702's "helpfulness" standard requires a valid scientific connection to the pertinent inquiry as a precondition to admissibility.

That these requirements are embodied in Rule 702 is not surprising. Unlike an ordinary witness, see Rule 701, an expert is permitted wide latitude to offer opinions, including those that are not based on first-hand knowledge or observation. *See* Rules 702 and 703. Presumably, this relaxation of the usual requirement of first-hand knowledge—a rule which represents "a 'most pervasive manifestation' of the common law insistence upon 'the most reliable sources of information,' " Advisory Committee's Notes on Fed.Rule Evid. 602 (citation omitted)—is premised on an assumption that the expert's opinion will have a reliable basis in the knowledge and experience of his discipline.

C.

Faced with a proffer of expert scientific testimony, then, the trial judge must determine at the outset, pursuant to Rule 104(a),[10] whether the expert is proposing to testify to (1) scientific knowledge that (2) will assist the trier of fact to understand or determine a fact in issue.[11] This entails a preliminary assessment of whether the reasoning or methodology underlying the testimony is scientifically valid and of whether that reasoning or methodology properly can be applied to the facts in issue. We are confident that federal judges possess the capacity to undertake this review. Many

---

10. Rule 104(a) provides:

"Preliminary questions concerning the qualification of a person to be a witness, the existence of a privilege, or the admissibility of evidence shall be determined by the court, subject to the provisions of subdivision (b) [pertaining to conditional admissions]. In making its determination it is not bound by the rules of evidence except those with respect to privileges." These matters should be established by a preponderance of proof. *See* Bourjaily v. United States, 483 U.S. 171, 175–76 (1987).

11. Although the *Frye* decision itself focused exclusively on "novel" scientific techniques, we do not read the requirements of Rule 702 to apply specially or exclusively to unconventional evidence. Of course, well-established propositions are less likely to be challenged than those that are novel, and they are more handily defended. Indeed, theories that are so firmly established as to have attained the status of scientific law, such as the laws of thermodynamics, properly are subject to judicial notice under Fed.Rule Evid. 201.

factors will bear on the inquiry, and we do not presume to set out a definitive checklist or test. But some general observations are appropriate.

Ordinarily, a key question to be answered in determining whether a theory or technique is scientific knowledge that will assist the trier of fact will be whether it can be (and has been) tested. "Scientific methodology today is based on generating hypotheses and testing them to see if they can be falsified; indeed, this methodology is what distinguishes science from other fields of human inquiry." Green, at 645. *See also* C. HEMPEL, PHILOSOPHY OF NATURAL SCIENCE, 49 (1966) ("[T]he statements constituting a scientific explanation must be capable of empirical test"); K. POPPER, CONJECTURES AND REFUTATIONS: THE GROWTH OF SCIENTIFIC KNOWLEDGE, 37 (5th ed. 1989) ("[T]he criterion of the scientific status of a theory is its falsifiability, or refutability, or testability").

Another pertinent consideration is whether the theory or technique has been subjected to peer review and publication. Publication (which is but one element of peer review) is not a *sine qua non* of admissibility; it does not necessarily correlate with reliability, *see* S. JASANOFF, THE FIFTH BRANCH: SCIENCE ADVISORS AS POLICYMAKERS, 61–76 (1990), and in some instances well-grounded but innovative theories will not have been published, *see* Horrobin, *The Philosophical Basis of Peer Review and the Suppression of Innovation*, 263 J.AM.MED.ASSN. 1438 (1990). Some propositions, moreover, are too particular, too new, or of too limited interest to be published. But submission to the scrutiny of the scientific community is a component of "good science," in part because it increases the likelihood that substantive flaws in methodology will be detected. *See* J. ZIMAN, RELIABLE KNOWLEDGE: AN EXPLORATION OF THE GROUNDS FOR BELIEF IN SCIENCE, 130–33 (1978); Relman & Angell, *How Good Is Peer Review?*, 321 NEW ENG.J.MED. 827 (1989). The fact of publication (or lack thereof) in a peer-reviewed journal thus will be a relevant, though not dispositive, consideration in assessing the scientific validity of a particular technique or methodology on which an opinion is premised.

Additionally, in the case of a particular scientific technique, the court ordinarily should consider the known or potential rate of error, *see, e.g.,* United States v. Smith, 869 F.2d 348, 353–54 (7th Cir. 1989) (surveying studies of the error rate of spectrographic voice identification technique), and the existence and maintenance of standards controlling the technique's operation. *See* United States v. Williams, 583 F.2d 1194, 1198 (2d Cir. 1978) (noting professional organization's standard governing spectrographic analysis), *cert. denied*, 439 U.S. 1117 (1979).

Finally, "general acceptance" can yet have a bearing on the inquiry. A "reliability assessment does not require, although it does permit, explicit identification of a relevant scientific community and an express determination of a particular degree of acceptance within that community." United States v. Downing, 753 F.2d, at 1238. *See also* WEINTSTEIN & BERGER, 702–41 to 702–42. Widespread acceptance can be an important factor in ruling particular evidence admissible, and "a known technique that has been able to attract only minimal support within the community," Downing, *supra*, at 1238, may properly be viewed with skepticism.

The inquiry envisioned by Rule 702 is, we emphasize, a flexible one.[12] Its overarching subject is the scientific validity—and thus the evidentiary relevance and reliability—of the principles that underlie a proposed submission. The focus, of course, must be solely on principles and methodology, not on the conclusions that they generate.

Throughout, a judge assessing a proffer of expert scientific testimony under Rule 702 should also be mindful of other applicable rules. Rule 703 provides that expert opinions based on otherwise inadmissible hearsay are to be admitted only if the facts or data are "of a type reasonably relied upon by experts in the particular field in forming opinions or inferences upon the subject." Rule 706 allows the court at its discretion to procure the assistance of an expert of its own choosing. Finally, Rule 403 permits the exclusion of relevant evidence "if its probative value is substantially outweighed by the danger of unfair prejudice, confusion of the issues, or misleading the jury...." Judge Weinstein has explained: "Expert evidence can be both powerful and quite misleading because of the difficulty in evaluating it. Because of this risk, the judge in weighing possible prejudice against probative force under Rule 403 of the present rules exercises more control over experts than over lay witnesses." Weinstein, 138 F.R.D., at 632.

III.

We conclude by briefly addressing what appear to be two underlying concerns of the parties and *amici* in this case. Respondent expresses apprehension that abandonment of "general acceptance" as the exclusive requirement for admission will result in a "free-for-all" in which befuddled juries are confounded by absurd and irrational pseudoscientific assertions. In this regard respondent seems to us to be overly pessimistic about the capabilities of the jury, and of the adversary system generally. Vigorous cross-examination, presentation of contrary evidence, and careful instruction on the burden of proof are the traditional and appropriate means of attacking shaky but admissible evidence. *See* Rock v. Arkansas, 483 U.S. 44, 61 (1987). Additionally, in the event the trial court concludes that the scintilla of evidence presented supporting a position is insufficient to allow a reasonable juror to conclude that the position more likely than not is true, the court remains free to direct a judgment, Fed.Rule Civ.Proc. 50(a), and likewise to grant summary judgment, Fed.Rule Civ.Proc. 56. *Cf., e.g.,* Turpin v. Merrell Dow Pharmaceuticals, Inc., 959 F.2d 1349 (6th Cir. 1992) (holding that scientific evidence that provided foundation for expert testimony, viewed in the light most favorable to plaintiffs, was not sufficient to allow a jury to find it more probable than not that defendant caused

---

12. A number of authorities have presented variations on the reliability approach, each with its own slightly different set of factors. *See, e.g., Downing,* 753 F.2d at 1238–39 (on which our discussion draws in part); WEINSTEIN & BERGER, 702–41 to 702–42 (on which the *Downing* court in turn partially relied); McCormick, *Scientific Evidence: Defining a New Approach to Admissibility,* 67 IOWA L.REV. 879, 911–12 (1982); and *Symposium on Science and the Rules of Evidence,* 99 F.R.D. 187, 231 (1983) (statement by Margaret Berger). To the extent that they focus on the reliability of evidence as ensured by the scientific validity of its underlying principles, all these versions may well have merit, although we express no opinion regarding any of their particular details.

plaintiff's injury), *cert. denied*, 506 U.S. 826; Brock v. Merrell Dow Pharmaceuticals, Inc., 874 F.2d 307 (5th Cir. 1989) (reversing judgment entered on jury verdict for plaintiffs because evidence regarding causation was insufficient), *modified*, 884 F.2d 166 (5th Cir. 1989), *cert. denied*, 494 U.S. 1046; Green 680–81. These conventional devices, rather than wholesale exclusion under an uncompromising "general acceptance" test, are the appropriate safeguards where the basis of scientific testimony meets the standards of Rule 702.

Petitioners and, to a greater extent, their *amici* exhibit a different concern. They suggest that recognition of a screening role for the judge that allows for the exclusion of "invalid" evidence will sanction a stifling and repressive scientific orthodoxy and will be inimical to the search for truth. *See, e.g.,* Brief for Ronald Bayer et al. as *Amici Curiae*. It is true that open debate is an essential part of both legal and scientific analyses. Yet there are important differences between the quest for truth in the courtroom and the quest for truth in the laboratory. Scientific conclusions are subject to perpetual revision. Law, on the other hand, must resolve disputes finally and quickly. The scientific project is advanced by broad and wide-ranging consideration of a multitude of hypotheses, for those that are incorrect will eventually be shown to be so, and that in itself is an advance. Conjectures that are probably wrong are of little use, however, in the project of reaching a quick, final, and binding legal judgment—often of great consequence—about a particular set of events in the past. We recognize that in practice, a gatekeeping role for the judge, no matter how flexible, inevitably on occasion will prevent the jury from learning of authentic insights and innovations. That, nevertheless, is the balance that is struck by Rules of Evidence designed not for the exhaustive search for cosmic understanding but for the particularized resolution of legal disputes.[13]

IV.

To summarize: "general acceptance" is not a necessary precondition to the admissibility of scientific evidence under the Federal Rules of Evidence, but the Rules of Evidence—especially Rule 702—do assign to the trial judge the task of ensuring that an expert's testimony both rests on a reliable foundation and is relevant to the task at hand. Pertinent evidence based on scientifically valid principles will satisfy those demands.

The inquiries of the District Court and the Court of Appeals focused almost exclusively on "general acceptance," as gauged by publication and the decisions of other courts. Accordingly, the judgment of the Court of Appeals is vacated and the case is remanded for further proceedings consistent with this opinion.

It is so ordered.

---

13. This is not to say that judicial interpretation, as opposed to adjudicative fact-finding, does not share basic characteristics of the scientific endeavor: "The work of a judge is in one sense enduring and in another ephemeral.... In the endless process of testing and retesting, there is a constant rejection of the dross and a constant retention of whatever is pure and sound and fine." B. CARDOZO, THE NATURE OF THE JUDICIAL PROCESS, 178, 179 (1921).

■ CHIEF JUSTICE REHNQUIST, with whom JUSTICE STEVENS joins, concurring in part and dissenting in part.

The petition for certiorari in this case presents two questions: first, whether the rule of *Frye v. United States,* 293 F. 1013 (D.C. Cir. 1923), remains good law after the enactment of the Federal Rules of Evidence; and second, if *Frye* remains valid, whether it requires expert scientific testimony to have been subjected to a peer-review process in order to be admissible. The Court concludes, correctly in my view, that the *Frye* rule did not survive the enactment of the Federal Rules of Evidence, and I therefore join Parts I and II–A of its opinion. The second question presented in the petition for certiorari necessarily is mooted by this holding, but the Court nonetheless proceeds to construe Rules 702 and 703 very much in the abstract, and then offers some "general observations."

"General observations" by this Court customarily carry great weight with lower federal courts, but the ones offered here suffer from the flaw common to most such observations—they are not applied to deciding whether or not particular testimony was or was not admissible, and therefore they tend to be not only general, but vague and abstract. This is particularly unfortunate in a case such as this, where the ultimate legal question depends on an appreciation of one or more bodies of knowledge not judicially noticeable, and subject to different interpretations in the briefs of the parties and their *amici.* Twenty-two *amicus* briefs have been filed in the case, and indeed the Court's opinion contains no less than 37 citations to *amicus* briefs and other secondary sources.

The various briefs filed in this case are markedly different from typical briefs, in that large parts of them do not deal with decided cases or statutory language—the sort of material we customarily interpret. Instead, they deal with definitions of scientific knowledge, scientific method, scientific validity, and peer review—in short, matters far afield from the expertise of judges. This is not to say that such materials are not useful or even necessary in deciding how Rule 703 should be applied; but it is to say that the unusual subject matter should cause us to proceed with great caution in deciding more than we have to, because our reach can so easily exceed our grasp.

But even if it were desirable to make "general observations" not necessary to decide the questions presented, I cannot subscribe to some of the observations made by the Court. In Part II–B, the Court concludes that reliability and relevancy are the touchstones of the admissibility of expert testimony. Federal Rule of Evidence 402 provides, as the Court points out, that "[e]vidence which is not relevant is not admissible." But there is no similar reference in the Rule to "reliability." The Court constructs its argument by parsing the language "[i]f scientific, technical, or other specialized knowledge will assist the trier of fact to understand the evidence or to determine a fact in issue ... an expert ... may testify thereto...." Fed.Rule Evid. 702. It stresses that the subject of the expert's testimony must be "scientific ... knowledge," and points out that "scientific" "implies a grounding in the methods and procedures of science," and that the word "knowledge" "connotes more than subjective belief or unsupported speculation." From this it concludes that "scientific knowledge" must be "derived by the scientific method." Proposed testimony, we are told, must be supported by "appropriate validation." Indeed, in footnote 9, the Court decides that "[i]n a case involving scientific evidence, *evidentiary reliability* will be based upon *scientific validity." Ibid.,* n. 9 (emphasis in original).

Questions arise simply from reading this part of the Court's opinion, and countless more questions will surely arise when hundreds of district judges try to apply its teaching to particular offers of expert testimony. Does all of this *dicta* apply to an expert seeking to testify on the basis of "technical or other specialized knowledge"—the other types of expert knowledge to which Rule 702 applies—or are the "general observations" limited only to "scientific knowledge"? What is the difference between scientific knowledge and technical knowledge; does Rule 702 actually contemplate that the phrase "scientific, technical, or other specialized knowledge" be broken down into numerous subspecies of expertise, or did its authors simply pick general descriptive language covering the sort of expert testimony which courts have customarily received? The Court speaks of its confidence that federal judges can make a "preliminary assessment of whether the reasoning or methodology underlying the testimony is scientifically valid and of whether that reasoning or methodology properly can be applied to the facts in issue." The Court then states that a "key question" to be answered in deciding whether something is "scientific knowledge" "will be whether it can be (and has been) tested." Following this sentence are three quotations from treatises, which speak not only of empirical testing, but one of which states that "the criterion of the scientific status of a theory is its falsifiability, or refutability, or testability."

I defer to no one in my confidence in federal judges; but I am at a loss to know what is meant when it is said that the scientific status of a theory depends on its "falsifiability," and I suspect some of them will be, too.

I do not doubt that Rule 702 confides to the judge some gate-keeping responsibility in deciding questions of the admissibility of proffered expert testimony. But I do not think it imposes on them either the obligation or the authority to become amateur scientists in order to perform that role. I think the Court would be far better advised in this case to decide only the questions presented, and to leave the further development of this important area of the law to future cases.

NOTES AND QUESTIONS

1. The Supreme Court's consideration of the *Daubert* case attracted enormous interest. Not only was the continued vitality of *Frye* a matter of controversy, but there was a growing concern on the part of some that federal courts had begun to allow juries to hear too much unreliable "junk science." *See* PETER HUBER, GALILEO'S REVENGE: JUNK SCIENCE IN THE COURTROOM (1991).

2. Scientists filed *amicus* briefs on both sides in *Daubert.* Their arguments largely tracked the concerns of the parties, and, to a considerable extent, focused on the role of the judge as a "gatekeeper" who decides what the jury is allowed to hear. To some scientists, a strong gatekeeper is needed so that juries will not be misled; to others, science that is not accepted by mainstream scientists might nonetheless be valid and should be considered by the jury. Neither theory, of course, perfectly fits the trial context: if a strong gatekeeper of valid science is needed, it is not clear a judge is the right choice, and if a decision has to be made about the validity of an unconventional theory, it is far from obvious that a lay jury is the best group to make it. In the end, the Court rejected both extremes and laid down very general guidelines under which judges exercise some control over what juries hear. The *Daubert* decision was such that after it was announced, lawyers for both sides claimed victory. Paul Houston, *High Court Relaxes Curbs on Expert Witness Testimony*, L.A. TIMES, June 29, 1993, at A14.

3. The court compromised as well on the subordinate question of the relevance of peer review, holding that publication in a peer reviewed journal is relevant but not dispositive on the issue of admissibility. We have discussed the use of peer review in determining who receives research grants, see Sec. II. B.3, *supra*. As we noted there, the use of peer review by scientific publications is similar—technical journals send submitted articles to leading figures in the field who make recommendations on whether the piece should be published. Peer review is a central mechanism through which the scientific community determines what is good science; indeed, peer review has been called "a mirror of science." STEPHEN LOCK, A DIFFICULT BALANCE: EDITORIAL PEER REVIEW IN MEDICINE, 4 (1985). But the Court maintains that the goals and needs of a trial are not identical to those of the scientific community. Do you agree?

4. The general nature of the Court's analysis of admissibility in *Daubert* has left much room for commentary. For an argument that *Daubert* can be interpreted to "require a deeper and more detailed preliminary review of scientific claims than most courts have theretofore undertaken," see Bert Black, Francisco J. Ayala & Carol Saffran–Brinks, *Science and the Law in the Wake of Daubert: A New Search for Scientific Knowledge*, 72 TEX. L. REV. 715, 721 (1994). For an argument that a restrictive reading of *Daubert* is questionable and that restrictive admissibility standards are ill-advised, see Joseph Sanders, *Scientific Validity, Admissibility, and Mass Torts After Daubert*, 78 MINN. L. REV. 1387 (1994). Beyond the law reviews, there is a rich commentary on *Daubert* on the law and science literature. *See, e.g.,* SHEILA JASANOFF, SCIENCE AT THE BAR: LAW, SCIENCE, AND TECHNOLOGY IN AMERICA, 62–68 (1995); DAVID L. FAIGMAN, LEGAL ALCHEMY: THE USE AND MISUSE OF SCIENCE IN THE LAW, 60–66 (1999); SUSAN HAACK, DEFENDING SCIENCE—WITHIN REASON: BETWEEN SCIENTISM AND CYNICISM, 240–44 (2003).

In the years following *Daubert*, the Supreme Court followed up with the following two decisions, creating the *Daubert* trilogy that now dominates all discussions of the admissibility of technical evidence in federal court.

General Electric Company v. Joiner

Supreme Court of the United States, 1997.
522 U.S. 136, 118 S.Ct. 512, 139 L.Ed.2d 508.

■ CHIEF JUSTICE REHNQUIST delivered the opinion of the Court.

We granted certiorari in this case to determine what standard an appellate court should apply in reviewing a trial court's decision to admit or exclude expert testimony under *Daubert v. Merrell Dow Pharmaceuticals, Inc.*, 509 U.S. 579 (1993). We hold that abuse of discretion is the appropriate standard. We apply this standard and conclude that the District Court in this case did not abuse its discretion when it excluded certain proffered expert testimony.

I.

Respondent Robert Joiner began work as an electrician in the Water & Light Department of Thomasville, Georgia (City), in 1973. This job required him to work with and around the City's electrical transformers, which used a mineral-oil-based dielectric fluid as a coolant. Joiner often had to stick his hands and arms into the fluid to make repairs. The fluid would sometimes splash onto him, occasionally getting into his eyes and mouth. In 1983 the City discovered that the fluid in some of the transformers was contaminated with polychlorinated biphenyls (PCB's). PCB's are widely considered to be hazardous to human health. Congress, with limited exceptions, banned the production and sale of PCB's in 1978. *See* 90 Stat.2020, 15 U.S.C. § 2605(e)(2)(A).

Joiner was diagnosed with small-cell lung cancer in 1991. He sued petitioners in Georgia state court the following year. Petitioner Monsanto manufactured PCB's from 1935 to 1977; petitioners General Electric and Westinghouse Electric manufactured transformers and dielectric fluid. In his complaint Joiner linked his development of cancer to his exposure to PCB's and their derivatives, polychlorinated dibenzofurans (furans) and polychlorinated dibenzodioxins (dioxins). Joiner had been a smoker for approximately eight years, his parents had both been smokers, and there was a history of lung cancer in his family. He was thus perhaps already at a heightened risk of developing lung cancer eventually. The suit alleged that his exposure to PCB's "promoted" his cancer; had it not been for his exposure to these substances, his cancer would not have developed for many years, if at all.

Petitioners removed the case to federal court. Once there, they moved for summary judgment. They contended that (1) there was no evidence that Joiner suffered significant exposure to PCB's, furans, or dioxins, and (2) there was no admissible scientific evidence that PCB's promoted Joiner's cancer. Joiner responded that there were numerous disputed factual issues that required resolution by a jury. He relied largely on the testimony of expert witnesses. In depositions, his experts had testified that PCB's alone can promote cancer and that furans and dioxins can also promote cancer. They opined that since Joiner had been exposed to PCB's, furans, and dioxins, such exposure was likely responsible for Joiner's cancer.

The District Court ruled that there was a genuine issue of material fact as to whether Joiner had been exposed to PCB's. But it nevertheless granted summary judgment for petitioners because (1) there was no genuine issue as to whether Joiner had been exposed to furans and dioxins, and (2) the testimony of Joiner's experts had failed to show that there was a link between exposure to PCB's and small-cell lung cancer. The court believed that the testimony of respondent's experts to the contrary did not rise above "subjective belief or unsupported speculation." 864 F. Supp. 1310, 1326 (N.D.Ga.1994). Their testimony was therefore inadmissible. The Court of Appeals for the Eleventh Circuit reversed. 78 F.3d 524 (1996). It held that "[b]ecause the Federal Rules of Evidence governing expert testimony display a preference for admissibility, we apply a particularly stringent standard of review to the trial judge's exclusion of expert testimony." *Id.*, at 529. Applying that standard, the Court of Appeals held that the District Court had erred in excluding the testimony of Joiner's expert witnesses. The District Court had made two fundamental errors. First, it excluded the experts' testimony because it "drew different conclusions from the research than did each of the experts." The Court of Appeals opined that a district court should limit its role to determining the "legal reliability of proffered expert testimony, leaving the jury to decide the correctness of competing expert opinions." *Id.* at 533. Second, the District Court had held that there was no genuine issue of material fact as to whether Joiner had been exposed to furans and dioxins. This was also incorrect, said the Court of Appeals, because testimony in the record supported the proposition that there had been such exposure.

We granted petitioners' petition for a writ of certiorari, 520 U.S. 1114 (1997), and we now reverse.

II.

Petitioners challenge the standard applied by the Court of Appeals in reviewing the District Court's decision to exclude respondent's experts' proffered testimony. They argue that that court should have applied traditional "abuse-of-discretion" review. Respondent agrees that abuse of discretion is the correct standard of review. He contends, however, that the Court of Appeals applied an abuse-of-discretion standard in this case. As he reads it, the phrase "particularly stringent" announced no new standard of review. It was simply an acknowledgment that an appellate court can and will devote more resources to analyzing district court decisions that are dispositive of the entire litigation. All evidentiary decisions are reviewed under an abuse-of-discretion standard. He argues, however, that it is perfectly reasonable for appellate courts to give particular attention to those decisions that are outcome determinative.

We have held that abuse of discretion is the proper standard of review of a district court's evidentiary rulings. Old Chief v. United States, 519 U.S. 172, 174 n. 1 (1997); United States v. Abel, 469 U.S. 45, 54 (1984). Indeed, our cases on the subject go back as far as *Spring Co. v. Edgar*, 99 U.S. 645, 658 (1879), where we said that "[c]ases arise where it is very much a matter of discretion with the court whether to receive or exclude the evidence; but the appellate court will not reverse in such a case, unless the ruling is manifestly erroneous." The Court of Appeals suggested that *Daubert* somehow altered this general rule in the context of a district court's decision to exclude scientific evidence. But *Daubert* did not address the standard of appellate review for evidentiary rulings at all. It did hold that the "austere" *Frye* standard of "general acceptance" had not been carried over into the Federal Rules of Evidence. But the opinion also said:

> That the *Frye* test was displaced by the Rules of Evidence does not mean, however, that the Rules themselves place no limits on the admissibility of purportedly scientific evidence. Nor is the trial judge disabled from screening such evidence. To the contrary, under the Rules the trial judge must ensure that any and all scientific testimony or evidence admitted is not only relevant, but reliable. 509 U.S., at 589 (footnote omitted).

Thus, while the Federal Rules of Evidence allow district courts to admit a somewhat broader range of scientific testimony than would have been admissible under *Frye,* they leave in place the "gatekeeper" role of the trial judge in screening such evidence. A court of appeals applying "abuse-of-discretion" review to such rulings may not categorically distinguish between rulings allowing expert testimony and rulings disallowing it. *Compare* Beech Aircraft Corp. v. Rainey, 488 U.S. 153, 172 (1988) (applying abuse-of-discretion review to a lower court's decision to exclude evidence), *with* United States v. Abel, 469 U.S. at 54 (applying abuse-of-discretion review to a lower court's decision to admit evidence). We likewise reject respondent's argument that because the granting of summary judgment in this case was "outcome determinative," it should have been subjected to a more searching standard of review. On a motion for summary judgment, disputed issues of fact are resolved against the moving party-here, petitioners. But the question of admissibility of expert testimony is not such an issue of fact, and is reviewable under the abuse-of-discretion standard.

We hold that the Court of Appeals erred in its review of the exclusion of Joiner's experts' testimony. In applying an overly "stringent" review to that ruling, it failed to give the trial court the deference that is the hallmark of abuse-of-discretion review. *See, e.g.,* Koon v. United States, 518 U.S. 81, 98–99 (1996).

III.

We believe that a proper application of the correct standard of review here indicates that the District Court did not abuse its discretion. Joiner's theory of liability was that his exposure to PCB's and their derivatives "promoted" his development of small-cell lung cancer. In support of that theory he proffered the deposition testimony of expert witnesses. Dr. Arnold Schecter testified that he believed it "more likely than not that Mr. Joiner's lung cancer was causally linked to cigarette smoking and PCB exposure." App. 107. Dr. Daniel Teitelbaum testified that Joiner's "lung cancer was caused by or contributed to in a significant degree by the materials with which he worked." *Id.,* at 140.

Petitioners contended that the statements of Joiner's experts regarding causation were nothing more than speculation. Petitioners criticized the testimony of the experts in that it was "not supported by epidemiological studies ... [and was] based exclusively on isolated studies of laboratory animals." 3 Record, Doc. No. 46 (Defendants' Joint Memorandum in Support of Summary Judgment 3). Joiner responded by claiming that his experts had identified "relevant animal studies which support their opinions." 4 Record, Doc. No. 53 (Plaintiffs' Brief in Opposition to Defendants' Motion for Summary Judgment 47). He also directed the court's attention to four epidemiological studies on which his experts had relied.

The District Court agreed with petitioners that the animal studies on which respondent's experts relied did not support his contention that exposure to PCB's had contributed to his cancer. The studies involved infant mice that had developed cancer after being exposed to PCB's. The infant mice in the studies had had massive doses of PCB's injected directly into their peritoneums or stomachs. Joiner was an adult human being whose alleged exposure to PCB's was far less than the exposure in the animal studies. The PCB's were injected into the mice in a highly concentrated form. The fluid with which Joiner had come into contact generally had a much smaller PCB concentration of between 0–to–500 parts per million. The cancer that these mice developed was alveologenic adenomas; Joiner had developed small-cell carcinomas. No study demonstrated that adult mice developed cancer after being exposed to PCB's. One of the experts admitted that no study had demonstrated that PCB's lead to cancer in any other species.

Respondent failed to reply to this criticism. Rather than explaining how and why the experts could have extrapolated their opinions from these seemingly far-removed animal studies, respondent chose "to proceed as if the only issue [was] whether animal studies can ever be a proper foundation for an expert'sopinion." 864 F. Supp., at 1324. Of course, whether animal studies can ever be a proper foundation for an expert's opinion was not the issue. The issue was whether *these* experts' opinions were sufficiently supported by the animal studies on which they purported to rely. The studies were so dissimilar to the facts presented in this litigation that it was not an abuse of discretion for the District Court to have rejected the experts' reliance on them.

The District Court also concluded that the four epidemiological studies on which respondent relied were not a sufficient basis for the experts' opinions. The first such study involved workers at an Italian capacitor plant who had been exposed to PCBs. Bertazzi et al., *Cancer Mortality of Capacitor Manufacturing Workers*, 11 Am. J. of Indus. Med. 165 (1987). The authors noted that lung cancer deaths among ex-employees at the plant were higher than might have been expected, but concluded that "there were apparently no grounds for associating lung cancer deaths (although increased above expectations) and exposure in the plant." *Id.,* at 172. Given that Bertazzi et al. were unwilling to say that PCB exposure had caused cancer among the workers they examined, their study did not support the experts' conclusion that Joiner's exposure to PCB's caused his cancer.

The second study followed employees who had worked at Monsanto's PCB production plant. J. Zack & D. Musch, *Mortality of PCB Workers at the Monsanto Plant in Sauget, Illinois* (Dec. 14, 1979) (unpublished report), 3 Record, Doc. No. 11. The authors of this study found that the incidence of lung cancer deaths among these workers was somewhat higher than would ordinarily be expected. The increase, however, was not statistically significant and the authors of the study did not suggest a link between the increase in lung cancer deaths and the exposure to PCB's.

The third and fourth studies were likewise of no help. The third involved workers at a Norwegian cable manufacturing company who had been exposed to mineral oil. Ronneberg et al., *Mortality and Incidence of Cancer Among Oil–Exposed Workers in a Norwegian Cable Manufacturing Company*, 45 Brit. J. of Indus. Med. 595 (1988). A statistically significant increase in lung cancer deaths had been observed in these workers. The study, however, (1) made no mention of PCB's and (2) was expressly limited to the type of mineral oil involved in that study, and thus did not support these experts' opinions. The fourth and final study involved a PCB-exposed group in Japan that had seen a statistically significant increase in lung cancer deaths. Kuratsune et al., *Analysis of Deaths Seen Among*

Patients with Yusho—A Preliminary Report, 16 CHEMOSPHERE, Nos. 8/9, p. 2085 (1987). The subjects of this study, however, had been exposed to numerous potential carcinogens, including toxic rice oil that they had ingested.

Respondent points to *Daubert*'s language that the "focus, of course, must be solely on principles and methodology, not on the conclusions that they generate." 509 U.S., at 595. He claims that because the District Court's disagreement was with the conclusion that the experts drew from the studies, the District Court committed legal error and was properly reversed by the Court of Appeals. But conclusions and methodology are not entirely distinct from one another. Trained experts commonly extrapolate from existing data. But nothing in either *Daubert* or the Federal Rules of Evidence requires a district court to admit opinion evidence that is connected to existing data only by the *ipse dixit* of the expert. A court may conclude that there is simply too great an analytical gap between the data and the opinion proffered. *See* Turpin v. Merrell Dow Pharmaceuticals, Inc., 959 F.2d 1349, 1360 (6th Cir. 1992), *cert. denied*, 506 U.S. 826. That is what the District Court did here, and we hold that it did not abuse its discretion in so doing.

We hold, therefore, that abuse of discretion is the proper standard by which to review a district court's decision to admit or exclude scientific evidence. We further hold that, because it was within the District Court's discretion to conclude that the studies upon which the experts relied were not sufficient, whether individually or in combination, to support their conclusions that Joiner's exposure to PCB's contributed to his cancer, the District Court did not abuse its discretion in excluding their testimony. These conclusions, however, do not dispose of this entire case.

Respondent's original contention was that his exposure to PCB's, furans, and dioxins contributed to his cancer. The District Court ruled that there was a genuine issue of material fact as to whether Joiner had been exposed to PCB's, but concluded that there was no genuine issue as to whether he had been exposed to furans and dioxins. The District Court accordingly never explicitly considered if there was admissible evidence on the question whether Joiner's alleged exposure to furans and dioxins contributed to his cancer. The Court of Appeals reversed the District Court's conclusion that there had been no exposure to furans and dioxins. Petitioners did not challenge this determination in their petition to this Court. Whether Joiner was exposed to furans and dioxins, and whether if there was such exposure, the opinions of Joiner's experts would then be admissible, remain open questions. We accordingly reverse the judgment of the Court of Appeals and remand this case for proceedings consistent with this opinion.

It is so ordered.

■ JUSTICE BREYER, concurring.

The Court's opinion, which I join, emphasizes *Daubert's* statement that a trial judge, acting as "gatekeeper," must " 'ensure that any and all scientific testimony or evidence admitted is not only relevant, but reliable.' " *Ante,* at 517 (*quoting* Daubert v. Merrell Dow Pharmaceuticals,

Inc., 509 U.S. 579, 589 (1993)). This requirement will sometimes ask judges to make subtle and sophisticated determinations about scientific methodology and its relation to the conclusions an expert witness seeks to offer— particularly when a case arises in an area where the science itself is tentative or uncertain, or where testimony about general risk levels in human beings or animals is offered to prove individual causation. Yet, as *amici* have pointed out, judges are not scientists and do not have the scientific training that can facilitate the making of such decisions. *See, e.g.,* Brief for Trial Lawyers for Public Justice as *Amicus Curiae* 15; Brief for New England Journal of Medicine et al. as *Amici Curiae* 2 ("Judges . . . are generally not trained scientists").

Of course, neither the difficulty of the task nor any comparative lack of expertise can excuse the judge from exercising the "gatekeeper" duties that the Federal Rules of Evidence impose—determining, for example, whether particular expert testimony is reliable and "will assist the trier of fact," Fed. Rule Evid. 702, or whether the "probative value" of testimony is substantially outweighed by risks of prejudice, confusion or waste of time, Fed. Rule Evid. 403. To the contrary, when law and science intersect, those duties often must be exercised with special care.

Today's toxic tort case provides an example. The plaintiff in today's case says that a chemical substance caused, or promoted, his lung cancer. His concern, and that of others, about the causes of cancer is understandable, for cancer kills over one in five Americans. *See* U.S. DEPT. OF HEALTH AND HUMAN SERVICES, NATIONAL CENTER FOR HEALTH STATISTICS, HEALTH, UNITED STATES 1996–97 AND INJURY CHARTBOOK 117 (1997) (23.3% of all deaths in 1995). Moreover, scientific evidence implicates some chemicals as potential causes of some cancers. *See, e.g.,* U.S. DEPT. OF HEALTH AND HUMAN SERVICES, PUBLIC HEALTH SERVICE, NATIONAL TOXICOLOGY PROGRAM, 1 SEVENTH ANNUAL REPORT ON CARCINOGENS v-vi (1994). Yet modern life, including good health as well as economic well-being, depends upon the use of artificial or manufactured substances, such as chemicals. And it may, therefore, prove particularly important to see that judges fulfill their *Daubert* gate-keeping function, so that they help assure that the powerful engine of tort liability, which can generate strong financial incentives to reduce, or to eliminate, production, points toward the right substances and does not destroy the wrong ones. It is, thus, essential in this science-related area that the courts administer the Federal Rules of Evidence in order to achieve the "end[s]" that the Rules themselves set forth, not only so that proceedings may be "justly determined," but also so "that the truth may be ascertained." Fed. Rule Evid. 102.

I therefore want specially to note that, as cases presenting significant science-related issues have increased in number, *see* JUDICIAL CONFERENCE OF THE UNITED STATES, REPORT OF THE FEDERAL COURTS STUDY COMMITTEE, 97 (Apr. 2, 1990) ("Economic, statistical, technological, and natural and social scientific data are becoming increasingly important in both routine and complex litigation"), judges have increasingly found in the Rules of Evidence and Civil Procedure ways to help them overcome the inherent difficulty of making determinations about complicated scientific, or otherwise technical, evidence. Among these techniques are an increased use of

Rule 16's pretrial conference authority to narrow the scientific issues in dispute, pretrial hearings where potential experts are subject to examination by the court, and the appointment of special masters and specially trained law clerks. *See* J. Cecil & T. Willging, Court-Appointed Experts: Defining the Role of Experts Appointed Under Federal Rule of Evidence 706, 83–88 (1993); J. Weinstein, Individual Justice in Mass Tort Litigation 107–10 (1995); *cf.* Kaysen, *In Memoriam: Charles E. Wyzanski, Jr.,* 100 Harv.L.Rev. 713, 713–715 (1987) (discussing a judge's use of an economist as a law clerk in United States v. United Shoe Machinery Corp., 110 F. Supp. 295 (Mass. 1953)), *aff'd,* 347 U.S. 521.

In the present case, the New England Journal of Medicine has filed an *amici* brief "in support of neither petitioners nor respondents" in which the Journal writes:

> [A] judge could better fulfill this gatekeeper function if he or she had help from scientists. Judges should be strongly encouraged to make greater use of their inherent authority ... to appoint experts.... Reputable experts could be recommended to courts by established scientific organizations, such as the National Academy of Sciences or the American Association for the Advancement of Science.

Brief, *supra,* at 18–19. Cf. Fed. Rule Evid. 706 (court may "on its own motion or on the motion of any party" appoint an expert to serve on behalf of the court, and this expert may be selected as "agreed upon by the parties" or chosen by the court); *see also* Weinstein, *supra,* at 116 (a court should sometimes "go beyond the experts proffered by the parties" and "utilize its powers to appoint independent experts under Rule 706 of the Federal Rules of Evidence"). Given this kind of offer of cooperative effort, from the scientific to the legal community, and given the various Rules-authorized methods for facilitating the courts' task, it seems to me that *Daubert's* gatekeeping requirement will not prove inordinately difficult to implement, and that it will help secure the basic objectives of the Federal Rules of Evidence, which are, to repeat, the ascertainment of truth and the just determination of proceedings. Fed. Rule Evid. 102.

■ Justice Stevens, concurring in part and dissenting in part.

The question that we granted certiorari to decide is whether the Court of Appeals applied the correct standard of review. That question is fully answered in Parts I and II of the Court's opinion. Part III answers the quite different question whether the District Court properly held that the testimony of plaintiff's expert witnesses was inadmissible. Because I am not sure that the parties have adequately briefed that question, or that the Court has adequately explained why the Court of Appeals' disposition was erroneous, I do not join Part III. Moreover, because a proper answer to that question requires a study of the record that can be performed more efficiently by the Court of Appeals than by the nine Members of this Court, I would remand the case to that court for application of the proper standard of review.

. . .

Kuhmo Tire Co. v. Carmichael

Supreme Court of the United States, 1999.
526 U.S. 137, 119 S.Ct. 1167, 143 L.Ed.2d 238.

■ Justice Breyer delivered the opinion of the Court.

In *Daubert v. Merrell Dow Pharmaceuticals, Inc.,* 509 U.S. 579 (1993), this Court focused upon the admissibility of scientific expert testimony. It pointed out that such testimony is admissible only if it is both relevant and reliable. And it held that the Federal Rules of Evidence "assign to the trial judge the task of ensuring that an expert's testimony both rests on a reliable foundation and is relevant to the task at hand." *Id.,* at 597. The Court also discussed certain more specific factors, such as testing, peer review, error rates, and "acceptability" in the relevant scientific community, some or all of which might prove helpful in determining the reliability of a particular scientific "theory or technique." *Id.,* at 593–94.

This case requires us to decide how *Daubert* applies to the testimony of engineers and other experts who are not scientists. We conclude that *Daubert's* general holding—setting forth the trial judge's general "gatekeeping" obligation—applies not only to testimony based on "scientific" knowledge, but also to testimony based on "technical" and "other specialized" knowledge. *See* Fed. Rule Evid. 702. We also conclude that a trial court may consider one or more of the more specific factors that *Daubert* mentioned when doing so will help determine that testimony's reliability. But, as the Court stated in *Daubert,* the test of reliability is "flexible," and *Daubert's* list of specific factors neither necessarily nor exclusively applies to all experts or in every case. Rather, the law grants a district court the same broad latitude when it decides *how* to determine reliability as it enjoys in respect to its ultimate reliability determination. *See* General Electric Co. v. Joiner, 522 U.S. 136, 143 (1997) (courts of appeals are to apply "abuse of discretion" standard when reviewing district court's reliability determination). Applying these standards, we determine that the District Court's decision in this case—not to admit certain expert testimony—was within its discretion and therefore lawful.

I.

On July 6, 1993, the right rear tire of a minivan driven by Patrick Carmichael blew out. In the accident that followed, one of the passengers died, and others were severely injured. In October 1993, the Carmichaels brought this diversity suit against the tire's maker and its distributor, whom we refer to collectively as Kumho Tire, claiming that the tire was defective. The plaintiffs rested their case in significant part upon deposition testimony provided by an expert in tire failure analysis, Dennis Carlson, Jr., who intended to testify in support of their conclusion.

Carlson's depositions relied upon certain features of tire technology that are not in dispute. A steel-belted radial tire like the Carmichaels' is made up of a "carcass" containing many layers of flexible cords, called "plies," along which (between the cords and the outer tread) are laid steel strips called "belts." Steel wire loops, called "beads," hold the cords together at the plies' bottom edges. An outer layer, called the "tread," encases the carcass, and the entire tire is bound together in rubber, through the application of heat and various chemicals. *See generally, e.g.,* J. DIXON, TIRES, SUSPENSION AND HANDLING 68–72 (2d ed.1996). The bead of the tire sits upon a "bead seat," which is part of the wheel assembly. That assembly contains a "rim flange," which extends over the bead and rests against the side of the tire. *See* M. MAVRIGIAN, PERFORMANCE WHEELS & TIRES 81, 83 (1998) (illustrations). [Graphic omitted; see printed opinion.]

Carlson's testimony also accepted certain background facts about the tire in question. He assumed that before the blowout the tire had traveled far. (The tire was made in 1988 and had been installed some time before the Carmichaels bought the used minivan in March 1993; the Carmichaels had driven the van approximately 7,000 additional miles in the two months they had owned it.) Carlson noted that the tire's tread depth, which was 11/32 of an inch when new, App. 242, had been worn down to depths that ranged from 3/32 of an inch along some parts of the tire, to nothing at all along others. *Id.,* at 287. He conceded that the tire tread had at least two punctures which had been inadequately repaired. *Id.,* at 258–61, 322.

Despite the tire's age and history, Carlson concluded that a defect in its manufacture or design caused the blowout. He rested this conclusion in part upon three premises which, for present purposes, we must assume are not in dispute: First, a tire's carcass should stay bound to the inner side of the tread for a significant period of time after its tread depth has worn away. *Id.,* at 208–09. Second, the tread of the tire at issue had separated from its inner steel-belted carcass prior to the accident. *Id.,* at 336. Third, this "separation" caused the blowout. *Ibid.*

Carlson's conclusion that a defect caused the separation, however, rested upon certain other propositions, several of which the defendants strongly dispute. First, Carlson said that if a separation is *not* caused by a certain kind of tire misuse called "over-deflection" (which consists of under-inflating the tire or causing it to carry too much weight, thereby generating heat that can undo the chemical tread/carcass bond), then, ordinarily, its cause is a tire defect. *Id.,* at 193–95, 277–78. Second, he said that if a tire has been subject to sufficient over-deflection to cause a separation, it should reveal certain physical symptoms. These symptoms include (a) tread wear on the tire's shoulder that is greater than the tread wear along the tire's center, *id.,* at 211; (b) signs of a "bead groove," where the beads have been pushed too hard against the bead seat on the inside of the tire's rim, *id.,* at 196–97; (c) sidewalls of the tire with physical signs of deterioration, such as discoloration, *id.,* at 212; and/or (d) marks on the tire's rim flange, *id.,* at 219–20. Third, Carlson said that where he does not find *at least two* of the four physical signs just mentioned (and presumably where there is no reason to suspect a less common cause of separation), he concludes that a manufacturing or design defect caused the separation. *Id.,* at 223–24.

Carlson added that he had inspected the tire in question. He conceded that the tire to a limited degree showed greater wear on the shoulder than in the center, some signs of "bead groove," some discoloration, a few marks on the rim flange, and inadequately filled puncture holes (which can also cause heat that might lead to separation). *Id.,* at 256–57, 258–61, 277, 303–

04, 308. But, in each instance, he testified that the symptoms were not significant, and he explained why he believed that they did not reveal over-deflection. For example, the extra shoulder wear, he said, appeared primarily on one shoulder, whereas an over-deflected tire would reveal equally abnormal wear on both shoulders. *Id.,* at 277. Carlson concluded that the tire did not bear at least two of the four over-deflection symptoms, nor was there any less obvious cause of separation; and since neither over-deflection nor the punctures caused the blowout, a defect must have done so.

Kumho Tire moved the District Court to exclude Carlson's testimony on the ground that his methodology failed Rule 702's reliability requirement. The court agreed with Kumho that it should act as a *Daubert*-type reliability "gatekeeper," even though one might consider Carlson's testimony as "technical," rather than "scientific." *See* Carmichael v. Samyang Tires, Inc., 923 F. Supp. 1514, 1521–22 (S.D.Ala. 1996). The court then examined Carlson's methodology in light of the reliability-related factors that *Daubert* mentioned, such as a theory's testability, whether it "has been a subject of peer review or publication," the "known or potential rate of error," and the "degree of acceptance . . . within the relevant scientific community." 923 F. Supp., at 1520 (*citing Daubert*, 509 U.S., at 589–95). The District Court found that all those factors argued against the reliability of Carlson's methods, and it granted the motion to exclude the testimony (as well as the defendants' accompanying motion for summary judgment).

The plaintiffs, arguing that the court's application of the *Daubert* factors was too "inflexible," asked for reconsideration. And the court granted that motion. *Carmichael*, 923 F. Supp. 1514 (S.D.Ala. 1996), App. to Pet. for Cert. 1c. After reconsidering the matter, the court agreed with the plaintiffs that *Daubert* should be applied flexibly, that its four factors were simply illustrative, and that other factors could argue in favor of admissibility. It conceded that there may be widespread acceptance of a "visual-inspection method" for some relevant purposes. But the court found insufficient indications of the reliability of

> the component of Carlson's tire failure analysis which most concerned the Court, namely, the methodology employed by the expert in analyzing the data obtained in the visual inspection, and the scientific basis, if any, for such an analysis. *Id.,* at 6c.

It consequently affirmed its earlier order declaring Carlson's testimony inadmissible and granting the defendants' motion for summary judgment.

The Eleventh Circuit reversed. *See* Carmichael v. Samyang Tire, Inc., 131 F.3d 1433 (1997). It "review[ed] . . . *de novo* 'the "district court's legal decision to apply *Daubert*.' " *Id.,* at 1435. It noted that "the Supreme Court in *Daubert* explicitly limited its holding to cover only the 'scientific context,' " adding that "a *Daubert* analysis" applies only where an expert relies "on the application of scientific principles," rather than "on skill-or experience-based observation." Id., at 1435–1436. It concluded that Carlson's testimony, which it viewed as relying on experience, "falls outside the scope of *Daubert*," that "the district court erred as a matter of law by applying *Daubert* in this case," and that the case must be remanded for further (non-*Daubert*-type) consideration under Rule 702. 131 F.3d, at 1436.

Kumho Tire petitioned for certiorari, asking us to determine whether a trial court "may" consider *Daubert's* specific "factors" when determining the "admissibility of an engineering expert's testimony." Pet. for Cert. i. We granted certiorari in light of uncertainty among the lower courts about whether, or how, *Daubert* applies to expert testimony that might be characterized as based not upon "scientific" knowledge, but rather upon "technical" or "other specialized" knowledge. Fed. Rule Evid. 702; *compare, e.g.,* Watkins v. Telsmith, Inc., 121 F.3d 984, 990–91 (5th Cir. 1997), *with e.g.,* Compton v. Subaru of America, Inc., 82 F.3d 1513, 1518–19 (10th Cir. 1996), *cert. denied,* 519 U.S. 1042.

II.

A.

In *Daubert*, this Court held that Federal Rule of Evidence 702 imposes a special obligation upon a trial judge to "ensure that any and all scientific testimony ... is not only relevant, but reliable." 509 U.S., at 589. The initial question before us is whether this basic gatekeeping obligation applies only to "scientific" testimony or to all expert testimony. We, like the parties, believe that it applies to all expert testimony. See Brief for Petitioners 19; Brief for Respondents 17.

For one thing, Rule 702 itself says:

> If scientific, technical, or other specialized knowledge will assist the trier of fact to understand the evidence or to determine a fact in issue, a witness qualified as an expert by knowledge, skill, experience, training, or education, may testify thereto in the form of an opinion or otherwise.

This language makes no relevant distinction between "scientific" knowledge and "technical" or "other specialized" knowledge. It makes clear that any such knowledge might become the subject of expert testimony. In *Daubert* the Court specified that it is the Rule's word "knowledge," not the words (like "scientific") that modify that word, that "establishes a standard of evidentiary reliability." 509 U.S., at 589–90. Hence, as a matter of language, the Rule applies its reliability standard to all "scientific," "technical," or "other specialized" matters within its scope. We concede that the Court in *Daubert* referred only to "scientific" knowledge. But as the Court there said, it referred to "scientific" testimony "because that [wa]s the nature of the expertise" at issue. *Id.,* at 590, n. 8.

Neither is the evidentiary rationale that underlay the Court's basic *Daubert* "gatekeeping" determination limited to "scientific" knowledge. *Daubert* pointed out that Federal Rules 702 and 703 grant expert witnesses testimonial latitude unavailable to other witnesses on the "assumption that the expert's opinion will have a reliable basis in the knowledge and experience of his discipline." *Id.,* at 592 (pointing out that experts may testify to opinions, including those that are not based on firsthand knowledge or observation). The Rules grant that latitude to all experts, not just to "scientific" ones.

Finally, it would prove difficult, if not impossible, for judges to administer evidentiary rules under which a gatekeeping obligation depended upon a distinction between "scientific" knowledge and "technical" or "other specialized" knowledge. There is no clear line that divides the one from the others. Disciplines such as engineering rest upon scientific knowledge. Pure scientific theory itself may depend for its development upon observation and properly engineered machinery. And conceptual efforts to distinguish the two are unlikely to produce clear legal lines capable of application in particular cases. *Cf.* Brief for National Academy of Engineering as *Amicus Curiae* 9 (scientist seeks to understand nature while the engineer seeks nature's modification); Brief for Rubber Manufacturers Association as *Amicus Curiae* 14–16 (engineering, as an " 'applied science,' " relies on "scientific reasoning and methodology"); Brief for John Allen et al. as *Amici Curiae* 6 (engineering relies upon "scientific knowledge and methods").

Neither is there a convincing need to make such distinctions. Experts of all kinds tie observations to conclusions through the use of what Judge Learned Hand called "general truths derived from . . . specialized experience." Hand, *Historical and Practical Considerations Regarding Expert Testimony*, 15 Harv. L.Rev. 40, 54 (1901). And whether the specific expert testimony focuses upon specialized observations, the specialized translation of those observations into theory, a specialized theory itself, or the application of such a theory in a particular case, the expert's testimony often will rest "upon an experience confessedly foreign in kind to [the jury's] own." *Ibid.* The trial judge's effort to assure that the specialized testimony is reliable and relevant can help the jury evaluate that foreign experience, whether the testimony reflects scientific, technical, or other specialized knowledge.

We conclude that *Daubert's* general principles apply to the expert matters described in Rule 702. The Rule, in respect to all such matters, "establishes a standard of evidentiary reliability." 509 U.S., at 590. It "requires a valid . . . connection to the pertinent inquiry as a precondition to admissibility." Id., at 592. And where such testimony's factual basis, data, principles, methods, or their application are called sufficiently into question, see Part III, infra, the trial judge must determine whether the testimony has "a reliable basis in the knowledge and experience of [the relevant] discipline." 509 U.S., at 592.

B.

Petitioners ask more specifically whether a trial judge determining the "admissibility of an engineering expert's testimony" may consider several more specific factors that *Daubert* said might "bear on" a judge's gatekeeping determination. Brief for Petitioners i. These factors include:

— Whether a "theory or technique . . . can be (and has been) tested";

— Whether it "has been subjected to peer review and publication";

— Whether, in respect to a particular technique, there is a high "known or potential rate of error" and whether there are "standards controlling the technique's operation"; and

— Whether the theory or technique enjoys " 'general acceptance' " within a " 'relevant scientific community.' " 509 U.S., at 592–94.

Emphasizing the word "may" in the question, we answer that question yes.

Engineering testimony rests upon scientific foundations, the reliability of which will be at issue in some cases. *See, e.g.,* Brief for Stephen N. Bobo et al. as *Amici Curiae* 23 (stressing the scientific bases of engineering disciplines). In other cases, the relevant reliability concerns may focus upon personal knowledge or experience. As the Solicitor General points out, there are many different kinds of experts, and many different kinds of expertise. *See* Brief for United States as *Amicus Curiae* 18–19, and n. 5 (citing cases involving experts in drug terms, handwriting analysis, criminal *modus operandi,* land valuation, agricultural practices, railroad procedures, attorney's fee valuation, and others). Our emphasis on the word "may" thus reflects *Daubert's* description of the Rule 702 inquiry as "a flexible one." 509 U.S., at 594. *Daubert* makes clear that the factors it mentions do *not* constitute a "definitive checklist or test." *Id.,* at 593. And *Daubert* adds that the gate-keeping inquiry must be " 'tied to the facts' " of a particular "case." *Id.,* at 591 (*quoting* United States v. Downing, 753 F.2d 1224, 1242 (3d Cir. 1985)). We agree with the Solicitor General that "[t]he factors identified in *Daubert* may or may not be pertinent in assessing reliability, depending on the nature of the issue, the expert's particular expertise, and the subject of his testimony." Brief for United States as *Amicus Curiae* 19. The conclusion, in our view, is that we can neither rule out, nor rule in, for all cases and for all time the applicability of the factors mentioned in *Daubert* nor can we now do so for subsets of cases categorized by category of expert or by kind of evidence. Too much depends upon the particular circumstances of the particular case at issue.

Daubert itself is not to the contrary. It made clear that its list of factors was meant to be helpful, not definitive. Indeed, those factors do not all necessarily apply even in every instance in which the reliability of scientific testimony is challenged. It might not be surprising in a particular case, for example, that a claim made by a scientific witness has never been the subject of peer review, for the particular application at issue may never previously have interested any scientist. Nor, on the other hand, does the presence of *Daubert's* general acceptance factor help show that an expert's testimony is reliable where the discipline itself lacks reliability, as, for example, do theories grounded in any so-called generally accepted principles of astrology or necromancy.

At the same time, and contrary to the Court of Appeals' view, some of *Daubert's* questions can help to evaluate the reliability even of experience-based testimony. In certain cases, it will be appropriate for the trial judge to ask, for example, how often an engineering expert's experience-based methodology has produced erroneous results, or whether such a method is generally accepted in the relevant engineering community. Likewise, it will at times be useful to ask even of a witness whose expertise is based purely on experience, say, a perfume tester able to distinguish among 140 odors at a sniff, whether his preparation is of a kind that others in the field would recognize as acceptable.

We must therefore disagree with the Eleventh Circuit's holding that a trial judge may ask questions of the sort *Daubert* mentioned only where an expert "relies on the application of scientific principles," but not where an expert relies "on skill-or experience-based observation." 131 F.3d, at 1435.

We do not believe that Rule 702 creates a schematism that segregates expertise by type while mapping certain kinds of questions to certain kinds of experts. Life and the legal cases that it generates are too complex to warrant so definitive a match.

To say this is not to deny the importance of *Daubert's* gatekeeping requirement. The objective of that requirement is to ensure the reliability and relevancy of expert testimony. It is to make certain that an expert, whether basing testimony upon professional studies or personal experience, employs in the courtroom the same level of intellectual rigor that characterizes the practice of an expert in the relevant field. Nor do we deny that, as stated in *Daubert*, the particular questions that it mentioned will often be appropriate for use in determining the reliability of challenged expert testimony. Rather, we conclude that the trial judge must have considerable leeway in deciding in a particular case how to go about determining whether particular expert testimony is reliable. That is to say, a trial court should consider the specific factors identified in *Daubert* where they are reasonable measures of the reliability of expert testimony.

C.

The trial court must have the same kind of latitude in deciding *how* to test an expert's reliability, and to decide whether or when special briefing or other proceedings are needed to investigate reliability, as it enjoys when it decides *whether or not* that expert's relevant testimony is reliable. Our opinion in *Joiner* makes clear that a court of appeals is to apply an abuse-of-discretion standard when it "review[s] a trial court's decision to admit or exclude expert testimony." 522 U.S., at 138–39. That standard applies as much to the trial court's decisions about how to determine reliability as to its ultimate conclusion. Otherwise, the trial judge would lack the discretionary authority needed both to avoid unnecessary "reliability" proceedings in ordinary cases where the reliability of an expert's methods is properly taken for granted, and to require appropriate proceedings in the less usual or more complex cases where cause for questioning the expert's reliability arises. Indeed, the Rules seek to avoid "unjustifiable expense and delay" as part of their search for "truth" and the "jus[t] determin[ation]" of proceedings. Fed. Rule Evid. 102. Thus, whether *Daubert's* specific factors are, or are not, reasonable measures of reliability in a particular case is a matter that the law grants the trial judge broad latitude to determine. *See Joiner,* 522 U.S. at 143. And the Eleventh Circuit erred insofar as it held to the contrary.

III.

We further explain the way in which a trial judge "may" consider *Daubert's* factors by applying these considerations to the case at hand, a matter that has been briefed exhaustively by the parties and their 19 *amici*. The District Court did not doubt Carlson's qualifications, which included a masters degree in mechanical engineering, 10 years' work at Michelin America, Inc., and testimony as a tire failure consultant in other tort cases. Rather, it excluded the testimony because, despite those qualifications, it initially doubted, and then found unreliable, "the methodology employed by the expert in analyzing the data obtained in the visual inspection, and the scientific basis, if any, for such an analysis." Civ. Action No. 93–0860–CB–S (S.D.Ala., June 5, 1996), App. to Pet. for Cert. 6c. After examining the transcript in "some detail," 923 F. Supp., at 1518–19, n. 4, and after considering respondents' defense of Carlson's methodology, the District Court determined that Carlson's testimony was not reliable. It fell outside the range where experts might reasonably differ, and where the jury must decide among the conflicting views of different experts, even though the evidence is "shaky." *Daubert,* 509 U.S., at 596. In our view, the doubts that triggered the District Court's initial inquiry here were reasonable, as was the court's ultimate conclusion.

For one thing, and contrary to respondents' suggestion, the specific issue before the court was not the reasonableness *in general* of a tire expert's use of a visual and tactile inspection to determine whether overde-flection had caused the tire's tread to separate from its steel-belted carcass. Rather, it was the reasonableness of using such an approach, along with Carlson's particular method of analyzing the data thereby obtained, to draw a conclusion regarding *the particular matter to which the expert testimony was directly relevant.* That matter concerned the likelihood that a defect in the tire at issue caused its tread to separate from its carcass. The tire in question, the expert conceded, had traveled far enough so that some of the tread had been worn bald; it should have been taken out of service; it had been repaired (inadequately) for punctures; and it bore some of the very marks that the expert said indicated, not a defect, but abuse through overdeflection. *See id.,,* at 595. The relevant issue was whether the expert could reliably determine the cause of *this* tire's separation.

Nor was the basis for Carlson's conclusion simply the general theory that, in the absence of evidence of abuse, a defect will normally have caused a tire's separation. Rather, the expert employed a more specific theory to establish the existence (or absence) of such abuse. Carlson testified precise-ly that in the absence of *at least two* of four signs of abuse (proportionately greater tread wear on the shoulder; signs of grooves caused by the beads; discolored sidewalls; marks on the rim flange), he concludes that a defect caused the separation. And his analysis depended upon acceptance of a further implicit proposition, namely, that his visual and tactile inspection could determine that the tire before him had not been abused despite some evidence of the presence of the very signs for which he looked (and two punctures).

For another thing, the transcripts of Carlson's depositions support both the trial court's initial uncertainty and its final conclusion. Those transcripts cast considerable doubt upon the reliability of both the explicit theory (about the need for two signs of abuse) and the implicit proposition (about the significance of visual inspection in this case). Among other things, the expert could not say whether the tire had traveled more than 10, or 20, or 30, or 40, or 50 thousand miles, adding that 6,000 miles was "about how far" he could "say with any certainty." *Joiner,* 522 U.S., at 265. The court could reasonably have wondered about the reliability of a method of visual and tactile inspection sufficiently precise to ascertain with some certainty the abuse-related significance of minute shoulder/center relative tread wear differences, but insufficiently precise to tell "with any certainty" from the tread wear whether a tire had traveled less than 10,000 or more than 50,000 miles. And these concerns might have been augmented by Carlson's repeated reliance on the "subjective[ness]" of his mode of analysis in response to questions seeking specific information regarding how he could differentiate between a tire that actually had been overdeflected and a tire that merely looked as though it had been. *Id.*, at 222, 224–25, 285–86. They would have been further augmented by the fact that Carlson said he had inspected the tire itself for the first time the morning of his first deposition, and then only for a few hours. (His initial conclusions were based on photographs.) *Id.*, at 180.

Moreover, prior to his first deposition, Carlson had issued a signed report in which he concluded that the tire had "not been . . . overloaded or under-inflated," not because of the absence of "two of four" signs of abuse, but simply because "the rim flange impressions . . . were normal." *Id.*, at 335–36. That report also said that the "tread depth remaining was 3/32 inch," *id.*, at 336, though the opposing expert's (apparently undisputed) measurements indicate that the tread depth taken at various positions around the tire actually ranged from .5/32 of an inch to 4/32 of an inch, with the tire apparently showing greater wear along *both* shoulders than along the center, *id.*, at 432–33.

Further, in respect to one sign of abuse, bead grooving, the expert seemed to deny the sufficiency of his own simple visual-inspection methodology. He testified that most tires have some bead groove pattern, that where there is reason to suspect an abnormal bead groove he would ideally "look at a lot of [similar] tires" to know the grooving's significance, and that he had not looked at many tires similar to the one at issue. *Id.*, at 212–13, 214, 217.

Finally, the court, after looking for a defense of Carlson's methodology as applied in these circumstances, found no convincing defense. Rather, it found (1) that "none" of the *Daubert* factors, including that of "general acceptance" in the relevant expert community, indicated that Carlson's testimony was reliable, 923 F. Supp., at 1521; (2) that its own analysis "revealed no countervailing factors operating in favor of admissibility which could outweigh those identified in *Daubert*," App. to Pet. for Cert. 4c; and (3) that the "parties identified no such factors in their briefs," *ibid.* For these three reasons *taken together,* it concluded that Carlson's testimony was unreliable.

Respondents now argue to us, as they did to the District Court, that a method of tire failure analysis that employs a visual/tactile inspection is a reliable method, and they point both to its use by other experts and to Carlson's long experience working for Michelin as sufficient indication that that is so. But no one denies that an expert might draw a conclusion from a set of observations based on extensive and specialized experience. Nor does anyone deny that, as a general matter, tire abuse may often be identified by qualified experts through visual or tactile inspection of the tire. See Affidavit of H.R. Baumgardner 1–2, cited in Brief for National Academy of Forensic Engineers as *Amicus Curiae* 16 (Tire engineers rely on visual examination and process of elimination to analyze experimental test tires). As we said before, *supra,* at 1977, the question before the trial court was specific, not general. The trial court had to decide whether this particular expert had sufficient specialized knowledge to assist the jurors "in deciding the particular issues in the case." 4 J. McLaughlin, Weinstein's Federal Evidence ¶ 702.05[1], p. 702–33 (2d ed.1998); *see also* Advisory Committee's Note on Proposed Fed. Rule Evid. 702, Preliminary Draft of Proposed Amendments to the Federal Rules of Civil Procedure and Evidence: Request for Comment, 126 (1998) (stressing that district courts must "scrutinize" whether the "principles and methods" employed by an expert "have been properly applied to the facts of the case").

The particular issue in this case concerned the use of Carlson's two-factor test and his related use of visual/tactile inspection to draw conclusions on the basis of what seemed small observational differences. We have found no indication in the record that other experts in the industry use Carlson's two-factor test or that tire experts such as Carlson normally make the very fine distinctions about, say, the symmetry of comparatively greater shoulder tread wear that were necessary, on Carlson's own theory, to support his conclusions. Nor, despite the prevalence of tire testing, does anyone refer to any articles or papers that validate Carlson's approach. *Cf.* Bobo, Tire Flaws and Separations, in Mechanics of Pneumatic Tires 636–37 (S. Clark ed.1981); C. Schnuth et al., *Compression Grooving and Rim Flange Abrasion as Indicators of Over–Deflected Operating Conditions in Tires*, presented to Rubber Division of the American Chemical Society, Oct. 21–24, 1997; J. Walter & R. Kiminecz, *Bead Contact Pressure Measurements at the Tire–Rim Interface*, presented to the Society of Automotive Engineers, Inc., Feb. 24–28, 1975. Indeed, no one has argued that Carlson himself, were he still working for Michelin, would have concluded in a report to his employer that a similar tire was similarly defective on grounds identical to those upon which he rested his conclusion here. Of course, Carlson himself claimed that his method was accurate, but, as we pointed out in *Joiner*, "nothing in either *Daubert* or the Federal Rules of Evidence requires a district court to admit opinion evidence that is connected to existing data only by the ipse dixit of the expert." 522 U.S., at 146.

Respondents additionally argue that the District Court too rigidly applied *Daubert's* criteria. They read its opinion to hold that a failure to satisfy any one of those criteria automatically renders expert testimony inadmissible. The District Court's initial opinion might have been vulnerable to a form of this argument. There, the court, after rejecting respondents' claim that Carlson's testimony was "exempted from *Daubert*-style scrutiny" because it was "technical analysis" rather than "scientific evidence," simply added that "none of the four admissibility criteria outlined by the *Daubert* court are satisfied." 923 F. Supp., at 1521. Subsequently, however, the court granted respondents' motion for reconsideration. It then explicitly recognized that the relevant reliability inquiry "should be 'flexible,' " that its " 'overarching subject [should be] . . . validity' and reliability," and that "*Daubert* was intended neither to be exhaustive nor to apply in every case." App. to Pet. for Cert. 4c (*quoting Daubert*, 509 U.S., at 594–95). And the court ultimately based its decision upon Carlson's failure to satisfy either *Daubert's* factors or any other set of reasonable reliability criteria. In light of the record as developed by the parties, that conclusion was within the District Court's lawful discretion.

In sum, Rule 702 grants the district judge the discretionary authority, reviewable for its abuse, to determine reliability in light of the particular facts and circumstances of the particular case. The District Court did not abuse its discretionary authority in this case. Hence, the judgment of the Court of Appeals is

Reversed.

■ JUSTICE SCALIA, with whom JUSTICE O'CONNOR and JUSTICE THOMAS join, concurring.

I join the opinion of the Court, which makes clear that the discretion it endorses—trial-court discretion in choosing the manner of testing expert reliability—is not discretion to abandon the gatekeeping function. I think it worth adding that it is not discretion to perform the function inadequately. Rather, it is discretion to choose among *reasonable* means of excluding expertise that is *fausse* and science that is junky. Though, as the Court makes clear today, the *Daubert* factors are not holy writ, in a particular case the failure to apply one or another of them may be unreasonable, and hence an abuse of discretion.

■ JUSTICE STEVENS, concurring in part and dissenting in part.

The only question that we granted certiorari to decide is whether a trial judge "[m]ay ... consider the four factors set out by this Court in Daubert v. Merrell Dow Pharmaceuticals, Inc., 509 U.S. 579 (1993), in a Rule 702 analysis of admissibility of an engineering expert's testimony." Pet. for Cert. i. That question is fully and correctly answered in Parts I and II of the Court's opinion, which I join.

Part III answers the quite different question whether the trial judge abused his discretion when he excluded the testimony of Dennis Carlson. Because a proper answer to that question requires a study of the record that can be performed more efficiently by the Court of Appeals than by the nine Members of this Court, I would remand the case to the Eleventh Circuit to perform that task. . . .

NOTES AND QUESTIONS

Today, the *Daubert, Joiner, Kumho* trilogy governs the admission of expert testimony in federal court. The central theme is the importance of the trial judge. That judge acts as a "gatekeeper" who determines whether or not experts are allowed to testify before the jury. This power extends not only to scientific experts, but to other technical experts, including engineers. The jury, of course, is free to believe or disbelieve what an expert says, but if the judge bars an expert altogether that often determines the outcome of the case, particularly when it is the plaintiff's expert who is excluded. Under the trilogy the judge is to apply a variety of factors, such as the presence of peer review and the rate of error, in determining if an expert is reliable. The trial judge is accorded considerable deference in making this decision; reversal is possible only under an abuse of discretion standard. And this standard is to apply not only to whether an expert's testimony is reliable, but to how to test an expert's reliability, since not all of the factors identified by the Supreme Court in *Daubert* are relevant in every case.

Are federal trial judges up to the job? Justice Breyer suggested in his *Joiner* concurrence that perhaps they could use their power to appoint independent experts to help them weigh the conflicting claims of the parties' experts. Subsequently, the Justice has endorsed a demonstration project undertaken by the American Association for the Advancement of Science to make neutral scientific experts available to aid judicial proceedings. *See Science in Court*, Wash. Post, Feb. 19, 1998, at A16. Is this approach consistent with the adversary system? Are some experts more neutral than others?

Professor Michael Gottesman, who argued the *Daubert* and *Joiner* cases in the Supreme Court on behalf of the plaintiffs, argues that trial judges are not really able to focus on whether an expert is reliable, but that they do believe they have a sense of whether an expert is honest. Gottesman writes that his "untested hypothesis is that trial judges find the gatekeeper role assigned by *Daubert* a handy instrument for excluding expert testimony they believe to be dishonest, and that the Supreme Court fully intended this result." Michael Gottesman, *From* Barefoot *to* Daubert *to* Joiner: *Triple Play or Double Error?*, 40 Ariz. L. Rev. 753, 759 (1998). This argument raises the question of whether judges or juries are better at determining honesty in this context and whether assigning this task to judges is consistent with the Seventh Amendment. *See id.* at 759–769.

The *Daubert* trilogy governs federal courts, but the states are free to devise their own approach. Many states never adopted *Daubert* itself, preferring to remain with the *Frye* general acceptance test or some other approach. Moreover, some of the states that adopted *Daubert* have declined to adopt *Joiner* or *Kumho Tire*, suggesting that the admissibility of technical evidence remains a difficult and controversial area. *See* David E. Bernstein & Jeffrey D. Jackson, *The* Daubert *Trilogy in the States*, 44 Jurimetrics J. 351–366 (2004).

Despite the challenges our court system faces when it confronts highly technical information—whether the setting is judicial review of agency action or the admissibility of evidence at trial—we continue to rely heavily on rather traditional judicial models, including the use of non-expert judges. Dramatic alternatives have at times been suggested, but they have failed to win wide acceptance. The "science court" idea, which involved submitting scientific claims to a panel of neutral scientists, is illustrative. There was a good deal of discussion of science courts, but in the end the idea "[l]ike a sky rocket ... got a lot of attention as it ascended but just as quickly fell downward to crash and burn." Thomas G. Field, Jr., *Pursuing Transparency Through Science Courts*, 11 Risk 209, 211 (2000). Are there ways to harness expertise in policymaking that do not replicate existing administrative agencies and advisory panels?

CHAPTER 5

ARTIFICIAL INTELLIGENCE, HUMAN VALUES, AND THE LAW

Computers, as a vital modern technology, play an important role in the lives of attorneys. Clients have computer-related problems ranging from intellectual property protection for software, see Chapter 4, Sec. II. D., *supra*, to the negotiation of complex contracts involving the sale and maintenance of hardware. Moreover, attorneys working on these problems increasingly use computerized databases for legal research, a development with implications for how we think and talk about the law. *See* Ethan Katsh, *Law in a Digital World*, 38 VILL. L. REV. 403 (1993).

Yet the greatest impact of computers on lawyers and on the law may lie ahead. The field of artificial intelligence has the potential to transform profoundly how lawyers do their work as well as the legal categories they work with. Artificial intelligence has been defined in a variety of ways. To some it is the art of building machines that can do intelligent tasks presently done by humans, while to others it is the never-ending job of making computers do more than the previous generation of computers could do. *See* RAYMOND KURZWEIL, THE AGE OF INTELLIGENT MACHINES 14 (1990). In practical terms, the artificial intelligence movement has produced not only extraordinary chess-playing machines, but working expert systems that are used, for example, in diagnosing medical problems in humans and mechanical problems in automobiles. *Id*. at 294–303.

This chapter explores some of the implications of artificial intelligence for the law. We begin with an examination of the current legal approach towards privacy and computers, so that we can consider whether that approach will be adequate for developments that may lie ahead as artificial intelligence systems become more ubiquitous.

I. COMPUTERS AND PRIVACY

Whalen v. Roe

Supreme Court of the United States, 1977.
429 U.S. 589, 97 S.Ct. 869, 51 L.Ed.2d 64.

■ JUSTICE STEVENS delivered the opinion of the Court.

The constitutional question presented is whether the State of New York may record, in a centralized computer file, the names and addresses of all persons who have obtained, pursuant to a doctor's prescription, certain drugs for which there is both a lawful and an unlawful market.

The District Court enjoined enforcement of the portions of the New York State Controlled Substances Act of 1972 which require such recording on the ground that they violate appellees' constitutionally protected rights of privacy. We noted probable jurisdiction of the appeal by the Commissioner of Health, 424 U.S. 907, and now reverse.

Many drugs have both legitimate and illegitimate uses. In response to a concern that such drugs were being diverted into unlawful channels, in 1970 the New York Legislature created a special commission to evaluate the State's drug-control laws. The commission found the existing laws deficient in several respects. There was no effective way to prevent the use of stolen or revised prescriptions, to prevent unscrupulous pharmacists from repeatedly refilling prescriptions, to prevent users from obtaining prescriptions from more than one doctor, or to prevent doctors from over-prescribing, either by authorizing an excessive amount in one prescription or by giving one patient multiple prescriptions. In drafting new legislation to correct such defects, the commission consulted with enforcement officials in California and Illinois where central reporting systems were being used effectively.

The new New York statute classified potentially harmful drugs in five schedules. Drugs, such as heroin, which are highly abused and have no recognized medical use, are in Schedule I; they cannot be prescribed. Schedules II through V include drugs which have a progressively lower potential for abuse but also have a recognized medical use. Our concern is limited to Schedule II, which includes the most dangerous of the legitimate drugs.

With an exception for emergencies, the Act requires that all prescriptions for Schedule II drugs be prepared by the physician in triplicate on an official form. The completed form identifies the prescribing physician; the dispensing pharmacy; the drug and dosage; and the name, address, and age of the patient. One copy of the form is retained by the physician, the second by the pharmacist, and the third is forwarded to the New York State Department of Health in Albany. A prescription made on an official form may not exceed a 30–day supply, and may not be refilled.

The District Court found that about 100,000 Schedule II prescription forms are delivered to a receiving room at the Department of Health in Albany each month. They are sorted, coded, and logged and then taken to another room where the data on the forms is recorded on magnetic tapes for processing by a computer. Thereafter, the forms are returned to the receiving room to be retained in a vault for a five-year period and then destroyed as required by the statute. The receiving room is surrounded by a locked wire fence and protected by an alarm system. The computer tapes containing the prescription data are kept in a locked cabinet. When the tapes are used, the computer is run "off-line," which means that no terminal outside of the computer room can read or record any information. Public disclosure of the identity of patients is expressly prohibited by the statute and by a Department of Health regulation. Willful violation of these prohibitions is a crime punishable by up to one year in prison and a $2,000 fine. At the time of trial there were 17 Department of Health employees with access to the files; in addition, there were 24 investigators with authority to investigate cases of overdispensing which might be identified by the computer. Twenty months after the effective date of the Act, the computerized data had only been used in two investigations involving alleged overuse by specific patients.

A few days before the Act became effective, this litigation was commenced by a group of patients regularly receiving prescriptions for Schedule II drugs, by doctors who prescribe such drugs, and by two associations of physicians. After various preliminary proceedings, a three-judge District Court conducted a one-day trial. Appellees offered evidence tending to prove that persons in need of treatment with Schedule II drugs will from time to time decline such treatment because of their fear that the misuse of the computerized data will cause them to be stigmatized as "drug addicts."

. . .

Appellees contend that the statute invades a constitutionally protected "zone of privacy." The cases sometimes characterized as protecting "privacy" have in fact involved at least two different kinds of interests. One is the individual interest in avoiding disclosure of personal matters, and another is the interest in independence in making certain kinds of important decisions. Appellees argue that both of these interests are impaired by this statute. The mere existence in readily available form of the information about patients' use of Schedule II drugs creates a genuine concern that the information will become publicly known and that it will adversely affect their reputations. This concern makes some patients reluctant to use, and some doctors reluctant to prescribe, such drugs even when their use is medically indicated. It follows, they argue, that the making of decisions about matters vital to the care of their health is inevitably affected by the statute. Thus, the statute threatens to impair both their interest in the nondisclosure of private information and also their interest in making important decisions independently.

We are persuaded, however, that the New York program does not, on its face, pose a sufficiently grievous threat to either interest to establish a constitutional violation.

Public disclosure of patient information can come about in three ways. Health Department employees may violate the statute by failing, either deliberately or negligently, to maintain proper security. A patient or a doctor may be accused of a violation and the stored data may be offered in evidence in a judicial proceeding. Or, thirdly, a doctor, a pharmacist, or the patient may voluntarily reveal information on a prescription form.

The third possibility existed under the prior law and is entirely unrelated to the existence of the computerized data bank. Neither of the other two possibilities provides a proper ground for attacking the statute as invalid on its face. There is no support in the record, or in the experience of the two States that New York has emulated, for an assumption that the security provisions of the statute will be administered improperly. And the remote possibility that judicial supervision of the evidentiary use of particular items of stored information will provide inadequate protection against unwarranted disclosures is surely not a sufficient reason for invalidating the entire patient-identification program.

Even without public disclosure, it is, of course, true that private information must be disclosed to the authorized employees of the New York Department of Health. Such disclosures, however, are not significantly different from those that were required under the prior law. Nor are they meaningfully distinguishable from a host of other unpleasant invasions of privacy that are associated with many facets of health care. Unquestionably, some individuals' concern for their own privacy may lead them to avoid or to postpone needed medical attention. Nevertheless, disclosures of private medical information to doctors, to hospital personnel, to insurance companies, and to public health agencies are often an essential part of modern medical practice even when the disclosure may reflect unfavorably on the character of the patient. Requiring such disclosures to representatives of the State having responsibility for the health of the community, does not automatically amount to an impermissible invasion of privacy.

Appellees also argue, however, that even if unwarranted disclosures do not actually occur, the knowledge that the information is readily available in a computerized file creates a genuine concern that causes some persons to decline needed medication. The record supports the conclusion that some use of Schedule II drugs has been discouraged by that concern; it also is clear, however, that about 100,000 prescriptions for such drugs were being filled each month prior to the entry of the District Court's injunction. Clearly, therefore, the statute did not deprive the public of access to the drugs.

. . .

A final word about issues we have not decided. We are not unaware of the threat to privacy implicit in the accumulation of vast amounts of personal information in computerized data banks or other massive government files. The collection of taxes, the distribution of welfare and social security benefits, the supervision of public health, the direction of our Armed Forces, and the enforcement of the criminal laws all require the orderly preservation of great quantities of information, much of which is personal in character and potentially embarrassing or harmful if disclosed. The right to collect and use such data for public purposes is typically accompanied by a concomitant statutory or regulatory duty to avoid unwarranted disclosures. Recognizing that in some circumstances that duty arguably has its roots in the Constitution, nevertheless New York's statutory scheme, and its implementing administrative procedures, evidence a proper concern with, and protection of, the individual's interest in privacy. We therefore need not, and do not, decide any question which might be presented by the unwarranted disclosure of accumulated private data—whether intentional or unintentional—or by a system that did not contain comparable security provisions. We simply hold that this record does not establish an invasion of any right or liberty protected by the Fourteenth Amendment.

Reversed.

■ JUSTICE BRENNAN, concurring.

I write only to express my understanding of the opinion of the Court, which I join.

The New York statute under attack requires doctors to disclose to the State information about prescriptions for certain drugs with a high potential for abuse, and provides for the storage of that information in a central computer file. The Court recognizes that an individual's "interest in avoiding disclosure of personal matters" is an aspect of the right of privacy, *ante*, at 876–877, and nn. 24–25, but holds that in this case, any such interest has not been seriously enough invaded by the State to require a showing that its program was indispensable to the State's effort to control drug abuse.

The information disclosed by the physician under this program is made available only to a small number of public health officials with a legitimate interest in the information. As the record makes clear, New York has long required doctors to make this information available to its officials on request, and that practice is not challenged here. Such limited reporting requirements in the medical field are familiar, ante, at 878 n. 29, and are not generally regarded as an invasion of privacy. Broad dissemination by state officials of such information, however, would clearly implicate constitutionally protected privacy rights, and would presumably be justified only by compelling state interests. *See, e.g.*, Roe v. Wade, 410 U.S. 113, 155–56 (1973).

What is more troubling about this scheme, however, is the central computer storage of the data thus collected. Obviously, as the State argues, collection and storage of data by the State that is in itself legitimate is not rendered unconstitutional simply because new technology makes the State's operations more efficient. However, as the example of the Fourth Amendment shows, the Constitution puts limits not only on the type of information the State may gather, but also on the means it may use to gather it. The central storage and easy accessibility of computerized data vastly increase the potential for abuse of that information, and I am not prepared to say that future developments will not demonstrate the necessity of some curb on such technology.

In this case, as the Court's opinion makes clear, the State's carefully designed program includes numerous safeguards intended to forestall the danger of indiscriminate disclosure. Given this serious and, so far as the record shows, successful effort to prevent abuse and limit access to the personal information at issue, I cannot say that the statute's provisions for computer storage, on their face, amount to a deprivation of constitutionally protected privacy interests, any more than the more traditional reporting provisions.

In the absence of such a deprivation, the State was not required to prove that the challenged statute is absolutely necessary to its attempt to control drug abuse. Of course, a statute that did effect such a deprivation would only be consistent with the Constitution if it were necessary to promote a compelling state interest. Roe v. Wade, *supra*; Eisenstadt v. Baird, 405 U.S. 438, 464, (1972) (White, J., concurring in result).

■ Justice Stewart, concurring.

In *Katz v. United States*, 389 U.S. 347, the Court made clear that although the Constitution affords protection against certain kinds of government intrusions into personal and private matters, there is no "general constitutional 'right to privacy.' . . . [T]he protection of a person's *general* right to privacy—his right to be let alone by other people—is, like the protection of his property and of his very life, left largely to the law of the individual States." *Id.*, at 350–351 (footnote omitted).

Mr. Justice Brennan's concurring opinion states that "[b]road dissemination by state officials of [the information collected by New York State] . . . would clearly implicate constitutionally protected privacy rights. . . ." *Ante*, at 880. The only possible support in his opinion for this statement is its earlier reference to two footnotes in the Court's opinion, *ibid.*, *citing ante*, at 876–877, and nn. 24–25 (majority opinion). The footnotes, however, cite to only two Court opinions, and those two cases do not support the proposition advanced by Mr. Justice Brennan.

The first case referred to, *Griswold v. Connecticut*, 381 U.S. 479, held that a State cannot constitutionally prohibit a married couple from using contraceptives in the privacy of their home. Although the broad language of the opinion includes a discussion of privacy, see *id.*, at 484–485, the constitutional protection there discovered also related to (1) marriage, see *id.*, at 485–486; *id.*, at 495 (Goldberg, J., concurring); *id.*, at 500 (Harlan, J., concurring in judgment), citing *Poe v. Ullman*, 367 U.S. 497 (Harlan, J., dissenting); 381 U.S., at 502–503 (White, J., concurring in judgment); (2) privacy *in the home,* see *id.*, at 484–485 (majority opinion); *id.*, at 495 (Goldberg, J., concurring); *id.*, at 500 (Harlan, J., concurring in judgment), *citing Poe v. Ullman, supra,* at 522 (Harlan, J., dissenting); and (3) the right to use contraceptives, see 381 U.S., at 503 (White, J., concurring in judgment); see also *Roe v. Wade*, 410 U.S. 113 (Stewart, J., concurring). Whatever the *ratio decidendi* of *Griswold,* it does not recognize a general interest in freedom from disclosure of private information.

The other case referred to, *Stanley v. Georgia*, 394 U.S. 557, held that an individual cannot constitutionally be prosecuted for possession of obscene materials in his home. Although *Stanley* makes some reference to privacy rights, *id.*, at 564, the holding there was simply that the *First* Amendment—as made applicable to the States by the Fourteenth—protects a person's right to read what he chooses in circumstances where that choice poses no threat to the sensibilities or welfare of others, *id.*, at 565–568.

Upon the understanding that nothing the Court says today is contrary to the above views, I join its opinion and judgment.

NOTES AND QUESTIONS

1. As *Whalen* indicates, the constitutional concept of privacy has uncertain application to databases. In other words, it is unclear whether the Constitution protects informational privacy. Do you agree with Justice Brennan or Justice Stewart on this matter? What relevance, if any, do the views of the Framers of the Constitution have on an issue involving, in part, a technology they never imagined? The Supreme Court has not resolved this question. It may be worth noting, however, that in a non-constitutional setting involving a privacy exemption to the Freedom of Information Act, Justice Stevens (the author of *Whalen*) wrote for the Court, "Plainly there is a vast difference between the public records that might be found after a diligent search of courthouse files, county archives, and local police stations throughout the country and a computerized summary located in a single clearinghouse of information." United States Dep't of Justice v. Reporters Comm. for Freedom of the Press, 489 U.S. 749, 109 S.Ct. 1468, 103 L.Ed.2d 774 (1989).

In the absence of constitutional protection, there are numerous state and federal statutes that seek to protect privacy in a variety of specific settings, such as health care information, financial data, and the like. Two useful collections of statutes and regulations that are updated regularly are THE PRIVACY LAW SOURCE-BOOK: UNITED STATES LAW, INTERNATIONAL LAW, AND RECENT DEVELOPMENTS (Marc Rotenberg ed., 2003), and ROBERT ELLIS SMITH, COMPILATION OF STATE AND FEDERAL PRIVACY LAWS (2002).

2. Notwithstanding these legislative efforts, three modern developments have made many people pessimistic about any individual having control over information about herself, the central idea of informational privacy. First, there are expert systems, a form of artificial intelligence, that enable information in various places to be combined and mined to create profiles of individuals and their preferences. Secondly, there is the growth of online professional, commercial, and recreational activity by millions of people, activity that leaves a digital trail. And finally, there is governmental interest in law enforcement and national security, an interest that has intensified since September 11, 2001. With powerful private and public desires to learn about people in an increasingly digital world, many have come to agree with the mantra of Scott McNealy, the founder of Sun Microsystems: "You . . . have zero privacy. Get over it." Edward C. Baig et al., *Privacy: The Internet Wants Your Personal Info . . . What's in It for You?*, BUS. WKLY., Apr. 5, 1999, at 84.

But not everyone has given up on the idea of informational privacy in the modern world. *See, e.g.*, Will Thomas DeVries, *Privacy: Protecting Privacy in the Digital Age*, 18 BERKELEY TECH. L.J. 283 (2003). One reason is that the very technologies that threaten privacy can also enhance it through mechanisms such as encryption. *See* Herbert Burkert, *Privacy-Enhancing Technologies: Typology, Critique, Vision, in* PHILIP E. AGRE & MARC ROTENBERG, TECHNOLOGY AND PRIVACY: THE NEW LANDSCAPE 125 (1997).

3. The emerging filed of biometrics provides an illustration of the two-sided nature of this problem. Biometric technologies identify people by their unique physical characteristics. Biometrics might, for example, enable you to gain access to your ATM without a personal identification number. You would first provide the bank with your fingerprint, which would be digitized, encrypted, and filed in a database. When you went to use your ATM card, you would present your finger to be scanned, and the resulting data would be compared with the database to make sure the owner of the card was the one using it. Biometric identification is possible not only with fingerprints, but with retinal scans, measurements of hand geometry, and a variety of other physical characteristics.

In principle, biometric identifiers could be accurate, cost-effective and convenient. They would free you, for example, from memorizing personal identification numbers, or carrying identification cards for admission to a health club. But what about the impact on privacy? From one point of view, biometrics enhance privacy. The Chief Executive Officer of one biometrics company puts the argument this way:

> Biometric technology makes the task of stealing identity much harder. Passwords and codes can be guessed, replicated, or passed along, but due to the unique qualities of biometrics, it is a much better way of ensuring positive identity. You cannot easily copy a fingerprint or retinal scan, but you can crack passwords.

Jon Halpin, *Bio–Identity*, 19 COMPUTER SHOPPER 390 (1999) (quoting Clint Fuller, CEO of SAFLink). On the other hand, some privacy advocates worry about biometric data being misused or falling into the wrong hands. An ACLU official asks:

> Who's entitled to gather this information? Can there be a secondary use? . . . [W]e enter the brave new world without any rules. There are no legal controls over how biometrics can be used—whether the information can be sold, whether it can be turned over to law enforcement without a warrant.

Guy Gugliotta, *Bar Codes for the Body Make It to the Market; Biometrics May Alter Consumer Landscape*, WASH. POST, June 21, 1999, at A1 (quoting Barry Steinhardt, associate director, ACLU). To date, public reaction has been mixed when companies have introduced biometrics. *See id*. For a thorough analysis of how biometrics could be regulated to maximize the benefits while reducing privacy risks, *see e.g.*, JOHN D. WOODWARD, NICHOLAS M. ORLANS, & PETER T. HIGGINS, BIOMETRICS (2003); John D. Woodward, *Biometric Scanning, Law & Policy: Identifying the Concerns—Drafting the Biometric Blueprint*, 59 U. PITT. L. REV. 97 (1997).

4. So the fate of traditional privacy in the context of modern technology remains unclear. These matters are increasingly working their way into traditional legal disputes. In 2004, the U.S. Supreme Court was presented with a case that raised informational privacy concerns in a routine law enforcement setting. The case arose when a police officer made a *Terry* stop of an individual, that is, the officer did not have probable cause to believe the individual had committed a crime, but he did have reasonable suspicion of criminal activity. Terry v. Ohio, 392 U.S. 1, 88 S.Ct. 1868, 20 L.Ed.2d 889 (1968). When the individual refused the officer's request that he identify himself, he was arrested. The question before the Court was whether an individual has a constitutional right to decline to identify himself under these circumstances. Below is an excerpt from an amicus brief filed in the Court by privacy advocates, followed by the Court's decision.

Brief of Amici Curiae, Electronic Privacy Information Center (EPIC) and Legal Scholars and Technical Experts

Hiibel v. Sixth Judicial District Court of Nevada, et al., 542 U.S. 177, 124 S.Ct. 2451, 159 L.Ed.2d 292 (2004).
(Brief No. 03–5554).

. . .

A name is now no longer a simple identifier: it is the key to a vast, cross-referenced system of public and private databases, which lay bare the most intimate features of an individual's life. If any person can be coerced by the state to hand over this key to the police, then the protections of the Fourth and Fifth Amendments have been rendered illusory.

The compelled disclosure of personal identification is central to the Court's consideration of this case. Critical to understanding the full consequences of providing identifying information to the police in the modern era is a close examination of the government databases and legal authority that now exists in the United States. Today the police have the ability to peruse increasingly sophisticated computer databases containing information wholly unrelated to the reason for an initial police stop.

Information systems that are currently available to the police, or may soon become available, include the National Crime Information Center ("NCIC"), the Multi–State Anti–Terrorism Information Exchange ("MA-TRIX"), the United States Visitor and Immigrant Status Indicator Technology System ("US–VISIT"), the Driver And Vehicle Information Database ("DAVID"), and the Transportation Workers Identification Credential ("TWIC").

Routine police access to these systems present a range of potential problems. Specifically, the record inaccuracies in the NCIC have been further compounded by the recent decision of the Department of Justice to exempt the record system from the data quality requirements of the Privacy Act, even after the Court's opinion in *Arizona v. Evans*, 514 U.S. 1 (1995), which raised concern about police reliance on faulty data systems.

The MATRIX system raises such troubling privacy concerns, for example, by integrating information from private sector and public sector record systems apparently without regard to the application of state privacy law, that several of the original state partners have withdrawn from the multi-state network project.

US–VISIT, a system of biometric identification originally intended for use by border control officials at ports of entry to the United States, will now enable law enforcement officers routinely to identify individuals, including students on university campuses, within the country.

DAVID, a record system built on motor vehicle information, gives the police rapid access to information that is subject to state and federal privacy law. The DAVID system is evolving rapidly from a government database intended to enforce motor vehicle laws to a general purpose system of identification that could be used routinely in police stops.

Finally, TWIC is an elaborate identification system that will provide police an extensive database of information about individuals who work in the transportation sector.

These systems raise significant Fourth Amendment and Fifth Amendment concerns and implicate individual liberty. The compelled production of personal identification now permits the government to engage in a far more extensive search of personal information stored in government databases than was ever contemplated in *Terry v. Ohio*, 392 U.S. 1 (1968). Further, the mere fact of a police stop may now create a transaction record that will be stored in government record systems, regardless of whether an arrest occurs. While it may be appropriate in the context of a lawful stop of a motor vehicle for the police to determine whether the vehicle is lost or stolen or whether there are outstanding warrants for the driver, it would not be appropriate for the police to conduct such a search of an individual prior to an arrest.

It should be anticipated that the police will obtain ever more efficient systems to monitor and track individuals through interconnected databases. The Supreme Court has repeatedly cautioned that there may come a time when clear safeguards, rooted in the Fourth and Fifth Amendments, on the use of such systems should be established. *See, e.g.,* Whalen v. Roe, 429 U.S. 589, 607 (1977) (Brennan, J., concurring) ("The central storage and easy accessibility of computerized data vastly increase the potential for abuse of that information, . . .''). That time has now come.

Given the extraordinary scope and capability of these new systems, which could easily become systems of mass public surveillance, amici believe it is critical for the Court to oppose the coerced disclosure of identity and to ensure that the police do not use a Terry stop for an unbounded fishing expedition of government computer databases.

. . .

. . . The Multi–State Anti–Terrorism Information Exchange (MATRIX)

The Multi–State Anti–Terrorism Information Exchange (''MATRIX'') is a state-run database system intended to allow law enforcement agencies in participating states to analyze information from multiple criminal and public record sources in near-real time, through a single web-based query. It is an example of the type of record system that seeks to link together a wide range of public and private record systems that will then be made available to law enforcement agents in the field. So little attention has been given to privacy concerns that several of the original state partners recently have withdrawn from the MATRIX project.

MATRIX uses a data mining system called ''Factual Data Analysis'' to analyze public and private data sources. MATRIX was developed by the Florida Department of Law Enforcement (''FDLE'') and a private company, SeisInt, Inc., and is already utilized by 1,000 law enforcement agency users in Florida. Letter from Fla. Dep't of Law Enforcement Commissioner Guy Tunnel to Fla. Today Editorial Editor John Glisch (Oct. 30, 2003).

FDLE Commissioner James Moore has hailed MATRIX as the first step in developing ''a national (not federally controlled) intelligence network.'' FDLE Commissioner James Moore, Remarks to Fla. Sheriffs Winter Conference (Jan. 26, 2003).

. . . Operation of MATRIX

MATRIX is implemented over a criminal justice network, the Regional Information Sharing System Network (''RISSNET''). RISSNET connects 5,700 law enforcement agencies in fifty states and the District of Columbia. MATRIX and ATIX: Information Programs Developed in Response to September 11, 2001, Ga. Homeland Security Bulletin No. 2003 (Ga. Office of Homeland Security), Aug. 1, 2003 at 1; Institute for Intergovernmental Research, MATRIX Program Objectives #2. MATRIX will provide access to other web-enabled ''document storage systems'' similar to those found on RISSNET. *Id.*

MATRIX is operated by a private company, SeisInt, Inc. The personal data is stored on computers owned and operated by SeisInt. This has raised significant concerns about compliance with state privacy laws. *See, e.g.,* Press Advisory, Thurbert Baker, Ga. Attorney General, Attorney General Baker Declares Transfer of Driver information to MATRIX Database Illegal (Oct. 20, 2003).

The MATRIX database includes personal information obtained from public information and private databases. The combined database provides access to an extraordinary range of personal information. Available documentation indicates that the MATRIX system currently includes:

1. Criminal history
2. Driver license information
3. Vehicle registration
4. Incarceration/corrections records
5. Digitized photographs
6. Investigative data
7. Property ownership
8. Address history
9. Marine vessel registration
10. U.S. directory assistance
11. Public utility service connections
12. Bankruptcies
13. Liens and judgments
14. UCC filings
15. U.S. domain names
16. Concealed weapons permits
17. DEA controlled substances licenses
18. FAA aircraft and pilots licenses
19. Federal firearms and explosives licenses
20. Hunting and fishing licenses
21. Professional licenses
22. Voter registration

Ga. Office of Homeland Security, *supra*; Institute for Intergovernmental Research, MATRIX Program Objectives #1; *see* Press Release, SeisInt, Inc., AccurInt Arms Law Enforcement.

MATRIX also includes searchable image data. These digitized images are associated with personal information. FDLE Planning Consultant Hopkins, supra. MATRIX image data include visual mapping data and individuals' pictures. MATRIX can generate "photo 'line-ups'" from an investigative query. Ga. Office of Homeland Security, supra. MATRIX may also be used for visual mapping, which means that an investigator would find a list of all persons who had lived at a requested address. *Id.*

MATRIX is funded partially by the Department of Justice, Office of Justice Programs, Bureau of Justice Assistance through a $4 million grant. Data Mining: Current Applications and Future Possibilities. Hearing before the House Subcomm. on Tech., Info. Policy, Intergovernmental Relations and the Census, Comm. on Gov't Reform, 108th Cong. (2003) (testimony of Hon. Paula B. Dockery, Fla. State Senator) at 5. The grant to the Florida-led state consortium was for database integration, hardware, software, and network support. Institute of Intergovernmental Research, MATRIX Overview. The Department of Homeland Security has pledged a further $8 million towards the project. Robert O'Harrow, Jr., *U.S. Backs Florida's*

New Counterterrorism Database: "Matrix" Offers Law Agencies Faster Access to Americans' Personal Records, WASH. POST, Aug. 6, 2003, at A1 ("Police in Florida are creating a counterterrorism database designed to give law enforcement agencies around the country a powerful new tool to analyze billions of records about both criminals and ordinary Americans.")

. . . Privacy Concerns Have Led States to Withdraw from MATRIX

Thirteen states originally agreed to participate in MATRIX: Alabama, Connecticut, Florida, Georgia, Kentucky, Louisiana, Michigan, New York, Oregon, Pennsylvania, South Carolina, Ohio, and Utah. Ga. Office of Homeland Security, supra; *see* Fla. State Senator Dockery, *supra* at 5. Six states (Alabama, Georgia, Kentucky, Louisiana, Oregon, South Carolina) have dropped out citing a variety of privacy and budget concerns. Ariel Hart, *National Briefing: South: Georgia Pulling Out of Terror Database*, N.Y. TIMES, Oct. 23, 2003, at A26; *see also* Press Release, Ga. Governor Sonny Perdue, Statement of Governor Perdue Regarding the MATRIX Database (Oct. 21, 2003).

Georgia has ceased participation in MATRIX specifically because of privacy concerns over compliance with state privacy laws. Ga. Att'y Gen. Baker, *supra*. Georgia Attorney General Thurbert Baker found that regular transfer of Georgia driver information to FDLE would violate Georgia state laws limiting transfer of data in the driver information database. *Id*. Under Georgia state law, driving records may be transferred only in response to a specific allegation of criminal conduct or unlawful activity. Id (applying O.C.G.A. § 40–5–2(c)(1)(D)). In a public statement ending Georgia's participation in MATRIX, Governor Sonny Perdue also expressed "serious concerns about the privacy interests involved" and withheld further transfer, even if lawful, of any state records to MATRIX. Ga. Governor Perdue, *supra*; *see also* Ga. Att'y Gen. Baker, *supra*.

. . . MATRIX Data Will Be Available to Police Officers on the Street

According to the planning documents, MATRIX will provide a "mechanism for local officers to share important information they collect 'on the street' with other law enforcement agencies." Institute for Intergovernmental Research, MATRIX Program Objectives #3. The Georgia Homeland Security Bulletin describes the MATRIX as being able to identify and locate persons "with minimal input and the push of a button." Ga. Office of Homeland Security, supra. Further, "investigative queries and analyses may be done in 'real time,'" and "requests that previously took hours, days or week [sic] now take seconds." Ga. Office of Homeland Security, *supra*; *see* Fla. State Senator Dockery, *supra* at 5; Ga. Bureau of Investigation Director Keenan, *supra*. *See generally*, Institute of Intergovernmental Research, MATRIX Home. Further, the Georgia Homeland Security Bulletin states that use of the MATRIX system in Florida provided "breakthroughs at speeds that otherwise would not have been possible." Ga. Office of Homeland Security, *supra*.

Officials explain that MATRIX is not a surveillance system, and safeguards exist to protect privacy. But there is no probable cause requirement in the FDLE Guidelines for use of MATRIX. FDLE Guidelines require only reasonable suspicion for releasing analyzed data for investigation. *Id*. at 3. Moreover, reasonable suspicion is not required for the MATRIX system to analyze data internally, since some analysis processes run automatically. *Id*. at 4. In applying the "Factual Data Analysis" component of MATRIX towards terrorist investigation, Florida uses private data mining entities to analyze public data records using law enforcement-defined criteria to produce a "probability score for criminal behavior." Fla. State Senator Dockery, *supra* at 4. These scores direct law enforcement officials to "locate, target, and monitor" subjects. *Id*. at 4. The same process is used by the FDLE Financial Crime Analysis Center to analyze data to identify suspicious financial activity for further investigation. *Id*. at 3.

Web sites are being developed to disseminate MATRIX data to law enforcement agencies and local officers. FDLE Commissioner James Moore, Remarks to Information Processing Interagency Conference (March 4, 2003); MATRIX Program Objectives #3.

. . .

CONCLUSION

The technology of government databases has changed dramatically since the Court held in 1968 that police may detain a person and conduct an investigatory stop with less than probable cause. Today, the police have within their electronic reach access to an extraordinary range of government databases. Moreover, every interaction with the police now raises the possibility that a more extensive personal profile will be established, regardless of whether any criminal conduct has occurred.

In recognition of the extraordinary consequences that may flow from police access to government databases, the Court should make clear that the failure to provide personal identification absent probable cause cannot provide the basis for an arrest. In the twenty-first century, significant Constitutional interests are implicated when the government compels the disclosure of personal identification.

Hiibel v. Sixth Judicial District Court of Nevada, et al.

Supreme Court of the United States, 2004.
542 U.S. 177, 124 S.Ct. 2451, 159 L.Ed.2d 292.

■ JUSTICE KENNEDY delivered the opinion of the Court.

The petitioner was arrested and convicted for refusing to identify himself during a stop allowed by *Terry v. Ohio,* 392 U.S. 1 (1968). He challenges his conviction under the Fourth and Fifth Amendments to the United States Constitution, applicable to the States through the Fourteenth Amendment.

I.

The sheriff's department in Humboldt County, Nevada, received an afternoon telephone call reporting an assault. The caller reported seeing a man assault a woman in a red and silver GMC truck on Grass Valley Road. Deputy Sheriff Lee Dove was dispatched to investigate. When the officer arrived at the scene, he found the truck parked on the side of the road. A man was standing by the truck, and a young woman was sitting inside it. The officer observed skid marks in the gravel behind the vehicle, leading him to believe it had come to a sudden stop.

The officer approached the man and explained that he was investigating a report of a fight. The man appeared to be intoxicated. The officer asked him if he had "any identification on [him]," which we understand as a request to produce a driver's license or some other form of written identification. The man refused and asked why the officer wanted to see identification. The officer responded that he was conducting an investigation and needed to see some identification. The unidentified man became agitated and insisted he had done nothing wrong. The officer explained that he wanted to find out who the man was and what he was doing there. After continued refusals to comply with the officer's request for identification, the man began to taunt the officer by placing his hands behind his back and telling the officer to arrest him and take him to jail. This routine kept up for several minutes: the officer asked for identification 11 times and was refused each time. After warning the man that he would be arrested if he continued to refuse to comply, the officer placed him under arrest.

We now know that the man arrested on Grass Valley Road is Larry Dudley Hiibel. Hiibel was charged with "willfully resist[ing], delay[ing], or obstruct[ing] a public officer in discharging or attempting to discharge any legal duty of his office" in violation of Nev.Rev.Stat. (NRS) § 199.280 (2003). The government reasoned that Hiibel had obstructed the officer in carrying out his duties under § 171.123, a Nevada statute that defines the legal rights and duties of a police officer in the context of an investigative stop. Section 171.123 provides in relevant part:

> "1. Any peace officer may detain any person whom the officer encounters under circumstances which reasonably indicate that the person has committed, is committing or is about to commit a crime.
>
> . . .
>
> "3. The officer may detain the person pursuant to this section only to ascertain his identity and the suspicious circumstances surrounding his presence abroad. Any person so detained shall identify himself, but may not be compelled to answer any other inquiry of any peace officer."

Hiibel was tried in the Justice Court of Union Township. The court agreed that Hiibel's refusal to identify himself as required by § 171.123 "obstructed and delayed Dove as a public officer in attempting to discharge his duty" in violation of § 199.280. App. 5. Hiibel was convicted and fined $250. The Sixth Judicial District Court affirmed, rejecting Hiibel's argument that the application of § 171.123 to his case violated the Fourth and Fifth Amendments. On review the Supreme Court of Nevada rejected the Fourth Amendment challenge in a divided opinion. 59 P.3d 1201 (2002). Hiibel petitioned for rehearing, seeking explicit resolution of his Fifth Amendment challenge. The petition was denied without opinion. We granted certiorari. 540 U.S. 965, 124 S.Ct. 430, 157 L.Ed.2d 309 (2003).

II.

NRS § 171.123(3) is an enactment sometimes referred to as a "stop and identify" statute. *See* Ala.Code § 15–5–30 (West 2003); Ark.Code Ann.

§ 5–71–213(a)(1) (2004); Colo.Rev.Stat. § 16–3–103(1) (2003); Del.Code Ann., Tit. 11, §§ 1902(a), 1321(6) (2003); Fla. Stat. § 856.021(2) (2003); Ga.Code Ann. § 16–11–36(b) (2003); Ill. Comp. Stat. Ch. 725, 5/107–14 (2004); Kan. Stat. Ann. § 22–2402(1) (2003); La.Code Crim. Proc. Ann., Art. 215.1(A) (West 2004); Mo.Rev.Stat. § 84.710(2) (2003); Mont.Code Ann. § 46–5–401(2)(a) (2003); Neb.Rev.Stat. § 29–829 (2003); N.H.Rev. Stat. Ann. §§ 594:2 and 644:6 (Lexis 2003); N.M. Stat. Ann. § 30–22–3 (2004); N.Y.Crim. Proc. Law § 140.50(1) (West 2004); N.D. Cent.Code § 29–29–21 (2003); R.I. Gen. Laws § 12–7–1 (2003); Utah Code Ann. § 77–7–15 (2003); Vt. Stat. Ann., Tit. 24, § 1983 (Supp.2003); Wis. Stat. § 968.24 (2003). *See also* Note, *Stop and Identify Statutes: A New Form of an Inadequate Solution to an Old Problem*, 12 RUTGERS L.J. 585 (1981); Note, *Stop-and-Identify Statutes After* Kolender v. Lawson: *Exploring the Fourth and Fifth Amendment Issues*, 69 IOWA L.REV. 1057 (1984).

Stop and identify statutes often combine elements of traditional vagrancy laws with provisions intended to regulate police behavior in the course of investigatory stops. The statutes vary from State to State, but all permit an officer to ask or require a suspect to disclose his identity. A few States model their statutes on the Uniform Arrest Act, a model code that permits an officer to stop a person reasonably suspected of committing a crime and "demand of him his name, address, business abroad and whither he is going." Warner, *The Uniform Arrest Act*, 28 VA. L.REV. 315, 344 (1942). Other statutes are based on the text proposed by the American Law Institute as part of the Institute's Model Penal Code. *See* ALI, Model Penal Code, § 250.6, Comment 4, pp. 392–393 (1980). The provision, originally designated § 250.12, provides that a person who is loitering "under circumstances which justify suspicion that he may be engaged or about to engage in crime commits a violation if he refuses the request of a peace officer that he identify himself and give a reasonably credible account of the lawfulness of his conduct and purposes." § 250.12 (Tentative Draft No. 13) (1961). In some States, a suspect's refusal to identify himself is a misdemeanor offense or civil violation; in others, it is a factor to be considered in whether the suspect has violated loitering laws. In other States, a suspect may decline to identify himself without penalty.

Stop and identify statutes have their roots in early English vagrancy laws that required suspected vagrants to face arrest unless they gave "a good Account of themselves," 15 Geo. 2, ch. 5, § 2 (1744), a power that itself reflected common-law rights of private persons to "arrest any suspicious night-walker, and detain him till he give a good account of himself. . . ." 2 W. Hawkins, Pleas of the Crown, ch. 13, § 6, p. 130. (6th ed. 1787). In recent decades, the Court has found constitutional infirmity in traditional vagrancy laws. In *Papachristou v. Jacksonville,* 405 U.S. 156 (1972), the Court held that a traditional vagrancy law was void for vagueness. Its broad scope and imprecise terms denied proper notice to potential offenders and permitted police officers to exercise unfettered discretion in the enforcement of the law. *See id.*, at 167–71.

The Court has recognized similar constitutional limitations on the scope and operation of stop and identify statutes. In *Brown v. Texas,* 443 U.S. 47, 52 (1979), the Court invalidated a conviction for violating a Texas stop and identify statute on Fourth Amendment grounds. The Court ruled that the initial stop was not based on specific, objective facts establishing reasonable suspicion to believe the suspect was involved in criminal activity. *See id.*, at 51–52. Absent that factual basis for detaining the defendant, the Court held, the risk of "arbitrary and abusive police practices" was too great and the stop was impermissible. *Id.*, at 52. Four Terms later, the Court invalidated a modified stop and identify statute on vagueness grounds. *See* Kolender v. Lawson, 461 U.S. 352 (1983). The California law in *Kolender* required a suspect to give an officer " 'credible and reliable' " identification when asked to identify himself. Id., at 360. The Court held that the statute was void because it provided no standard for determining what a suspect must do to comply with it, resulting in "virtually unrestrained power to arrest and charge persons with a violation." *Id.*, at 360 (quoting *Lewis v. New Orleans,* 415 U.S. 130 (1974) (Powell, J., concurring in result)).

The present case begins where our prior cases left off. Here there is no question that the initial stop was based on reasonable suspicion, satisfying the Fourth Amendment requirements noted in *Brown* Further, the petitioner has not alleged that the statute is unconstitutionally vague, as in *Kolender* Here the Nevada statute is narrower and more precise. The statute in *Kolender* had been interpreted to require a suspect to give the officer "credible and reliable" identification. In contrast, the Nevada Supreme Court has interpreted NRS § 171.123(3) to require only that a suspect disclose his name. *See* 59 P.3d, at 1206 (opinion of Young, C.J.) ("The suspect is not required to provide private details about his background, but merely to state his name to an officer when reasonable suspicion exists"). As we understand it, the statute does not require a suspect to give the officer a driver's license or any other document. Provided that the suspect either states his name or communicates it to the officer by other means—a choice, we assume, that the suspect may make—the statute is satisfied and no violation occurs. *See* id., at 1206–07.

III.

Hiibel argues that his conviction cannot stand because the officer's conduct violated his Fourth Amendment rights. We disagree.

Asking questions is an essential part of police investigations. In the ordinary course a police officer is free to ask a person for identification without implicating the Fourth Amendment. "[I]nterrogation relating to one's identity or a request for identification by the police does not, by itself, constitute a Fourth Amendment seizure." INS v. Delgado, 466 U.S. 210, 216 (1984). Beginning with *Terry v. Ohio,* 392 U.S. 1 (1968), the Court has recognized that a law enforcement officer's reasonable suspicion that a person may be involved in criminal activity permits the officer to stop the person for a brief time and take additional steps to investigate further. . . .

. . .

Obtaining a suspect's name in the course of a *Terry* stop serves important government interests. Knowledge of identity may inform an officer that a suspect is wanted for another offense, or has a record of violence or mental disorder. On the other hand, knowing identity may help clear a suspect and allow the police to concentrate their efforts elsewhere. Identity may prove particularly important in cases such as this, where the police are investigating what appears to be a domestic assault. Officers called to investigate domestic disputes need to know whom they are dealing with in order to assess the situation, the threat to their own safety, and possible danger to the potential victim.

Although it is well established that an officer may ask a suspect to identify himself in the course of a *Terry* stop, it has been an open question whether the suspect can be arrested and prosecuted for refusal to answer. *See Brown*, 443 U.S., at 53, n.3. Petitioner draws our attention to statements in prior opinions that, according to him, answer the question in his favor. In *Terry*, Justice White stated in a concurring opinion that a person detained in an investigative stop can be questioned but is "not obliged to answer, answers may not be compelled, and refusal to answer furnishes no basis for an arrest." 392 U.S., at 34. The Court cited this opinion in dicta in *Berkemer v. McCarty*, 468 U.S. 420, 439 (1984), a decision holding that a routine traffic stop is not a custodial stop requiring the protections of *Miranda v. Arizona*, 384 U.S. 436 (1966). In the course of explaining why *Terry* stops have not been subject to *Miranda*, the Court suggested reasons why *Terry* stops have a "nonthreatening character," among them the fact that a suspect detained during a *Terry* stop "is not obliged to respond" to questions. See *Berkemer, supra*, at 439, 440. According to petitioner, these statements establish a right to refuse to answer questions during a *Terry* stop.

We do not read these statements as controlling. The passages recognize that the Fourth Amendment does not impose obligations on the citizen but instead provides rights against the government. As a result, the Fourth Amendment itself cannot require a suspect to answer questions. This case concerns a different issue, however. Here, the source of the legal obligation arises from Nevada state law, not the Fourth Amendment. Further, the statutory obligation does not go beyond answering an officer's request to disclose a name. *See* NRS § 171.123(3) ("Any person so detained shall identify himself, but may not be compelled to answer any other inquiry of any peace officer"). As a result, we cannot view the dicta in *Berkemer* or Justice White's concurrence in *Terry* as answering the question whether a State can compel a suspect to disclose his name during a *Terry* stop.

The principles of *Terry* permit a State to require a suspect to disclose his name in the course of a *Terry* stop. The reasonableness of a seizure under the Fourth Amendment is determined "by balancing its intrusion on the individual's Fourth Amendment interests against its promotion of legitimate government interests." Delaware v. Prouse, 440 U.S. 648, 654 (1979). The Nevada statute satisfies that standard. The request for identity has an immediate relation to the purpose, rationale, and practical demands of a *Terry* stop. The threat of criminal sanction helps ensure that the request for identity does not become a legal nullity. On the other hand, the Nevada statute does not alter the nature of the stop itself: it does not change its duration, [United States v. Place, 462 U.S. 696, 709 (1983)] or its location, [Dunaway v. New York, 442 U.S. 200, 212 (1979)]. A state law requiring a suspect to disclose his name in the course of a valid *Terry* stop is consistent with Fourth Amendment prohibitions against unreasonable searches and seizures.

. . .

IV.

Petitioner further contends that his conviction violates the Fifth Amendment's prohibition on compelled self-incrimination. The Fifth Amendment states that "[n]o person . . . shall be compelled in any criminal case to be a witness against himself." To qualify for the Fifth Amendment privilege, a communication must be testimonial, incriminating, and compelled. *See* United States v. Hubbell, 530 U.S. 27, 34–38 (2000).

Respondents urge us to hold that the statements NRS § 171.123(3) requires are nontestimonial, and so outside the Clause's scope. We decline to resolve the case on that basis. "[T]o be testimonial, an accused's communication must itself, explicitly or implicitly, relate a factual assertion or disclose information." Doe v. United States, 487 U.S. 201, 210 (1988). *See also Hubbell,* 530 U.S., at 35. Stating one's name may qualify as an assertion of fact relating to identity. Production of identity documents might meet the definition as well. As we noted in *Hubbell,* acts of production may yield testimony establishing "the existence, authenticity, and custody of items [the police seek]." Id., at 41. Even if these required actions are testimonial, however, petitioner's challenge must fail because in this case disclosure of his name presented no reasonable danger of incrimination.

The Fifth Amendment prohibits only compelled testimony that is incriminating. *See* Brown v. Walker, 161 U.S. 591, 598 (1896) (noting that where "the answer of the witness will not directly show his infamy, but only *tend* to disgrace him, he is bound to answer"). A claim of Fifth Amendment privilege must establish:

> [ ] reasonable ground to apprehend danger to the witness from his being compelled to answer. . . . [T]he danger to be apprehended must be real and appreciable, with reference to the ordinary operation of law in the ordinary course of things,—not a danger of an imaginary and unsubstantial character, having reference to some extraordinary and barely possible contingency, so improbable that no reasonable man would suffer it to influence his conduct.[]

Id., at 599–600 (*quoting* Queen v. Boyes, 1 Best & S. 311, 321 (1861) (Cockburn, C.J.)).

As we stated in *Kastigar v. United States,* 406 U.S. 441, 445 (1972), the Fifth Amendment privilege against compulsory self-incrimination "protects against any disclosures that the witness reasonably believes could be used in a criminal prosecution or could lead to other evidence that might be so used." Suspects who have been granted immunity from prosecution may, therefore, be compelled to answer; with the threat of prosecution removed, there can be no reasonable belief that the evidence will be used against them. *See id.*, at 453.

In this case petitioner's refusal to disclose his name was not based on any articulated real and appreciable fear that his name would be used to incriminate him, or that it "would furnish a link in the chain of evidence needed to prosecute" him. Hoffman v. United States, 341 U.S. 479, 486 (1951). As best we can tell, petitioner refused to identify himself only because he thought his name was none of the officer's business. Even today, petitioner does not explain how the disclosure of his name could have been used against him in a criminal case. While we recognize petitioner's strong belief that he should not have to disclose his identity, the Fifth Amendment does not override the Nevada Legislature's judgment to the contrary absent a reasonable belief that the disclosure would tend to incriminate him.

The narrow scope of the disclosure requirement is also important. One's identity is, by definition, unique; yet it is, in another sense, a universal characteristic. Answering a request to disclose a name is likely to be so insignificant in the scheme of things as to be incriminating only in unusual circumstances. *See* Baltimore City Dept. of Social Servs. v. Bouknight, 493 U.S. 549, 555 (1990) (suggesting that "fact[s] the State could readily establish" may render "any testimony regarding existence or authenticity [of them] insufficiently incriminating"); *Cf.* California v. Byers, 402 U.S. 424, 432 (1971)(opinion of Burger, C. J.). In every criminal case, it is known and must be known who has been arrested and who is being tried. *Cf.* Pennsylvania v. Muniz, 496 U.S. 582, 601–602 (1990) (opinion of Brennan, J.). Even witnesses who plan to invoke the Fifth Amendment privilege answer when their names are called to take the stand. Still, a case may arise where there is a substantial allegation that furnishing identity at the time of a stop would have given the police a link in the chain of evidence needed to convict the individual of a separate offense. In that case, the court can then consider whether the privilege applies, and, if the Fifth Amendment has been violated, what remedy must follow. We need not resolve those questions here.

The judgment of the Nevada Supreme Court is

Affirmed.

■ Justice Stevens, dissenting.

The Nevada law at issue in this case imposes a narrow duty to speak upon a specific class of individuals. The class includes only those persons detained by a police officer "under circumstances which reasonably indicate that the person has committed, is committing or is about to commit a crime"—persons who are, in other words, targets of a criminal investigation. The statute therefore is directed not "at the public at large," but rather "at a highly selective group inherently suspect of criminal activities." Albertson v. Subversive Activities Control Bd., 382 U.S. 70, 79 (1965).

Under the Nevada law, a member of the targeted class "may not be compelled to answer" any inquiry except a command that he "identify himself." Refusal to identify oneself upon request is punishable as a crime. Presumably the statute does not require the detainee to answer any other question because the Nevada Legislature realized that the Fifth Amendment prohibits compelling the target of a criminal investigation to make any other statement. In my judgment, the broad constitutional right to remain silent, which derives from the Fifth Amendment's guarantee that "[n]o person ... shall be compelled in any criminal case to be a witness against himself," U.S. Const., Amdt. 5, is not as circumscribed as the Court suggests, and does not admit even of the narrow exception defined by the Nevada statute.

"[T]here can be no doubt that the Fifth Amendment privilege is available outside of criminal court proceedings and serves to protect persons in all settings in which their freedom of action is curtailed in any significant way from being compelled to incriminate themselves." Miranda v. Arizona, 384 U.S. 436, 467 (1966). It is a "settled principle" that "the police have the right to request citizens to answer voluntarily questions concerning unsolved crimes," but "they have no right to compel them to answer." Davis v. Mississippi, 394 U.S. 721, 727, n. 6 (1969). The protections of the Fifth Amendment are directed squarely toward those who are the focus of the government's investigative and prosecutorial powers. In a criminal trial, the indicted defendant has an unqualified right to refuse to testify and may not be punished for invoking that right. See Carter v. Kentucky, 450 U.S. 288, 299–300 (1981). The unindicted target of a grand jury investigation enjoys the same constitutional protection even if he has been served with a subpoena. See Chavez v. Martinez, 538 U.S. 760, 767–768 (2003). So does an arrested suspect during custodial interrogation in a police station. Miranda, 384 U.S., at 467.

There is no reason why the subject of police interrogation based on mere suspicion, rather than probable cause, should have any lesser protection . . . .

The Court correctly observes that a communication does not enjoy the Fifth Amendment privilege unless it is testimonial. Although the Court declines to resolve this question, ante, at 2460, I think it clear that this case concerns a testimonial communication. Recognizing that whether a communication is testimonial is sometimes a "difficult question," Doe v. United States, 487 U.S. 201, 214–215 (1988), we have stated generally that "[i]t is the 'extortion of information from the accused,' the attempt to force him 'to disclose the contents of his own mind,' that implicates the Self–Incrimination Clause," id., at 211 (citations omitted). While "[t]he vast majority of verbal statements thus will be testimonial and, to that extent at least, will fall within the privilege," id., at 213–214, certain acts and physical evidence fall outside the privilege. In all instances, we have afforded Fifth Amendment protection if the disclosure in question was being admitted because of its content rather than some other aspect of the communication.

Considered in light of these precedents, the compelled statement at issue in this case is clearly testimonial. It is significant that the communication must be made in response to a question posed by a police officer. As we recently explained, albeit in the different context of the Sixth Amendment's Confrontation Clause, "[w]hatever else the term ['testimonial'] covers, it applies at a minimum ... to police interrogations." Crawford v. Washington, 124 S.Ct. 1354, 1374 (2004). Surely police questioning during a *Terry* stop qualifies as an interrogation, and it follows that responses to such questions are testimonial in nature.

Rather than determining whether the communication at issue is testimonial, the Court instead concludes that the State can compel the disclosure of one's identity because it is not "incriminating." *Ante,* at 2460. But our cases have afforded Fifth Amendment protection to statements that are "incriminating" in a much broader sense than the Court suggests. It has "long been settled that [the Fifth Amendment's] protection encompasses compelled statements that lead to the discovery of incriminating evidence even though the statements themselves are not incriminating and are not introduced into evidence." United States v. Hubbell, 530 U.S. 27, 37 (2000). By "incriminating" we have meant disclosures that "could be used in a criminal prosecution or could lead to other evidence that might be so used," Kastigar v. United States, 406 U.S. 441, 445 (1972)—communications, in other words, that "would furnish a link in the chain of evidence needed to prosecute the claimant for a federal crime," Hoffman v. United States, 341 U.S. 479, 486 (1951). Thus, "[c]ompelled testimony that communicates information that may 'lead to incriminating evidence' is privileged even if the information itself is not inculpatory." *Hubbell,* 530 U.S., at 38, (*citing Doe,* 487 U.S., at 208, n. 6).

Given a proper understanding of the category of "incriminating" communications that fall within the Fifth Amendment privilege, it is clear that the disclosure of petitioner's identity is protected. The Court reasons that we should not assume that the disclosure of petitioner's name would be used to incriminate him or that it would furnish a link in a chain of evidence needed to prosecute him. *Ante,* at 2461. But why else would an officer ask for it? And why else would the Nevada Legislature require its disclosure only when circumstances "reasonably indicate that the person has committed, is committing or is about to commit a crime"? If the Court is correct, then petitioner's refusal to cooperate did not impede the police investigation. Indeed, if we accept the predicate for the Court's holding, the statute requires nothing more than a useless invasion of privacy. I think that, on the contrary, the Nevada Legislature intended to provide its police officers with a useful law enforcement tool, and that the very existence of the statute demonstrates the value of the information it demands.

A person's identity obviously bears informational and incriminating worth, "even if the [name] itself is not inculpatory." *Hubbell,* 530 U.S., at 38. A name can provide the key to a broad array of information about the person, particularly in the hands of a police officer with access to a range of law enforcement databases. And that information, in turn, can be tremendously useful in a criminal prosecution. It is therefore quite wrong to suggest that a person's identity provides a link in the chain to incriminating evidence "only in unusual circumstances." *Ante,* at 2461.

The officer in this case told petitioner, in the Court's words, that "he was conducting an investigation and needed to see some identification." *Ante,* at 2455. As the target of that investigation, petitioner, in my view, acted well within his rights when he opted to stand mute.

Accordingly, I respectfully dissent.

■ JUSTICE BREYER, with whom JUSTICE SOUTER and JUSTICE GINSBURG join, dissenting.

Notwithstanding the vagrancy statutes to which the majority refers, see *ante,* at 2456–2457, this Court's Fourth Amendment precedents make clear that police may conduct a *Terry* stop only within circumscribed limits. And one of those limits invalidates laws that compel responses to police questioning.

In *Terry v. Ohio,* 392 U.S. 1 (1968), the Court considered whether police, in the absence of probable cause, can stop, question, or frisk an individual at all. The Court recognized that the Fourth Amendment protects the "right of every individual to the possession and control of his own person." *Id.,* at 9 (quoting Union Pacific R. Co. v. Botsford, 141 U.S. 250, 251 (1891)). At the same time, it recognized that in certain circumstances, public safety might require a limited "seizure," or stop, of an individual against his will. The Court consequently set forth conditions circumscribing when and how the police might conduct a *Terry* stop. They include what has become known as the "reasonable suspicion" standard. 392 U.S., at 20–22. Justice White, in a separate concurring opinion, set forth further conditions. Justice White wrote: "Of course, the person stopped is not obliged to answer, answers may not be compelled, and refusal to answer furnishes no basis for an arrest, although it may alert the officer to the need for continued observation." *Id.,* at 34.

. . .

There is no good reason now to reject this generation-old statement of the law. There are sound reasons rooted in Fifth Amendment considerations for adhering to this Fourth Amendment legal condition circumscribing police authority to stop an individual against his will. *See ante,* at 2461–2464 (STEVENS, J., dissenting). Administrative considerations also militate against change. Can a State, in addition to requiring a stopped individual to answer "What's your name?" also require an answer to "What's your license number?" or "Where do you live?" Can a police officer, who must know how to make a *Terry* stop, keep track of the constitutional answers? After all, answers to any of these questions may, or may not, incriminate, depending upon the circumstances.

Indeed, as the majority points out, a name itself—even if it is not "Killer Bill" or "Rough 'em up Harry"—will sometimes provide the police with "a link in the chain of evidence needed to convict the individual of a separate offense." *Ante,* at 2461. The majority reserves judgment about whether compulsion is permissible in such instances. *Ibid.* How then is a police officer in the midst of a *Terry* stop to distinguish between the majority's ordinary case and this special case where the majority reserves judgment?

The majority presents no evidence that the rule enunciated by Justice White and then by the *Berkemer* Court, which for nearly a generation has set forth a settled *Terry* stop condition, has significantly interfered with law enforcement. Nor has the majority presented any other convincing justification for change. I would not begin to erode a clear rule with special exceptions.

I consequently dissent.

NOTES AND QUESTIONS

1. As the Court notes, not every state has a statute requiring you to identify yourself if a police officer asks you to do so. Would you vote for or against such a statute?

2. Dissenting in *Hiibel,* Justice Stevens expresses concern about "law enforcement databases ... [that] can be tremendously useful in a criminal prosecution," while Justice Breyer also notes that "a name itself ... will sometimes provide the police with 'a link in the chain of evidence needed to convict the individual of a separate offense.'" Do these constitutional considerations capture the privacy risks of modern databases?

3. The amicus brief notes inaccuracies in some of the databases available to the police. If the databases are accurate is the invasion of privacy reduced? Shortly after *Hiibel* was decided, the Matrix system described in the amicus brief was sold to LexisNexis. Civil liberties advocates warned that the combination of Matrix and LexisNexis databases "could be massively intrusive if used in the wrong way," while LexisNexis replied that it will protect the privacy of its users. Robert O'Harrow, *LexisNexis To Buy Seisint for $775 Million: Data Firm's Matrix Tool Generated Controversy,* WASH. POST, July 15, 2004, at E1.

4. *Hiibel* demonstrates an intersection between law and technology that is similar to the application of free speech to the Internet or, years ago, of negligence to aircraft. A different kind of intersection comes into play when we turn to the use of artificial intelligence to do jobs presently done by attorneys.

II. COMPUTERS AND LEGAL REASONING

Edwina L. Rissland, *Artificial Intelligence and Law: Stepping Stones to a Model of Legal Reasoning*

99 YALE L.J. 1957, 1957–61, 1963–64, 1971–73, 1980–81 (1990).

This Comment discusses developments in the twenty-year-old interdisciplinary field of Artificial Intelligence (AI) and law. This field is important for both AI and law because it is directed at improving our understanding and modeling of legal reasoning.

. . .

AI is the study of cognitive processes using the conceptual frameworks and tools of computer science. As a distinct subfield of computer science, AI had its beginnings in the mid-fifties. In 1968 Marvin Minsky, one of the founders of AI, said it well: AI is "the science of making machines do things that would require intelligence if done by man." Thus, all manner of intelligent behavior is in the realm of AI, including playing chess, solving calculus problems, making mathematical discoveries, understanding short stories, learning new concepts, interpreting visual scenes, diagnosing diseases, and reasoning by analogy. Any discussion of AI must note that tasks involving "common sense" reasoning or perception, such as language understanding, are by far the most difficult for AI. More technical tasks, like solving calculus problems or playing chess, are usually much easier. That is because the latter can be framed in well-defined terms and come from totally black-and-white domains, while the former cannot and do not. What distinguishes the AI approach from other studies of cognition and knowledge, such as psychology or philosophy, is its insistence on grounding the analysis in computational terms—preferably in a successfully running computer program that embodies the analysis.

AI is pursued for at least two reasons: to understand the workings of human intelligence and to create useful computer programs and computers that can perform intelligently. Most workers in the field of AI pursue these goals simultaneously. For instance, in the course of designing a computer program for commercial purposes like making credit card approval decisions, the program designer needs to examine how experienced people make such decisions, since they are usually the best, and often the only, source of information about how the job is done. Likewise, in engaging in AI for the sake of understanding or modeling cognition, it is far more satisfying to exhibit a running program: to some degree success is a working computational model.

In the context of law, these twin rationales translate into the twin goals of understanding certain key aspects of legal reasoning and building computational tools useful for legal practice, teaching, or research. An example of the former is the development of an AI model for reasoning based upon the doctrine of precedent. The process of developing an AI model causes one to learn about legal reasoning. Modeling involves elucidating key ingredients of precedent-based reasoning, such as making assessments of the relevance of precedents to new situations, distinguishing contrary cases, and drawing connections between relevant cases; then describing them in detail and building a program to execute them.

An example of the second, more applications-oriented goal, is construction of a set of computational tools (a lawyer's workbench, so to speak) to assist in the preparation of a brief. These may include functions to assist in gathering relevant precedents from data bases, sorting them according to their doctrinal approaches, and "Shepardizing" them. Building a practical system, like one to assist with writing a brief, requires developing analytical models. Typically, satisfaction with an analytical model increases if it offers insights leading to the practical advances.

The desire to develop a model of legal reasoning is not new. Certainly key aspects of legal reasoning, such as the analysis of precedent, have been the subject of many discussions. However, for the most part, previous studies have not provided the level of detail required of an AI model; that is, they have not provided enough detail to indicate how they could be implemented as a computer program. In AI, one is forced to be detailed. For instance, law has been described as "reasoning by example." This may be an appropriate level of description for some purposes, but for AI, it leaves too many questions unanswered. To take advantage of invaluable insights offered by legal scholars about legal reasoning, an AI researcher needs to specify both how the reasoning is to happen and what information and methods are required.

The AI approach forces one to be relentlessly analytic and specific. It advocates that one use ideas and methods of computer science to develop conceptual and computational frameworks.

. . .

[W]e can enumerate several goals that we would like an ideal AI and law program to achieve. It should be able, among other things, to:

1. Reason with cases (both real and hypothetical) and analogies;

2. Reason with rules;

3. Combine several modes of reasoning;

4. Handle ill-defined and open-textured concepts;

5. Formulate arguments and explanations;

6. Handle exceptions to and conflicts among items of knowledge, like rules;

7. Accommodate changes in the base of legal knowledge, particularly legal concepts, and handle non-monotonicity, that is, changes in which previous truths no longer hold as more becomes known;

8. Model common sense knowledge;

9. Model knowledge of intent and belief;

10. Perform some aspects of natural language understanding.

We are a long way from such an ideal. There is, however, activity on all of these important fronts, and impressive progress on a few.

In fact, one can today speculate about which of these desiderata can be expected now, in the near future, someday, or probably never. Presently, AI is actively pushing back the boundaries on case-based reasoning (goal 1), has well-understood methodologies in rule-based reasoning (goal 2), and is exploring multi-paradigm reasoning (goal 3). Reasoning with open-textured predicates (goal 4) has had an admirable first cut, but it will require further contributions from other AI specialities like case-based reasoning (CBR) and machine learning. Major contributions have been made to precedent-based argumentation, and progress is being made on explanation (goal 5). Thus one can be optimistic that someday AI will be able to deal with many of the key goals for an AI and law program in at least a rudimentary manner. I would go so far as to say that the first five desiderata are attainable now or in the near future.

The next two desiderata—handling exceptions and conflict (goal 6) and accommodating to change in the base of knowledge (goal 7)—presently are being addressed broadly in AI, particularly in machine learning. It is reasonable to expect AI programs to be able to handle gradual change soon, but not abrupt or rapid change. Non-monotonicity is being vigorously explored by an active cohort of researchers, primarily using approaches grounded in sophisticated logics. Thus, these two desiderata might be met someday.

As for the last three desiderata, I am much less optimistic. Modeling common sense reasoning, knowledge of intent and belief, and natural language capabilities are by far the hardest tasks. With regard to language, some capabilities like interactive dialogue and understanding of short summaries can be achieved in narrowly circumscribed domains; fuller capabilities are far off. Widely applicable general "solutions" are very distant. Some, like the understanding of written appellate opinions—the ultimate fantasy—I expect never to see.

. . .

[One] landmark AI project was Kevin Ashley's, which was done in this author's research group at the University of Massachusetts. Ashley developed a program called HYPO to model certain aspects of case-based reasoning as exemplified by appellate-style argumentation with precedents. The problem area of this project was trade secret law. The task was to produce elements of precedent-based argument. The HYPO project focused solely on reasoning with cases, and was the first project—not only in AI and law, but also in AI in general—to attack squarely the problem of reasoning with cases and hypotheticals in a precedent-based manner.

HYPO performs as follows: Given a fact situation, HYPO analyzes it according to its model of trade secret law and then retrieves relevant cases from its knowledge base of cases. It then determines which relevant cases are most on point, or potentially so, for whose point of view, and from which analytic approach. HYPO then generates the skeleton of an argument. In such an argument snippet, HYPO first argues for side one (plaintiff or defendant) by making a legal point and citing its best, most on point cases; then it argues for side two by responding with a counterpoint, citing a most on point case supporting side two's point of view or also by distinguishing the current facts from side one's cases; and finally, HYPO argues again for side one with a rebuttal of side two's position, which may include distinguishing side two's cases and strengthening the relationship of side one's analysis to the current facts. At various points in the argument, HYPO may generate and employ hypotheticals—for instance, to refute a claim when no actual counter-example case exists in HYPO's knowledge base of cases.

HYPO is able to: assess relevancy of cases; decide for each side which relevant cases are most on point and which of these are best to cite in argument; analogize and distinguish cases; generate and reason with hypotheticals; cite various types of counterexamples to a point; and construct the skeleton of a case-citing argument. HYPO does not in any way attempt to bring in policy-level concerns or argumentation; rather, it sticks to arguing with cases, on their facts, in a technical way. HYPO also does not include other aspects of legal reasoning, such as reasoning with rules.

A key feature of HYPO is a kind of case index, called a "dimension," which it uses to retrieve and analyze cases. Dimensions represent important legal factors. They encode the knowledge that the presence of certain facts enables a case to be addressed from a certain point of view. A dimension enables HYPO to retrieve a set of cases that support the same analytic approach and to compare and assess the relative strength of the cases within this group.

HYPO uses dimensions to define concepts like "relevant," "most on point" and "best" cases. In HYPO, a case is considered "relevant" if it shares at least one dimension with the fact situation. HYPO ranks cases according to how on point they are by examining the overlap between the set of dimensions present in the fact situation and the sets of dimensions present in the cases. If the overlapping set of dimensions of one case, B, is contained within that of another case, A, then A is defined as more on point than B, the rationale being that A has more lines of analysis in common with the fact situation than does B.

By then taking into account which cases support or cut against a party, their relative strength along shared dimensions, and the dimensions not shared, HYPO is able to analogize, distinguish, and otherwise manipulate cases to construct snippets of precedent-citing argument. For instance, to distinguish a case that the opposing party, say the plaintiff, has cited as controlling the outcome of the current fact situation, HYPO looks at the cited case for the existence of dimensions unshared with the current situation. HYPO then argues, for the defendant, that the presence or absence in the current factual setting of these dimensions diminishes the applicability of the cited case; in other words, these are differences that really make a difference.

To summarize, the HYPO project models some of the key ingredients of reasoning with precedents. The model provides computational definitions of relevant cases, on point cases, and best cases to cite. Because of the precision of HYPO's model, a researcher can examine specific details and assumptions. By providing an analysis and computational model for reasoning with cases, perhaps the most vital aspect of legal reasoning, Ashley's work is a giant step toward the goal of understanding legal argumentation.

. . .

I have tried to show how AI and law researchers are pursuing their twin goals of analytic and practical advances, and how past and ongoing research can be viewed as a coherent attempt to model legal reasoning, particularly argumentation. Even though we may be a long way from some vision of the ideal legal reasoning AI program, and in fact may never be able to achieve certain aspects of human expertise, we can already accomplish very interesting and useful projects. We can use the fine lens of AI to explicate the process of legal reasoning, for instance the creation of case-based arguments; to shed light on questions in legal philosophy, such as the nature of open-textured predicates; and to provide practical, even socially beneficial, applications, such as expert systems in certain administrative areas. The insistence on using computational methods in the AI approach provides a useful discipline for considering longstanding issues in legal reasoning.

Although I have not discussed it here, this body of research can also be fruitfully applied to the law school curriculum. For instance, we can provide our law students with environments in which to examine their own legal knowledge. The conceptual framework of AI can also provide a way to describe our own expertise, such as posing of artful hypotheticals, and show students how they may also possibly acquire it. AI provides a set of tools, based on detailed models of representation and process.

By this discussion, I hope both to encourage those wishing to attempt AI-style projects, and also to reassure those unsure of whether we should.

For instance, some might be concerned that the use of AI models will somehow trivialize legal reasoning by making it seem too simple, undermine the importance of lawyers and judges by relegating them to the role of mere users of systems which do all of the interesting reasoning, or dehumanize us by describing intelligent behavior in well-defined terms. I think AI research shows just the opposite: The more we understand human reasoning, the more we marvel at its richness and flexibility, the more questions we ask as we try to understand its workings, and the more we require of a computer program exhibiting intelligence.

Legal reasoning is complex. Our current AI models, albeit too simple, are but steps to more subtle and complete models, and at each step we understand more. There will always be a need for human lawyers and judges. The goal is to assist, not to replace. Demystification of some of the most precious qualities of human intelligence is not to be feared; understanding does not destroy or diminish that which is understood. We should not be afraid to know how we know.

Cass R. Sunstein, *Of Artificial Intelligence and Legal Reasoning*

8 U. Chi. L. Sch. Roundtable 29 (2001).

I.   HYPO and Analogy

The computer on which I am now writing is capable of many impressive feats. Sometimes it talks to me. It can recognize spelling errors and point them out to me. It is astonishing how many words it seems to know. My computer can also find (some) bad writing, and it lets me know when I should rewrite (some) bad sentences. Everyone knows that the best computer chess player can beat the best human chess player. Fewer people know that an onboard computer system from Carnegie Mellon University has driven a van almost all of the 2,849 miles from Washington, D.C., to San Diego, California, both day and night, in the rain, at an average of sixty-three miles per hour. And this is only the barest tip of the iceberg.

Can computers engage in legal reasoning too? Can they do it well? Even better than people? Some grounds for an affirmative answer might emerge from the simple observation that much of legal reasoning is analogical in nature. In ordinary life, analogical reasoning often takes the form White House is to President as X is to Congress, with the solution consisting of a judgment that X is the Capitol Building. The task of identifying good analogies—the kind of task imposed on high school students—seems to be the sort of thing at which computers can excel. If this is right, perhaps computers can do well in law too, simply because legal reasoning is pervasively analogical and based on close attention to past cases. An understanding of the relationship between artificial intelligence and legal reasoning might well illuminate both of these endeavors.

It is best to anchor the discussion in an illustration. Suppose that the rule in State A is that employers can discharge employees "at will," that is, for any reason or for no reason at all. Suppose that an airline then discharges a copilot for refusing to fly a plane that the copilot believes to be unsafe to fly. Is the discharge lawful?

Let us assume that there are many analogies in the relevant jurisdiction. Suppose that the courts in State A have created a series of public policy exceptions to the at will rule—that they have said that an employer cannot be discharged for refusing to commit a crime, or for obtaining workers' compensation benefits, or for cooperating with the police about potential criminal activity on the part of the employer. Suppose too that courts have limited the reach of the public policy argument by allowing employers to discharge employees for smoking on the premises, for reporting to the Community Credit Bureau about possible regulatory violations by a bank, and for engaging in political activity outside of the workplace on behalf of candidates of whom the employers disapprove. Might it be possible for a computer to find, or show, which cases are "most" analogous to the discharge of the copilot, and which cases are "least" analogous to it?

A number of people have attempted to answer this question in the affirmative—to show the potential role of artificial intelligence in assisting lawyers, and perhaps even in engaging in legal reasoning. I will use as an illustration an extremely interesting book by Kevin Ashley, which makes some striking claims about the role of computer programs in analogical reasoning in law.[4] Ashley has created a computer program, HYPO, which appears to excel at providing assistance in trade secrets cases. If HYPO is told about a case, HYPO will, among other things, draw up a set of analogous cases, tell you how they are similar and how they might be distinguished, rank them in order of analogousness, and even give you arguments about how to meet the claim that the cases are different from the case at hand, with citations. Ashley suggests that HYPO is far more useful, in many ways, than LEXIS and Westlaw, insofar as the latter simply rely on "keywords" in past cases.

More strikingly, he shows that HYPO's performance, when confronted with a fact pattern, is not so different from the performance of actual judges. HYPO tends to refer to the same cases and to make the same arguments about how they are similar and different; HYPO even makes similar responses to claims that cases are similar and different. But Ashley's conclusion is still more ambitious: "If lawyers argue with precedents precisely because it is not feasible to prove the right answer by deductive logic, then the goal of a theory of analogical legal argument should not be to explain what the right answer is. Precedential reasoning is interesting precisely because, even without logical necessity, there still may be an ordering to the persuasiveness of arguments. The appropriate goal for a theory of arguing from precedents is to describe that order accurately ... HYPO is a step toward such a theory."

How does HYPO provide "a step" toward a theory of accurately describing the "order" of the persuasiveness of arguments? How would we know if artificial intelligence is actually engaging in legal reasoning?

4. KEVIN D. ASHLEY, MODELING LEGAL ARGUMENT (1990).

II.   Weak and Strong

A.   Hypotheses

What I am going to urge here is that there is a weak and a strong version of the claims for artificial intelligence in legal reasoning, that we should accept the weak version, and that we should reject the strong version, because it is based on an inadequate account of what legal reasoning is. We should reject the strong version not because artificial intelligence is, in principle, incapable of doing what the strong version requires (there is no way to answer that question, in principle), but because there is no evidence that, at the present time, any computer program is in a position to do what is necessary. To the question, can computer programs engage in legal reasoning, the best answer is therefore: Not yet.

According to the weak version, artificial intelligence can serve as a large improvement on existing computerized services such as LEXIS and Westlaw, because well-designed programs are able to assemble an array of relevant cases, to suggest similarities and differences, and to sketch arguments and counterarguments. This is a true and important point. In the strong version, artificial intelligence can now engage in legal reasoning, because a well-designed program can tell a lawyer, or even a judge, what cases are really closest to the case at hand and what cases are properly distinguished from it. I believe that the strong version is wrong, because it misses a central feature of analogical reasoning: its inevitably evaluative, value-driven character.

What is legal reasoning? Let us agree that it is often analogical. In his classic discussion of legal reasoning,[a]. Edward Levi rightly emphasizes this point. But in doing so, Levi makes a serious mistake: He suggests that when engaging in reasoning by example, courts ask what case is "more" similar to the case at hand. It is much more accurate to say that analogizers in law have to ask which case has relevant similarities to the case at hand. It is more accurate still to say that whether a case has relevant similarities to the case at hand depends on the principle for which the initial case is said, on reflection, to stand. It follows that the crucial step in analogical reasoning consists, not in a finding of "more" similarities, not in establishing "many" distinctions, and not even in showing "relevant" similarities and differences, but instead in the identification of a principle that justifies a claim of similarity or difference. Because the identification of that principle is a matter of evaluation, and not of finding or counting something, artificial intelligence is able to engage in analogical reasoning only to the extent that it is capable of making good evaluative judgments.

. . .

We can therefore venture a hypothesis: Since HYPO can only retrieve cases and identify similarities and differences, HYPO cannot really reason analogically. The reason is that HYPO has no special expertise in making

---

a.   [Eds.—EDWARD H. LEVI, AN INTRODUC-
TION TO LEGAL REASONING (1949), Chapter 1, I.
D., *supra*.]

good evaluative judgments. Indeed, there is no reason to think that HYPO can make evaluative judgments at all.

B. An Example

Consider the problem with which I began. Is an airline permitted to discharge a copilot who refuses to fly a plane on the ground that it is unsafe to fly? Let us see how HYPO might be helpful on this question. HYPO might show that, in a way, this case is like a case in which an employer discharges someone for refusing to commit perjury. In both cases, the employer's action threatens to injure third parties. On the other hand, HYPO might add, the cases are distinguishable: The discharge by the airline does not threaten to produce a crime, and in any case the airline seems to have a legitimate interest in ensuring that safety judgments are made by pilots rather than copilots. Perhaps HYPO will note that, in a way, the airline case is "most" like the decision allowing employees to be fired for reporting possible regulatory violations by a bank. In the airline case, however, the discharge would have more serious consequences, including many deaths. Doesn't this distinction make a difference?

The only way to answer these questions, and to come to terms with the universe of analogies, is to settle on a principle that explains why the case at hand should fall on one or another side of the line. We might say, for example, that an employer is never permitted to discharge an employee as a result of an objectively reasonable judgment by the employee that a certain course of action is necessary to save lives. This principle does not conflict with any of the precedents. Or we might say that an employer is always permitted to discharge an employee when the employee has refused to accept a reasonable order from a hierarchical superior, if that order (a) is job-related and (b) would not require the employee to commit a crime. This principle does not conflict with any of the precedents.

How should a court choose between the two possible principles? How should a lawyer persuade a court to make that choice? It is not helpful to say that the question is which precedent is "closer" to the case at hand. Whether a precedent is closer depends not on a factual inquiry, but on identification of a (normative) principle by which "closeness" can be established. It is more helpful to proceed by asking which principle is actually better. How can we figure that out? An important question is whether the pro-employee principle in the airline case would actually improve safety on balance (or instead perhaps impair safety, as the Court of Appeals suggested in the case). Another important question is whether the pro-employee principle would disrupt airplane operations by giving copilots a right to veto flights when safety is not much of an issue. It is worthwhile to note that these are empirical issues. Judges may not know how to answer them. But my guess is that HYPO, with its admittedly excellent database, knows even less.

There is yet another avenue for progress, involving an assessment of the proposed principle by seeing if it is inconsistent from the normative point of view with anything else that we believe, or to which the legal system has committed itself or would likely commit itself. Here HYPO is not entirely unhelpful, but it can hardly do what needs to be done. I think that Dworkin is correct to suggest that legal reasoning often consists of an effort to make best constructive sense out of past legal events. If analogical reasoning is understood in this light, the analogizer attempts to make best constructive sense out of a past decision by generating a principle that best justifies it, and by bringing that principle to bear on the case at hand. Why should we think that HYPO has any skill at that endeavor?

My conclusion is that artificial intelligence is, in the domain of legal reasoning, a kind of upscale LEXIS or Westlaw—bearing, perhaps, the same relationship to these services as LEXIS and Westlaw have to Shepard's. . . .

III.   Three Qualifications

There are three qualifications to what I have said thus far. First, precedents will sometimes sharply constrain the law's room to maneuver. . . . An upscale version of LEXIS, one that has a full stock of precedents on hand, should be able to identify and resolve problems of this kind.

The second qualification is that we cannot exclude the possibility that, eventually, computer programs will be able both to generate competing principles for analogical reasoning and to give grounds for thinking that one or another principle is best. Perhaps computers will be able to engage in the kind of empirical testing that is often a crucial (though overlooked) basis for good legal outcomes. Perhaps computers will be able to say whether a particular normative principle fits well with the normative commitments of most people in the relevant community. I have hardly suggested that these are unimaginable possibilities. The possibilities for growth in the domain of artificial intelligence cannot be predicted at this exceptionally early stage.

The third qualification is that the weak and strong versions of the claims for artificial intelligence in law, as I have described them, are really poles on a continuum, not a dichotomy, and there is reason to hope for movement from the weak to the strong. . . .

I have emphasized that those who cannot make evaluative arguments cannot engage in analogical reasoning as it occurs in law. Computer programs do not yet reason analogically. But this proposition should not be confused with the suggestion that in the nature of things, evaluative arguments are uniquely the province of human beings, or that computer programs will never be able to help human beings with it, or even to engage in it on their own.

NOTES AND QUESTIONS

1. Sunstein leaves open the question of whether computers could someday make "evaluative arguments . . . on their own." Do you think that day will come during your lifetime as an attorney? If it does, how will it affect your work? For an effort to explain how artificial intelligence can incorporate analogical and evaluative reasoning, see Kevin D. Ashley, *An AI Model of Case–Based Legal Argument from a Jurisprudential Viewpoint*, 10 ARTIFICIAL INTELLIGENCE & LAW 163 (2002).

2. If you were writing a program to perform a legal task, you would probably question outstanding attorneys about how they proceed. What kinds of questions might you ask a criminal defense lawyer to help you in writing a program that would advise a client as to when to plead guilty? Is there any skill the defense lawyer has that could not be explained in response to probing questions from you? Are there limits on expert systems other than those identified by Sunstein?

Expert systems already on the market include a virtual Patent Advisor that General Electric has developed for its own use in conjunction with Jnana Technologies Corporation. *See* Krysten Crawford, *Robot, Esq.*, FORBES, Oct. 2, 2000, at 90. A variety of legal web advisors are already shaping portions of the law practice landscape. *See, e.g.*, Richard Gruner, *Thinking Like a Lawyer: Expert Systems for Legal Analysis*, 1 HIGH TECH. L.J. 259 (1987); Darryl R. Mountain, *Could New Technologies Cause Great Law Firms to Fail*, 52 SYRACUSE L. REV. 1065 (2002). Scholars and practitioners have devoted particular attention to the question of how artificial intelligence can illuminate proof issues in court. *See* Symposium, *Artificial Intelligence and Judicial Proof*, 22 CARDOZO L. REV. 1365 (2001).

3. The question of the extent to which computer programs could perform tasks presently done by attorneys and judges is, of course, a subset of a much larger question. There are those who believe that all problems solvable by a human being are, in principle, reducible to a set of algorithms that can be solved by a machine, while others contend that human beings often use intuitive, unconscious approaches highly dependent on context that could never be duplicated mechanically. *See, e.g.*, HUBERT L. DREYFUS & STUART E. DREYFUS, MIND OVER MACHINE (1986). In practice, the predictions made by artificial intelligence supporters of what tasks will be taken over by machines have often proved overly optimistic. IGOR ALEKSANDER & PIERS BURNETT, THINKING MACHINES: THE SEARCH FOR ARTIFICIAL INTELLIGENCE 195 (1987).

4. One way to test the outer limits of computer capability in the legal world is to consider the work of judges in difficult cases. In a United States Supreme Court case involving review of a trial court decision in Puerto Rico, Justice Oliver W. Holmes wrote for the Court:

> This Court has stated many times the deference due to the understanding of the local courts upon matters of purely local concern. . . . This is especially true in dealing with the decisions of a Court inheriting and brought up in a different system from that which prevails here. When we contemplate such a system from the outside it seems like a wall of stone, every part even with all the others, except so far as our own legal education may lead us to see subordinations to which we are accustomed. But to one brought up within it, varying emphasis, tacit assumptions, unwritten practices, a thousand influences gained only from life, may give to the different parts wholly new values that logic and grammar never could have got from the books.

Diaz v. Gonzales, 261 U.S. 102, 43 S.Ct. 286, 67 L.Ed. 550 (1923).

5. Could a computer ever be taught the "thousand influences gained only from life" of which Holmes speaks? If Holmes is right, is a wealthy judge able to understand a dispute involving poor people? Indeed, if judging as presently practiced involves unspoken assumptions, is that cause for celebration? Suppose, for example, that a judge has unspoken, perhaps even unconscious, sexist assumptions. Would it be better to replace such a judge with a more mechanical decisionmaker— one that is clearly unprejudiced? Or would the machine have prejudices of its own?

III.   COMPUTERS, RIGHTS AND THE DEFINITION OF LIFE

Bruce Mazlish, *The Fourth Discontinuity*
8 TECH. & CULTURE 1, 1–8 (1967).

A famous cartoon in *The New Yorker* magazine shows a large computer with two scientists standing excitedly beside it. One of them holds in his hand the tape just produced by the machine, while the other gapes at the message printed on it. In clear letters, it says, "Cogito, ergo sum," the famous Cartesian phrase, "I think, therefore I am."

My next cartoon has not yet been drawn. It is a fantasy on my part. In it, a patient, wild of eye and hair on end, is lying on a couch in a psychiatrist's office talking to an analyst, who is obviously a machine. The analyst-machine is saying, "Of course I'm human—aren't you?"[1]

These two cartoons are a way of suggesting the threat which the increasingly perceived continuity between man and the machine poses to us today. It is with this topic that I wish to deal now, approaching it in terms of what I shall call the "fourth discontinuity." In order, however, to explain what I mean by the "fourth discontinuity," I must first place the term in a historical context.

In the eighteenth lecture of his *General Introduction to Psychoanalysis*, originally delivered at the University of Vienna between 1915 and 1917, Freud suggested his own place among the great thinkers of the past who had outraged man's naive self-love. First in the line was Copernicus, who taught that our earth "was not the center of the universe, but only a tiny speck in a world-system of a magnitude hardly conceivable." Second was Darwin, who "robbed man of his peculiar privilege of having been specially created, and relegated him to a descent from the animal world." Third, now, was Freud himself. On his own account, Freud admitted, or claimed, that psychoanalysis was "endeavoring to prove to the 'ego' of each one of us that he is not even master in his own house, but that he must remain content with the veriest scraps of information about what is going on unconsciously in his own mind."

A little later in 1917, Freud repeated his sketch concerning the three great shocks to man's ego. In his short essay, "A Difficulty in the Path of Psychoanalysis," he again discussed the cosmological, biological, and now psychological blows to human pride and, when challenged by his friend Karl Abraham, admitted, "You are right in saying that the enumeration of

---

1. After finishing the early drafts of this article, I secured unexpected confirmation of my "fantasy" concerning an analyst-machine (which is not, in itself, critical to my thesis). A story in the *New York Times,* March 12, 1965, reports that "a computerized typewriter has been credited with remarkable success at a hospital here in radically improving the condition of several children suffering an extremely severe form of childhood schizophrenia.... What has particularly amazed a number of psychiatrists is that the children's improvement occurred without psychotherapy; only the machine was involved. It is almost as much human as it is machine. It talks, it listens, it responds to being touched, it makes pictures or charts, it comments and explains, it gives information and can be set up to do all this in any order. In short, the machine attempts to combine in a sort of science-fiction instrument all the best of two worlds—human and machine. It is called an Edison Responsive Environment Learning System. It is an extremely sophisticated 'talking' typewriter (a cross between an analogue and digital computer) that can teach children how to read and write.... Dr. Campbell Goodwin speculates that the machine was able to bring the autistic children to respond because it eliminated humans as communication factors. Once the children were able to communicate, something seemed to unlock in their minds, apparently enabling them to carry out further normal mental activities that had eluded them earlier."

my last paper may give the impression of claiming a place beside Copernicus and Darwin."

There is some reason to believe that Freud may have derived his conviction from Ernst Haeckel, the German exponent of Darwinism, who in his book *Natürliche Schöpfungsgeschichte* (1889) compared Darwin's achievement with that of Copernicus and concluded that together they had helped remove the last traces of anthropomorphism from science. Whatever the origin of Freud's vision of himself as the last in the line of ego-shatterers, his assertion has been generally accepted by those, like Ernest Jones, who refer to him as the "Darwin of the Mind."

The most interesting extension of Freud's self-view, however, has come from the American psychologist, Jerome Bruner. Bruner's version of what Freud called his "transvaluation" is in terms of the elimination of discontinuities: where discontinuity means an emphasis on breaks or gaps in the phenomena of nature—for example, a stress on the sharp differences between physical bodies in the heavens or on earth or between one form of animal matter and another—instead of an emphasis on its continuity. Put the other way, the elimination of discontinuity, that is, the establishment of a belief in a continuum of nature, can be seen as the creation of continuities, and this is the way Bruner phrases it. According to Bruner, the first continuity was established by the Greek physicist-philosophers of the sixth century, rather than by Copernicus. Thus, thinkers like Anaximander conceived of the phenomena of the physical world as "continuous and monistic, as governed by the common laws of matter."[5] The creating of the second continuity, that between man and the animal kingdom was, of course, Darwin's contribution, a necessary condition for Freud's work. With Freud, according to Bruner, the following continuities were established: the continuity of organic lawfulness, so that "accident in human affairs was no more to be brooked as 'explanation' than accident in nature"; the continuity of the primitive, infantile, and archaic as co-existing with the civilized and evolved; and the continuity between mental illness and mental health.

In this version of the three historic ego-smashings, man is placed on a continuous spectrum in relation to the universe, to the rest of the animal kingdom, and to himself. He is no longer discontinuous with the world around him. In an important sense, it can be contended, once man is able to accept this situation, he is in harmony with the rest of existence. Indeed, the longing of the early nineteenth-century romantics, and of all "alienated" beings since, for a sense of "connection" is fulfilled in an unexpected manner.

---

5. For Bruner's views, see his "Freud and the Image of Man," Partisan Review, XXIII, No. 3 (Summer 1956), 340–47. In place of both Bruner's sixth-century Greek physicists and Freud's Copernicus, I would place Galileo as the breaker of the discontinuity that was thought to exist in the material world. It was Galileo, after all, who first demonstrated that the heavenly bodies are of the same substance as the "imperfect" earth and subject to the same mechanical laws. In his *Dialogue on the Two Principal World Systems* (1632), he not only supported the "world system" of Copernicus against Ptolemy but established that our "world," i.e., the earth, is a natural part of the other "world," i.e., the solar system. Hence, the universe at large is one "continuous" system, a view at best only implied in Copernicus. Whatever the correct attribution, Greek physicists, Copernicus, or Galileo, Freud's point is not in principle affected.

Yet, to use Bruner's phraseology, though not his idea, a fourth and major discontinuity, or dichotomy, still exists in our time. It is the discontinuity between man and machine. In fact, my thesis is that this fourth discontinuity must now be eliminated—indeed, we have started on the task—and that in the process man's ego will have to undergo another rude shock, similar to those administered by Copernicus (or Galileo), Darwin, and Freud. To put it bluntly, we are now coming to realize that man and the machines he creates are continuous and that the same conceptual schemes, for example, that help explain the workings of his brain also explain the workings of a "thinking machine." Man's pride and his refusal to acknowledge this continuity, is the substratum upon which the distrust of technology and an industrialized society has been reared. Ultimately, I believe, this last rests on man's refusal to understand and accept his own nature—as being continuous with the tools and machines he constructs. Let me now try to explain what is involved in this fourth discontinuity.

. . .

The evidence seems strong today that man evolved from the other animals into humanity through a continuous interaction of tool, physical, and mental-emotional changes. The old view that early man arrived on the evolutionary scene, fully formed, and then proceeded to discover tools and the new ways of life which they made possible is no longer acceptable. As Sherwood L. Washburn, professor of anthropology at the University of California, puts it, "From the rapidly accumulating evidence it is now possible to speculate with some confidence on the manner in which the way of life made possible by tools changed the pressures of natural selection and so changed the structure of man." The details of Washburn's argument are fascinating, with its linking of tools with such physical traits as pelvic structure, bipedalism, brain structure, and so on, as well as with the organization of men in co-operative societies and the substitution of morality for hormonal control of sexual and other "social" activities. Washburn's conclusion is that "it was the success of the simplest tools that started the whole trend of human evolution and led to the civilizations of today."

Darwin, of course, had had a glimpse of the role of tools in man's evolution. It was Karl Marx, however, who first placed the subject in a new light. Accepting Benjamin Franklin's definition of man as a "tool-making animal," Marx suggested in *Das Kapital* that "the relics of the instruments of labor are of no less importance in the study of vanished socio-economic forms, than fossil bones are in the study of the organization of extinct species." As we know, Marx wished to dedicate his great work to Darwin—a dedication rejected by the cautious biologist—and we can see part of Marx's reason for this desire in the following revealing passage:

Darwin has aroused our interest in the history of *natural technology,* that is to say in the origin of the organs of plants and animals as productive instruments utilised for the life purposes of those creatures. Does not the history of the origin of the productive organs of men in society, the organs which form the material basis of every kind of social organisation, deserve equal attention? Since, as Vico [in the New Science (1725)] says, the essence of the distinction between human history and natural history is that the former is the work of man and the latter is not, would not the history of *human technology* be easier to write than the history of natural technology? Technology reveals man's dealings with nature, discloses the direct productive activities of his life, thus throwing light upon social relations and the resultant mental conceptions.

Only a dogmatic anti-Marxist could deny that Marx's brilliant imagination had led him to perceive a part of the continuity between man and his tools. Drawn off the track, perhaps, by Vico's distinction between human and natural history as man-made and God-made, Marx might almost be given a place in the pantheon of Copernicus, Darwin, and Freud as a destroyer of man's discontinuities with the world about him. Before our present-day anthropologists, Marx had sensed the unbreakable connection between man's evolution as a social being and his development of tools. He did not sense, however, the second part of our subject, that man and his tools, especially in the form of modern, complicated machines, are part of a theoretical continuum.

.   .   .

The *locus classicus* of the modern insistence on the fourth discontinuity is, as is well known, the work of Descartes. In his *Discourse on Method,* for example, he sets up God and the soul on one side, as without spatial location or extension, and the material-mechanical world in all its aspects, on the other side. Insofar as man's mind or soul participates in reason—which means God's reason—man knows this division or dualism of mind and matter, for, as Descartes points out, man could not know this fact from his mere understanding, which is based solely on his senses, "a location where it is clearly evident that the ideas of God and the soul have never been."

Once having established his God, and man's participation through reason in God, Descartes could advance daringly to the very precipice of a world without God. He conjures up a world in imaginary space and shows that it must run according to known natural laws. Similarly, he imagines that "God formed the body of a man just like our own, both in the external configuration of its members and in the internal configuration of its organs, without using in its composition any matter but that which I had described [i.e., physical matter]. I also assumed that God did not put into this body any rational soul [defined by Descartes as 'that part of us distinct from the body whose essence . . . is only to think']."

Analyzing this purely mechanical man, Descartes boasts of how he has shown "what changes must take place in the brain to cause wakefulness, sleep, and dreams; how light, sounds, odors, taste, heat, and all the other qualities of external objects can implant various ideas through the medium of the senses . . . I explained what must be understood by that animal sense which receives these ideas, by memory which retains them and by imagination which can change them in various ways and build new ones from them." In what way, then, does such a figure differ from real man? Descartes confronts his own created "man" forthrightly; it is worth quoting the whole of his statement:

> Here I paused to show that if there were any machines which had the organs and appearance of a monkey or of some other unreasoning animal,

we would have no way of telling that it was not of the same nature as these animals. But if there were a machine which had such a resemblance to our bodies, and imitated our actions as far as possible, there would always be two absolutely certain methods of recognizing that it was still not truly a man. The first is that it could never use words or other signs for the purpose of communicating its thoughts to others, as we do. It indeed is conceivable that a machine could be so made that it would utter words, and even words appropriate to physical acts which cause some change in its organs; as, for example, if it was touched in some spot that it would ask what you wanted to say to it; if in another, that it would cry that it was hurt, and so on for similar things. But it could never modify its phrases to reply to the sense of whatever was said in its presence, as even the most stupid men can do. The second method of recognition is that although such machines could do many things as well as, or perhaps even better than, men, they would infallibly fail in certain others, by which we would discover that they did not act by understanding, but only by the disposition of their organs. For while reason is a universal instrument which can be used in all sorts of situations, the organs have to be arranged in a particular way for each particular action. From this it follows that it is morally impossible that there should be enough different devices in a machine to make it behave in all the occurrences of life as our reason makes us behave.

Put in its simplest terms, Descartes' two criteria for discriminating between man and the machine are that the latter has (1) no feedback mechanism ("it could never modify its phrases") and (2) no generalizing reason ("reason is a universal instrument which can be used in all sorts of situations"). But it is exactly in these points that, today, we are no longer able so surely to sustain the dichotomy. The work of Norbert Wiener and his followers, in cybernetics, indicates what can be done on the problem of feedback. Investigations into the way the brain itself forms concepts are basic to the attempt to build computers that can do the same, and the two efforts are going forward simultaneously, as in the work of Dr. W.K. Taylor of University College, London, and of others. As G. Rattray Taylor sums up the matter: "One can't therefore be quite as confident that computers will one day equal or surpass man in concept-forming ability as one can about memory, since the trick hasn't yet been done; but the possibilities point that way." In short, the gap between man's thinking and that of his thinking machines has been greatly narrowed by recent research.

Descartes, of course, would not have been happy to see such a development realized. To eliminate the dichotomy or discontinuity between man and machines would be, in effect, to banish God from the universe. The rational soul, Descartes insisted, "could not possibly be derived from the powers of matter ... but must have been specially created." Special creation requires God, for Descartes' reasoning is circular. The shock to man's ego, of learning the Darwinian lesson that he was not "specially created," is, in this light, only an outlying tremor of the great earthquake that threatened man's view of God as well as of himself. The obstacles to removing not only the first three but also the fourth discontinuity are, clearly, deeply imbedded in man's pride of place.

How threatening these developments were can be seen in the case of Descartes' younger contemporary, Blaise Pascal. Aware that man is "a thinking reed," Pascal also realized that he was "engulfed in the infinite immensity of spaces whereof I know nothing, and which knows nothing of me." "I am terrified," he confessed. To escape his feeling of terror, Pascal fled from reason to faith, convinced that reason could not bring him to God. Was he haunted by his own construction, at age nineteen, of a calculating machine which, in principle, anticipated the modern digital computer? By his own remark that "the arithmetical machine produces effects which approach nearer to thought than all the actions of animals"? Ultimately, to escape the anxiety that filled his soul, Pascal commanded, "On thy knees, powerless reason."

Others, of course, walked where angels feared to tread. Thus, sensationalist psychologists and epistemologists, like Locke, Hume, or Condillac, without confronting the problem head on, treated the contents of man's reason as being formed by his sense impressions. Daring thinkers, like La Mettrie in his *L'Homme Machine* (1747) and Holbach, went all the way to a pure materialism. As La Mettrie put it in an anticipatory transcendence of the fourth discontinuity, "I believe thought to be so little incompatible with organized matter that it seems to be a property of it, like Electricity, Motive Force, Impenetrability, Extension, etc."

On the practical front, largely leaving aside the metaphysical aspects of the problem, Pascal's work on calculating machines was taken up by those like the eccentric nineteenth-century mathematician Charles Babbage, whose brilliant designs outran the technology available to him. Thus it remained for another century, the twentieth, to bring the matter to a head and to provide the combination of mathematics, experimental physics, and modern technology that created the machines that now confront us and reawaken the metaphysical question.

NOTES AND QUESTIONS

1.   Mazlish has expanded on these views in his book, *The Fourth Discontinuity* (1993). As Mazlish notes, Darwinian theory has long posed a challenge to human uniqueness. This may explain some of the opposition to the teaching of evolution—opposition that has led to a good deal of litigation. *See* Chapter 4, Sec. I. B., *supra*. In recent years, new arguments have been raised that suggest further continuities between humans and other animals. Cognitive ethologists have contended that some non-human animals, including birds and rhesus monkeys, possess consciousness. *See* Alison Jolly, *A New Science That Sees Animals as Conscious Beings*, Smithsonian, Mar. 1985, at 66. Of course, animal consciousness need not be identical to our own. *See* Ray Jackendoff, Consciousness and the Computational Mind 325–26 (1987). Moreover, some theorists have contended that traits such as altruism, previously thought to be uniquely human, are in fact present in humans as a result of evolutionary processes and do not distinguish us from other primates. This linking of evolutionary theory to human behavior could have broad consequences for the social sciences. *See, e.g.,* Roger Masters, *Evolutionary Biology and Political Theory*, 84 Am. Pol. Sci. Rev. 195 (1990). In particular, there is a growing interest in the use of evolutionary analysis in law. Scholars have argued that understanding the evolutionary roots of human behavior is often a necessary precondition for developing sensible legal rules. *See, e.g.,* Owen D. Jones, *Evolutionary Analysis in Law: An Introduction and Application to Child Abuse*, 75 N.C. L.

REV. 1117 (1997); Owen D. Jones & Timothy H. Goldsmith, *Law and Behavioral Biology*, 104 COLUMBIA L. REV. (forthcoming 2004).

2. But Mazlish's central point is that another discontinuity—that between humans and machines—is breaking down. Here too, the pressure on human uniqueness comes from several directions. There are, of course, the sophisticated artificial intelligence programs discussed in Section II., *supra*, that can perform complex tasks. But there also is the artificial life movement which uses computers to model simple biological entities and then lets those entities evolve behavior patterns as the program runs. Thus computer-generated "birds," given certain initial features, gradually begin to "flock." *See* Christopher Langton, *Artificial Life, in* ARTIFICIAL LIFE: THE PROCEEDINGS OF AN INTERDISCIPLINARY WORKSHOP 1 (Christopher G. Langton ed., 1989). Combining the concepts of evolution and machine intelligence can lead to strong contentions: Geoff Simons, from the National Computing Center in England, argues that computers are an evolving life-form that will eventually develop free will, emotions and an aesthetic capacity. GEOFF SIMONS, THE BIOLOGY OF COMPUTER LIFE: SURVIVAL, EMOTION AND FREE WILL (1985).

3. These contentions have hardly gone unchallenged. Prominent philosophers and scientists have argued in recent years that the ability of computers to mimic human behavior hardly proves that computers can think as humans do. The starting point of this debate is the so-called Turing Test for whether computers can think. In essence, Alan Turing contended that if a computer could convince a human interrogator, in a fair test, that it was answering questions just as a human would, the computer can think. *See* Alan Turing, *Computing Machinery and Intelligence*, 59 MIND, No. 536 (1950). To date, although some computers have fooled human judges in discussions of specific topics, no machine has passed an unrestricted Turing Test. John Markoff, *Can Machines Think? Humans Match Wits*, N.Y. TIMES, Nov. 9, 1991, at A1. Moreover, the philosopher John Searle has asserted that passing the Turing Test proves only that a machine can manipulate symbols, not that it understands what it is doing in the way that a human does. *See* JOHN SEARLE, MINDS, BRAINS AND SCIENCE (1984). The scientist Roger Penrose has attacked the Turing Test from another angle, contending that humans can intuit as true propositions that cannot be reached by a computer's step-by-step approach. ROGER PENROSE, THE EMPEROR'S NEW MIND 110–11 (1989).

4. It may be, however, that regardless of how one resolves the philosophical debate over the capacities of modern digital computers, the apparent continuity between machines and humans stressed by Mazlish will continue to grow. After all, both Searle and Penrose reject Cartesian dualism, and they accept the possibility that some artificially constructed entity, though not a digital computer, could attain consciousness. *See* Searle, *supra* at 35–36; Penrose, *supra* at 416. The article that follows speculates about the implications for the legal definition of life and death if society gradually came to believe that machines could be self-aware in the sense that humans are. Earlier portions of the article note that development of the ability to maintain respiration and a heartbeat with machines led to the current view that cessation of the functioning of the whole brain constitutes death. Steven Goldberg, *The Changing Face of Death: Computers, Consciousness, and Nancy Cruzan*, 43 STAN. L. REV. 659, 664–65 (1991). Moreover, when the higher brain, and therefore the capacity for consciousness, is destroyed, we generally permit the withdrawal of treatment so that whole brain death results. In particular, we typically withdraw treatment from individuals in a persistent vegetative state, and those individuals then die. *Id.* at 667–73. Thus consciousness is central to our view of life. But what if consciousness were no longer seen as a uniquely human trait?

Steven Goldberg, *The Changing Face of Death: Computers, Consciousness, and Nancy Cruzan*

43 STAN. L. REV. 659, 680–83 (1991).

What if a consensus ever grows in our society that computers are self-aware in the same sense that humans are? Such a consensus might arise concerning digital computers or it might accompany the development of other machines, such as those discussed by Searle and Penrose. Perhaps we would finally cease trying to find distinctions between ourselves and our machines. Western history suggests, however, that we would not give in so easily. More likely we will react by seeking some new trait we do not share with conscious computers. If the artificial heart did not faze us for long, perhaps the artificial mind will not either. One candidate for a uniquely human characteristic beyond self-awareness is already available. Some ethicists have described the capacity for social interaction as an essential human trait that is very different from mere consciousness. This capacity is central to one observer's view of why playing chess with the grandmaster program Deep Thought is not the same as playing with a human:

> My father taught me chess when I was six or seven years old. We played often during winters when little work could be done at the farm. Comfortably encamped in front of the living-room stove, a large bowl of freshly popped corn nearby, we engaged in mortal combat as snow fell outside and cold winds howled.
>
> I just cannot envision so relaxing and enjoyable a scene were "Deep Thought's" monitor substituted for my father....
>
> More recently, on the evening I learned my grandparents were seriously ill, a friend invited me to play chess so I would not have to be alone just then, but also wouldn't be compelled to talk much if I didn't feel like it.
>
> "Deep Thought" is incapable of a simple act of friendship and kindness such as that. Nor could the machine have given me the emotional support I needed at that difficult time....
>
> Give me ... mere mortals ... with whom to play chess—for the simple pleasures by which they enrich my life—win, lose, or stalemate. Surely the machine has not been nor ever can be invented to improve upon that.

Computers force us to see chess playing, once regarded as a remarkable intellectual feat requiring introspection and intuition, more importantly as an occasion for human interaction. Even if Deep Thought knows it is playing chess, it cannot perceive how its human opponent feels about the game. At least until computers are built that can provide solace for humans, this step would give us some psychological distance from machines.

But if we know anything from recent history, moving the essence of humanity toward a "social interaction" standard would have profound implications for the legal definition of death. If computers push our sense of uniqueness away from self-awareness toward social interaction, the definitions of life and death may eventually follow. The groundwork has already been laid—without reference to machine self-awareness. Two recent law review articles have already proposed that human interaction should supplant mere consciousness as the legal standard for life. Kevin

Quinn [at 76 Cal.L.Rev. 897 (1988)] suggests that the definition of life should be set at a "threshold ... higher than minimal consciousness"; the standard he puts forth is "a minimum capacity for interpersonal relationships." When that capacity is irretrievably lost, Quinn argues, a surrogate may elect to remove life-sustaining treatment. Nancy Rhoden at 102 Harv.L.Rev. 375 (1988) contends that when "analysis of the patient's capacities shows that she is unable to enjoy the distinctly human pleasures of relating to her environment and to others, then family discretion [on whether to end treatment] is warranted." Rhoden states explicitly that such patients have capacities beyond those of an individual in a persistent vegetative state.

The adoption of these views is much more likely to come about if a consensus grows that computers can be self-aware. Of course, such a consensus, if it developed at all, would grow slowly and would never be complete. Absolute proof that another human, let alone a machine, is self-aware is not available; consciousness is intrinsically a subjective phenomenon. But we treat other humans as though they were conscious and we may come to act that way toward certain machines. It would be a gradual process as we came to think of particular devices as not merely doing things but as knowing they were doing things. As we have seen, nothing that Searle or Penrose proposes suggests that machines *must* lack self-awareness. If consciousness is merely a product of a machine—indeed, if, as Searle himself says, consciousness is to brains as digestion is to stomachs—consciousness may come to be viewed as no more unique to human life, and hence to the definition of human life, than respiration or circulating blood.

A diminished sense of the uniqueness of consciousness would most likely engender a corresponding broadening of the category of those regarded as dead. We might begin by continuing to label "alive" those who lack the capacity for social interaction, yet nevertheless tolerate removal of their means of existence, as we do now for those who lack consciousness. Other pressures pushing toward the same end increase the probability that this change will occur. Many have long predicted or feared, for example, that social worth and economic considerations could force withdrawal of treatment from ill geriatric patients. We must now recognize that the emergence of an increasingly rarefied sense of what it means to be human could have the same impact. This new pressure may prove to be the most important. One can discuss rationally the social justice issues involved in deciding which people are entitled to expensive treatment. But when one begins to view the subjects of treatment not as people, but as entities indistinguishable from machines, the outcome of the debate is likely to be foreordained: treatment will be withdrawn.

A view of what this future would look like is provided by Quinn's and Rhoden's analyses of the leading case of *In re Conroy* [486 A.2d 1209 (N.J. 1985)]. In *Conroy*, the Supreme Court of New Jersey, the court that decided the *Quinlan* case [355 A.2d 647 (N.J. 1976)], considered whether a feeding tube could be removed from an elderly brain-damaged woman who was hospitalized with a variety of serious permanent ailments and who had a limited life expectancy. Conroy could not speak or interact with other people, but she appeared to retain some sort of consciousness—she would, for example, scratch herself, pull at her bandages, and smile when her hair was combed or when she received a "comforting rub." The court explicitly noted that she was not in a persistent vegetative state. The court concluded that the feeding tube could not be removed since Conroy had not made clear that she wanted such a result. The court was not satisfied that either the burdens of her life outweighed the benefits or that her pain rendered treatment inhumane.

Quinn challenges this result on the ground that because an individual in Conroy's situation cannot engage in "interpersonal relationships," she has "no possibility of personal life" and thus there should be no obligation to maintain "biological life." Rhoden explains her support for removing Conroy's feeding tube in somewhat different terms. Conroy, she suggests, is not "able to experience or enjoy life." The court in *Conroy,* when it said feeding could not be terminated, "in essence reduced Ms. Conroy, or the person that she was, to an object that passively experienced physical sensations." It is easy to see how this view would gain strength from the development of machines we regard as self-aware. Viewing Conroy, a conscious individual, as "an object" is a tendency that can only be strengthened when we have "objects," such as thinking machines, that we view as conscious.

NOTES AND QUESTIONS

1. Developments in artificial intelligence could impact on the law in a variety of ways apart from the definition of death. It may be, for example, that an increasingly mechanistic view of how the human mind functions could profoundly affect legal doctrines that turn on intent. *See, e.g.*, Rebecca Dresser, *Review Essay: Making Up Our Minds: Can Law Survive Cognitive Science?*, 10 CRIM. JUST. ETHICS 27 (1991).

2. Perhaps the ultimate legal question raised by artificial intelligence is whether machines could ever have rights. *See, e.g.*, Phil McNally & Sohail Inayatullah, *The Rights of Robots*, 20 FUTURES 119 (1989). After all, the demonstration of similarities between humans and other animals has been a key part of the argument for animal rights. *See, e.g.*, PETER SINGER, ANIMAL LIBERATION 9–17 (2d ed. 1990). If machines, like humans, can be conscious, perhaps it would be unfair to deny them certain rights. Decades ago, the philosopher Hilary Putnam, in a discussion of the "minds of machines," concluded that he could not prove whether or not robots could, in principle, be conscious, but that it seemed better to him "to extend our concept so that robots are conscious—for 'discrimination' based on the 'softness' or 'hardness' of the body parts of a synthetic 'organism' seems as silly as discriminatory treatment of humans on the basis of skin color." Hilary Putnam, *Robots: Machines or Artificially Created Life?*, 61 J. PHIL. 668, 691 (1964).

3. For others, the legal status of machines would turn not on whether the machine could think or be conscious, but rather on whether it could feel. How would you decide if a robot had feelings? Professor Michael Gemignani posits that a robot could "be designed to express sympathy and show emotions and the human might even come to 'love' the machine. . . . If we cannot tell the difference between the responses of a sentient being and a machine, then is the machine entitled to the same respect and rights as the sentient being?" Michael Gemignani, *Laying Down the Law to Robots*, 21 SAN DIEGO L. REV. 1045, 1059 n.40 (1984); *see also* Robert A. Freitag, *End Note*, STUDENT LAW., Jan. 1985, at 54. For a general discussion of the legal and moral status of "unconventional entities generally, not merely lakes and mountains, but robots and embryos, tribes and species, future generations and artifacts . . .," see Christopher Stone, *Should Trees Have Standing? Revisited: How Far Will Law and Morals Reach? A Pluralist Perspective*, 59 S. Cal. L. Rev. 1, 8 (1985). If fiction is any guide, remarkable issues lie ahead: one prize-winning science fiction novel describes a robot rights movement led by a machine that has the capacity to disobey human orders and to do evil as well as good. JOHN SLADEK, TIK-TOK (1985).

4. Even the conventional idea of a robot as a mechanical creature is beginning to break down. Bioengineers have linked neurons from snails, leeches, and other living organisms to silicon chips to create primitive "bio-computers." The ultimate goals of these efforts include more intelligent computers as well as artificial retinas and the like. *See, e.g.*, Shankar Vedantam, *Brain Cells, Silicon Chips Are Linked Electronically: Part–Mechanical, Part–Living Circuit Created*, WASH. POST, Aug. 28, 2001, at A3; Eric Niiler, *New Bio–Circuit Technology Presents Intriguing Medical and Military Possibilities: When Electron Meets Neuron*, SAN DIEGO UNION-TRIBUNE, Jan. 19, 2000, at E1. Does your view of the nature or rights of a machine turn on whether it incorporates biological materials?

5. Could the merging of humans with other entities lead not to an increased number of rights-bearers but rather to a dilution of the concept of human rights? Are there other reasons to strive to maintain a sense of human uniqueness? Must such uniqueness ultimately depend on religious or spiritual principles?

INDEX

References are to pages.

†